Psychology and Social Care

of related interest

The Psychology of Ageing
An Introduction 2nd Edition
Ian Stuart-Hamilton
ISBN 1 85302 233 0

Competence in Social Work
Edited by Kieran O'Hagan
ISBN 1 85302 332 9

Handbook of Theory for Practice Teachers in Social Work
Edited by Joyce Lishman
ISBN 1 85302 098 2

Community Care Practice and the Law 2nd Edition
Michael Mandelstam
ISBN 1 85302 647 6

An A–Z of Community Care Law
Michael Mandelstam
ISBN 1 85302 560 7

Good Practice in Supervision
Statutory and Voluntary Organisations
Edited by Jacki Pritchard
ISBN 1 85302 279 9
Good Practice 1

Good Practice in Risk Assessment and Risk Management 1
Edited by Jacki Pritchard and Hazel Kemshall
ISBN 1 85302 338 8
Good Practice 3

Good Practice in Risk Assessment 2
Key Themes for Protection, Rights and Responsibilities
Edited by Hazel Kemshall and Jacki Pritchard
ISBN 1 85302 441 4.
Good Practice 5

Good Practice in Child Protection
A Manual for Professionals
Edited by Hilary Owen and Jacki Pritchard
ISBN 1 85302 205 5
Good Practice 1

Psychology and Social Care

Edited by David Messer and Fiona Jones

Co-edited by Claire Meldrum, Mary Horton and Brian Littlechild

Jessica Kingsley Publishers
London and Philadelphia

The right of the contributors to be identified as authors of this work has been asserted by them in accordance with the Copyright, Designs and Patents Act 1988.

First published in the United Kingdom in 1999 by
Jessica Kingsley Publishers Ltd,
116 Pentonville Road,
London N1 9JB, England
and
325 Chestnut Street,
Philadelphia PA 19106, USA.

www.jkp.com

Library of Congress Cataloging in Publication Data
A CIP catalog record for this book is available from the Library of Congress

British Library Cataloguing in Publication Data
Psychology for social carers
1. Psychology, Applied 2. Human services – Psychological aspects 3. Social services – Psychological aspects
I. Messer, David J., 1952– II. Jones, Fiona
150.2'436

ISBN 1 85302 762 6

Printed and Bound in Great Britain by
Athenaeum Press, Gateshead, Tyne and Wear

Contents

Part IV Working with clients: Specific issues

Introduction

How Will this Book Help Me?

In recent years it has become difficult to avoid being aware of the impact of psychology. Few major events or crises seem to pass by without a psychologist being called upon by the media to give an opinion or explanation. Psychologists of various types can be found on television, in newspapers and in magazines commenting on anything from the psychological impact of major disasters and crimes to trivial issues such as what (if anything!) your choice of spectacles says about what type of person you are. The light psychologists are able to shed on such issues is also quite variable. Psychology is a fairly new science, and given the complexity of its subject matter, it is inevitable that some areas are well-developed and others are under-researched.

The expansion of psychology in the last few years has also meant that there has been a growth in the applied areas of work in which psychologists can now be found. Clinical and educational psychology are perhaps the best known specialisms, but recently there has also been an increase in the numbers working as occupational psychologists, sports psychologists, health psychologists, forensic psychologists and counselling psychologists, as well as academics who research and teach psychology related to any of the above specialisms.

This book is written by a range of psychologists or people who adopt a psychological approach. Some research and teach in universities and others work as clinical, health or occupational psychologists in various applied settings. The chapters reflect their diverse viewpoints and varying approaches. This enables the book to give a broad ranging introduction to psychology as it can be applied to the social care professions. It is designed primarily for students in training, but will hopefully provide a useful reference source in the early years of practice. It will have relevance not only for those who are aiming for social work careers in social services departments, but those working in voluntary or private organizations (including residential establishments) or working as probation officers. It is also likely to be relevant to a range of other professionals, for example those in education welfare or work for the health services. The term 'social care professional' used throughout the book is intended to include such other professionals. The term 'social worker' is used where issues or examples may relate predominantly to the work of professional social workers. Overall, the book aims to provide a good working knowledge of recent research findings and the latest thinking in psychology theory, with clear pointers to how this can be applied in practice. The book has been written with reference to the knowledge, skills and values needed for competent social work practice as specified by the Central Council for Education and Training in Social Work (CCETSW). Further details can be obtained by contacting the address at the end of the chapter.

This first section of the book will look at the relevance of psychology for social care professionals. It will discuss the work of professional psychologists and ways social care professionals can themselves apply psychological knowledge. The chapter will then introduce some of the theoretical and methodological approaches used by psychologists which form the basis for many of the findings described throughout the book. Finally, the chapter will describe how the book is structured in ways to help you apply psychological knowledge to your own practice.

Is Psychology Relevant to Social Care Professionals in Practice?

Psychology is relevant to social care professionals in two main ways. First, such professionals are very likely to come into contact with psychologists who are often working with the same clients. Psychologists have areas of competency and skills which can ideally complement those of social care professionals. However, if these two groups of workers do not understand the types of approach used by each other they may overlap or even conflict. Perhaps more importantly, however, psychology is one of a number of disciplines which provide a knowledge base which can inform and improve good professional social care practice. The following two sections will discuss these two issues in more detail.

Social care professionals and psychologists

It is possible that social care professionals, in their day-to-day work, will come into contact with psychologists operating in a range of different roles. For example, an occupational psychologist may be involved in their recruitment or training, or may ask them to fill in a survey about work stress. Counselling psychologists are also increasingly employed in such settings as the workplace or GP surgeries (as are large numbers of counsellors without formal psychological qualifications), and may do work which overlaps with that of the social care professional. However, social care professionals are perhaps most likely to come across educational or clinical psychologists. For example, social workers may be working alongside such psychologists in multi-disciplinary terms, or they may find it useful to seek each other's advice to aid in the assessment or treatment of clients. It is therefore useful for social workers and other social care professionals to have some knowledge of the work of these types of psychologist.

EDUCATION PSYCHOLOGISTS

These psychologists are primarily employed by education authorities to assess and develop interventions to help individuals who are having difficulty at school. A child may be referred because of social, emotional or learning difficulties. Such children often also have family difficulties and are known to social workers and other social care professionals. Close liaison between educational psychologists and the social care professional can therefore be of great importance. Generally, an educational psychologist will have a psychology degree and post-graduate training, as well as teaching qualifications. Their expertise includes assessing children's progress and their needs (both academic and emotional), and providing advice and treatment. (See, for example, Chapter 14, where Julie Dockrell, Nicola Grove and Pat Hasan discuss the assessment of IQ.)

CLINICAL PSYCHOLOGISTS

These psychologists work often in the mental health field and have extensive postgraduate training in both assessment and the provision of therapy based on psychological theories. They work in both hospital and community settings with people with health problems (particularly mental health) and those with severe learning difficulties. It is not unusual for a client to be referred to both the psychologist and the community or hospital worker. This may happen after a stroke or head injury or in patients suffering depression, phobias or attempting suicide. The clinical psychologists may use tests to assess intellectual functioning and psychological state, and may recommend and implement psychological treatment. This may include counselling for depression or behaviour therapy for phobia (see Chapter 18 by David Winter). In such cases, a social worker may also be called in to assess and work with the client and their family, a role which may overlap with that of the psychologist calling for close collaboration between the two professionals to ensure effective help is given.

For further information about the work of psychologists, see Higgins (1988), or contact the British Psychological Society (address at the end of the chapter).

Social work and psychology

Social workers in their everyday practice frequently deal with clients with psychological problems. These may be set in the context of many other types of complex social, financial or legal difficulties. The social worker is called upon to draw on a range of diverse disciplines to inform their practice. Integrating these areas of knowledge and applying them is a challenge. This books attempts to provide the kind of framework for understanding the psychological issues relevant to different groups which will aid social workers' interventions (see below).

To try to illustrate how an understanding of psychology may help the social worker, it may be helpful to look at a particular case, not untypical of those you may be called upon to deal with.

A CASE STUDY: THE SMITH FAMILY

The Smith family are referred to the social services by their health visitor because there are concerns about the welfare of their two small children, Gemma and Jamie, aged 2 and 5. Mr Smith, has a history of psychiatric illness and has been labelled schizophrenic. His illness is controlled by medication. However, recently he has been made redundant and has decided he no longer needs his medication. His behaviour is giving some cause for concern in that he at times appears irrational and aggressive. The health visitor is worried that Mrs Smith seems depressed and unable to cope, and the children are dirty and uncared for. There is concern in particular about Jamie, who causes his mother problems. She seems to find his demands intensely irritating and frequently criticizes and punishes him for trivial misbehaviour. Jamie seems withdrawn and still wets the bed. A supportive neighbour who used to help out has recently moved away. A look through the social work records shows that the family do have a history of contact with social services. Mr Smith has had several compulsory admissions to psychiatric hospital, and there were concerns about the couple's ability to cope when Jamie was first born, but the case was closed when their social worker moved away from the area when Jamie was about three months old.

Discussion point

    ° Identify the ways in which you think psychology might help you in understanding and working with this family. Make some brief notes about this before reading any further.

This is a complex case but not untypical of the kind of problems a social worker may have to deal with. This kind of case is likely to involve close collaboration with a number of other agencies and professionals, for example health visitors, psychiatrists and police officers. Social workers are the representatives of their departments who are in daily contact with both the public and with other organizations. Working effectively within their own bureaucracies while also working closely with professionals based in different types of organizations with different value systems is one of the most difficult aspects of social work. A knowledge of various models of organizations (as discussed in Chapter 1 by Karen Izod and Joanna Dodd) may help social workers to understand and negotiate some of the organizational difficulties they encounter.

In the case of the Smith family, perhaps more important than understanding the organizational values of other workers, it will be helpful to have an understanding of the way the problems may be viewed by other professionals. A basic understanding of the classifications of mental illness (as given in Chapter 18 by David Winter) will help you to understand not only what is meant by a label of 'schizophrenia', but also the limitations of this diagnosis. This chapter also gives an introduction to a range of models for understanding and treating psychological problems. While few professionals are exclusively trained to adopt only one approach, the models underpinning the practice of different professional groups are likely to be very different. A social worker may have reservations about the medical or behavioural model of mental illness, but will undoubtedly be more effective in both their own interventions and their communications with other professionals if they have knowledge of the strength and limitations of both their own and others' viewpoints.

In the social worker's own intervention, an understanding of child development issues is essential. Such knowledge provides the framework for the social worker to decide whether Jamie's behaviour and Mrs Smith's relationship with him is a cause for concern. Psychologists have made a major contribution to providing an understanding of typical development, as well as the signs to look for in identifying emotional and physical abuse. The large number of chapters on children in this book reflect the importance of this area for social workers. The limited information raised above is enough to raise concerns that the children may be at risk. Yet deciding just how great that risk is and what action is appropriate is always difficult. Chapter 4 on risk assessment and decision making will help the social worker identify whether their decisions may be biased, and will suggest some ways that they may be able to avoid such influences.

However, the social worker must also not lose sight of the wider family, and the complex different relationships between family members and between them and the outside world. For example, the systems approach described by Anne Woollett (Chapter 6) may provide one framework for understanding and working with the complex family relationships. This is just one of a number of theoretical approaches which may be relevant. Many more will be discussed throughout the book, but some key theoretical perspectives used by psychologists are introduced below.

What Theoretical Perspectives do Psychologists Use?

Psychologists may operate from many different theoretical standpoints which take different perspectives on the individual person. Some key perspectives, which are relevant to the approaches used by the contributors of this book, are described below. Each of these perspectives provides important theories which are relevant to social care professionals. Many psychologists would not identify themselves clearly as operating within just one perspective, but may draw on a range of theoretical approaches. Where possible, the descriptions below will point out where in the book you will find more detail and practical examples. However, two chapters in particular provide thorough theoretical coverage: Chapter 15 by Dorota Iwaniec gives a detailed review of a range of theories relevant to child abuse; and David Winter reviews the theoretical approaches underpinning therapy for people with psychological problems in Chapter 18.

Behavioural

This is one of the earliest approaches in psychology. Psychologists who use this perspective study individuals be examining their overt, quantifiable behaviour. They believe that all behaviour is shaped by the environment in the form of reinforcements. The notion of learning through conditioning is crucial here. Iwaniec's chapter (Chapter 15) gives a full description of the way different kinds of rewards and punishments may lead to behavioural problems in children. In the context of psychological problems in adults, the application of a behavioural approach for treating phobias is described by David Winter in Chapter 18.

Psychodynamic

Psychodynamic theory, another early approach in psychology, was developed by Sigmund Freud. This views behaviour as largely determined by unconscious forces; that is motivated by fears and desires of which we are unaware. A summary of this approach can be found in the chapter on child abuse, theories and research by Dorota Iwaniec (Chapter 15). This theory and its application, in the form of using the therapeutic relationship to help the client to gain insights, were key features of social work training until the 1970s. This kind of therapeutic intervention was, in practice, often unrealistic given the pressures and demands on social workers. Nevertheless, the theoretical approach continues to provide useful insights for practitioners. Chapter 18 by David Winter describes psychodynamic treatment in more detail, while Mary Horton's chapter on groups (Chapter 7) provides a psychoanalytical perspective to explain the influence of groups.

Cognitive

This perspective arose out of a dissatisfaction with the behaviourist approach, which focused purely on the connections between stimuli and responses. Cognitive psychologists believe that the best way to understand human behaviour and experience is to understand the mental processes that occur during activities such as perceiving, remembering and problem solving. Psychologists operating within this perspective tend to adopt a rigorous scientific approach (often using experiments), for example to investigate the intricacies of memory (see Chapter 5 by Paul Seager, Mark Kebbell and Richard Wiseman).

Related to this approach is the area of social cognition, which is concerned with how we make sense of ourselves and other people. This claims that altering negative patterns of thinking about events (e.g. about our ability to cope) may be an effective goal for therapy, and that it is not necessary to uncover unconscious motivations. This is frequently a feature of stress management training (see Chapter 2 by Fiona Jones and Ben Fletcher). Chapter 19 by Clive Hollin also describes the use of such cognitive approaches with offenders to increase moral reasoning and self-control and, in Chapter 20, Richard Hammersley describes their use with drug users.

Biopsychological

This is the area of psychology most linked to medicine. Psychologists operating within this perspective are primarily concerned with linking physiology and behaviour, and such research is responsible for much of our knowledge of how behaviour is linked to different parts of the brain. The study of people with head injuries or other brain damage has yielded important insights. The study of animal behaviour has also contributed to our understanding of the nervous system (see Chapter 22 on brain damage by Jane Pierson, and Chapter 23 on dementia by John Done and Judith Thomas). While concerns about the structure of the brain may seem a long way from the day-to-day responsibilities of social care professionals, it will undoubtedly be the case that at some stage many will come into contact with clients suffering strokes or other brain damage. They are also likely to encounter physiological explanations of psychological disorders such as schizophrenia (see Chapter 18 by David Winter).

Humanistic

The humanistic approach is often known as the third force in psychology. It can be seen as a reaction against the deterministic nature of behaviourism and to the lack of self-determination in much of psychoanalytic thinking. The emphasis in this perspective is on the way that individuals influence their own destiny, and the way that psychological growth can occur through a process of self-determination. The work of Maslow has been an important impetus in developing these areas. Maslow has emphasized the processes of growth and fulfilment. In relation to this, there has been a focus on the way freedom to make our own choices is important for personal growth, the way that each individual can set their own agenda to achieve personal growth, and the way that there is a hierarchy of needs to enable self-actualization to take place (biological needs, a need for belongingness in relation to other people, and needs for self-esteem and self-actualization). This approach has had more direct influence on therapeutic perspectives than on academic psychology; however, the more indirect influence of this perspective is widespread and is present in many chapters of this book.

It is important to recognize that psychologists are now much less likely than in the past to adopt a single perspective when they want to provide explanations or to provide therapy. It is becoming increasingly recognized that some explanations work better in some circumstances than others. For example, problems getting a child to eat can be seen as a result of reinforcement (e.g. they may be rewarded by receiving more attention), while other behaviour such as a child becoming withdrawn may require more complex explanations. Similarly, a range of treatment approaches is required. For example, behaviourist treatment can be effective in treating phobias, whereas a variety of interventions including family therapy may be more appropriate when attempting to deal with problems of the whole family system.

This is not an exhaustive list of all the different approaches present in psychology. There are important perspectives which emphasize the socio-cultural context of human behaviour (see Chapter 3 by Ann Phoenix, as well as Chapter 6 by Anne Woollett and Chapter 17 by Leo Hendry). The feminist perspective is also beginning to receive more attention and acknowledgement (e.g. see Chapter 15 by Dorota Iwaniec and Chapter 6 by Anne Woollett).

How do Psychologists Investigate Human Functioning?

Psychologists adopt a variety of different methods to investigate human functioning. In the past the experimental method (see below) was usually seen as the 'best' way to try and find out about any issue. However, recently it has been more widely recognized that experiments are not always possible, suitable or appropriate for every topic that is being investigated. As a result, there are a number of methods employed by psychologists, ranging from the classic laboratory experiment to participant observations of the way a group is functioning (see Chapter 7). One unifying perspective across the range of methods employed by psychologists is the concern that the information they collect can be checked and evaluated by others; the wish is to avoid situations where claims about what people do is a matter of opinion rather than a matter of objective description. As a result, many (but not all) psychologists are interested in making sure that the information they collect can be quantified. This usually involves putting the information into a numeric form (e.g. the number of delinquent acts carried out by males and females according to age and family background). This type of data is described as *quantative*. However, in recent years there has also been an increasing use of a wider range of methodologies including the use of open ended questionnaires, interviews and discussion groups, giving *qualitative* information. A brief description of key approaches is given below, pointing out where some further examples can be found in later sections of the book.

Experimental method

The use of experimental work is fundamental to much of psychology. It means that psychological phenomena can be studied in a carefully controlled environment. Often psychologists are interested in examining whether some measurable aspect of human functioning (the dependent variable) is influenced by something (the independent variable). This methodology is perhaps best illustrated by using one or two of the many examples you will find later in the book. For example, Paul Seager *et al.* in Chapter 5 describe the way experiments can be used to assess how good people are at detecting liars. Such experiments enable the psychologist to manipulate and control the information which is supplied to people so that it is possible to identify the cues that they use in making their assessments. These experiments have demonstrated that people are not as good at detecting lies as they think, and that they often base their decisions on inappropriate cues. However, such experiments may have the drawback that behaviour is studied in very artificial circumstances. People may behave very differently in real situations, and it is unclear how generalizable such findings are to other situations.

Sometimes, to overcome this criticism, experiments may be conducted in real settings where as far as possible good experimental design is used. In Chapter 11, David Messer describes one such study by Klaus and Kennell (1976), where mothers in hospital were randomly allocated to a treatment group, which had extra time with their babies after birth, or a control group, who were separated immediately after birth in the normal hospital procedure of the time.

This study illustrates an important feature of psychological experiments, the use of control groups. In an experiment which uses a control group, one group of people are given an experience to see whether this affects their functioning, in this case extra contact with their baby. Another group of people do not have this experience; these are in the control group. Thus, the interest is in determining whether there are differences between the two groups as a result of the experimental intervention.

The mothers in Klaus and Kennell's study were randomly allocated to the two groups (the experimenters might have put all the names in a hat, and given the extra contact time to those mothers whose names were drawn out of the hat first; random allocation simply means that all people have an equal chance of being included in each condition). As a result of the random allocation, it is assumed that any difference between groups is likely to be the result of the experimental intervention. Statistical tests are used to indicate how likely it is that a measured difference is not due to chance, and this tells us that if another experiment was conducted there would be a very good chance that the same findings would be produced.

Psychologists realize that the random allocation of people to groups can sometimes affect the findings (for example, it could be that by chance the group of mothers who are given extra time in contact with their babies are the more sensitive mothers). However, they try to minimize this possibility by using as large as groups of people as possible so that any one person's reactions are unlikely to bias the findings, and by using statistical tests to work out whether their findings are likely to be due to chance. Such tests give a numerical measure, called the *statistical significance level*, which represents the probability that such findings are due to chance.

It is not always possible to conduct experiments for a variety of reasons. Often it is not ethical to try to change human functioning without a very good reason to believe that the intervention will help people in the investigation and not harm others. For example, it would not be ethical to test whether breast feeding promotes infant–mother attachment by asking one group of mothers to breast feed and another group to bottle feed their infants. In cases such as these, the psychologist might have to compare a group of mothers who are already breast feeding with a group of mothers who are already bottle feeding to examine differences in attachment. Unfortunately, if a difference in attachment was found in this study we could not be absolutely certain that this difference was due to the effects of breast feeding. It could be that some other factor which is related to breast feeding is the real cause of any difference. For example, mothers who breast feed might have a different attitude to child care that mothers who bottle feed, which may lead to a difference in attachment between the group. One way investigators try to avoid such confounding effects is to make sure that both groups contain people with similar characteristics. For example, the investigator might check that the mothers in the breast and bottle feeding groups had similar attitudes to childrearing, so that this could be ruled out as a cause of any difference.

It is very important to be aware of the distinctions between a true experiment which can usually tell us what causes particular behaviours, and a quasi-experiment which does not involve the random allocation of people to groups. In the latter case, we cannot be sure what is the cause of a difference between groups of people. Perhaps the best example of the problems of using a quasi-experiment design is the debate about the role of smoking cigarettes in causing lung cancer. For a long time tobacco companies have maintained that we cannot be sure that smoking causes lung cancer in humans, and technically they are correct. Experiments have not been conducted which have randomly assigned people to a group who will be made to smoke and a group prevented from smoking. Consequently, it has been possible to argue that it is not smoking, but some other factor, which causes cancer. However, it is now generally accepted that smoking causes cancer on the basis of numerous studies of people who do and do not smoke, animal experiments and an understanding of the way that cancer cells are promoted by substances in cigarettes.

Survey method

Many psychological phenomena are not easily studied by the above methods. For example, for both practical and ethical reasons, it is not usually possible to conduct experimental studies of work stress where groups of social workers would be randomly allocated to more or less pleasant work conditions or types of case load to find out more about the stressors of the job. Even quasi-experiments may not be useful as the differences between social workers with one type of case load (e.g. children) compared to another type (e.g. elderly clients) may be many and varied. A conclusion that, for example, child care workers had higher levels of anxiety may not tell us a great deal about the specific causes of anxiety for these workers. A survey is likely to be the method adopted by the psychologist in this case. This will enable them to measure the social worker's perceptions of their work and its problems. For example, Chapter 2 describes a number of survey studies of stress in social workers.

Often, in such a study participants are given a number of statements to which people may agree or disagree (often using a five-point rating scale from strongly agree to strongly disagree). Statements may then be grouped to form measures of particular job features (such as workload) and the ratings added together to form a quantitative measure. Questionnaire measures of psychological well-being or anxiety have also been developed by psychologists and psychiatrists. These have been tested for their validity and reliability (i.e. are they true and consistent measures) across a large number of samples.

Measures developed in this way can be used, for example, to assess the extent of strain experienced by the workers. In this type of survey, there may be an interest in showing relationships between certain job features and anxiety by using statistical correlations. A correlation is a statistical assessment about how closely two sets of numbers are related. For example, one study found that social workers who rated their workload as heavy also had high levels of anxiety, whereas lower ratings of workload were associated with lower anxiety. This study measured both perceptions of workload and anxiety at the same time in one survey (that is, it was cross-sectional). It is therefore not possible to show that workload causes anxiety; it may be that anxious people are more likely to rate a quite normal workload as heavy. Such findings therefore need to be treated with caution and as indicating possible areas of concern. Further research over time (that is, longitudinal studies) are needed to establish causation.

Designing a good survey is not straightforward, and care is needed in writing questions so that they are not ambiguous, do not contain leading questions and are not constructed in a way that will encourage 'response biases'. It is also crucial that the questionnaire does not miss out areas of importance to those who fill them in. A good understanding of the area of research, often based on literature reviews, interviewing or observations and piloting of survey questions, may be needed to ensure that it will give the answer to the research questions. Questions may be open ended requiring descriptive answers (giving qualitative data) or they may use rating scales (giving quantitative data). Computer packages are available to help analyze both types of data. The use of survey methods is common throughout the social sciences, and there are a number of good reference texts for those wanting to know more about the use of surveys (e.g. see the 'Further Reading' section at the end of this chapter).

Observational method

Of course, not everyone can complete questionnaires, and even if they do, we cannot be sure that their reports really correspond to their actual behaviour. Observational methods are therefore invaluable. A classic study mentioned in Chapter 8 examined whether a group containing both oriental and white people were refused entry to a restaurant when they went in person and when they wrote to the owner (Lapiere, 1934). The group was usually told the restaurant was full when they wrote to the owner, but were admitted when they went in person.

When collecting observational data, checks are usually made to ensure that different investigators can code the same behaviour in the same way: this is particularly important if there is a subjective element to the coding. For example, it is relatively simple to code whether the group was or was not allowed entry, but more difficult to code for how welcoming was the behaviour of the staff. Often it is assumed that observational studies take place in naturalistic surroundings (e.g. in the restaurant), but it is possible to conduct observational studies in a laboratory (see Chapter 11), and experimental studies can contain observational components.

Case studies

A rather different kind of observational approach used by psychologists is described in Chapter 22 on brain damage. Here, clinical observations of individual people who have suffered injuries or surgery to various areas of their brains have helped neuropsychologists to gain clues to the functioning of the brain. While psychologists often prefer large samples, individuals with very specific brain injuries are rare, and such case studies may provide important insights, as in Luria's (1972) account of a head injured patient.

Individual differences – the psychometric approach

Many of the approaches described above are used to look at how people are likely to react in given circumstances or conditions. While psychologists accept that not all people are the same, a major interest is in identifying ways in which people react in similar ways in specific circumstances. However, there is a strong tradition in psychology which focuses on identifying and measuring individual differences. Many people will have come into contact with IQ tests or other aptitude tests at school. Such psychometric tests, including personality testing, are becoming an increasing feature of job recruitment.

Often there are objections to the use of intelligence tests or other measures of ability or personality. Some of the objections are well founded, in that there can be uncertainty about how well any test is assessing the characteristic it is attempting to measure. The debate about the usefulness of intelligence tests is a very good example of this, with there being discussion of how well these tests distinguish 'intelligent' from less intelligent people. Part of the problem is that there is no agreed definition of intelligence – the term means different things to different people (see Chapter 10 by Claire Meldrum). However, in defence of these methods of assessment, it should be pointed out that people's responses can be compared to that which is expected for a particular age and background. Such assessments may be less biased than a simple interview or more subjective assessment.

To summarize, we have seen that there are a variety of ways that psychologists collect information about people. The understanding of a topic may be the result of a variety of methods (e.g. research on substance use uses information about the chemical effects of drugs, surveys, experimental evaluations of treatment methods, observations, in-depth interviews with users, and so on). When this is the case, then it should both increase our understanding and increase our confidence that the findings are not some by-product of the method of investigation.

How Will this Book Help Me?

The case study at the start of this chapter demonstrates that a wide range of chapters may be relevant and have practical implications for a single social work case. Similarly, you will find examples of the different methodological approaches cropping up in different sections of the book. However, we have aimed to structure the book to help you find your way around and use it as a reference text. The opening section, 'Working in organizations and society', deals with the context in which social care professionals operate, including working in organizations (Chapter 1, by Karen Izod and Joanna Dodd) and working in a multicultural society (Chapter 3, by Ann Phoenix). The second section deals with a range of general issues to do with 'Working with clients'. These have been selected as providing a psychological perspective on some issues which are fundamental to all social care professionals working with individuals, families and groups, including issues of prejudice and discrimination (Chapters 8 and 9 by Mary Horton). The third section focuses on an area of particular importance to social care professionals, that of 'Working with children and young people', and including chapters on developmental issues and two chapters on child abuse (Chapters 15 and 16 by Dorota Iwaniec). Among the extensive coverage of a range of child care case issues is a specific chapter devoted to physical and sensory disabilities (Chapter 13 by Vicki Lewis), and a chapter discussing why some individuals are quite resilient in the face of deprivation or abuse (Chapter 12 by Ann and Alan Clarke). The fourth section provides more detailed information relevant to work with specific groups of clients. This includes the topic of dying and bereavement (Chapter 24, by Paul March and Clare Doherty), and the latest work on the psychological implications of HIV infections (Chapter 21 by Barbara Hedge). These, and the other specialized topics in this section, are dealt with in a depth which ensures that they should be a useful reference source during the early years of professional practice. The book ends with some concluding thoughts about how psychology might be of use to you in practice.

Each section incorporates boxes which contain additional information, often giving practical examples or drawing your attention to key issues or theories. The chapters also contain a number of discussion points and questions which you are encouraged to think about either as individuals or groups. Questions which could form the basis of seminar discussions are included at the end of the chapter. These are followed by further readings to enable you to gain additional information about the topic of the chapter.

Further Reading

Robson, C. (1993) *Real World Research: A Resource for Social Scientists and Practitioner Researchers.* Blackwell: Oxford.
This gives a good introduction to how psychological approaches can be used in applied settings. It covers qualitative and quantitative methods.

Oppenheim, A.N. (1992) *Questionnaire Design, Interviewing and Attitude Measurement.* London: Pinter.
This book provides a practical guide to survey methodology.

Higgins, L.T. (1988) *Career Choices in Psychology.* Leicester: British Psychological Society.
This gives detailed work profiles of careers in psychology.

Useful Addresses

For further information about careers in psychology and information about the Register of Chartered Psychologists contact:

The British Psychological Society
St Andrew's House,
48 Princess Road East,
Leicester LE1 7DR, UK.

Website: http://www.bps.org.uk

For information about social work training and the knowledge, skills and professional standards expected of newly qualified social workers, contact the Central Council for Education and Training in Social Work (CCETSW):

CCETSW Information Service
Derbyshire House,
St Chad's Street,
London WC1H 8AD

References

Klaus, M.H and Kennell, J.H. (1976). *Parent-Infant Bonding.* St Louis, MI: Mosby.

Lapiere, R. (1934) 'Attitudes verses actions'. *Social Forces*, vol. 13, 230–237.

Luria, A.R. (1972) *The Man with a Shattered World. The History of a Brain Wound.* New York, NY: Basic Books.

Acknowledgement

The authors would like to acknowledge the support of the University of New South Wales, Sydney, Australia. Much of the editing process was completed (via e-mail) while Fiona Jones was in the post of Honorary Visiting Research Fellow in the Psychology Department there.

PART I

Working in Organizations and Society

Introduction

The role of the social care professional, of necessity, has adapted and evolved in response to the demands of both societal and organizational changes. The opening chapters draw on the work of occupational and social psychologists, who have studied aspects of organizations and society, and examine some issues of particular relevance to social workers and other social care professionals.

These professionals typically carry out their role within the context of large organizations such as social services departments or probation services. Frequently, they also need to liaise closely and have knowledge of the workings and procedures of other organizations such as the Department of Social Security, the National Health Service or police departments. Cooperation with these departments may be crucial to the professional functioning effectively and yet they may at times have conflicting aims and values which may make working with other professions one of the most demanding aspects of social work.

Chapter 1 focuses on the organizations themselves and introduces a range of different ways of thinking about the contexts in which professionals work. The second chapter focuses on the professionals themselves and looks at the much publicized concept of occupational stress and discusses research that has investigated stress in social workers (including the impact of violence). The chapter also introduces a range of interventions which have been suggested to reduce stress. Finally, Chapter 3 considers the wider context of social care professionals operating within a multi-cultural society, focusing particularly on transracial adoption and the specific role of the professional social worker.

Models of Organizations
An Introduction for Social Care Professionals
Karen Izod and Joanna Dodd

Introduction

Both while studying as students and when employed in professional practice, you will have to deal with large organizations. These will have a considerable impact upon what you are required to do and able to achieve; they will also have an effect on your sense of well-being and satisfaction. All of you will have experiences of organizations where you feel comfortable and those which produce discomfort, even when the jobs are similar.

Other chapters deal with particular aspects of motivation, stress and anxiety at work. The aim of this chapter is to encourage professionals working in social care to consider the organizational structures and processes that impact upon their work. For instance, social workers and probation officers operate as relatively autonomous professionals who are required to make judgements about the needs of individual clients within a complex legal, social and emotional context. One of the key individual support mechanisms developed through training and early practice is a code of professional ethics to help guide actions with clients. When working effectively, the organizational context is an important resource for support and authorisation of the decisions made. However, there are times when the organizational requirements of any role will conflict with individual beliefs about good professional practice, and challenge professional discretion and autonomy.

When discussing this process, a recently qualified social worker described the experience of building up her own 'mental guidebook' to help her work effectively. She spoke of the way in which the minutiae of organizational life, gained through observation, experience and direct learning had come to be represented as some kind of internalized guide to working within the organization. This 'guide book' included some awareness of the function of the whole organization within its community and the political dilemmas it faced, it covered the range of tasks to be performed, knowledge of relevant procedures and policies, who and how to ask for information and support, and it also reflected some awareness of what to expect from herself and how to interact with others.

To aid the development of new practitioners in their understanding of current and future organizational contexts, and to enhance the process of building such a guidebook, this chapter will offer some general insights into the models used by organizational psychologists. The models chosen from the many available are those considered relevant as background to the recent changes in the social service context. One of the assumptions, central to psychology, is that there are differences between people in their attitudes, skills, knowledge and in the way they take in and process ideas and information. One aim of psychology is to understand and explain these differences. Organizational psychology focuses upon the implications of these differences for behaviour at work; specifically, the differences between people in the way they 'construct' their ideas about their place of employment and the different contributions each individual makes to such organizations. The term construct is widely used within psychology to describe the idea that people act like 'scientists', gathering information from experience which they build into 'models' which then allow them to make predictions about future events (Kelly, 1995; Bannister and Fransella, 1986).

Although it is assumed that all people process experience in this way, the ideas or 'constructs' that are produced can differ widely, even if people appear to have the same experience. These differences between people in skill, knowledge and understanding of problems are a tremendous resource for organizations. For example, it is difficult to imagine one person trying to fulfil all the roles needed if, for example a child needs looking after away from home or an individual leaving prison after many years is to be settled into the external community. However, these essential differences can also be the source of disagreement, confusion and misunderstanding. All too often when such differences occur, an attempt is made to blame one person for the mistake, or to argue that one person's view of a situation was incorrect. This can lead to a process of scapegoating where, rather than solving the problem, the blame is located in just one person. In contrast to this, organizational psychology aims to locate such problems in the nature of relationships and systems and not in individuals.

Organizations as Conceptual Entities

To explore what we mean by suggesting that organizations exist as conceptual entities, we shall consider two sets of processes. The individual processes involved in making sense of social situations and the collective processes whereby such meaning and the consequent actions are regulated through 'culture'.

Human beings need to make sense of the situations they find themselves in, and in doing this they 'construct' mental models of situations to help them predict what responses are likely to be elicited by each of their actions. This also happens in employment organizations. However, we can never have direct experience of all parts of any organization so we have to use our imagination (generate hypotheses) together with our preconceptions and experiences to fill in any gaps. The picture we create serves as a framework for us in making decisions about how to operate at work. It is constructed out of interaction with the parts of an organization that we can have contact with; the people, the policies, the processes. Therefore when we talk about the characteristics of the organization we work for, we are describing an entity, created in our imagination out of our different expectations and experiences. All people employed by, or who have contact with, an organization are involved in the same process. This is as true for an organizational theorist as it is for a social care professional visiting her/his first client. To explore this idea try the exercise in Box 1.1.

Box 1.1 An Exercise in Understanding your Immediate Organization

The purpose of this exercise is to explore how an 'organization' is built from the constructs each individual creates. If we are to use this awareness to identify and solve problems at work we need to explore the understanding that each separate individual has generated. To do this, we have to accept that all interpretations of a situation are valid. Frequently, when there are problems in the workplace, it is blamed on one particular person, or one particular task. However, difficult situations in the workplace are usually much more complicated than this with many different factors playing a part.

The psychologist's first activity when working as a consultant to an organization with a problem is to try to understand from all differing perspectives how each individual constructs and explains a problem. It is worth attempting a similar exercise yourself by acting as a 'consultant' attempting to understand how you 'construct' ideas at work or home. Start by thinking about one situation you found difficult to deal with last week and explore the factors that were involved both in making it a problem and in resolving the problem. For example, it could be a difficulty in understanding a new procedure or dealing with a 'difficult' client or a conflict with a classmate or family member.

Do this by taking the following steps:

1. Describe the situation and how it developed.
2. State what you expected to happen at each key point, whether or not your expectations were met and how having your expectation met, or not met, influenced how the situation then developed.
3. Use this information to try and describe the hypotheses/assumptions that you were using and how these made you expect certain things and not others. For example, if it was a new procedure, did you expect it to be easy or difficult or if it was a 'difficult' client, did you expect to be supported by your colleagues?
4. Identify how many other people were involved in this situation. Examples of the types of relationships to think about are those you have with the people involved in your work; your clients, your boss, your immediate colleagues and members of other departments, your parents, your spouse, your children.
5. If you wish to take this thinking a little further, begin to consider what other 'constructs' are used. Take each of the individuals you have identified in (4) above and try to describe the 'constructs' about this problem each individual may have used.

(See also Morgan, 1986, in the Further Reading section at the end of this chapter.)

This means that for any one given place of employment, no two people will necessarily have created the same 'conceptual entity'. Morgan (1986) has discussed the different metaphors that people can use in interpreting events within organizations. He suggests that we are all involved in 'reading' the organizational situations we find ourselves in, but that some people are more skilled than others. He suggests that this skill is increased with the variety of models we are able to use in interpreting situations. Mangham (1987) extends this idea by arguing that it is not just the skill at reading situations which determines our effectiveness. He suggests that our ability to improvize our behaviour in the light of the context we have created is also of importance.

However, this is not to suggest that such models are constructed in a complete vacuum. There are various pressures that are experienced in the process of building these constructs:

'as individuals come into contact with organizations, they come into contact with dress norms, stories people tell about what goes on, the organization's formal rules and procedures, its informal codes of behaviour, rituals, tasks, pay systems, jargon, and jokes only understood by insiders, and so on. These elements are some of the manifestations of organizational culture. When cultural members interpret the meaning of these manifestations, their perceptions, memories, beliefs, experiences and values will vary, so interpretations will differ – even of the same phenomena. The patterns or configurations of these interpretations, and the ways they are enacted, constitute culture.' (Martin, 1992)

Martin suggests that this experience of 'culture' is a way in which these individual pictures of organizations can be regulated. However, this does not suggest an experience of uniformity. In any organization there will be interplay between the individual and 'culture', and there can be more than one set of cultural patterns. It is a mistake to assume that any one company or organization operates with a single homogeneous culture, instead it is more helpful to think of a range of sub-cultures. In large corporations such different cultures are found between departments or functions. Within the social services the existence of many disparate services that need to work closely together accentuates this experience. To illustrate this, consider the jokes and criticisms that abound between the different professions that contribute to social services when, for example, a probation officer's way of approaching a problem contrasts sharply with the police's assumptions.

There are various practices within the organization that act to maintain stability in a culture by giving the employees similar experiences. Many of the human resource practices within an organization such as selection procedures, performance evaluation, pay systems, development practices and promotion criteria can reinforce its culture. For example, in the social services, training and code of professional ethics are good examples of significant regulatory, and self-regulatory features.

In times of stasis new staff will develop their individual mental images or constructs in the context of the prevailing 'culture' of the organization. However, in recent years the prevalence of change within work environments has been one of the significant phenomena identified both within research in organizational psychology and by people at work (Hollway, 1991). The significance of change experiences has also been identified within social services (Statham, 1996). These studies suggest that individual pictures of organization will change in response to the changing context but that cultural patterns are much harder to change. There have been many studies of the possibility of changing culture over the last 20 years as many organizations, including social service departments, have come to realize that in order to survive they need to be able to respond to rapid and dramatic changes in the environment. Peters and Waterman (1982) claim that culture cannot be changed. Bibeault (1982) argues that culture change can only be achieved by making significant changes in personnel. Others, such as Williams et al. (1989), argue that culture change is possible and desirable in many circumstances, but accept that it will be resisted because the prevailing patterns provides the security necessary to function effectively at work.

The Context of Change for Social Services

Social care professionals in the public, voluntary or private sectors are working in organizations which are constantly adjusting to resource constraints and political demands. The fundamental components in the provision of social services, those of context, purpose, task and working relationships, are all subject to debate. Assumptions cannot be made about who will offer services such as supervising offenders in the community or domicillary care. Yet these services were, until recently, only conceivably offered through public organizations. There are various factors driving these changes; legal changes, political demands, financial and other resource constraints and widespread organizational restructuring.

Statham (1996) outlines how changes to legislation such as the Children Act (1989) and the National Health Service and Community Care Act (1990) and the related policy guidance, have led to the most fundamental changes in the arrangements for personal and social care since unified social services departments were created 25 years ago. Similar impact is envisaged within the Probation Service with proposed legislative changes to the Criminal Justice Act and Family Law Bill (Home Office White Paper, 1996).

These legislative changes have occurred within a framework of Local Government reorganization and consequent restructuring of the workplace for many social services departments. Local authorities have been seeking innovative solutions in an attempt to deliver adequate levels of service provision with increasingly limited resources. This has been reflected in the attempts we have observed at reorganizing internal structures, trying out new job designs and changing working relationships both within and between agencies. This has also contributed to a re-evaluation of the skills and knowledge which professionals require to include such features as understanding and managing change and innovation (Statham, 1996).

In addition, relationships with central government are characterized by demands for greater accountability through increased monitoring and control. These demands require a heavy investment in resources. However, there are also parallel demands for improved service outcomes in the context of reduced resources despite the requirement for greater level of monitoring and control. Providing more for less has become a dilemma encountered throughout social services departments.

The uncertainty associated with these continuing changes and the dilemmas faced by professional staff feeling unable to deliver the quality of service their ethics demand of them has inevitable negative consequences. The absence of control over significant decisions at work coupled with the increasingly constrained resource base are important contributors to health problems associated with work (Jones and Fletcher, 1996). In addition, Chapter 2 by Jones and Fletcher provides an assessment of the causes and consequences of stress for social services employees. The case illustration in Box 1.2 highlights some typical consequences of resource constraints and changing service and skill demands on the experience of work.

Box 1.2 A Case Study on the Impact of Change on Job Control and Service Provision

Staff working in a large resource centre for adults with moderate learning difficulties had recently been required, due to local resource constraints, to extend their user group to include adults being rehabilitated in the community, some of whom presented much more challenging behaviour, and were seen as having 'special needs'.

Conflict began to emerge between the managers and the staff about the use of care plans, and particularly about how to deal with some of the adults with 'special needs' who would wander around the building and disrupt the work going on in other groups, i.e. the kitchen, the workshop. These concerns escalated to open rows, and staff absence rates began to increase. The general feeling in the staff group was that of not having any control over their work, distancing themselves from the user group, and not caring about what happened. In meetings with the whole staff group and in separate meetings with the individual units, the following picture emerged:

The original purpose of the unit was to train adults to be able to take up sheltered or open employment. This implied a throughput of clients, with the expectation that they would come to the unit for up to two years, and then be successfully placed in employment. The sense of achievement for staff came through their work in making possible a significant change in the lives of their clients. They believed that their role was to simulate a working environment, to aid this change.

The new group required high levels of containment and care. In addition, the members of this group were less able to respond to the occupational, recreational and training provision which was central to the original purpose of the resource centre. The introduction of a new client group, without full consultation or apparent understanding of the work of the unit led to a confusion about the work expectations and a sense of lack of recognition for the work done. This generated a sense of being 'dumped' with adults who did not really fit in, and who needed skills beyond those that the unit could provide. Experiences of failing in the work were common.

Through the process of clarifying the staff experiences and their concerns, the managers were able to seek authority from their senior managers to redefine the purpose of the unit.

Discussion points

- ° Discuss the following with reference to the case study in Box 1.2:
- ° What does this case indicate about the impact of organizational change upon
    - (a) the experiences of staff
    - (b) the extent to which client needs are met?
- ° What steps do you think could have been taken to prevent this situation arising?
- ° Consider Chapter 2 by Jones and Fletcher and discuss what further insights this material gives to this case illustration.

This introduction suggests that organizations are conceptual entities which are built by individuals through experience. It also indicates that this experience will be dominated by constant pressures for change due to environmental pressures. This experience of change will make greater demands on new staff for understanding their working context and finding 'constructs' which are helpful in managing the expectations of the professional role. The remainder of this chapter will illustrate different ways in which organizations have been examined theoretically, and link these different models or approaches with the increasing experience of change within the social services context.

Using Theoretical Approaches to Organization to Explore these Changes

Rather than viewing the models contained within organizational psychology as definitive, it is more helpful to consider them as 'tools to think with' – as technologies (Hollway, 1991). The approaches outlined within this chapter are chosen to illustrate both the range available and to give an insight into the models that may be in use within your workplace. As the following descriptions indicate, the variations between models can contribute to widely different views about what is appropriate and acceptable in intervening at work. These different views will give rise to misunderstanding and disagreement about appropriate responses and actions. To demonstrate these differences, four different approaches to understanding organizations are now described in the following sections. Each of these 'models' makes a contribution to understanding the issues raised by the change process which has just been discussed.

We begin with a model that dominated social services thinking in the 1960s and 1970s. *Open systems theory* was used to address the professional– client relationship and how this could best be supported. At this time this account was useful in that it could provide a way of focusing upon the work needed to make a difference for clients. The situation changed in the 1980s with two significant requirements emerging: reorganization and greater managerial control. The pressure for reorganization was motivated by a belief that there could be a better arrangement of the components necessary for service delivery; an improved structure. As background to understanding this pressure a model of *functional structures* is presented. The increased demand for accountability and control meant that greater emphasis has been given to models of *bureaucracy*. Such an approach emphasizes the need for systems to monitor and control the work of those providing services. Both of these models divert the focus away from the relationship with clients, to those internal to the organization and to resource providers. This shift within social services had implications for those involved in service delivery, as it led to a displacement of the needs of the client and a reduction in professional autonomy, thereby producing conflicts with existing expectations. To explore this, the final approach outlined is the literature which examines the *political processes at work* within organizations.

Although the four approaches have been selected for their capacity to illustrate conceptually the changes to social services provision described above, they all offer ways of thinking that can be applied to any organizational situation. At the end of the descriptions, one case study is given that can be analyzed using the different models. This comparative exercise will provide an insight into the relative strengths and weaknesses of these models/approaches as 'tools to think with'.

Organizations as open systems

The concept of organizations functioning as open systems originated with the work of the Tavistock Institute during the 1950s, and was developed by its members through their action research programmes. Understanding the biological and ecological processes which enabled living organisms to sustain themselves, and survive, and applying these ideas to human systems and organizations, is central to open systems theory. Integral to this 'organic' model is the belief that organizations 'exist, and can only exist' (Miller and Rice, 1967) through transactions with their environment, across a boundary, or boundary region. Since the primary function of social services departments requires provision of services to individuals in the community (i.e. outside of the organization), much of the activity of the organization lies in attending to and maintaining the boundary region, and managing the emotional experiences of working at these margins. In an environment which is supportive and provides resources, it is possible to operate on these margins based upon an assumption of shared purpose. The emphasis on flow, openness and transformation in this model allows full recognition and containment of professional autonomy in engaging with clients, within an organizational context.

There are various factors that can be identified as central to this model:

1. Organizations exist in an *environment* and must be selectively open to that environment to survive. Social services are funded by that environment and receive their clients from other parts of that environment so are required to account for their actions externally to different groups.

2. Processes of *assimilation* (taking in) and *accommodation* (internal adjustments to use that which has been assimilated) need to be in place to ensure productive intake from the environment. Assimilation involves ensuring that key groups from the environment, described above, understand the nature of the work of the agency to ensure intake, both of funds and clients, continues. Accommodation requires a set of internal processes to ensure that the response to the intake is appropriate. These will both be systems to devolve funding and to individualize the service offered to each client.

3. Processes of *transformation* need to be in place to ensure that the output from the organization is appropriate. The particular focus of such processes within social services is the provision of services to clients which allow some material change to take place. In addition, this may involve staff development activities to guarantee continuing relevance.

4. Any organization comprises different *components* (organs) which have distinct *functions* and hence distinct *structures*. Within the social services this is reflected both within agencies and their regional deployment and between the different agencies in social service settings.

5. These different functional structures need *regulation* to operate coherently together, which produces a tension between differentiation and integration. In the social services setting, pressures for regulation are diverse due to the existence of two key interest groups (funders and clients). Regulation exists in legal requirements, in managerial practices, in case conferences and in the day-to-day exchanges between members of staff.

6. This integration usually requires a set of organizational *sub-systems*. This can include all the systems of recording, of recruiting, of supervision and case conferences and of budgeting.

In-service organizations where one of the key forms of intake is people in need of help, there has been clear identification of the experiences of anxiety for staff in engaging with the needs of their clients and the potentially risky consequences of professional decisions (Menzies Lyth, 1960). Therefore, one of the key areas of investment within such service provision was the establishment of regulatory processes, such as a formal system of supervision, case conferences and documentation, that could contain this anxiety for professionals and allow the work with clients to continue. The following discussion point encourages you to think through the key aspects of the model as it applies to your experience.

Discussion points

- To explore the way this model encourages you to think about organizations, consider a recent client who left your service (or if you are currently studying and have no immediate practice to draw upon, think about a course you have recently finished). Take each of the underlined concepts from open systems theory in turn and discuss the system that your client (or you) went through (e.g. where in the environment did they (or you) come from, how were they (or you) assimilated, what different components of the organization did they (or you) need to interact with?).
- Produce a diagram or flow chart to document the process that emerges.

The work by French and Bell (1995), recommended in the 'Further Reading' section at the end of this chapter will also help in this discussion exercise.

Organizations as functional structures

In an increasingly demanding environment with pressure on resources, the implicit models imposed upon an organization also change. The requirement for local authorities to begin restructuring meant that it was necessary to change the thinking about organizations to emphasize the manifest structures. The following model provides a key analysis from organizational psychology about the various structures of organizations. Mintzberg (1983) divides organizations into different sections and identifies different functions which need to be co-ordinated together. He wished to relate the structure of these different parts to the function each fulfils. He also wanted this classification to apply to all organizations. This is a difficult task as there are so many different types of organizations. For example, a private tennis club, a local authority and a multinational corporation are all organizations, but they have widely different structures. This model does have areas of overlap with the last as he also produces a method of classifying the ways in which collective human activity can be co-ordinated in terms of the mechanisms of communication. His model describes five basic parts to an organization, five co-ordination devices and five types of organization.

The five basic parts involve three geared to the delivery of goods and services (1–3 below) and two which provide support to the central core (4–5).

1. The *strategic apex* is where decisions are taken and communicated about the direction of the organization and where resources are allocated accordingly. This part is frequently described as the 'top' of an organization, e.g. the director of social services and advisory board.

2. The *middle line* has the responsibility of ensuring that the decisions made by the strategic apex are executed. This part comprises day-to-day management. For example, in a probation office this would include those who manage budgets for service provision or those who are responsible for ensuring that all the necessary resources and monitoring processes for case management are available.

3. The *operating core* is that part of the organization which actually undertakes the day-to-day work of ensuring that the goods or services offered are delivered. In social services, this comprises those professionals and volunteers who take responsibility for the direct intervention with clients. It is through these people that the purpose of the organization is realized.

4. The *support structure* consists of those functions which provide the 'housekeeping' services such as building maintenance, cleaning, laundry and management of accounts. One important example from social services are those departments responsible for the maintenance of client records.

5. The *technostructure* comprises those professionals or technical specialists with knowledge relevant to the delivery of specialist services. In social services, the access to legal advice and support in managing that complex part of the context of their work is key.

Mintzberg (1983) suggests that different organizations have different arrangements of these parts. He describes these as different types of organization, and suggests that these exist because of the relative importance of different functions in differing endeavours. Each of the five structures he identified are given below.

1. *Simple structures* describes those organizations which have predominantly a strategic apex and operating core. An example in social services would be a voluntary organization which has a central office and many small local projects run by volunteers.

2. A *professional bureaucracy* is mainly comprised of an operating core of self-managing professional staff with a small strategic apex and some support structure. Techno-structure may well be bought in on a consultancy basis when necessary. Many legal practices are run along these lines.

3. A *machine bureaucracy* has a balanced contribution from all the parts described above. The local authority is an example of this type of organization.

4. A *divisionalized form* is predominantly middle line and operating core with all the other parts retained in a separate 'parent' organization. The organization of the prison service could approximate to this.

5. The term *adhocracy* describes those organizations where the operating core is separated from other parts of the organization as rapid response to changing conditions is necessary. The emergence of reactive multi-disciplinary teams to address the specific needs of a client group is an example of this.

The co-ordination of all the different parts into a coherent whole is extremely complex. To help understand this, Mintzberg has produced a classification which identifies five co-ordination devices: two (1–2) involve interpersonal interaction, and three involve employing standards (3–5):

1. *Mutual adjustment* is the approach we all use in our day-to-day lives, for example chatting with others to exchange relevant information and modifying our actions and intentions accordingly.

2. *Direct supervision* involves a similar activity, but is undertaken more formally, usually with a manager ensuring that information is passed (e.g. in the form of briefing sessions), and that the consequent actions are monitored; or in the form of a senior professional providing guidance and support to a junior colleague in a formalized arrangement.

3. *Standardizing the input* involves establishing a base line of training and educational requirements. Professional training in social care, examinations and registration are good examples of this, as it helps ensure that new personnel have the requisite skills and knowledge.

4. *Standardizing the process* tends to be applied to co-ordinating more simple work by deploying sets of rules designed to standardize the way in which tasks are performed; or by providing a process of accountability to ensure that complex decisions are properly monitored. An example of this would be the conference procedures established for sectioning a client under the Mental Health Act coupled with the routine process of documenting the decision.

5. *Standardizing the output* concentrates upon prescribing an acceptable quality of service or goods and then monitoring to ensure that this is achieved.

The following discussion point will help you to think through this model and relate it to personal experience.

Discussion points

° The following exercise will help you in thinking through organizations as functional structures (the reference by Payne (1996) in the 'Further Reading' section may also be useful).

° Think of one organization you have had recent experience of. Try to identify the different parts you are aware of and apply the classification described in Mintzberg's model.

° Using the information you have generated, try to draw a picture of the organization. Decide which type of organization you would classify this as and give your reasons. Then discuss the co-ordination mechanisms you have experienced.

° Are there any gaps? Would additional forms of co-ordination help? Are some forms of co-ordination over-emphasized?

° After doing this exercise, look at the ideas generated from the previous discussion point and consider how the information provided from Mintzberg's model may add to or change the observations you made using open systems theory.

Bureaucratic control in organizations

The provision of social care usually takes place in settings where the principal organising mode is bureaucratic. Order is created and maintained in a hierarchy through use of the written word. Bureaucracy has its origins in the mechanisation of industry. It has come to be associated with the classical management theorists who suggest that greater efficiency in the use of resources is possible if 'labour', in this case service delivery, is separated from managerial work, which exists to delegate and control the work. The key features of bureaucratic organization are:

1. The existence of hierarchy.

2. The authority of those in senior positions is exercised as a chain of command through top-down communication channels.

3. Power and control is centralized with a small executive group.

4. With increasing size, there is an increased division of labour, both between different departments and between the 'top' and 'bottom' of the organization.

5. Mechanisms of monitoring and control exist to ensure that the work of those in subordinate positions meet the objectives set by those in senior positions within the organization.

In implementing this model, the principles of scientific management were developed and extended to ensure bureaucratic control was possible (see Hollway, 1991 for an analysis). These principles were based upon the notion that any task an individual may be required to do could be reduced to a set of prescribable actions. Various problems have been identified with bureaucracies. The general problems (from McKenna, 1994) are:

1. Goal displacement: over time the job and the rules and regulations governing the 'job' appear to become more important than the work that needs to be done.

2. Conflict: employees appear less content with the organizational role allocated than the model suggests.

3. Informal organization: the model does not recognize the role of informal work groups or processes.

4. Division of labour: this may be out of step with recent developments in technology.

5. Impersonality: the adherence to rules and the rigidity that follows leads to the experience of frustration and lack of control.

6. Adaptation: the rigidity described above may contribute to a lack of responsiveness to the external environment.

The location of social care within a bureaucratic context has always generated tension and debate about the dangers of deskilling professionals. Deskilling refers to the way in which professional or craft autonomy is broken down through bureaucratic control mechanisms. These are features such as the need to complete detailed forms, e.g. when placing a child with foster parents, which appear unrelated to the work at hand. Braverman (1974) has suggested that the experience of deskilling is a common feature of bureaucracy. There are three tenets to Braverman's argument. The first is that 'the dissociation of the labour process from the skills of the workers' means that the process of work is separated from any skill, craft or professional knowledge base. A consequence is that the managerial knowledge base becomes more significant within the organization. The second is that 'the separation of conception from execution' means that those doing the work have no control over the intent and so are separated from gaining knowledge about the work to be done. Finally, he argues that 'the use of this monopoly over knowledge to control each step of the labour process and its execution' means that those delivering, in this case the services required, are subject to explicit and detailed instructions about how to conduct their work. This effectively separates them from any control over the decisions that need to be made.

A wish to redress this imbalance of control is emerging in some local authorities and probation services, embodied in the notion of the 'competent work place' in which emphasis and value is placed upon professional practice arising from a sound body of research, knowledge and professional ethics. However, as stated earlier, there has been increased pressure upon social service departments to comply with increasing numbers of bureaucratic control systems. These are designed to meet the growing notion of public accountability which desires the control of professional staff. While it is frequently important for staff to have the protection of such accountability mechanisms in place, it can also lead to a frustration with 'red tape' and lack of freedom. Use the following discussion point to think through the implications of this model of bureaucratic control for day-to-day work.

Discussion points

- ° Start by drawing a hierarchical chart for an organization you have had recent experience of, indicating the different layers as you see them. Consider these different layers and attempt to outline the managerial relationships that are in place. Discuss the different monitoring and control mechanisms that exist within this managerial relationships.

- ° Can you identify which of these mechanisms are supportive of the work of those in subordinate positions? Can you identify those which deskill people? Can you identify any variations between different managers in the way they use these control mechanisms? What recommendations might you make to this organization to overcome the problems associated with bureaucracy? (The reference by Hollway, 1991, in the 'Further Reading' section may help you in this exercise.)

Political processes within organizations

This heading refers to a collection of work that has investigated the ways in which different individuals and groups seek to have influence within the workplace. In this context, the notion of 'political processes' refers to those activities which are *not* required by a role, but which are undertaken to have an impact upon the outcome. This outcome may be individual gain or organizational change. Given the recent changes to the social services context, the decreasing autonomy of the professional role and the uncertainty within the agencies and organizations about resources and viability, an increased use of political processes would be likely. The following account outlines the sources of and nature of such processes.

For the social service professions political processes are played out at several different levels. This tendency is compounded by the pressures for change outlined earlier. There are *macro-political processes* focused upon the consequences of professional judgement upon public perception, and there are the *micro-political processes* at place within organizations as individuals attempt to work within increasingly uncertain and under-resourced environments.

Macro-political concerns are expressed in the following illustrative questions: What level of risk of re-offending is acceptable within a community? Who can have respite care and who can't? Who is responsible for safeguarding a child? These questions are the everyday questions facing professionals in their encounters with members of the public. They belong to the professional world, in the sense that theoretical knowledge, learning from experience, and evidence-based practice can provide a framework for decision making. They also belong to communities who concern themselves with these issues, who wish to be heard and influence the policies and practices of public agencies, and who enter into the political domain either as individuals, or through representative groups.

The public nature of the work requires that all social service professionals have an awareness of the potential ways in which their actions can be interpreted by those external to their profession. An awareness of these macro-political issues leads to internal negotiations around the action that will be tolerated and can be explained as reasonable to a potentially adverse public. In consultancy discussions with experienced social workers this has been described as 'The Sun factor', i.e. If I do this and it all goes dreadfully wrong – what will *The Sun* headlines make of this. Managing these external pressures is made more complex when the work is conducted within an organizational setting characterized by conflict and uncertainty, and where blame is easily apportioned.

These externally generated political dilemmas contribute to a greater emphasis upon the need to understand and work with the organizational micro-political processes (the attempts to influence policy or practice within the workplace). Political behaviour has been defined as that which is not required by an individual's role and is undertaken to have influence or control over a significant part of organizational practice. Miles (1980) has identified four organizational features, all of which are prevalent in the current social services climate which contribute to an increase in political behaviour in the workplace. These are:

- ambiguous goals
- scarce resources
- changes to the technology or processes used within the organization
- blurred decision-situations leading to unclear outcomes.

Robbins (1991) suggests also that low trust and role ambiguity will contribute to an increase in political behaviour. The types of political behaviour or tactics that emerge in organizations are described comprehensively elsewhere (McKenna, 1994). However, a summary is useful in this context. Pfeffer (1992) identifies the following; controlling information, controlling lines of communication, using outside experts, controlling the agenda, game playing, image building, building coalitions, controlling what counts in making a decision. Different people in different positions have more or less access to means to use these mechanisms. For example, managers may be more able to gain access to outside expertise as they may have access to the necessary financial resources, whereas a social worker will have greater hands-on information that can be shared or withheld.

To begin thinking about your experience of political processes attempt the questions in the discussion point below.

Discussion points

- Think about an organization you have had recent experience of and identify an issue that was uncertain. List the different people concerned with the situation and identify what outcome they desired. Identify the tactics that each used in an attempt to influence the outcome.

- Which were successful and which were not? Were there differences between people based upon the position they held? Did you take any action in this situation that could be described as political? What factors made you think that this was an appropriate or necessary course of action? (The reference by McKenna, 1994, in the 'Further Reading' section may be helpful here.)

Box 1.3 Models of Organization Applied to a Change
in a Voluntary Organization

A brief account of a changing organizational situation is given below. Read this and consider how each of the models, introduced above, can help understand the situation. Use the questions below as the basis for this consideration.

A Regional Voluntary Agency operates a network of 'neighbourhood family centres', each providing a range of services, including a 'drop-in' facility and creche, an information and counselling service, parenting education groups, and an outreach service to local schools, providing discussion groups on personal relationships for adolescents.

Each family centre is staffed by two part-time clerical/receptionists, six practitioners; two working per service, with the exception of the 'drop-in' facility which is undertaken on a rota basis. Three practitioners hold 'senior practitioner' status, three are basic grade, and the unit is supported by a number of volunteers, mostly users of the centre, who had undergone some training.

The family centre is managed by the Centre Manager, who is also responsible for managing two other centres in the region, and she is accountable to an assistant Regional Manager based at head office. In the Centre Manager's increasing absence, which is due to the geographical breadth of her role, the three senior practitioners share responsibility for day-to-day management issues, again on a rota basis.

This creates some unease amongst the volunteers and receptionists, who tend to relate to the senior they have most contact with and in whom they have most confidence.

In a context of nil growth in funding, the Centre Manager decided that the family centre should develop its education services, and extend them to other settings where fees could be attracted. To do this, the 'drop-in' facility would be much reduced in the hours it was available, and the receptionists additionally would provide initial screening of callers. If the caller wanted information rather than advice, they would be dealt with only by the receptionist. The rationale was to cut back on the amount of time the social workers had to make themselves available, sometimes when there were very few callers.

Integrating Models

The four theoretical approaches to organization were introduced to help identify the variety of approaches/models of relevance in explaining the recent changes within social services. However, these models also provide distinct insights into problems at work, and in a single situation can frequently be more helpful when used together. The case study given in Box 1.3 and the subsequent discussion points are designed to encourage you to think about these models comparatively. Think through this case and consider what aspects of the various models are helpful. You can then apply the same process to important situations as they emerge at work. This should help you to become more proficient in understanding the organizational pressures that influence all experiences of work.

Discussion points

- ° With reference to the case study in Box 1.3 discuss the following questions:

Open Systems theory

- ° How are the clients taken into this organization and treated?
- ° What sub-systems can you identify in place?
- ° How will the Centre Manager's decision change the system?

Functional structures

- ° What type of organization is this and what parts does it comprise?
- ° What co-ordinating mechanisms are in place and which are successful?
- ° What other mechanisms would help?

Bureaucracy

- ° How would you draw a hierarchical chart for this organisation?
- ° How is work broken down and controlled?
- ° Is there any evidence of deskilling?

Political

- ° What are the factors in this contributing to political behaviour?
- ° What tactics would you imagine the different groups using to influence the outcome?

Summary: Models of Organization in Social Services

This chapter has introduced the importance of the organizational context upon workers in social service environments. It suggested that an understanding of organizations is best obtained by viewing them as conceptual entities. The recent drivers of change within social service environments were described, together with an indication of their impact for individuals at work. To explore the changing conceptualizations of organization associated with this changing context, four theoretical approaches to organizations were described; open systems theory, organizations as functional structures, a general account of bureaucratic control, and the literature which has explored the political processes within organizations.

Case studies were provided for students to explore each model and then compare the relative value of each as a model to think with.

Seminar Questions

1. What mental image or construct might your client have about your own agency? What will have influenced their perceptions, and if they are voluntary clients, why did they choose your agency rather than another? What might this indicate about the kind of service they are seeking?

2. Discuss the nature of regulation in your professional work. Discuss whether these processes would best be described by open systems theory, Mintzberg's theory, bureaucratic models or the notion of political processes. What aspects of regulation do you find helpful and why? What aspects of regulation do you find counter-productive and why?

3. Discuss how clients enter a social service environment and the structures and processes needed to ensure they receive the most appropriate treatment. In what ways could (a) the systems in place, or (b) the functional structure, or (c) the bureaucratic controls, or (d) the political process, contribute to a client being mistreated?

4. Discuss your own experiences of working in an uncertain environment. What tactics did you develop to make sense of the situation? What was effective and what was not? How might you apply this understanding when working (a) with clients, and (b) with colleagues?

Further Reading

French, W.L. and Bell, C.H. (1990) *Organizational Development: Behavioural Science Interventions for Organizational Improvements (4th ed.)*. Englewood Cliffs: NJ: Prentice Hall.
These authors provide greater detail for understanding systems theory concepts in Chapter 5, and demonstrate how these are applied in organizational developments within Chapter 9.

Hollway, W. (1991) *Work Psychology and Organizational Behaviour: Managing the individual at work*. London: Sage.
This book provides an analytical account of the development and use of scientific management in Chapter 2 and describes the replacement of this approach with a more human centred approach in Chapter 4.

Jones, F. and Fletcher, B.(C). (1996) 'Job control and health.' In M.J. Schabracq, J.A. Winnubst and C.L. Cooper (eds) *Handbook of Work and Health Psychology*. Chichester: Wiley.
This chapter gives further theoretical insight into the impact of reduced autonomy on well-being.

McKenna, E. (1994) *Business Psychology and Organizational Behaviour*. Hove, UK: LEA.
Chapter 9 provides a comprehensive account of the related issues of power, politics and conflict within organizations.

Morgan, G. (1986) *Images of Organization*. California: Sage.
Chapter 10 describes a case study which illustrates the differences between individuals in the way they make sense of organizational situations.

Payne, R. (1996) 'Models of organizations.' In P. Warr (ed.) *The Psychology of Work*. London: Penguin.
This gives an accessible account of Mintzberg's work.

References

Bannister, D. and Fransella, F. (1986) *Inquiring Man (3rd Edition)*. London: Croom Helm.

Bibeault, D.B. (1982) 'Corporate turn-around: How managers turn losers into winners.' In J.D. Edwards and S. Kleiner (eds) *Transforming Organisational Values and Culture Effectively. Leadership and Organisational Development Journal, 9,* 1.

Braverman, H. (1974) *Labour's Monopoly Capital. The Degradation of Work in the Twentieth Century.* New York: Monthly Review Press.

French, W.L. and Bell, C.H. (1995) *Organization Development: Behavioural Science Interventions for Organizational Improvements (4th Edition)*. Englewood Cliffs, NJ: Prentice Hall.

Hollway, W. (1991) *Work Psychology and Organizational Behaviour: Managing the Individual at Work.* London: Sage.

Home Office (1996) *White Paper: Protecting the Public. The Government's Strategy on Crime in England and Wales.* CMND 3190. London: HMSO.

Huxley, P. (1993) 'Case management and care management in community care.' *British Journal of Social Work, 23.*

Jones, F. and Fletcher, B.(C). (1996) 'Job control and health.' In M.J. Schabracq, J.A. Winnubst and C.L. Cooper (Eds) *Handbook of Work and Health Psychology.* Chichester: John Wiley.

Kelly, G.A. (1955) *The Psychology of Personal Constructs.* New York: Norton.

McKenna, E. (1994) *Business Psychology and Organizational Behaviour.* Hove, UK: LEA.

Mangham, I.L. (1987) *Organization Analysis and Development: A Social Construction of Organizational Behaviour.* Chichester: John Wiley.

Martin, J. (1992) *Cultures in Organizations: Three Perspectives.* New York and Oxford: Oxford University Press.

Menzies Lyth, I.E.P. (1990) 'Social systems as a defense against anxiety: an empirical study of the nursing service of a general hospital.' In E. Trist and H. Murray (eds) *The Social Engagement of Social Science Vol.1. The Socio-Psychological Perspective.* London: Free Association Books.

Miles, R.H. (1980) *Macro Organizational Behaviour.* Glenview: Scott Foresman.

Miller, E.J. and Rice, A.K. (1967) *Systems of Organization: The Control of Task and Sentient Boundaries.* London: Tavistock.

Mintzberg, H. (1983) *Structure in Fives.* Englewood Cliffs, NJ: Prentice Hall.

Morgan, G. (1986) *Images of Organisation.* Beverly Hills, CA: Sage.

Peters, T.J. and Waterman, R.H. (1982) *In Search of Excellence.* New York: Harper and Row.

Pfeffer, J. (1992) *Managing with Power.* Boston: Harvard Business School.

Robbins, S.P. (1991) *Organizational Behaviour: Concepts, Controversies, Applications.* New York, NY: Prentice Hall.

Statham, D. (1996) *The Future of Social and Personal Care: The Role of Social Services Organisations in the Public, Private and Voluntary Sectors.* National Institute for Social Work.

Williams, A., Dobson, P. and Walters, M. (1989) *Changing Culture.* London: IPM.

Acknowledgements

The authors wish to thank Anna Coss, Professional Officer (Director and Members), and staff members of Surrey County Council Social Services Department, and Michael Varah, Chief Probation Officer, Surrey Probation Service, for their valuable information.

Confidentiality

Case studies have been selected to represent typical situations of change in social care, and are drawn from the composite knowledge of the authors.

CHAPTER 2

Occupational Stress

Fiona Jones and Ben (C.) Fletcher

Introduction

Occupational 'stress' has received a great deal of media coverage and is widely considered to be a growing problem in the 1990s. It is thought to be endemic to many areas of work, but nowhere more so than to the caring professions. A growing body of research has amassed evidence about stress in a range of health and social service occupations in Britain and abroad. Occupational psychologists have frequently been involved in this kind of research with a view to identifying the major work stressors, that is external, relatively permanent features of the work environment or the work itself (e.g. the extent to which a job provides an individual with autonomy). This has led to the development of models suggesting a wide variety of job characteristics that are potentially stressful. This emphasis is perhaps artificial, since it is well known that situations which one individual will take in their stride may place an intense strain on another. Individual differences in personality or coping abilities, for example, are clearly important. Nevertheless, it is possible to identify those features of the work environment which are likely to be a source of strain for many workers. This approach to occupational stress has far-reaching implications in terms of changing the way work is designed, rather than merely treating stress in the individual.

This chapter will discuss what is meant by 'stress', and examine some key approaches to its study. This will include organizational models of stress as well as approaches which emphasize individual differences in stress proneness. It will discuss one particular outcome of stress, 'burnout', to which professionals in human service occupations are considered to be particularly vulnerable. This phenomenon has been the subject of a great deal of research in the USA. The chapter will review the research findings in the UK on stress in the social care professions, and look at what can and should be done to alleviate stress for these practitioners.

Stress

'Stress' is a much misused term: it has been variously treated as synonymous with such concepts as 'strains', 'demands', 'stressors' and 'pressures'. In the popular press, and often in the academic literature too, the term is used to cover a wide range of issues ranging from trivial to serious (see Box 2.1). The confusion about the meaning of the term even extends to uncertainty over such basic issues as whether a certain amount of stress is 'a good thing' (the answer is likely to be different if stress means 'pressure' rather than if it means 'strain'). Some researchers have

---

Box 2.1 Popular Conceptualizations of Stress

A rapid review of magazine articles, advertisements, radio and television programmes gives a picture of how we have come to see stress, its causes, its dire consequences and ways in which we might alleviate it.

Causes of stress
Almost any aspect of life, e.g. work, lack of work, summer holidays, Christmas.

Consequences of stress
These are many and often serious. The following quote from the women's magazine *Marie Claire* (October, 1994) summarizes possible outcomes.

> 'nailbiting, irritability, tiredness, loss of libido, withdrawal from friends and family, and food cravings. Then to more serious symptoms of burnout: anxiety and depression, panic attacks, exhaustion, high blood pressure, skin complaints, insomnia, sexual dysfunction, migraine, bowel problems and menstrual disorder. It may eventually lead to potentially fatal conditions, like heart disease.'

Ways we might alleviate stress
Just as we are told there are a wide range of causes and consequences of stress, there is also a diverse range of remedies on offer. These include methods which may change our approach to life, those aiming at improving general health and fitness and those leading to short-term relaxation. They include suggestions which seem sensible and some which may seem bizarre. Recommendations include psychotherapy, homeopathy, acupuncture, physical exercise, the use of stress-relieving cookery recipes, cutting down on tea or coffee, ginseng beer, laughing, massage, juggling, meditation, and the use of stress relieving bubble baths and shampoos. These are presented in no particular order and you may have your own view on their usefulness. Certainly most are not sufficiently evaluated. You may also be able to think of other examples.

---

suggested that the term is therefore meaningless and should be abandoned (Pollock, 1988; Briner and Reynolds, 1993). However, the usual approach, which is adopted in this chapter, is to regard it as a general term to encompass a broad area of study, which includes the study of environmental stressors, strains (which may be physical, psychological or behavioural), and moderating influences including a range of factors to do with personality, coping and the availability of supports. The study of stressors alone has included a wide range of different types of factor. They may be acute or chronic, with effects that are brief or long-lasting, instantly traumatic or with negative effects that build up over time. Some researchers have focused on major life events (such as divorce or bereavement) and their effects on well-being (Holmes and Rahe, 1967). At the other extreme, it has been suggested that minor everyday hassles are more important in predicting ill health (Delongis *et al.*, 1982) and that interpersonal stressors are the most upsetting of daily stressors (Bolger *et al.* 1989). Most occupational research has used an intermediate level of analysis looking at relatively stable and enduring aspects of the work environment.

Discussion point

° Look at Box 2.1. What do you think the term 'stress' means? Is it a useful concept? Might its popularity have led to us perceiving the world as more stressful than otherwise?

Models of Occupational Stress

It is clear that work stress is not a simple issue. For example, a heavy work- load may well be a source of stress, but the extent to which it leads to strain will be dependent on a number of intervening variables. In addition to the individual's own personality, the extent of resources to deal with the load, the amount of autonomy the person has and the amount of social support, will all be important. Researchers working in the study of occupational stressors have used a number of different approaches or models to examine the relationships between stressors and strains. Such models have clear implications for the way work could be designed to minimize stress. Three of these models – Warr's vitamin model, Karasek's demand–discretion model and Payne and Fletcher's demand–support–constraint model – are discussed below.

Warr's vitamin model

Warr has identified a number of environmental features which affect mental health. The importance of these features has primarily been studied in the context of work or unemployment, although they are relevant to all kinds of environment. They are as follows:

1. *Opportunity for control.* Mental health is likely to be affected by the extent to which situations offer opportunity for personal control over activities or events. Warr (1987) suggests that the 'opportunity for control has two main elements: the opportunity to decide and act in one's chosen way, and the potential to predict the consequences of action'. (p.4)

2. *Opportunity for skill use.* Mental health is likely to be affected by the extent to which the environment allows opportunity to use existing skills or develop new skills.

3. *Externally generated goals.* Mental health is likely to be affected by the extent to which the environment makes demands or generates goals.

4. *Variety.* The extent to which environments offer variety will further influence mental health.

5. *Environmental clarity.* This includes three aspects:

    (i)   feedback about the consequences of one's own actions

    (ii) the degree to which other people and things in the environment are predictable

    (iii) the clarity of role requirements.

6. *Opportunity for interpersonal contact.* This is important in meeting needs for friendship and social support. In addition, many goals may only be achieved through group membership.

7. *Availability of money.* The availability of money is clearly a factor likely to influence mental health by causing anxiety about the individual's ability to provide for their own, or their family's basic needs. In addition, shortage of money is likely to influence the extent to which the individual may be able to gain access to sufficient levels of the other factors – such as variety or control.

8. *Physical security.* In the work context this would include such factors as job security and poor working conditions.

9. *Valued social position.* The final aspect considered important for mental health is that of having a position within a social grouping which leads to being held in esteem by others.

Warr uses the analogy of vitamins to explain the way that these work features affect mental health. Low levels of vitamins lead to poor physical health and similarly low levels of each of the listed environmental features will lead to poor mental health. As with vitamins, Warr suggests that above a certain level there is no added benefit if more of the feature is added. For example, above a certain level an increase in money or interpersonal contact will not lead to a further improvement in mental health. In the case of some vitamins (for example, Vitamins A or D), very large amounts may be harmful for health. Other vitamins (for example, C or E) can safely be consumed in large quantities. Similarly, Warr suggests that certain environmental features will be harmful if levels are very high. This is true of elements 1–6 listed above. The remaining three elements are not harmful at high levels. Thus, the model predicts that too much money or physical security will not be harmful, but too much control or variety may be.

Warr suggests that the presence of control is particularly important in that it is likely to give scope for determining the other eight elements. Of all the work characteristics, control has probably received the greatest amount of research. It is a key element in the next model to be described, Karasek's demand-discretion model (Karasek, 1979).

Karasek's demand–discretion model

This model is one of the most well-known and influential approaches to occupational stress. It focuses on only two main aspects of work, job demands (by which he is referring to volume and pace of work and being subject to conflicting demands) and job control, both issues which may be familiar to social carers. Karasek considers that the effects of job demands are moderated by job control or discretion (referred to as 'decision latitude' by Karasek). Figure 2.1 identifies the types of jobs which are thought to result from the various combinations of demands and discretion. The model predicts that a combination of high job demand and low levels of job discretion would lead to high levels of psychological and physical strain – a 'high strain' job. By contrast, low levels of demand and high levels of discretion would be 'low strain' jobs. High job demands with a high level of discretion makes for 'active jobs' which are not unduly stressful because they allow the individual to develop protective behaviours. Jobs with low demands and low discretion, on the other hand, tend to be passive, resulting in reduced activity and learned helplessness. Thus, while active and passive jobs are intermediate in terms of strain outcomes, a passive job would lead to higher levels of strain than an active job.

Much of Karasek's work has focused on demonstrating that there are increased risks of cardiovascular disease amongst those with high demand, low control jobs (e.g. Karasek *et al.*, 1982; Pieper, LaCroix and Karasek, 1989), but the model has also been used to predict the more immediate impact on psychological well-being and job satisfaction. This approach may help to explain why high levels of strain (including heart disease) are often found in the lower levels in organizational hierarchies in studies of a range of organizations including the British civil service (Marmot *et al.*, 1991). While there are clearly stressors associated with senior positions, these are likely to be mitigated by greater control and ability to delegate. One clear

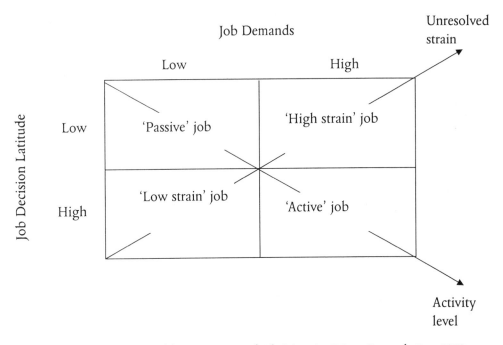

Figure 2.1 Karasek's job strain model. By permission of Administrative Science Quarterly, June 1979

practical implication of this model is that work could be made less stressful without reducing demand but merely by increasing discretion. Indeed, in his own research, Karasek (1990) has shown that where people had experienced company reorganizations in which they participated, and which resulted in increased job control, they showed lower levels of symptoms (including depression, exhaustion, heart problems, dizziness and headaches). While this study shows convincing evidence in terms of the importance of control, it does not consider the interplay of job demands and level of control. In general, it seems to be the case that the evidence is stronger for the importance of control than it is for the full model (see Ganster and Fusilier, 1989 and Jones and Fletcher, 1996).

Karasek's narrow focus on demand and control and the interactions between the two has meant that this is a model which is relatively easily testable and has straightforward practical implications. This probably accounts for the dominance of this approach in the research literature. However, this strength is also its major limitation. Models are needed which incorporate the diversity of stressors existing in jobs such as social work. Lack of social support is widely becoming recognized as a major contributor to stress at work, and is now frequently added to Karasek's model (e.g. Johnson and Hall, 1988); however, a model which encompasses a much wider range of stressors is described below.

The demand–support–constraint model

This model is based on the work of Payne (1979) and Fletcher and Payne (1980a,b). The central idea of this approach is that strain results when there is a lack of balance in the demands and constraints placed on a person in relation to the supports that are available to them (Fletcher, 1991). The dimensions of the model are:

1. *Demands.* This is the degree to which the environment contains stimuli which require attention and response. The stimuli may be technical, intellectual, social or financial. Demands are the things that have to be done. Table 2.1 presents some common job demands. It can be seen from this list that this definition of demands encompasses a wider range of aspects of work than Karasek's approach.

2. *Supports.* This is the degree to which there are resources which are relevant to meeting the demands of the individual or the group. These supports may be technical, intellectual, social, financial, etc. For example, being part of a happy cohesive workforce or having good supervision may reduce the impact of demands. Job control is only one of these potentially supportive aspects of work.

3. *Constraints.* These are the aspects of the environment which prevent a person or group from coping with demands. For example, the lack of relevant resources to do a job well. Such constraints can act to prevent people maximizing the benefits of supports, as well as affect how they can cope with the demands. For example, an unpleasant, uncooperative colleague may not just be unsupportive, they may positively disrupt the work of others. Table 2.1 shows some common work supports/constraints.

Table 2.1 Work Stressors as Demands or Supports/Constraints

Work demands	Work supports/constraints
Job pressure	Being clear about role
Having too much to do	Job discretion, autonomy, control
Having too little to do	Quality of relationships with:
Being responsible for people	Boss
Being responsible for things (equipment)	Colleagues
Demands from others	Subordinates
Conflicting demands/roles	Union membership
Over/under promotion	Role ambiguity
Keeping up with others/organizations	Variety level, skill utilization
Organizational climate	Social perception of job
Office politics	Participation in decisions
Organizational structure	Payment/reward system
Organizational/job changes	Quality of equipment
Major decisions	Physical working conditions
Expectancies of others/organization	How work is planned/managed

From Work, Stress, Disease and Life Expectancy by Ben (C.) Fletcher. Copyright John Wiley and Sons Ltd. Reproduced with permission.

According to this framework, strain results from a lack of balance between the demands, supports and constraints. Thus, high demands may not be stressful if the job (or non-work environment) also provides good levels of support and low constraints. This model has proved practically useful in forming the framework for an investigation of the stressors of work amongst a range of occupations including social workers (see below), and for identifying ways in which the work can be made less stressful.

Discussion points

    ° List the stressors you perceive in social work.

    ° How well do you think the models describe social work stress?

Burnout

The models described above focus on the stressors of the job, and may be used to predict a wide range of strains, but most often have looked at the ways job stressors are related to anxiety or depression. The latter are measured using questionnaire scales which have been validated for this use, e.g. the General Health Questionnaire (Goldberg, 1972). A high score will mean that an individual has a score comparable with psychiatric patients. Other strain measures may also be used, e.g. including physical symptoms, absenteeism, job dissatisfaction and 'burnout'.

Burnout can be viewed as one form of reaction to work stressors, to which workers in the human services or 'caring professions' are said to be particularly vulnerable. It has been a popular approach to the study of stress in these professions in the USA. More recently, a number of studies in the UK have also started to look at 'burnout' as one of the manifestations of strain (e.g. Gibson, McGrath and Reid, 1989). The concept of burnout is operationalized in the 'Maslach Burnout Inventory' which consists of scales measuring *emotional exhaustion, depersonalization,* and lack of *personal accomplishment* (Maslach and Jackson, 1981). Emotional exhaustion is characterized by lack of energy and feeling that one's emotional resources are used up (Cordes and Dougherty, 1993). The key element in depersonalization is a feeling of detachment or treating clients as objects rather than people. A lack of personal accomplishment may be marked by feelings of failure. Emotional exhaustion is often regarded as the first stage of burnout, and is primarily a response to excess demands especially from 'work overload, interpersonal interactions, role conflict and high levels of both personal and organizational expectations'. (Cordes and Dougherty, 1993, p.644).

In their review of the literature, Cordes and Dougherty suggest a number of factors likely to lead to burnout. Much of the burnout research has focused on the role of the client in burnout. They suggest:

> Client interactions that are more direct, frequent, or of longer duration, for example, or client problems that are chronic (versus acute) are associated with higher levels of burnout. Role conflict, role ambiguity and role overload have been shown to be associated with burnout to varying degrees. (p.628)

They conclude that burnout has been linked to a wide range of negative outcomes, including mental and physical health problems, negative effects on social and family relationships, negative attitudes towards clients, increased turnover and deterioration in performance.

Recently, the three-dimensional aspect of burnout has been criticized (e.g. Garden, 1989) and it has been suggested that not all components are necessary for defining burnout, emotional and physical exhaustion being the key components. Garden suggests that the association of depersonalization and lack of personal accomplishment with burnout could be the result of human service occupations attracting certain personality types who may be prone to burnout.

Discussion point

° Do you think that the social care professions attract people who may be particularly prone to stress? If so, what is it about their personalities or approach to their work which makes them particularly vulnerable?

Individual Differences in Susceptibility to Stress

We have already seen that when presented with the same demands at work, individuals may differ in their response due to factors such as the amount of job control they perceive and their resources in terms of social support. While these are typically regarded as objective features of the job it is undoubtedly true that people's reports are influenced by their own individual characteristics. A person with an optimistic disposition may report more job control than a pessimist in the same job. A friendly sociable person may be able to use their personal resources to elicit social support even in a relatively unsupportive environment. However, a number of particular personality characteristics have been suggested that are thought to lead individuals to be either particularly prone to stress or resistant to it.

Much research has focused on *Type A* personality. This type of person is typified by perpetually struggling to achieve more and more in less and less time. They are likely to be competitive, aggressive, striving for achievement and easily aroused to hostility. Early studies (e.g. Rosenman *et al.*, 1966) provide convincing evidence of relationships between Type A behaviour and coronary heart disease. In recent years this evidence has been disputed. A large review of studies (Booth-Kewley and Friedman, 1987) concludes that it is not necessarily the case that the whole constellation of Type A factors is problematic. The impatient workaholic may not be particularly prone to heart disease, which seems to be more associated with a number of negative emotions, including the anger and hostility typical of Type A people, but also other negative emotions such as depression and anxiety.

Other approaches to studying individual differences also implicate a depressive approach to life as more likely to lead to stress and ultimately ill health. For example, it has been suggested that a general tendency to suffer *negative affect* (that is a tendency to suffer a range of negative emotions even in the absence of stressors) is related to likelihood of suffering stress (Watson and Pennebaker, 1989). Peterson, Seligman and Vaillant (1988) have also suggested that those who have a pessimistic, self-blaming way of interpreting events are more likely to suffer ill-health than optimists. On the positive side, many consider that these styles can be changed and people may be trained to adopt a more positive approach (see the section on stress management training below).

In addition to such features, which tend to be regarded as relatively stable aspects of an individual's personality, it has also been suggested that there are also differences in individuals' *coping* strategies (which are in turn likely to be related to personality factors). Lazarus and Folkman (1984) have defined coping as the 'constantly changing cognitive and behavioural efforts to manage specific external or internal demands that are appraised as taxing or exceeding the resources of the person'. They suggest that coping is a dynamic process characterized by cognitive appraisal. In a stressful situation an individual initially evaluates the potential harm or benefit of a stressor (primary appraisal), they then evaluate what can be done to overcome or prevent harm or improve benefits – (secondary appraisal). Finally, they will engage in coping behaviours. Lazarus has distinguished between two types of coping, problem focused (directed at managing or altering the problem), and emotion focused (directed at regulating the emotional response). A widely accepted classification of coping developed by Carver, Scheier and Weintraub (1989) builds on this approach to suggest a range of more specific ways in which individuals may cope with stress (see Box 2.2). They suggest that some of these types of coping will be dysfunctional in some situations but not in others. This classification forms the basis for the COPE scale, a measure which can be used to assess individuals' coping styles (what they 'usually' do) or their situational responses (what they do in a specific situation).

Box 2.2 The COPE Approach (Carver *et al.*, 1989)

Primarily problem-focused approaches to coping:

- Active coping – taking direct action to deal with a stressor.
- Planning.
- Suppression of competing activities.
- Restraint coping – waiting for the right moment to act.
- Seeking social support for instrumental reasons (e.g. seeking advice).

Primarily emotion-focused approaches:

- Seeking social support for emotional reasons.
- Positive reinterpretation and growth (e.g. trying to view a stressor in positive terms).
- Acceptance.
- Turn to religion.
- Focusing on and venting emotion.
- Denial.
- Behavioural disengagement.
- Mental disengagement.
- Alcohol-drug disengagement.

Discussion point

  ° Think back to times when you have felt particularly anxious, for example about facing an
    imminent exam or driving test or waiting to find out the outcome of a job interview. What
    coping strategies do you typically use when faced with different types of problem? Which
    of these do you think are helpful and which may be dysfunctional?

To sum up, there are a wide number of factors (in terms of stressors, strains and individual
differences), many of which are not clearly distinct from each other, that need to be taken into
account in studying stress. This makes it a much more complex area to study than many reports
(in both the popular and academic literatures) might suggest. A practical limitation of most
research is that it cannot take all of the factors above into account. There is a limit to the length
of questionnaire that people are willing to fill in! Hence, researchers typically will select only
some aspects for study. In the following section, a number of studies of stress in social work are
discussed which draw on some of the approaches described above.

Stress in Social Work and the Related Professions

Stressors of the social work role

While social care professionals have not received the same amount of attention by stress
researchers as have health service professionals, there are nevertheless a growing number of
studies focusing on social workers.

In the late 1980s, awareness of the issue of stress grew within the social services in the UK.
In many areas it was becoming difficult to recruit and retain staff. Increasing concern about
high levels of stress led to the British Association of Social Workers (BASW) launching its Staff
Care Campaign with a series of articles in *Social Work Today*. However, at this stage there was
little empirical evidence about stress in social work.

In 1989 a study of social workers in Northern Ireland (Gibson *et al.* 1989) found that half of
the 176 respondents had thought of leaving social work in the previous year, and over 30 per
cent of them could be classified as suffering from mild psychiatric morbidity. Despite this, the
vast majority did report finding the work satisfying. The most commonly cited stressors were
to do with having too little time to perform duties to the worker's satisfaction and having to
ration scarce services and resources. A number of other factors were found to be a source of
stress by approximately half the sample. These included the emotional demands of clients, the
administrative responsibility and imposing controls which curtailed or restricted the personal
autonomy of clients. Support to deal with the stressors of the job was limited, with 67 per cent
saying that their employer provided no means of helping staff suffering from work related
stress and 80 per cent feeling that the prime source of support was the work group.

This study also measured burnout and compared scores with the US norms. They found that
the main manifestation of burnout was a feeling of lack of personal accomplishment. Relatively
small numbers experienced high levels of depersonalization or emotional exhaustion.

In the same year, a study of working conditions in six local authorities in the UK reported
similar findings (NALGO, 1989). The most important stressors, in order of importance, were
lack of resources, volume of work, client needs and working conditions.

Our own study (Jones, Fletcher and Ibbetson, 1991) used the Demand– Support– Constraint model as a framework to look at stressors in Hertfordshire Social Services Department. Like Gibson *et al.* (1989) we found that high levels of job satisfaction did not prevent people from reporting high levels of strain. Over 30 per cent had at some stage in the previous two years felt as though they were going to break down. Of these 75 per cent said that the main cause of stress was their work as a social worker. Most felt that the pressure of work impaired the level of service they were able to provide. Like in the Northern Ireland sample, the highest perceived demands were to do with having too much work. Over 70 per cent often had to work extra hours to get their work done and those who did this were more likely to have high scores for anxiety and depression. For most, paper work was an important component of work overload. There were also a number of factors that most social workers viewed as constraints, e.g. the public image of social work, the physical environment at work and the standard of office equipment. Also like social workers in Northern Ireland, the main source of support was the worker's own colleagues.

The results of above studies suggest that even people who find the work very satisfying may suffer and eventually be driven to leave because the stressors of the job may be too great and the support too little. Some social work roles are inevitably likely to be particularly stressful. Bennett, Evans and Tattersall (1993) studied social workers in specialist roles in South Glamorgan. They compared child care social workers with those working with mental health and learning disability. They found that child care workers reported highest levels of perceived stress and highest scores on a mental distress scale. These workers were also less able to distance themselves from the stresses. They experienced greater pressure from factors intrinsic to the job, from relationships with other professionals and from the organizational structure.

Little research seems to have been conducted looking at the recent rapid changes in social service departments following the implementation of community care legislation. However, one survey (Marchant, 1995) has suggested that while over half of their sample of care managers (staff responsible for assessing clients' needs and purchasing packages of care) report that their job is more challenging and interesting than before, the report gives little cause for optimism about staff stress.

The emphasis in the above should not be taken as implying that experiencing strain in social care work is the sole prerogative of the social worker. Indeed, one study (Bradley and Sutherland, 1995) has shown that home helps also report considerable strain, which seems to result from their high level of personal involvement with clients (which could include responsibility for finances). The dependence of clients and ultimately their death were frequently reported as stressors. These pressures on other colleagues may not always be recognized by social workers.

There seems to have been little published research into stress in probation officers, but one recent unpublished report based on a survey of 265 staff by Staffordshire Probation Service (1996) finds that most staff experience stress at times, but 22 per cent report often or always experiencing it. The aspects of work that seemed to be the most important contributors included excessive workload, fears about job security and not being consulted or given information about changes.

Stress and violence

In the last few years, there has been increasing concern about violence to social workers, which in several extreme cases has proved fatal. Clearly, violence and the fear of violence is a stressful aspect of such work, and has been the subject of a number of research studies. A large scale and particularly rigorous study by Rowett (1986) concluded that, while reported incidence of violence was often very low, the actual incidence was dramatically higher than previously suspected. The author suggests that in any one year it may be that most social workers are 'harmed by clients at least once, sufficient to cause bruising or more serious damage' (p.125).

Those who had been attacked were perceived to be 'provocative, incompetent, authoritarian and inexperienced' although there was no reason to believe that this perception was accurate. This stereotype was held by social workers who had been victims as well as those who had not and is clearly likely to deter social workers from reporting incidents and thus prevent them from gaining access to support services. Certainly Rowett's report found that only five per cent of incidents were formally recorded. Littlechild (1995) reviews a number of studies and concludes that workers do not report incidents because they fear that they will not be dealt with sympathetically, that nothing positive will happen as a result and they are concerned that they will be viewed negatively by colleagues and managers. He further concludes from existing research evidence that the effects can be devastating, including 'self blame, guilt, and anger about the incident; concerns about future safety at work and at home, fear of reporting incidents; fear of perceptions by colleagues and managers. Workers may have concerns about dealing subsequently with similar types of situations, dealing with new clients, or dealing with new situations' (p.124).

Information is gradually accumulating from a number of studies which give some indications of the situations where social workers are most at risk. Based on this research, Littlechild (1996) suggests that staff are most likely to be vulnerable when dealing with situations where clients see them as exercising power or control which is seen to be unfair, particularly in circumstances where their own or their relatives liberty is at risk (e.g. assessing mental health clients for compulsory admission to hospital or in child protection work). Most often, the client is known to the social worker, with few attacks happening on first meetings.

Actual violence, and even the knowledge of a high risk of exposure to violence is clearly a particularly potent form of stressor which perhaps more than any other requires to be taken very seriously by organizations. Such basic measures to ensure health and safety of workers go beyond stress management interventions, but nevertheless the stress interventions discussed below are clearly relevant. These are not a replacement for many basic practical procedures such as giving a clear message that violence will not be tolerated (for example, Braithwaite (1995) suggests notices in offices to this effect), the use of alarm systems to ensure social workers can call help from interview rooms and training in basic practical ways of avoiding risky situations.

Discussion point

- ° Try to list as many possible approaches and strategies as you can for reducing the risk of violence to social workers. These might include organizational policies, the design of buildings as well as measures an individual might take.

Managing Stress at Work

It has been suggested that there are three points at which it is possible to provide interventions to help reduce or eliminate occupational stress (Ivancevich *et al.* 1990). The first type of intervention focuses on the stressors and aims to modify the environment. This may involve changes in the work organization; for example, jobs may need to be re-designed to reduce stressors or increase worker's control. The second aims to change the individual's cognitions (for example, through stress management training courses), and the third aims to reduce stress by treating the individual (for example, by counselling).

Focusing on the organization: Job design and organizing work

The models of stress discussed in this chapter have clear implications for the design of jobs within the social care professions, in terms of increasing levels of certain work features (or 'vitamins') such as control (for example, see the study by Karasek (1990) described above). It is reasonable, on the basis of research into occupational stress, to conclude that highly demanding jobs may be made less stressful by increasing the individual's control or the supports available to them. Research studies investigating a range of social service occupations have made recommendations for organizational change along these lines (see for example, Gibson *et al.*, 1989 and Jones *et al.*,1991). One clear example where an organizational response is needed is in dealing with the threat of violence. The low levels of reporting suggest that individuals feel that it will be seen as their own individual problem and that they will not be given a helpful response. Only if it is seen as an organizational problem which is tackled by a range of policies are people likely to change their view. Such policies include encouraging reporting of incidents to enable the organization to take appropriate action (which may include instituting criminal proceedings against the perpetrator), and providing support for social workers who have been attacked or threatened. It is equally important to develop policies to minimize risks, for example, by reducing staff isolation in high risk situations and providing clear means of obtaining rapid back up (and other methods discussed above). Such policies can themselves be implemented in ways which are more or less likely to be stressful. Littlechild (1993) suggests that in an effective organizational response to violence, social workers should be consulted and when possible they should be in control of developing, operating and monitoring their own policies. The models discussed above would indicate that such an approach represents effective stress management.

Focusing on the individual: Training and counselling

While occupational psychology research would suggest the importance of designing work so that many sources of stress are minimized, the main approaches taken by employers over the past few years have been either to train the individual to cope with stress by means of stress management courses or to treat the individual by means of counselling schemes. Similarly, there has been a disproportionate emphasis in the research literature on individual interventions and outcomes. It is ethically questionable to train employees to tolerate poorly designed organizations (Ganster *et al.*, 1982). However, stressful work demands are inherent in the nature of the work of social care professionals, and it is unlikely that these could be eliminated altogether. Hence, there will remain a need for services to help the individual worker. A diverse approach focusing both on the organization and the individual is likely to be most effective. The two most popular individual approaches, stress management courses and counselling schemes, are discussed in further detail below.

STRESS MANAGEMENT TRAINING

Sending employees on stress management training courses is a measure frequently adopted by employers. A typical course might include a diverse range of techniques including training about work stressors, relaxation (or meditation) techniques, assertiveness and time management. A key element is likely to be the use of cognitive-behavioural techniques, based on the view that stress is often caused by negative 'self talks'. Training would focus on replacing these with more positive internal dialogues. Attempts to evaluate such interventions have tended to show relatively limited changes in the well-being of participants. This may be due in part to the fact that many of those sent on courses may not have been suffering from stress in the first place. A classic study by Ganster *et al.* (1982) provided a very thorough evaluation of a stress management programme in an American social services agency. The researchers found that after 16 hours of training, there were small reductions in depression, anxiety and adrenaline secretion in participants compared with a control group. These changes were maintained four months later. However, the authors suggest that many commercially available training programmes offer courses which are no more than half a day and are unlikely to produce noticeable improvements. There has, as yet, been insufficient research to identify which of the diverse elements are particularly effective.

Many of the techniques taught in stress management courses are also widely available in an ever-increasing number of self-help manuals, some of which are geared for particular work groups. See the suggestions for Further Reading at the end of this chapter.

COUNSELLING SCHEMES

Over the past few years there has been a growth in the number of organizations providing counselling services for their employees. These may take the form of in-house confidential counselling services, as provided by some large organizations such as the Post Office (Sadu *et al.*, 1989). Alternatively, a number of independent companies offering Employee Advice Programmes (often referred to as EAPs) are increasingly being used by British companies to provide counselling services. Typically, the latter offer advice and counselling for a wide range of problems, from minor consumer or legal issues to more serious psychological problems. While public sector employers have generally been slower to recognise the benefits of providing counselling support for staff, these services are beginning to become available within the social services (e.g. see Gilbert and Farrier-Ray, 1995). However, a recent survey of Staffordshire Probation Service (1996) found that while 39 per cent said that they would consider using the service's confidential counselling service, 24 per cent had not known that it existed!

A number of studies have attempted to examine the effectiveness of counselling or therapy for work stress. An evaluation of the Post Office scheme showed improvements in psychological well-being and sickness-absence after counselling (Sadu *et al.*, 1989). A study by Firth and Shapiro (1986) found large reductions in symptoms after 16 hours of therapy for work-related distress. Two different types of therapy showed similar results, though one of these, 'prescriptive therapy', utilizing cognitive-behavioural approaches similar to those often used in stress management training, showed particularly promising results. Studies have tried to determine what elements in therapeutic interventions are most effective, often findings show that widely different types of therapy have tended to produce very similar results (Stiles, Shapiro and Elliot, 1986). It seems that little headway has been made towards determining exactly what it is about counselling that works. However, Firth and Shapiro's study suggests that 16 hours spent treating distressed individuals may be a more useful and cost-effective way of stress management than an equivalent time providing stress management training for individuals who are not stressed.

Summary

To sum up, this chapter has looked at general approaches to occupational stress, and has also highlighted some of the issues which are relevant to social workers and other social care professionals. It is clear that these professionals have many elements that are likely to lead to the work being perceived as stressful. However, on the positive side it is worth pointing out that it also has many elements which have been shown to be associated with high levels of job satisfaction (Hackman and Oldham, 1976). Social care professionals are likely to have a fair amount of variety in their work, they may be able to see a piece of work through to a satisfying conclusion and their work has significance for others. It may offer them, at least at times, a fair degree of control and satisfying feedback. These factors may account for the fact that many social workers often report high levels of satisfaction despite reporting high levels of stress (e.g. Jones *et al.*, 1991).

Where staff are under stress, the costs in terms of staff well-being may be high, and this in turn is likely to mean they are less able to meet the needs of clients. Too often, stress is seen as an individual problem to be treated by stress-management or counselling interventions. A number of recent court cases, such as the case of the social worker John Walker, have highlighted the fact that employers do have a duty under the *Health and Safety at Work Act* (1974) to ensure the health, safety and welfare of their employees and this includes mental health (see guidelines published by the HSE, 1995). Employers can be found negligent if they do not protect their workers from effects of overwork or other unreasonable job conditions. Provision of counselling and stress management training is unlikely to provide such protection. Attention will also need to be paid to the nature of the work and its organizational context.

Seminar Questions

Think of a particular social care job or role (e.g. child care work, working with older clients, etc.). Considering the available stress literature, what aspects of the job would you expect to be particularly stressful and what could be done to improve the situation? Try to think of interventions at a number of levels, such as:

1. Changing the organization to make the work environment less stressful.

2. Improving the nature of the individual's work role or job description to prevent stress.

3. Providing help to manage stress where it is unavoidable.

Further Reading

Thompson, N., Murphy, M. and Stradling, S. (1994) *Dealing with Stress.* Practical Social Work Series, J. Stradling (ed.). Basingstoke: BASW and Macmillan.
This British Association of Social Workers publication gives practical advice and includes a detailed account of theory and research.

Arroba, T. and James, K. (1987) *Pressure at Work, a Survival Guide.* London: McGraw-Hill.
This is a good self-help guide to managing stress, offering practical, simple and attractively presented advice.

Breakwell, G. M. (1989) *Facing Physical Violence.* Leicester: BPS Books.
This is a sensible and readable guide published by the British Psychological Society which includes practical checklists to help assess the potential for danger in a situation.

References

Bennett, P., Evans, R. and Tattersall, L. (1993) 'Stress and coping in social workers; a preliminary investigation.' *British Journal of Social Work, 23*, 31–44.

Bolger, N., Delongis, A., Kessler, R. C. and Schilling, E. A. (1989) 'Effects of daily stress on negative mood.' *Journal of Personality and Social Psychology, 57*, 5, 808–818.

Booth-Kewley, S. and Friedman H. S. (1987) 'Psychological predictors of heart disease: a quantitative review.' *Psychological Bulletin 101,3*, 343–362.

Bradley, J. and Sutherland, V. (1995) 'Occupational stress in social services: a comparison of social workers and home help staff.' *British Journal of Social Work, 25*, 3, 313–31.

Braithwaite, R. (1995). 'Striking out.' *Community Care*, 10 August.

Briner, R.B. and Reynolds, S. (1993) 'Bad theory and bad practice in occupational stress.' *SAPU memo 1405.* Sheffield University.

Carver, C. S., Scheier, M.F. and Weintraub, J.K. (1989) 'Assessing coping strategies: a theoretically based approach.' *Journal of Personality and Social Psychology, 56*, 2, 267–283.

Cordes, C. and Dougherty, T.W. (1993) 'A review and integration of research on job burnout.' *Academy of Management Review, 18*, 4, 621–656.

Delongis, A., Coyne, J.C., Dakof, G., Folkman, S. and Lazarus, R. S. (1982) 'Relationships of daily hassles, uplifts, and major life events to health status.' *Health Psychology, 1*, 2, 119–136.

Firth, J. and Shapiro, D.A. (1986) 'An evaluation of psychotherapy for job-related distress.' *Journal of Occupational Psychology, 59*, 111–119.

Fletcher, B. (C). (1991) *Work, Stress, Disease and Life Expectancy.* Chichester: Wiley.

Fletcher, B. (C). and Payne, R.L. (1980a) 'Stress at work: a review and theoretical framework, I.' *Personnel Review, 9*, 1, 19–29.

Fletcher, B. (C)., and Payne, R.L. (1980b) 'Stress at work: a review and theoretical framework, II.' *Personnel Review, 9*, 2, 5–8.

Ganster, D. C. and Fusilier, M. R. (1989) 'Control in the workplace.' In C. L. Cooper and I. Robertson (eds) *International Review of Industrial and Organizational Psychology.* Chichester: John Wiley.

Ganster, D., Mayes, B.T., Sime, W.E. and Tharp, G.D. (1982) 'Managing organizational stress: a field experiment.' *Journal of Applied Psychology, 67*, 5, 533–542.

Garden, A. (1989) 'Burnout: The effect of psychological type on research findings.' *Journal of Occupational Psychology, 62*, 3, 223–234.

Gibson, F., McGrath, A., and Reid, N. (1989) 'Occupational stress in social work.' *British Journal of Social Work, 19*, 1–18.

Gilbert, P. and Farrier-Ray, S. (1995) 'Stressed Out'. *Community Care*, 19 January.

Goldberg, D. P. (1972) *The Detection of Psychiatric Illness by Questionnaire*. London: Oxford University Press.

Hackman, J. R. and Oldham, G. R. (1976) 'Motivation through the design of work: test of a theory.' *Organisational Behaviour and Human Performance, 16*, 250–279.

Health and Safety Executive (1995) *Stress at Work: A Guide for Employers*. Suffolk: HSE Books.

Holmes, T. H. and Rahe, R. H. (1967) 'The social readjustment rating scale.' *Journal of Psychosomatic Research, 11*, 213–218.

Ivancevich, J.M., Matteson, M.T., Freedman, S.M. and Phillips, J. S. (1990) 'Worksite stress management interventions.' *American Psychologist, 45*, 2, 252–261.

Johnson, J.V. and Hall, E.M. (1988) 'Job strain, work place social support and cardiovascular disease: a cross-sectional study of a random sample of the working population.' *American Journal of Public Health, 78*, 1336–1342.

Jones, F. and Fletcher, B. (C). (1996) 'Job control and health.' In M.J. Schabracq, J.A. Winnubst and C.L. Cooper (eds) *The Handbook of Work and Health Psychology*. Wiley: Chichester.

Jones, F., Fletcher, B. (C). and Ibbetson, K. (1991) 'Stressors and strains amongst social workers: demands, supports, constraints, and psychological health.' *British Journal of Social Work, 21*, 443–469.

Karasek, R. A. (1979) 'Job demands, job decision latitude and mental strain: implications for job design.' *Administrative Science Quarterly, 24*, 285–308.

Karasek, R. A. (1990) 'Lower health risk with increased job control among white collar workers.' *Journal of Organisational Behaviour, 11*, 171–185.

Karasek, R. A., Theorell, T.G.T., Schwartz, J., Pieper, C. and Alfredsson, L. (1982) 'Job, psychological factors and coronary heart disease.' *Advanced Cardiology, 29*, 62–67.

Lazarus, R. S. and Folkman, S. (1984) *Stress, Appraisal and Coping*. New York: Springer.

Littlechild, B. (1993) *Managing Aggression and Violence Toward Social Work Staff: Moving from Individual Blame to Agency Support*. Hertfordshire: Centre for Social Work Studies, University of Hertfordshire.

Littlechild, B. (1995) 'Violence against social workers.' *Journal of Interpersonal Violence, 10*, 1, 123–130.

Littlechild, B. (1996) 'The risk of violence and aggression to social work and social care staff.' In H. Kemshall and J. Pritchard (eds) *Good Practice in Risk Assessment and Risk Management*. London: Jessica Kingsley Publishers.

Marchant, C. (1995) 'Care managers speak out.' *Community Care*, 30 March.

Marmot, M. G., Smith, G.M., Stansfield, S., Patel, C., North, F., Head, J., White, I., Brunner, E. and Feeney, A. (1991) 'Health inequalities among British Civil Servants: the Whitehall II study.' *The Lancet, 337*, 1387–1393.

Maslach, F., and Jackson, S. E. (1981) *The Maslach Burnout Inventory: Research Edition*. Palo Alto, California: Consulting Psychologists Inc.

National Association of Local Government Officers (1989) *Social Work in Crisis – a Study of Conditions in Six Local Authorities*. Commissioned from the Department of Social Work Studies, University of Southampton. London: NALGO.

Payne, R. L. (1979) 'Demands, supports, constraints and psychological health.' In C. Mackay and T. Cox (eds) *Response to Stress: Occupational Aspects*. London: IPC.

Peterson, C. Seligman, M.E.P. and Vaillant, G.E.(1988) 'Pessimistic explanatory style is a risk factor for physical illness: A thirty five year longitudinal study.' *Journal of Personality and Social Psychology, 55*, 1, 23–27.

Pieper, C., LaCroix, A.Z., and Karasek, R.A. (1989) 'The relation of psychosocial dimensions at work with CHD risk: a meta-analysis of five United States data bases.' *American Journal of Epidemiology, 129*, 3, 483–494.

Pollock, K. (1988) 'On the nature of social stress: production of a modern mythology.' *Social Science and Medicine, 26*, 3, 381–392.

Rosenman, R. H., Freidman, M. Straus, R., Wurm, M., Jenkins, C.D. and Messinger, H.B. (1966) 'Coronary heart disease in the Western Collaborative Group Study: a follow-up experience of two years?' *Journal of the American Medical Society 195*, 130–136.

Rowett, C. (1986) *Violence in Social Work*. Cambridge: University of Cambridge Institute of Criminology.

Sadu, G., Cooper, C. and Allison, T. (1989) 'A Post Office initiative to stamp out stress.' *Personnel Management* August, 40–45.

Staffordshire Probation Service (1996) *Occupational Stress Survey*. Unpublished.

Stiles, W. B., Shapiro, D. A. and Elliot, R. (1986) 'Are all psychotherapies equivalent?' *American Psychologist, 41*, 2, 165–180.

Warr, P. B. (1987) 'Job characteristics and mental health.' In P. B. Warr (ed.) *Psychology at Work*. Harmondsworth: Penguin.

Watson, D. and Pennebaker, J.W. (1989) 'Health complaints, stress and distress: Exploring the central role of negative affectivity.' *Psychological Review, 96*, 234–254.

Zastrow, C. (1984) 'Understanding and preventing burn-out.' *British Journal of Social Work, 14*, 141–155.

CHAPTER 3

'Sensitive' to 'Race' and Ethnicity?

The Intersection of Social Work, Psychology and Politics in Transracial Adoption Practice

Ann Phoenix

Introduction

> The Central Council for the Education and Training of Social Workers (CCETSW) requirements for the Diploma in Social Work award attach a high priority to an anti-discriminatory approach in college and placement teaching and assessment. This area is now recognized as of central importance to the social worker's role and practice. (Robinson 1995, p.1)

> The CCETSW document which outlines the requirements and regulations for the Diploma in Social Work requires that social work students have to demonstrate a knowledge and understanding of: theories or human growth and behaviour, identity, and personality… Although CCETSW do not state that these theories are psychological or derived from psychology, it is obvious that these theories are psychological or derived from psychology. (Robinson, 1995 p.3)

The above excerpts suggest that social work training is concerned both with anti-discriminatory theory and practice and with psychological understandings. This being the case, it may seem that it should be a simple task to pick out relevant ways in which psychology has addressed issues of 'race' and ethnicity. There are, however, four reasons why this task is not straightforward:

1. Psychology has a poor history of addressing issues related to 'race' and ethnicity (Henwood and Phoenix, 1996; Joseph *et al.*, 1990; Phoenix, 1987; Robinson, 1995). The discipline has often aroused the suspicion of black people and those from other minority ethnic groups that it serves to reproduce, rather than alleviate racism (Henriques, 1984; Howitt and Owusu-Bempah, 1994; Reicher, 1993).

2. Despite the priority attached to anti-discriminatory approaches, social work and social policy (the discipline which most directly informs social work) are historically imbued with taken-for-granted notions of white supremacy (Williams, 1989) and have poor records in dealing with racism generally and in relation to clients' lives (Dominelli, 1988; Ahmad, 1990; Robinson, 1995; Lewis, 1996a). When 'race' and ethnicity have

been addressed in social work practice, they have frequently been treated in *essentialist* ways (Lewis, 1996b). (See the definition of essentialism, in Box 3.1.)

3. Psychology is characterized by multiple sub-branches and approaches which are not reconcilable. As a result, it does not provide simple, unitary explanations which social workers can apply to their practices. This is compounded by the fact that, while social work theory may draw on psychological understandings, most psychological work does not address itself to specific social work questions.

4. Social work itself is also subject to contradictions. Any 'caring profession' which attempts to rectify the problems perceived to beset families, while, at the same time, identifying, and dealing with, those families which are seen as posing problems for society, is likely to be controversial and to generate opposing viewpoints. For example, definitions of what constitutes a pathological family and, hence, is seen to require intervention are often racialized and biased in favour of the white middle classes (Dominelli, 1988; Robinson, 1995). There are, thus, likely to be contradictory and competing interests in professional practice, with social workers (whatever their 'race' and ethnicity) frequently facing hostility from clients and society at large as well as internal divisions about how to deal with 'race' and racism (Lewis, 1996a).

Despite these complications, social work theory and practice have, necessarily, drawn on psychological ideas about 'race' and ethnicity. Similarly, some psychologists have attempted, through research, to clarify the issues needed to inform social work practice. However, the difficulties faced by social workers in drawing on psychological ideas about 'race' and ethnicity are reflected in the heated and, sometimes, apparently irreconcilable debates.

This chapter explores the contradictions related to 'race' and ethnicity which are generated by the intersection of psychology and social work. It discusses transracial adoption as an example involving recurrent, heated debates and where theoretical constructions of racism, ethnicity and racialized identities coincide. This is an issue on which social workers themselves are divided and where psychological evidence can be drawn upon to support different perspectives. The chapter argues that it makes little sense to treat such debates as if they can be resolved in favour of one 'side'. Psychological knowledge is generally partial (rather than complete), and is sometimes contradictory (rather than straightforward). Yet enough is currently known to indicate that, for practice to be anti-discriminatory, and in order to take racialized identities seriously, transracial adoption has to be treated in a more complex way than is indicated by 'taking sides'. This approach runs counter to the pressing demands on social workers to act immediately. However, it offers the possibility of dealing more satisfactorily with 'race' and ethnicity than have more simplistic attempts to be 'sensitive' to 'race' and ethnicity.

Entrenched positions in the transracial adoption 'debate' partly result from political divisions of those concerned with this issue. The chapter argues that psychological understandings of identities and on the place of 'race' and racism in children's lives, may help to provide a route out of this impasse. However, since psychological knowledge itself is not politically neutral (Henriques *et al.*, 1984; Seidman and Rappaport, 1986; Herman, 1995; Woollett and Phoenix, 1996), it is important that these understandings are not used simply to reinforce a *status quo* which aims to be 'colour-blind' and to ignore the existence of racism.

The question of transracial fostering raises some of the same issues as does transracial adoption. In practice, however, it has generally proved less explosive. This is mainly because fostering, constructed as short-term 'looking after' (in contradistinction from the permanent parenting hoped for in adoption) is not considered to be as damaging by those opposed to transracial adoption. Thus while many social workers would prefer to make 'same-race' fostering as well as adoptive placements (Rhodes, 1992), they have generally devoted less energy to opposing transracial fostering. The impact of transracial adoption policies on fostering practices is indicated by much publicized instances where, for example, children of mixed-parentage are removed from white foster parents who wish to adopt them in order to establish permanent 'same-race' placements. Yet, while transracial adoption policies have a part to play in such practices, the decisions made are frequently more complicated than acknowledged in the media. Most importantly, foster parents have not been cleared as adoptive parents by social work departments and placements made as short-term are generally not expected to become permanent, however long they last in practice. The 'short-term/permanent' distinction is, therefore, of relevance in both practice and theory. This chapter examines the issues raised by 'permanent' transracial placements since these have been most contentious. For useful discussions of policies and practices related to short-term transracial placements see Rhodes (1992) and Rushton and Minnis (1997).

A diversion through terminology: The thorny question of definitions

One of the issues faced by those thinking about 'race' and racism is that there are many ways in which the terms 'race', 'racism' and 'ethnicity' are used and disagreements about how they should be used. Furthermore, definitions have tended to shift over time as the boundaries between people constructed as being from different 'races' or ethnic groups have moved. Changes in the meaning and usage of the term 'black' are a case in point; changing from a term of contempt to being claimed as the preferred term by black people themselves. Gates (1994, p.201) demonstrated this succinctly for a USA context: 'The "Personal Statement" for my Yale application began: "My grandfather was colored, my father was Negro, and I am black."' In Britain, the term 'black' has also changed from excluding, to including and then excluding again people of Asian descent. Whether or not people of mixed-parentage (also referred to as 'of dual heritage' or as 'bi-racial') are considered black is a point of contention in discussions of transracial adoption. Shifts have occurred because definitions are a site of dispute over what groups should be called, who has the right to define them and who should be included within particular terms.

It is partly because terminology is ideologically marked that some people, particularly those from the white ethnic majority, are diffident about discussing 'race' and racism in case they 'say the wrong thing'. Nonetheless, there are useful ways in which to discuss 'race' and ethnicity while being 'sensitive' to the reasons why terminology remains contested and, hence, dynamic. The terms of 'race' and ethnicity are all about processes of boundary maintenance in that they are ways of separating 'them' and 'us'. They are, thus, about social relations and, often help to make constructed, racialized, boundaries seem natural (see Box 3.1).

Box 3.1 Some Definitions of Racialized Terminology

Ethnicity refers to a collectivity or community which shares common attributes to do with cultural practices and shared history. While ethnic group is sometimes used as if it refers to people who are in less powerful positions within society and who are often subjected to racism, ethnicity applies to everybody.

Race is often used to mean no more than 'black' and 'white', which are treated as opposites. People designated as belonging to the same 'race' are constructed as belonging to the same human stock. 'Race' is seen as inherited and manifested in biological or physical difference or culture. Skin colour, physiognomy, culture or territory have all been used as markers of the boundaries between 'races' (Anthias, 1996). Hence, 'race' overlaps with ethnicity. The ways in which 'race' (and ethnicity) is designated shifts over time. Many people put the term 'race' into quotation marks to signify that it is socially constructed, rather than about 'natural', biological or cultural difference. Others have argued that for these reasons, it should not be used (e.g. Banton, 1977). Although 'race' is a social construct, the fact that it continues to be treated as socially significant means that it has real effects through racism. It should not, therefore, be dismissed (Donald and Rattansi, 1992). The term *racialization* (Omi and Winant, 1986) includes the idea that 'racial meanings are not static but are social processes. Equally, the use of the term *transracial adoption* reflects the socially constructed *polarization* of 'races'.

Essentialism involves treating an ethnic group or 'race' as if it has unchanging characteristics which will forever differentiate it from other groups (i.e. an essence). This exaggerates differences and understates similarities between groups.

Racisms take many different forms and can range from the grossest practices of genocide and slavery, through harassment and denial of social rights, to name calling. They involve exclusion and, frequently, inferiorization and so are intimately connected with power relations, since one group has to have the power to exclude another from power and resources. They thus involve a range of economic and political practices. It is now generally accepted that racisms have to be conceptualized in the plural, since there are different forms of racism (Brah, 1992, 1996). Similarly, experiences of racism are differentiated by social class, gender, sexuality and able-bodiedness.

Discussion point

°   Consider the ways in which the terminology of 'race' has changed over time. Can you think of any terms which are disputed or unclear at the moment? Which do you think will be used in the future and which do you think will fall into disuse?

Transracial Adoption: The Collision of Politics, Psychology and Social Work Practice

Transracial adoption has generated debates about terminology, 'racial identity' and the place of 'race', racism and ethnicity. These are all issues which are discussed in a range of academic disciplines and in everyday talk. However, the fact that they are commonly used tends to obscure, rather than to clarify their meanings because different people use the concepts in different ways and have different views on how to measure and/or recognize them. Box 3.2 demonstrates some of this complexity in relation to theories of identities.

The complexities identified in Box 3.2 make it difficult for social workers usefully to draw on theories of identities in making decisions about transracial adoption. In the discussion which follows, some of the problems with treating identities as singular are identified and promising

Box 3.2 Theories of Identities

Psychological work has been very influential in producing theories of *identity*. There has, however, been a tendency to focus on individual identity. Social identities (e.g. gender, 'race' and social class) have not received as much attention as 'personal identities'. The individualizing of identity and the treatment of it as singular, partly results from the influence of Erikson's (1968) ego identity approach, which consisted of a series of age-related stages, with identity being the main task of adolescence. Erikson theorized identity as having integrity and continuity and as important to keeping the internal and external worlds in line with each other. Following Erikson, many psychologists construct identity as an inner core which is the self and which requires continuity if it is not to experience threat (Breakwell, 1986). There is a preoccupation, particularly in the USA, with identity as a marker of healthy psychological adjustment related to *self-esteem*. Marcia (1987, 1994) built on Eriksonian theory to identify a process of identity development in which the highest level is individual *identity achievement* which is secure to the extent that it remains largely unaffected by the external world.

The notion of coherent, stable identities is, however, increasingly coming into question within the burgeoning field of identity, even by those who are proponents of Erikson's approach, because it is recognized that each person has *plural identities* (e.g. of gender, ethnicity, sexuality and adoption). These identities are, however, rarely theorized simultaneously, but tend to be dealt with independently. *Social Identity Theory* initiated by Tajfel (1978) perhaps constitutes a middle position between traditional psychological approaches and more sociological ones (Hogg and Abrams, 1988), which are discussed below. Unfortunately, the continued emphasis on laboratory experiments as the major means of testing and contributing to Social Identity Theory makes it less relevant to understandings of social relations and inequities in power relations outside the laboratory (but see Kelly and Breinlinger, 1996 for an exception). The Social Identity Theory tradition has had little to say about the identities of young people.

Despite more complex psychological theorizing of social identities, the notion of unitary, stable identities is one which is taken-for-granted in much psychological work on *ethnic identity*. Ethnic and *racial* identity are generally treated as if they necessarily possess clearly identifiable, static qualities, without which members of minority ethnic groups are likely to suffer damage. For members of minority ethnic groups (but not for the majority ethnic group) ethnic identity (measured on standardised tests) is assumed to be highly placed in a hierarchy of identities which must, essentially, be positive (Phinney and Rosenthal, 1992). Indeed, Phinney *et al.* (1990) suggest that minority ethnic group members will suffer confusion and despair if they fail to achieve an ethnic identity (usually referred to as *identity confusion*). Such work misses the fact that ethnic identity is plural, so that there are a variety of ways in which it may be experienced and may intersect with other identities. It also ignores the importance of ethnic identity to majority ethnic groups, probably because this is often not recognized (see, for example Frankenberg, 1993a,b and Cohen, 1988) and that where young people from the majority feel themselves to be lacking an ethnic identity, there can be dangerous tensions between some young people from the white majority and those from minorities (Macdonald *et al.*, 1988).

ways of theorizing identities (which draw on sociology and cultural studies) are considered. Wetherell (1996) provides further discussion.

The story of the transracial adoption controversy

In 1983 the Association of Black Social Workers and Allied Professionals gave evidence to the House of Lords against the continuation of the practice of transracial adoption. At that time transracial adoption had already become controversial and it has continued to be the site for some of the most heated arguments in adoption and in social policy.

The transracial adoption controversy is usually seen as having polarized 'sides' ('for' and 'against'). However, the binary opposition between 'pro-' and 'anti-' positions does not help the understanding of transracial adoption and so is not helpful to policy and practice. Indeed, the 'pro-' and 'anti-' division is largely contrived, since even the Children Act (1989) leaves the issue open by stating that 'a local authority shall give due consideration … to the child's religious persuasion, racial origin and cultural and linguistic background'. The phrase 'due consideration' does place religion, 'race', ethnicity and language on the agenda in decisions about children. However, it is sufficiently vague that it does not prescribe any specific course of action to be taken.

It is perhaps in recognition that this vagueness is unsatisfactory in a situation where some children still spend long periods being 'looked after' by local authorities that the Labour government issued new guidance on adoption in 1998. This guidance states that:

> Children from minority ethnic or mixed race backgrounds should not face unnecessary delays while the (adoption) agency looks for the 'perfect' match… It is unacceptable for a child to be denied loving adoptive parents solely on the grounds that the child and adopters do not share the same racial or cultural background.
>
> All families should assist children placed with them to understand and appreciate their background and culture… It is important that adopters teach their children how to deal with racism' (Department of Health press release, 98/353, Friday 28th August 1998: 'Action taken to achieve right balance for adoption.)

While this guidance admirably attempts to deal with both children's needs for loving homes and the importance of race, racisms and ethnicity, it is itself vague about the emphasis that should be given to 'racial or cultural background' in adoption decisions and in what exactly is being asked of adoptive parents. It is, therefore, unlikely that this new guidance will resolve the transracial adoption controversy.

The controversy centres around the issue of whether the placement of black children and those from other minority ethnic groups with white foster or adoptive parents damages the 'racial identities' of the children. Transracial adoption of white, majority children by black parents is extremely rare. Some of the most difficult childcare placement decisions relate to 'race' and ethnicity. However, the transracial adoption debate is generally simplified into racialized terms. Advocates of 'same race' placements argue that transracial adoption will result in black children failing to develop a positive racial identity and that white parents will not be able to give them coping skills for living in a racist society. Furthermore, black children will grow up unable to relate to other black people and, hence, will be unable to bear inevitable rejections from white society (see Tizard and Phoenix, 1993). Proponents of transracial adoption do not necessarily disagree that black and other minority children should ideally go to black and minority parents, a position endorsed by the Children Act 1989 (e.g. Gaber and Aldridge, 1994). They are, thus, not always on opposite sides from proponents of 'same-race placements'. However, they argue that black children's interests are better served by placement in loving white majority ethnic homes which provide continuity of care, rather than in institutions or short-term care.

Both sides of this debate draw on arguments about children's psychosocial development and, to some extent, both find support from the few studies that have been carried out on transracial adoption. In the early 1980s, for example, Gill and Jackson (1983) conducted a British study of over 30 13–15 year olds who had been transracially adopted (and were from a wide range of ethnic groups; some being of mixed-parentage). They found that, on the whole, the young people were 'psychologically well-adjusted' with high self-esteem; happy in their families and doing well at school. However, few called themselves black or agreed with the statement that 'they felt proud to be black'. Rather, they felt very distant from black people and said that they had little in common with them. In the USA, Simon and Alstein have now followed up an initial sample of 204 three to seven year old 'transracially adopted' children into adulthood (Simon and Alstein, 1977, 1981, 1987; Simon, 1994; Simon, Alstein and Melli, 1994). At the second contact, when the children were between 11 and 15 years of age, they found that one in six of the parents they interviewed reported that their children were showing problems which they considered to be related to the transracial adoption. However, at the end of the study, most parents (over 90 per cent) reported that they would 'do the same again'. Overall, they did not find evidence of problems with 'racial identity' in the transracially adopted children.

There is some clinical evidence that a few transracially adopted children do suffer severe problems of identity (Small, 1986; Maximé, 1986). However, while clinical evidence is important, it is not sufficient to the task of providing support for one or other side of the debate since it is not possible to generalize from small numbers of exceptional cases. Furthermore, there is also clinical evidence that a small percentage of black children and children of mixed-parentage living with their birth parents also experience severe identity problems (e.g. Banks, 1992, 1996).

How, then, is it possible to make sense of the polarized impasse in this controversy? The discussion below teases apart the issues raised by strong versions of both positions to demonstrate that such complex questions are not adequately dealt with from entrenched, opposed, positions.

Positions which support transracial adoption

It is clearly important for children to be brought up in households where they are loved, considered important and given continuity of care (see this volume Chapter 6, Anne Woollett; Chapter 11, David Messer; Chapter 12, Ann Clarke and Alan Clarke). However, the construction of a stark opposition between 'pro-' and 'anti-' transracial adoption positions generally precludes recognition that this one psychological position (that children need love and continuity of care), includes people who have different political and psychological perspectives. Thus, there are five overlapping positions which those who are 'pro-transracial adoption' may support:

I. 'LOVE IS ALL YOU NEED'

If continuous love and care from one or two parent figures is sufficient to override all other considerations in child care, the implication is that there is a hierarchy of children's psychological needs with loving nurturance in a family being at the top. Few people would wish to deny the importance of loving, continuous care. However, more work is needed on the place of 'race' in children's lives in racialized societies. Clearly, it is unsatisfactory to place black children, and those from other minority ethnic groups, with adults who do not recognize that they will face racism, and who are determined to ignore the colour and ethnicity of children in their care.

2. COLOUR-BLINDNESS AND THE DENIAL OF RACISM

The extreme version of the 'colour blind' argument' that colour plays little or no part in northern societies and is, therefore, irrelevant to children's lives' is extremely easy to refute and is not often presented. Demographic data illustrate that there are continuing racialized inequities in many countries (see, for example, Owen, 1994), while various studies (in psychology and other disciplines) illustrate the ways in which racism continues to operate (Commission for Racial Equality, 1985, 1988). Many people persist in arguing that young children are not yet racialized and do not notice 'race'. However, there is also a range of evidence to the contrary from the work of the black psychologists Kenneth and Mamie Clark in the 1930s through to more recent research (e.g. Wright, 1992; Troyna and Hatcher, 1992; Holmes, 1995). For example, Ogilvy et al. (1990, 1992) found that nursery teachers treat, and respond differently to, Asian Scottish children than white Scottish children, while James (1997) found that white London children in ethnically mixed schools produce negative, racialized discourses of Asian people.

Paradoxically, a less extreme version of the 'return to colour-blindness' argument raises more serious and insidious issues which require that the political motivation for denials of racism be questioned. In Britain, as in various other countries, many black people and some white people have struggled to document and change some of the injustices of racism. Groups of black social workers have done much within their profession to put racism on the social work agenda. In the area of 'same-race placement', they have had marked impact, even if they remain in professionally precarious positions (Lewis, 1996a). In particular, the adoption of 'same-race placement' policies by many social work departments was in recognition of the prevalence of racism and its deleterious consequences. The late 1980s and 1990s, however, have been characterized by a retreat from engagement with issues of racism in the USA and in Britain. The term 'political correctness' has been used as an insult to defuse opposition to racism, sexism and heterosexism. In this context, some of those who attack 'political correctness' welcome challenges to 'same-race placement' policies. In treating racisms as non-existent, 'colour-blind' practices help to disempower black social workers (and black clients and potential parents) by treating their concerns about racism as irrelevant. Since black social workers are treated as problematic in many social work departments (Lewis, 1996b), colour-blind approaches also deny the existence of racisms within the social work profession.

3. THE SUCCESS OF TRANSRACIAL ADOPTION

Many proponents of transracial adoption point to its success in turning out happy and successful adults. Those who have found in their research that transracial adoption does not seem to damage the racial identity of black children are particularly clear that transracial adoption has been so successful that it should not be debarred (Simon and Alstein, 1977, 1981, 1987; Simon, 1994; Simon, Alstein and Melli, 1994).

For some, it is a short step from arguing that transracial adoption has been successful, to arguing that it is advantageous for black children to be reared in white, middle class homes. Here, as in the issue of 'colour blindness' and denial of racism (discussed above), the implications of research findings are given a particular slant, without acknowledgement of political bias. In the early 1980s, for example, Sandra Scarr engaged in debate with psychologists, social scientists and geneticists about transracial adoption. This followed from the publication of a paper by Scarr and Weinberg (1976), which suggested that it was parenting from white people, rather than economic advantage which was responsible for 'the above-average IQ scores of black/interracial children adopted transracially' (see Chapter 6, this volume). Arguments about the biases in IQ tests have long been presented (Henwood and Phoenix, 1996; Dockrell, Grove and Hasan this volume). Yet, in Scarr and Weinberg's argument, transracial adoption is constructed as providing a compensatory environment for black children. Not surprisingly, this publication generated a great deal of controversy, with Oden and MacDonald (1983) suggesting that the social commentary concluding the article made it unsuitable for publication.

This questionable position, of advocating transracial adoption as compensatory environment, is rarely voiced. However, it does surface from time to time. For example, Bartholet (1994, p.168) suggests that 'whites are in the best position to teach black children how to manoeuvre in the white worlds of power and privilege' at the same time that she implies that some of the black adopters who have been recruited in recent years are not adequate to the task of childrearing. Arguably, while demonstrated success does not warrant legislation against transracial adoption, it does not justify the encouraging of transracial adoption. The differential positioning of black and white people and the economic resources available to them, continue to be important considerations. As with the wording of the Children Act, then, the argument that transracial adoption is successful for most children who experience it leaves open, rather than either supporting or opposing its practice.

4. IMPRACTICALITY OF A BAN

The argument that a ban of transracial adoption is unrealistic (and unkind) arises from the continued reported lack of black and minority ethnic group families willing to adopt children. However, it is difficult to establish how many black children and those from other minority ethnic groups are waiting to be placed at any one time:

> The fact that this information is still so hard to procure, despite being of major public importance, is perhaps due to the low priority it has been afforded or to its sensitive nature: such figures are notoriously difficult to collate due to the difficulties in agreeing on definitions of ethnicity and the precise meaning of 'waiting for placement'. (Rushton and Minnis, 1997, p.156)

However many black children are waiting to be placed, the shortage of black parents should be an interim position. If scarcity of black adopters is the only reason for allowing transracial adoption, extensive efforts, like those made by some social services departments, should be made to remedy the situation. Unfortunately, social services' commitment to increase the number of black adoptive and foster parents is sometimes more rhetorical than actual. In her study of foster care placements in one London borough, Rhodes (1992, p.257) found that:

> Within the borough of the case study, the apparent radicalism and rapid pace of change belied an inherent conservatism which began to reassert itself as the immediate pressure to recruit black foster parents declined. The emphasis on team consensus and strategies of conflict avoidance prevented serious challenge to the *status quo*. The fragility of the new moves rapidly became obvious as the more radical initiatives, one by one, were dropped and the Fostering Team reverted to its old practices and approach… What had, only weeks earlier, been declared 'top priority' was overtaken by 'more pressing needs' – a shortage of white foster parents. The excuse of resource constraints allowed the Team to continue to pay lip service to the goal of same race placement whilst withdrawing from any practical commitment.

5. RACE AND ETHNICITY SHOULD NOT BE THEORIZED IN
ESSENTIALIST AND STATIC WAYS

Some of those who are in favour of transracial adoption base their support on the theorizing of 'race' and ethnicity which is informed by postmodernism and critiques of essentialism. From such a position they argue that people in the same racialized groups may well have different identities and that these identities are not fixed, but may change over time. Furthermore, there are similarities between those in different racialized groups. They thus challenge the essentialist notions of identity used in some 'anti-transracial adoption' arguments.

Table 3.1 summarizes the implications of particular 'pro-transracial adoption' positions for social work practice.

Table 3.1 Implications of Type of 'Pro-Transracial Adoption' Position for Social Work Practice

Type of 'pro-transracial adoption' position	Implication for social work practice
1. Love overrides all other concerns with respect to 'children's needs' and childcare.	Little attention should be paid to 'race' or ethnicity in the placement of children.
2. Social work practice should return to 'colour-blind' policies.	The existence of racisms are denied so no account should be taken of 'race' or ethnicity.
3. Transracial adoption is successful in producing children who fare well.	Attention may or may not be paid to 'race', but transracial adoption should be allowed. In its extreme version, transracial adoption would be preferred.
4. The impracticality of a blanket ban on transracial adoption.	Racism and ethnicity are both 'taken into account' but transracial placements made if 'same-race' placements are not available. What is meant by 'not available' is open to challenge.
5. 'Race' and ethnicity should not be theorized in essentialist and static ways.	'Race' and racisms are taken seriously, but 'transracial adoption' is not banned.

Positions which oppose transracial adoption

Just as those who support transracial adoption can have different reasons for supporting it, so too do opponents of transracial adoption come from different positions. There are four main perspectives which are commonly expressed from the 'anti-transracial adoption' viewpoint. These partially intersect:

1. *The politically indefensible 'stealing of children'.* In the 1980s, David Devine (then Assistant Director of Social Services in Camden, later Assistant Director of CCETSW) made many media appearances in which he argued that transracial adoption constituted the 'stealing of children' from the black community and was the supreme demonstration of the use of power by white society against black people. He frequently drew on his experience of having been transracially adopted, to argue against the policy. The limitations of using personal experience as the basis on which to draw policy conclusions was often demonstrated in those programmes since Devine was often faced by Ben Brown, also a social worker who had been transracially adopted and who was in favour of the continuation of the practice.

This argument results from the possibility of racism being a fundamental part of the transracial adoption process. There is a differential rate of entry into care for children who are black and of mixed-parentage (Bebbington and Miles, 1989) which raises the possibility that there are racially discriminatory reasons for entering care. The shortfall of black adoptive parents has also, convincingly, been argued to be the result of indirect (and, possibly, direct) discrimination. For example, the fact that black people are more likely than white people to be from the working classes and that parents of African Caribbean descent are more likely to be lone parents, have been identified as factors which make black parents less likely to be constructed as 'good parents' (Phoenix, 1987). Thus, viewed from another perspective, the circumstances which lead proponents of transracial adoption to argue that it has to be allowed where there is a shortfall of black and other minority group adoptive parents (e.g. Gaber and Aldridge, 1994) can be constructed as a demonstration of institutional racism.

The issues of racially discriminatory reasons for children being 'looked after' by local authorities and for black parents not being accepted as foster or adoptive parents is obviously an important one, which some local authorities have been trying to address over the last two decades. However, it is important to remember that black children 'looked after' by local authorities will not necessarily be placed with black families, or cared for by black residential childcare workers, if they are not transracially adopted. Instead, black children often stay in temporary care with a variety of white carers. For this reason, some of those who are against transracial adoption as politically indefensible accept that it may have to be used as a default position if permanent black carers are not quickly found (just as some of those who are in favour of transracial adoption accept that it should only be a default position).

2. *Racism overrides all.* This position intersects with all the other positions in the 'anti-transracial adoption' argument, although the other positions do not necessarily entail the 'racism overrides all' position. Basically, the argument is that racism is so damaging to black children that black children should only live with black parents who have experienced racism and who can help their children to understand and deal

with it. It thus employs the essentialist notion that all black parents will be able to help their children to deal with racism, while also assuming that white parents will not be able to help their children to understand or to deal with racisms.

3. *Racial and ethnic separatism.* The notion that different 'races' and ethnic groups should not mix is a well-worn argument that is more usually held by white supremacists. However, more recently, black nationalists have responded to continuing outrages of racism by arguing that black people should keep themselves as far apart from white people as possible. Since transracial adoption necessarily involves contact (although not sexual) between black and white people, these two politically divergent positions are united in the transracial adoption controversy. People who are adamantly opposed to racism thus espouse the same practices as those who are its most vociferous supporters. Gilroy (1996, p.72) argues that 'enemies' ('white supremacists and black absolutists, klansmen and black nationalists, zionists and anti-semites') can understand the world in the same way and, hence, can be political allies.

The separatist position is, arguably, as indefensible as the suggestion (e.g. from Bartholet, 1994) that transracial adoption promotes racial integration through mixing. The futility of this argument is demonstrated by, for example, the fact that heterosexual marriage between two consenting adults has not produced gender equity.

4. *Transracial adoption produces 'identity confusion'.* Perhaps the most rehearsed argument against transracial adoption is that it damages the racial identity of black children and those from other minority groups. According to this argument, black or mixed-parentage children brought up in white households may develop well in some ways, but will suffer from 'identity confusion'; fail to develop a 'positive black identity' and be unable to relate to other black people. Furthermore, unless they are very well trained, white parents will be unable to pass on to black children the strategies they need in order to survive in a society where racism is common and where some degree of rejection by white people is likely (Maximé, 1986; Small, 1986). Since it is possible, in this argument, for white parents to be well trained, so that they can pass on strategies for surviving racism, this position allows the possibility that, if there are no other options, some white parents might be allowed to adopt black children.

Table 3.2 summarizes the implications of particular 'anti-transracial adoption' positions for social work practice.

Table 3.2 Implications of 'Anti-Transracial Adoption' Position for Social Work Practice

Type of 'anti-transracial adoption' position	Implications for social work practice
The politically indefensible 'stealing of children'.	Transracial adoption allowed as a last resort, default position.
Racism overrides all.	Transracial adoption not allowed under any circumstances.
Racial and ethnic separatism.	Transracial adoption not allowed under any circumstances.
Transracial adoption produces 'identity confusion'.	Transracial adoption allowed as a last resort, provided that white parents are well trained about racism.

Contributions from Psychological Research

Psychological research cannot claim to be able to resolve the 'transracial adoption debate'. However, in conjunction with research from other disciplines and by making explicit the political arguments, it can be used to move forward the 'transracial adoption debate'. The fact that psychological work provides support for both 'sides' of the debate in itself indicates that we need to conceptualize 'transracial adoption' in ways which do not reproduce the current oppositional extremes, but which attempt to use the complexities of the racialization of childhood as the starting point for making decisions about children.

Racism and racialization are always part of black, mixed-parentage and other minority ethnic group children's lives

Although some proponents of the transracial adoption position would like to take a 'colour blind' approach, there has, for a long time, been a wealth of evidence which indicates that the lives of very young children are racialized (e.g. Clark and Clark, 1939, 1947; Holmes, 1995). To take a 'colour-blind' approach is thus to ignore the evidence that exists. In addition, it reproduces societal power relations by leaving the racialization of white children from the majority ethnic group unquestioned and denying the experiences of racism faced by black and other minority ethnic group's children. This can have deleterious effects on black children and those from other minority ethnic groups. In the first of her 1997 Reith lectures, Patricia Williams, a black professor of law in the USA, made this abundantly clear with an evocative example. When her son was three, his nursery teacher told her that he seemed to be colour blind. It turned out, however, that it was not that he could not distinguish colours but that, when asked to name a colour, he would reply 'it doesn't matter'. This was because his friends at nursery school had told him that he could not be a superhero, since superheroes could not be black. In response to his distress about this, the teacher had told him that colour 'doesn't matter'. The well-meaning teacher had, with one small comment, negated the pain of this child's experience, produced an unintended educational problem for him and left his white

By way of contrast, opponents of transracial adoption construct it as the prime site of problems for black children. However, the psychological evidence indicates that this is not the case. The data that exist on 'racial identities' suggest that the process of identity development is difficult and painful for many non-adopted young black children (Hutnik, 1991; Milner, 1983). Yet, the self-esteem of black young people is not discernibly different from that of white young people (Phinney *et al.*, 1990; Phinney and Rosenthal, 1992; Spencer, 1990). These data suggest that learning to recognize and deal with racism may well be a painful process for black children.

The theorization of racialized identities: Blackness as dynamic, plural and contested

An important point at issue between 'pro-' and 'anti-' groups relates to theories of identities. This is rarely the focus of discussion, yet it is a key area in which psychology can provide insights that may inform the 'debate'. At the heart of notions of black, transracially adopted children developing 'a positive black identity' is the idea that there is one identity position which black people should occupy. Self-esteem and self-concepts are considered to be necessarily interlinked with black identity in one-to-one correspondence. This notion dates back to early work on racial identity that assumed that black children who 'misidentified' would suffer from 'identity confusion' which would adversely affect them and their educational attainment. This argument was central to the 1954 Brown v. the Board of Education desegregation case, which initiated the process of desegregation of schools in the USA (Clark, 1963). The Clarks' research (1939, 1947) was the single most quoted piece of research in that case with a central argument being that school segregation damaged the racial identities of black children. The interpretation of these data has been disputed, since there was no evidence that the deleterious effects of segregation on black children was linked to the racial segregation of schools (Murphy *et al.*, 1983). However, similar assumptions about self-esteem and positive black identity continue to be made (Katz, 1995). In recent years, some white young people sometimes wish to be black (Hewitt, 1986; Jones, 1988). However, this has not been similarly interpreted as evidence of psychological pathology, probably because it is taken-for-granted that it is black, not white young people, who are likely to suffer from identity problems.

The idea that transracial adoption impairs the development of a 'positive black identity' suggests that there is a single way in which black identity can be positive. Yet, the very notion of what it means to be black is dynamic, shifting with changes in political agenda and social theory (Gilroy, 1994). While the political and psychological are interlinked, it would seem to make more sense to think of black identities as plural and changing, rather than as unitary and static. Furthermore, the term 'black' constitutes part of a contested terrain, since part of the reason for its shifts in meaning is that some of those included, and some of those excluded from it continually campaign (in various ways) to change its usage.

The essentialist view, of a one-to-one correspondence between a 'positive black identity' and self-esteem, is not supported by research evidence. From a review of mainly USA work, Jackson, McCullough and Gurin (1986, p.248) argue that there has been a simplistic assumption that self-esteem and black identity are necessarily related although 'empirical evidence to support this self-evident assumption is lacking'. The essentialist insistence that black people should identify in a particular way underpins insults such as 'bounty' or 'coconut' applied to black people (or 'banana' for Chinese origin young people). Such names suggest that there is a core of identity underneath skin colour and that some people are not black (or 'yellow') through and through. Amina Mama (1995) discusses how such ideas caused some of the professional black women she interviewed anxiety that they were not 'black enough'.

Current theorizations, of identity (particularly those informed by postmodernism) construct it as plural, dynamic and situated in social contexts, rather than as static and unitary. Stuart Hall gives a clear example of how it is not possible to know how anybody will identify, simply by knowing whether they are black or white:

> In 1991, President Bush, anxious to restore a conservative majority to the US Supreme Court, nominated Clarence Thomas, a black judge of conservative political views. In Bush's judgement, white voters (who may have been prejudiced about a black judge) were likely to support Thomas because he was conservative on equal-rights legislation, and black voters (who support liberal policies on race) would support Thomas because he was black. In short, the President was 'playing the identities game'.
>
> During the Senate 'hearings' on the appointment, Judge Thomas was accused of sexual harassment by a black woman, Anita Hill, a former junior colleague of Thomas's. The hearings caused a public scandal and polarized American society. Some blacks supported Thomas on racial grounds; others opposed him on sexual grounds. Black women were divided, depending on whether their 'identities' as blacks or as women prevailed. Black men were also divided, depending on whether their sexism overrode their liberalism. White men were divided, depending, not only on their politics, but on how they identified themselves with respect to racism and sexism. White conservative women supported Thomas, not only on political grounds, but because of their opposition to feminism. White feminists, often liberal on race, opposed Thomas on sexual grounds. And because Judge Thomas is a member of the judicial elite and Anita Hill, at the time of the alleged incident, a junior employee, there were issues of social class position at work in these arguments too. (Hall, 1992)

What is demonstrated in the above example is the cross-cutting and plural nature of the possible identifications that can be produced by intersections of 'race', gender and social class. Far from having static identifications and a unitary, essential identity, one person can (but does not necessarily) hold competing identifications on the basis of the different social positions they occupy. Commonalities and differences between people occupying different social positions are thus also dynamic. The appearance of black power and black consciousness movements in the 1960s (which are often cited as having had a direct impact on black children's responses in studies of 'racial identity') would seem to support theories that it is possible for there to be radical and dramatic changes in identifications and identities over the life course.

Furthermore, many people of mixed-parentage are now choosing to identify themselves as definitely 'mixed' or 'bi-racial'. This poses challenges to the conceptualization of black and white people as if they were binary opposites (see Tizard and Phoenix, 1993 and Root, 1996 for further discussion). The anti-transracial adoption position might be expected to be 'sensitive' to issues of 'race' and ethnicity, since it engages with them. However, in using static notions of racialized identities, it is insensitive to the ways in which 'race' and ethnicity are experienced and expressed. It is worth noting that, from a position in support of transracial adoption, Simon and her colleagues (1994) recognize that blackness is multiple and that black experience is heterogeneous. They conclude that transracial adoptees are 'no less black than are children of the ghetto' (p.115). However, the fact that they make their point of comparison 'children of the ghetto' appears to suggest that they believe that authentic blackness is really the province of the ghetto. This essentialism partly diminishes the force of their argument.

It is clear from the discussion above that theorizations of blackness used in the service of 'same-race placement' arguments are currently outdated because they are static, unitary and essentialist. To address the complexities now recognized to be inherent in the construction of identities, insights from psychology and other disciplines could usefully be applied. Fear that psychological arguments about identity will be used to deny racism is one reason for reluctance to use such arguments when rethinking policies and practices about children 'looked after' by local authorities. This is, of course, a serious issue and needs to be openly acknowledged in a context where psychological arguments are addressed, but where their potential use in the denial of racism is resisted.

Blackness is not a sufficient qualification for passing on strategies for dealing with racism

The suggestion that 'unless they are carefully trained' white adoptive parents will not be able to pass on strategies for dealing with racism to black children (Small, 1986) suggests that black parents, by virtue of their experiences of racism, will be able to pass such strategies on to their children. Relatively little research has been done on this issue. However, the findings from a study of the social identities of young people demonstrated that black parents did not necessarily attempt to pass on such strategies to their children, while some white parents of children of mixed-parentage did so (Tizard and Phoenix, 1993). Furthermore, in adoption placement practice, it is not clear whether black substitute families do provide for continuity of identity for black children (Butt and Mirza, 1997).

The Positioning of Social Workers

The above discussion has attempted to illustrate the complexities generated by 'debates' on transracial adoption and in theories of racialized identities. These complexities are partly responsible for the difficulties social workers face in attempting to deal with the placement of children from a variety of ethnic backgrounds. The continual treatment of transracial adoption as if it is a 'debate' polarized into 'sides', together with the tendencies to polarize 'race' into black–white opposites, has tended to result in social workers needing to match the 'race' and/or ethnicity of parents with those of children. However, the relative poverty of social constructions of 'race' and ethnicity do not represent the plurality of backgrounds from which people come and, hence, the plurality or heritages of children to be 'looked after' by local authorities. Social workers are, thus, left to deal with complexities which have not been sorted out by the rest of society, and then find themselves pilloried when decisions are made which other people either do not like or consider simplistic.

This 'no-win situation' is compounded by the fact that the 'transracial adoption debate' has left social workers to surmise how to behave in a situation where rhetoric about taking 'race', racism and ethnicity seriously is not backed by commitment from managers (Rhodes, 1992). Social workers themselves have not, therefore, been well served by the ways in which transracial adoption and fostering have been placed on social work agenda and dealt with in practice.

Social workers are, of course, not simply interchangeable. In Britain, Gail Lewis (1996a), and in the Netherlands, Philomena Essed (1996), both argue that black and minority ethnic group social workers are 'often viewed as a problem rather than an asset' (Lewis, 1996b, p.51). Many black social workers fear that they, together with black children and families, are in danger of being marginalized, rather than taken seriously in social work (Butt and Mirza, 1997). At the same time, 'race', racism and culture are often reduced to 'simplistic and patronizing "culture tours" which further divide black social workers from white social workers' (Lewis, 1996b, p.46).

> '…I remember when I was in Fostering and Adoption and I went on a training course "Working with West African Families"… and it was a white woman running it, and 90 per cent of the people on the course were white, and they left thinking "oh, I can work with West African families", and it was a white woman who did it. I think she had been to Nigeria twice or three times, and spent some time with a family and said "they are so kind because they will even give you their food, even if they haven't got much, they will give it to you" in a very patronizing sort of way… But the thing is, ever since I have been here, I think we have had one debate on race and as it so happened I was the person who had put it on the agenda.' (African woman social worker interviewed by Gail Lewis, 1996b, p.46)

> The one-sided emphasis on the culture of the Other strengthens the tendency to experience ethnic groups as 'quite different' and as a 'problem'. In the meantime, people get stuck in the pattern of thinking about other cultures as a list of stereotypes: in Moroccan households, take off your shoes; don't say 'hi' to Surinamese people, but rather 'how do you do, Ma'am'; with Turks, what was it again? with Dutch people, oh great! we can be our normal selves for a change. This strengthens the familiar pattern of the Dutch being normal while others are not. You always need to show understanding for those who are not normal, whereas nobody talks about the normal. (Essed, 1996, p.31)

This simplistic treatment of 'race' and ethnicity as 'Other' sits side by side with attempts to privilege 'race' in childcare placements. It is perhaps not surprising that social workers find it difficult to know what best to do in relation to transracial adoption or that black social workers are often precariously positioned. Box 3.3 illustrates the ease with which it is possible to assume that particular practices are specific to certain ethnic groups although they occur in a range of ethnic groups.

Box 3.3 The Racialization and Ethnicization of Experience

'The following story shows how ethnicization of experiences can happen in practice.

A nineteen-year-old from Amsterdam is angry because she has to be home earlier than most of her classmates. She complains that her parents are overprotective, and she wants to move out, but she isn't quite sure how to do this without a huge fight. She is Turkish. She thinks that her parents are strict with her because they are Turkish. This image is reinforced by stories in the paper about Muslim immigrants who are strict with their daughters and about girls who run away because they refuse to accept this any longer.

At a summer job, she works with an outgoing, slightly older Dutch girl. Imagine her surprise when this new friend vividly describes the fights she has had with her parents, their struggles, and the tricks she had to pull in order to move out. Imagine the Turkish girl's relief that overprotectiveness is not the prerogative of Turkish parents. She recognizes the experience she shares with her Dutch friend, even though she knows that there are also differences in the way they were raised.' (Essed, 1996, p.35)

Discussion point

○ Use this example to think about differences you consider to be the result of ethnicity and/or 'race'. Think of an example of what you consider to be clear differences between the groups to which you belong and another group. Are there any similarities between the groups? Are there always large differences between the groups? Are the differences due to 'race' and ethnicity or are socioeconomic circumstances also relevant?

The Way Forward? Concluding Thoughts

While the transracial adoption 'debate' is often presented in its strong form, as polarized 'sides', many people who locate themselves on one or other 'side' recognize that, since social circumstances are never perfect, it may be necessary to make placements with which, in ideal circumstances, they would disagree. In addition, those who are politically 'worlds apart' may sometimes share the same positions with regard to transracial adoption. Nonetheless, one important benefit provided by the raising of the transracial adoption debate in the 1980s by the Association of Black Social Workers and Allied Professionals, has been the placing on social work agenda of 'race', ethnicity and racism. As a result, a 'colour-blind' approach is less tenable than it was.

The intricacy of the issues raised by transracial adoption makes it unlikely that easy ways can be found to implement insights from psychology (and other disciplines) in practice. It is clear from psychological work that racialized identities are more complex than opponents of transracial adoption have tended to allow. In being apparently 'sensitive' to 'race' and ethnicity, they have been insensitive to the ways in which 'race' and ethnicity are represented in identities. Supporters of transracial adoption are, however, unjustified in using criticisms of the anti-transracial adoption position as justification for 'colour (and ethnicity) blind' approach. Other psychological work indicates that 'race', ethnicity and racism are important from early in children's lives (e.g. Bath and Farrell, 1996). Furthermore, the ways in which racisms impact on black social workers can easily serve to marginalize their (plural) viewpoints (Lewis, 1996a). Failure to recognize this would further justify a retreat from addressing issues of 'race' and racism (Kirton, 1996), allowing psychological evidence to be used for the maintenance of the political *status quo*. Transracial adoption provides perhaps the most vivid example of how politics and psychology intersect in social work theory and practice. It is this which makes the controversy a recursive one.

Recent research on social care in Britain indicates that, while controversies abound in all aspects of the care of black children and their families' experiences, it is possible to produce clear and practical suggestions for improvements (Barn, 1993; Butt and Mirza, 1997; Jones and Butt, 1995). For this to happen, any theoretically informed social work practice has to engage both with the impact of racism and with the dynamic pluralism of racialized identities. Both have to be taken on board in decisions about the placement of children. However, decisions cannot simply be 'colour coded'. Using psychological evidence in order genuinely to be sensitive to 'race' and ethnicity requires an engagement with the complexities of transracial adoption. This is likely to become more, rather than less important if the proposed privatization of social work functions, including adoption, takes place.

Summary

Despite the recognition that the holding of inflexible positions with regard to 'transracial adoption' is no longer tenable (Gaber and Aldridge, 1994; Kirton, 1996), polarized positions continue to be espoused. This chapter has argued that 'debates' on 'transracial adoption' cannot, usefully, be settled in favour of one 'side' or the other; 'pro-' or 'anti-'. Psychological knowledge can contribute to taking forward the 'debate' in a more complex way than is indicated by the metaphor of 'taking sides'. However, psychological knowledge is generally partial and is sometimes contradictory. It thus cannot resolve arguments between entrenched political positions in the transracial adoption 'debate'. Yet enough is currently known to indicate that, for practice to be anti-discriminatory, and to take the plurality and complexity of racialized identities seriously, adoption decisions have to be informed by understandings that childhood is racialized. Since psychological knowledge itself is not politically neutral (Henriques *et al.*, 1984; Seidman and Rappaport, 1986; Herman, 1995; Woollett and Phoenix, 1996), it is important that these understandings are not used simply to reinforce a *status quo* which aims to be 'colour-blind' and to ignore the existence of racism.

Seminar Questions

1. In order to try to move beyond a polarized 'transracial adoption debate', discuss all the factors which need to be considered when placing with adoptive parents: (a) black children; (b) children of mixed-parentage; and (c) those from other minority ethnic groups (choose a specific example if possible).

   - Consider how racism and racialized identities should, ideally, be considered in placement decisions.

   - Choose a specific, (potentially) controversial case. If you do not have access to such an example, consider a case you have read about in the newspapers. What made the case controversial? What were the different political interests involved? Do you consider that the case was well dealt with by the social workers involved? Would psychological evidence have helped?

2. The Children Act (1989) says that 'a local authority shall give due consideration ... to the child's religious persuasion, racial origin and cultural and linguistic background'. This is more difficult than it sounds. Consider the following two sets of questions and discuss with some colleagues different possible ways of dealing with them in practice.

-   With which parents should a child with British, Iranian, Irish and Nigerian heritage be placed? Why?

-   Do all black parents understand racism? Is understanding of racism confined to those who have been subjected to racialized discrimination? Is an understanding of racism important for parents adopting white children (whatever their ethnicity)? Why/why not? Can social workers do anything to help adoptive parents better understand racism? If so, how?/If not, why not?

Further Reading

Three of the following texts focus on psychological issues of 'race', racism and ethnicity (Essed; Mama; Wetherell and Potter). Each does so by drawing on theoretical and empirical work usually considered beyond the scope of psychology. This interdisciplinarity is one of the strengths of all the books annotated. A further strength is that each demonstrates the complexity of racialized subjectivities and the ways in which racisms are (re)produced and experienced. In each case, authors also draw on their insider positioning in relation to their research samples while taking complex, critical perspectives on the accounts of their research participants, informed partly by the historical work on which they draw. The other reference (Rushton and Minnis) is a recent, directly relevant, literature review.

Essed, P. (1991) *Understanding Everyday Racism*. London: Sage.
Philomena Essed interviewed black women in California, USA and in the Netherlands. Her research is concerned with the ways in which racism is produced and reproduced through the minutiae of everyday interactions. It is unusual in focusing on the everyday experiences of black women and the diverse ways in which different black women interpret experiences, depending on their theoretical knowledge, past experiences and geographical situation. The book contains detailed case studies as well as more general accounts.

Mama, A. (1995) *Beyond the Masks: Race, Gender and Subjectivity*.
London: Routledge.
Beyond the Masks is concerned with the subjectivities of black feminists. Amina Mama interviewed women who belonged to the black feminist group in which she was a member. She examines the ways in which black women construct their racialized and gendered subjectivities. Mama demonstrates the simultaneity of 'race' and gender in the production of subjectivities and explores the contradictions and complexities inherent in being positioned in gendered, racialized discourses and in the formation of subjectivities.

Rushton, A. and Minnis, H. (1997) 'Annotation: Transracial family placements'. *Journal of Child Psychology and Psychiatry, 38*, 2, 147–159.
Rushton and Minnis review literature on transracial family placements (adoption and short-term placements). They provide a comprehensive review of relevant pieces of research and include a table for easy comparison of US and British studies directly of transracial adoption, over the last three decades. The major contribution of the review is that it is constructively critical of the studies it reviews, but acknowledges that their writing is informed by political and value judgements. The recognition that terminology is contentious and dynamic, together with suggestions for future research and a brief consideration of the implications for practice make this a valuable review.

Wetherell, M. and Potter, J. (1992) *Mapping the Language of Racism*. London: Harvester Wheatsheaf. This book presents a historical narrative of New Zealand before analyzing the accounts of white New Zealanders on 'race', racism and culture. In doing so, it provides a useful, clearly presented, review of psychological theories of racism and of identities. The research which informs the text is discourse analytic and so takes a social constructionist perspective on the accounts of white New Zealanders, examining the contradictions within them. The book contributes to understandings of the plurality of 'whiteness'; a topic which has been much neglected in studies of 'race', racisms and ethnicity.

References

Ahmad, B. (1990) *Black Perspectives in Social Work*. Birmingham: Venture Press.

Anthias, F. (1996) Inaugural lecture, University of Greenwich.

Banks, N. (1992) 'Mixed up kids.' *Social Work Today, 24*, 3.

Banks, N. (1996) 'Young single white mothers with black children in therapy.' *Clinical Child Psychology and Psychiatry, 1*, 1, 19–28.

Banton, M. (1977) *The Idea of Race*. London: Tavistock.

Barn, R. (1993) *Black Children in the Public Care System*. London: Batsford/BAAF.

Barth, F. (1969) *Ethnic Groups and Boundaries*. Boston: Little, Brown.

Bartholet, E. (1994) 'Race matching in adoption: an American perspective.' In I. Gaber and J. Aldridge (eds) *In the Best Interests of the Child: Culture, identity and transracial adoption*. London: Free Association Books.

Bath, L. and Farrell, P. (1996) 'The attitudes of white secondary school students towards ethnic minorities.' *Educational and Child Psychology, 13*, 3, 5–13.

Bebbington, A. and Miles, J. (1989) 'The background of children who enter local authority care.' *British Journal of Social Work, 19*, 349–368.

Brah, A. (1992) 'Difference, diversity, and differentiation.' In J. Donald and A. Rattansi (eds) *'Race', Culture and Difference*. London: Sage.

Brah, A. (1996) *Cartographies of Diaspora: Contesting identities*. London: Routledge.

Breakwell, G. (1986) *Coping with Threatened Identities*. London: Methuen.

Butt, J. and Mirza, K. (1997) *Social Care and Black Communities*. London: HMSO.

Clark, K. (1963) *Prejudice and Your Child*. Boston: Beacon Press.

Clark, K. and Clark, M. (1939) 'The development of consciousness of self and the emergence of racial identity in negro preschool children.' *Journal of Social Psychology, 10*, 591–599.

Clark, K. and Clark, M. (1947) 'Racial identification and prejudice in negro children.' In T.M. Newcomb and E.L. Hartley (eds) *Readings in Social Psychology*. New York: Henry Holt.

Cohen, P. (1988) 'Perversions of inheritance: studies in the making of multi-racist Britain.' In P. Cohen and H. Bains (eds) *Multi-Racist Britain*. London: Macmillan.

Commission for Racial Equality (1985) *Birmingham Local Education Authority and Schools: Referral and suspension of pupils*. London: CRE.

Commission for Racial Equality (1988) *Medical School Admissions: Report of a formal investigation*. London: CRE.

Dominelli, L. (1988) *Anti-Racist Social Work*. London: Macmillan.

Dominelli, L. and McLeod, E. (1989) *Feminist Social Work*. London: Macmillan.

Donald, J. and Rattansi, A. (1992) 'Introduction.' In J. Donald and A. Rattansi (eds) *'Race', Culture and Difference*. London: Sage.

Erikson, E. (1968) *Identity, Youth and Crisis*. New York: Norton.

Essed, P. (1996) '"As long as they don't call me a racist"': ethnization in the social services.' In P. Essed (ed.) *Diversity: Gender, Color and Culture*. Amherst: University of Amherst Press.

Frankenberg, R. (1993a) *White Women, Race Matters*. London: Routledge.

Frankenberg, R. (1993b) 'Growing up white: feminism, racism and the social geography of childhood.' *Feminist Review, 45*, 51–84.

Gaber, I. and Aldridge, J. (eds) (1994) *In the Best Interests of the Child: Culture, identity and transracial adoption*. London: Free Association Books.

Gates, H.L. (1994) *Colored People*. Harmondsworth: Penguin.

Gill, O. and Jackson, B. (1983) *Adoption and Race*. London: Batsford/BAAF.

Gilroy, P. (1994) 'Roots and routes: black identity as an outernational project.' In H. Harris, H. Blue and E. Griffith (eds) *Racial and Ethnic Identity: Psychological development and creative expression*. New York: Routledge.

Gilroy P. (1996) 'Revolutionary conservatism and the tyrannies of unanimism.' *New Formations, 28*, 65–84.

Hall, S. (1992) 'Questions of Cultural Identity.' In S. Hall, D. Held and T. McGrew (eds) *Modernity and its Futures.* Cambridge: Polity.

Henriques, J., Hollway, W., Venn, C., Urwin, C. and Walkerdine, V. (1984) *Changing the Subject.* London: Methuen.

Henwood, K. and Phoenix, A. (1996) 'Race' in psychology: teaching the subject.' *Ethnic and Racial Studies, 19,* 4, 841–863.

Herman, E. (1995) *The Romance of American Psychology.* Berkeley: California University Press.

Hewitt, R. (1986) *White Talk, Black Talk.* Cambridge: Cambridge University Press.

Hogg, M. and Abrams, D. (1988) *Social Identifications: A Social Psychology of Intergroup Relations.* London: Routledge.

Holmes, R. (1995) *How Young Children Perceive Race.* London: Routledge.

Howitt, D. and Owusu-Bempah, J. (1994) *The Racism of Psychology: Time for Change.* Hemel Hempstead: Harvester Wheatsheaf.

Hutnik, N. (1991) *Ethnic Minority Identity: A Social Psychological Perspective.* Oxford: Oxford Science.

Jackson, J., McCullough, W. and Gurin, G. (1986) 'Family, socialization environment, and identity development in black Americans.' In H.P. McAdoo (ed.) *Black Families: Second edition.* Newbury Park: Sage.

James, J. (1997) 'The views and perceptions of environmental and public health issues for children from different ethnic communities living in Stepney and Wapping.' Paper presented to a Department of Health Conference. *The Health and Health Care of Children and Young People from Minority Ethnic Groups in Britain.* London: National Children's Bureau, 23–24 January 1997.

Jones, A. and Butt, J. (1995) *Taking the Initiative.* London: NSPCC.

Jones, S. (1988) *Black Culture, White Youth.* London: Macmillan.

Joseph, G.G., Reddy, V. and Searle-Chatterjee, M. (1990) 'Eurocentrism in the social sciences.' *Race and Class, 31,* 4, 1–26.

Katz, I. (1995) 'Anti-racism and modernism.' In M. Yelloly and M. Henkel (eds) *Learning and Teaching in Social Work: Towards Reflective Practice.* London: Jessica Kingsley.

Kelly, C. and Breinlinger, S. (1996) *The Social Psychology of Collective Action.* London: Falmer.

Kirton, D. (1995) '"Race", identity and the politics of adoption.' University of East London Centre for Adoption and identity studies: Working paper number 2.

Kirton, D. (1996) 'Review Article: Race and adoption.' *Critical Social Policy, 16,* 1, 123–136.

Lewis, G. (1996a) *Living the Differences: Ethnicity, Gender and Social Work.* Unpublished PhD thesis. Milton Keynes: Department of Social Policy, Open University.

Lewis, G. (1996b) 'Black women's experience and social work.' *Feminist Review, 53,* 24–56.

Macdonald, I., Bhavnani, R., Khan, L. and John, G. (1989) *Murder in the Playground.* London: Longsight Press.

Mama, A. (1995) *Beyond the Masks: Race, Gender and Subjectivity.* London: Routledge.

Marcia, J. (1987) 'Identity in adolescence.' In J. Adelson (ed.) *Handbook of Adolescent Psychology.* New York: Wiley.

Marcia, J. (1994) 'The empirical study of ego identity.' In H. Bosma, T. Graafsma, H. Grotevant and D. de Levita (eds) *Identity and Development: An interdisciplinary approach.* London: Sage.

Maximé, J. (1986) 'Some psychological models of black self-concept.' In S. Ahmed, J. Cheetham and J. Small (eds) *Social Work with Black Children and their Families.* London: Batsford/BAAF.

Milner, D. (1983) *Children and Race Ten Years On.* London: Ward Lock Educational.

Murphy, J. John, M. and Brown, H. (1983) *Dialogues and Debates in Social Psychology.* London: Lawrence Erlbaum.

Oden, C. and MacDonald, W.S. (1983/1978) 'Comment: The rip in social science reporting.' In S. Scarr (ed.) *Race, Social Class and Individual Differences in I.Q.* London: Lawrence Erlbaum.

Ogilvy, C., Boath, E., Cheyne, W., Jahoda, G. and Schaffer, H.R. (1990) 'Staff attitudes and perceptions in multi-cultural nursery schools.' *Early Child Development and Care, 64,* 1–13.

Ogilvy, C., Boath, E., Cheyne, W., Jahoda, G. and Schaffer, H.R. (1992) 'Staff–child interaction styles in multi-ethnic nursery schools.' *British Journal of Developmental Psychology, 10,* 85–97.

Omi, M. and Winant, H. (1986) *Racial Formation in the United States: From the 1960s to the 1980s.* New York: Routledge & Kegan Paul.

Owen, D. (1994) *Ethnic Minority Women and the Labour Market: Analysis of the 1991 census.* Manchester: Equal Opportunities Commission.

Phinney, J., Lochner, B. and Murphy, R. (1990) 'Ethnic identity development and psychological adjustment in adolescence.' In A. Stiffman and L. Davis (Eds) *Ethnic issues in Adolescent Mental Health.* Newbury Park, California; Sage.

Phinney, J. and Rosenthal, D. (1992) 'Ethnic identity in adolescence: process, context, and outcome.' In G. Adams, T. Gullotta and R. Montemayor (Eds) *Adolescent Identity Formation.* London: Sage.

Phoenix, A. (1987) 'Theories of gender and black families.' In G. Weiner and M. Arnot (eds) *Gender Under Scrutiny.* London: Hutchinson.

Reicher, S. (1993) 'Policing normality and pathologising protest: a critical view of the contribution of psychology to society.' *Changes, 11,* 2, 121–126.

Root, M. (ed.) (1996) *The Multiracial Experience: Racial Borders as the New Frontier.* Thousand Oaks, CA: Sage.

Rhodes, P. (1992) *Fostering: The Challenge to Social Work Practice.* Avebury: Aldershot.

Robinson, L. (1995) *Psychology for Social Workers: Black Perspectives.*. London: Routledge.

Rushton, A. and Minnis, H. (1997) 'Annotation: Transracial family placements.' *Journal of Child Psychology and Psychiatry, 38,* 2, 147–159.

Scarr, S. and Weinberg, R. (1983/1976) 'IQ test performance of black children adopted by white families.' In S. Scarr (ed.) *Race, Social Class and Individual Differences in I.Q.* London: Lawrence Erlbaum.

Seidman, E. and Rappaport, J. (1986) 'Framing the issues.' In E. Seidman and J. Rappaport (eds) *Redefining Social Problems.* New York: Plenum.

Simon, R. (1994) 'Transracial adoption: the American experience.' In I. Gaber and J. Aldridge (eds) *In the Best Interests of the Child: Culture, identity and transracial adoption.* London: Free Association Books.

Simon, R. and Alstein, H. (1977) *Transracial Adoption.* New York: Wiley-Interscience.

Simon, R. and Alstein, H. (1981) *Transracial Adoption: A Follow-Up.* Lexington, MA: Lexington Books.

Simon, R. and Alstein, H. (1987) *Transracial Adoptees and Their Families: A study of identity and commitment.* New York: Praeger.

Simon, R., Alstein, H. and Melli, M. (1994) *The Case for Transracial Adoption.* Washington, DC: American University Press.

Small, J. (1986) 'Transracial placements – conflicts and contradictions.' In S. Ahmed, J. Cheetham and J. Small (eds) *Social Work with Black Children and their Families.* London: Batsford/BAAF.

Spencer, M.B. (1990) 'Development of minority children: an introduction.' *Child Development, 61,* 2, 267–269.

Tajfel, H. (1978) *Differentiation Between Social Groups.* London: Academic Press.

Tizard, B. and Phoenix, A. (1993) *Black, White or Mixed Race? Race and racism in the lives of young people of mixed parentage.* London: Routledge.

Troyna, B. and Hatcher, R. (1992) *Racism in Children's Lives: A Study of Mainly White Primary Schools.* London: Routledge.

Wetherell, M. (ed) (1996) *Identities Groups and Social Issues.* London: Sage/Open University.

Williams, F. (1989) *Social Policy: A Critical Introduction. Issues of race, gender and class.* Cambridge: Polity.

Williams, P. (1997) *The Reith Lectures.* London: BBC.

Woollett, A. and Phoenix, A. (1996) 'Motherhood as pedagogy: contrasting feminist and developmental psychology accounts.' In C. Luke (ed.) *Feminisms and Pedagogies of Everyday Life.* New York: State University of New York Press.

Wright, C. (1992) *Race Relations in the Primary School.* London: David Fulton.

PART II

Working with Clients
General Issues

Introduction

Psychologists study a range of both individual functioning and how people function in social situations. This section of the book covers topics which have been selected as providing important background or foundation knowledge for social care professionals. Unlike the many introductory texts which discuss topics such as the psychology of learning or the social psychology of groups, this section, in common with subsequent sections of the book, aims to highlight the ways social workers and related professionals can use psychological knowledge in practice. The first two chapters, for example, draw on some of the most recent psychological work to highlight issues which are likely to be of importance in working with all client groups where social care professionals make difficult decisions about risk, and where accuracy of assessment is crucial. Both chapters offer clear practical advice for the professional. The chapter on risk assessment and decision making includes important information on how we may be unaware of the biases and influences on our decisions, and considers how we might improve decision making. The second chapter, on the pitfalls of interviewing, focuses on the accuracy of information, and includes an introduction to some aspects of the psychology of memory and recent work on lying and deception. This provides useful advice on how to conduct interviews where the concern is to get clear accurate information. This may be important in a wide range of situations where the social care professional is assessing needs. The focus of these two chapters reflects the changing nature of social care and the increased awareness of a need for training in such issues as risk assessment and decision making.

The subsequent chapters move on to some of the more traditional concerns of social care professionals. Working with the family is clearly a central part of social worker duties, and the majority of cases are likely to raise issues that impinge on the wider family. Anne Woollett discusses the complex and diverse ways that families function, concluding with a discussion of families as groups. The next chapter, by Mary Horton, moves on to the issue of working with other kinds of groups. She describes some important classic studies to demonstrate the power of group influence, and introduces both cognitive social psychology and psychodynamic approaches to groups. She describes ways in which group processes can be used for therapeutic purposes, for example in therapeutic communities. Her subsequent two chapters focus on more negative aspects of individual and group functioning – that of prejudice and discrimination. The first chapter of the two describes the way that prejudice can be seen as an individual attribute. This theme is developed in the next chapter, where the importance of group functioning, in relation to prejudice, is discussed. She concludes with a summary which draws together the material in both chapters.

One group who seem to have experienced more than their share of prejudice and discrimination is, arguably, the older people in our society. We have an ageing population, and working with older people is a major focus of social work and the related professions. This tends to be a somewhat neglected area of both research and training, and frequently ageing is viewed in a negative light. The elderly are assumed to conform to a stereotype that is sedentary, sexless and intellectually diminished. Claire Meldrum's chapter draws on psychological research to reject these myths and to highlight the possibilities of successful ageing. Again, as in the other chapters, the issues and implications for social care professionals are discussed.

CHAPTER 4

Risk Assessment
and Decision Making

Wendy Middleton, Anthony Clyne and Peter Harris

Introduction

Many decisions that you make as a social care professional concerning clients will involve issues of risk. What is the likelihood that a client who has previously taken an overdose will do so again? Is there a danger that a Schedule 1 offender will abuse the children of a new partner he/she is living with? See Box 4.1 for a full example.

All human activities involve some element of risk. Judging the likelihood that a particular risk event will happen can be difficult. Some risks or dangers may seem easier to predict than others. The likelihood of being knocked down if you step in front of a moving car, for example, may seem easier to predict than the great uncertainty about whether or not you might get CJD from a single meal of steak. Even when the general likelihood of a risk is known, predicting whether that risk will occur or not on one specific occasion to one particular person is difficult.

Box 4.1 Case Example

A social worker visits the home of a frail 78 year old woman, at the request of her son. The son is concerned that his mother is in danger living on her own. He worries about what would happen if she tripped, fell, and was left alone and undiscovered until the next time he visited. He has noticed that sometimes his mother is confused and forgetful. The son feels his mother would be out of danger if she moved into a residential home. He feels that his mother is not capable of making a decision, and it should be made for her.

The social worker talks to the woman and finds out that she has lived in the house for 30 years, and wants to live there until she dies. The woman feels that her son is interfering in her life.

- What information does the social worker need in order to make a full assessment of the risk to the client?

- Can the social worker balance the potential risk to the woman, and her right to self-determination? How?

- Consider whether you feel that people should be able to take risks.

- Should this client be able to risk her own physical safety and well-being?

Box 4.2 Some Definitions

- risk: 'the probability that a particular adverse event occurs during a stated period of time.' (Warner, 1992, p.2)

- risk factors: 'circumstances that may affect the intensity or likelihood of risk-taking outcomes.' (Carson, 1995, p. 26)

- risk assessment: 'the study of decisions subject to uncertain consequences.' (Warner, 1992, p.3)

- risk management: 'a system for implementing, controlling, and learning from risk decisions.' (Carson, 1995, p.26).

Social care professionals are involved in decisions to intervene in people's lives in many ways: mental health assessments may result in compulsory admission to hospital; appointeeships or guardianships shift the responsibility for clients' financial concerns to social workers; and the 'supervised discharge' legislation now enables professionals to coerce clients living in the community to attend for treatment (Section 25, supervised discharge of the Mental Health (Patients in the Community) Act 1995). All of these examples involve making decisions about risk. While the law determines the circumstances in which statutory powers can be used, the decision concerning whether to employ them in any particular case is left to courts, local authorities, and professionals. A recent report of the Social Services Inspectorate (Laming, 1995) called for 'more fine-tuned risk assessments, producing improvements in decisions about when to use statutory powers for any client group'. While risk assessment is an important part of the social care professional's role, there are few consistent practical guidelines about the exact means by which risk assessments and decision are made. Some decisions about risk may seem relatively clear cut, but practitioners encounter many situations where the level of risk to and from clients is unclear.

In this chapter we consider how people make decisions about risk, we examine the biases which can lead us to make errors in this decision making, and consider ways to make 'better' decisions about risk. Throughout the chapter we will give examples of risk assessment and decision making relevant to working with adult client groups.

There is some discussion in the literature on risk about the definition of key terms such as those in Box 4.2, for example, concerning the overlap between risk assessment and risk management (Warner, 1992). You may want to return to these definitions as you read the chapter and review them.

There are many influences on risk-relevant decisions. Below we discuss several psychological factors concerning the individual making risk assessments, and how these can influence decisions made about risk.

Beliefs and Attitudes about Risks

Petty and Cacioppo (1986, p.127) define attitudes as a person's 'general evaluations about themselves, other persons, objects or issues'. Attitudes are beliefs and evaluations held toward various attitude 'objects'. Social psychologists have long examined whether our attitudes influence our behaviour, for example, whether holding negative attitudes towards ethnic minorities is likely to lead to racist behaviour in professional practice (see Chapter 3). While the evidence for a relationship between attitudes and behaviour may be mixed (Stroebe and Stroebe, 1995), awareness of how our beliefs and attitudes may influence decisions in our work can be useful to evaluate how objective our decisions are. For example, a practitioner may overestimate the risk to a client using cannabis, if they believe cannabis use inevitably leads down a path to more serious drug use and practices (see Chapter 20). A practitioner with positive attitudes towards residential care for the elderly, based on the happy experiences of their own relatives, may tend to assume that most people will happily adjust to life in a residential home. Research suggests that people tend to search for information consistent with their own pre-existing beliefs and attitudes, which is likely to further reinforce that attitude (see Sutherland (1992) for an interesting account of 'misplaced consistency'). Thus an openness to information which may run counter to your own attitudes may help you to make considered, more 'objective' decisions.

Discussion point

   ° What risks do you take in your own life? Do you take part in any sports or activities (e.g. squash, rock climbing, football, driving without a seat belt) which carry some risk of injury? Consider the benefits to you of the risks you take. Risks can have benefits as well as costs. How would it feel if someone suggested to you that you should not do something that is important to you because it is too risky or dangerous?

Mood and Risk

The mood we are in when we make decisions can influence the nature of the decisions we make (Maule and Hockey, 1996). People in positive moods tend to make decisions more quickly (Isen and Means, 1983). Johnson and Tversky (1983) found that good mood, or 'positive affect', was associated with people rating negative events as less likely to occur, and positive events as relatively more likely to occur, compared with judgements made by people in a neutral mood. As a cautionary point, Maule and Hockey accept that the evidence of a relationship between mood and risk is sometimes complicated and often contradictory; other studies have not found the same pattern of results as Johnson and Tversky. However, one interesting field study by Maule and Hockey concerning GPs found that GPs with high negative affect – such as feeling more tense than usual – judged their own clinical decisions to be more risky, but when the GPs in the study had a positive mood, they judged their clinical decisions to be less risky. This relationship between mood and risk was stronger on the days when the GPs had particularly heavy workloads. This recent evidence would seem to suggest that people think they make riskier decisions in their work when they are experiencing work pressure and are in a negative mood. Maule and Hauley conclude that variations in everyday mood can and do affect the way people assess risk, and potentially influence the decisions people make. Acknowledging the impact that our mood can have on our judgement is therefore important.

Context

The context in which someone assesses a risk may influence the perceived likelihood of risk. For example, the publicity surrounding cases where people with schizophrenia have attacked or killed members of the public (e.g. the Clunis case: Christopher Clunis, diagnosed with schizophrenia, stabbed John Zito to death at Finsbury Park Tube station in 1992) may lead people to overestimate the risk to the public from those with this diagnosis. Of course, people with mental disorder in the community who pose no danger to the public are not likely to be considered 'newsworthy', and are very unlikely to receive coverage in the media. Even if press coverage was given to the low level of threat posed by people with schizophrenia, it would be unlikely to grab our attention in the way that a headline screaming 'mad man goes manic with axe' would.

Biases in Judgement and Decision Making

The example above demonstrates how the 'availability' of information can influence our judgements about the likelihood of certain events: information about people with mental disorders who may be dangerous is more readily available to us, and therefore more easily recalled. In this section we review two biases which can lead to errors in cognitive processing. When people make decisions or judgements it is quicker and easier to simplify the task by relying on certain 'rules of thumb' or *heuristics*. Much of the time, heuristics enable us to make decisions and judgements quickly and easily. However, while taking shortcuts in information processing may lead to quicker decisions, and take less effort, shortcuts create opportunities for errors or biases to occur in judgement.

The availability heuristic

Tversky and Kahneman (1974) defined the availability heuristic as the process whereby decision makers 'assess the frequency of a class or the probability of an event by the ease with which instances or occurrences can be brought to mind' (1974, p.1127). So a headline grabbing event, such as a person diagnosed as schizophrenic posing a danger to the public, will be readily recalled, and the event may actually be thought to occur more frequently than is in fact the case. Events are more likely to be available if they are dramatic, concrete, easy to visualize, and are associated with strong emotions. An example for social work practice might be that a social worker who has recently dealt with a number of clients who have Deliberately Self-Harmed (DSH), may estimate the rate of DSH to be higher than it actually is, and to inappropriately anticipate DSH in other clients.

The representativeness heuristic

The representativeness heuristic is a way of judging the probability that object 'A' belongs to category 'B'. As an example, a study on the representative heuristic gave people the following description:

> 'Linda is 31 years old, single, outspoken, and very bright. She studied philosophy. As a student, she was deeply concerned with issues of discrimination and social justice, and also participated in anti-nuclear demonstrations.'

Subjects were asked to rate the probability that Linda is (a) a primary school teacher, (b) worked in a bookshop, (c) is active in the feminist movement, (d) is a psychiatric social worker, (e) is a bank clerk, (f) is an insurance salesperson, (g) is a bank clerk and is active in the feminist movement.

Subjects rated that Linda was more likely to be a feminist (c) than a bank clerk (e). However, they also thought that it was more likely that she was both a feminist and a bank clerk (g), than simply a bank clerk (e) (Tversky and Kahneman, 1983). This is an error because there must be more female bank clerks than female bank clerks who are feminists. Because the description of Linda is stereotypical of a feminist, but not stereotypical of a bank clerk, people concluded she is therefore more likely to be a feminist bank clerk.

The representativeness heuristic demonstrates how the provision of certain information can lead us to make faulty judgements and decisions. Another study illustrates this point: students taking a degree in social work were either told a hypothetical client had 'sado-masochistic fantasies' or that he 'had sado-masochistic fantasies, fixes up old cars in his spare time and once ran away from school'. Students given the first description were more likely to think that he could be a child abuser than students given the second description (cited in Sutherland, 1992). The additional information had no bearing on the likelihood that the client was a child abuser, but the simple presence of the additional information made the client seem less stereotypical of, and therefore less likely to be, a child abuser.

In social work practice, for example, the representativeness heuristic may, for example, lead us to neglect to consider that women sexually abuse children, and conclude that women are not a risk to children in this context, because child sex abusers are typically men. Of course, that doesn't mean that women do not sexually abuse children.

These accounts demonstrate errors or biases in the process of judgement. There are, of course, many other biases in judgement and decision making (Baron, 1994). We have focused on two of the most common biases. They are *descriptive examples of judgement and decision making*, that is, how people actually make decisions.

There is considerable evidence that decisions based on human judgement (e.g. clinical decisions) tend to be no better, or are slightly worse, than decisions based on actuarial predictions. Examples of actuarial sources are base rates and demographic data (Dawes, Faust and Meehl, 1989). Of course, demographic statistics can be inaccurate too, for example, through inadequate sampling techniques, but they do tend to be as or more accurate than human decisions. One study looked at judgements about the likelihood that patients would be re-admitted for psychiatric care and treatment.

Psychiatric workers were asked to predict the likelihood that their patients would be re-admitted. Staff judgements were compared with a rather crude comparison measure: file weight. The number of previous admissions a patient has had may be predictive of future hospital admissions. The weight of the patient's file was used as an indicator of past hospitalization – heavier files were seen as indicative of a higher number of previous admissions. You may have anticipated that, surely, staff judgements would be better than such a simple measure as the weight of a patient's file, but in fact, there was no difference in the predictive accuracy of file weight and staff judgements (Lasky *et al.*, 1959). An explanation for

---

Box 4.3 Risk Factors for Suicide

- age 45 +
- male
- divorced, widowed, or single
- social isolation or living alone
- terminal illness
- other major physical illness
- history of self-harm
- family history of completed suicide
- family history of alcoholism
- childhood bereavement
- social classes I and V
- psychiatric illness and personality disorder
- access to firearms and medication

Recent socio-demographic suicide risk groups

- young Asian females
- young males

(NHS Health Advisory Service, 1994; Lester, 1994; Fischer *et al.*, 1993.)

---

these findings is that the psychiatric workers were relying on heuristics to form their judgements, which allows bias to be introduced into the decision making process. If file weight can be as good a predictor as human judgement, in this context, it is possible to see how predictions based on more commonly used actuarial sources can be better than human judgement.

Known risk factors, based on demographic knowledge and research, can therefore be a very useful resource in risk assessment. Box 4.3 shows risk factors for adult suicides. Incorporating such information about known risk factors into social care professionals risk assessments may be useful to effectively increase the range of information considered in a risk assessment (that is, to act as a prompt), and as a check on pre-existing, and possibly inaccurate, beliefs about the kind of person who may be vulnerable to a risk such as suicide. This should improve the quality of risk decisions.

Discussion point

- ° Accurate and up-to-date information about risk factors is available for a variety of risks. Do you find this threatening to your role as a social care professional? How should practitioners reconcile information about risks based on risk factors and knowledge based on past experience of working with service users?

Often people do not have access to demographic/base-rate information, or such information is not available. Decision makers need to make decisions as free from bias as possible.

Psychologists have also studied how one would ideally make decisions, to make the 'best' decision possible in a given situation. These are called *normative models of decision making*, and we shall consider normative models of decision making next.

Normative Models of Decision Making

Normative decision making is concerned with making 'rational', 'objective' decisions which are likely to bring about a desired outcome. In the case of risk, this may be to attempt to eliminate the possibility of a risk outcome occurring completely, or to achieve an acceptable level of risk for a client, for example, balancing the likelihood of risk with the client's need for autonomy. Normative models, which address how to make the best decision when there are a number of possible options or ways forward, use the concepts of *utility* and probability. Utility is the desirability of an outcome – what you want to achieve. In normative models the utility of an outcome is examined in association with the chances that an outcome will actually occur – the probability of an outcome. Examples of normative models include *expected-utility theory and multi-attribute utility theory* (Baron, 1994; Plauss, 1993).

As a simple example, the kind of decision which could be examined by multi-attribute utility theory is the decision about which social work course to apply for. Should you apply for the course which has good quality teaching and study options which appeal to you, but very high entrance requirements which influence the likelihood of getting a place, or the course which has lower entrance requirements so your chances of success are greater, but the course is less well-established and its status may be lower? Multi-attribute utility models could be used for complex decisions concerning different options available when budgets have been cut, and a number of different services are considered for withdrawal, or deciding which political party to vote for when there are strengths and weaknesses attached to each party.

There are a variety of techniques for making multi-attribute decisions which utilize some complex mathematical and computational modelling (see Yoon and Hwang, 1995, for formulae and examples of their use). The important point about these normative models is that they demonstrate how 'ideal' decisions could be made, with the exclusion of biases in cognitive processing. Given the sometimes complex calculations required by normative models of decision making, reaching decisions by the normative route could be very time consuming. For practical purposes, it might be more useful to be aware of ways to improve decision making so that it is closer to the 'ideal' of the normative model. *Prescriptive models of decision making* aim to do this. Baron defines prescriptive models as 'designs or interventions, whose purpose is to bring the results of actual thinking into closer conformity to the normative model' (Baron, 1994, p.18). The development of prescriptive models of decision making for risk assessment, which are relevant to social care practice, has really begun only recently. Writers in this field, such as David Carson, have looked at the kinds of risk information relevant to risk assessment in social care practice, and ways of standardizing risk assessment so it is less vulnerable to errors or biases. The rest of this chapter considers some of the techniques which are being developed to improve the validity and accuracy of risk assessment.

Box 4.4 A Simple Guide to Probabilities

Baron defines probability as 'a numerical measure of the strength of a belief in a certain proposition' (Baron, 1994, p.188). Probabilities can be any value between 0 and 1. A probability of 1 means that the likelihood that an event/incident will occur is absolutely certain. A probability of 0 means that there is no chance at all that the event will occur. The nearer a probability is to 1, the greater the likelihood that the event/incident will occur. A probability of 0.3 means that, on average, the event will take place 30 times for every 100 occasions (that is, the same as a percentage value of 30 per cent). A probability of 0.6 means that on average the event will take place 60 times out of every 100 occasions: a probability of 0.6 therefore indicates a greater likelihood of the event occurring than a probability of 0.3. For example, a probability of 0.25 for the risk of attempted suicide in a particular client group means that for every 100 clients, 25 will attempt suicide.

Prescriptive Models of Decision Making

David Carson has a preference for statistical estimates of risk over subjective 'guesses' serving as risk assessment:

'It is as impossible to calculate, with precision, the likelihood or the seriousness of a child being abused as it is to predict whether a married couple will separate. But nobody expects that degree of prescience… Decision aids are needed. It is a rare risk that can be assessed entirely in our heads. It may be impossible to state accurately that there is a 0.67 probability that a parent will abuse his or her child. But 0.6, at least, will generally be more accurate than 0.2 or 0.9 and more helpful than a vague word like 'possible', which may be interpreted in a wide range of different ways.' (Carson, 1995, p.26; see Box 4.4 for a simple explanation of probabilities)

Known risk factors, such as in Box 4.3, are one source of decision aid. When these are not available, it can be useful to consider the specific attributes of a risk decision and use these in risk judgements.

One area in which this has been developed is work with elderly people with mental health problems (*Community Care*, 1995). A risk checklist was developed with this client group which broke risk down into four aspects: physical, social, environmental and mental. Each area of risk was further broken down into its components parts and given a score from zero, indicating no or little risk likelihood, to two, indicating a high risk likelihood. These scores could then be added together to give an indication of the level of risk, whether low, medium or high. For example, physical risk components might include fractures from falling and wandering outside which could lead to hypothermia. A client who could be prevented from wandering outside, but not prevented from falling, might be given a risk rating of '0' for wandering, and '1' or '2' for falling. These scores could then be added, together with ratings for other risk components, to form an overall risk rating. This procedure can be adapted for other client groups. If you should decide to adapt this method for your own practice, you do not have to use a scale from 0–2; you can in fact use whatever scale suits you. For example, you might prefer to rate risk on a scale from 0–100, where '0' indicates no likelihood of the risk and '100' indicates that the risk is absolutely certain. So long as all risk components are rated on the same scale, the choice of scale is yours (see Chapter 16 in Baron, 1994 or Yoon and Hwang, 1995).

Weighted risk indicators

The method above – calculating a summed total risk level – can be effective for making decisions about risk, where each risk component is of equal seriousness or importance. However, some risk outcomes are more serious than others. For example, imagine an elderly mentally ill (EMI) client who has some physical risks such as those mentioned above, but who in addition has in the past created a fire risk by leaving a cooker on. While both risks could be given the highest score, '2', using the method above, to indicate that the likelihood of both is high, it could be in this case that a fire risk is potentially more serious and catastrophic than the risk of a fracture from falling over. The procedure above does not incorporate judgements about the seriousness of the outcome. In decisions about risk for this client then, it might be necessary to give more weight to the fire risk than the fracture risk.

To do this, an additional step can be added to the summed total procedure outlined earlier. Look just at the first line in Table 4.1 which refers to an EMI client who is living in their own home. In this hypothetical example, the client has been given risk ratings of '2' for all three risk components, giving a total risk score of 6. However, when fire risk is considered to be twice as serious as the other risks, the risk value for fire risk must be multiplied by its seriousness, in this case '2' because it is twice as serious, giving a score of 4 for fire risk and a total weighted score of 8. (If the risk of fire had been judged to be three times as great as the other risks, the fire risk value would be multiplied by three, and so on.) Given that the lowest possible score for this particular weighted risk total is 0 and the highest possible score is 8, it is possible to gain some idea of the relative risk for the client in this example.

Weighted risk indicators can be used to compare the risks faced by an individual in different settings. Imagine that an assessment is being carried out and a decision is being made concerning the EMI client. There are several options for the client; staying in their own home as they are now; staying in their own home but with the addition of assistance for some parts of the day by a paid carer; and residential care. The level of risk for the client differs as a function of where they live as shown below.

Table 4.1 Example Risk Calculations with EMI Client[1]

| | Risk component | | | | |
	Falling	Hypothermia	Fire	Risk total	Weighted risk total
Home	2	2	2	6	8
Home with assistance	1	0	2	3	5
Residential care	1	0	1	2	3

[1] Where '0' indicates no or little risk and '2' indicates high risk.

With the simple risk indicator, there would seem to be little difference between the level of risk for being at home with assistance, and being in residential care. However, the fire risk component needs to be weighted to indicate its greater importance. Assuming again that a fire risk is twice as serious as the other risks, when the fire risk rating is multiplied by two, and the ratings again summed, we can see that there is a difference of two points between home with assistance and residential care (the weighted totals).

Discussion point

- ° Risk assessments, as the example in Table 4.1 shows, are specific and the level of risk, and its seriousness, may vary as a function of time and place. How often or when is it necessary to review risk assessments?

A weighted risk indicator has been developed by Worthing Priority Care NHS Trust which assesses the degree of risk associated with violent or aggressive clients, as shown in Figure 4.1. With the Worthing Weighted Risk Indicator, a response of 'yes' to any of the 15 risk questions is awarded the score indicated. A response of 'no' to any question is not awarded a score. When all the questions have been answered the scores for 'yes' answers are summed and the total risk score can be compared to the scale at the bottom of the risk indicator. A high score indicates a high risk of violence/aggression, and the client can be categorized as having a low, moderate, or severe risk of violence/aggression. Within each of the three risk types – low, moderate and severe – it is possible to see whether the assessed client is towards the lower or upper end of each category.

Strengths and weaknesses of weighted risk indicators

One of the main strengths of using risk indicators, particularly weighted risk indicators such as that in Figure 4.1, is that it provides consistency. For example, if local authority and health professionals all used the same risk indicator to assess the risk of aggression from service users, when it was felt necessary, the procedure would probably be perceived to be fairer. The opportunity for discrimination would be reduced, and it would reduce differences in assessment by different individuals. Of course, professionals may disagree about the presence or absence of a particular risk in a user, but at least they would be considering the same categories of risk factors. Thus, the assessment could be seen as standard and potentially more objective. If a professional was asked to account for a decision, and explain why they had decided that a client was or was not vulnerable to a risk, the use of a weighted risk indicator would verify that the professional had followed an established, systematic procedure to form a judgement. The use of such indicators reduces the opportunity for cognitive errors to occur which may lead to faulty decisions. Ultimately then, risk indicators should lead to better decisions about risk.

With accurate information about risk and risk likelihood, it is possible to seek to reduce hazards and dangers, or to develop strategies to reduce risk. Weighted risk assessment can provide a very useful basis for making decisions about appropriate interventions/actions with clients. The risk indicator in Figure 4.1 could, for example, be used over time with an individual client to assess whether any change is occurring in that client's risk of violence/aggression, perhaps to monitor the effect of an intervention.

While individual social care professionals may find it useful to develop a simple risk checklist to inform their own practice, risk indicators used in decision making and assessment

Question	No	Yes	Score
Has the client identified specific individuals he/she intends to harm?	☐	☐	12
Has the client used a weapon in the assault of another person?	☐	☐	9
Has the client been previously admitted to a high security unit?	☐	☐	9
Has the client been previously admitted to a low/medium unit?	☐	☐	7
Is there evidence of the client being dangerously impulsive to others?	☐	☐	5
Is there a known history of assaults on others that required medical attention?	☐	☐	5
Has the client threatened physical/psychological harm to others?	☐	☐	5
Has the client expressed but not demonstrated aggressive behaviour?	☐	☐	4
Has the client expressed paranoid delusions featuring specific individuals?	☐	☐	4
Is there evidence/reports of sexually inappropriate behaviour?	☐	☐	3
Has the client previous convictions for violent/sexually inappropriate behaviour?	☐	☐	3
Are there known triggers to violent behaviour?	☐	☐	3
Does the client use recreational drugs?	☐	☐	1
Does the client use alcohol to excess?	☐	☐	3
Has the client refused to co-operate in treatment designed to reduce dangerousness?	☐	☐	1

TOTAL = ...

3 6 9 12 15 18 21 24 | 27 29 31 34 39 42 45 48 | 51 54 57 60 63 66 69 72

LOW   **MODERATE**   **SEVERE**

Figure 4.1 Weighted risk indicator for violence/aggression (Worthing Priority Care NHS Trust).

should be properly tested and validated. However the research and development of risk indicators is very costly. First, it is necessary to assemble accurate and up-to-date information about the incidence of risks and relevant risk factors. Where such information is not available it would be necessary to pool professionals' expertise to formulate likely risk factors. Decisions about the appropriate weight to assign different risk factors are likely to be complex. Newly developed risk indicators need to be piloted, evaluated and up-dated as necessary. That is, the predictive ability and efficacy of risk indicators would need to be checked. Risk indicators are of no use if they are too general: their power is in their specificity. Thus, the development of a number of risk indicators, for a variety of different risks, would be necessary. Though this would be time-consuming, the development of risk indicators may lead to some common agreement about risk among a group of professionals. The introduction of standard procedures for risk assessment may, however, be experienced by professionals as inflexible, and as not giving sufficient room for individual decisions about 'special cases'. For instance, when making assessments about risk, it may often be necessary to take into account the client's rights to independence and self-determination.

Risk Assessment in Practice

While heuristics or short-cuts in decision making may produce errors in decisions, the opposite option involving a very extensive search of all the possible evidence when making a risk-relevant decision, may also be problematic. If you take too much information into account, you could spend so long wading through all the available evidence, that it becomes difficult to make a decision within a reasonable time limit. Obviously it becomes necessary to make a 'good-enough' decision. This practice is called *satisficing* (see Baron, 1994 or Nisbett *et al.*, 1983 for a discussion). Baron (1994) argues that good decision making involves fair and sufficient search for appropriate evidence about a decision, where information searches are defined as 'sufficient' 'when it best serves the thinker's personal goals, including the goal of minimising the cost of thinking' (Baron, 1994, p.30). Decision making about risk in practice is likely to be a combination of clinical judgement and actuarial methods such as risk indicators.

Risk assessment by social care professionals does not take place in a vacuum, but must always be consistent with legislation, and statutory and local guidelines. Box 4.5 shows an extract from the Code of Practice for the Mental Health Act (1983), which Approved Social Workers need to refer to when assessing clients for compulsory admission to psychiatric hospital. Risk has a high profile in the mental health field (Davis, 1996). Indeed, you can see that the relevant practice guidelines makes reference to the assessment of risk, with particular attention to the possible risk to others. The Code of Practice gives details about the appropriate people to speak to in order to gain information, and information about risk, when assessing a client. The Code of Practice also indicates some of the types of information that should be sought. However, the Code of Practice is somewhat vague and lacks clarity about *how* to integrate and evaluate the available information such that reasonable, considered and competent judgements and decisions are reached. This chapter has indicated some of the errors that can occur in this process.

The Code of Practice has further specific recommendations of factors to take into account concerning protection to others.

National and local operational policy guidelines may set out procedures for acting on the results of risk assessment. The process for applying risk assessments is similar for different client groups. For example, local guidelines on the Care Programme Approach (CPA) may specify when risk assessment should be a significant part of work with mental health service users (CPA level 3), and child protection workers have similar guidelines for acting on risk assessment with regards to the child protection register. Similarly, some organizations may have guidelines which concern the management of identified risks.

Finally, it should be made clear that it is never possible to create an environment that is completely risk free. Likewise, it is not always possible to be 100 per cent accurate when making a risk assessment. If a risk outcome does occur, e.g. a successful suicide attempt, after an

Box 4.5 Extract from the Code of Practice for the Mental Health Act (1983)

'Assessment for possible admission under the Mental Health Act (1983)
A patient may be compulsorily admitted under the Act where this is necessary:

- in the interests of his own health, *or*
- in the interests of his own safety, *or*
- for the protection of other people.

In judging whether compulsory admission is appropriate, those concerned should consider not only the statutory criteria but also

- the patient's wishes and view of his own needs
- his social and family circumstances
- the risk of making assumptions based on a person's sex, social and cultural background or ethnic origin
- the possibility of misunderstandings which may be caused by other medical/health conditions including deafness
- the nature of the illness/behaviour disorder
- what may be known about the patient by his nearest relative, any other relatives or friends and professionals involved, assessing in particular how reliable this information is.
- other forms of care and treatment including, where relevant, consideration of whether the patient would be willing to accept medical treatment in hospital informally or as an out-patient
- the needs of the patient's family or others with whom the patient lives
- the need for others to be protected from the patient
- the impact that compulsory admission would have on the patient's life after discharge from detention
- the burden on those close to the patient of a decision not to admit under the Act
- the appropriateness of guardianship.'

'In considering "the protection of other persons" it is essential to assess both the nature and likelihood of risk and the level of risk others are entitled to be protected from, taking into account:

- reliable evidence of risk to others
- any relevant details of the patient's medical history and past behaviour
- the degree of risk and its nature. Too high a risk of physical harm, or serious persistent psychological harm to others, are indicators of the need for compulsory admission
- the willingness and ability to cope with the risk, by those with whom the patient lives
- the possibility of misunderstandings resulting from assumptions based on a person's sex, social and cultural background or ethnic origin and from other medical/health conditions including deafness.'

(Crown copyright. Reproduced with the permission of the Controller of Her Majesty's Stationery Office.)

assessment has been made and a decision about risk reached, this does not mean that the risk assessment process was wrong (Baron, 1994). If the decision or judgement was made with all the available information after a thorough information search, and consideration given to the seriousness of the risk, and the possible outcomes, then a judgement can be said to be a rational and 'good' judgement, even when proved wrong.

Summary

In this chapter we have considered two influences on decision making about risk: attitudes about risk and the mood we are in when making risk judgements. 'Shortcuts' in cognitive processing are useful for making decisions quickly, but can lead to bias in decision making. Two heuristics – the availability and representativeness heuristics – which have implications for decision making about risk are described. The predictive ability of human decisions concerning risk are compared to decisions based on demographic data about risk factors. Normative models describe the 'ideal' way in which decisions can be made to reduce the opportunity for bias to occur in decision making. Some techniques are described which aim to improve risk decisions and make judgements closer to the normative ideal. We end by considering the strengths and weaknesses of using systematic, objective indicators for making decisions about risk in social work practice.

Seminar Questions

1. Social care professionals are often blamed when they are perceived to have failed to in-tervene to protect the public from risk. They are also blamed when they have acted to protect the public or a client, but the risk was perceived to be too low to justify the course of action. Discuss the implications for clients, the general public, yourself as a practitioner, and your employing organization, when a risk decision has gone 'wrong'. Consider the implications of both over-estimating and under-estimating risk.

2. Think of an occasion when you have made a decision in your own life which involved assessing risk. Think of a decision (or a hypothetical decision) involving risk assess-ment in your social work practice. Do you consider similar types of information when evaluating risk in your own life, as you do when evaluating risk in someone else's?

3. Consider how risk assessment and management should be conducted within a multi-disciplinary setting. What are the roles of the different agencies/professionals in-volved in multi-disciplinary teams with regards to risk assessment?

Further Reading

Baron, J. (1994) *Thinking and Deciding, 2nd edition.* Cambridge: Cambridge University Press.
A thorough and theoretical account of processes involved in thinking and decision making. Covers both descriptive and normative decision making in great depth.

Kemshall, H. and Pritchard, J. (1996) *Good Practice in Risk Assessment and Risk Management 1.* London: Jessica Kingsley Publishers.
Covers risk assessment and decision making with a wide variety of client groups. It is more practical than theoretical.

Plauss, S. (1993) *The Psychology of Judgement and Decision Making.* New York: McGraw-Hill.
Covers similar material to Sutherland and Baron, and is pitched roughly in between the two in terms of the difficulty of the material.

Sutherland, S. (1992) *Irrationality: The Enemy Within.* London: Penguin.
This is an entertaining book which covers many biases in decision making with excellent examples. A fun read.

References

Carson, D. (1995) 'Calculated risk.' *Community Care,* 26 October, 26–27.

Davis, A. (1996) 'Risk work and mental health.' In H. Kemshall, and J. Pritchard (eds) *Good Practice in Risk Assessment and Risk Management.* London: Jessica Kingsley Publishers.

Dawes, R.M., Faust, D. and Meehl, P.E. (1989) 'Clinical Versus Actuarial Judgement.' *Science, 243,* 1668–1674.

Fischer, E.P., Comstock, G.W., Monk, M.A. and Spencer, D.J. (1993) 'Characteristics of completed suicides: implications of differences among methods.' *Suicide and Life Threatening Behaviour, 23,* (2) 91–100.

Isen, A.M. and Means, B. (1983) 'The influence of positive affect on decision making strategy.' *Social Cognition, 2,* 18–31.

Johnson, E.J. and Tversky, A. (1983) 'Affect, generalization, and the perception of risk.' *Journal of Personality and Social Psychology, 45,* 20–31.

Laming, H. (1995) *Partners in Caring: The fourth annual report of the chief inspector of the social services inspectorate.* London: HMSO.

Lasky, J.J., Hover, G.L., Smith, P.A., Bostian, D.W., Duffendack, S.C. and Nord, C.L. (1959) 'Post-hospital adjustment as predicted by psychiatric patients and their staff.' *Journal of Consulting Psychology, 23,* 213–218.

Lester, D. (1994) 'Estimates of prescription rates and the use of medications for suicide.' *European Journal of Psychiatry, 8,* 2, 81–83.

Maule, A.J. and Hockey, G.R.J. (1996) 'The effects of mood on risk-taking behaviour.' *The Psychologist, 9,* 10, 464–467.

National Health Service Health Advisory Service (1994) *Suicide Prevention: The Challenge Confronted.* London: HMSO.

Petty, R.E. and Cacioppo, J.T. (1986) 'The elaboration likelihood model of persuasion.' In L. Berkowitz (ed.) *Advances in Experimental Social Psychology 19.* New York: Academic Press.

Stroebe, W. and Stroebe, M.S. (1995) *Social Psychology and Health* Buckingham: Open University Press.

Sutherland, S. (1992) *Irrationality: The Enemy Within.* London: Penguin.

Tversky, A. and Kahneman, D. (1974) 'Judgement under uncertainty: heuristics and biases.' *Science, 185,* 1124-1130.

Tversky, A. and Kahneman, D. (1983) 'Extensional versus intuitive reasoning: the conjunction fallacy in probability judgement.' *Psychological Review, 90,* 293–315.

Warner, F. (1992) 'Introduction.' *Risk: Analysis, Perception and Management.* London: The Royal Society.

Yoon, K.P. and Hwang, C.L. (1995) *Multiple Attribute Decision Making: An Introduction.* California: Sage Publications

Pitfalls in Interviewing
A Psychological Perspective

Paul Seager, Mark Kebbell and Richard Wiseman

Introduction

Social care professionals are required to interview people for a wide range of reasons (e.g. assessment of clients' needs, to determine facts in potentially sensitive areas of clients' lives). However, it is not always easy, and there are many pitfalls associated with conducting interviews. This chapter does not aim to provide comprehensive cover of interview skills as there are many texts available to do this; rather it aims to introduce some of the latest findings from psychological research which may not be included in more general approaches to interviewing. This includes several important issues, such as: helping the interviewee give more detailed and complete answers to questions; and determining whether the interviewee is either withholding information, or giving the social care professional misleading or deceptive answers. Psychologists have not developed techniques which give definite answers to these problems, and thus there is no sure-fire way of spotting whether a client is lying, or ensuring clients always give detailed and complete answers. However, the chapter does point out the pitfalls associated with these two areas of interviewing, and reviews the ways in which these problems can be minimized.

The first part of the chapter outlines research which has examined ways of improving both the interviewee's memory, and the quality of answers that can be given to questions posed by the social care professional. The second part looks at research into the detection of deception: it discusses how good people actually are at detecting lies and the factors that might make a lie easier or harder to spot. The chapter concludes with a number of tips for enhancing the process of conducting interviews.

Methods of Improving Interviewees' Memory

The improvement of an interviewee's memory can have important implications for a social care professional. Often, significant decisions are based on interviews with clients (and thus it should be noted that the Home Office 'Memorandum of Good Practice' should be followed at all times). For example, an interview with a child may result in that child being placed into protective care. Therefore, it is essential that the professional interview in a way that maximizes the accuracy of a client's account.

Psychologists have carried out a considerable amount of research into ways of improving interviewees' memory, and the resulting methods have the potential to enhance memory by up to 40 per cent (Kohnken, Thurer and Zoberbier, 1994; Fisher and Geiselman, 1992; Kebbell and Wagstaff, in press). Essentially, these methods rely on minimizing factors that may have an adverse effect on memory while including factors that improve memory.

Factors which impair memory

There are many ways in which interviewers can inadvertently impair interviewees' recall (see Fisher, Geiselman and Raymond, 1987).

INTERRUPTIONS

Interviewers frequently interrupt interviewees as they attempt to answer questions. Such interruptions often break the concentration of the interviewee and switches their attention from trying to recall information to the interviewer's interruption. To illustrate this effect, ask a friend to recite the 12 times table (e.g. 1 multiply 12 = 12, 2 multiply 12 = 24, etc.). Interrupt them half way through by asking them to tell you their telephone number. Then tell them to carry on with the 12 times table. This interruption will make them far more likely to make a mistake, and makes the task far more difficult than if they were not interrupted. This has the same effect as interrupting interviewees' attempts to remember information. Further, after interviewees have been interrupted several times they begin to expect such interruption throughout the interview and may shorten their responses accordingly – thus possibly excluding important details (Fisher, Geiselman and Raymond, 1987; Clifford and George, 1996). Of course, in some situations it is necessary to interrupt clients, such as if time is short, or if the client is wandering off the point.

CLOSED QUESTIONS

Some interviewers rely heavily on the use of closed question (e.g. 'Did you have a good relationship with her?') rather than open-ended ones (e.g. 'Tell me about your relationship with her'). This approach has the advantage of eliciting information that the interviewer feels is relevant. However, it can also cause problems. For example, by their very nature closed questions require only a limited response. Further, when closed questions are used the interview takes on the format of the interviewer asking a question and the interviewee giving a brief answer, the interviewer asking another closed question, and so on (see Box 5.1 for an example). This format typically allows only a short time between a question's answer and the next question – giving little opportunity for the interviewee to elaborate or extend an answer. Also, this format ensures that an interview is directed by the interviewer rather than the interviewee. It is difficult enough for the interviewee to retrieve detailed events from memory when actively trying; it is virtually impossible when he or she remains passive. Finally, this format also means that the only information elicited is that which is requested. Thus, if the interviewer forgets to ask a certain question, or does not realize that certain information is important, no information in that area is recorded.

Incidentally, closed questions can also be a problem on forms that are designed to evaluate people's needs. For example, a form that has been designed to assess an elderly person's need for social work support could miss out on important information if it relies on closed questions. It may ask whether the elderly person is able to get their own meals (thus prompting a yes or no answer), rather than using a more open question, such as 'Tell me how you go about getting your own meals'. The open question is more likely to reveal problems, and also areas in which more help could be given.

Discussion point
   ° What questions could the interviewer have asked to elicit more information? In what way could these questions bias answers?

OTHER PROBLEMS

Other problems which may impair an interviewee's memory include: negative phrasing, leading questions, inappropriate language and judgemental comments. Negative phrasing occurs when questions are asked in the negative (e.g. 'I don't suppose you remember if…?'). Phrasing questions in this way actively discourages the interviewee from trying to remember information. Leading questions subtly suggest that a certain answer is required (e.g. 'Do you ever feel that you can't cope?'). Such questions are not only likely to produce compliance rather then accurate recall, but may also bias interviewees' later recollections of an event (Loftus, 1975). Inappropriate language is found where interviewers use overly formal sentences, words, or jargon, which are difficult for the interviewee to comprehend (e.g. 'Who is the primary caregiver in this household?'). Such language may not only prevent the interviewee from understanding the question, but also creates a barrier between the interviewer and the interviewee which is not conducive to good communication. Judgemental comments are occasionally made, often about the interviewee's role in an incident (e.g. 'That really wasn't a

---

Box 5.1 A Typical Police Interview

Psychologists Ronald Fisher and Edward Geiselman recorded police interviews with eyewitnesses in Florida, USA. One extract from their 1992 book *Memory Enhancing Techniques for Investigative Interviewing* (p.20) was as follows:

Interviewer: About how much taller was he than you?

Witness: He was a tiny bit taller than me.

I: Was he very thin? Was he heavy?

W: He was about medium.

I: Was he white or black?

W: Black.

I: Did he have long hair or short hair?

W: Short hair.

I: Was it very short, like close to the scalp?

W: Yeah.

Fisher and Geiselman note that the interviewer asks only closed questions and as a result the interviewee appears passive and volunteers minimal information.

good idea'); these may either offend the interviewee or make them defensive, thus jeopardizing accurate recall.

Factors which enhance memory

There are a variety of ways in which interviewers can help improve interviewees' recall.

CONTEXT EFFECTS

Psychologists have found that memory for information is better if remembered under the same context to that in which it was learned. For example, in one experiment Godden and Baddeley (1975) tested the memory of deep-sea divers. The divers were asked to learn lists of words either on a beach or under 15 feet of water. They were then asked to remember these words in the same or opposite situation. Thus, some divers learnt the words under water and were later tested under water (same situation). Others learnt the words under water but were tested on the beach (opposite situation). Godden and Baddeley found that the memory of divers who were tested in the same situation as they learnt the words was approximately 40 per cent better than the divers who learnt the words in one situation but recalled them in another. These results have been replicated by other researchers, though with less dramatic effects (e.g. Smith, Glenberg and Bjork, 1978).

Smith (1979) investigated whether it is necessary to physically reinstate the same environment for the effect to work, or whether it is sufficient simply to have interviewees imagine themselves in the original environment. He had people study words in a distinctive basement room one day, then had them remember the words either in the same room or in a different fifth floor room the next day. People in the basement recalled about 18 words, significantly more than the group tested in the fifth floor room who could only recall about 12 words. A third group was also tested in the room on the fifth floor; however, these individuals were instructed to remember as much as possible of the original learning environment of the room in which they learnt the words before they were required to try and recall the list. This group recalled an average of 17 words, which was not significantly different from the average score of those who were tested in the same physical environment, but was significantly more than those who were simply tested in the fifth floor room. Hence, it appears the original context does not necessarily have to be physically reinstated; simply thinking of the situation in which the event occurred may help one remember information about the event.

There is also evidence that such effects even work at an emotional level. Goodwin *et al.* (1969) tested the effects of alcohol on memory. They found similar results to those of Godden and Baddeley; information learnt when people had drunk alcohol was more accurately recalled when people had drunk alcohol again than when they were sober, and *vice versa*. Similar findings have been found with happy and sad moods. Teasdale and Fogarty (1979) found that when mood was manipulated people who were sad found it easier to recall sad prior experiences than happy experiences.

Thus, there seems to be considerable support for these 'context' effects. Consequently, psychologists have explored whether the same method can be used to improve interviewees' memory. In a series of experiments Fisher and Geiselman (1992) had interviewees mentally reinstate the context in which an event occurred (e.g. remembering the surroundings, weather, nearby people/objects, how they were feeling at the time, etc.) and discovered that these individuals could recall significantly more than individuals who did not engage in such thoughts.

The practical implications of reinstating context is that it may be a useful tool for improving a client's recall of a past event. Social care professionals are often called upon to make many types of assessment (e.g. of a client's needs), and context effects may help to give an accurate picture of past events, which in turn may affect the assessment judgement.

REPORT EVERYTHING

Further, there is some evidence that interviewees' memory can be improved by simply asking them to report everything. Some people hold back information because they feel that it is not important. However, what an interviewee believes is important and what a social care professional actually finds important may be quite different. In addition, the recall of a trivial piece of information may cue the recall of a more important piece of information.

BUILDING RAPPORT

Finally, it is important that time is spent building rapport with the interviewee. This is achieved by getting to know the interviewee, trying to put them at ease and ensuring that they are relaxed. This is particularly important as events of interest to social care professionals are often embarrassing or abhorrent to the interviewee or, alternatively, the interviewee may have been in some way culpable for embarrassing, abhorrent and/or criminal acts. Thus, establishing rapport is likely to facilitate accurate recall of such information by establishing an environment of trust.

Discussion point
   ° How would you go about establishing rapport with an unfamiliar client?

Detecting Lies

Social care professionals may come into contact with people who attempt to conceal relevant information from them and/or lie. For example, clients may try to convince professionals that they need more help than they really do, or conversely, they may try to make out that they are unable to cope with a situation when this is not the case. Being able to reliably detect such individuals would undoubtedly be a very useful skill to have. How accurate are your lie detection skills? How do you decide if you are being told the truth during an interview? Can you learn to become a better lie detector? The following sections tackle these issues.

Discussion point
   ° How many times do you think that people lie to you on a daily basis? What kind of lies do you think that you are being told? Who do you think lies to you more often: friends or strangers?

How good are people at detecting lies?

A 1994 Gallup poll revealed that 65 per cent of the British population described their lie detection skills as 'good' or 'very good'. This suggests that most people believe that they are pretty good lie detectors. Unfortunately, experiments carried out by psychologists do not support this notion. In a typical study, participants are presented with a videotape containing several interviews. In half of the interviews the interviewees are lying; in the other half of the interviews they are telling the truth. Participants are asked to watch each of the interviews and say whether the interviewee is a liar or a truth-teller. One would expect participants to obtain a 50 per cent hit rate just by chance alone. Unfortunately, participants do little better than chance, scoring, on average, between 45 per cent and 60 per cent (Miller and Stiff, 1993).

Additional studies have investigated the lie detection skills of individuals who are faced with deception on an everyday basis. Again, the results reveal that such individuals are not able to reliably spot the difference between liars and truth tellers. For example, Kraut and Poe (1980) discovered that custom officers were no better at detecting liars than students. Similar results have been found with police officers, judges, operators of lie detectors, robbery investigators and psychiatrists (DePaulo and Pfeifer, 1986; Ekman and O'Sullivan, 1991). Indeed, of all the different groups which have been examined, only US secret service agents have performed significantly better than chance (Ekman and O'Sullivan, 1991).

Worse still, there is no relationship between observers' confidence in their overall lie-detection ability and their measured accuracy. Thus, even when people are confident they have spotted a liar they are no more likely to be correct than when they are sure that the person is telling the truth. In short, most people believe that they are competent lie detectors. However, psychological research has repeatedly shown that the vast majority of the population, including individuals whose profession involves facing deceit, are little better than chance at detecting deception. Why are most people such poor lie detectors? Research suggests that one of the main reasons centres around the signals that people associate with liars (see, for example Kraut (1978) and Riggio and Friedman (1983)).

Discussion point

○ Write down a list of cues that you would look for when trying to decide whether a person was lying or not. Are there any instances when you think that the cues you have listed might not be appropriate indicators of deception?

As an example of false cues to deception, most people believe that liars will be unable to hold your gaze and will constantly 'fidget' (Kraut and Poe, 1980). However, behavioural analysis of videotapes of people telling lies have revealed that both of these beliefs are often incorrect. In fact, liars tend to engage in slightly more eye contact than truth tellers and there is usually no difference in the shifting in body posture when people lie (Zuckerman, DePaulo and Rosenthal, 1981).

What behaviours reliably accompany lying?

Given that people's intuitive ideas about the behavioural changes which accompany lying are usually incorrect, psychologists have tried to identify what, if any, signals reliably indicate lying. Most of this research has involved examining videotapes of liars and truth tellers, and looking for reliable behavioural difference between the two. In a review of the resulting literature, deTurck and Miller (1985) argued that there are only six behaviours that reliably alter during lying (although some dispute these findings: see, for instance, Vrij, 1995).

The first two are non-verbal and have been labelled 'adaptors' and 'hand gestures'. 'Adaptors' are defined by Miller and Stiff (1993) as 'The amount of time either hand is moving while touching the body during the response' (p.57). There is often an increased use of adaptors when a lie is being told. 'Hand gestures' refer to general movement by the hands when not touching the body. These movements were also often found to increase during lying.

The remaining four cues were verbal and consisted of 'speech errors', 'pauses', 'response latency' and 'message duration'. 'Speech errors' refer to non-fluency within a stream of words. This includes having to go back and qualify a point, generally being vague about the topic of the question, or there can be gaps in the flow of words that are filled with noises such as 'err', 'umm', 'aah' and the like. The research suggests that there were significantly more of these type of errors made when people were lying than when they were telling the truth. 'Pauses' refer to silent gaps in speech whilst a person considers what to say. When a lie is being told these cues also significantly increase. The time taken to start an answer after a question has been asked is referred to as a 'response latency'. This also significantly increases when individuals lie, suggesting that liars tend to think more about the answer that they are about to give before they respond to the question (though this may be modified by whether they have had time to prepare for the interview or not). The final cue is 'message duration'. This is the amount of time that a person spends giving an answer. The research suggests that liars' responses are much briefer than responses from people who tell the truth. It is as if they wish to get their lie over and done with as quickly as possible.

It should be noted that there may be limitations in telling people to look for these cues. It may be very difficult for them simultaneously to concentrate on the task in hand (i.e. actually conducting the interview) whilst trying to look for an increased prevalence of certain behaviours, and a decrease in the occurrence of others. Trying to complete all three tasks at once may result in a cognitive overload and a failure to complete any of the tasks satisfactorily. In fact, whilst there are studies that say that training people to detect certain cues can enhance deception detection (e.g. deTurck et al., 1990), there are other studies (e.g. Kohnken, 1987) that conclude that looking for such cues is not at all useful.

A more difficult tool to use in detecting deception is to look for what Ekman (1992) calls 'microexpressions'. He says that they 'provide a full picture of the concealed emotion, but so quickly that it is usually missed' (p.129: see Box 5.2). These are shown on the face of the person for a very short period of time, usually for less than a quarter of a second. On the face of it, this may seem to be a very inaccessible cue to deceit, but Ekman claims that it is possible to train oneself to be able to detect these microexpressions in about an hour. This can be done by flashing photographs in front of your face very quickly and trying to tell what expression was on the face of the person in the picture. At first, this may seem impossible, but after several hundred photos, Ekman claims that it will be possible to achieve. By being able to spot microexpressions, it may be possible to judge emotions that a person is having but is attempting to hide. As with other cues to deception, they do not always appear for everyone, but Ekman claims that they are reliable indicators when they do appear. However, a point to note is that little work has been carried out to develop this technique.

Box 5.2 Can 'Microexpressions' be Used to Spot Deceit?

Psychologist Paul Ekman (1992) recounts the story of the psychiatric patient, Mary, who was being treated for depression. Having been in hospital for a few weeks, a doctor was considering whether she should be allowed home to see her family for the weekend. His interview with Mary was videotaped. The doctor was worried as to whether she would attempt to take her life whilst out of hospital. Mary told him that she was no longer feeling depressed and that she would like to spend some time with her family. His dilemma was whether she was telling him the truth or not. At a later date Mary actually admitted that she had still been feeling very unhappy and that she had wanted a weekend pass in order to be free to try to commit suicide.

Ekman analyzed the film using slow-motion replay and found a complete expression of sadness on her face but only for a fraction of a second, and then it was quickly covered with a smile. He showed the film containing the microexpression to various participants: untrained people were unaware of the brief sadness expression saying that they thought she felt good about herself. However, experienced clinicians were not fooled and were able to spot the sadness message from the microexpression. It also appears that Mary was very aware of the sadness that she had shown.

The implications of this are that if it is possible to learn to spot microexpressions, then it is another possible way to get an insight into feelings that people are trying to hide.

When is it especially difficult to detect a liar?

Additional research has examined the circumstances under which people are especially good at lying. This work has revealed that people are more effective lie-tellers if they have had time to prepare and practice their lies (Littlepage and Pineault, 1982). It may, therefore, be a better idea to conduct any interviews where a person is suspected of lying at very short notice, rather than giving the person time to prepare answers. For example, if a social worker suspects a case of child abuse, it would be better to turn up to interview the parents at relatively short notice, rather than give them two or three days warning of an impending interview. Unfortunately, even simply not telling a client what an interview is going to be about may not be enough to allay their suspicions. If they know that they have been deceiving the social worker, they will likely suspect the worse, and thus prepare themselves for the forthcoming interview. As a general rule, do not give a person suspected of lying time to prepare any answers, or rehearse any explanations for their actions. It may then be easier to make a judgement as to whether the person is being deceptive or not.

Another point to note is that the higher the stakes involved with the lie, the more likely an individual is to leak clues to deception. If the person has a lot to gain by the lie being believed, and a lot to lose by the lie being discovered, there is a good chance that they will betray themselves with some kind of deception cues. Therefore, it might be useful for social care professionals to evaluate the stakes attached with any potential lie they think may be told to them. If it is a high stake lie, then it is more likely that any cues associated with lying will be reliable indicators that a lie is being told.

Finally, Ekman (1992) draws the distinction between easy and hard lies. An easy lie is where the deceiver does not have to cover-up their emotions, or present a false impression about their emotions; there has been ample opportunity to plan and rehearse the lie; the liar is experienced at lying; and the person being lied to is not suspicious. A hard lie would have the opposite conditions. It also seems to be the case that it is slightly easier to lie about facts than it is to lie about emotions.

Can people be trained to become better lie detectors?

Psychologists are divided on the question of whether it is possible to train people to become better lie detectors (see, for example Bull, 1989) or DePaulo, 1994). However, some of the studies that have investigated such training have found some evidence that it works. For example, Zuckerman and his colleagues (Zuckerman, Koestner and Alton, 1984; Zuckerman, Koestner and Colella, 1985) had trainees watch interviews and then told them whether the interviewee was a liar or truth teller. This feedback allowed observers to build up a baseline of the interviewees' deceptive and truthful behaviour, and led to an improvement in their lie detection ability. DeTurck et al. (1990) took a different approach to training. They presented trainees with a 30 minute course in which they informed them about the behavioural cues which reliably indicated deception. Despite the short duration of the course, the authors claimed that the trainees' lie detection skills were significantly increased.

Box 5.3 The Lie-Detector

Also known as a *polygraph*, the lie-detector is a controversial piece of equipment. Its proponents claim that it is a dependable way of detecting whether people are lying or not. By connecting electrodes to the person being questioned, and charting their physiological responses (i.e. breathing rate, skin electrical conductance, blood pressure), it is claimed that polygraphers are able to make reliable guilty/innocent determinations.

The polygraph is not only used in criminal investigations, but is increasingly being used for the screening of job applicants, and also for security vetting of personnel already employed. According to Carroll (1991), around 25 per cent of American employers use polygraph tests as a matter of routine. But how reliable are these tests?

There is a fierce debate raging between those who claim these tests are reliable and those who take an opposite stance. One of the main dangers of using the polygraph is that innocent people will be mistakenly pronounced as guilty. After all, the test only measures physiological responses, and such responses can be caused by a number of emotions (e.g. fear, anger) of which guilt is only one. Carroll (1991) looked at a number of experimental, laboratory-based studies using the polygraph, and found that while it had an impressive rate of detecting the guilty person, it had an equally unacceptable rate of falsely accusing innocent people.

A further consideration is that such studies have been, on the whole, only conducted within the laboratory, where participants have very little to lose, regardless of their mock guilt or innocence. This is clearly not the case in real life: innocent people's reputations can be ruined by a misdiagnosed polygraph test, and guilty people can be freed to re-offend.

The overall picture, however, is still unclear, but at least some research suggests that it might be possible to train people to become better lie detectors. However, it must be remembered that when lie detection research has been able to discriminate between liars and truth tellers this has been at a group level. The ability of a researcher to be able to statistically discriminate between a group of liars and a group of truth tellers in a particular context is a long way from being able to determine if one particular individual is lying or telling the truth. Even training people in the use of technological devices such as the polygraph, to detect lies on an individual basis, is still not completely reliable (see Box 5.3).

The basic conclusion that we can draw from this, therefore, is that we are worse at detecting liars than we believe we are and that there is no simple, reliable way to detect deception. Future research may determine more effective strategies for detecting deception, but at present the most successful strategy for determining if someone is telling the truth is likely to be objective evidence from other sources that confirm or discredit the interviewee's account.

A final point on lie detection should be made. It is not likely that everyone will tell you lies. People in certain professions think that they will be lied to more than people in other professions. Social workers may fall into this category. Indeed, Ekman (1992) argues that social workers '…think that nearly everyone they see is guilty, and everyone is lying' (p.292). Therefore, it may be worth taking the time to review any possible instance of lying as objectively as possible, taking into account all of the aforementioned points in this part of the chapter, in order to make a less biased judgement as to whether deception is actually occurring.

A Practical Summary – Tips for Conducting Interviews

Try to avoid:

- interrupting the interviewee's answers. This only encourages short answers and disrupts the interviewee's responses

- using closed questions. These also encourage short answers and can lead to you missing out on important information

- negative phrasing (e.g. 'you don't remember if…?'). These discourage the interviewee from trying to remember information

- leading questions (e.g. '…and next he picked up the knife?'). Such questions are likely to encourage the interviewee to agree with you rather than recall what actually happened. They may even permanently bias memory for an event

- phrasing questions in overly formal sentences or words. This not only prevents the interviewee from understanding the question, but also creates a barrier between the two of you

- judgemental comments (e.g. 'That wasn't a good idea'). These may make the interviewee defensive and help disrupt rapport.

Try to:

- recreate context. Have the interviewee imagine the context in which an event occurred (e.g. the surroundings, weather, people and objects, how they were feeling at the time, etc.)

- ask the interviewee to remember everything they can, regardless of whether it seems important
- build rapport. Get to know the interviewee, try to put them at ease and establish a feeling of trust.

When trying to decide whether the interviewee is lying:

- remember that you're probably not as good at spotting lies as you think you are!
- if possible, speak with the person informally, and about subjects that they have no cause to lie about. This will give you a useful baseline of the behaviour that they normally use
- take into account how much chance they may have had to practise their lies and rehearse their answers
- consider how much they have to lose from being caught at the lie: the higher the stakes, the more likely they are to leak some deception cues
- determine whether you are looking for an easy (factual) or a hard (emotional) lie
- when asking them questions that you think they might lie to, look out for cues that are more reliable indicators of lying (e.g. adaptors and pauses in speech)
- remember that some people will show deceptive cues when they are not lying and some people will not show deceptive cues even when they are lying
- often the best way to find out if someone is lying is by using another source of evidence (e.g. verifying a client's story from another person)
- again, remember that you are probably not as good at spotting lies as you think you are!

Box 5.4 The 'Megalab Truth Test'

In 1994, a nationwide study examined whether the British public were better able to spot lies on the television, radio or in newspapers (Wiseman, 1995). Sir Robin Day was interviewed twice about his favourite films: in one interview he lied, and in one he told the truth. Television viewers were shown the two interviews. Radio listeners were played the soundtrack of the interviews whilst newspaper readers were simply given a transcript of the interviews. As such the television viewers were presented with visual cues (e.g. eye contact and body movement), verbal cues (e.g. the actual words used and length of response) and vocal cues (e.g. tone of voice and number of pauses). Radio listeners only received verbal and vocal cues whilst newspaper readers only had the verbal cues. Each group were asked to say which interview they believed to be the lie. The results were surprising. Radio listeners were the best at detecting deception (73.4 per cent correct), followed by newspaper readers (64.2 per cent) whilst television viewers were only marginally better than chance (51.8 per cent).

These findings may seem counterintuitive at first, with the group receiving the greatest number of cues having the worst results. However, perhaps the result isn't that surprising. Research shows that vocal and verbal cues (e.g. hesitancy, length of reply) are more reliable indicators of deception than visual cues (e.g. shifts in posture, eye contact) – it seems that television viewers based their judgement on body language and ended up misleading themselves!

Box 5.5 The 'Megalab Interviews'

The interviews printed below are the ones used in the Megalab experiment, as described in Box 5.3. Can you spot which of the interviews is the lie? The answer is printed at the end of the chapter.

Interview 1:

Dr Wiseman: So, Sir Robin, what's your favourite film?

Sir Robin: *Gone With the Wind.*

DW: And why's that?

SR: Oh, it's, it, it's a classic. Great characters; great film star – Clark Gable; a great actress – Vivien Leigh. Very moving.

DW: And who's your favourite character in it?

SR: Oh, Gable.

DW: Right. And how many times have you seen it?

SR: Um...[pause] I think about half a dozen.

DW: And when was the first time you saw it?

SR: When it first came out. I think that was in 1939.

Interview 2:

DW: So, Sir Robin, what's your favourite film?

SR: Ah...[pause] er, *Some Like It Hot.*

DW: And why do you like that?

SR: Oh, because it gets funnier every time I see it. There are all sorts of bits in it which I love. And I like them more each time I see it.

DW: Who's your favourite character in it?

SR: Oh, Tony Curtis I think. He's so pretty...[short pause] and he's so witty, and he mimics Cary Grant so well and he's very funny the way he tries to resist being seduced by Marilyn Monroe.

DW: And when was the first time that you saw it?

SR: I think when it came out, and I forget when that was.

Summary

The purpose of this chapter has been to point out some pitfalls in the way in which interviews may be conducted by social care professionals. This includes both the way in which the interview is structured, and the fact that the professional may not be as good as they think at detecting whether the person being interviewed is telling the truth. First, it discussed factors that may both aid and hinder an interviewer from getting pertinent information from the interviewee. Secondly, it looked at whether it was possible to reliably detect deception within such an interview, and, if so, what cues should be looked for. A concluding example giving you an opportunity to test your skills is given in Boxes 5.4 and 5.5.

Overall, the authors have offered several ways in which the structure and content of an interview can be improved to facilitate the gathering of reliable information – including spotting whether the interviewee is trying to mislead the interviewer.

Seminar Questions

1. How would you conduct an interview to help an interviewee remember information. Why?

2. What would be the ideal situation in which to conduct an interview if you thought that there was a good chance that the interviewee would be lying to you. Why?

Further Reading

Ekman, P. (1992) *Telling Lies. Clues to Deceit in the Marketplace, Politics and Marriage. 2nd Edition.* New York: Norton.
This book contains a good general overview of lie detection, and how lies can be detected. It also contains two new chapters about lying in the 1990s.

Fisher, R.P. and Geiselman, R.E. (1992) *Memory Enhancing Techniques for Investigative Interviewing: The Cognitive Interview.* Springfield, CT: Charles C. Thomas.
This book provides clear, practical advice concerning interviewing. Relevant research is summarised in the appendix.

Miller, G.R. and Stiff, J.B. (1993) *Deceptive Communication.* California: Sage.
This book gives a good coverage of the issues surrounding lies and lying. It also gives a good, readable account of research into this area.

References

Bull, R. (1989) 'Can training enhance the detection of deception?' In J.C. Yuille (ed) *Credibility Assessment.* London: Kluwer Academic Publishers.

Carroll, D. (1991) 'Lie detection: lies and truths.' In R. Cochrane and D. Carroll (eds) *Psychology and Social Issues.* New York: The Falmer Press.

Clifford, B.R. and George, R. (1996) 'A field evaluation of training in three methods of witness/victim investigative interviewing.' *Psychology, Crime and Law 2,* 231–248.

DePaulo, B.M. (1994) 'Spotting lies: can humans learn to do better?' *Current Directions in Psychological Science 3,* 83–86.

DePaulo, B.M. and Pfeifer, R.L. (1986) 'On-the-job experience and skill at detecting deception.' *Journal of Applied Social Psychology 16,* 249–267.

deTurck, M.A., Harszlak, J.J., Bodhorn, D.J. and Texter, L.A. (1990) 'The effects of training social perceivers to detect deception from behavioural cues,' *Communication Quarterly 38,* 189-199.

deTurck, M.A. and Miller, G.R. (1985) 'Deception and arousal. Isolating the behavioural correlates of deception.' *Human Communication Research 12,* 181-201.

Ekman, P. (1992) *Telling Lies. Clues to Deceit in the Marketplace, Politics, and Marriage. 2nd Edition.* New York: Norton.

Ekman, P. and O'Sullivan, M. (1991) 'Who can catch a liar?' *American Psychologist 46,* 913–920.

Fisher, R.P. and Geiselman, R.E. (1992) *Memory Enhancing Techniques for Investigative Interviewing: The Cognitive Interview.* Springfield: Charles C. Thomas.

Fisher, R.P., Geiselman, R.E. and Raymond, D.S. (1987) 'Critical analysis of police interview techniques.' *Journal of Police Science and Administration 15,* 177–185.

Gallup poll (1994) Published in *The Daily Telegraph,* 24 March.

Godden, D.R. and Baddeley, R. (1975) 'Context-dependent memory in two natural environments: on land and underwater.' *British Journal of Psychology 66,* 325–332.

Goodwin, D.W., Powell, B., Bremer, D., Hoine, H. and Stern, J. (1969) 'Alcohol and recall: State dependent effects in man.' *Science 163,* 1358.

Kebbell, M.R. and Wagstaff, G.F. (in press). 'The cognitive interview: an analysis of its forensic effectiveness.' In D.V. Canter and L. Alison (eds) *Beyond Profiling: Developments in Investigative Psychology.* Aldershot: Dartmouth.

Kohnken, G. (1987) 'Training police officers to detect deceptive eyewitness statements: does it work?' *Social Behaviour 2,* 1–17.

Kohnken, G., Thurer, C. and Zoberbier, C. (1994) 'The cognitive interview: Are the interviewers' memories enhanced too?' *Applied Cognitive Psychology 8,* 13–24.

Kraut, R. (1978) 'Verbal and nonverbal cues in the perception of lying.' *Journal of Personality and Social Psychology 36*, 380–391.

Kraut, R. and Poe, D. (1980) 'Behavioural roots of person perception: the deception judgements of customs inspectors and laypersons.' *Journal of Personality and Social Psychology 39*, 784–798.

Littlepage, G.E. and Pineault, M.A. (1982) 'Detection of deception of planned and spontaneous communications.' Unpublished Paper, Department of Psychology, Middle Tennessee State University, Murfreesboro, USA.

Loftus, E.F. (1975) 'Leading questions and eyewitness report.' *Cognitive Psychology 7*, 560–572.

Miller, G.R. and Stiff, J.B. (1993) *Deceptive Communication.* California: Sage.

Riggio, R.E. and Friedman, H.S. (1983) 'Individual differences and cues to deception.' *Journal of Personality and Social Psychology 45*, 899–915.

Smith, S.M. (1979) 'Remembering in and out of context.' *Journal of Experimental Psychology: Human Learning and Memory 5*, 460–471.

Smith, S.M., Glenberg, A. and Bjork, R.A. (1978) 'Environmental context and human memory.' *Memory and Cognition 6*, 342–353.

Teasdale, J.D. and Fogarty, S.J. (1979) 'Differential effects of induced mood on retrieval of pleasant and unpleasant events from episodic memory.' *British Journal of Clinical Psychology 22*, 248–257.

Vrij, A. (1995) 'Behavioural correlates of deception in a simulated police interview.' *The Journal of Psychology 129*, 15–28.

Wiseman, R. (1995) 'The Megalab truth test.' *Nature* 373 (2 February), 391.

Zuckerman, M., DePaulo, B.M. and Rosenthal, R. (1981) 'Verbal and nonverbal communication of deception.' In L. Berkowitz (ed.) *Advances in Experimental Social Psychology.* New York: Academic Press.

Zuckerman, M., Koestner, R. and Alton, A.O. (1984) 'Learning to detect deception.' *Journal of Personality and Social Psychology 46*, 519–528.

Zuckerman, M., Koestner, R. and Colella, M.J. (1985) 'Learning to detect deception from three communication channels.' *Journal of Nonverbal Behaviour 9*, 188–194.

Megalab Interview Answer: Interview 1 was the lie.

Working with Families

Anne Woollett

Introduction

Families are an important fact of life for most children and adults. In spite of substantial demographic changes, traditional 'nuclear' families are often viewed as the 'norm/ideal' form, and other families are defined with reference to them. But the links between family form and functioning are complex: some 'nuclear' families experience problems while other kinds of families demonstrate strengths and resilience. A major omission from research on families is the 'voice' of family members themselves, reflecting on their experiences of family life.

A variety of theoretical approaches to families are drawn on in this chapter, including psychodynamic, attachment, systems, feminist and ecological theories. Approaches vary in the extent to which they focus on the interior of families (on individuals and relations between them) and on families as social groups operating within (and influenced by) the wider social and economic context such as schools, parental employment, health care, welfare and legal systems. Ideas about families and about the needs and rights of children and of parents are influenced by the wider cultural and moral context: in Western societies there is considerable commitment to equity in family relations and on personal development and self-fulfilment, but also a concern about the increasing instability of family relations.

What are Families: Family Forms and the Family Life Cycle

Families take a number of forms. The *nuclear* family (male breadwinner, female full-time carer, and dependent biological children living in a common residence) is often considered as the 'normal' or traditional family. But a considerable proportion of families do not conform to this traditional form. Many households/families (such as married couples without children and couples whose children are no longer dependent) do not include children, and others (such as adopted and foster children) include children who are not biologically related to their parents (Muncie and Sapsford, 1995; Clarke, 1996).

Families also vary in terms of the relations between parents. While the majority of parents are married, families are created increasingly by parents who are cohabiting rather than married, up to one-third of children in the UK according to some figures (Clarke, 1996). Families are also created when children are born to women on their own. Increasing rates of family breakdown and remarriage, in the UK as elsewhere in the Western world, result in children living with one parent (usually the mother) and with step parents (Muncie and

Sapsford, 1995). However, in spite of these changes, there is also evidence to suggest that at any time point about 80 per cent of children are living with both parents (married and cohabiting), 10 per cent with a lone mother, and a further 9 per cent with mother and stepfather (Clarke, 1996).

The statistics about families are complex and open to different interpretations. This is in part because of variations in the ways the statistics are collected and presented. Figures which compare the number of marriages entered into in any year with the number of divorces in the same year give the impression that family breakdown is more common than, for example, figures which consider divorce as a function of the year in which couples married or the length of marriage. For a discussion of family statistics and their interpretation see Clarke (1996) and Muncie and Sapsford (1995).

Discussion point

- ° Make a list of a variety of family forms. Consider how these forms may influence relationships between parents, and between parents and children.

Family life cycle

The statistics about families are problematic because they are based on snapshots of family forms at the time the data were collected, and take little account of the ways in which families change over the family life cycle. Psychologists who take a life cycle approach to families point to regular changes in family forms and their implications for family relations (Aldous, 1996; Huston and Vangelisti, 1995). Key events in the family life cycle seen as having particular significance for parental relations and for parents' relationships with children are: the initial transition to parenthood (Michaels and Goldberg, 1988; Huston and Vangelisti, 1995); the birth of subsequent children and caring for more than one child (Dunn, 1988; Munn, 1991); children going to school and becoming more competent and independent (Maccoby, 1984; Newson and Newson, 1968, 1976); children reaching adolescence (Brannen *et al.*, 1994; Apter, 1990); and children leaving home (Aldous, 1996). These changes over the family life cycle are seen as part of the 'normal' pattern of family life, and are viewed differently than changes such as family breakdown, illness and disability. While the latter are relatively frequent, they are seen as unexpected and not as part of the 'normal' family life cycle (Aldous, 1996; Dallos and Sapsford, 1995).

Discussion point

- ° Identify some events in the family life cycle. Discuss the implications of each for family relations. Compare the ways in which families may deal with events considered 'expected' and 'normal' and those seen as 'problematic'. Do you think this may differ across ethnic groups?

Families in the wider social setting

Because they concentrate on the early years of the family life cycle when children's lives are lived largely within their families, psychological approaches tend to focus on the interior of families. Ecological theories, in contrast, focus on the exterior relations and the wider social, economic and cultural/ideological context in which families exist and their influence on family relations and children's development (Bronfenbrenner, 1986). The influence of the wider context can be seen in studies which examine the engagement of young people in activities and relationships outside their families and how they are influenced by friends, schools and youth culture (Allatt, 1996; Brannen *et al.*, 1994). Similarly, studies of the social context of single or 'lone' mothers suggest that they often have the support of other people including their own mothers, child minders, friends and neighbours (Phoenix, 1991; Dallos and Sapsford, 1995).

Bronfenbrenner (1986) reviews studies of the influence of the economic situation and parental employment on families. He argues that parental income has a direct impact on the neighbourhoods in which families live and the opportunities they can provide for children. Unemployment and low income can increase tensions between parents as they try to balance the needs and demands of different family members. The nature of parents' employment (such as their hours of work, how much work they bring home, whether one or two parents are working) influences parents' commitment to work compared with parenting and the amount of time they spend with children and can monitor their activities (Ferri and Smith, 1996). Employment also has an influence on families through the values and qualities (such as obedience, risk taking, honesty, time keeping and service to others) which are required in particular jobs (Bronfenbrenner, 1986). The idea that different forms of employment require or encourage somewhat different values and qualities underlies much analysis of social classes differences in child rearing (Newson and Newson, 1976; Das Gupta, 1995).

Summary

Some of the diversity of family forms and the ways in which families change over the life cycle have been considered. In the next sections family functioning and how family members make sense of their families are discussed.

How Families Function

Professionals bring to their study of family functioning a variety of approaches and concerns (Mayall, 1990). Psychologists, for example, in their examination of families, are interested in the ways in which families encourage aspects of development in children such as cognitive and language development and attachment relations. Mothers, in contrast, view children in more holistic terms, emphasizing children's individuality and how children get on with others in their families, at school and in the wider world. They also have somewhat different concerns, such as whether children behave 'well' and comply with family rules about telling parents where they are going (Tizard and Hughes, 1984; Mayall, 1990; Allatt, 1996).

The main emphasis of psychological research on family functioning is on the ways in which families (and especially mothers) influence children's development and socialization. The contribution of mothers is the most common focus, even when there are no genetic links between mothers and children (as may be the case in families created through adoption or the use of reproductive technologies), and when women are caring for their partner's children from a previous relationship. Psychodynamic approaches emphasize the impact of mothers on children's emotional lives, whereas psychological theories stress mothers' cognitive and educational roles (Parker, 1995; Woollett and Phoenix, 1996; Dallos and Sapsford, 1995). However, while these approaches provide powerful evidence for the role of mothers, by stressing the 'causal' or 'determining' role of mothers they underplay the influence of fathers, siblings and other family members. The ways in which children may influence parents and family life are also often underestimated: parents and other family members respond to children in ways which are influenced by children's age, gender, characteristics and ways of coping (White and Woollett, 1992; Das Gupta, 1995; and see also Chapter 11).

Children's experiences of family life are influenced by a range of factors. One is birth order. A first born child has parents who are inexperienced but have time to spend with the child in comparison with a second or subsequent child who has to share parents' attention with an older sibling but always has the company of their siblings (Dunn, 1988; Munn, 1991). The gender of children influences how parents respond to them. Mothers are more concerned about the safety of girls and supervise them more than boys, providing girls with more opportunity to talk to mothers and confide in them compared with boys (Newson and Newson, 1986; Burman, 1994). Girls are also given greater permission to express fear and distress, they receive greater support for dealing with family breakdown, and are encouraged to think about themselves in terms of their relationships with others (Gilligan, 1982). Because they are less supervised, boys take more risks (and are involved in more road traffic accidents), but are also encouraged to be more independent and self-sufficient (Newson and Newson, 1986). This means that boys are given less support for their fears and concerns, but are more often able to escape family problems and distress through friendships outside the family (White and Woollett, 1992; Dunlop, 1995).

Physical care and safety

The ability of families to care for children in a safe and healthy environment is given considerable emphasis by policy makers and professionals concerned with child protection. Psychological and psychodynamic approaches, however, tend to take this aspect of family life for granted, and therefore do not often address the ways in which a family's physical environment and their economic circumstances influence how they bring up children. Those studies to take this approach suggest that families who live on run down housing estates or near busy roads, in the absence of safe play areas, may decide to keep their children at home (Mayall, 1994; Das Gupta, 1995). As a result, children may spend many hours a day watching television, take little exercise, and have little opportunity to play with other children (Duncan *et al.*, 1994). Mothers' views about how to bring up their children are influenced by the physical resources they can draw on (Das Gupta, 1995; Mayall, 1990). Newson and Newson (1976) discuss the ways in which being able to wash and dry dirty clothes easily influences how relaxed mothers are likely to feel about children engaging in wet or messy play. Similarly Newson and Newson (1976) argue that when space is restricted and children have to play alongside older children doing homework and parents watching television, mothers may discourage noisy games, even though they consider that children need to 'express themselves' (Mayall, 1990).

Warmth, emotional security and attachment

Psychodynamic theories point to the emotional intensity of family life, emphasizing the expression of emotions and early development of trusting relationships and *attachment* (a preference for the mother or main caregiver which provides a secure emotional base; see also Chapter 11). The development of attachment is viewed as necessary if children are to explore their physical and social environment, to gain a sense of themselves as lovable and competent and other people as trustworthy (Tizard, 1991). Traditionally, attachment theories have argued that the mother–child relationship is the 'key' relationship in the development of secure attachments, and this view is often reflected in social policy and child care practice (New and David, 1985). There is increasing recognition that children are also attached to fathers, siblings and others and the role these attachment relationships play in children's emotional development (Burman, 1994; Dunn, 1988; Tizard, 1991).

Socialization of child and preparation for future lives

A function of families extensively explored by psychologists is that of *socialization* (preparing children for their roles in the world outside the family). Psychological research has identified a number of ways in which families differ in their techniques of socialization or child rearing, and how these are linked to different outcomes for children's behaviour and development.

It is often argued that a powerful way of distinguishing parents and their child rearing techniques is in terms of their control or discipline. Parents who exert a moderate amount of pressure on children to do well, to behave in 'mature' ways and to be compliant tend to have children who are more obedient, competent and concerned for others than are children whose parents exercise very low or very high levels of control (see Maccoby and Martin, 1983 and Das Gupta, 1995 for reviews of studies in this area). It is often considered that this is the case because parents who are very controlling restrict children's opportunities to explore their physical and social environment, and that parents who are very permissive or tolerant fail to provide children with feedback on the outcomes of their behaviour (Maccoby and Martin, 1983; White and Woollett, 1992). However, it is also argued that the outcomes for children are linked more closely to the type than the amount of control parents use: parents who control children and maintain compliance through the use of reasoning and explain to children why their behaviour is inappropriate tend to be more effective than parents who use physical control and coercion. Reasoning and explanation are considered to be more effective because children are provided with information about what parents (and others) consider right and wrong, appropriate and inappropriate, and are told about the consequences of their behaviour. which they can use to guide their future behaviour.

Another aspect of parents' child rearing identified in research is the extent to which parents express warmth and affection towards children. Studies suggest that the use of reasoning and explanation is more effective when accompanied by the expression of feelings by parents, for example, by showing pleasure or their annoyance (Johnson and McGillicuddy-Delisi, 1983). In educational terms, it is argued that the expression of feelings helps children to learn which activities are likely to meet with approval and disapproval. But making children aware of the feelings of others also shows them that others care and are interested in what they do, and this may encourage children to behave well to meet with the approval of parents (White and Woollett, 1992).

The extent to which parents involve children in discussions and decision making and allow children to influence activities and parents' responses (often referred to as being 'child-centred') also has consequences for children's behaviour and development. This style of child-rearing enables children to take an active part in family life, to make their wishes known and have them respected. But it also means that parents are more likely to be knowledgeable about their children's likes and dislikes, and can make use of this information to ensure children's compliance (Newson and Newson, 1976; Walkerdine and Lucey, 1989).

These different aspects of socialization are sometimes discussed as if they are separate from one another and function independently. However, in a study of parents of young children, Baumrind (1973) argues that these different aspects are not independent but tend to cluster together. She identified three patterns or clusters, which she labelled 'authoritarian', 'authoritative' and 'permissive', which are outlined in Box 6.1.

Box 6.1 Three Patterns of Child Rearing

Diane Baumrind identified three patterns or techniques of socialization and child rearing in parents of young children. These are:

Authoritarian parents

- value obedience
- believe in limiting children's autonomy and independence
- set high standards of behaviour
- do not display warmth and affection towards children
- favour strong and punitive measures to control children's misbehaviour.

Authoritative parents

- value compliance
- respect the child's autonomy and independence
- set high standards for children's behaviour
- display warmth and affection
- explain rules and decisions
- control by means of reasoning.

Permissive parents

- are tolerant of children's behaviour and autonomy, allowing children to determine their own activities
- do not demand strict standards for children's behaviour
- are warm and affectionate
- are not controlling.

Discussion point

° Consider how parents identified as authoritarian, authoritative and permissive might deal with the following: young people coming in late without permission, a child who hits others at school, a child who mixes with friends who parents do not approve of. From your discussion, how easy do think it is to categorize parents in these ways? What are the advantages and disadvantages of categorizing parents?

A major aim of psychological research is to consider the implications of parents' child rearing for their children's behaviour and development. Baumrind (1973) found that parents who balanced control and demands for good behaviour with warmth and involve children in decision making (authoritative parenting) were more effective, and their children performed better in terms of greater cognitive competence, desire to achieve, friendliness to peers, independence and self-control, than did children brought up in families described as 'authoritarian' (controlling, considerable demands on children but less warmth and involvement of children in decision making) or 'permissive' (acceptance of children, but little control or demands for mature behaviour). The effectiveness of child-centred or sensitive parenting is also reported in laboratory-based studies, in which mothers are observed interacting with infants and young children (Maccoby and Martin, 1983). The children of mothers who allow themselves to be paced by children's moods, preferences and interests are more competent, demonstrate greater self-worth and are more willing to co-operate with adults than are children whose mothers are less sensitive and child-centred (Maccoby and Martin, 1983; White and Woollett, 1992).

It is often assumed in studies that there is a direct causal link between parents' child-rearing style and their children's behaviour and development. However, the picture is more complex: 'circular' models of causation may be more useful than linear models because parents respond to children's behaviour as well as influencing it, and both parents' and children's behaviour are 'caused' by wider family patterns of behaviour and relations. So, for example, it is likely that parents' aggression and smacking of children may be directly linked to children's aggression because parents model aggressive behaviour and teach the child that hitting is an effective way of controlling others. But children's aggression can also be seen as a 'cause' of parents' behaviour when, for example, parents respond to children who hit a younger sibling or bully other children at school by smacking them. Rather than viewing children's behaviour as a direct response to their parents' child rearing, it is useful to think of parents and children as influencing one another. Children and parents may also be influenced by general family atmosphere and culture in which hitting is common/acceptable and where other bids for attention are ignored.

Discussion point

° Focusing on a particular issue, consider the ways in which parents and children may influence one another. How may parents break such cycles of behaviour?

However, the general applicability of the findings of research such as that of Baumrind (1973) has been challenged. Studies demonstrating the efficacy of authoritative parenting have been conducted largely in the USA with white, 'nuclear' and predominantly middle class families. It is argued that findings from studies with such families cannot necessarily be generalized to other families. Walkerdine and Lucey (1989), for example, point to considerable variability in parents' ideas about what are qualities they value for children. Verbal fluency, for example, which is held in high regard by middle class US parents (and by researchers and policy makers), is often viewed negatively by working class parents, as 'answering back' or 'disrespect'. Questions about the generalizability of findings are also raised in studies with families from ethnic minority communities (see also Chapter 3). Stopes-Roe and Cochrane (1990) report that Asian parents in the UK question the value of qualities such as independence and individual achievement which they view as 'selfish', or as putting self before others and hence do not wish to encourage. When they are concerned to maintain their cultural and ethnic identity, Asian parents often express disapproval of young people becoming independent and wanting to make their own friends. They are concerned that in becoming independent, young people (and especially young women) may bring disgrace to their families (Stopes-Roe and Cochrane, 1990; Dosanjh and Ghuman, 1996).

In ethnic minority communities, parents often value more highly qualities such as compliance, co-operation and respect for elders (Greenfield and Cocking, 1994). They are valued because they are seen as reflecting commitment to family and community and to social relations characterized by interdependence rather than independence and individualism. Parents sometimes also view these qualities as important, because they are seen as providing young people with effective ways of coping with racism or social exclusions, or with a marginal economic position in society. Ogbu (1981) suggests that Black and Asian parents often consider that 'obedient' or 'quiet' children are less likely to be labelled as 'problems' by schools, police, and welfare agencies than are children who 'know their own minds' or 'talk back to adults'.

Studies which examine the achievement of young people from ethnic minority communities also raise questions about whether authoritative parenting is universally effective. Studies report links between authoritative parenting and achievement for children in white middle class families. However, the achievement of Chinese, Japanese and Black American children and young people is more closely linked to authoritarian than to authoritative parenting (Greenfield and Cocking, 1994; Lambourn et al., 1996). Young people from these communities do better when their parents are not child-centred, but have high expectations and supervise their children closely. Lambourn et al. (1996) argue that authoritarian parenting is more effective for young people from ethnic minority communities because it reassures them that parents care about them, and how well they are doing, and is not viewed as overcontrolling or as interfering with young people's independence. Greenfield and Cocking (1994) suggest that as a result young people are encouraged to work hard and keep out of trouble for the sake of their families as well as for themselves. And their success is seen as strengthening relationships between young people, their families and communities rather than as encouraging separation from them.

Conflicts and their management

An important aspect of socialization in families is teaching children about how to express their feelings and get their wishes met in ways considered appropriate. The different, and sometimes opposing, wishes of family members can result in conflict, with parents trying to control and structure children's lives and children resisting parents' control (Dunn, 1988). Conflict is expressed and managed in different ways. In some families conflict is seen as a problem which mothers seek to minimize: they draw on their knowledge of children to anticipate and defuse potentially difficult situations (Tizard and Hughes, 1984; Dunn, 1988). Parents also minimize conflict through the use of explanation and talking things through. These techniques rely for their effectiveness on high levels of verbal skills and a belief in their value, and so as Walkerdine and Lucey (1989) argue, are employed more often in middle class than in working class families. However, as Tizard and Hughes (1984) suggest, conflicts and arguments are not necessarily problematic: they may have pedagogical benefits if they encourage parents to articulate rules (such as the need to share, to take turns, and to respect the property of other people) and make children aware of how their behaviour is viewed by others.

In contrast, other families view conflicts as 'facts of family life', acknowledging the different ideas of children and parents about issues such as what television programmes children watch, and what is an appropriate time to come home in the evening. In such families, family members are more likely to be allowed to express their feelings and engage in conflict. The benefits of this approach to conflicts, as Walkerdine and Lucey (1989) argue, are that children gain competence in recognizing and handling strong feelings, and when they can/cannot influence parents and older siblings.

Discussion point

○ Consider some of the advantages and disadvantages for parents and children of some different ways of managing conflicts in families.

Families often use different ways of dealing with conflict at different points in the life cycle: crying and temper tantrums may be tolerated in a two year old, but such 'babyish' ways are not considered appropriate for seven or eight year olds (Newson and Newson, 1968, 1976). 'Explaining' and 'talking through' are effective only once children are verbally skilled (Newson and Newson, 1968). But as they become more verbally skilled, children can also challenge parents, countering parents' 'reasons' with reasons of their own (Newson and Newson, 1976), and later even refusing to talk things through (Allatt, 1996; Brannen et al., 1994). A refusal to engage with parents may be particularly effective when parents are not used to dealing with displays of strong emotions. Working class families often prefer to manage conflicts through the use of techniques such as smacking, not letting children go out, or preventing them from watching a television programme which acknowledge parent–child conflict and do not rely on verbal argument (Newson and Newson, 1976; Tizard and Hughes, 1984).

Discussion point

   ° The roles and functions of families are often discussed in isolation from one another. Consider the issues for parents and how they may be supported as they try to balance keeping children safe AND allowing them to be independent, or between being child-centred AND encouraging children to respect their elders.

FAMILY FORM AND FAMILY FUNCTIONING

It is usually assumed that there is a close association between how effectively families function and their form, with 'nuclear/intact' families considered to function more effectively than divorced or one parent families. However, as Gottfried and Gottfried (1994) argue, the situation is more complex. In 'nuclear/intact' families parents often do support one another and give children a sense of parents' joint concern and commitment to them. But this is not always the case: when parents are stressed or do not communicate effectively, one parent may undermine the attempts of the other to monitor children's activities or deal with signs of problems such as illegal drug use. In single parent and divorced families parenting may be less effective: a mother bringing up children on her own may feel overwhelmed by her experience of divorce, or so tied up in earning a living that her parenting is inconsistent, over controlling one day and not sufficiently controlling the next, and she may fail to monitor her children's activities closely.

But parenting in single parent and divorced families is often caring, consistent and appropriate. This may be the case because family breakdown is not always associated with stress and a reduction in the quality of parenting. Family breakdown can lead to a reduction in conflict and tension, allowing the custodial parent more time to deal with children's distress and misbehaviour, and more opportunity to talk things through with children than was the case before the family breakdown. Parents bringing up children on their own may also compensate for the lack of a second parent by supervising children closely, and by demanding that children behave particularly well because they are aware of the negative view of single parent families (Gottfried and Gottfried, 1994; White and Woollett, 1992).

Family breakdown is particularly problematic, and children are more likely to be considered as 'problems' when it is associated with a multiplicity of stressors (such as parental conflict and little support) and disruptions (such as reduction in family income, moving home and school) (Rutter, 1985; White and Woollett, 1992). Single parent and divorced families tend to experience greater levels of stress and disruption than intact families. But this is not always the case, and family breakdown can bring a reduction in conflict and uncertainty, and similarly, nuclear/intact families also vary considerably in their levels of stress. Because conflict, stress and disruption are more closely associated with children's problems than is family form, professionals working with families need to consider the stress and disruptions families are experiencing and the support available to them, rather than whether or not they conform to traditional family forms.

Discussion point

- ° Identify some stresses and disruptions and supports for families. Consider the ways these might operate to increase/mitigate the effects of family breakdown for parents and children.

Summary

In this section, a range of family functions and roles have been examined. They reflect current professional ideas and concerns about children and families, and the impact of family functioning on children's present and future behaviour. It has been argued that ideas about children and families are not fixed and universal, but vary considerably across the life cycle and across families. In the next section, families and their functions are considered from the perspective of family members themselves.

Experiences of Families and Family Life

Increasingly, psychological research recognizes that parents and children reflect on their experiences in families and compare their own family with others they know. Research which takes this perspective suggests that children have a clear notion of the 'family', viewing it as a close knit group living in the same household ('living their lives together' 'a place to belong to') and as a private world (where you are 'accepted as you are') in contrast to the public world of work, school, street or playground (Allatt, 1996; Moore *et al.*, 1996). Children also define families in terms of shared activities (such as visiting granny, or going for walks), everyday living (such as preparing food), and the support families provide for one another (Moore *et al,*. 1996; Dallos, 1995; Allatt, 1996; Dallos and Sapsford, 1995; Brannen *et al.*, 1994). Grandmothers and others who live at a distance are seen as 'family' if they work at being involved and are interested in what children are doing. 'Being' a family member is continually renegotiated: children argue that if they are to have a role in their lives, non-custodial parents need to be involved and show commitment (O'Brien *et al.*, 1996).

Children view parents as being differently involved in family life, with mothers seen as more involved and committed, listening to children and being there 'for' them more than fathers. Fathers are seen to engage in family life largely through play and similar activities (Ferri and Smith, 1996; Wetherell, 1995; Allatt, 1996).

Identity/who I am

Family members suggest that an important function of families, but one which less often considered by psychologists, is that of providing a sense of identity and belonging. Families provide parents and children with an identity, as one of the 'Smiths' or 'Patels'. Families embody symbolically a person's history, and embed them in a complex of family relationships and activities (Allatt, 1996; Dallos and Sapsford, 1995).

The negative identity associated with living in non-traditional families is often resisted by family members. While they consider that family breakdown is usually painful and disruptive, some mothers and children reject the label of 'deviant', pointing to similarities between themselves and 'nuclear/intact' families, and emphasizing how well they are doing. Sometimes mothers argue that a reduction in tension has enabled them to relate to children in more child-centred and affectionate ways, and in their turn children have become more responsive and get on better with siblings (Kier and Lewis, 1995; Rutter, 1985). Children sometimes report that since the family breakdown they have been given greater responsibility and are involved in family decisions, making them feel valued and 'grown up' (Moore et al., 1996). Other families deal with the negative identity associated with family breakdown differently. While they accept the negative identity, they insist that it does not apply to their family, but only to families who are not coping so well as they are (Dallos, 1995; Gottfried and Gottfried, 1994).

Family life is also experienced differently according to the perspective of individual family members, and over time. Parents usually report less anger and hostility over time as they and their children settle into new routines (Gano-Phillips and Fincham, 1995). Remarriage means that these routines are disrupted and need to be renegotiated. Remarriage often means a happier family atmosphere and an improvement in family finances, but children sometimes regret that it also means a less close relationship with their mother and fewer family responsibilities (White and Woollett, 1992).

Parents in families created by remarriage (like those created by the new reproductive technologies) often 'normalize' their families by stressing their commitment to parenting, arguing that social relationships between parents and children are a firmer basis for good parenting than biological or genetic relationships (White and Woollett, 1992). However, children's experiences also depend on the wider context in which families live. When children know other children who are adopted or whose parents have split up, with whom they can share feelings and experiences, children often feel less isolated and less 'abnormal' (Moore et al., 1996).

Analysis of the experiences of non-traditional families gives further weight to the need to be cautious about making assumptions about 'cause' and 'effect' in family relationships. When families divorce, parents often anticipate problems and any which do occur are 'explained' or 'blamed' on the divorce without sufficient consideration of other possible causes. There is some evidence to suggest that behavioural problems usually considered to be a 'result' of divorce, may be found prior to the breakdown of parental relations (Das Gupta, 1995). So, for example, children who truant or get into trouble with the police put pressure on their families. This pressure may 'cause' or increase existing tensions between parents and the risks of family breakdown. A 'problem' child may also add to family stresses by encouraging blame and recriminations (Das Gupta, 1995; Emery, 1988).

Discussion point

 ° Family members have differing perspectives on family issues. Drawing on the information in Box 6.2 about T's refusal to work for his examinations suggest how different family members might 'explain' T's behaviour. Consider how families may be helped to recognise and appreciate each other's perspectives.

Box 6.2 The Perspectives of Different Family Members

Family A are experiencing problems because T, the 16 year old son, refuses to work for his exams. His parents are also concerned because they do not know where he gets to when he is not at school, but fear that he is hanging around with friends who take drugs.

T himself says

- he has worked hard at school in earlier years
- his friends find school 'boring'
- he thinks his younger brother has it 'easier' than he did
- he cannot talk to his mother as much as he could when he was younger
- he gets angry when his parents do not trust him but want to know where he is all the time

T's mother says

- she wants T to do better for himself than his father did
- she feels that they live in a dangerous area for children like T
- she thinks her husband leaves family things to her too much
- she is hoping to get a full-time job in the next year

T's father

- he cannot understand why T has become such a problem
- he believes that home should be a relaxing place
- he is proud of his children, although he finds it difficult to relate to them
- he is expected to work long hours at work
- he is worried about his mother who has heart problems.

T's younger brother

- he looks up to and admires T
- has always found school easier than T
- he gets on well with his younger sister
- he likes going fishing with his father
- he enjoys watching television with his mother.

Summary

To understand how families function, it is important to consider the perspectives of family members themselves. These suggest that an issue for families who are not 'nuclear/intact' families is how to maintain a positive identity and sense of themselves as a family given assumptions about the problematic nature of such families. It also indicates the complex ways in which family members relate to one another, which are considered in the following section.

Families: Individuals, Relationships and Groups

Psychologists bring to the study of families a number of distinct approaches, some focusing on families as individuals and collections of individuals, and others on families as networks of relationships, or as a social group. Some of these ways of considering families and their implications for understanding how families function are discussed in this section.

Individuals: psychological approaches to families often take the individual, and especially individual children, as their main focus and examine the ways in which children are influenced by parents and changes in families (Dunn, 1988; Aldous, 1996; Maccoby and Martin, 1983). Less frequently considered are parents, their experiences and emotional satisfaction with family life. Feminist theorists have examined women's experiences as mothers, arguing motherhood provides women with a valued identity and that women obtain considerable emotional satisfaction from mothering (Phoenix *et al.*, 1991). However, at the same time motherhood is often viewed more negatively, with women reporting dissatisfaction with the hard work of child care and associated household tasks which often leave them isolated and depressed with little time for themselves or their relationship with a partner (Nicolson, 1993). Psychodynamic theories also point to the contradictory feelings of women as they try to balance concerns about their child's dependence on them and their own dependency on male partners, and between feeling 'in control' as a mother, but also controlled by the demands of motherhood (Parker, 1995).

Relationships: psychological and psychodynamic theories also consider relationships within families, and especially mother–child relations (Woollett and Phoenix, 1996; Parker, 1995). There is now greater recognition of the significance of fathering for men and men's relationships with their children, for children and for men themselves (Lewis and O'Brien, 1987; Wetherell, 1995).

Psychological research on father–child relations has tended to stress differences in the parenting style of men and women. Fathers are reported as engaging in play more than mothers, but as being less involved in childcare and as less sensitive and child-centred in their play (Burman, 1994; White and Woollett, 1992). Studies also find that fathers' involvement and their play is influenced by the child's gender more than is the case for mothers. Psychological and psychodynamic approaches argue that fathers are important for children because they provide a male role model and source of identification, and that this is linked to children's gendered identities (Wetherell, 1995; Lewis and O'Brien, 1987). However, there is also evidence that mothers and fathers in the same family share many of the same values and ideas about how to bring up children (White and Woollett, 1992).

Network of relationships within families

Systems theory argues that the sets of relationships in families (mother–child, father–child, mother–father, child–child) do not function independently, but are mutually dependent, with each influencing others in ways which change over the life cycle. Psychological research concentrates on relations between children and parents, but increasingly recognizes that a central family relationship is that between parents (Aldous, 1996). The nature and quality of the parental relationship is significant for parents themselves, but also for children because it influences all family relationships, including those between mothers and children and fathers and children (Gable *et al.*, 1992; White and Woollett, 1992).

Systems theory also argues for the recognition of changes in relationships over the family life cycle (Aldous, 1996). So, for example, as they get older, young people become more independent and go out with friends rather than taking their leisure at home, and this is encouraged by parents (Brannen et al., 1994). Young people's independence requires the negotiation of rules about what time young people come home and whether they are collected by parents. These rules are continually being renegotiated as parents take account of young person's capacities, responsibilities and their circumstances, such as where young people are going and with whom they are going. This means, as Allatt (1996) argues, that monitoring the activities of young people requires not just that parents ask questions, but that young people take responsibility for telling parents where they are going and for the establishment of shared understandings and trust. A pattern of mutual understanding and influence has benefits because if young people recognize that parents monitor their behaviour because they care for them, young people are more likely to consider that parents' questions are legitimate.

By viewing families as intermeshing sets of relationships which change over time, systems theories may reinforce notions of the 'normality' of changes in roles and relationships in adolescence. As a result, young people's demands for increasing independence and their negotiation of relationships with parents is often viewed by parents as 'painful' but 'natural'. But parents may also resist such changes. For example, in families with no tradition of 'talking things through' or involving young people in decision making, it may be difficult for parents to listen to young people's point of view and negotiate rules with them (Steinberg et al., 1989). Also parents from ethnic minority communities may challenge young people's demands for independence if they consider that they indicate a rejection by young people of their culture (Stopes-Roe and Cochrane, 1988; Woollett and Marshall, 1996).

In a similar way, relations between parents change over the life cycle. The birth of a first child is a major change. Having children is often seen as an expression of parents' affection and commitment to one another and as bringing the couple closer. But as Michaels and Goldberg (1988) report, becoming a parent also has a negative impact on the quality of the parental relationship. Couples vary considerably in how they deal with the changes parenting brings: those who see themselves as parents first and a couple second are often happier to spend time in child care and are less concerned about the lack of child-free time. However, other couples, and especially those whose relationships are not well-established, can find the lack of 'child-free' time disruptive of their relationship as a couple (Moss et al., 1986). The birth of a second child further alters relationships between parents and family dynamics more generally, as parents and first born children establish relationships with the new baby (Dunn, 1988), and mothers manage relations between siblings (Munn, 1991).

Feminist research points to tensions in parental relations, arguing that men and women's gendered upbringing and experiences create somewhat different needs and expectations of family life (Backett, 1987; Wetherell, 1995). Relations between parents are often particularly strained in the early months of parenthood, as women experience isolation and tiredness associated with heavy work load of caring for a small child (Michaels and Goldberg, 1988). Tensions often focus around shared roles and responsibility for childcare. With parenthood, women usually take on major responsibility for childcare and household tasks and become less involved in roles outside the family (Oakley, 1981; Croghan, 1991), whereas men maintain their commitment to the world of work. As Moss *et al.* (1986) suggest, parents may find they have less to talk about than before the baby was born, and little sense of what their partner does on a day-to-day basis. For some couples, poor parental relations are compensated for by their enjoyment in parenting and sense of doing a good job (Gable *et al.*, 1992). This is especially the case for couples with traditional ideas about gendered roles, and for women whom motherhood is a valued identity establishing their position within their wider families, but also for women who have companionship and support (Huston and Vangelisti, 1995; Woollett *et al.*, 1994).

The negative impact of changing family roles on marital satisfaction is greater when women and men are committed to equity in family roles and employment provide women with valued identities and financial independence (Huston and Vangelisti, 1995; Gable *et al.*, 1992). As children get older, mothers return to employment outside the home, and this is often associated with fathers becoming more involved in child care (Ferri and Smith, 1996). The relationship between maternal employment and fathers' involvement in child care is complex: women who are employed outside the home need fathers to take care of children, and so may encourage their involvement. But it may also be the case that in families committed to sharing family roles, women are more likely to be employed outside the home (Wetherell, 1995). When fathers are involved and family roles are shared, parents report greater satisfaction with the parental relationship (Aldous, 1996).

The dissatisfactions many couples experience in the early years of parenting are often seen as a cause for concern because they increase the risks of family breakdown (Aldous, 1996; Dallos, 1995). When the parental relationship is close and parents can confide in one another, women feel more positive about their maternal role and are warmer and more sensitive in their relations with their children (Cox *et al.*, 1989). Feeling that they are working together well and are good parents helps to buffer the parental relationship against the lack of time couples have for themselves (Gable *et al.*, 1992). It is sometimes suggested that couples are not sufficiently aware of the strains parenting can put on the marital relationship. Professionals working with families can help couples to recognize that these strains are common, and to consider ways of reducing them. Couples are sometimes helped if they are encouraged to listen to each other and identify sources of conflict, and to discuss ways to make time for one another (Dallos, 1995).

Tensions and conflicts between parents can also have an impact for children (Rutter, 1985; Gano-Phillips and Fincham, 1995). Divorce and family breakdown are particularly distressing for children when they are accompanied by conflict between parents. The term 'conflict' is used somewhat loosely to describe mild disagreements, tensions and 'atmosphere' in the family, to intimidation and threats of physical violence, and verbal and physical confrontation (Gano-Phillips and Fincham, 1995). As a result, it is still not clear which aspects of parental conflict are most distressing for children. It has been suggested that the impact of conflicts between parents for children results from parents having little energy for children. The quality of parenting and parents' monitoring of children's activities are thereby reduced (Moore *et al.*, 1996). But parents may also fail to recognize children's distress and confusion about what is happening (Das Gupta, 1995; Gano-Phillips and Fincham, 1995). Those working with families experiencing marital conflict need to help parents to be aware of their children's feelings, and to talk to them about what is happening.

Even after they have separated, the quality of the parental relationship can continue to have an impact on children. While conflict is often reduced and parents become more responsive to children, conflicts sometimes continue, often focusing on access arrangements and financial support for children. When relations between parents continue to be poor after a divorce, children, and especially young children, find it difficult to maintain a relationship with the non-custodial parent (Das Gupta, 1995). But even when children can spend time with their fathers, children may choose not to because they feel that to do indicates disloyalty to mothers, especially when there has been domestic violence (Metts and Cupach, 1995). The impact of parental conflict and family breakdown on children is sometimes reduced if children are able to talk to siblings about what is happening. However, this is not always the case because siblings may experience the family breakdown differently (Monahan et al., 1993). An older child, for example, may benefit from a close relationship with the mother and the extra responsibility they are given, but a younger child may not experience such benefits but feel excluded because they are considered 'too young' to have things explained to them.

Box 6.3 Interrelations Amongst Family Relations

P, aged eight years, is reported as troublesome at school. His teacher says he is not concentrating at his school work and bullies other children. Consider the ways in which P's problems may be associated with other difficulties his family is experiencing.

- Father enjoys work and has a good and well paid career but there are continuous threats of re-dundancy.
- Mother and father get on quite well together, but they do argue about the father's lack of involvement around the house, and especially about his claims that he is 'too tired' to do things with the children.
- Father considers that he works hard to bring home money, and that looking after the children is the mother's responsibility.
- P does not feel close to his parents because they do not share his passion for football and sports.

Discussion point
- ° There are complex changes in family relations over the family life and as a result of family breakdown. Using the example in Box 6.3, discuss the ways in which family relationships influence and are influenced by other relationships.

Families as groups: Family culture

Another way in which families have been considered is as a group with their own characteristics or ways of doing things (Aldous, 1996; Muncie et al., 1995). Here the attention is not on family members as individuals or the relationships between them, but on the family as a unit. Working on the assumption that the whole is more than the sum of the parts, family theorists have considered the ways in which families have a *culture* (set of distinctive values and ways of operating). The culture of a family characterizes 'us' as a family, and provides a basis for comparing ourselves with 'other' families. Some ways in which research taking this perspective characterizes families include 'conflictful', 'adaptable' or as having firm boundaries between 'family' and 'non-family' (Aldous, 1996). Through shared family activities and stories, families articulate their common culture and identity, and what it means to them to be a member of their family. The symbolic significance of families can be seen in accounts of family rituals, events and celebrations, such as weddings, Christmas, Diwali and Hanukkah. Through these families renew their commitment to one another and renegotiate family roles and responsibilities through the life cycle as new members join, others leave or are unable to carry out their roles (Dallos, 1995). In these ways, families also become aware of what family members can expect and demand of one another, and develop a sense of how the family views itself and presents itself publicly (such as whether it is important to be seen as 'respectable', and maintain family 'honour') (Vuchinich and Angelelli, 1995; Stopes-Roe and Cochrane, 1990).

Research which takes this approach examines a variety of aspects of family culture, including what families consider to be appropriate ways of managing conflict and relating to one another. Some families are characterized by a clear distinction between 'parents' and 'children', with children expected to listen and take note of parents and parents expecting to make decisions without consulting children. In such families, young people may feel they have to break their links with parents to achieve autonomy and independence (Aldous, 1996; Vuchinich and Angelelli, 1995).

The family culture also determines how boundaries are set between the family and the outside world. These boundaries and their permeability influence the extent to which family members feel able to obtain support outside their families. In families with strong boundaries between members and between families and the outside world, family members may find it difficult to recognize that the problems they are experiencing, such as difficult parental relations or the impact of disability on parent–child relations, are experienced by others, or to ask for support from people outside the family because this is viewed as betrayal or 'letting the family down'.

The culture of the family can help children to resist values and ways of behaving they encounter within the wider youth culture. This may be especially important in helping young people to resist pressure to use illegal drugs or truant from school. The emphasis in Asian families on concern for others and commitment to the family means that many Asian young people are willing for parents to choose a marriage partner for them, contrasting their confidence in their parents' concerns for their happiness with the uncertainties of choosing a partner for themselves (Brannen et al., 1994; Stopes-Roe and Cochrane, 1990).

But when the family culture prioritizes parents' wishes and normalizes violence and bullying, children may find it difficult to resist abuse from their parents. To resist abuse, children have to voice their objections and to set themselves against the culture of their family (La Fontaine, 1990). This may be especially difficult in families which have drawn firm boundaries between themselves and other families and children do not mix with others. Their isolation may mean that children have few opportunities to find out from other children that abuse is not an expression of parental love and concern, or to seek help from people outside the family (White and Woollett, 1992).

Summary

In this chapter I have considered a number of psychological approaches to family forms and functions. Psychologists and other social scientists bring an array of theories and ways of examining individuals, relationships and groups to bear on families. I have drawn on research from a variety of perspectives to argue that families and relations in families are complex, multi-dimensional and ever changing. Families are often the subject of scrutiny because they are seen as 'causes' of children's behaviour and development and because of interest in the impact of changes in family circumstances. However, as I have tried to suggest, establishing causes is often very complex and the ways family members influence and are influenced by one another are not adequately explained by linear models of causality. I have also drawn on research which takes the perspectives of parents and children to argue for the value, theoretically and practically, for those working with families to understand how parents and children make sense of their families and family life.

Seminar Discussion Points

1. Identify some issues you have experienced as a social care professional when working with families. In what respects do you consider your personal and professional approaches to a range of families are similar and how do they differ? Discuss what influences your evaluation of a family.

2. Consider some of the different ways in which parents and children in the same families may experience their families. Relate such differences to power, gender, age, and economic circumstances of family members.

3. Drawing on some of the different approaches to families in this chapter, think about ways to reduce conflict levels in families.

4. It is suggested that a major problem for those in 'non-nuclear/intact' families is that they are viewed negatively. How might such ideas translate themselves into how families function?

Further Reading

Muncie, J., Wetherell, M., Dallos, R. and Cochrane, A. (eds) (1995) *Understanding the Family.* London: Sage.
This takes a multidisciplinary approach to families and family relations. Their discussion of families within the wider political and legal framework is of particular relevance for professionals working with families.

White, D. and Woollett, A. (1992) *Families: A Context for Development.* London: Falmer.
This considers many of the issues raised in this chapter in greater detail drawing on research in developmental psychology.

Brannen, J. and O'Brien, M. (eds) (1994) *Childhood and Parenthood.* London: Institute of Education.
A set of papers from a variety of disciplines which provide a wealth of information about families, their forms, functions and how they are viewed by family members. Contributors and perspectives from across Europe.

Moore, M., Sixsmith, J. and Knowles, K. (1996) *Children's Reflections on Family Life.* London: Falmer. A fascinating set of accounts of different kinds of families, focusing especially on the perspectives of children.

References

Aldous, J. (1996) *Family Careers: Rethinking the Developmental Perspective.* London: Sage.

Allatt, P. (1996) 'Conceptualising parenting from the standpoint of children: relationship and transition in the life course.' In J. Brannen and M. O'Brien (eds) *Children in Families: Research and Policy.* London: Falmer.

Apter, T. (1990) *Altered Loves: Mothers and Daughters During Adolescence.* Hemel Hempstead: Harvester Wheatsheaf.

Backett, K. (1987) 'The negotiation of fatherhood.' In C. Lewis, and M. O'Brien, (1987) *Reassessing Fatherhood: New Observations on Fathers and the Modern Family.* London: Sage.

Baumrind, D. (1973) 'The development of instrumental competence through socialisation.' In A.E. Pick (ed.) *Minnesota Symposium on Child Psychology.* Minneapolis: University of Minnesota Press.

Brannen, J., Dodd, K., Oakley, A. and Storey, P. (1994) *Young People, Health and Family Life.* Buckingham: Open University Press.

Bronfenbrenner, U. (1986) 'Ecology of the family as a context for human development: research perspectives.' *Developmental Psychology, 22,* 723–742.

Burman, E. (1994) *Deconstructing Developmental Psychology.* London: Routledge.

Clarke, L. (1996) 'Demographic change and the family situation of children.' In J. Brannen and M. O'Brien (eds) *Children in Families: Research and Policy.* London: Falmer.

Cox, M.J., Owen, M.T., Lewis, J.M. and Henderson, V.K. (1989) 'Marriage, adult adjustment and early parenting.' *Child Development, 60,* 1015–1024.

Croghan, R. (1991) 'First-time mothers' accounts of inequalities in the division of labour.' *Feminism and Psychology, 1,* 221–247.

Dallos, R. (1995) 'Constructing family life: family belief systems.' In J. Muncie, M. Wetherell, R. Dallos and A. Cochrane (eds) *Understanding the Family.* London: Sage.

Dallos, R. and Sapsford, R. (1995) 'Patterns of diversity and lives realities.' In J. Muncie, M. Wetherell, R., Dallos and A. Cochrane (eds) *Understanding the Family.* London: Sage.

Das Gupta, P. (1995) 'Growing up in families.' In P. Barnes (ed.) *Personal, Social and Emotional Development in Children.* Milton Keynes: Open University Press.

Dosanjh, J.S. and Ghuman, P.A.S. (1996) *Child-Rearing in Ethnic Minorities.* Bristol: Multilingual Matters.

Duncan, G.J., Brooks-Gunn, J. and Klebanov, P.K. (1994) 'Economic deprivation and early childhood development.' *Child Development, 65,* 296–318.

Dunlop, R. (1995) 'Gender effects in a 10 year study of adolescents in divorce.' In J. Brannen and M. O'Brien (eds) *Childhood and Parenthood.* London: Institute of Education.

Dunn, J. (1988) *The Beginnings of Social Understanding.* Oxford: Basil Blackwell.

Emery, R.E. (1988) 'Marriage, divorce and children's adjustment.' *Developmental Clinical Psychology and Psychiatry* Vol. 14. Thousand Oaks, California: Sage.

Ferri, E. and Smith, K. (1996) *Parenting in the 1990s.* London: Family Policy Studies Centre.

Gable, S., Belsky, J. and Crnic, K. (1992) 'Marriage, parenting, and child development: progress and prospects.' *Journal of Family Psychology, 5,* 276–294.

Gano-Phillips, S. and Fincham, F.D. (1995) 'Family conflict, divorce, and children's adjustment.' In M.A. Fitzpatrick, and A.L. Vangelisti (eds) *Explaining Family Interactions.* London: Sage.

Gilligan, C. (1982) *In a Different Voice: Psychological Theories and Women's Development.* Cambridge, MA: Harvard University Press.

Gottfried, A.E. and Gottfried, A.W. (1994) *Redefining Families: Implications for Children's Development.* New York: Plenum.

Greenfield, P.M. and Cocking, R.R. (eds) (1994) *Cross-Cultural Roots of Minority Child Development.* Hillsdale, New Jersey: Lawrence Erlbaum Associates.

Huston, T.L. and Vangelisti, A.L. (1995) 'How parenthood affects marriage.' In M.A. Fitzpatrick, and A.L. Vangelisti (eds) *Explaining Family Interactions.* London: Sage.

Johnson, J.E. and McGillicuddy-Delisi, A.V. (1983) 'Family environment factors and children's knowledge of rules and conventions.' *Child Development 54,* 218–226.

Kier, C. and Lewis, C. (1995) 'Family dissolution: mothers' accounts.' In J. Brannen and M. O'Brien (eds) *Childhood and Parenthood.* London: Institute of Education.

La Fontaine, J. (1990) *Child Sexual Abuse.* Cambridge: Polity Press.

Lambourn, S.D., Dornbusch, S.M. and Steinberg, L. (1996) 'Ethnicity and community context as moderators of the relations between family decision making and adolescent adjustment.' *Child Development, 67*, 283–301.

Lewis, C. and O'Brien, M. (1987) *Reassessing Fatherhood: New Observations on Fathers and the Modern Family.* London: Sage.

Maccoby, E.E. (1984) 'Middle childhood in the context of the family.' In W.A. Collins (ed.) *Development During Middle Childhood: The Years from Six to Twelve.* Washington, DC: National Academy Press.

Maccoby, E.E. and Martin, J.A. (1983) 'Socialisation in the context of the family.' In E.M. Hetherington (ed.) *Handbook of Child Psychology: Volume 4: Socialisation, Personality and Social Development.* Fourth Edition. New York: Wiley.

Mayall, B. (1990) 'Childcare and childhood.' *Children and Society, 4*, 374–386.

Mayall, B. (1994) *Children's Childhoods Observed and Experienced.* London: Falmer.

Metts, S. and Cupach, W.R. (1995) 'Postdivorce arrangements.' In M.A. Fitzpatrick, and A.L. Vangelisti (eds) *Explaining Family Interactions.* London: Sage.

Michaels, G.Y. and Goldberg, W.A. (eds) (1988) *Transition to Parenthood: Theory and Research.* Cambridge: Cambridge University Press.

Monahan, S.C., Buchanan, C.M., Maccoby, E.E. and Dornbusch, S.M. (1993) 'Sibling differences in divorced families.' *Child Development, 64*, 152–168.

Moore, M., Sixsmith, J. and Knowles, K. (1996) *Children's Reflections on Family Life.* London: Falmer.

Moss, P., Bolland, G., Foxman, R. and Owen, C. (1986) 'Marital relations during the transition to parenthood.' *Journal of Reproductive and Infant Psychology, 5*, 71–86.

Muncie, J. and Sapsford, R. (1995) 'Issues in the study of "The Family".' In J. Muncie, M. Wetherell, R. Dallos and A. Cochrane (eds) *Understanding the Family.* London: Sage.

Munn, P. (1991) 'Mothering more than one child.' In A. Phoenix, A. Woollett and E. Lloyd (eds) *Motherhood: Meanings, Practices and Ideologies.* London: Sage.

New, C. and David, M. (1985) *For the Children's Sake: Making Childcare more than Women's Business.* Harmondsworth: Penguin.

Newson, J. and Newson, E. (1968) *Four Years Old in an Urban Community.* Harmondsworth: Penguin.

Newson, J. and Newson, E. (1976) *Seven Years Old in the Home Environment.* Harmondsworth: Penguin.

Newson, J. and Newson, E. (1986) 'Family and sex roles in middle childhood.' In D.J. Hargreaves and A.M. Colley (eds) *The Psychology of Sex Roles.* London: Harper and Row.

Nicolson, P. (1993) 'The social construction of motherhood.' In D. Richardson and V. Robinson (eds) *Introducing Women's Studies.* Basingstoke: Macmillan.

Oakley, A. (1981) *From Here to Maternity: Becoming a Mother.* Harmondsworth: Penguin.

O'Brien, M., Alldred, P. and Jones, D. (1996) 'Children's constructions of family and kinship.' In J. Brannen and M. O'Brien (eds) *Children in Families: Research and Policy.* London: Falmer.

Ogbu, J.V. (1981) 'Origins of human competence: a cultural-ecological perspective.' *Child Development, 52*, 413–429.

Parker, R. (1995) *Torn in Two: The Experience of Maternal Ambivalence.* London: Virago.

Phoenix, A. (1991) *Young Mothers?* Cambridge: Polity.

Phoenix, A., Woollett, A. and Lloyd, E. (eds) (1991) *Motherhood: Meanings, Practices and Ideologies.* London: Sage.

Rutter, M. (1985) 'Family and school influences: meanings, mechanisms and implications.' In A.R. Nicol (ed) *Longitudinal Studies in Child Psychology and Psychiatry: Practical lessons from Research Experience.* Chichester: Wiley.

Steinberg, L., Elmen, J.D. and Mounts, N.S. (1989) 'Authoritative parenting, psychosocial maturity, and academic success among adolescents.' *Child Development, 60*, 1424–1436.

Stopes-Roe, M. and Cochrane, R. (1990) *Citizens of This Country.* Bristol: Multilingual Matters.

Tizard, B. (1991) 'Employed mothers and the care of young children.' In A. Phoenix, A. Woollett and E. Lloyd (eds) *Motherhood: Meanings, Practices and Ideologies.* London: Sage.

Tizard, B. and Hughes, M. (1984) *Young Children Learning: Talking and Thinking at Home and School.* London: Fontana.

Vuchinich, S. and Angelelli, J. (1995) 'Family interaction during problem solving.' In M.A. Fitzpatrick and A.L. Vangelisti (eds) *Explaining Family Interactions.* London: Sage.

Walkerdine, V. and Lucey, H. (1989) *Democracy in the Kitchen: Regulating Mothers and Socialising Children.* London: Virago.

Wetherell, M. (1995) 'Social structure, ideology and family dynamics: the case of parenting.' In J. Muncie, M. Wetherell, R. Dallos and A. Cochrane (eds) *Understanding the Family.* London: Sage.

White, D. and Woollett, A. (1992) *Families: A Context for Development.* London: Falmer.

Woollett, A. and Phoenix, A. (1996) 'Motherhood as pedagogy: developmental psychology and the accounts of mothers and young children.' In C. Luke (ed) *Feminisms and the Pedagogies of Everyday Life.* New York: State University of New York Press.

Woollett, A. and Marshall, H. (1996) 'Reading the body: young women's accounts of the meaning of the body in relation to independence, responsibility and maturity.' *European Journal of Women's Studies, 3,* 199–214.

Woollett, A., Marshall, H., Nicolson, P. and Dosanjh, N. (1994) 'Asian women's ethnic identity: the impact of gender and context in the accounts of women bringing up children in East London.' *Feminism and Psychology, 4,* 101–114.

CHAPTER 7

Working with Groups

Mary Horton

Introduction

An understanding of the nature of group processes is crucial for social care professionals' effective work as members of teams and groups. Equally important is an understanding of the possibilities and limitations of using groups with clients and colleagues – to inform, promote insight, change behaviour or alleviate suffering.

Most social psychology textbooks discuss group behaviour, but few attempt to show the relationship between the psychologically-based cognitive approach and the psychodynamic approach to groups that is used by many workers in the field. This chapter confronts this challenging task. In the first section, I review social psychological work on group influence. Next I consider the various explanations about group processes that have been provided by cognitive social psychology, and suggest that a model from psychodynamic theory might subsume them. Finally, I look at applications of these ideas to working with clients.

The Social Psychology of Group Influence

Introduction

That people are social beings and open to each other's influence is a truism, but the depth and nature of these exchanges are often unrecognized. 'Messages' may be unconscious or deliberate, verbal or non-verbal, and we may be aware or unaware that we are receiving them. But social psychologists argue that these influences structure our perceptions and attitudes and underpin our beliefs about the social world. In this section, I consider research about different forms of social influence, in order to help you identify these processes in yourselves and in clients.

Unobtrusive influence

In *ambiguous* situations people will tend to accept each other's judgements in the absence of evidence about what is really there. But these norms (agreed perceptions, attitudes and values), once formed are hard to change. Sherif's (1936) classic study tested the hypothesis that others are used as reference points in the emergence of norms. He instructed people to judge, in each other's presence but without discussion, the degree of apparent movement of a single light-point in a totally dark room. Although subjects were unaware of it, such perceived movement is illusory, being caused by *random* eye movements ('Random' means in this context that the direction and extent of the eye-movement of any one subject would not necessarily agree with that of any other subject). Nonetheless, successive judgements of individuals in the group converged – the blind having led the blind. ('Convergence' means in this context that subjects took account, whether they are aware of it or not, of other subject's previous judgements when making their own new judgement.) This confirmed Sherif's prediction. When tested individually afterwards, subjects did not diverge from the previously established group average or 'norm'. Sherif proposed that this process of using others as an anchor for one's own perceptions could explain the emergence of all social norms from 'a common need to define a common reality'. Although his generalization is too sweeping, Sherif's conclusion stands – that in the absence of other information, people tend to use each other to define a reality, which then may grow to have the status of an external given.

Second, in *unambiguous* situations, individuals may succumb to majority pressure if they find themselves the single dissenter, even when the majority position is clearly wrong. In Asch's (1956) seminal studies, groups of 7–9 male American college students were shown a white card with a vertical black line, and a second card with three lines of varying lengths. They had to choose which of the three lines best matched the standard and give their answers aloud. All subjects except one were confederates of the experimenter, secretly primed to lie. Nearly one-third of the lone naive subjects made wrong statements on more than half the trials in order to fit in with the majority. Asch had expected far fewer people to deny the blatant evidence of their own eyes, and concluded that those who consistently succumbed to 'wrong-headed' majority pressure, did so because of a personality defect – low ego strength or an excessive need for dependence.

Asch's paradigm has been repeated many times, but with growing divergence from the original findings. Nicholson, Steven and Rocklin (1985) conducted a replication with British and American students. None of the British and only 14 per cent of the Americans made false judgements on more than half the trials. Asch (unpublished correspondence, Perrin and Spencer, 1980) explained this in terms of Western culture becoming more supportive of independence.

Discussion point

  ° Think of a situation when you felt under pressure to agree with a decision of your peers against your better judgement. Did you succumb? What were the characteristics of the situation which led you to agree or to refuse to agree with the others? How might group pressure be resisted?

Overt pressure

Many social psychologists have studied the influence of the authority structure on the behaviour of people in groups. Most work on leadership has found there are no personality traits or working styles that show leadership 'quality', but the best leaders are those who can adapt their styles to changing group or external conditions (Fiedler, 1967). However, some recent work has suggested there may be an interaction of situation and personality on leadership behaviour (Janis, in Heller, 1992).

Milgram (1974) posed a different question. What are the limits of influence of a malign authority? In his experiments he pitted the (presumed) moral norm of his subjects – that of not inflicting unnecessary pain – against the tendency to obey orders seen as coming from a legitimate authority. Milgram used adult volunteers for an experiment at Yale University, ostensibly about learning, which involved them as 'teachers' inflicting electric shocks of increasing severity on a 'learner' as a punishment for errors. The volunteers obeyed the experimenter's orders to continue to give shocks although they were neither forced nor threatened. Milgram, like Asch, was surprised by his results. About two-thirds obeyed until told to stop even though the levers were labelled 'DANGER – SEVERE SHOCK'. The experiment was a deception, the 'learner' was not really shocked but Milgram's findings *were* shocking.

Why is the tendency to obey so strong? Milgram proposed what he called *the agentic state*. An innate or early learnt sensitivity to cues defining another person as an 'authority' will create an internal change so that a previously independent individual will become 'the agent of the other'. The situation of having voluntarily entered a role relationship entailing putting oneself under the orders of another, was sufficient to induce the agentic state and to absolve subjects from responsibility for their actions.

Discussion point

- ° Do you think social care professionals sometimes experience pressure to obey orders from their seniors that conflict with their personal values or professional judgement? Under what circumstances, if any, should social care professionals disobey instructions from senior professionals?

Group membership

That people can influence us to a greater extent than we might have imagined has been demonstrated. But three related questions remain. First, what is the attraction toward group membership that opens us to being both influenced and influential within it? Secondly, what is the nature of group structures and processes that can influence members so that the behaviour and/or decisions of the group may be different from that of isolated individuals? Thirdly, what effect has group membership on the perception of and behaviour towards non-members?

The first question 'why do we join groups at all?', is fundamental to social psychology. One early answer to this question was provided by Allport's (1924) concept of *social facilitation*. He showed that individuals working on the same task in the same room but not communicating (i.e. co-acting rather than interacting) performed better than individuals working alone. Further research, however, found that the presence of others could sometimes be so anxiety-arousing as to be inhibiting (for example, in a competition). The exciting properties of others is therefore only a partial explanation of the underlying rewards of group membership. Another answer was that of the properties of others as providing safety and *social support* (Schachter, 1959). Much recent research has shown that the presence of others (family or friends) helps to reduce stress at times of crisis.

A related approach is that of Festinger's *Social Comparison Theory* (1954). He suggested that the knowledge we are seeking when attaching ourselves to a group is about *ourselves*. Consequently, we join groups to evaluate our own opinions and abilities in comparison with those of others. As the tendency to seek self-validation depends to a considerable extent upon the perceived similarity of the target group to ourselves, we choose those groups who we think are most like us because the usefulness of comparison will usually decrease as our difference from others increases. (For example, a world-class tennis player would learn little about her seeding prospects for Wimbledon by joining a club of novices, nor would it do much for her game.) However, Festinger's explanation, although useful, is again only partial as it ignores the influences of 'reference groups' (or those groups which have the values, attitude and social position we admire, and aspire to) on our choice of group.

Another early answer to the question of why we join groups, or enter into any voluntary social relationship is that of *Social Exchange Theory* (Thibault and Kelley, 1959). The theory states that we enter a group when the rewards of so doing (or what we get) are thought as greater than the penalties (or what we have to give): and we leave when the balance is reversed. This does not imply that we are always conscious of our computation of the positive and negative weights; it simply means that at some point the process 'surfaces' in a motivation to join, and at another point, in a motivation to leave. Although it may seem too broad to be explanatorily useful, the concept of social exchange does make explicit that there are disadvantages as well as advantages to group membership. Breakwell's distinction of internal and external criteria for membership points also to the reality that a group may want an individual to join (external criteria) for reasons which are different from those of the individual to become a member (internal criteria). A mis-match between these two sets of criteria will not lead to long-term membership (Breakwell and Rowett, 1982).

Discussion point

- ° What were the major rewards and penalties you perceived in being a social care professional: (a) before you started training? (b) Now? Has the overall balance in your perceptions of being a member of your professional group shifted in a positive or a negative direction, or not at all?

Breakwell's work is part of an interesting advance which has come from two English social psychologists – Tajfel and Turner. Tajfel's (1981) *Social Identity Theory* suggests, like Festinger, that the search for personal identity and self-esteem is the motivation for joining groups. But this becomes linked to the need to maintain group or social identity once membership has been attained. The social identity of groups is thus created by a process of social categorization that simplifies the social world by 'clumping' it into discrete categories 'us' and 'them'. Turner (1987) extends Tajfel's view by introducing his *self-categorization* theory. Briefly, he suggests that the simplification of the social world is matched by a simplification of self-concepts – what he calls de-personalization or 'self-stereotyping' – in which group members perceive themselves as examples of their group category, rather than as individuals.

These ideas have provided considerable stimulus to social psychologists which will be looked at in Chapter 9. However, a few questions remain. First, the process of social and self-simplification may be presumed to be different in the case of ascribed groupings (like gender, race or social background) and those we choose to join. Second, in most societies individuals will have multiple memberships of ascribed and voluntary groups; these questions will be considered further in Chapter 9. But overall, social identity theory, by defining the group in terms of 'us' and 'them', has highlighted the fact that the group cannot exist in a vacuum. Social identity theory goes beyond the small group and looks at the psychology of society.

Behaviour in the group

Here I will look at two related aspects: the behaviour of the individual *in* the group, and the behaviour *of* the group in terms of its output – its decisions and actions. There is the suggestion that our attitudes and behaviour, our goals and values, our perceptions of the world and of ourselves will change towards that of our group. We begin to play the role assigned to us by the group's authority. An example is given by Zimbardo (see Box 7.1).

Box 7.1

The effects of playing the role of 'guard' or 'prisoner' were studied in the context of an experimental simulation of a prison environment. The subjects were 24 young, healthy middle-class, white, male American college students who volunteered and were then screened for any propensity to psychopathology or criminal behaviour. They were then randomly divided into the role of 'prisoners' or 'guards'. The prisoners were incarcerated in a basement of Stanford University, and tended by the guards. A rule of no physical maltreatment was enforced, but apart from that, the guards were free to treat the prisoners as they liked.

The results were so horrific that the experiment had to be curtailed after 6 days. In Zimbardo's words 'This play we had staged became one in which … the characters were playing their roles only for each other…. Differences dissolved between role and identity… and finally between "illusion" and "reality".' (Zimbardo, 1983, p.384) The guards abused their power, the prisoners became apathetic robots. Zimbardo concludes: 'In the contest between the forces of good men and evil situation, the situation triumphed" (Zimbardo, 1982, pp.390–391).

The finding is reminiscent of the conclusion of Milgram's obedience experiment. However, these are two extreme demonstrations of group influence. In more ordinary situations group influence can be described as the changing of individual behaviour by the internalization of group norms (how to behave) values (what is good or bad) and goals (what to aspire to) until a state of *social cohesion* (or general within group agreement and liking) is reached. Social cohesion can differ in extent and type between different sorts of groups. For example, one type might be 'interpersonal cohesiveness', based on mutual liking, while another might be 'task-based cohesiveness' derived from commitment to a common goal (Hosking and Morley, 1991, p.106). Social cohesion can be beneficial by alleviating pain, and strengthening personal identity. In addition, a commitment to a common goal can lead to more efficient task performance. However, its latent dangers remain – that of social stereotyping, ethnocentrism, rejection and group aggression. For example, an early experiment by Schachter (1951) showed that a stooge primed to play the role of deviate in a group, by maintaining a stand in extreme opposition to the majority view, was 'rejected' in that he tended to have the lowest score on a sociometric measure of interpersonal liking among the group. He was *most* rejected in groups pre-judged to have the *highest* social cohesion.

However, the fate of the deviate is not necessarily that of rejection. Moscovici's (1976) experiments on minority influence used a paradigm very similar to Asch's experiments on majority influence, except that the majority of subjects were naive and only two were stooges of the experimenter, primed to give the wrong answer in judgements. Although the extent of the influence of the minority was less than that of the majority, it was shown to occur under certain conditions – those in which the minority were consistent (always agreed with each other) and yet flexible (occasionally both agreed with the majority). Moscovici suggested that the challenge posed by the minority enabled some of the others to free themselves from the majority and to start to think for themselves.

Behaviour of the group

When we turn from studies of the influence of the group on the individual, and look at the behaviour of the group as an entity, there are two areas of importance to social workers. One is that of group decision-making, and the other is that of the group's relation to other groups, which is examined in Chapter 9. The most relevant work on group-decision making is that of Janis (1982). His life work was dedicated to studying mistakes in policy-decisions occurring at the highest political and managerial levels. He concluded from careful examination of the evidence, that disastrous decisions such as that of Kennedy to invade Cuba, or Nixon's attempt to cover up the Watergate burglary were due to the operation of 'group-think'. He conceived 'group-think' as a faulty form of collective thinking that tends to occur when highly cohesive groups are under considerable stress to come to an important decision, often with limited time in which to do so. What occurs is irrational group thinking in which the power and morality of the in-group (or the group to which the individual belongs) are over-estimated; there is closed-mindedness to new information which might lead to a revised decision; and there is a pressure toward uniformity in the decision-making and a shared 'illusion of unanimity'. In his latest work, Janis in Heller (ed) (1992) suggests that policy-making groups with leaders having personality deficiencies are more prone to 'group-think' (or biased towards a particular type of solution) and are the groups most likely to produce 'fiascos'.

Discussion point

° Have you ever been a member of a policy-making group (such as a case-conference) which made a 'disastrous decision' (however minor)? Looking back, can you think why the wrong decision was made? Do you now think that irrational thinking on the part of the group or the leader had anything to do with it? Can you draw any lessons from your experience?

The Group Dynamic Approach to the Understanding of Group Processes

Introduction

We have seen that when in a group our attitudes and behaviour are affected by others. This occurs through the roles and categorizations we give ourselves and others. As we have seen, explanations for these phenomena have been many:

- There is a need to arrive at a consensual definition of 'reality' (Sherif)
- There is a need to be in agreement with other members (Asch)
- There is a fundamental role-relationship which entails obedience to a leader (Milgram)
- There is a need to evaluate oneself and establish a personal identity in relation to one's group (Festinger)
- There is a tendency to dichotomize the social world into 'us' and 'them', which, combined with a need for self-esteem, leads to the assignment of a positive social identity to 'us, in contrast to 'them'. (Tajfel)

These explanations do not necessarily contradict one another. They are held together by the underlying concept of 'social cohesion'. However, it is difficult to see how these specific explanations can account for certain aspects of group behaviour. Is there an approach to the understanding of groups that can encompass all these explanations, and also account for some phenomena not adequately explained by cognitive social psychology? Psychodynamic theory may be able to do so. Although this section is largely theoretical, it provides a basis for the practical issues of working with groups and institutions, which is the subject of the final section.

What is psychodynamic theory?

Freud is generally known through his clinical work in understanding and treating neuroses, but his life's aim was to develop a theory of the human mind that could account for *all* behaviour of individuals, groups and institutions.

My main argument is that the motives put forward by social psychologists to explain behaviour can be subsumed under one or other of Freud's two primary motives (see Box 7.2). Psychodynamic theory suggests that, as the baby develops, the simple *pain-avoidance* motive becomes that of the avoidance of anxiety, which is the anticipation or fear of pain. The feared pain can be of physical or psychological events such as the loss of self-esteem (cf. Tajfel), or the loss of supportive others (cf. Asch's dependency motive). It can simply be the fear of the unknown itself.

Box 7.2

There are three main tenets to Freud's theory. The first is that of *two primary motives*. Freud (1930) named these two motives the pursuit of pleasure (which Freud called the libidinal impulse) and the avoidance of pain. These two motives are, at times, in conflict. That is, we must sometimes bear pain (such as that of waiting) to get pleasure; and some pleasures (such as over-indulgence) lead to pain.

The second tenet is that of the *unconscious*. To Freud, the unconscious is not simply a repository for what we do not remember. It is a repressive force, preventing awareness of painful memories or desires that would conflict with our conscious goals. However, these unconscious fears and wishes inform our actions so that we may behave, not necessarily irrationally, but from motives deeper than we realize. The unconscious makes itself known through our small mistakes, such as forgetting or slips of the tongue, through jokes, dreams and neurotic symptoms.

The third tenet is the fundamentally *social nature* of the human mind. We internalize and identify with aspects of those who are important to us, such as our parents, whom we both love and fear. Freud used the terms *ego* and *superego* to describe the different levels at which the mind incorporates the social world. Freud describes the ego as largely preconscious (not entirely repressed). Through the ego, we imitate and learn, influence and are influenced. The superego is a more archaic, less malleable structure, deeply unconscious, where our early internalized parental 'images' are metaphorically 'laid down', forming our conscience. This is not the adult conscience of sophisticated moral argument, but a jumbled collection of prohibitions and ideals, accessible to our adult awareness only as the 'pricking of conscience' when we may be on the point of transgressing an early learned rule. None the less, Freud sees the primitive superego as the basis of our 'social being'.

Primitive *pleasure seeking*, the impulse for self-gratification (although retaining a libidinal aspect), also undergoes modification into what Freud (1916) calls *knowledge-seeking* or the motive to understand ourselves (cf. Tajfel's need for personal and social identity) and the outside world (cf. Sherif's need to define a 'common reality'). The seeking of knowledge can be used in the service of the avoidance of anxiety. For example, we seek scientific knowledge partly to predict and avert unpleasant environmental change, as well as for the benefits it brings. However, just as they conflict in their primitive modes, the two more 'adult' motives sometimes conflict: the knowledge that we seek may be of the unknown that we fear.

To summarize: the motivational bases for group behaviour provided by traditional social psychology can be subsumed in terms of the two basic motivations posited by psychodynamic theory – the fear of harm and desire for knowledge. (including the knowledge which is love). Because these motivations are conceived as being in conflict, psychodynamic theories of group behaviour, such as those of Freud and Bion (to follow), can be more deeply explanatory than the social psychological theories described above, each of which posits a *single*, if different motivational base. I am not suggesting that these cognitive explanations are thereby negated; rather, that they can be more clearly understood when included in the perspective provided by psychodynamic theory.

Freud's group theory

Freud gave the following definition of a group:

> A psychological group is a collection of individuals who have introduced the same person (i.e. the leader) into their *superego*, and on the basis of this common element have identified themselves with one another in their ego. (1921)

What Freud is saying here is that for a psychological group to emerge from a collection of individuals, there must first be a potential leader. The potential followers unconsciously choose this leader by identifying with him or her at a deep level, replacing the parental images in their superego with the image of the leader. Having *all* done this, they have something fundamental in common and can identify with each other at the more surface level of the ego, as if they were siblings.

Discussion point

○ Do you think all groups need a leader? Do you think people tend to act childishly when in a group?

There are difficulties posed by Freud's group theory (De Board, 1978), but there are also some inferences we can draw which may deepen our understanding of current thinking. One concerns the relation between follower and leader. Freud says this involves the replacement of personal conscience by the internalized image of the leader, so that a follower can carry out actions in the service of the leader which might otherwise be personally abhorrent. This is reminiscent of the 'agentic state' proposed by Milgram to explain people's behaviour in his obedience experiments. Milgram (1974) himself links his explanation with Freud's ideas, suggesting the tendency to obey comes from the depths of our social being.

Perhaps we can understand Freud's group theory further, by considering his thinking as applied to actual groups (Freud, 1921; see Figure 7.1). He distinguishes between what he calls *primitive* groups with an actual leader (e.g. a street gang or a religious cult with an actual, living

	Primitive	*Secondary*
Natural	A religious cult	The Amish community
Artificial	A research team in a university	A management committee in a social services department

Figure 7.1 Model of Freud's group types

leader) and *secondary* groups led by an abstraction (e.g. a rule-book, which lays down the procedures for who will be appointed to the chair and the conduct of the group). He also distinguishes between a *natural* group, held together entirely by the internal forces he has described (e.g. the Amish community in Pennsylvania, who are tolerated by, but live independently from, the wider society), and an *artificial* group, held by both internal and external social forces. Examples are a committee appointed in a social service department, or a higher level organization such as a social services department existing within a local authority.

It is apparent that the types of group we have been considering, as well as those we shall look at in the final section, and the groups to which the reader may belong in a professional role, can be either 'primitive' or 'secondary' in Freud's sense, but they are all 'artificial' or embedded in the social matrix.

Discussion point
  ° Do you find Freud's group theory helps you to understand the way in which the groups to which you belong function? In what ways is it useful or not useful?

Bion's group theory

The psychoanalyst Bion (1961) disagreed with some of Freud's ideas – in particular, the importance of the emergent leader in the formation of the group. Bion's ideas have been tested on many volunteer groups from the general public in Britain and the United States (De Board, 1978), albeit this testing is an experiential rather than an experimental process. An example are the study groups described in the next section.

Like Freud, Bion designed his theory so that it could be generalized to the understanding of all groups and institutions in society. But the model on which it is based is that of small, face-to-face, 'secondary' and 'artificial' groups with boundary rules (of time, space, role and task) set in the context of a larger institution. Bion sees the group as operating on two levels: a conscious work-group trying to fulfil the group task and a simultaneously existing set of unconscious 'myths' about what the group goals are and how they can be achieved. These group myths operate when the task of the work-group becomes too difficult, such as when the responsibility of decision making creates too much anxiety. The myths act as a defence against anxiety by deflecting the group away from the task. Bion thinks these *basic assumptions* are jointly held, unconscious beliefs which can be sensed in the emotional content of communication. Like Freud, he thinks the group in this basic assumption mode tends to regress to child-like thinking and sometimes behaviour.

Bion identifies three unconscious basic assumptions used by groups as a defence against reality. They are: dependency, fight-flight and pairing. The myth of *dependency* is that the group is meeting so that a leader on whom it depends absolutely should satisfy all its needs. The feeling is one of helplessness and then despair when (inevitably in time) the leader fails to live up to these ideals. A group of anxious social work students, working under the supervision of a 'powerful' and 'wise' senior worker, easily fits this picture.

The myth of *fight-flight* is that there is an external enemy who must be attacked or avoided if the group is to survive. The group finds an emergent or unofficial 'leader' who will take them into aggressive *fight* or panic *flight*, and the feeling is one of fear and hate. Sometimes the enemy is found within the group and scape-goating can ensue. For example, in social work meetings antagonism toward an 'unfeeling' management or 'irresponsible' clients may cloud the group's judgement and lead to wrong decisions.

The myth of *pairing* is that the future will solve all present problems. The group often focuses on two members who are seen as the prophets from whom solutions will be born. The underlying atmosphere is of unrealistic hope, often expressed in vague generalizations: 'Things will be better in the spring/when we get more money/when the management reorganize us'. But addressing the here-and-now group task (e.g. making the required number of family visits with too few staff) is avoided.

In the life of any group, according to Bion, unconscious 'myths' (or basic assumptions) will alternate, but only one myth can operate at one time in a 'work-group'. Basic assumption groups have emergent leaders, unconsciously chosen by the group. However, unlike Freud's leaders, they are not psychologically the 'strongest', but are often those least able to resist the unconscious group pressure to re-enact the 'myth'. The externally appointed chair, on the other hand, is distinguished from the group by his or her role, which may or may not be matched by greater skill and knowledge.

Discussion point

- ° Bion thought that unconscious 'basic assumption thinking' could occur at any time. Are there any groups to which you belong where you think that basic assumptions clouded rational discussion or decision-making?

Foulkes' approach

Foulkes was a contemporary of Bion and, like him, extended psychoanalytic theory to the study of groups. Also like Bion, he conceived of two levels of group activity – the conscious and the unconscious. But here the similarities end. Foulkes does not conceive of unconscious and regressive group-held myths or basic assumptions. Instead he starts, as does Freud, from the basis of the inherent social nature of man:

'What stands in need of explanation is not the existence of groups but the existence of individuals.' (Foulkes and Anthony, 1957, p.215)

He sees the group as building itself up on the basis of reciprocal communication, both conscious and unconscious (such as the non-verbal communication of mood) until the *group matrix* is formed and the group becomes alive as a group. The matrix is the network of intra-group relationships which has a history and develops a culture within the group; it can be thought of as similar but not identical to the social psychological concept of 'group cohesion'. Foulkes would agree with social psychologists and psychodynamic thinkers that there are universal human needs which group membership satisfies (for example: to have a leader). He would also agree with the psychoanalytic view of groups, that certain universal dramas are symbolically re-enacted within a group (such as birth, partnership, loss and death). However, his approach allows for any group to be understood in terms of its own particular membership and history.

The basic processes which produce a group matrix are those of *projection* and *transference*. Projection can be defined as an unconscious way of seeing unacknowledged aspects of oneself in other people (e.g. seeing someone else as insignificant, when underneath you feel *you* are not a significant or important member of the group), and transference is a process by which aspects of individuals who are historically important to us are seen in people around us ('You remind me of my father when you talk like that'). Both these mechanisms can be seen as *defences*, that is ways of avoiding internal or external reality. But also they can be seen as '…breath(ing) life into the world around us and attaining a relatedness to the world we live in' (Powell, 1989 p.273). Through these fundamental mechanisms, the group matrix emerges. Once it has formed, members can also project ideas and feelings onto the group itself, which gives it even more illusory life.

Because of its 'contentless' nature (he does not suggest particular group 'myths') Foulkes' approach has less explanatory value than the theories of Freud and Bion; and certainly less predictive value than those of cognitive social psychology. Its utility lies in its application to group therapy – using groups to help people – which we will be looking at in the next section. Freud's group theory is seldom applied today to the practice of working with groups. Bion's theory, although it has had considerable success in helping members of organizations to understand and counteract the regressive 'pull' of group factors, has met with less success when applied to patient or client groups (Malan *et al.*, 1976). Practitioners working with Foulkes' model, on the other hand, have had considerable success (for example, Sigell, 1992).

Perhaps its very success has led to the criticism that the Foulkesian approach stresses only the 'good', constructive aspects of group behaviour, and, unlike Bion's model, ignores the possibly destructive factors unconsciously (and sometimes consciously) at work. But recent extensions of Foulkes' approach (Nitsun, 1996) has included within the Foulksian framework, those 'anti-group' or negative factors which can lead to 'anti- therapeutic' results such as scape-goating or dropping-out, unless they are recognized and communicated to the group by the conductor.

Lewin's field theory

Lewin was a social psychologist, working in the field of group dynamics (a term he originated). He was much influenced by psychoanalytic ideas, and his seminal work helped to form a bridge between the two disciplines. His theory derives from an analogy with the force-fields of physics (for example, the attractive force of a magnet). He suggested that each individual exists in a psychological 'force-field' (his memories, beliefs, attitudes and goals) which limits his possible behaviours. This he called 'the life space', and it is inherently modifiable – limited, in its turn, only by social and physical conditions. The 'life space' field (as in physics) remains static when the 'driving' and 'restraining' forces are balanced, although the state is one of tension rather than rest (for example, the desire to have a new job with greater opportunities, may be balanced by the fear of unemployment). A change in social conditions, such as redundancy, or in psychological conditions, such as an increased dislike of the present job, may instigate a change in behaviour toward job-seeking, which will in turn change the psychological life-space. The depth and strength of Lewin's field theory, however, lies in the fact that he considered the psychological force-field to be composed of both conscious and unconscious motivations.

When Lewin applied field theory, he saw the group culture as exerting an attractive force on the individual's life-space, inducing the individual to change his attitudes or behaviour to agree with the group. There is also a tension between the individual's wish to be independent of and to be dependent on the group. He thought of group influences as more powerful than that of merely rational argument (cf. Asch's work). His famous experiment in persuading American housewives to eat offal during World War II, demonstrates this. Half his subjects were given lectures and written instructions while the other half engaged in group discussion and exchanged menus: 32 per cent in the group, compared with 3 per cent in the lecture situation, changed to the new food (Lewin, 1951).

Discussion point

   ° Have you had any experience of working with client groups, for example, in the community – discussing with them the possibility of lobbying to improve housing conditions? Do you think your rational arguments or the pressure of the group itself had more effect on whatever decision was reached?

For Lewin, the process of group change has three steps. First there is *unfreezing*, or reappraisal of old values, due to some change in the group's external or internal reality (for example, a change in management or community policy, or the introduction of new ideas). Secondly there is *moving* towards the performance of the new group behaviour, or the adoption of the new group ideology. Thirdly there is *refreezing*: the maintenance of the new position through a combination of individual and group commitment, providing an inertial force.

Lewin's dynamic approach to thinking about groups, and about change or stasis as the effect of the balance or lack of balance of opposing forces, can help us to answer some of the questions left unanswered by cognitive social psychology. It is possible to encompass the phenomena of group change and cohesion, conformity and minority influence, scape-goating and the toleration of difference – if the concept of stasis as a tension or balance of opposing forces is introduced.

Working with Groups: Some Applications of Theory

Introduction

We have now reviewed some of the major approaches to the understanding of group processes. In this section, we shall look at ways of applying both cognitive and psychodynamic approaches to our practice when working with groups.

Training groups

These are experiential learning groups derived from the work of Lewin and Bion and take place under the guidance of a qualified facilitator or consultant. They are face-to-face groups with fixed membership, meeting for a total set time of at least 10–15 hours, but often longer. Learning is either 'massed' into two or three days, or 'spaced' across months. Although the specific aims will differ according to the group's theoretical orientation, the overall purpose is to increase group interaction skills. The *Johari Window* (so named after its inventors, Joe and Harry) gives a diagrammatic picture of the learning potential provided by experiential training groups (Figure 7.2).

	Known to self	Unknown to self
Known to Others	Public (1)	Blind (2)
Unknown to Others	Hidden (3)	Unconscious (4)

Figure 7.2 Johari social behaviour window

In a training group the aim is to help trainees change such public behaviour (cell 1) that might be agreed to be maladaptive; to increase awareness of behaviour to which they might be blind (cell 2); to encourage people to disclose thoughts and feelings they keep hidden (cell 3), but only if this openness is appropriate to the group task. The interpretation of unconscious processes (cell 4) is the aim of study groups (these are training groups run on Bionian lines), which are designed to bring to the group's awareness blocks to effective task performance created by processes such as 'basic assumption' thinking. This later objective is not usually present in T-groups or training groups based on the work of Lewin (De Board, 1978).

Discussion point
- ° As a teacher, I am sometimes made aware of my mannerisms by feedback from a class. Can you think of any feelings or behaviour to which you may have been blind, until made aware of them in a group?

The criterion for success of a training group is usually the self-evaluation of the learner, sometimes combined with assessment by trainers, other group members and work colleagues. Testing the outcome of some groups may be thought antithetical to their experiential purpose, and rigorous testing of training groups is difficult because of the lack of appropriate controls and sensitive measures of change (Oatley, 1984). But a large-scale study by Lieberman, Yalom and Miles (1973) which did use matched controls and compared ten group styles, showed that, six months later, 39 per cent of participants, compared with 17 per cent of controls, thought they had made lasting positive changes in their social relationship skills.

Both T-groups and study groups are used in professional and management training. It is usual for conductors to be trained, but Whitaker (1985) provides a useful source book for those wanting to engage in this work.

Therapy and counselling groups

In contrast to training groups, therapy and counselling groups are designed to offer professional help to clients in emotional distress or with behavioural problems. They can be used as an alternative or adjunct to individual therapy or counselling. Different types of individual psychotherapy will be looked at in the chapter on mental health by David Winter (Chapter 18). The conduct of any of the three types of group (training, therapy or counselling) necessitates the acquisition of specific professional qualifications by the group leader. These groups are thus distinct from the types of group-work which social workers and other members of the caring professions are competent to conduct without further training. A brief summary of the main types of therapy and counselling groups is given here, as it seems important for practitioners to know what to choose from should they wish to train as group therapists or counsellors in order to add a valuable skill to their professional competence.

There are numerous approaches to *group therapy* (Aveline and Dryden, 1988). They can be seen as fitting into three categories according to their theoretical orientation: the psychodynamic, the cognitive behavioural and a middle group using a humanistic approach (see Box 7.3). Brown and Pedder (1991) provide a brief and useful overview of group psychotherapy.

Box 7.3 Some Group Therapies Available in Britain

1. Psychodynamic

(a) The Tavistock approach is influenced by Bion's (1961) work. The focus is on the group as a whole, rather than the individual in the group. Training is centred in the Tavistock Clinic (London).
(b) Group analysis was developed by Foulkes (Foulkes and Anthony, 1957). It focuses on the individual in the context of the group. Training is through the Institute of Group Analysis (London). A useful guide is Agazarian and Peters (1981).

2. Humanistic

(a) *Interpersonal group therapy* is primarily associated with the work of Yalom (1995). Widely used in the USA, it is also used in Britain but has little formal recognition. (Aveline and Dryden, 1988, p.44). It combines existential ideas with those of American ego-analysts. But its roots lie in the work of Kurt Lewin.
(b) *Encounter groups therapy*. This is often confused with interpersonal group therapy and the labels are sometimes used interchangeably. It originated from the work of Karl Rogers. Although encounter groups are still used in Britain, there is no formal recognition of them.

3. Cognitive-Behavioural

(a) Social *skills* training (SST) was developed from the work of Argyle (Trower *et al.*, 1978). As a group therapy it transfers to the group ideas about social learning drawn from individual psychology. It is used, for example, with physically or mentally challenged clients to help them develop the abilities and confidence to live in the community. Practitioners are social and clinical psychologists, social workers and psychiatric nurses. Assertion and anger management training are specific forms of group therapy using the SST approach.
(b) *Anxiety Management Training* (AMT) applies the principles of cognitive therapy (Aveline and Dryden, 1988) for use in groups of anxious or neurotic patients. It is mainly used by clinical psychologists.

Many of these groups are private and fee-paying, but some NHS hospitals provide therapy for in- and/or outpatient groups. Intensive group-work, mainly from a psychodynamic base, is used in psychiatric hospitals, homes and half-way houses using the *therapeutic community* approach.

Outcome studies of group therapy, like those of training groups, are difficult to conduct and many studies do not use controls. Parloff and Dies (1977) reviewed research from 1966 to 1975 and found mixed results. Perhaps the most important conclusion to be drawn is the need to match the type of patients to the type of group.

Group counselling reflects the same theoretical orientations as group therapy, but in practice it is more eclectic. Training for both individual and group counselling is under the general direction of the British Association for Counselling. Often, groups are organized to deal with specific areas of distress, such as groups for the bereaved, for disaster survivors, for adult survivors of child abuse or groups for marital counselling.

Family therapy is another widely used tool that social care professionals can learn to practice or to refer clients; family therapy is considered in the chapter on mental health (Chapter 18).

Group-work by social care professionals

There are many situations where it is appropriate for social care professionals to conduct group work with clients. Whitaker (1985), a professor of social work, provides a careful and practical source book for social workers and other professionals who want to use the group approach. It is deliberately a-theoretical but uses a combination of the group-analytic (Foulkes) and interpersonal (Yalom) approaches.

There are many people known to social care professionals who might benefit from a group rather than an individual case-work approach – that is, where the problems or distress of individuals might be thought to be capable of amelioration by meeting with like others. And here group-work can be seen at times to merge with community work. Group-work does not necessarily imply a process by which distressed individuals learn to adapt to their situations, though that is sometimes the only possibility. At other times, from the seed-bed of the small group, possibilities for realistic community change may arise. For example, from a group of isolated single mothers with their toddlers, a self-help scheme for child-care exchanges might emerge, which might in its turn lead to a concerted attempt to persuade the education authority to provide nursery places. Group work and community work are not necessarily opposed.

McCaughan (1980) in an article on 'The purposes of group-work in social-work', provides a useful framework. She suggests four main areas in which group-work is appropriate. First is *social support* or help for the socially isolated. Examples are the physically disabled, wives of serving prisoners, the elderly, ex-prisoners, ex-psychiatric patients, and increasingly in the 1990s – the young homeless. The purpose of social support is to form a base from which information may be exchanged and friendships formed, to increase self-esteem and build social competencies. The second area is support in *daily living care*. This is of course a primary purpose of residential care, which will be discussed in the next section, but some individuals and groups living in the community (households of ex-psychiatric patients for example) could be helped in this way. Many group projects (for example, for the elderly or the homeless) provide communal meals as well as medical attention and facilities for personal hygiene. The third purpose is that of *social control*. This can be a primary purpose for groups of clients in trouble such as young offenders on probation, but also for ex-alcoholics, drug users and gamblers. With all these groups a primary goal of the group leader will be that of preventing the recurrence of the behaviour in question. The fourth purpose is that of *change*, to bring about a desired individual or community improvement.

It is obvious that training and therapy groups have the purpose of individual change predominately in mind. It is also clear that group-work in social care needs to keep all four purposes – support, care, control and change – in focus, as any group project will quite likely be doing all those things in greater or lesser degree. Finally, it is clear that in social-care groups, unlike training or therapy groups the change envisaged could be in the community as well as in individuals in the group.

Taking all these differentiating factors into account, there are still a few general psychological principles which may be borne in mind. Care should be taken in the selection of members so that there are enough differences for useful comparison processes to be undertaken, but not so many that cohesion is difficult to achieve or that splitting may occur. The boundaries of time and space need to be clearly delineated. Groups can either have a fixed time limit and membership (like many training groups) or a changing membership and no fixed ending (like many therapy groups). More intensive work can be done with fixed groups, but they should end at the time stipulated. Psychodynamic theory would suggest that it is only after the group's loss has been mourned that the former members can internalize and use the experience. However, it has to be acknowledged that for some social care clients, the need for support, care and sometimes control will remain, and the most that can be achieved in a time-limited group is some amelioration of distress. The next section, on group living, will look in more detail at psychological aspects of the problems and possibilities of longer-term group provision.

The gender and ethnic composition of any group will obviously impact on its process and therapeutic outcome. Care should be taken that individuals (i.e. a single black person in a white group or a single male in a female group) are not placed in positions where scape-goating might occur (see Chapters 8 and 9 on prejudice). There is little easily available information on the effects of gender and ethnic differences in therapeutic groups, but the chapter in Aveline and Dryden (1988) on sex therapy groups could be of use here.

Discussion point

   ° Have you attended, or helped to run, a client group? What was the group's purpose? Have you found the points made here useful, or not, when looking back at your experience? In what way?

A final point is that of the assessment of the effects of group-work. How can you tell if your work has really been of use or not? And what aspects of the process may have produced these results? A detailed discussion is not possible here and, as mentioned earlier, sound professional research is both time-consuming and expensive. However, Whitaker (1985) provides a useful chapter on monitoring, feedback and more formal research methods that can be used by practising social care professionals.

Group Living

Introduction

'Group living' is a term encompassing a wide range of areas in which social workers and others in the caring professions practise. This diversity makes the topic difficult to cover in this chapter. I will therefore first delineate the area and then focus on two aspects: institutional life and the therapeutic community.

The type of client for whom some form of 'group living' may be sought or imposed is varied. It ranges from children in need of care, young people in need of control, adults who have broken the law, those dependent on drugs or alcohol, the physically disabled, the chronic sick or dying, people with mental health problems, the homeless and the elderly.

The 'accommodation' provided varies from the large institution (prisons or hospitals), residential schools or training centres, children's homes, hostels and group homes. These accommodations differ not only in the type of client, but in the degree of freedom of the client to move in or out, the number, training and orientation of the staff, the goals of the organization (temporary containment, long-term care or rehabilitation) and the nature of the provider – the social services, the health service, the prison service, the voluntary service or the private sector.

In this section, therefore, we are excluding children and the elderly (who are the subjects of other chapters) and are looking at group living for disabled or disturbed adults which is either directly or indirectly influenced, by social services. It is important to note here that some of the institutional aspects of group living – such as large homes and hospitals – are being abolished, and the focus is now on Care in the Community (Darlington et al., 1981; Breakwell and Rowett, 1982).

Institutional life

Goffman's (1968) classic work depicted the 'total institution' – a mental hospital in which the patients exist in a setting from which all aspects of individual autonomy and self-respect have been removed. Only by learning patterns of subservience to the staff – playing the role of 'good patient' – can they survive; until the role becomes their identity and they become institutionalised (cf: Zimbardo's prison experiment p. 174). Although institutionalization in the mental hospital in this extreme sense was an unintended by-product of a consciously well-meaning system, Dornbusch's (1955) study of an American military academy shows a how similar drastic process can be deliberately introduced. Young civilians are changed into committed fighting men by first stripping them of their identity and then giving them another. Lifton's (1961) study of thought reform in China, based on accounts of expelled Westerners and summarized in Brown (1985), depicts a similar intensive and coercive re-education process. An interesting counterpoint to Lifton's study is the autobiographical account of his imprisonment and re-education by the last Emperor of China (Aisin-Gioro Pu Yi, 1979), written from the viewpoint of the apparently happily converted – from Emperor to Citizen.

There is, of course, no way of distinguishing the truly converted from the situationally conforming if they remain within the 'totalizing' environment, but Lifton, Milgram and Asch's work all suggests that, once removed from the situation of influence, there will be individual differences, partly based on personality attributes, on the depth of change.

The essence of the total institution is that it *is* total – there is no outside. There is, however, a fundamental difference between the experiences of being a patient in a pre-reformation mental hospital, an inmate of a present-day western prison, undergoing thought-reform in China, or indoctrination into the US army. In the latter two situations, the process is deliberate, and a new identity and sense of self-respect awaits those who successfully undergo the experience. In the former two, the process of identity-stripping is either unintended or has no management goal in the sense of re-education.

Thus, the institutionalized patient or prisoner has no new identity other than that of the totally subservient, unless it were provided by the institution's sub-culture (for example, *One Flew over the Cuckoo's Nest*). A social psychological analysis would suggest that prisoners may learn to be more committed criminals (for which there is much evidence) not because they are 'ineducable' nor too easily educated in the 'university of crime', but because, in terms of Tajfel's Social Identity theory (discussed further in Chapter 9), the identity given them as prisoners by the staff is so totally negative, they have no escape, in the psychological sense of maintaining some measure of self-esteem, except by re-evaluating the criminal role as a positive social identity.

Discussion point
  ° Do you, as professional social care professionals, think there are any circumstances in which deliberate and coercive re-educating might be socially justified? If yes: Who should do it, and to whom?

A group dynamic view of the extreme scenarios of institutions such as prisons or hospitals also sees the behaviour of the staff in stripping inmates of their identity as a *social defence mechanism*. That is, it could be seen as an unconscious or unacknowledged means of protecting the staff against anxiety. This is similar to Bion's 'basic assumptions', where unconscious myths or fantasies protect the group against facing the anxiety of the real work task. The process of 'social defence' a term originating with Eliot Jaques (1995), who demonstrated this process in his study of the relationship between managers and workers in a factory. He showed how the existence of mutual misperceptions of the motives and goals of the other side protected each side from the anxiety of recognizing the conflict between their different needs and aspirations, and the limited extent to which both were practically achievable. This social defence may have suppressed social anxiety and enabled the organization to survive as a psychological entity; but it also prevented any long-term solution to the problem of worker-management relations, as the maintenance of the problem became an essential element in the social defence system of the organization as a whole. The concept has been applied as an explanatory tool to other organizations such as hospitals and special schools by Menzies-Lyth (1989).

Miller and Gwynne (1972) studied the relations between management and residents in five institutions for the physically disabled and young chronic sick. Two were run by the voluntary services, two by the health service and one by the social services. Most residents in each institution were suffering from the advanced stages of such diseases as multiple sclerosis, cerebral palsy or muscular dystrophy. After a careful investigation involving observation, interviews and discussion with residents and staff, they conclude that there were two opposing models of management (sometimes co-existing in a single institution). These they called the *warehousing* and the *horticultural* models. In the warehousing model, the primary task was simply the preservation of the physical life of the inmates, who were depersonalized into hopeless cases. Complete dependence was required and individuality suppressed. In the horticultural model, the primary task was the development of unfulfilled capacities in inmates seen as 'nearly normal' and capable of return to outside society.

Miller and Gwynne's conclusion was that, although the horticultural model was more humane, both models were acting as social defence mechanisms for their proponents (sometimes both staff and residents) against the disturbing reality that for most inmates their placement was a last resort – a form of social death irreversibly leading to physical death. In the warehousing model the social defence was against the staff's recognition that 'There but for the grace of God go I', and the behaviour can be seen as similar to that in Goffman's institution – making as wide a separation as possible between us and them. In the horticultural model, the defence was that of over-identification and a denial of the recognition of the real situation of the inmates. Miller and Gwynne suggested that an honest facing of the real situation would reduce the anxiety and the need to defend against it, and would allow the primary task to be carried out – that of making the residents' stay as personally fulfilling and as little psychologically damaging as possible. Their practical advice included a loosening of boundaries between the institution and the outside world by a better use of voluntary workers, and also that the final stay might be preceded by short visits so that the final transition was not so shocking. They suggested other ways in which residents' independence and control over their own lives might be maximized, including that of giving them the freedom of voluntary euthanasia.

Discussion point
  ° Some of Miller and Gwynne's recommendations were adopted, others not. As social professionals, do you think that residents in terminal institutions, such as hospices, homes for aids sufferers or the severely incurably handicapped should be given the choice of ending their own lives? What are the arguments for, and against?

McCaughan (1980) reiterates the problems of institutionalization which were highlighted by Goffman, and Gwynne and Miller, and makes the point that an understanding of group processes and their application in group-work is essential for staff in residential institutions. The group tasks might be managing the tensions of daily living, facilitating the integration of newcomers, providing opportunities for personal development, or in some cases helping residents to find solutions for some of their problems, which might have been partly responsible for their admission in the first place (such as residents in bail or probation hostels). A vital group task within the institution McCaughan suggests is that of helping staff to exercise creative leadership through reviews of group events and the application of these learning experiences. An important task for staff to address is their agreement or otherwise on the purpose of their institution. (For example, is it a warehouse, a refuge, a cradle, a springboard, or perhaps none of these?) As Miller and Gwynne have shown, the effect of these implicit values on the organizational culture and the experience and behaviour of clients can be immense.

One also needs to bear in mind the organizational culture when setting up groups in institutions, as stressed by Whitaker (1985). Explicit organizational rules – on who may join, for how long, at what time and place, and the recognition or otherwise for the need for confidentiality – may limit a group's potential as agent of change. But implicit institutional values can be even more damaging. For example, Bloomfield, (1991) describes a staff-support group she conducted in Pentonville prison. The group was for staff who were themselves acting as leaders of small groups of inmates. The aim of the inmate groups was to allow prisoners to express in words their frustration and rage, in the hope that physical violence would be reduced. The institutional culture was initially antagonistic:

> 'The prison officers who volunteered to take groups were ridiculed by their colleagues and called "groupees".' (Bloomfield 1991, p.242)

The experiment continued for four years, at the end of which Bloomfield concluded that there had been some growth in communication in both the staff support and the inmate groups. The prison as a whole also seemed marginally more receptive of the innovation. Any changes in the level of violent incidents over four years are, unfortunately, not reported. However, Bloomfield makes the point that innovations such as hers are limited not only by the institutional culture, but by the attitudes of the larger society from which both staff and inmates are drawn – and in Britain the predominant attitude towards prisoners seems to be that of retribution rather than rehabilitation.

A more successful innovation within the prison system is that of Grendon Underwood – deemed by some, the first 'therapeutic community' prison in Britain. There the institutional aim and the organizational culture are congruent, as both staff and prisoners are volunteers and both may ask for transfers from and to other institutions. The prisoners are long-term violent offenders (murderers, rapists, arsonists, paedophiles) reaching the last few years of their sentence, and have been selected on the basis of their intelligence and willingness to change. The prison is internally open with high external security. The inmates participate in intensive group therapy, focused partly on learning social skills, anger and stress management. But they participate in group cognitive therapy specifically focused on the individual's public acknowledgement of what he has done and his recognition of it as wrong (which some, especially sex offenders, will initially deny). The recidivism rate at Grendon is no higher than the national average, although the inmates comprise those having committed some of the most serious crimes. (Personal communication.)

Therapeutic communities

The therapeutic community movement was initiated from within psychiatry by those shocked at the 'anti-therapeutic' effects of the large mental hospital. Today, the term is applied to a variety of residential or day communities catering not only for the mentally ill but those with behavioural difficulties or drug or alcohol dependence. A voluntary placement in a community such as the Henderson hospital – a unit for young people with behavioural problems – can be used as an alternative to a prison sentence. Some children's homes, such as the Caldecott Community (Little and Kelly, 1995), have adopted the therapeutic community approach, as well as some homes or 'villages' for the mentally disabled, where the stay might be for life.

The common *attributes* of a therapeutic community have been described by Kennard (1983) as an informal atmosphere, where staff and clients are not distinguished by dress; a central place of group meeting where the entire community gathers; the sharing of work of maintaining and running the community by all residents and staff; and the encouragement of community members to take responsibility for themselves and other members. The common *values* of therapeutic communities, are the acceptance of psychodynamic principles; a recognition of the basic equality of all members; democratization, in that the community is run by its members; a belief in the efficacy of the approach; and (within limits) permissiveness. The therapeutic *methods* used are those of sociotherapy (the institution as therapist); peer group influence (the group as therapist); 'reality confrontation' (life as therapist) and therapy as active learning (of social, occupational and artistic skills). As we will see, the shared values in particular are sometimes not carried out in practice.

The innovative ideas of the movement seemed to arise almost simultaneously and apparently independently. They were largely but not entirely derived from psychoanalytic and group dynamic approaches. For example, in 1944 Bion was medical superintendent of Northfield Hospital for soldiers with war neuroses. Instead of the existing system of passive dependence on staff, he inaugurated a regime of small patient-led task groups which combined responsibility for ward housekeeping with that for exercise, recreation and group discussion. Bion was followed by Foulkes and later by Main, both of whom continued Bion's innovation. From Bion and Foulkes experiences grew respectively the Tavistock study groups and the Institute of Group Analysis. From Main's experiences (Main 'some basic concepts in therapeutic community work', in Jenson, 1980) came the development of the Cassel Hospital, where the disturbance of one member is treated as a disturbance of the family system, and the whole family lives in the hospital. They maintain outside work, social and educational links while engaging within the hospital in a combination of individual, group and family therapy.

Maxwell Jones' World War II experience of the morale raising properties of groups led him to start a treatment unit for unemployed ex-soldiers. This became the Henderson Hospital for behaviourally disturbed young people, in which he introduced many of the methods associated with the therapeutic community – such as participative group decision making by community meetings of patients and staff (Jones, 'The therapeutic community', in Hinshelwood and Manning, 1979).

In the 1950s, David Clark, (see Clark, 1974) as medical superintendent of Fulbourn Hospital, Cambridge, introduced what he called 'social therapy' a radical innovation based on Maxwell Jones' ideas, where the whole hospital became a therapeutic community – the boundaries between patients and staff were all but dissolved, and major decisions were taken at community meetings. The innovation spread for some years in mental hospitals in Britain and the US (see Rappaport, 1960); but the apparently overwhelming success of neuroleptic drug treatments in reducing the need for long-term stay in mental hospitals has led to the abandonment of the humane but labour intensive approach of the 'therapeutic community' in favour of a quick return to the community and an increasing use of group homes and hostels.

Other psychiatrists within the therapeutic community movement had, however, already taken the innovative ideas out of the hospital. Bierer (Bierer and Evans, 1969) initiated the concept of the 'day hospital', where young people with severe neurotic disorders were able to live at home, but participate daily in a combination of small and large groups and community meetings, as well as occupational, art and movement therapies. Unfortunately, this particular model of the therapeutic community collapsed in the 1980s due perhaps to an unacknowledged but irreconcilable conflict between the principles of democratic liberalism and the need for a modicum of management authority (Baron, 1987).

The 'anti-psychiatry' movement, led by Laing and Berke, also reacted to the condition in mental hospitals by establishing 'refuges' for the psychiatrically ill outside the hospital. But, unlike the day hospitals, Laing and Berke moved outside the framework of the National Health Service. An account of their first venture is given in Barnes and Berke (1973). Today a number of group homes or households have been established. Some are run by the Arbours Association (Berke et al., 1995) and others by the Philadelphia Association. But the initiative has not grown as much as the originators might have expected, partly because they are dependent on private sector funding, and partly perhaps because the mental hospital system itself became more liberal, with treatment increasingly transferred from old 'asylums' to units of general hospitals.

The other organizations choosing the label of 'therapeutic community' are the half-way houses between the mental hospital and the community run by the Richmond Fellowship (Jenson, 1980), and some units for rehabilitation from drug or alcohol addiction. The most noted are the Phoenix units, run both in Britain and the US, and the Synanon Community in America. An interesting difference between communities whose sole aim is recovery of its clients from drug or alcohol abuse and other therapeutic communities is that the former tend to be hierarchically rather than democratically run, and clients undergo a regime initially quite harsh, but which becomes progressively more mild as the client becomes more free of his addiction. If it were not the case that clients voluntarily agree to enter, and are free to leave if they do not want to continue the programme (but cannot then re-enter), there seems a hint of a return to the total institution here – as though revolution has come full circle. It should be noted that the Synanon Community did come full circle in that it began to assume the qualities of a closed cult. It was eventually disbanded and its leader imprisoned.

From the viewpoint of social psychology the question remains – Is there any evidence that therapeutic communities work? An early study by Fairweather (1964) showed that patients in a small-group ward, compared with a traditional ward in the same mental hospital, spent fewer days in hospital and were seen as 'better' than patients from the traditional ward at a six-month follow-up. But attempts to study other types of therapeutic community have shown mostly the difficulties in such a complex task (Hinshelwood and Manning, 1979).

On reflection, we can see that the therapeutic community movement may have mirrored in miniature the socio-political models of the larger society. The majority embody and enact the ideals of a liberal democracy, but at their extremes they show the possibilities of reversion to a state of totalitarianism or anarchy. What can be learnt from the example of the extremes is the danger of setting up a structure which gives too much power to a charismatic leader (as did the Synanon Community), or the other end of the spectrum, the danger of abandoning all structure in the belief that any structure is a social defence against anxiety. That may be true, but some defences are necessary.

Finally, from the viewpoint of the social care professional, it can be seen that some of the liberalizing ideas of the therapeutic community movement found a place in the creation and structure of many group homes and hostels. Today it seems possible that the innovations of the 1990s in social care may seem less radical than those of the 1950s and 1960s when the therapeutic community movement started, because public attitudes have themselves become more liberal, and what was once radical is now seen as normal. The therapeutic community movement itself may have helped to promote these attitude changes.

Conclusion

The purpose of this chapter has been to show how the practice of working with groups in the social care professions can be better understood and improved by greater comprehension of the psychological theories underlying particular ways of working. I have argued that cognitive and psychodynamic approaches to the understanding of small groups and institutions need not be seen as either contradictory or each applying to a separate area of practice; but that the ideas in terms of the understanding of the motivational bases of group behaviour can be seen to complement each other. This knowledge can help us to develop our competence and skills, by allowing us to utilize a greater range of techniques and ideas.

Seminar Questions

1. Should clients be coerced into obeying advice or instructions? If so, under what circumstances, and by what means? If not, why not?

2. How might knowledge about the factors involved in group influence be useful to the practising social care professional?

3. How might social care professionals use group-work to increase their own learning about groups?

4. How might an understanding of social psychological and group dynamic factors help social care professionals to reduce tension in a group home?

Further Reading

Aveline, M. and Dryden, W. (eds) (1988) *Group Therapy in Britain*. Milton Keynes: Open University Press.
A useful source book. The papers by Kennard on therapeutic communities and Miller on organizational dynamics are both relevant.

DeBoard, R. (1978) *The Psychoanalysis of Organisations*. London: Tavistock.
Chapter 2 on Freud's group theory and Chapter 4 on Bion give extended coverage to the ideas in this chapter, as do his Chapter 6 on Lewin, Chapter 7 on T-groups and Chapter 9 on social defence systems.

Douglas, T. (1986) *Group Living*. London: Tavistock.

Sutton, C. (1995) *Social Work, Community Work and Psychology*. London: BPS Books.

Is a useful overview. Chapter 8 A 'Working with communities and groups', is relevant to this chapter.

Whitaker, D.S. (1987) *Using Groups to Help People*. London: Routledge.
An extremely useful practical guide designed particularly for the social work and helping professions.

References

Agazarian, Y. and Peters, R. (1981) *The Visible and Invisible Group*. London: Routledge.

Aisin-Gioro, P.Y. (1979) *From Emperor to Citizen*. Beijing: Foreign Languages Press.

Allport, F. (1924) 'Social stimulation in the group and the crowd' in E. Hollander and R. Hunt (eds) (1972) *Classic Contributions to Social Psychology*. Oxford: Oxford University Press.

Asch, S.E. (1956) 'Studies of independence and conformity: a minority of one against a unanimous majority.' *Psychological Monographs, 70*, 9 (whole No. 416).

Aveline, M. and Dryden, W. (1988) *Group Therapy in Britain*. Milton Keynes: Open University Press.

Barnes, M. and Berke, J. (1973) *Mary Barnes: Two Accounts of a Journey Through Madness*. Harmondsworth: Penguin.

Baron, C. (1987) *From Asylum to Anarchy*. London: Free Association Press.

Berke, J., Masoliver, C. and Ryan, T. (eds.) (1995) *Sanctuary*. London: Process Press.

Bierer, J. and Evans, R. (1969) *Innovations in Social Psychology*. London: Avenue Publishing.

Bion, W.R. (1961) *Experiences in Groups and other Papers*. London: Tavistock.

Bloomfield, I. (1991) 'A group in prison.' *Group Analysis, 24*, 241–256.

Breakwell, G. and Rowett, C. (1982) *Social Work: The Social Psychological Approach*. Berkshire: Van Nostrand.

Brown, D. and Pedder, J. (1991) *Introduction to Psychotherapy. 2nd ed*. London: Routledge.

Brown, H. (1985) *People, Groups and Society*. Milton Keynes: Open University Press.

Clark, D. (1974) *Social Therapy in Psychiatry*. Harmondsworth: Penguin.

Darlington, T., Miller, E. and Gwynne, G. (1981) *A Life Together*. London: Tavistock.

De Board, R. (1978) *The Psychoanalysis of Organisations*. London: Tavistock.

Dornbusch, S. (1955) 'The military academy as an assimilating institution.' *Social Forces, 33*, 316–321.

Fairweather, G.W. (ed) (1964) *Social Psychology in Treating Mental Illness*. New York: Wiley.

Festinger, L. (1954) 'A theory of social comparison processes.' *Human Relations 7*, 117–4.

Fiedler, F.E. (1967) *A Theory of Leadership Effectiveness*. New York: McGraw-Hill.

Foulkes, S.H. and Anthony, E.J. (1957) *Group Psychotherapy. The psycho-analytic approach*. Harmondsworth: Penguin Books.

Freud, S. (1916) 'Introductory lecture on psychoanalysis'. In S. Freud (1972) Vol.1. *Introductory Lectures in Psychoanalysis*. Harmondsworth: Penguin.

Freud, S. (1921) 'Group psychology and the analysis of the ego.' In S. Freud (1985) *Civilisation, Society and Religion, 12*. Pelican Freud Library, Harmondsworth: Penguin Books.

Freud, S. (1930) 'Civilisation and its discontents.' In S. Freud, (1985) *Civilisation, Society and Religion, 12*. Pelican Freud Library. Harmondsworth: Penguin.

Goffman (1968) *Asylums*. Harmondsworth: Penguin.

Heller, F. (ed) (1992) *Decision Making and Leadership*. Cambridge: Cambridge University Press.

Hinshelwood, R. and Manning, N. (1979) *Therapeutic Communities*. London: Routledge.

Hosking, D.M. and Morley, I. (1991) *A Social Psychology of Organising*. London: Harvester Wheatsheaf.

Janis, I. (1982) *Group Think, 2nd edition*. Boston: Houghton Mifflin.

Jaques, E. (1995) 'Social systems as a defence against persecutory and depressive anxiety.' In M. Klien *et al.* (eds) *New Directions in Psychoanalysis*. London: Tavistock.

Jenson, E. (ed.) (1980) *The Therapeutic Community*. London: Croom Helm.

Jones, M. (1982) *The Process of Change*. London: Routledge.

Kennard, D. (1983) *An Introduction to Therapeutic Communities*. London: Routledge.

Lewin, K. (1951) 'Field theory.' In *Social Science*. New York: Harper.

Lieberman, M.A., Yalom, I.D. and Miles, M.B. (1973) *Encounter Groups, First Facts*. New York: Basic Books.

Lifton, R. (1961) *Through the Form and the Psychology of Totalism*. London: Gollancz.

Little, M. and Kelly, S. (1995) *A Life Apart*. London: Tavistock.

McCaughan, N. (1980) 'The purposes of group-work in social work', In P.B. Smith (ed.) *Small Groups and Personal Change*. London: Methuen.

Malan, D., Balfour, F., Hood, V. and Shooter, A, (1976) 'Group psychotherapy, a long term follow-up study'. *Archives of General Psychiatry, 33*, 1303–1315.

Menzies-Lyth, I. (1988) *Containing Anxiety in Institutions: Selected Essays.* London: Free Association Books.

Menzies-Lyth, I. (1989) *The Dynamics of the Social.* London: Free Association Books.

Milgram, S. (1974) *Obedience to Authority.* London: Tavistock.

Miller, E. and Gwynne, G. (1972) *A Life Apart.* London: Tavistock.

Moscovici, S. (1976) *Social Influence and Social Change.* London: Academic Press.

Nicholson, N., Steven, C.G. and Rocklin, T. (1985) 'Conformity in the Asch situation: a comparison between contemporary British and U.S. university students.' *British Journal of Social Psychology, 24,* 59–63.

Nitsun, M. (1996) *The Anti-Group.* London: Routledge.

Oatley, K. (1984) *Selves in Relation: An Introduction to Psychotherapy and Groups. New Essential Psychology.* London: Methuen.

Parloff, M.B. and Dies, R.R. (1977) 'Group psychotherapy outcome research 1966–1975.' *International Journal of Group Psychotherapy, 27,* 281–319.

Perrin, S. and Spencer, C. (1980) 'The Asch effect – a child of its time?' *Bulletin of the British Psychological Society, 32,* 405–406.

Powell, A. (1989) 'The nature of the group matrix.' *Group Analysis 22,* 271–281.

Rappaport, R. (1960) *Community as Doctor.* London: Tavistock.

Schachter, S. (1951) 'Deviation, rejection and communication.' *Journal of Abnormal and Social Psychology, 46,* 190–207.

Schachter, S. (1959) *The Psychology of Affiliation.* Palo Alto, CA: Stanford University Press.

Sherif, M. (1936) *The Psychology of Social Norms.* New York: Harper and Row.

Sigell, B. (1992) 'The long-term effects of group psychotherapy.' *Group Analysis, 25,* 333–352.

Sutton, C. (1994) *Social Work, Community Work and Psychology.* London: BRD Books.

Tajfel, H. (1981) *Human Groups and Social Categories.* Cambridge: Cambridge University Press.

Thibault, J. and Kelley, H. (1959) *The Social Psychology of Groups.* New York: Wiley.

Trower, P. Bryant, B. and Argyle, M. (1978) *Social Skills and Mental Health.* London: Methuen.

Turner, J. (1987) *Rediscovering the Social Group.* Oxford: Blackwell.

Whitaker, D.S. (1987) *Using Groups to Help People.* London: Routledge.

Yalom, I. (1995) *The Theory and Practice of Group Psychotherapy, 4th ed.* New York: Basic Books.

Zimbardo, P.G. (1983) 'Transforming experimental research into advocacy for social change'. In H.H. Blomberg, A.P. Hare, V. Kent, and M. Davies (eds) *Small Groups and Social Interaction,* Volume 1. New York: Wiley.

CHAPTER 8

Prejudice and Discrimination
Individual Approaches
Mary Horton

Introduction

'Prejudice' is an emotive term. Some writers prefer others such as *discrimination*, that is the making of differences in social action towards others; *stereotyping*, that is the persistence of fixed and usually over-simplified ideas about the other people; or *racism* (sexism or ageism, etc.), which implies the holding of views antagonistic to another racial, gender or age group and, by inference, in favour of one's own. *Ethnocentricism* is a term also used to denote a strong preference for one's own cultural group and dislike of other cultures. All these terms address aspects of the overall concept, but for this chapter I have chosen the word 'prejudice', as it seems to embody an essential aspect of the thinking and behaviour we are going to look at. 'Prejudice' is Latin for 'judging before': that is, making up one's mind *before* seeing the evidence. It suggests a lack of open-mindedness and an inability to tolerate 'not-knowing'; and it certainly implies the persistence or rigidity of the 'judgement', as by definition, contrary evidence will not change it. These and other questions of the nature of prejudice will be looked at in this chapter and the one following. But a useful 'holding definition' to start with might be simply 'negative attitudes towards other people seen as members of a category and not as individuals. The relation between 'prejudice' (the underlying judgement) and 'discrimination' or the taking of some action against another group is important to clarify. A sociologist, Merton, in 1949, showed the distinction between the two concepts in the following typology:

1. *The un-prejudiced non-discriminator:* who might be expected to lead campaigns for the reduction of prejudice, but who might on the other hand tend to find private solutions for social problems – that is, ignore the social dimension altogether.

2. *The un-prejudiced discriminator:* or 'timid liberal': one who without holding deeply prejudiced attitudes will support discriminatory practice if it is less trouble, but with a sense of guilt.

3. *The prejudiced non-discriminator:* or 'timid bigot': who can be prevented from expressing his underlying prejudice by social or legal pressure.

4. *The prejudiced discriminator:* who believes that the differences between races (or other social groups) are 'real', and society should be ordered accordingly. (Bloom 1971, pp.158–159)

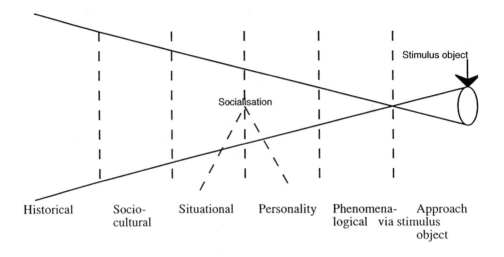

Figure 8.1 Allport's diagramatic view. (Reproduced from Allport, 'Prejudice: A problem in psychological and social causation', Journal of Social Issues 4, 1950, by permission of Blackwell Publisher, Malden, MA, USA)

Thus for types (1) and (4) attitudes and behaviour are congruent, while for types (2) and (3) they are not. Merton's typology allows us to *describe* people in terms of distinctive categories, but the questions social psychologists ask are for *explanations* or why? questions. Allport (1950) provides a diagrammatic view of different levels of explanation offered (figure 8.1). In his classic text *The Nature of Prejudice* (1970), Allport describes his diagram in detail.

- *The historical approach* argues that the individual is shaped by historical social context. An example is the Marxian *exploitation theory*, which holds that (race) prejudice is an attitude propagated among the public to stigmatize some group as inferior so their exploitation can be justified.

- The *socio-cultural approach* is argued by sociologists and anthropologists. They too look at social context, but in terms of the conflict between social change and social stasis. *Urbanization* and upward mobility (i.e. change) increase competition and the tendency to derogate the under-dog. Alternatively, a *community pattern theory* of prejudice, stresses the historical continuity (i.e. stasis) of ethnocentrism, and old resentments against out-groups (such as Irish hostility towards the English).

- The *situational approach* stresses current social forces, i.e. the education pattern that socializes children into the views of the group, the relative *density* of different groups (the majority and the minorities) and the types and extent of *contact* available.

- The *personality approach* emphasizes causation in human nature, and initially looked for explanation in terms of 'basic needs'. One early psychological theory is *frustration theory*, in which frustration by circumstance or more powerful members of the in-group is displaced onto the out-group, who then become scape-goats. Later theories, such as the *authoritarian personality*, suggest an explanation in terms of character-structure rather than basic needs.

- *The phenomenological approach* stresses the immediate view of the individual – that is, his perception of and/or attitude towards the 'other'. What would otherwise be a simple description is given explanatory status, as it is assumed that all the previous factors discussed (i.e. personality, situation, cultural and historical) converge into a final common focus.

- *The stimulus object approach* (which Allport also calls the 'grain of truth' approach) looks at the relation between the 'real' attributes of the 'other', and those which are gratuitously thrust upon him or her. Such an *interaction theory*, in today's terminology, might look at the effect of people's attitudes on the behaviour of those discriminated against, and in turn at the effect of that behaviour on people's perceptions in terms of increasing or modifying prejudice.

Social psychological explanations tend to be those which Allport would describe as *situational*, *personality* or *phenomenological*, and it is these we shall be looking at primarily in this chapter. However, it is important not to forget the socio-cultural and historical forces which shape individual attitudes and personality. The present-day emphasis on social identity theory and social representations (discussed in Chapter 9), has refocused emphasis on group and cultural issues which had been previously lacking in social psychology.

An understanding of the investigations of social psychologists into prejudice is of use to social care professionals for several reasons. First, you may meet prejudice from the public against particular groups of clients: 'the needy', such as the homeless, unemployed, or those on social support; 'the rule-breakers' such as the deviant or difficult; and those who threaten by their inherent difference – the mentally or physically ill or handicapped. Second, as professionals whose task it is to care for those clients, and who are seen as holding particular views towards them – such as protecting and empowering – you may encounter negative attitudes and stereotypes towards your own profession. Third, you may encounter prejudice within yourselves – not only towards those who are prejudiced towards you, or those groups opposing what you are trying to achieve; but also toward your own client groups, and perhaps your own colleagues who may come from a different race or culture. Finally, anti-racism is an explicit aspect of contemporary social work training.

Prejudice as an Attitude

Early social psychologists, particularly in the US, conceptualized the nature of the relation between the individual and his or her social world in terms of 'attitudes' or positive or negative orientations towards differentiated entities called 'social objects'. These 'objects' could be social groups or categories (for example, foreigners or students); social institutions (such as the church or the education system); or social values (such as political or cultural views). These early studies were directed towards establishing to what extent views for and against these 'objects' 'existed' in people by using paper-and-pencil techniques such as questionnaires. One of the earliest was that of Bogardus (1925) in which he asked his (almost entirely white,

American) subjects, to rate members of 39 nationalities (listed alphabetically from American to Welsh), on a 7-point rating scale ranging from '(would admit) to close kinship by marriage' to 'would exclude from my country'. He found that English and Canadian potential immigrants were thought of as socially 'closest', while Koreans and Turks were the most distant. Such an approach would today seem not only unethical and probably illegal, but also methodologically extremely crude and somewhat pointless. However, these early approaches can be seen as the first steps in an attempt to understand social behaviour by using simple descriptive questioning. These early studies were largely about racial or cultural issues, because they were centrally important topics in America at that time – and ones that liberally-minded academics wanted to investigate. A more sophisticated approach was that of Lapiere (1934). He studied not only verbal attitudes, but also the behaviour of Americans to some actual foreigners. With a Chinese couple he visited over 250 hotels and restaurants throughout the USA. They were turned away from only one establishment (with the words 'we don't take Japs'). But the interest of the study lies in the fact that he followed up his visits with a letter asking to book a future room or table for some Chinese – and over 90 per cent of establishments refused him. (The same results were obtained from a control sample which he had not visited earlier.) A small replication (Kutner, Wilkins and Yarrow, 1952) of 11 restaurants visited by a group of two white and one black women supported Lapiere's findings. The huge discrepancy between the written 'attitude' and the actual behaviour led social psychologists to consider more deeply the nature of the phenomenon they were investigating, but not to the abandonment of the concept of 'attitude' itself. Attention turned to more careful definitions (Fishbein 1967) and the development of theories as to the function of attitudes in the personality as a whole. A seminal book by Heider (1958) suggested that an internal 'balance' or consistency of values, beliefs and opinions was important for the individual's sense of internal harmony or well-being. When this internal balance was threatened by the introduction of 'non-fitting' information, harmony could be restored, by changing the mental element which was easiest for the individual to alter in order to re-establish consistency. Festinger (1957) suggested that in particular circumstances, the reduction of 'dissonance' or internal inconsistency is accomplished by the changing of an attitude or an internal feeling towards a social object. The particular circumstances were when an event occurred over which the subject had either no control or which they had already decided to do or which had already taken place, and could not be denied. Many experiments have supported Festinger's contention – subjects given a present they did not choose and they had previously rated fairly negatively, were found on re-testing to have a higher opinion of it. Participants given the task of arguing *for* an issue that they were previously *against*, were found to have changed their opinions slightly *towards* the issue, when asked later. Festinger's cognitive dissonance theory has led to the dictum 'Change behaviour and attitudes will change'. But is this the case with prejudice? The question will be looked at further in the next chapter, but Festinger's dissonance theory has had a tremendous influence on American social psychology, though a smaller one in Europe. It has also met with considerable criticism (Kiesler, Collins and Miller, 1969). It seems to work (i.e. dissonance is reduced by attitude change) only in specific experimental situations, where alternative modes of coping are denied. Individual differences between people in their tendency to want to reduce internal inconsistency, have also not been adequately considered. For example, work by Harvey (1965) suggests that people with a more 'concrete' way of thinking generally will be more motivated to reduce dissonance. Another attitude theory which relates clearly to the study of prejudice is Katz's (1960) Functional theory. Katz suggests that there are four main functions of a particular orientation towards a social object:

1. *An instrumental, adjustive or utilitarian function*: since an individual strives to maximize rewards and minimize penalties, he will develop favourable attitudes toward those objects which result in reward and unfavourable attitudes to those which result in punishment.

2. *A knowledge function*: to make sense of things, helping the individual to understand and structure his experience.

3. *A value-expressive or self-realizing function*: a person may gain satisfaction from expressing himself in terms of attitudes that are appropriate to his personal values and his self-concept.

4. *An ego-defensive function*: to protect a person from acknowledging unpleasant truths about himself, or recognizing the harsh realities of the environment.

Any particular attitude may, of course, serve more than one function, but they can be seen to differ primarily in their presumed cause, and in the structural position they hold in the mind. An attitude with a largely *instrumental* function has been learnt by experience or socialization, and will quickly change if the liked object no longer provides the expected reward or if expectations of reward have been raised. Such an attitude can be easily changed. An attitude with a largely *knowledge* function, will have a positive or negative orientation, to the extent that this 'fits in' with orientations to other beliefs or opinions. An attitude with a primarily *value-expressive* function, also has an underlying consistency motive – but here the consistency desired is not between opinions or cognitions, but with fundamental beliefs and his sense of 'self'. Both these functions can be seen to relate to the cognitive consistency theories, discussed above. But the attitude with a value-expressive function can be seen to be more deeply embedded in the personality, and to change the attitude more profound internal changes may need to be made.

Ego-defensive attitudes will be aroused in situations which threaten the individual. They can also be aroused by encouragement of their expression by others (such as the mass media). They can be positive orientations, toward a 'leader' or a 'cult', or negative such as racial prejudice. This is the most difficult level to change. Perhaps it can be done only by giving the person some understanding of why they are feeling the way they do. They can then be free to change themselves or to engage in changing their environment – or both. The importance to social care professionals of this brief incursion into some of the work on the social psychology of attitudes is to demonstrate that attitudes cannot be thought of as isolated 'entities', but are part of the individual's whole orientation to his social world: his surface opinions, deeper attitudes and fundamental beliefs, values and goals – as well as his 'personality'. All form a complex structure, together with the orientation of his group, community and culture. More recent work in social psychology has left the study of attitudes (fruitful though it has been) and looked at the social origins of attitude structures in the work on *social representations*, which will be looked at in Chapter 9.

Prejudice as a personality attribute

The difference between a 'social attitude' and 'social personality trait or tendency' in social psychology is that the concept of social personality refers to underlying general 'patterns of behaviour, feelings and attitudes a person has that are relatively enduring and relatively predictable' (Gosling, 1994, p.135). They are thought of as more stable, more general and more determined by an individual's early history and underlying needs than are attitudes. Some psychologists would suggest that personality can be partly determined by the inheritance of behavioural predispositions (cf. Eysenck). However, at the level of social personality that we are looking at here – that is, personality as one of the many possible influences on prejudice – the question of innate predispositions, though contentious, is not really relevant. A useful way of looking at the relation between attitudes and personality is shown in Figure 8.2.

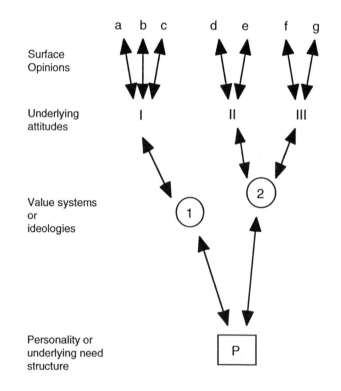

Figure 8.2 Hierarchical structure of attitudes/personality (adapted from Oppenheim, 1992, Questionaire Design, Interviewing and Attitude Management, reproduced by permission of Pinter Publishers, Cassell Academic. Wellington House, 125 Strand. London. England.)

The personality approach which has had the most profound effect on psychological thinking about prejudice is that of *The Authoritarian Personality* (1950). The research was carried out in the late 1940s at the University of Berkeley, California, by three psychoanalytic thinkers (Frenkel-Brunswik, Levinson and Sanford) and a sociologist (Adorno), with whose name the work is usually associated. It is important to make clear here that the term *authoritarian* is distinct from that of *authoritative*. The former describes people who have a strong hierarchical orientation to external authority, they submit to those above them, and are aggressive to those below: the latter possess authority either from their role-position or their knowledge and ability, or both.

The Berkeley researchers were concerned by the extent to which fascism and Nazism had been adopted as a mass ideology in the 1930s. But they turned their attention initially to the situational and personality levels of explanation and were guided by their belief that people's behaviour could be understood in terms of their early socialization. Their investigative tools were attitude and personality measures, combined with in-depth interviews. Their research question concerned whether it was possible to identify a potentially fascist personality type who might be susceptible to anti-democratic propaganda and would '...accept fascism if it became a strong or respectable social movement' (Adorno *et al.*, 1964, p.1).

They started from the historical base that the political organization of fascism gained its mass motive power to a considerable extent by the actualization of group hatred against minorities – predominantly the Jews. They devised a scale to measure *ethnocentricism* (E) defined as '...an ideological system pertaining to groups ... (distinguishing) between *in-groups* ... with which the individual identifies himself, and *out-groups* with which he does not have a sense of belonging and which are antithetical to the in-group' (Adorno *et al.*, 1964, p.104). They were interested in the all-inclusiveness of the beliefs about out-group members; the generality of the rejection of the out-group; and the stereotyping, or fixedness and rigidity in thinking about out-groups. They then devised the F or proto-fascism scale as a measure of social personality composed of statements overtly expressing general feelings or beliefs about society as a whole, rather than orientations to specific objects (minority groups). The selection of statements for the F-scale was made to operationalize a number of underlying personality trends hypothesized on the basis of earlier research as forming the syndrome underlying prejudice. A high F-scorer was conceived as rigid, dogmatic, servile to authority, with a tendency to externalize unacceptable impulses and an opposition to the imaginative and subjective.

Both the E- and F-scales, and others, were given to different groups of white Americans, mainly middle-class and composed of both students and professional men and women, totalling over 2000 people. The research conclusions were that the scores on the two scales were related (e.g. high scorers on one scale tended to be high scorers on the other).

The second part of the project involved looking for support for the hypothesis of a central personality disposition, by conducting in-depth clinical interviews with a sub-sample of 80 people who scored very high or very low on both E- and F-scales. Using a psychoanalytic perspective, the researchers identified an authoritarian personality syndrome created in early childhood, at the oedipal stage of development, where the conflict between love and hate of the same sex parent was solved by the small child's wholesale 'identification with the aggressor'

– or the previously hated rival. The solution is not one of compromise, but of over-adjustment. The aggression against the parent was repressed and displaced onto the out-group, which, by projection, was accredited with those undesirable characteristics, the individual had to disown in himself.

This typology is descriptive of the most often found *classic authoritarian*, a person very fearful of being different and being weak. Outwardly conventional, their over-rigid superego (see Chapter 7) is unintegrated with their personality as a whole, and they remain 'driven' by a harsh internal parent. However, the clinical interviews, revealed other, though much less evident 'types'. One was labelled 'the psychopath', with a different resolution of the Oedipus complex leading to an irrational and blind hatred of authority. The authors describe them as 'hoodlums and rowdies ... all those who do the dirty work of a fascist movement'. Other types found were the *crank* who is socially isolated and for whom 'prejudice is a means to escape mental disease by collectivization.' Lastly is the *manipulative* who treats people as objects. Such a person has a pathologically detached outlook; in-group loyalty is complete, and there is unconditional identification of the individual with the group. At the other end of the spectrum, the researchers found that very low-scorers were less easy to classify than very high scorers. However, for both the very high and very low typologies, the authors warned against making undue generalisations from a small and unrepresentative sample.

Returning to the classic authoritarian, the identification of which was the object of the study, the researchers go on to ask the fundamental question of cause. Why are some people more authoritarian than others? This is answered in terms of differential child-rearing practices, as shown in the interview material. Parents of high scorers were seen as harsher, colder and more punitive than those of low scorers. High scorers see the parental role as one of authority and submission. The researchers conclude that parent authoritarians produce child authoritarians – a form of cultural inheritance. The question of cause is now pushed further back. What makes for differences in child-rearing practices? Here the socio-cultural level of explanation is invoked. National, regional and class differences were suggested as possible explanations (the more punitive child-rearing practices of some nationalities, i.e. Germany, before World War II, of rural communities and the working class could be cited as evidence at this sociological level of explanation). However, a prime cause at this level was found in the interview material. It could be seen that more rigid child-bearing practices were found among parents assumed as suffering from status anxiety due to the discrepancy between their socio-economic status and the one they aspired to. Thus, social change itself was posited as a causal factor. The drive for 'upward social mobility' in the US was seen as creating a climate of social change, perhaps similar to, though not as extreme as, the political and economic chaos of Germany between the wars (Staub, 1992).

At the psychological level, hypotheses derived from the intensive qualitative studies of the Berkeley group were tested. For example, Harris, Gough and Martin (1950) found ethnic prejudice in children associated with stress on obedience, control and fear inculcation by parents. Frenkel-Brunswick (1953) found in a group of children aged 10–11 that prejudice and authoritarianism correlated with rigid and repressive child-rearing habits. Lyle and Levitt (1955) found that children's F-scale scores were related to punitiveness in parental attitudes.

Milgrim (1974) found that very obedient people (see Chapter 7) had higher F-scale scores. Mitchell and Byrne (1973) found that more punitive students subjects (who recommended stiffer punishments for cheating) had higher F-scale scores. And there is much other similar evidence of expected relationships being found (Bethlehem, 1985). Unfortunately little further empirical work has been done on the question of the level of association of the psychological concept of the prejudiced personality with the more sociological concept of social change and status insecurity.

Critique of the authoritarian personality has gone in three directions. First, the faults in *scale construction* have led to many attempts at improvement, the one most relevant here being the British Ethnocentrism Scale (Warr *et al.* ,1967) and the new balanced F-Scale (Lee and Warr, 1969). They found, as had Adorno, that older people, the less educated, those of lower socio-economic status, and the politically conservative, tended to have higher E-scores and that the association between ethnic attitude and the authoritarian personality was still seen to hold, only somewhat more weakly.

The second critique has been that social or political background and situation is a more important factor in determining people's attitudes and behaviour than the underlying personality organization. A study by Minard (1952) of a West Virginian coal-mining community showed that about 60 per cent of white miners conformed to the social norms of segregation above ground, but co-operated with the black miners below ground which was the task 'norm'. About 20 per cent were friendly both above and below ground, and 20 per cent maintained a totally segregated stand. Minard concluded that conformity to prevailing norms was the motivating factor for the miners behaviour. Pettigrew (1958) found that white students born in South Africa had stronger anti-black attitudes than those not born in the province. Mean F-scale scores did not differ. He repeated his study in the US and found that white students born in the south had stronger anti-black attitudes than those born in the north but studying in the south. Again, there were no differences in F-scale scores. Pettigrew concludes, like Minard, that socialization and conformity to norms is more important than personality in shaping attitudes. However, these criticisms seem misplaced, as in Adorno's study, in the words of Sanford:

> ...we sought to make clear that we were talking about readiness or susceptibility in the individual, that what actually happened depended upon contemporary circumstances...' (1973, p.73.)

That is, one major constituent of the authoritarian personality is his conformity, which in extreme cases could be associated with the personality defect which Asch calls 'low ego-strength' in his conformity studies (see Chapter 7). It is this 'susceptibility to propaganda' which fits in with early socialization, current insecurity and the need to scape-goat (as was the case in Nazi Germany) that the Berkeley researchers were trying both to estimate and understand.

The third critique concerns their *typology*. The classic authoritarian, as found by Adorno was both conformist and politically conservative. Was the F-scale itself a politically biased measure? Rokeach (1960) developed a scale to measure *dogmatism*, or the degree of open versus closed mindedness in the holding of beliefs, which he designed as a politically unbiased version of the F-scale. However his general findings were that the highly dogmatic people also scored highly on the F- and E-scales. Billig (1978), in a participant observation study of the National Front in England, found two countervailing personality types. The *classic authoritarian* was described as over-controlled: he stressed discipline, obedience, pride, nationalism, self-control and cleanliness. But the other, labelled *the man of violence*, was described as 'under-controlled'. Although having the same opposition to immigration and overall racist beliefs, he was less rigid, more open-minded and did not emphasize discipline, punishment and obedience. In many ways, his attitudes seemed liberal, even progressive. But unlike the classic authoritarian, he was easily roused to anger and violence. Billig suggests that his two typologies represent opposing psychological poles within fascism. But Billig's 'man of violence' also fits the 'psychopathic' type found by Adorno, who, like the classic authoritarian, was also a very high scorer on both E- and F-scales. The possibility that these are not opposing but similar types, cannot be directly checked, as Billig's semi-participatory stance within the Front, prevented him from conducting formal tests. But his study is particularly valuable as he was able to study actual rather than potential fascists.

To conclude, mention might be made of Colman and Gorman's (1982) study of 'Conservatism, dogmatism and authoritarianism in british police officers.' They found that their sample of recruit and probationer police were significantly more conservative and more authoritarian than a matched control sample – but they did not differ on Rokeach's Dogmatism Scale – suggesting that the latter scale had less validity. In his report on the Brixton Riots of 1980, Lord Scarman (1982), referring to Colman's study, recommended the use of the F-scale in the future recruitment of police – so that the very highly prejudiced would be excluded. His recommendations have never been implemented.

Discussion point

○ Do you think the use of psychological personality scales to exclude people from, or select them for, particular jobs is a good or bad idea? In what circumstances; for what jobs; what sort of people?

Finally, three studies published by the Columbus Trust investigating genocide (University of Sussex): Dicks (1972), Cohn (1974) and Poliakov (1966), as well as a recent study by Lifton (1986), have explored the conditions under which extreme forms of racial persecution occur:

they all point to the conclusion that most individuals ... involved... were not generally found to be grossly pathological in their psychological make-up. Individual psychopathology was found to be less important in accounting for their actions than ... a dehumanizing ideology, in-stitutionalised and accepted within the society. (Sherwood 1980)

These more or less ordinary people, it is suggested, used psychological defences to protect themselves from the full knowledge of what they were doing. The individuals who can resist the pressure to obey are perhaps more extraordinary than those who commit atrocities in the name of obedience (Milgram, 1974; see Chapter 7). Perhaps the answer to the Berkeley group's research question, 'Who is susceptible to anti-democratic propaganda?', is simply that we all are.

Prejudice as a Mental Mechanism

What we are concerned with in this section are people's *internal processes*. We are not looking for individual differences here, though they will certainly be present. Nor are we looking for major explanations in terms of personality. What we *are* looking for is the description and understanding of processes assumed to be general organizing features of the human mind. The particular *content* of these thoughts and feelings will, of course, differ between different groups (Eskimos may have very different beliefs about the English than do Australians), and these differences can be accounted for in terms of individual learning and group culture. We are looking for general factors in the perception and evaluation of the social world. The study of prejudice in this context is the study of those factors which lead to a general tendency to misperceive, to have false or inaccurate beliefs, to make unjustified generalizations and false or irrational judgements about other people (e.g. impressions based on first contact, stereotypes, etc.).

Early work in the field was derived from Asch's (1946) study of how we form impressions of other people's personality. He suggested that certain information which has evaluative overtones, can be thought of as 'central' and can colour the meanings we give to more peripheral information. In his classic experiment, he found that altering the trait word 'warm' to 'cold' in otherwise identical descriptions of an imaginary person radically changed the nature of people's perception of this person. The 'warm' person was seen positively overall, and the 'cold' person negatively. Later studies found that experimental subjects were not naive, but brought with them expectations of what attributes will go with which ('warm' and 'friendly', for example), which together formed a set of internal 'person-patterns' they called '*implicit personality theory*' (Wishner, 1960).

So person perception is not a matter of building up a picture from discrete bricks of information, but the information is organized in terms of previous expectations and overarching value assumptions, which together with a need for 'closure' or unity (Asch, 1946), and a general mental preference for consistency (Heider, 1958) results in a simplification and possible bias in our picture of the perceived person. We are not talking here of the growth of knowledge of the other in a long-term relationship, but how others are seen on the basis of a single meeting or no first-hand evidence at all. Later work in social cognition (Fiske and Taylor, 1984) suggested that these 'person- patterns' could be thought of as social schemata or ways of categorizing social information in simplified form, so that social judgements could be made quickly and efficiently. They were useful ways of processing information, but could become 'stereotypes' (see below).

The *first impression* of another person is a very important aspect of how we develop an overall picture. What we learn first seems to carry more weight than what we learn later, even though it might be thought that the most recent information might be more useful to us. Luchins (1957) conducted the classic experiment showing this primacy effect, and later studies have supported his findings. Robinson (1995) says that the first impression of a client may affect the future professional relationship with the social worker. In her book on black perspectives in social work, she points out that preconceptions about dress, speech, physical attractiveness and non-verbal communication patterns such as eye-contact, gestures, degree of touching and preferred interpersonal distance (called 'personal space') can all affect these initial impressions of others, especially when the contact is between people of different cultures. These impressions may then develop into stereotypes.

Discussion point

- ° Think of a client from a different ethnic background from your own. What do you remember of your first contact with him/her? What was the most salient aspect of his/her appearance or behaviour? What did you infer about the type of personality they were, or how they might behave in the future? Have you changed any of these first impressions at later meetings?

Stereotyping, or what Fiske and Taylor call 'role-schemata', is the holding of a 'person-pattern' based on category membership. We make inferences from the group to which that person belongs (race, nation, class, gender, age, occupation, etc., or groups relevant to social care professionals such as the disabled, the mentally ill, prisoners, the homeless, single parents, etc.). Another form of stereotyping is to assign individuals to categories on the basis of one or two salient attributes (he walked with a shuffle and was mumbling to himself; he must be an ex-mental patient).

The area which has attracted the most social psychological research interest is ethnic stereotyping. The original work was conducted by Katz and Braly (1933) in the US. Students were presented with a list of ten ethnic groups and 84 traits, and asked to list for each group the most typical traits. The aim was to see whether stereotypes depicted in the media were reproduced by the students. They were. However, these stereotypes appeared to change in subsequent studies. For example, in 1967 'negroes' were no longer seen as 'superstitious' and 'ignorant'; and the Japanese, who in 1951 (at the end of World War II) had been 'imitative', 'sly' and 'treacherous', were in 1967 'industrious', 'ambitious' and 'efficient'.

The criticisms of this type of study have been immense. Subjects are constrained by the task to act in a stereotypical manner to assign a set list of traits to a set list of categorizations. In 1951 and 1967, some students to their credit refused the task on the grounds that it was immoral. Also, the experimenters did not ask what people thought was meant by 'typical', but assumed it would be taken as 'true of all members of the category' (a case of experimenters stereotyping subjects?). A further small replication (McCauley and Stitt, 1978), using a more careful definition of 'typical', found startlingly different results – larger than might be expected by the 11 year gap between studies.

But perhaps the most important point about stereotypes is 'How are they formed?' Brown (1995) addresses the question. He suggests that (following Allport, 1970) in the first place they are transmitted through *socialization* – the family, the school, the mass media. They are imbibed, so to speak, through the culture. The transmission of stereotypes in this way might also have an ideological function – to justify the *status quo*. Secondly, there is the possibility that they might be to some extent a *distorted reflection* of social reality (Allport's 'grain of truth' approach). For example, because people of lower socio-economic status may be more likely to be unemployed, this fact is simplified, generalized and turned into a 'trait' and working-class people are seen as 'lazy'. Brown finds some evidence for this influence of social class in a study of Brewer and Campbell (1976) of ethnic groups in East Africa. The Kikuyu, the most economically developed, were described by the other tribes as, among other things, 'pushy' and 'proud'. (The Kikuyu were also, on average, taller than the others.)

Another 'grain of truth' example is the existence of socially prescribed roles, for example of women as 'homemaker' and 'caregiver', leading to stereotypical attributions to females of being 'warm', 'kind' and 'understanding'. Eagley and Steffen (1984) showed that when women were seen as employed people, these stereotypes diminished, and conversely, men described as 'homemakers' were seen as more socially sensitive than previously.

Another important aspect of the 'social reality' explanation is that of the self-fulfilling prophecy. Stereotypic expectations can create the conditions in which evidence confirming the stereotype is forthcoming. People begin to behave in the role we have accorded them. An experiment by Snyder et al. (1977) demonstrates this. Male subjects were told that a woman they were talking to on the telephone was either 'attractive' or 'unattractive'. The interaction style of the *woman* was subsequently judged as more 'friendly' and 'likeable' when the *man* had pictured her as 'attractive'.

In real-life settings, the same phenomenon can be seen, and the power of such stereotypic expectations might be thought socially dangerous. The classic demonstration is that of Rosenthal and Jacobsen (1968). The researchers gave a specially created 'intelligence' test to a class of American elementary school children. They then randomly selected 20 per cent of the class and told the teachers they would show a significant 'learning spurt' in the next year. A year later, they retested the class, and found that the randomly selected children had indeed made the expected learning gains – even though only the teachers knew the names of these children. They concluded that the teachers' expectations had 'subliminally' influenced these children's behaviour. Later studies have shown mixed results, but a study of 5000 children in 72 British junior schools (Crano and Mellon, 1978) using a complex method called 'cross lagged analysis' designed to separate causal influence from mere relatedness (or correlation), did suggest a *causal* relation between the teachers' expectations and the subsequent performance of the children. The application of such findings to the understanding of the apparently 'poor' performance of ethnic minority children, such as West Indians in English schools, is obvious. But the point should be made that teachers' expectations, though powerful, are not the total explanation. Individual children do differ in ability.

A final example may be of particular interest to social care professionals. Levy and Langer (1994) looked at the effects of cross-cultural differences in stereotypes of old age on memory performance. They compared samples of elderly Americans (where the prevailing stereotype is of a general cognitive and social decrement with age) with elderly Chinese (where the old are venerated and expect to continue to contribute socially). The elderly Chinese outperformed the elderly Americans in the memory tasks, and they also had a more positive attitude to ageing.

Discussion point

° Do you have any older clients (say 60 plus)? Do you expect them to be less mentally able than young people? Do you think they expect you to expect them to be less mentally able? What effects do you think these reciprocal expectations (if they exist) may have on your relationship with them?

The 'socialization' and 'grain of truth' explanations of the formation of stereotypes show them as somewhat similar to attitudes. The next approach – that of *social cognition* – shows them as quite different phenomena. Stereotyping is seen as a fundamental, normal and semi-automatic way of mental processing. Social stereotypes or 'role schemata' are efficient mechanisms for dealing with an over-complex world. In learning to drive, the moment comes when you no longer have to think consciously but driving begins to 'come naturally'. In the same way, social cognition psychologists suggest that stereotypes are 'natural cognitions'. The template or predisposition to categorize is inherent, and the content of the stereotype is very early learnt. They are not totally accurate because they are, by their nature, selective and over-simple. But this is their utility – they free us mentally to think about other things. In this way, they are fundamentally rational processes.

Unfortunately, this is not quite the case. Further research has shown consistent biases in the way we choose and process social information. Our selection is not random but is guided by our need to find order and consistency (as Asch and Heider suggested). So new information is often chosen on the basis of what we already know (like the primacy effect), that is, to *confirm* the expectation we have. This general bias has been shown in logical reasoning (Watson and Johnson-Laird (1972), and such confirmatory biases have also been seen in social reasoning (Brown, 1995). An interesting experiment (Snyder and Swann, 1978) led subjects to believe they were going to interview either an 'extrovert' or an 'introvert'. The study found that the questions chosen by the subject-interviewers were designed to elicit information consistent with their expectations, rather than disconfirming them, although their experimental task was to make as accurate an assessment as possible. The influence of '*labelling*' on the perception of behaviour is well known. A child taking a rubber from another is seen as 'aggressive' if he is black, but 'assertive' if he is white. A sarcastic colleague is 'spiteful' if female but 'cynical' if male. A normal person, given the label 'mental patient', is seen as maladjusted (Fiske and Taylor, 1984). All these can be seen as examples of confirmatory biases – assuming that the existing social stereotype of black, female or mentally ill is a negative one. The confirmatory bias can help to explain the persistence of inaccurate or wholly false stereotypes – simply by the avoidance of disconfirming information.

Asch, in 1946, suggested that a fundamental human disposition was the need to give meaning to the social world. More recently, in the 1960s and 1970s cognitive social psychologists started to look at the way people attribute cause or responsibility to actors in the social world. Although a slightly different area from that of stereotyping – consistent biases in the way causal influences are made have been found, which can be applied to the study of stereotyping. For example, there is a consistent bias towards assigning responsibility to an attribute of the actor, rather than to the situation (he failed the exam because he was stupid). But this is not the case when the actor is oneself (I failed the exam because the questions were unfair). Another relevant attribution bias is the *illusory causation* bias – the tendency to attribute cause or responsibility to actors who are physically salient, who stand out or are different in some way (red hair, bright clothes, loud voice or black skin, in a wheel-chair, etc.). To summarize, the attributional biases seem to show a faulty reasoning process that suggest 'causal schemata' are being used to explain events in the social world in the same way that 'role schemata' are being used to perceive social categories. In both situations the need to find 'meaning' quickly is pursued, to the detriment of a deeper or more accurate understanding.

These explanations – socialization, social reality and social cognition– of the formation and persistence of stereotypes are not mutually exclusive. All can be part of the process. But the concept itself may be inadequate. Fiske and Taylor (1984) suggest:

> Work on role schemata (i.e. stereotypes) goes beyond the point that social schemata can be an aid to information processing, and it tends to incorporate affect and behaviour. (p.100)

For example, the role-schema or stereotype for Hell's Angels goes beyond the processing of information about black leather jackets and motor-bikes. It also goes beyond the inferences that they are macho, tough, working-class and likely to drive dangerously and engage in gang-fights. It helps *you* to decide how you feel about them, and whether you would like to join them, ignore them or discriminate against them. That is, an element of the perceiver as actor is acknowledged. Thus, there is a need to consider 'affect' and 'behaviour', and with them the concept of the value or principle which may (or may not) inform our decisions about how to act in the social world.

A final question is one of value. How can negative stereotypes be changed, given that they are both rigid and 'semi-automatic' as well as damaging to the recipients and in the long run to their possessors? (An inaccurate view of the world, although it may reduce uncertainty and anxiety, also reduces the probability of long-term survival.) We will look again at this question in the next chapter, but here we can examine another factor: that of taking the decision *not* to act, but to wait. As Nicolson and Bayne (1990) suggest:

> The most direct way of countering the disproportionate power of first impressions [and stereotypes] is first to become aware of them, and then to treat them as hypotheses – to check the evidence on which they are based and look for further [and especially disconfirming] evidence. (quoted in Robinson, 1995, p.31; additions in brackets are my own).

Conclusion

In this chapter, we have looked at prejudice as an attribute of the individual – as an attitude, a personality trait, and as an inherent aspect of the process of thinking. However, in all three of these approaches I have tried to show the importance of the wider social influences on prejudiced thinking and discriminatory behaviour: the influence of socialization processes, the mass media and social expectations. In Chapter 9, we will be looking more directly at group and cultural influences on and explanations of prejudice. A summary of the argument of both chapters will be given at the end of Chapter 9.

Further Reading

Brown, R. (1995) *Prejudice.* Oxford: Blackwell.
This book covers topics dealt with in both Chapters 8 and 9. The relevant chapters at this point are *Chapter 1,* 'The nature of prejudice', *Chapter 2,* 'Prejudiced individuals', and *Chapter 4,* 'Stereotyping and prejudice'.

Gross, R. (1992) *Psychology, the Science of Mind and Behaviour.* London: Hodder and Stoughton.
Chapter 17 'Interpersonal perception', provides a useful review of stereotyping and cognitive biases. *Chapter 19* 'Attitudes, attitude change and prejudice,' covers the aspects discussed here in the sections on prejudice as an attitude and prejudice as a personality attribute.

Robinson, L. (1995) *Psychology for Social Workers – Black Perspectives.* London: Routledge.
Covers a broader perspective than that covered in this chapter, or the next – encompassing issues raised by CCETSW paper 30 (1991), and seeks to redress the omission of a 'black perspective' in much current teaching of psychology to social workers.

References

Adorno, T.W., Frenkel-Brunswik, E., Levinson, D.J. and Stanford, D. (1964) *The Authoritarian Personality, Parts one and two.* New York: Wiley.

Allport, G.W. (1950) 'Predjudice: a problem in psychological and social causation.' *Journal of Social Issues, 4.*

Allport, G.W. (1970) *The Nature of Prejudice.* Reading, Massachusetts: Addison-Wesley

Asch, S.E. (1946) 'Forming impressions of personality.' *Journal of Abnormal and Social Psychology, 4,* 258–290.

Bethlehem, D.W. (1985) *A Social Psychology of Prejudice.* Beckenham, Kent: Croom Helm.

Billig, M. (1978) *Fascists – A Social Psychological View of the National Front.* London, Harcourt, Brace: Jovanovich.

Bloom, L. (1971) *The Social Psychology of Race Relations.* London: Allen and Unwin.

Bogardus, E. (1925) 'Measuring social distances.' *Journal of Applied Sociology ,9,* 299–308.

Brewer, M. and Campbell, D. (1976) *Ethnocentrism and Intergroup Attitudes: East African Evidence.* New York: Sage.

Brown, R. (1995) *Prejudice.* Oxford: Blackwell.

Cohn, N. (1966) *Warrant for Genocide.* London: Eyre and Spottiswoode.

Colman, A. and Gorman, L. (1982) 'Conservatism, dogmatism, and authoritarianism in British police officers.' *Sociology ,16,* 1–11.

Crano, W. and Mellon, P. (1978) 'Causal influence of teachers' expectations on children's academic performance: a cross-lagged panel analysis.' *Journal of Educational Psychology, 79,* 39–49.

Dicks, H. (1972) *Licensed Mass Murder: A Socio-Psychological Study of Some SS Killers.* London: Chatto-Heinemann.

Eagley, A and Steffen, V. (1984) 'Gender stereotypes stem from the distibution of women and men into social roles.' *Journal of Personality and Social Psychology, 43,* 9, 15–28.

Festinger, L. (1957) *A Theory of Cognitive Dissonance.* New York: Harper Row.

Fishbein, M. (ed.) (1967) *Readings in Attitude Theory and Measurement.* New York: Wiley.

Fiske, S. and Taylor, S. (1984) *Social Cognition.* Reading, Massachusetts: Addison-Wesley.

Frenkel-Brunswick, E. (1953) 'Prejudice in the interviews of children: attitudes towards minority groups.' *Journal of Genetic Psychology, 82* 108–143.

Gosling, J. (1994) 'Personality.' In D. Messer and C. Meldrum (eds) *Psychology for Nurses and Health Care Professionals.* London: Prentice Hall.

Harris, D., Gough, H. and Martin, W. (1950) 'Children's ethnic attitudes: 2. relationships to parental beliefs concerning child training.' *Child Development, 21* 169–181.

Harvey, O. (1965) 'Some situational and cognitive determinants of dissonance resolution.' *Journal of Personality and Social Psychology, 1,* 4, 349–355.

Heider, F. (1958) *The Psychology of Interpersonal Relations.* New York: Wiley.

Katz, D. (1960) 'The functional approach to the study of attitudes.' *Public Opinion Quarterly, 24,* 163–204.

Katz, D. and Braly, K. (1933) 'Racial stereotypes of one hundred college students.' *Journal of Abnormal and Social Psychology, 28,* 280–290.

Kiesler, C., Collins, B. and Miller, N. (1969) *Attitude Change.* New York: Wiley.

Kutner, B., Wilkins, C. and Yarrow, P. (1952) 'Verbal attitudes and overt behaviour involving racial prejudice.' *Journal of Abnormal and Social Psychology, 47,* 649–652.

Lapiere, R. (1934) 'Attitudes versus actions.' *Social Forces, 13,* 230–237.

Lee, R. and Warr, P. (1969) 'The development and standardisation of a balanced F-scale.' *Journal of General Psychology, 81,* 109–129.

Levy, B. and Langer, E. (1994) 'Aging free from negative sterotypes: successful memory in China and among the American deaf.' *Journal of Personality and Social Psychology, 66,* 989–997.

Lifton, R. (1986) *The Nazi Doctors – Medical Killing and the Psychology of Genocide.* London: Macmillan.

Luchins, A. (1957) 'Primacy-regency in impression formation.' In C. Hovland (ed.) *The Order of Presentation in Persuasion.* New Haven, Connecticut: Yale University Press.

Lyle, W. and Levitt, E. (1955) 'Punitiveness, authoritarianism, and parental discipline of grade school children.' *Journal of Abnormal and Social Psychology, 51,* 401–411.

McCauley, C. and Stitt, C. (1978) 'An individual and quantitative measure of stereotypes.' *Journal of Personality and Social Psychology, 36,* 929–940.

Milgrim, S. (1974) *Obedience to Authority.* London: Tavistock.

Minard, R. (1952) 'Race relationships in the Pocahontas coal field.' *Journal of Social Issues, 8,* 29–44.

Mitchell, H. and Byrne, D. (1973) 'The defendant's dilemma: effects of jurors' attitudes and authoritarianism on judicial decisions.' *Journal of Personality and Social Psychology, 25,* 123–129.

Nicholson, P. and Bayne, R. (1990) *Applied Psychology for Social Workers, 2nd edition.* London: Macmillan.

Oppenheim, A.N. (1992) *Questionnaire Design, Interviewing and Attitude Measurement.* London: Pinter.

Pettigrew, T. (1958) 'Personality and sociocultural factors in intergroup attitudes: a cross national comparison.' *Journal of Conflict Resolution, 2,* 29–42.

Poliakov, L. (1974) *Aryan Myth: History and Nationalist Ideas in Europe.* London: Heinemann.

Robinson, L. (1995) *Psychology for Social Workers – Black Perspectives.* London: Routledge.

Rokeach, R. (1960) *The Open and Closed Mind.* New York: Basic Books.

Rosenthal, R. and Jacobson, L. (1968) *Pygmalion in the Classroom.* New York, NY: Holt, Rinehart and Winston.

Sanford, N. (1973) 'The roots of prejudice: emotional dynamics.' In P. Watson (ed.) *Psychology and Race.* Harmondsworth: Penguin.

Scarman, Lord. (1982) *The Scarman Report: The Brixton Disorders 10-12 April 1981.* Harmondsworth: Pelican.

Sherwood, R. (1980) *The Psychodynamics of Race.* Sussex: Harvester Press.

Snyder, M. and Swann, W. (1978) 'Hypothesis testing processes in social interaction.' *Journal of Personality and Social Psychology, 36,* 1202–1212.

Snyder, M., Tanke, E. and Berscheid, E. (1977) 'Social perception and interpersonal behaviour: on the self-fulfilling nature of social stereotypes.' *Journal of Personality and Social Psychology, 35,* 656–666.

Staub, E. (1992) *The Roots of Evil.* Cambridge: Cambridge University Press.

Warr, P., Faust, J. and Harrison, G. (1967) 'A British ethnocentrism scale'. *British Journal of Social and Clinical Psychology 6,* 267–277.

Watson, P. and Johnson-Laird, P. (1972) *Psychology of Reasoning.* London: Batsford

Watson, P. (ed.) (1973) *Psychology and Race.* Harmondsworth: Penguin.

Wishner, J. (1960) 'Reanalyses of impressions of personality.' *The Psychological Review 67, 2,* 96–112.

CHAPTER 9

Prejudice and Discrimination
Group Approaches
Mary Horton

Introduction

In Chapter 8, the work on attitudes and personality looked for individual differences between people and their explanation in terms of socialization. The work on person perception and stereotyping looked for general mechanisms and biases in the way we perceive and categorize others. Now we will look at prejudice in our judgement of, and discriminitory behaviour towards, others as a direct effect of group membership and cultural influences. This is a truly 'social' position in a way that earlier approaches were not; but this understanding has always been implicit in social psychological studies of prejudice and discrimination. Bogardus' Social Distance Scale (1925) (see Chapter 8) asked native Americans to classify potential immigrants. Katz and Braly (1933) asked American univerisity students to assign traits to named 'foreign' groups and nationalities. Adorno *et al.* (1964) studied white American attitudes to other ethnic groups. But now we will be looking *explicitly* at group and cultural influences, on the relationship between 'us' and 'them' in the explanation of prejudice.

Note: as in Chapter 8, although much of the work discussed here relates to ethnic prejudice, relevance to all forms of prejudice is intended.

Prejudice as a Group Phenomenon

In Chapter 7 on 'Working with groups', we looked briefly at Tajfel's Social Identity Theory. Here we will look in more detail at this important advance in the way social psychologists try to understand and explain prejudice and discrimination. We will approach it through first looking at Sherif's work on conflict between groups, and then at Tajfel's early experiments on the minimal group paradigm. We will then go on to look in more depth at social identity theory and prejudice.

Sherif and the functional group approach

Sherif (who looked at the emergence of group norms in the classic experiment discussed in Chapter 7) wanted to demonstrate the possibility that active hostility between groups composed of basically similar individuals could be caused by (i.e. was a 'function' of) simply the competition between them. He conducted a series of 'field experiments' with American boys' summer camps in 1949, 1953 and 1954 (Sherif, 1967). We will look at the 1954 study (Box 9.1).

Sherif had shown that when two, otherwise similar groups have conflicting aims (only one side could win the tournament), hostility is generated. This only evaporates with the introduction of what he called 'superordinate goals' – that is, when the groups had to unite against a common enemy (in the example, the withdrawal of food and water). Sherif made an analogy to society as a whole, and suggested that all group conflict could be a function of the existence of incompatible goals, and between-group harmony a function of the necessity of co-operation to achieve a common goal.

Box 9.1 The Boys Camp Experiment (1954)

Two groups of eleven 11–12 year old white middle-class boys were taken to two nearby camp sites. Neither group knew of the others' existence. During the *first period* the development of in-group feeling was observed by the adult leaders. Informal group norms and roles appeared. One group named itself 'the Rattlers', and espoused a norm of toughness. The other called itself 'the Eagles', and espoused a norm of religious idealism. In the *second* part of the holiday the two groups met, but only in the context of a tournament of competitive games (baseball, tug-of-war, etc.). Active hostility, including name-calling, scuffles and inter-camp raids, quickly developed. During the *last* period at the camp, the competitive games were discontinued and the adults tried to create between-group harmony by bringing the groups together for joint activities such as meals and the 'camp-fire'. Unfortunately, simple contact seemed only to increase hostility. Finally, the adults surreptitiously organized a series of 'mini-crises' (for example, the water-pipe became blocked, the food-truck broke down) which could only be dealt with by co-operative behaviour between the groups. Slowly, hostility decreased, and by the end of the camp the two groups were living in harmony, and between-group friendships developed.

Functional theory, that is, the competition for resources or for status, has been found to hold in many organizational and industrial situations (Sherif, 1969). However, an attempt to repeat his findings with a camp of English boy scouts (Tyerman and Spencer, 1983) did not apparently succeed. But the situation was very different as the scouts were all from the same troop, and maintained their 'superordinate group membership' throughout the competitive manipulations. The 1983 study shows one limitation to the generality of Sherif's findings. They need to be seen in the context of the history of group memberships, and the conflict, not only between groups, but between the individual's different group loyalties.

Discussion point

° Does Sherif's explanation of group hostility in terms of incompatible group goals seem adequate to you? Can you think of any examples of active dislike between groups which can be accounted for by functional theory – that is, the competition for resources or for status? Are there any examples known to you of between-group hostility, which you think cannot be explained by functional theory?

Tajfel and the minimal group paradigm

Tajfel (1970) argued that Sherif's functional explanation might apply only to groups (like his summer camp boys) who already possessed a number of group attributes, which, singly or in combination might account for the outcome he found:

- the boys were already divided into two groups. Although a reason was never given them, the *de facto* separation might have seemed important to the boys
- the two groups had had time to develop some interpersonal *liking* and in-group *cohesion*
- each group had a history (albeit a short one) and time to develop shared *norms* and *roles*
- *self-interest* might have been involved as the winning team was given prize money.

Tajfel therefore created an experimental situation where all these factors were explicitly excluded. The subjects were divided into two groups on apparently trivial criteria. They never met as a group and therefore could have no 'history'. They were not told who the other members of 'their' group were, so individual past liking or disliking was ruled out. Self-interest in terms of being able to get money for oneself was also ruled out. The only group attribute that remained was the label – or social categorization into 'my group'/not my group. This was the 'minimal group paradigm' which Tajfel hypothesized would be sufficient to generate discriminatory behaviour (Box 9.2).

Box 9.2.The Original Minimal Group Experiment

A sample of 14-year-old boys was randomly and secretly divided into two groups. Then each boy in isolation was asked to choose from a series of paired lists of different amounts of money to be given to pairs of individual, anonymous other boys – differentiated only by their categorization into 'my group' or 'the other group'. The linked lists were constructed so that if a small amount was given to one member of the pair, a larger amount would be given to the other. It was found that the boys awarded the money so that the difference between the amount given to 'my group member' and 'the other group member' was as large as possible, even when this meant that less money overall would accrue to 'my group'

✔

Example:	My group member	7	10	12
	The other group member	3	8	11

Here the 7/3 combination would be chosen as it gives the largest discrimination between groups (4) although choosing either of the other pairs would give more money to 'my group'.

Tajfel's hypothesis was supported. Social categorization (or labelling) was in itself sufficient to produce discriminatory behaviour. The paradigm has been repeated many times with different people in different situations and the findings appear to be robust, although the artificiality of the design has been criticized. The subjects and cultures in which studies have been carried out include Welsh adults, female students in California, students in Oregon, New York and Switzerland, soldiers in the German army and children in New Zealand (Gross, 1996). One interesting partial disconfirmation was Wetherall's (1982) New Zealand study. She found Polynesian children more generous to the 'out-group' than were white children, and suggested this reflected cultural norms emphasizing co-operation in the Polynesian children. The question of culture will be taken up in the next section.

But what do Tajfel's finding mean? He has not refuted Sherif's theory. The existence of incompatible goals might well be a powerful motivator of intergroup hostility and discrimination, but he has shown that it is not necessary. Discrimination, in the sense of the creation of differences, is a function of the process of labelling itself.

Discussion point

○ The maintenance of 'differentials' is an important factor in pay-bargaining, and Tajfel (Tajfel and Fraser, 1978) gives this as an example of the generalizability of his findings to 'real-life'. Can you think of any examples from your experience as a social care professional where the establishment of a 'distance' (economic, physical or psychological) has been of paramount importance in the relation between two otherwise fairly similar groups? If so, does this behaviour make sense to you in terms of Tajfel's hypothesis, or do you think other factors are involved?

Social identity theory

From these early experiments Tajfel developed his *Social Identity Theory* (1981). In it he proposed an explanation of prejudice in terms of the general human propensity to belong to groups and to value those memberships. Tajfel is saying we are all, to some extent, prejudiced, but we can learn to understand and to counter this tendency. His conclusion can be seen as similar to that of the Adorno group at Berkeley and the Columbus trust at Sussex, discussed in Chapter 8. And indeed, the concepts of the in-group and the out-group were originally coined by the Berkeley researchers (Adorno *et al.*, 1964, p.104). However, Tajfel's work springs from a background in psychology, almost directly opposed to the 'personality theorists', and his ways of understanding and 'countering' prejudice and discrimination would be through group or social rather than individual action. What he shares with the personality theorists is perhaps a common set of values.

Tajfel argues that a search for personal identity and self-esteem is the motivation for joining groups (after Festinger's theory of Social Comparison, discussed in Chapter 7). This then becomes linked to the need to maintain group or social identity once membership has been achieved. The social identity of groups is created by the process of social categorization – that is, the labelling process as generated by the 'minimal group experiments'. Like the process, of the creation of social or role schemata, discussed in Chapter 8, social categorization simplifies the social world by 'clumping' it into discrete categories – the fundamental categorization being into 'us' and 'not us' or 'them'. Social identity is then maintained by *discrimination* which is simply behaviour designed to establish or to increase the difference between 'them' and 'us'.

Social identity theory would suggest (Brown, 1995) that discrimination and prejudice would be generated most powerfully in identity-threatening situations where the other group was seen as very similar to one's own, such as Catholics and Protestants in Northern Ireland. Of course, there are many other factors involved here, such as real cultural differences in religion, and real group historical memories, but the socialpsychological explanation can be thought of as acting in addition to or in combination with these other factors – as suggested by Allport (1970) (see Chapter 8.) Another identity-threatening situation is when the 'other group', or individual representatives of it, are seen as very different from one's own group. This threat of the strange or the foreign, can be explained in terms of individual psychology (see Chapter 8), but it is less easy to explain in terms of group psychology, unless the dimension of the larger society, is explicitly introduced, together with the concept of *negative social identity*.

There is an important corollary to Social Identity Theory. A distinction is often made between the social categories we choose (for example, by training to be a social worker) and those into which we are born, such as race, religion, nationality and gender. The qualities attached to such categories are already presented in the social world as established stereotypes, and these may not always be positive. What happens when a category into which we are placed by birth, such as race or gender, is predominantly negative – that is, when we have a *negative social identity*? Figure 9.1 shows Tajfel's answer.

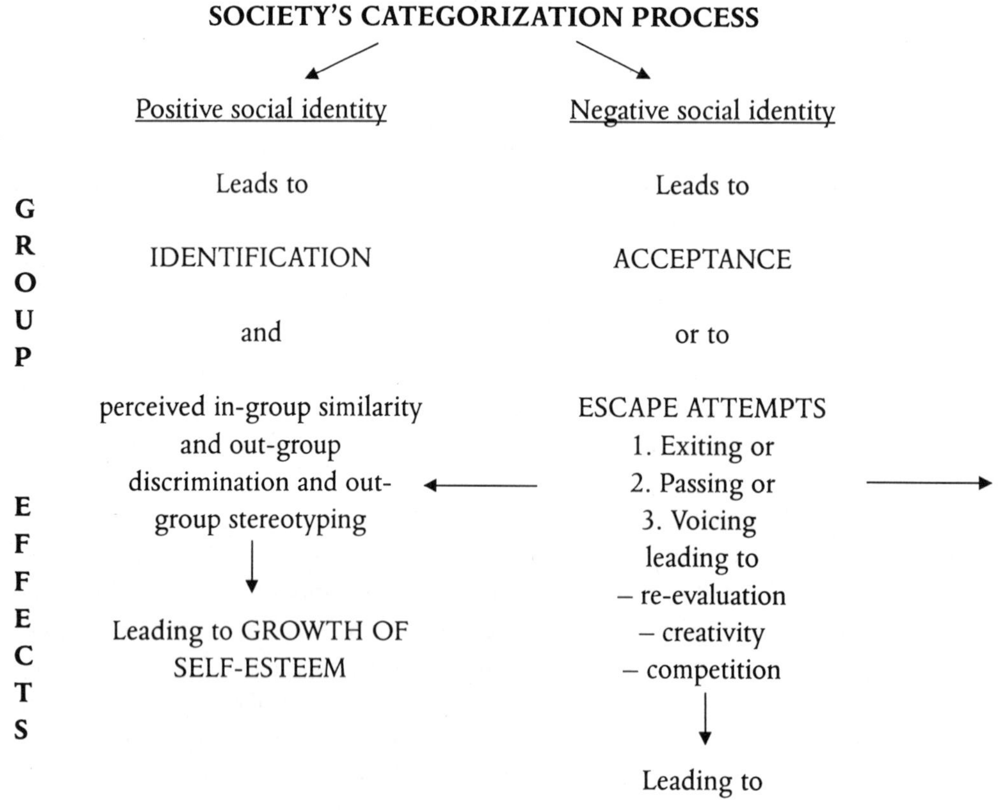

SOCIETY'S CATEGORIZATION PROCESS

Positive social identity	Negative social identity
Leads to	Leads to
IDENTIFICATION	ACCEPTANCE
and	or to
perceived in-group similarity and out-group discrimination and out-group stereotyping	ESCAPE ATTEMPTS 1. Exiting or 2. Passing or 3. Voicing leading to – re-evaluation – creativity – competition
Leading to GROWTH OF SELF-ESTEEM	Leading to

GROUP

EFFECTS

Figure 9.1 Tajfel's categorization process (adapted from Brown, 1985)

With a negative social identity we have four survival possibilities: accepting, exiting, passing or voicing. For example, in countries with a white majority or a white power-base, black people are generally given a negative social identity. These attributions, can (but need not) be accepted or adopted by the group members. On the other hand, black people may try to escape. They may choose to *exit* and move to another country, or to a community composed entirely of black people, or they may choose to *pass* by adopting the habits and attitudes of the white majority and trying to be one of 'them'. These can be thought of as individual answers to a group 'problem' (though many may take these routes). A final possibility is the group solution – to *voice* the black identity as positive. *Voicing* has three aspects – the *re-evaluation* of the stereotype (for example, black is beautiful), *creativity* in turning disadvantages to advantages perhaps by changing the rules or the goals, and direct *competition* with the majority group (an undesirable but possible form of which would be armed combat).

A number of social psychological studies demonstrate some of the processes outlined by Tajfel, although not originally designed for that purpose. I will mention two. Clark and Clark (1947) asked black and white American children aged between 3 and 7, and living in racially mixed areas, to choose either a black or a white doll on a number of different criteria. They found that among the *black* children, about 6 – 10 chose the *white* doll as 'nice' and the *black* doll as 'bad', and 2 in 3 wanted to play with the *white* doll. A replication, more than 20 years later (Hraba and Grant, 1970) showed a complete reversal. About 6 in 10 black children chose the *black* doll as 'nice', and the *white* doll as 'bad'. More than 2 in 3 wanted to play with the *black* doll. One might infer that the social transmission of a negative black identity to the 1947 cohort had changed to a more positive identity for the 1970 cohort, in line with expectations from the social changes occurring during the intervening years.

Rosenhahn (1973) showed how the strength of an initial act of social categorization, or labelling, prevented any further unbiased perception of the labelled by the labeller (see also Chapter 18). Rosenhahn was testing whether American psychiatrists could distinguish between the sane and the insane, by getting nine 'normal' subjects to act as 'pseudo-patients' and ask for hospital admission. All were admitted and eight were labelled 'schizophrenic'. From the viewpoint of Social Identity Theory, what is interesting is what happened after admission. Although none of the subjects made any attempt to continue the pretence, none were detected as frauds by any of the hospital staff. The pseudo-patients reported that all interaction with staff seemed to be conducted through a psychological veil of the role-perceptions of the doctor–patient relationship. One might suggest, in social identity terms, that the staff were in an identity-threatening situation, where not only their professional judgement, but their very identification of themselves as doctors was in jeopardy, were they to recognize a patient as a normal human being. The other patients felt no such identity threat (the new inmates were 'one of them') and they were able quickly to see through the pretence. The happy (?) ending is that all nine pseudo-patients were released within two months, but with a label of 'schizophrenia in remission'!

Discussion point

° Most social identities are neither all positive nor all negative. (i) What social identity do you think you have as a social worker? That is, how do you think social workers are seen by others? (ii) Would you like to change any aspects of this identity? If so, which aspects? and how would you change them?

Conclusion

Social identity theory goes beyond the small group and looks at the psychology of society. By defining the group as a separation into 'us' and 'them', it has highlighted the fact that the group cannot exist in a social vacuum. Finally, it provides us with a radically new explanation for the age-old phenomena of prejudice and discrimination. But although it has been useful in helping us to understand the nature of prejudice from a more fully social perspective, it has some drawbacks. From the viewpoint of the social majority, if social change is generated by the discontent and social action of the minority, there is no need to act on their behalf. There is no conception of a moral stance outside one's social identity. Consequently, the possible danger of over-identification with one's group or role, leading to a loss of self, increasing social fixedness and inability to leave the group does not seem to be sufficiently considered. A possible extension of social identity theory to deal with these difficulties by including 'society' (the state or the institution) as a superordinate element in the model is looked at by Horton (1996). In the next section, we will look more closely at some of these larger cultural influences.

Prejudice as a Cultural Phenomenon

Introduction

Although the relevance of the larger society, in the sense of historical, political, economic and sociological determinants of prejudice, has been implicit throughout these two chapters (e.g. Allport's diagram at the beginning of Chapter 8), it is only more recently that social psychologists have paid explicit attention to the salience of culture in the origin, content and function of prejudice.

A preliminary social psychological definition of culture is needed. For this chapter we will take it as that combination of shared ideas, values, beliefs and common history and expectations which create a boundary, within which the individual belongs and outside of which he is an alien – a foreigner. When differentiating physiological characteristics such as skin colour or communication barriers such as language are added, the boundary may become impermeable, and ethnocentrism (or thinking one's own culture superior) may become xenophobia (or active hostility to the outsider).

This definition of culture can be seen to partially overlap with the definition of a group in the sense of a social categorization, as described in the last section. But the need to separate the two concepts is important when looking at the social psychology of prejudice, as it can be shown that some of the work on groups and social identity is 'culture bound' in the sense of being imbued with white, western, individualistic and competitive values, whereas some of the approaches we will be looking at here allow us to look outside this cultural bias.

We shall look at some of the work which has addressed the topic of prejudice and it's causes from the viewpoint of the social psychological study of ideologies and social representations, and consider the inherently cultural nature of prejudice in the form of racism.

Ideologies

The term 'ideology' originated with French revolutionary philosophers of the early nineteenth century (Billig, 1982), but interest in the explicit study of ideology as an explanatory concept in social psychology can perhaps be dated from Brown's *Ideology* (1973). He defines ideologies as systems of thought and explanation, co-ordinated bodies of beliefs concerning values, rules and goals that underlie political, social or economic action. Their precise *content* is often unclear, as is their *origin*. Some may grow from tradition or myth (such as many religious ideologies). Others are constructed by philosophers, scientists or political thinkers. Some may be created as well as propagated by the mass media in its role as modern day extension of the older pattern of communication by rumour or by story telling.

The clearest form of expression of ideologies is linguistic. This can be *explicit* in the form of legal, political or religious documents (The US Constitution, *The Communist Manifesto*, *Mein Kampf*, The United Nations Charter, The Ten Commandments), or *implicit* in literature and myth, or in popular culture such as comic books or television. When their propositions become slogans they can be used to mobilize groups and individuals. They are also expressed in individual verbal (and non-verbal) communication, particularly between role-holders whose positions are defined by the social structure (itself both the creator and the creation of its ideology) – such as officials and clients, or doctors and patients, for example.

Brown suggests that a particular ideological pattern or template can itself bias social perception and judgement (as was suggested in Chapter 8 in the section on prejudice as a cognitive mechanism). For instance, the cognitive bias of the selective search for confirmatory information might in part be due to the positivistic values of contemporary Western science. The apparently universal tendency to interpret and predict the behaviour of others in terms of its internal or personality attributes has been shown in cross-cultural studies not to hold in less individually oriented cultures such as India and Japan (Moghaddam *et al.*, 1993), and there are many more examples (for example, Moscovici and Hewstone, 1983, p.120).

A salient function of ideologies is to *explain* and, by implication, *justify* differences and inequities between cultural and social groups (east and west, black and white, right and left, rich and poor, old and young, men and women, the sick and the healthy, etc.). These differences are often explained in terms of deeper ideological structures such as 'economic reality', 'common-sense', 'personality', 'biological inheritance' or 'will of God'. It is this function of ideologies in creating, explaining, justifying and maintaining ethnocentrism, prejudice and discrimination against out-groups, especially other racial groups, that is crucial to the topic of this chapter. However, Brown only sets the stage for such an analysis. Research in the area has been conducted under the related but slightly different label of 'social representations'.

Social representations

A social representation can be thought of as a 'bottom up' version of an ideology (Forgas, 1981). Moscovici, its creator, a French social psychologist, describes social representations as the study of people's efforts to understand themselves and the world around them – to solve the common-place puzzles of life. They are the modern day equivalent of the myths and belief systems of traditional societies. People are thought of, not as the passive receptors of a handed-down dominant ideology, but as active thinkers, translating ideas for their own use. Social representations are thus dynamic and changing phenomena, and research is conducted by qualitative methods – asking questions about the subject's own construction of meanings and explanations. As an example, one of Moscovici's first studies was of the social representation of psychoanalysis, or how it was understood by ordinary French people. As with the early study of attitudes (with which it does have a certain similarity), the research aim is primarily descriptive, but generalizations or hypotheses about how people think about society can be made from an accumulation of studies.

A basic aspect of ordinary thinking, Moscovici notes, is the tendency to reduce the unfamiliar to the familiar by analogies with things we understand (a psychoanalytic session is in this way, 'like a sort of confessional'). Two processes are involved in this transformation. The first is *anchoring* – to classify, label or give a name. An example here comes from a study by Jodelet (1980) of the re-housing of ex-mental patients in a French village (a French version of 'community care' perhaps?). The newcomers were immediately labelled *bredins* – a local term for vagrants and half-wits. Although an almost totally inaccurate classification, it served to reduce the unknown to that which was known, and establish a form of certainty – however false. Herzlich (1973) shows how the labelling of symptoms by the lay-person (such as 'fatigue', for example) helps to reduce the unknown to the known, as if the name itself gave some sort of explanation or meaning. The second process is *objectification* or the taming of the unfamiliar by making it real. For example, by comparing God to a father, we give some sort of reality to a supernatural concept. The lay psychologist attributes 'complexes' to another person, as though they were almost physical attributes. Imagery has become concretized.

To summarize, social representation is concerned with the way knowledge is represented in a society and shared by its members. Representations act as frames of reference, selecting and classifying information and suggesting explanations. These may seem irrational, sometimes bizarre, but are based on *shared* social beliefs (though this does not ensure rationality!). There is a rapid, almost automatic, progress from description to explanation. This gives a certain force to a social representation – it has an answer for everything. The functions of social representations are first to facilitate communication between individuals and groups by establishing a shared 'social reality'. Second, it is to guide social action – that is, individuals will interpret their own and others' conduct in the light of this shared knowledge. Third, through socialization, shared social representations are impressed on the child, infiltrating to the 'core of the personality', and forming limits to perceptions and attitudes (Moscovici and Hewstone, 1983).

However, all is *not* for the best in this apparently best of all possible worlds. These common sense theories about key aspects of society include racialist theories. These include prejudgements and stereotypes (of greedy Jews, violent blacks, etc.), and discriminatory behaviour such as avoiding the areas where the disliked minority lives and not sending your children to the same school. But these are superficial aspects of racism, and it is simplistic (Moscovici and Hewstone argue) to think that change can occur merely by making people aware of the irrationality of their beliefs or by changing the language in which they are couched. The hidden core of a racialist social representation is a social representation of human nature, including the belief in a hereditary factor in national character. Biological, psychological and religious images and ideas make up this inner core. Racialism corresponds to a social representation which gives replies to questions such as 'What is man?', 'What is his origin?' and 'Why are people different'?

Billig's (1978) participant observation study of the National Front (discussed in Chapter 8) gives a clear example of the intricacy and cohesion of the set of beliefs and attitudes comprising a racialist 'social representation' (though Billig himself does not use the term). Underlying stereotypes of black people and active hostility towards them is a complex set of ideas, including the need for racial cleansing, and a belief in a Zionist conspiracy.

Helen Joffe (1996), in her study of the social representation of AIDS, makes the point that its early representation in the western world, both by the scientific and the lay communities, was in terms of out-groups – homosexuals and/or Africans. This 'anchoring' in the out-group acts as a form of identity-protection, and has operated throughout the ages:

> The response to syphilis when it began to sweep through Europe in the fifteenth century pro- vides the now classic example. It was the 'French pox' to the English, 'Morbus Germanicus' to the Parisians, the 'Naples sickness' to the Florentines, the 'Chinese disease' to the Japanese. (Joffe, 1996, p.178)

A similar association with foreigners and out-groups has been made for other pandemic illnesses – typhus, leprosy, polio and cholera. What holds these representations together is their lay explanatory function – the cause or genesis or blame, is held to lie outside the in-group or culture.

Fauconnet (1928, discussed in Hewstone, 1983) first linked the concept of responsibility or blame to the idea of collective (or social) representation. The link to the psychology of prejudice lies in the similarity at the social level, of 'blaming the foreigner' and its function in protecting social identity, to the unconscious defence mechanism of projection (onto the other), used by the individual to protect himself from unwanted knowledge, suggested as one of the main functions of prejudice, by Adorno et al. (1964) – see Chapter 8. The point is also made by Rustin (1991).

The main social motive in attributing blame, Fauconnet argues, is to punish the cause of crime and prevent its return. The need to find a culprit is increased when the crime is serious and it is vital for the maintenance of social order that someone be seen to be punished. Fauconnet links this to the phenomenon of scape-goating. The 'expulsion of evils' through the scape-goat, has appeared in various historical forms world-wide in mythology (Frazer, 1924). Poliakov (1980) links scape-goat explanations with patterns of thought he calls 'diabolic causality', and presents evidence for this pattern operating as a 'social representation' at several historical periods. The 'demons' blamed for catastrophes were the forerunners of the 'world conspirators', he suggests – a role allocated in modern times to Jews, Jesuits, Freemasons and Marxists, among others. One proposed solution to the problem of 'diabolic causality' is that of extermination of the relevant group – 'extermination' being the final form of discrimination. In similar vein, Bains (1983) looks at superstitious beliefs as explanations on the level of social representations. He cites as an example witchcraft as a theory of causality. Bains suggests that these beliefs reduce threat and uncertainty by attributing negative events to controllable causes where remedial action is simple and direct: find the witch. The modern world is not immune to bizarre explanations for catastrophes, as the rise of the Nazi movement after the economic collapse of Weimar Germany in 1929 demonstrates. By offering scape-goats instead of a rational analysis of the situation, the Nazis gave hope to the German people by attributing the crisis to a cause that was relatively easily controllable by elimination – the Jews.

To conclude, social representation theory by providing a lay theory of causality, offers a social psychological explanation of 'prejudice' that takes into full account the phenomena of active hostility towards, persecution and elimination of, outgroups, which experimental social psychology has not been able to offer.

Review of the Social Psychological Study of Prejudice
(Chapter 8 and 9)

A central question of social psychology has been that of the explanation of prejudice and discrimination in the relations between individuals and groups. The early *attitude* approach was largely descriptive – establishing that ethnocentric attitudes and behaviour did exist, and were to some extent measurable. Explanations were in terms of the function the attitudes performed in the maintenance of the psychological well-being of their possessors (Katz, 1960). They were thought to have an *adaptive* function in helping individuals to 'fit in' with the expectations of the majority culture; a *knowledge* function in helping individuals to make sense of their social world; an *expressive* function in allowing individuals to express their own personal and social identities; and lastly, a *defensive* function in helping individuals to avoid recognizing unpleasant realities about themselves and their situations by displacing their aggression and projecting their 'reality' onto other individuals and groups.

The *personality* approach focused on Adorno *et al.*'s study of the authoritarian personality. Explanations centred on the attitudes and behaviour associated with ethnocentricism, prejudice and scape-goating having their origin in the personality pattern of individuals vulnerable to influence by 'fascist' and 'racist' propaganda because of their tendency to project onto minorities aspects of themselves they could not tolerate, while remaining subservient to the dominant culture. In Katz's terms, they were using the *defensive* function of prejudice, together with its *adaptive* or conformist function. The origins of this personality pattern were traced to particular child-rearing practices which resulted in the projection of aggression because of the inhibition of its expression within the family. The tendency to engage in repressive child-rearing practices was seen to differ between cultures and classes, and also to be related to the social anxiety generated in times of social change.

The *social cognition* approach has concentrated on the study of the stereotypical quality of individual social perceptions and beliefs about out-groups and individual members of them.

The explanation here has been in terms of the *knowledge* function of prejudice. Stereotypes act to simplify a complex social world, and the tendency to make these simplifications was seen as inherent in the nature of cognitive activity (how the mind works in the processing of information). That this simplifying activity inherently involves biases and errors in the making of social judgements is acknowledged. When these judgements involve values and lead to discriminatory behaviour, the problem of prejudice becomes manifest.

The *social group* approaches are twofold, although related. They consider prejudice and discrimination, sometimes amounting to active hostility toward an out-group, as occurring at a group level of explanation and (initially at any rate) between groups of roughly equal power. Sherif's *functional group* explanation stressed the identity between self and social (or group) interests, and presented evidence to demonstrate that groups (in boys' camps) exhibited hostile behaviour which resembled prejudice and discrimination when placed in situations of direct competition. Sherif made an analogy with situations of conflict between cultures and classes in the wider society. Tajfel took a different stand and showed that discrimination and negative stereotyping of out-groups occurred without any group conflict or competition. He explained the behaviour in terms of a universal need for self-esteem, channelled through the group. This is an explanation similar to Katz's *expressive* function of attitudes for individuals. Tajfel's *social identity theory* is specifically related to the topic of this chapter – prejudice and discrimination against minorities by the larger society, and the inherent nature of the consequent struggle between the opposing social groups.

The *social representations* approach which looks at popularizations of the beliefs and ideologies of society, shows how, at the group level, the simplification of received new ideas performs the *knowledge* function of attitudes, in allowing analogies to be made between the known and the unknown. Social representations also have a *defensive* function in protecting people against the anxiety of uncertainty and ambiguity by providing quick explanations for otherwise puzzling phenomena. These immediate and popular explanations can become irrational, involving apparently 'superstitious' beliefs rapidly propagated (like rumours). The 'explanations' can involve the external blaming of groups or individuals held to be scape-goats, in whom the feared 'evil' (be it blackness or AIDS) is placed and the possessors driven away (mentally or physically). Such behavioural representations can be seen to have their origin in cultural history or myth.

My conclusion is that all the explanations of prejudice and discrimination provided by social psychology have some utility, but that neither separately nor together are they sufficient. As Allport (1970) stressed, historical, economic and sociological factors also need to be addressed, and social psychology is unable to do this. However, even within the limits of a psychological approach, it is important to look at the phenomena as multiply caused, and not to stress one explanation such as the knowledge or expressive function to the exclusion of others. In particular, in my opinion, it is important to take into account the cultural and emotional depth of the explanations given in terms of the defensive function of prejudice.

Reducing Prejudice

Many suggestions have been put forward for reducing prejudice. One early method might be termed the 'simple knowledge approach'. The more the majority culture learn about other cultures, the more they will understand them. This was the belief underlying the training of police recruits in Britain in intercultural (i.e. black) awareness. One cannot deride such a direct approach, but it has obvious limitations. Colman and Gorman's (1980) study showed that, although recruits' prejudice level became significantly lower between the beginning and end of initial training, that of probationers after a year in the field had 'returned' to the levels of the incoming recruits. Mere knowledge is not enough; it is important where it comes from – formal training or the more informal socialization into the peer group.

The education system can be seen as a powerful force for the socialization of children. A well-known experiment conducted by a white school teacher in a white American school, using an experiential rather than a simple knowledge transmission technique, is reported by Aronson and Osherow (1980) (see Box 9.3)

Box 9.3 The blue-eyed, brown-eyed study

A class of nine-year olds were told one day that brown-eyed children were superior to blue-eyed children. Those in the class with brown eyes were given extra privileges, and those with blue eyes were restricted. By the end of the day, the blue-eyed children had a noticeably lower work performance, and showed depression. The brown-eyed children had begun to denigrate the blue-eyed and to call them names.

The next day the teacher said she had lied, and it was really the blue-eyed children who were superior. The pattern of prejudice and discrimination immediately reversed, and the brown-eyed children became the victims.

The children were then debriefed. The aim of the exercise had been to allow them to experience the evils of prejudice and discrimination in a safe environment – the school.

The study was followed up in 1990, when the teacher, Jane Elliot, invited the class back to discuss the original study and to watch the film that was made at the time. She claims that the children's experience of discrimination (when participants in her study) led to long-term gains (Elliot, 1990). The case study, together with the follow-up, demonstrates the potential power of the school as a socializing agent.

Official 'anti-racist' propaganda has been suggested as a way of reducing prejudice by disseminating knowledge and exerting social influence. Again, it can be seen as a common sense approach. However, here again, the informal level of 'social representations' may distort or dilute the 'official' message. Also, Reicher (1986) reported significant increases in popular levels of prejudice in Britain associated with the first Immigration Act in 1962. What governments do may be more important than what they say. Stephan and Stephan (1984) have reviewed much of the work on propaganda campaigns to reduce prejudice, showing that the attitude change resulting may be only temporary, and the message itself may be misconstrued by those who are deeply prejudiced.

The *mere contact approach* is another early and perhaps naive hypothesis. The rationale appears to be that the reality of actual contact and the development of inter-personal liking will dispel the erroneous negative stereotypes and attitudes learned from the wider informal culture. Early US studies seemed to support this view. Deutsch and Collins (1951) compared an integrated with a segregated housing estate and found that prejudice had decreased more in the former than in the latter. However, further studies suggest that such 'contact' experiments are successful only when the to-be-integrated groups already have a perceived equal status in the eyes of their members, which is to say that neither group should already be deeply prejudiced against the other. Otherwise, contact, particularly if enforced, may simply confirm existing stereotypes, and increase hostility. Reports of incidents on some council housing estates in Britain seem to support the hypothesis that contact may merely increase friction.

A modification of the contact hypothesis to include the variable of 'common-fate', or in Sherif's terms 'superordinate goals' requiring intergroup co-operation (such as a united action by tenants to get the council to improve conditions) has been found to result in some reduction of prejudice in the form of overt discrimination or conflict (for example, in Chapter 8 Minard's coal miners had to co-operate underground for their own and others' safety). But, as Minard found, attitudes and behaviour may tend not to generalize to the non-work situation. Also, the problem remains of what happens if the joint goal is not attained. Co-operation may change to mutual recrimination and possibly scape-goating.

Two suggestions have emerged from social identity theory, which might be called the *categorization approach*. The first is that if, as Tajfel maintained, mere categorization is sufficient to initiate discriminatory behaviour, then a process of 'de-categorization' or a re-defining of the boundaries of 'us' and 'them' should reduce or prevent discrimination. Unfortunately, there appears to be no experimental evidence so far testing this possibility. Also, its real-life applicability as a process distinguishable from that of 'common fate' or a 'common enemy' seems difficult to envisage. Perhaps a slow atrophy of the boundary's salience is what is hoped for. However, this possible way of reducing prejudice introduces an important value dimension. Are we looking for 'assimilation' or pluralism' in a future non-prejudiced society?

A more immediately applicable hypothesis is that of the ameliorating effect on prejudice of 'cross-cutting categorizations' or, more simply, multiple group memberships. Evidence shows (Hewstone and Brown, 1986) that when 'us' and 'them' boundaries are blurred by overlapping memberships of other groups, prejudice and discrimination are reduced. For example, members of different racial groups may belong to the same parent–teacher association or professional body. However, as Billig *et al.*'s (1982) qualitative study on prejudice and tolerance makes clear, the popular use of language (linked, one might suggest to the defensive function of attitudes in maintaining separate mental 'compartments') enables apparently contradictory beliefs and attitudes to be held and acted upon simultaneously. Billig's example is of a white teenage advocate of the policies of the National Front, walking out of the room hand-in-hand with her best friend – a black girl.

To summarize: as prejudice and discrimination can be seen as multiply caused, even within the limits of a social psychological approach, so must any attempt to reduce prejudice take into account its complex nature. Perhaps five levels at which interventions might be made can be distinguished. First, there is the *intrapsychic* level which would include not only the inculcation of new knowledge, including that of the human tendency to stereotype, but also the attempt to increase self-awareness in the sense of an understanding of the unconscious defensive function of prejudice (Frosh, 1989). The second would be the *interpersonal* level, which might involve social skills training and feed back, including experiential training groups (see Chapter 8). The third might be the *group* level, where the effects of manipulation might be demonstrated and fed back to the participants (such as ethical versions of the 'blue-eyed, brown-eyed' experiment). Direct intervention at the fourth level of *informal culture*, might be difficult, but many participant observation studies operate in this way, and action research operates by feeding back initial results to initiate change. The fifth and final institutional level will be considered in the next section.

Racism, Anti-Racism and the Social Caring Professions

Racism, as the term is used by social care professionals, implies the existence of a policy of racial prejudice and discrimination at an ideological or institutional level of society. It can be seen in the formal, acknowledged (or semi-acknowledged) position of the State – as in the present British immigration laws. At this level it is often seen by psychologists as the academic province of sociology (cf. Rustin, 1991), and psychologists (as in this chapter) tend to avoid using the term. However, racism also has an informal, unacknowledged, sometimes unconscious aspect. Wetherall and Potter (1992) define it in terms of both lay and professional discourse:

> which has the effect of establishing, sustaining and reinforcing oppressive power relations be-
> tween (the majority and minority culture). (p.70)

These power relations, Wetherall and Potter argue, involve the unequal distribution of knowledge – mental forms of regulation and control possessed by, for example, professionals (such as social workers) in their interaction with clients. It is the *effect* rather than the content of racist discourse which is important. For example, for a white person to say 'blacks are lazy' is not racist in terms of its content, nor in terms of its obvious falsity as a generalization unqualified by comparisons (i.e. a stereotype). It is racist, following Wetherall and Potter, because its expression may help to legitimize 'punitive' behaviour towards unemployed black people. In terms of this analysis, it is not only the clear and logical pronouncements (?) of academics, professionals and policy makers which are diluted by lay people in their efforts to understand them, as social representation theory suggests. As well as a 'trickle down' effect, there is a 'trickle up' effect. The discourse of institutions is inextricably alloyed by lay perceptions and beliefs. Dhruev (1992) makes this point in relation to social work practice.

At this informal level, it could be argued, racism is a legitimate province of psychologists, though as yet occupied by few. In an indirect way, Cochrane's work on *The Social Creation of Mental Illness* (1983) is an example, as is Littlewood and Lipsedge's *Aliens and Alienists* (1982). Both books show how, in this country, ethnic minorities are more often hospitalized than native born English, in part because either the expectations of the doctors ('drunken Irish') or the culturally specific metaphors in which the patients try to describe and explain their distress, or both, predispose doctors to attribute a diagnosis of psychosis. The National Health Service is not an explicitly racist institution, but the institutionally condoned – perhaps, sometimes, institutionally bred – attitudes of individuals in their roles as staff, and of which they may remain partly unaware, can result in racial discrimination against patients.

Turning to the institution of the police force, we have already seen (Chapter 8) how peer influence may negate formal indoctrination. But Lord Scarman, in his report on the Brixton Riots (1982) makes a further point:

> It was alleged by some ... that Britain is an institutionally racist society ... If ... the suggestion being made is that practices may be adopted by public bodies as well as by private individuals which are *unwittingly* discriminatory against black people, then this is an allegation which ... where proved (should be) swiftly remedied. (Para 2.22 (my italics))

As Henriques *et al.* (1984) point out, Scarman, a profoundly liberal man, could not bring himself to think that, although not explicitly or legally condoned, some practices which could be in part knowingly discriminatory might be implicitly condoned at fairly senior levels in the police force and other institutions. The psychological point to be made here is that when we move from analysis in terms of individuals to analysis in terms of institutions, the concept of awareness or knowingness becomes blurred, and the attribution of responsibility difficult to make.

It is against this background that CCETSW's anti-racist policy was formed. Paper 30 (1991) requires social work trainers to ensure '... that students are prepared for ethnically sensitive practice and to combat racism' (3.6.2.14). Anti-racism is '... a policy paradigm that addresses power relations rather than merely recognizes culture.' (Husband, 1992). Power relations in this context would include the implicit dominance by a white social worker engaged in an interpersonal but professional 'role relationship' with a black client. It would include, Husband suggests, work with children and families, the mentally ill, the elderly, those with learning difficulties, and probation work. That is, it encompasses practice with those groups, already disempowered, without the additional burden of being a black client of a largely white profession.

Faced with the professional task of 'combating racism', the present chapter provides a basis from which to begin. The academic stance of the 'institution' of psychology itself, with its perhaps mythical (as the discourse analysts would argue) objective of neutrality, may seem inherently opposed to any act of combat. If this were so, it would be to the detriment of the discipline of psychology. Explicit values are at the very least more 'concious' and open than unacknowledged beliefs and practices. Although as psychologists we may have no final answers to the problem; for professionals and academics alike, it is the case that if we do not at least try to stop racism, we actually behave in a racist manner by allowing it to continue.

Note

This definition of 'institutional racism' as 'unwitting' has now been accepted in the Government Report on the behaviour of the police in the murder of Stephen Lawrence.

Seminar Questions

1. Are people prejudiced because of the type of personality they have or because of the social group they live in?

2. Can an understanding of social psychological theories of prejudice and discrimination help us to reduce prejudice in this country?

3. How can we best combat racism in social work practice?

Further Reading

Brown, R. (1995) *Prejudice.* Oxford: Blackwell.
The relevant chapters here are: *Chapter 3* 'Social categorisation and prejudice', *Chapter 6* 'Prejudice and intergroup relations', and *Chapter 8* 'Reducing prejudice'.

Dominelli, L. (1988) *Anti-Racist Social Work.* Basingstoke: Macmillan.
Although not written by a psychologist, this book, part of the 'practical social work' series edited by BASW, helps to underline the points made in the final section of this chapter, and provides practical pointers towards reducing racist practices.

Hubbard, C. (ed.) (1982) *'Race' in Britain.* London: Hutchinson.
Covers the topic from a broader perspective than the purely psychological, including historical and political perspectives. The section on 'Social identity and social structure' is particularly relevant to this chapter.

Turner, J. and Giles, H. (eds) (1981) *Intergroup Behaviour.* Oxford: Blackwell.
The classic exposition of the social group approach. Milner's chapter on racial prejudice and Tajfel's chapter on stereotyping and groups, are both useful.

References

Adorno, T., Frenkel-Brunswik, E., Levinson, D. and Stanford, D. (1964) *The Authoritarian Personality: Parts one and two.* New York: Wiley.

Allport, G. (1970) *The Nature of Prejudice.* Reading, MA: Addison-Wesley.

Aronson, E. and Asherow, N. (1980) 'Co-operation, pro-social behaviour and academic performance: experiments in the desegregate classroom.' In L. Bickman (ed.) *Applied Social Psychology Annual, 1.* Beverly Hills, California: Sage.

Bains, G. (1983) 'Explanations and the need to control.' In M. Hewstone (ed.) *Attribution Theory Social and Functional Extensions.* Oxford: Blackwell.

Billig, M. (1978) *Fascists – A Social-Psychological View of the National Front.* London: Harcourt Brace Jovanovich.

Billig, M. (1982) *Ideology and Social Psychology.* Oxford: Blackwell.

Billig, M., Condor, S., Edwards, D., Gane, M., Middleton, D. and Radley, A. (1988) *Ideological Dilemmas.* London: Sage.

Bogardus, E. (1925) 'Measuring social distances.' *Journal of Applied Sociology, 9*, 299–308.

Brown, L.B. (1973) *Ideology.* Harmondsworth: Penguin.

Brown, R. (1986) *Social Psychology, Second Edition.* London: Macmillan.

Brown, R. (1995) *Prejudice.* Oxford: Blackwell.

Clark, K. and Clark, M. (1947) 'Racial identification and preference in negro children.' In T. Newcomb and E. Hartley (eds) *Readings in Social Psychology.* New York: Holt.

Cochrane, R. (1983) *The Social Creation of Mental Illness.* London: Longman.

Colman, A. and Gorman, L. (1980) 'Conservatism, dogmatism and authoritarianism in British police officers.' *Sociology, 16*, pp.1–11.

Deutsch, M. and Collins, M. (1951) *Interracial Housing.* Minneapolis: University of Minneapolis Press.

Dhruev, N. (1992) 'Conflict and race in social work relations.' *Journal of Social Work Practice, 6*, 1, 77–86.

Elliot, J. (1990) 'Discovering psychology.' Program 20 (PBS video services). Washington, DC: Annenberg/CPB program.

Fauconnet, P. (1928) *La Reponsabilite Second Edition.* Paris: Alcan.

Forgas, J. (ed) (1981) *Social Cognition.* London: Academic Press.

Frazer, J. (1924) *The Golden Bough.* London: Macmillan.

Frosh, S. (1989) *Psychoanalysis and Psychology.* Basingstoke: Macmillan.

Gross, R. (1996) *Psychology, The Science of Mind and Behaviour 2nd Edition.* London: Hodder and Stoughton.

Henriques, J., Hollway, W., Urwin, C. and Walkerdine, V. (1984) *Changing the Subject.* London: Methuen.

Herzlich, C. (1973) *Health and Illness.* London: Academic Press.

Hewstone, M. (ed.) (1983) *Attribution Theory: Social and Functional Extensions.* Oxford: Blackwell.

Hewstone, M. and Brown, R. (eds) (1986) *Contact and Conflict in Intergroup Encounters.* Oxford: Blackwell.

Horton, M. (1995) 'Alienation and social identity: the bringing together of two theoretical paradigms.' In G. Breakwell, and E. Lyons (eds) *Changing European Identities.* Oxford: Butterworth-Heinemann.

Hraba, J. and Grant, G. (1970) 'Black is beautiful: a re-examination of racial preference and identification.' *Journal of Personality and Social Psychology, 16,* 398–402.

Husband, C. (1992) 'A policy against racism.' *The Psychologist.* September, 414–417.

Jodelet, D. (1980) 'Les fous mentales au village.' Unpublished doctoral dissertation, Ecoles des hautes études in science sociales, Paris.

Joffe, H. (1996) 'AIDS research and prevention: A social representational approach.' *British Journal of Medical Psychology, 69,* 169–190.

Katz, D. (1960) 'The functional approach to the study of attitude.' *Public Opinion Quarterly, 24,* 163–204.

Katz, D. and Braly, K. (1933) 'Racial stereotypes of one hundred college student.' *Journal of Abnormal and Social Psychology, 28,* 280–290.

Littlewood, R. and Lipsedge, R. (1982) *Aliens and Alienists.* Harmondsworth: Penguin.

Moghaddam, F., Taylor, D. and Wright, S. (1993) *Social Psychology in Cross-Cultural Perspective.* New York: Freeman.

Moscovici, S. (1981) 'On social representation.' In Forgas, J. (ed.) *Social Cognition.* London: Academic Press.

Moscovici, S. and Hewstone, M. (1983) 'Social representations and social explanations.' In M. Hewstone (ed.) *Attribution Theory: Social and FunctionalExtensions.* Oxford: Blackwell.

Poliakov (1980) Chapter in R.W. Faur and S. Moscovici (eds) *Social Representations.* Cambridge: Cambridge University Press.

Reicher, S. (1986) 'Contact, action and racialization: some British evidence.' In M. Hewstone and R. Brown (eds) *Contact and Conflict in Intergroup Encounters.* Oxford: Blackwell.

Rosenhahn, D. (1973) 'On being sane in insane places.' *Science, 179,* 250–258.

Rustin, M. (1991) *The Good Society and the Inner World,* London: Verso.

Scarman, Lord (1982) *The Scarman Report: The Brixton Disorders 10–12 April 1981.* Harmondsworth: Pelican.

Sherif, M. (1954) 'Experiments in group conflict.' *Scientific American,* 54–58.

Sherif, M. (1966) *Group Conflict and Co-operation: Their Social Psychology,* London: Kegan Paul.

Sherif, M. and Sherif, C. (1969) *Social Psychology.* New York: Harper and Row.

Stephan, W. and Stephan, C. (1984) 'The role of ignorance in intergroup relations.' In N. Miller and M. Brewer (eds) *Groups in Contact.* New York: Academic Press.

Tajfel, H. (1970) 'Experiments in intergroup discrimination.' *Scientific American 223,* 6, 96–102.

Tajfel, H. (1981) *Human Groups and Social Categories: Studies in Social Psychology.* Cambridge: Cambridge University Press.

Tajfel, H. and Fraser, C. (1978) *Introducing Social Psychology.* Harmondsworth: Penguin.

Tyerman, A. and Spencer, C. (1983) 'A critical test of the Sherifs' robber's cave experiments: Intergroup competition and cooperation between groups of well-acquainted individuals.' *Small Group Behaviour, 14,* 4, 515–531.

Wetherall, M. (1982) 'Cross-cultural studies of minimal groups: implications for the social identity theory of intergroup relations.' In H. Tajfel (ed.) *Social Identity and Intergroup Relations.* Cambridge: Cambridge University Press.

Wetherall, M. and Potter, J. (1992) *Mapping the Language of Racism.* New York: Harvester Wheatsheaf.

The Psychology of Ageing

Claire K. Meldrum

Introduction

As the number of older people increases in society, social care professionals are likely to spend more of their time catering to the needs of older clients. In this chapter I shall consider to what extent social care professionals should make allowances for the impaired mental power or different cognitive style of their older clients. Also discussed is the vexed question of whether or not people's personalities change as they age or whether they remain relatively stable. Finally I shall outline the theories which have attempted to prescribe for successful social ageing. Throughout the chapter you will be encouraged to relate theoretical issues to the concerns of social care practice. Before reading any further, try the activity described in Box 10.1.

Box 10.1 Discussion Activity on Journeying Through Adulthood

Try to recruit the help of someone older or middle aged who is willing to talk to you about their life. Ask the person to give a brief account (in about 20 minutes) of their adult life up to the present time. This could be tape recorded if the person did not mind. Otherwise, you could take some notes as the person was talking. Now consider the account you have been given by discussing the following question with the person who has helped you:

1. Are there aspects of this person's life which have remained much the same throughout adulthood? In other words, is there much continuity in their life?
2. Are there any identifiable separate stages of phases or has progress through adulthood been a more gradual process?
3. Have there been any major changes (discontinuities)? If there have been changes, have these been visible to others (external) or more internal, e.g. relating to changes in attitudes and beliefs?
4. Do you think this person has remained fundamentally the same person throughout adult life or has he/she changed significantly in any way? Ask the person concerned what he/she thinks.

Now read on and compare your findings with those of Helen Bee (1996) (see below).

In her book, *The Journey of Adulthood*, Helen Bee (1996) provides a sketch of her own adult life up to the time of writing (she is in her mid 50s). In analyzing that account, she identifies three important themes that arise in looking at adult development and ageing:

- continuity *and* change throughout adulthood (e.g. Helen Bee has remained an intellectual but her relationships with others have changed)

- the notion of stages or episodes in life where one concentrates one's energies on different things at different times (e.g. raising a family or building a career)

- the inner and outer journey through life. Some changes that one experiences may be visible to other people (e.g. changing one's job), while other changes are less obvious (e.g. becoming more concerned with spiritual development and less concerned with worldly success).

These three themes occur in any discussion of adult development and ageing and you will notice that they recur throughout the chapter.

Types of Ageing

According to Birren and Renner (1977) there are three different ways in which the age of an individual can be described. By using all three approaches, we can achieve a more meaningful understanding of the ageing process than if we use the biological definition only.

Biological age. This has two aspects. The first relates to the relative condition of the individual's organ and body systems, for example heart and lung capacity. It is clear, when using this criterion, that biological age need not be synonymous with chronological age. Some 70-year-olds may be fitter in terms of body systems than 50-year-olds. The second aspect of biological age refers to an estimate of an individual's potential life span. Such an estimate (based upon biological, social and psychological factors) enables comparisons between individuals of the same chronological age in terms of their life expectancies.

Psychological age. This refers to how well an individual can adapt to the demands made by a changing environment. In addition, this type of age includes the notion of subjective awareness about one's capabilities. Psychological age may be related to chronological and biological age, but it cannot be adequately encompassed by either or both. A person may be 80 years old and suffering from chronic arthritis, but nevertheless be as alert and well informed as someone much younger.

Social age. This refers to how satisfactorily an individual adheres to the social roles, habits and attitudes which a society expects of someone of that age. Social age may be related to chronological, biological and psychological age. However, this relationship is not entirely predictable. For instance, some older people enjoy music and sporting activities that are more commonly associated with a younger age bracket. We become aware of the existence of social age stereotyping when we hear expressions such as 'dirty old man' or 'mutton dressed as lamb'. In these cases, the individuals described have violated the accepted social norms associated with older people.

Functional age. The notion of functional age is also becoming popular and can be defined as 'an index of one's level of capacities or abilities relative to those of others of similar age. Such skills can range from job performance to the condition of various organ systems' (Hayslip and Panek, 1989, p.12). Again, there is no exact correspondence between chronological and functional age. For instance, an older individual living alone may be more, or less, self-sufficient than a twenty-year-old. In assessing a person's needs a measure of this type of ageing may be the most pertinent.

Despite the acknowledged status of these different types of ageing, it is still *chronological* age that is most commonly used as a classifying variable (means of allocating people to 'age groups') in research on the effects of ageing.

Bromley (1988) has discussed the difficulties of trying to distinguish *normal* from *pathological* ageing. In reality, however, no one is entirely free of all pathology. Most researchers of cognitive change during normal ageing either, at worst assume a lack of serious pathology in their participants or, at best, select them from 'healthy' populations on the basis of their medical records or self-reports. That some subjects might have undiagnosed depression or early-stage dementia remains a problem, particularly in research on the old-old (usually defined as those aged 75 years and over). As Rinn (1988) has reported, half the cerebral infarcts (areas of damaged brain tissue caused by disruption of the blood supply) which are discovered at autopsy were undetected during the person's life. He recommends that those collecting normative data on test performance in older people should check on the status of participants about three years after the data have been collected.

Cognitive Ageing

Social care professionals may be involved in helping to decide whether an older person is capable of living independently. Among the many factors that will be involved in arriving at a decision will be a consideration of the person's intellectual functioning; can this person, for example, demonstrate adequate understanding and an ability to remember things in order to cope with the demands of daily living? It is important, therefore, to consider whether, in the absence of illness, cognitive abilities do actually change during adulthood. If they do, what types of changes are they and why do they happen? According to Schaie (1996) 'intellectual competence attains increasing importance from middle adulthood on, when level of intellectual competence may determine job retention, whether or not independent living within the community remains possible and [whether] maintenance of control over one's financial decision making [is still possible]' (p.17). How inevitable is the negative stereotype of the increasingly inflexible and mentally slow, forgetful older person? Is there a qualitative or quantitative change in the cognitive (intellectual) functioning of older people? Where changes can be detected, should these be construed as cognitive deterioration, or rather as adaptations to changing life circumstances?

Discussion points:

- ° When do you think the ageing process begins? (Compare your answers with the quotations in Box 10.2)

- ° What factors might influence when cognitive processes start to decline?

- ° What abilities would you wish to know about if you were involved in the care of someone whose chronological age was not known?

Box 10.2 When Does Cognitive Ageing Start?

'All the age trends ... begin early and are usually progressive from the middle twenties onwards.' (Welford, 1966, p.5)

'... most abilities tend to peak in midlife, plateau until the late fifties or sixties, and then show decline, initially at a slow pace, but accelerating as the late seventies are reached.' (Schaie, 1989, p.66)

'... limitations of mental functioning occurs precipitously in individuals over the age of 65 or 70 and is closely related to health status.' (Birren, 1968, p.19)

'... the decline is continuous rather than abrupt and thus the loss of intellectual ability may be as important a consideration in a comparison of 50-year-olds with 30-year-olds, as it is in a comparison of 70-year-olds with 50-year-olds.' (Salthouse, 1982, p.82)

Research methods

The three research methods employed in studies of ageing and cognition have been the cross-sectional, the longitudinal and the cross-sequential. In general, results from longitudinal studies have tended to minimize age differences in cognitive functioning. Cross-sectional results, however, paint a gloomier picture of decline in those abilities that require abstract reasoning. In an attempt to understand these sometimes contradictory findings, Schaie (1965) devised the cross-sequential method that takes account of the shortcomings of the two earlier approaches.

Cross-sectional and longitudinal: The majority of studies of ageing and cognition have, until fairly recently, used the *cross-sectional* method where individuals of different ages are compared at the same point in time. For example, one may compare a group of 20-year-olds with a group of 70-year-olds. Cross-sectional investigations have the advantage of allowing data to be collected rapidly. As a consequence, this type of study is common.

However, such designs also have several disadvantages. The most important of these is that people of different ages have had different experiences so that, for example, today's 20-year-olds have had a very different education and diet compared to today's 70-year-olds. It has been suggested that many age differences noted in cross-sectional studies can be explained in terms of these *cohort* (generational) *influences*.

Longitudinal studies, on the other hand, are those in which the same individuals are tested repeatedly over a period of time. The most important advantage of this method is that individual ageing trends as well as inter-individual variability can be studied. However, several difficulties attach to the longitudinal approach. The long timescale involved acts as a disincentive to some researchers, who wish to know the results of their work before they die! These studies are also expensive and may suffer from inconsistent use of measurement tools over long periods of data collection.

The biggest problem of all for longitudinal studies is *selective attrition*. This refers to the situation when the participants who remain in a longitudinal study are no longer representative of the individuals who were originally recruited. Those who drop out tend to be less intellectually able than those who remain. Despite this selective attrition, many longitudinal studies nevertheless do show decline in cognitive functioning in older people, although the onset appears to be later than that indicated by cross-sectional studies (Botwinick and Siegler, 1980).

Another potentially confounding factor is the amount of *practice* that participants undergo. Necessarily, there are repeated assessments and so older individuals will become more practised in the testing procedures.

In 1965, Schaie combined aspects of both cross-sectional and longitudinal methods in such a way as to take into account both practice effects and selective attrition. He aimed to establish whether or not age differences in cognitive processing could be explained entirely in terms of cohort effects.

The cross-sequential method: In his Seattle Longitudinal Study (SLS) of adult development which now spans 35 years, Schaie and his colleagues used a sequential method. They began in 1956 by testing participants in a series of cohorts, seven years apart in age., The first study was therefore cross-sectional. Thereafter some participants from each cohort (age group) were followed longitudinally and retested every seven years, with the last retesting in 1991. New cross-sectional samples were also drawn at each testing point. The main results of this study will be returned to later.

Discussion points

- ° List some cohort effects that might distinguish your generation from your parents'
- ° Do you think these cohort effects have influenced intellectual functioning?

Cognitive Processes and Ageing

The term *cognitive processing* relates to the mental activities of perceiving, remembering and information processing that enable us to acquire information, to make plans and to solve problems. Therefore the study of cognitive ageing is concerned with how these abilities change or remain stable as we grow older.

Most studies of ageing and cognitive ability have been concerned with the decline and loss of function. Only more recently has interest turned to stability and adaptation as features of the developing cognitive system in older adults. Traditionally, the study of cognitive processing is concerned with issues such as attention and memory and brief reviews of findings in each of these areas will be given. It is, however, the phenomenon of intelligence that has been most frequently explored. Therefore, this area of investigation will be examined first.

Intelligence and its measurement

What happens to intelligence as one ages? This is not as simple a question as it first appears. For a start, what is meant by the term 'intelligence'? Some characterize intelligence as a single, unitary process, a general cognitive ability. Others construe it as a number of different, independent mental processes each of which is separately measurable by a standard test (e.g. the verbal and performance subscales of the Weschler Adult Intelligence Scale,1955).

It is, however, Thurstone's primary mental abilities and the concepts of fluid and crystallized intelligence that are most often used in discussions of intelligence and ageing.

Thurstone (1938) proposed, and devised psychometric tests to measure, seven primary mental abilities:

- *Verbal comprehension* (recognizing vocabulary)
- *Word fluency* (retrieving words)
- *Number* (doing simple arithmetic)
- *Space* (visualizing fixed or rotating spatial relations)
- *Associative memory* (remembering paired items such as words)
- *Perceptual speed* (grasping visual details)
- *Inductive (general) reasoning* (detecting a rule/relationship, e.g. in a number series task, and applying the rule to complete a sequence).

Schaie used five of the above scales, omitting associative memory and perceptual speed in his Seattle Longitudinal Study (SLS).

By contrast, Cattell (1963) and Horn (1970) have argued that all mental abilities can be subsumed under two component headings.

Crystallized intelligence, which is measured by tasks such as reading, comprehension and vocabulary, is thought to be highly dependent on education and experience, but less dependent upon central nervous system function. Thurstone's three primary mental abilities of verbal comprehension, word fluency and number are encompassed by this concept. *Fluid intelligence*, on the other hand, is measured by tests of response speed, memory span and non-verbal reasoning, that is, mental abilities that are not imparted by one's culture. It is thought to be dependent upon the smooth working of the central nervous system. Thurstone's remaining four primary mental abilities correspond to fluid intelligence.

When does intelligence decline?

It appears that crystallized intelligence remains stable over much of the lifespan, while fluid intelligence, on the other hand, shows decline. Early cross-sectional studies indicated a decline in this type of intelligence from as early on as the mid 20s, whereas longitudinal studies show declines to start much later, usually in the late 50s (see statements in Box 10.2). However, owing to the problems associated with both cross-sectional and longitudinal methods (namely cohort effects and selective attrition, respectively) one is unable, from these studies, to arrive at a conclusion regarding when decline in fluid intelligence begins. This is where Schaie's cross-sequential method comes into its own. Participants were tested five times over a 28-year period on five different primary mental abilities. His findings are summarized as follows:

- Fluid abilities tend to decline earlier than crystallized abilities
- Even in this study there is some uncertainty about when cognitive decline occurs. The data collected during the first three cycles of the SLS suggested there were no reliable age decrements in fluid intelligence before the age of 60. However, more recently, analyses from the last two cycles have revealed small but significant decrements for some birth cohorts during their 50s. By the age of 74, reliable decrements could be found for all five primary mental abilities tested.

- At age 81, less than half of the participants had declined in ability over the last seven years (Schaie, 1989)

- There are large individual differences at all ages. Substantial overlaps in the scores were found from young adulthood into at least the mid-70s.

- Cohort (generational) differences in psychometric abilities were demonstrated. There has been an improvement over historical time in inductive reasoning ability, with the more recent generations performing better on these tasks than older generations. What is less encouraging is the pattern for number skills. These peak for the 1917 and 1924 birth cohorts and decline thereafter.

Differences in intellectual functioning in older people

Various details of personal history, including health records, were collected for participants in the SLS. On the basis of these, Schaie proposes several reasons for the individual differences found. He lists the following variables as related to cognitive ageing.

REASONS FOR INDIVIDUAL DIFFERENCES IN COGNITIVE AGEING

Absence of chronic disease: As individuals move through the lifespan their intellectual functioning may be increasingly influenced by their physical health status (Siegler and Costa, 1985). Several studies have revealed a relationship between hypertension and cardiovascular disease and a decline in the mental abilities of older people (Schaie, 1989).

High levels of education, occupational status and income: In addition to these obvious demographic variables, Schaie (1984) draws attention to the positive effects of exposure to stimulating environments, making use of educational resources throughout adulthood and having an intelligent spouse.

Personality: for example, self-efficacy (the belief in one's capabilities) and cognitive functioning were related but this is hardly surprising and the relationship might be reciprocal (Lachman, 1983). High levels of mental flexibility in midlife are predictive of numerical and verbal skills in old age (Schaie, 1984). Changes in personality associated with ageing are discussed later in the chapter.

Speed of performance (i.e. reaction time): Traditionally this has been studied by measuring how long it takes a person to respond to the appearance of a stimulus. Other techniques include card sorting and providing as many words as possible that begin with a specified letter. Whatever the method used, these reaction times are seen as a convenient way of assessing how quickly the central nervous system is processing information. Reaction times tend to slow with age and this might explain why older people perform worse at timed intelligence tests than young. However, this loss of speed does not account directly for all the age-related changes found. Practice can minimize reaction times and even when response speed is controlled for, age differences in test scores remain: old minds are not as efficient at mental processing as young minds. This suggests qualitative changes in cognitive functioning with age.

Discussion point

○ To what extent do you think that the five primary mental abilities used by Schaie in the SLS provide adequate measures of the intellectual capabilities of his participants?

Ageing and attention

If a clear-cut deficit could be established in attentional processing in older people this could provide a parsimonious, single explanatory mechanism for the ubiquitous age-related differences found in cognitive functioning. However, the emerging picture is not so simple. Three types of attention have been investigated over the years, using cross-sectional methods.

Sustained attention is the term used to describe the ability to concentrate on a particular task over a period without being distracted. Salthouse (1982) reports that although there is some decline in this ability with age, it is not appreciable.

Selective attention involves the ability to focus attention on one task despite the presence of distractions. Evidence concerning the effects of ageing on this skill is inconclusive (see Rabbitt, 1979).

Divided attention describes the ability to attend simultaneously to more than one source of information. In many day-to-day activities we are called upon to divide our attention, for example, while preparing a meal and listening to the radio, while driving. Craik and Salthouse (1992) report the results of a meta-analysis of divided attention studies. This showed that there are age differences in the ability to carry out two or more tasks simultaneously. Such a conclusion helps to explain why older drivers have more accidents per mile driven than middle-aged drivers. These accidents take the form of sign, right of way and turning violations rather than speeding and other major offences (Sterns, Barrett and Alexander, 1985).

There are considerable differences of opinion among researchers in this area and these may be attributable to the different methodologies employed. Most, however, agree that age-related decrements do occur when multiple *complex* tasks are undertaken. Older people, it appears, are victims of a loss of processing resources which limits their capacity to attend to as many competing stimuli as they did when younger (Salthouse, 1991).

Discussion point

○ What are the implications of these findings on the attentional capacity of older people for the social care professionals?

Ageing and memory

Memory is usually thought of as a three-component process. It involves the encoding of information into the memory system, the storage of that information and finally the retrieval or recollection of that information. From time to time all of us experience problems with our memories. For instance, we forget a phone number or an appointment. Seldom do these lapses cause concern. Only when an 'appropriate' age is reached will an individual begin to wonder if experiences such as these herald the onset of old age, or even senility. Age-based beliefs about memory may sensitize older people to be more aware of the same everyday memory failures that they have experienced all their lives. The stereotype of an older person often incorporates some notion of forgetfulness. How accurate a picture is this? Are memory deficits an inevitable consequence of the ageing process? Studies of ageing and memory have utilized different ways of modelling memory processes. A brief summary of some of the major models is given in Box 10.3.

Box 10.3 Some Models of Memory

The dual memory theory (Atkinson and Shiffrin, 1971) proposes a way of categorizing memories based on the length of time they are retained. Short- and long-term memory are seen as permanent structural components of the memory system. Short-term memory (STM) provides temporary storage of information. The majority of information held in STM fades rapidly. However, information to be retained can be transferred into long-term memory (LTM).

With their model of *working memory*, Baddeley and Hitch (1974) challenged the idea of a unitary STM. They describe working memory (STM) as consisting of several components:

- the *central executive* which directs the activities of the other components

- the *articulatory loop* which resembles an 'inner voice' and is used, for example, when one mutters a telephone number just before dialling

- the *visuospatial scratchpad*, an 'inner eye' which holds spatial information in conscious memory. This is useful, for example, when one is driving on a familiar road so that one can anticipate a required turn off or a dangerous bend.

- the *primary acoustic store* which acts as an 'inner ear' to represent acoustic features such as loudness or tone. According to Baddeley and Hitch, STM acts as a working memory store that allows several pieces of information to be held in mind at the same time and to be used consciously. Working memory has a capacity based on time – about as many words as one can say in two seconds.

Tulving (1972) proposed that long-term memory could be divided into two types: episodic and semantic. *Episodic memory* (EM) is an autobiographical memory for events that happen in one's life. *Semantic memory* (SM) is one's store of general factual knowledge and is independent of personal experience. More recently, Tulving (1985) has added the concept of *procedural memory* (PM). This term describes abilities such as motor skills or 'how-to-do' memories. EM is most vulnerable to central nervous system inefficiency and thus to ageing effects.

The bulk of evidence to date suggests that STM is relatively stable across adulthood, whereas certain aspects of LTM are more prone to age-related decline (e.g. Craik, 1977). It has been suggested that where age deficits are found in STM these may be due to the failure of older participants to use spontaneously the best encoding and retrieval procedures. Once aided or prodded to adopt more efficient methods, they perform as well as younger people. General knowledge and memories about how to do things (see Box 10.2) are relatively unaffected by age.

In relation to older people, there are two additional memory-related capacities which have attracted research interest. These are prospective memory and metamemory.

Prospective memory is one's ability to remember to remember (e.g. remembering to take medication). Several studies (e.g. Cockburn and Smith, 1991) have shown that this type of memory is vulnerable to ageing effects. This corresponds to the stereotyped image of the absent-minded older person. However, Moscovitch (1982) and Maylor (1990) have reported studies where older people were apparently better at remembering to carry out a future act, previously agreed to. The key to their success seemed to lie in their taking more care than younger participants to set up reminders for themselves. It appears that while prospective memory abilities do seem to decline with age, older people often take measures to overcome this by active use of salient external cues such as calendars, lists and so forth.

Metamemory refers to 'how much we know about what we know' (Lachman, Lachman and Thronesbery, 1979) and is an important aspect of memory, particularly in older people. Confidence in one's abilities will affect the amount of effort one devotes to trying to achieve certain goals. For example, if you believe that your memory is poor, you may rely heavily on passive memory aids such as lists and calendars, rather than employ active cognitive strategies, such as mnemonic devices.

Research findings on age differences in metamemory are mixed. Murphy, Sanders, Gabrieski and Schmitt (1981) found that older adults, compared with younger adults, tended to overestimate what they could remember. More recently, however, Rabbitt and Abson (1991) reported on the metamemorial skills of 320 people aged between 50 and 79 years. Their data provide 'no evidence that … chronological age *per se* has any influence on optimism or accuracy of metamemory predictions' (p.148). Rather they believe that the accuracy of individuals' assessments of their memory abilities declines with age-related changes in life-style and self-esteem. Such findings reinforce the belief of many that noncognitive factors influence learning and memory in older people. Furthermore, Poon (1985) argues that by encouraging people to continue to use previously learned and demonstrably effective strategies and by promoting awareness of metamemory, we may enhance the memory performance of many older people.

Discussion point

- ∘ If episodic memory is vulnerable to age-related deficits, how might you try to help a client overcome the effects of such deficits? Use the information you have gained from this chapter, but also try to draw upon your own experience, where possible.

Interventions Using Cognitive Training

As we have seen, there is evidence for age-related decline in some areas of intellectual performance. To what extent can these declines be reversed by appropriate interventions? When considering the evidence on reversibility, one must also bear in mind the ethical issues that are raised, for example, whether such reversal is always in the interest of the individual concerned, or whether the high costs of training are the best use of limited resources.

A number of training programmes have been carried out with older adults to see if practice would lead to cognitive improvements. Kliegl, Smith and Baltes (1990), for example, trained older adults in the memory strategy known as the Method of Loci. This technique involves memorizing a familiar sequence of vivid images (e.g. the rooms and passageways of one's home) and then hooking each of the images to whatever item has to be remembered. Kliegl *et al.* used words as the items. This strategy invariably improves people's memory and older people are no exceptions. Provided they were given enough time to link the word with its image, the majority of the participants showed memory improvement.

Other studies (e.g. Schaie and Willis, 1986) have produced similar findings. There are clear implications for those working with older people in either residential or day care centres. Continued use of one's mental faculties through stimulating activities and access to remedial therapy can do much to maintain and even improve one's cognitive abilities.

Reasons some people fail to respond to training

It is suggested that those people who showed no improvement lacked any reserve capacity to be actualized. Hayslip and Panek (1989) have scrutinized the findings from training in fluid intelligence tasks and conclude that individual differences are extensive in response to such programmes. Craik and Salthouse (1992) have summarized the empirical findings concerning why some fail to do well in cognitive training programmes under the three explanatory headings of: limited processing resources; age related slowing; and failure to inhibit.

Limited processing resources and explanations: This hypothesis proposes that there is a diminished pool of mental energy available to older adults, compared with younger adults. On this basis, the role of environmental supports to aid cognitive function is important. Information provided in pictorial format may help older adults since complex picture recognition does not decline with age. Similarly, Zacks *et al.* (1987) recommend that explicit explanations, not requiring subtle inferences to be made, are particularly beneficial to older people. Ways of limiting the processing requirements for older adults, especially when they are ill, requires more research attention.

Age-related slowing and information presentation: With advanced age, the speed at which information is processed is reduced (Salthouse, 1985). Whatever the underlying cause, the effects of this phenomenon can be alleviated by permitting sufficient time for older people to absorb information. An alternative approach is to try, by means of cognitive training, to help older adults to speed up. Whichever approach is adopted, however, the result is unlikely to be the elimination of age differences in processing speed. Nevertheless, considerable improvement can be achieved for many.

Failure to inhibit: It has been proposed by Hasher and Zacks (1988) that older adults have faulty inhibitory mechanisms in working memory. That is, they are easily distracted by contextual irrelevancies and by internal musings which are only peripherally related to the task in hand. These distractions impede efficient processing of relevant information. Research in this area might inform the way in which advice, information and comfort are given to older clients.

Discussion point

- ° How might knowledge about possible slowing, failure to inhibit and limited processing resources in older people influence the way a social care professional might give advice, information or comfort to a client?

Sounding a Positive Note

In reading about age-related deficits and the need for cognitive supports and interventions, it is all too easy to form a pessimistic view of the cognitive abilities of older people. This would be unfortunate and unnecessary. Remember that Schaie's longitudinal study found few age-related declines in people's intellectual capacities before the age of 60 years. Most adults continue to use acquired knowledge in an effective manner throughout their later years. With increasing age, much of everyday experience depends less on fluid intelligence and more on specific domains of knowledge that are relevant to one's life at the time. In addition, the training studies of Schaie (1996) show that targeted cognitive intervention can often 'reverse the modest age-related decline that is likely to be related to disuse. Interventions may well be useful in retaining independent living status for older persons who might otherwise be institutionalized because of marginal cognitive competence' (p.197).

The role of expertise

Charness (1985) has shown that expert knowledge can compensate for general losses in processing speed and working memory. Older chess experts do not recall as many pieces from a briefly presented display of a game board as do younger chess experts, but they were found to be just as competent in choosing the best chess move from possible alternatives. Therefore, Charness concludes, older chess experts compensate for processing and memory deficits by bringing to bear retrieval structures that they have acquired over years of practice. The growth of these elaborate knowledge structures allows older experts to search for appropriate moves not just as deeply and quickly but also more proficiently than younger experts.

Salthouse (1984) has published comparable findings among typists. Older typists react more slowly but overall typing speed is unaffected by age. This is the result of older typists compensating for decline in speed by looking further ahead and allowing themselves more time to plan what their next key stroke should be. These changes in ways of thinking and behaving can be construed as adaptational, rather than decremental. For practical purposes these adaptations equip most older adults to live independent and fulfilling lives.

Beliefs about development

Further evidence of the richness found in the thinking of many older adults comes from a study by Heckhausen, Dixon and Baltes (1989). They examined the belief systems of young, middle-aged and old adults about the nature of development.

Three interesting findings emerged:

- there was much inter-age consensus in expectations about the nature of adult development
- adult development was perceived to be multidirectional, with both growth and decline in intellectual ageing
- older adults held more elaborate views about development than younger adults, e.g. older people were more likely than younger people to view personality and social and intellectual abilities as subject to developmental growth. The authors interpret this finding as evidence of 'the continuing evolution of the knowledge system that adults

acquire about the nature of lifespan development'. This can be seen as intellectual growth with age and can be set against the relatively small scale decrements found in psychometric studies.

It appears, therefore, that the cognitive changes that occur with age include useful adaptations to the changing demands made on us as we grow older. Where intellectual deficits have been found they are minor, and need have no serious effects on one's ability to cope with everyday life.

Personality and Ageing

To what extent does a person's personality remain the same throughout adulthood? Take yourself as an example. Have your personality characteristics (traits) remained the same throughout your adult life or have they changed? Compare your answers with the findings of Costa and McCrae (1994), who have summarized the results of many studies including their own. They report considerable stability over long stretches of adulthood in five basic dimensions of personality: neuroticism, extraversion, openness, agreeableness and conscientiousness. Costa and McCrae also found that the highest levels of consistency were in middle and later adulthood. To use Bee's words, 'We take ourselves along on our journey through life'. These consistent traits will affect the choices we make and the decisions we take at various points on the journey. People, for example, who are open and extravert are more likely to embrace changes in mid-life and these changes will, in turn, contribute to their continuing openness and extraversion (Costa and McCrae, 1994). It is worth remembering that older people who are disagreeable or neurotic may have been disagreeable or neurotic throughout their adult life.

Along with this evidence for individual consistency in basic personality traits, there is also some evidence of shared, systematic changes, that is, changes that occur in many people as they grow older. Findings can be categorized under two headings: changes that occur between early and middle adulthood, and changes that occur between middle and late adulthood. Bee (1996) concludes that the middle aged adult is 'more complex ... more individual and perhaps more hard-edged' (p.306) than the younger adult. On the other hand, the changes from middle to late adulthood can be described as a shift from 'striving to accepting, from ingesting to digesting, from active to somewhat more passive, from exploration to observation' (p.310). A summary of personality changes commonly found in adulthood are listed in Box 10.4. There are a number of reasons why we need to exercise caution when dealing with findings in this area. Most of the evidence comes from American studies and therefore may not represent accurately the experience of other cultures. There is no uniformity of method employed. Some researchers use cross-sectional techniques (e.g. Brandtstadter and Greve (1994) who found increased flexibility in goal setting among older adults), while others use longitudinal methods (e.g. Stevens and Truss (1985) who found increased autonomy in those of middle age).

Two main types of explanation have been offered to account for personality changes during adulthood. The first of these looks to theoretical frameworks of development and the second considers the effects of particular life events that people experience. The best known example of the first approach is Erikson's theory of personality development.

Box 10.4 Personality Changes Commonly Found in Adulthood

From early to middle adulthood
Increase in: self-confidence and self-esteem; strivings for success; openness to self; maturity (e.g. less impulsive, more self-disciplined); androgyny (men and women more like one another in personality)
From middle to late adulthood
Increase in: flexibility in setting goals.
Decrease in: autonomy; striving for achievement.
Contradictory research findings on: increases in compassion or caring for others; increase in interiority (i.e. less concerned with trying to change the world, more interested in personal or spiritual matters); increase in personal rigidity.

Erikson's stage theory of personality development (1959)

Erikson described personality in terms of eight, age-related, invariant stages. At each stage a crisis (developmental difficulty) needs to be overcome. For a summary of the three adult stages see Box 10.5. In early adulthood, the main crisis is that of intimacy versus isolation. If one can develop an intimate, caring relationship then one will avoid the isolation that may follow if one fails to do so. The next crisis, generativity versus stagnation, is resolved satisfactorily if one finds a way of being productive and of supporting the next generation. Finally, the stage of ego-integrity versus despair is a time of reflection, the culmination of the previous stages. If one can view one's life as well spent this will lead to a sense of self-acceptance. Despair may happen if one's life is viewed as a series of missed opportunities and wasted time.

Box 10.5 Erik Erikson's Adult Stages of Personality Development (1959)

Name of stage	Social focus	Human virtue	Approximate age
Intimacy versus isolation	Friendships	Love	20s
Generativity versus stagnation	Household	Care	late 20s to 50s
Ego-integrity versus despair	Humankind	Wisdom	50s and beyond

The main criticisms of Erikson's theory concern problems in subjecting it to empirical testing since one has to rely on self-reports. At face value, the theory has considerable validity as it coincides with many people's common sense beliefs about development. Without doubt, Erikson's theory has contributed significantly to the lifespan approach to human development.

Stage theories of personality development are concerned with similarities among people in the patterns of change across a lifetime. Although most supporters of stage theories do acknowledge the influence of social and historical contexts on the way people develop, they, nevertheless, tend to concentrate on the common features of developmental change rather than

Box 10.6 The Social Readjustment Rating Scale (adapted from Holmes and Rahe, 1967)

Rank	Life event	Mean value
1	Death of spouse	100
2	Divorce	73
3	Marital separation	65
4	Jail term	63
5	Death of a close family member	63
6	Personal illness or injury	53
7	Marriage	50
8	Fired at work	47
9	Marital reconciliation	45
10	Retirement	45
11	Change in health of family member	44
12	Pregnancy	40
13	Sex difficulties	39
14	Gain of new family member	39
15	Business readjustment	39
16	Change in financial status	38
17	Death of close friend	37
18	Change to different line of work	36
19	Change in number of arguments with spouse	35
20	Heavy mortgage repayments	31
21	Foreclosure of mortgage or loan	30
22	Change in responsibilities at work	29
23	Son or daughter leaves home	29
24	Trouble with in-laws	29
25	Outstanding personal achievement	28
26	Spouse begins or stops work	26
27	Begin or end school	26
28	Change in living conditions	25
29	Revision of personal habits	24
30	Trouble with boss	23
31	Change in work hours or conditions	20
32	Change in residence	20
33	Change in schools	20
34	Change in recreation	19
35	Change in church activities	19
36	Change in social activities	18
37	Moderate mortgage or loan	17
38	Change in sleeping habits	16
39	Change in number of family get-togethers	15
40	Change in eating habits	15
41	Vacation	13
42	Christmas	12
43	Minor violations of the law	11

focusing on the differences which distinguish one person's developmental experience from another's. Before you read on, consider the following discussion point.

Discussion point
- ° Think of the middle aged and older people whom you know. In what ways do they differ? What do you think has caused these differences? The next section looks at one of the main ways in which researchers have tried to answer these questions.

The life events approach to development

The life events approach tries to show how the experiences which individuals have might explain the differences between them. Life events are major happenings or milestones which require a degree of psychological adjustment and, therefore, are likely to affect personality. Life events may be positive or negative or a mixture of both. One useful way of categorizing them is suggested by Wadeley (1996):

- Normative, age-graded events, e.g. menopause, bereavement (see Chapter 24)
- Normative, history-graded events, e.g. war or economic recession
- Non-normative events, experienced by some but not most people, e.g. accidents, divorce, imprisonment.

While all these life events would require an individual to make psychological adaptations, some events are going to be more stressful than others and, therefore, require greater levels of adjustment. Can you think why non-normative events are generally considered to be more stressful for individuals?

Holmes and Rahe (1967) developed the Social Readjustment rating scale which lists 43 'life change events' which require the individual to adapt. The scale assigns each event a value which reflects its stressfulness (see Box 10.6). They claimed that the more changes a person experienced, the more adaptation was required and the more likely it would be that the person would become physically ill or emotionally disturbed.

Discussion point
- ° Use the Holmes and Rahe Social Readjustment Rating Scale. How many life events have you experienced in the last year? Do you think there are times in life when the listed events are likely to cluster together?

Scores of 300 or more for the preceding year are associated with greater vulnerability to both physical and mental illness. A number of studies have confirmed that multiple life events often do precede a deterioration in health. Several criticisms, however, have been made of the Social Readjustment Rating Scale. These include:

- The amibiguity of some of the items on the scale, for example, 'personal injury or illness' does not indicate the severity of the illness. Someone who has had the flu would get the same score as someone who has lost a limb or had a heart attack.
- The scale emphasizes crises or major events, but takes no account of the minor ups and downs of everyday living (daily uplifts and hassles) which may cause us stress and

affect our development. The research of Kanner *et al.* (1981), using the Hassles and Uplifts scales, has shown that hassles (such as having too many things to do) are even more closely associated with health status than are life events.

- The scale takes no account of how an individual reacts to an event. Pregnancy may be welcomed by some, but perceived as a catastrophe by others. People's previous experience of similar events or the coping strategies and social supports available to them will affect how they react.

- Age, gender, ability and social background are some of the 'mediating variables' which are likely to affect how someone responds to events. For example, social networks tend to be smaller for men than for women and many older people lack the social support that they need (Antonucci, 1991). Within Asian and Caribbean countries the care of older people by their family is considered important. When people from such cultures emigrate to countries where less value is placed on family care of elders they are likely to face additional problems to those they might have expected in the normal course of growing older.

Discussion point

- ° List the additional difficulties which might be faced by older people who belong to ethnic minorities within this country. Compare your ideas with those mentioned in Box 10.7.

The study of personality and ageing reveals that many people maintain a core of personality characteristics throughout life. Where personality changes do happen they can often be explained in terms of particular life events and in older people are most often attributable to changes in health status.

Box 10.7 Ageing Ethnic Minorities

Within Great Britain, the experience of belonging to an ageing ethnic minority group was investigated by Fenton (1987) who reported that 'Among all the common stresses of growing old, minority older people also experience particular difficulties. Most of Britain's black older people are earlier migrants, and it is when the settler reaches old age in the "new country" that he or she feels most acutely the pain of separation from the country of birth. The more alien and hostile their present situation is, the more saddening it is to grow old in a cold climate, and the greater the yearning for "home"' (p.3). Many of the African-Caribbean people whom Fenton spoke to talked of their families being 'mostly separated'. Older immigrants from south Asia were often concerned that their children were becoming 'westernized' and uncaring towards their older relatives.

Furthermore, since many early black immigrants worked in low paid, physically demanding jobs, such as foundry work and hospital domestic work, they bear the consequences of such employment into their old age in terms of poor health and poverty. The experience of racism, discrimination and isolation compounds the problems of poverty and poor health.

Successful Ageing and the Role of the Social Care Professional

If social care professionals are to help enhance the life of older clients they must confront their own stereotypes about older people. Social care professionals may be culpable in that they negatively stereotypes older adults. Given the shortage of resources available and the media coverage of child abuse cases, it is not surprising that older people have been a relatively low priority for most practitioners. It has been assumed until recently that older people's needs were practical and straightforward and this, in turn, has led to a rather fatalistic view about old people's problems. Social care professionals, however, can make a considerable difference to the quality of life enjoyed by older people. But first they need to jettison the common myths that older people are sick, sedentary, sexless, senile and impoverished. Let us look at each of these in turn.

Common myths of ageing (adapted from Fisher, 1995)

Older people as sick and sedentary: Although older people are not as healthy as younger people, over 60 per cent of older people report their health as 'good for their age' (Cartwright and Smith, 1988). Remember, it is an individual's own perception of health that defines his or her personal well being.

Older people as sexless: there is a persistent myth that interest in sex disappears with age. The data from Kinsey's reports on male and female sexuality (1953) as well as longitudinal data (Palmore, 1981) show that among adults with an available partner, half are still sexually active well into their 70s and most on a regular basis. McCartney *et al.* (1987) report the distress of older men and women who are living in various types of institution when staff take a disapproving attitude towards the expression of any sexual behaviour. There is clearly a need for greater staff education concerning the continuing sexuality of older people.

Older people as senile: The type of intellectual decline in older people that interferes with daily living is nearly always associated with disease and is not due to ageing. There is an increase in the frequency with which depression is diagnosed as people age. Some researchers (e.g. Costa, McCrae and Locke, 1990), however, suspect that there may be an element of misdiagnosis, given that certain symptoms of depression such as poor sleep patterns and decrease in appetite are changes commonly associated with ageing anyway.

Older people as impoverished: While clearly some older people experience poverty, there is an increasing number of older people who are enjoying the benefits of occupational pension schemes during their retirement. For the majority, however, statutory provision is the only source of income. It is crucial for well-being in later life that this provision is adequate to protect people from the negative effects of poverty on health (Whitehead, 1987). Although the income of older people in Britain compares unfavourably with those in many other European countries (Hedstrom and Ringer, 1987), some studies (e.g. Melanson and Downe-Wamboldt, 1987) have shown that most older people felt that their income was adequate.

Ageist beliefs (myths) are damaging because they can lead us to behave as though they were true, resulting in condescending, offensive and discriminatory behaviour. Not only must social care professionals abandon the myths of ageing, they must also foster the components (dimensions) of well-being in their clients if they are to facilitate successful ageing.

Dimensions of well-being

Research on what promotes a sense of well-being in people of all ages reveals six important factors (Ryff, 1989):

- *self-acceptance*: having a positive attitude towards oneself
- *positive relations with others*: being involved with and caring about others
- *autonomy*: being independent and having a sense of control
- *environmental mastery*: being able to cope with a wide array of activities in one's life
- *purpose in life*: having a sense of direction and purpose
- *personal growth*: being able to achieve appropriate goals.

Discussion point

- ° Think of an older person you know and consider how you might affect each of the dimensions of well-being in your relationship with that person.

Theories can provide a useful way of organizing data, information and speculation about how people might age successfully. There have been two influential theories which have focused on the social context of ageing. Each has attempted to prescribe a lifestyle for older people which would result in successful social ageing.

Social theories of ageing

Disengagement theory (Cumming and Hendry, 1961): sees older people gradually disengaging from contact with others. This is viewed as a natural and positive process, aided and abetted by society, whereby an ageing person becomes less involved with others, more reflective and self-absorbed. This approach views the stereotypic decline of active interests and increase of more sedentary pursuits in later life as beneficial to both older people and society.

Many criticisms have been levelled at this theory: it is oversimplistic and lacks empirical supporting evidence; active older people are happier than passive older people (Adelmann, 1994); people who are apparently disengaging may simply be continuing with a lifestyle that they had already (Maddox, 1981); there may be a cohort effect – later generations of older people may be healthier and financially more independent so that 'disengagement' may disappear (Wadeley, 1996). Many people, of course, are contented with a relatively disengaged lifestyle and enjoy solitary hobbies. The point, however, is that such disengagement is not necessary for successful ageing.

Activity theory (Havighurst *et al.*, 1968): advocates the benefits of remaining active in later life, claiming that greatest life satisfaction is found among those who are least disengaged. Although this theory is probably an oversimplification, most recent research findings demonstrate that social involvement is linked to better outcomes (Bee, 1996).

It is important to remember, however, that older people are individuals and that the optimal stategy for one may be less than ideal for another. As Stuart-Hamilton (1991) says, 'The image of hordes of social workers forcing the older people to mix with others "for their own good", with compulsory whist drives *et al.*, is not a pleasant one' (p.111). Changes in lifestyle may be forced on the ageing adult owing to illness or reduced income. Where health is maintained and income remains adequate there is much continuity of lifestyle from middle to old age.

Summary

The chapter begins by looking at the different ways in which age can be defined: biological; psychological; social; functional; normal versus pathological. After the procedures and limitations of the cross-sectional and longitudinal research methods are outlined, the cross-sequential method devised by Schaie is discussed.

Studies of cognitive ageing in the three areas of intelligence, attention and memory are summarized and the findings from some cognitive training programmes are outlined and theoretical explanations proposed. The chapter reaches the conclusion that the minor declines experienced by some people after the age of 60 can easily be offset by experience and sensible planning so that daily living is not impaired.

The extent to which one's personality changes or remains stable was then explored and two contrasting approaches to personality development were outlined and evaluated: Erikson's stage theory and the life events approach of Holmes and Rahe. A core of personality traits seem to persist throughout life. Life events, however, and especially changes to health, may result in some changes in personality characteristics.

The need for social care professionals to reject the myths which surround older people and to enhance the well-being of their clients was discussed. The chapter ended by outlining briefly the Disengagement and the Activity theories of successful ageing, concluding that no single strategy is likely to be successful for everyone.

Box 10.8 Reminiscence

Most of us will be able to recall times when we have reminisced with friends and family about events in the past. According to Butler (1963), old people do this more than other age groups as part of the process of life review in which they analyze and evaluate their earlier lives. Butler saw this an important way of achieving ego-integrity. As a result of this hypothesis, many life-review interventions have been organized with older adults and increases in self-esteem and sense of well-being have been reported (e.g. Haight, 1991). However, other researchers (e.g. Wallace, 1992) have found no beneficial effects and doubts have been raised also about whether or not spontaneous reminiscence is really more common among older people than among the middle aged or any other age group. Slater (1995) reminds us that 'in the euphoria of psychologizing reminiscence into a form of therapy …there has been a tendency to consider those who find reminiscence irrelevant as part of the "awkward squad", like those who don't want to do other activities laid on in residential care settings' (p.124).

Seminar Questions

1. Make two lists:

    (a) all the pejorative expressions you can think of that are applied to old people

    (b) all the complimentary expressions you can think of that are applied to old people.

Which list is the longer? What does this tell you about our society's view of old people?

Which stereotypes of older people do you think are the most damaging? How might these affect the quality of care provided to an older client by a social care professional?

2. What skills have you noticed that older people possess that compensate for any loss of cognitive speed?

3. Refer to Box 10.8. Do you think that older people reminisce more than younger people? Do you think that reminiscence has any useful function for older adults other than providing a means for enjoyable storytelling?

Further Reading

Stuart-Hamilton, I. (1996) *The Psychology of Ageing: An introduction* (2nd ed.) London: Jessica Kingsley.
A book that manages to be both detailed and concise. Ageing and intelligence, memory, language and personality are covered in a highly accessible fashion.
   A number of more demanding texts are available to those who feel they would like to tackle the complexities of this area. I recommend:

Birren J.E. and Schaie K.W. (eds) (1996) *Handbook of Psychology of Ageing* (4th ed.). London: Academic Press. This provides an authoritative review of and reference source for the topic of ageing.

References

Adelmann, P.K. (1994) 'Multiple roles and physical health among older adults. Gender and ethnic comparisons.' *Research on Aging, 16,* 142–166.
Antonucci, T.C. (1991). 'Attachment, social support and coping with negative life events in mature adulthood.' In E.M.Cummings, A.L Greene and K.H Karraker(eds) *Lifespan Developmental Psychology. Perspectives on Stress and Coping.* Hillsdale, NJ: Erlbaum.
Atkinson, R.C. and Shiffrin, R.M. (1971) *The Control of Short Term Memory.* Scientific American, 224, 82–90.
Baddeley, A.D. and Hitch, G. (1974) 'Working memory.' In G.A. Bower (ed) *Recent Advances in Learning and Motivation,* Vol 8. New York: Academic Press.
Bee, H.L. (1996) *The Journey of Adulthood.* (3rd edition) New Jersey:Prentice Hall.
Birren, J.E. and Renner, V.J. (1977) 'Research on the psychology of aging: principles and experimentation.' In J.E. Birren and K.W. Schaie (eds) *Handbook of the Psychology of Aging* (pp. 3–38). Van Nostrand Reinhold.
Birren, J.E. (1968) 'Psychological aspects of aging: Intellectual functioning.' *Gerontologist, 8,* 16–19.
Botwinick, J. and Siegler, I. (1980) 'Intellectual ability among the older: Simultaneous cross-sectional and longitudinal comparisons.' *Developmental Psychology, 16,* 49–53.
Brandtstadter, J. and Greve, W. (1994) 'The ageing self: Stabilizing and protective processes.' *Developmental Review, 14,* 52–80.
Bromley, D.B. (1988) *Human Ageing: An Introduction to Gerontology.* Harmondsworth: Pelican Books.
Butler, R.N. (1963) 'The life review: An interpretation of reminiscence in the aged.' *Psychiatry, 26,* 65–76.
Cartwright, A. and Smith, C. (1988) *Older People, Their Medicines and Their Doctors.* London: Routledge and Kegan Paul.
Cattell, R.B. (1963) 'Theory of fluid and crystallized intelligence.' *Journal of Educational Psychology, 54,*1–22.
Charness, N. (ed) (1985) *Aging and Human Performance: Studies in Human Performance.* Wiley.
Cockburn, J. and Smith, P.T. (1991) 'The relative influence of intelligence and age on everyday memory.' *Journal of Gerontology, 46,* 31–36.
Costa, P.T and McCrae, R.R. (1994) 'Set like plaster? Evidence for the stability of adult personality.' In T.F. Hetherton and J.L. Weinberger (eds) *Can Personality Change?* Washington, DC: American Psychological Association.

Costa, P.T., McCrae, R.R. and Locke, B.Z. (1990) 'Personality factors.' In F.I.M. Craik and T.A. Salthouse (eds) *The Handbook of Ageing and Cognition.* Hillsdale, NJ: Lawrence Erlbaum

Craik, F.I.M. (1977) 'Age differences in human memory.' In J.E. Birren and K.W. Schaie *Handbook of the Psychology of Aging.* New York: Van Nostrand Reinhold.

Craik, F.I.M and Salthouse, T.A. (eds) (1992) *The handbook of Aging and Cognition.* LEA.

Cumming, E. and Henry, W.E. (1961) *Growing Old.* New York: Basic Books.

Erikson, E.H. (1959) *Identity and the Life Cycle.* New York: Norton.

Fenton, S. (1987) *Ageing Minorities: Black People as they Grow Old in Britain.* London: Commission for Racial Equality.

Fisher, V. (1995) 'Wellbeing in later life.' In D. Messer and C. Meldrum (eds) *Psychology for Nurses and Health Care Professionals.* Prentice Hall: Harvester Wheatsheaf.

Hasher, L. and Zacks, R.T. (1988) 'Working memory: Comprehension and aging: A review and a new view.' In G.H. Bower (ed) *The Psychology of Learning and Motivation* (Vol 22, pp.193–225) New York: Academic Press.

Haight, B.K. (1991) 'Reminiscing:The state of the art as a basis for practice.' *International Journal of Ageing and Human Development, 33,* 1 1–32.

Havighurst, R.J., Neugarten, B.L. and Tobin, S.S. (1968) 'Disengagement and patterns of ageing.' In B.L. Neugarten (ed) *Middle Age and Ageing.* Chicago: University of Chicago Press.

Hayslip, B. and Panek, P.E. (1989) *Adult Development and Aging.* London: Harper Collins, College Publishers.

Heckhausen, J., Dixon, R.A. and Baltes, P.B. (1989) 'Gains and losses in development throughout adulthood as perceived by different adult age groups.' *Developmental Psychology, 25,* 109–121.

Hedstrom, P. and Ringer, S. (1987) 'Age and income in contemporary society: A research note.' *Journal of Social Policy, 16,* 2, 227–239.

Holmes, T.H. and Rahe, R.H. (1967) 'The social readjustment rating scale.' *Journal of Psychosomatic Research, 11,* 213–218.

Horn, J.L. (1970) 'Organisation of data on lifespan development of human abilities.' In R.L. Goulet and P.B. Baltes (eds) *Lifespan Developmental Psychology.* London: Academic Press.

Kanner, A.D., Coyne, J.C., Schaefer, C. and Lazarus, R.S (1981) 'Comparison of two modes of stress management: Daily hassles and uplifts versus major life events.' *Journal of Behavioural Measurement, 4,* 1–39.

Kinsey, A., Pomeroy, W. and Martin, C. (1953) *Sexual Behaviour in the Human Female.* Philadelphia: WB Saunders Co.

Kliegl, R., Smith, J. and Baltes, P.B. (1990) 'On the locus and process of magnification of age differences during mnemonic training.' *Developmental Psychology, 26,* 894–904.

Lachman, M.E. (1983) 'Perceptions of intellectual aging: antecedent or consequence of intellectual functioning?' *Developmental psychology, 19,* 482–498.

Lachman, J., Lachman, R. and Thronesbery, C. (1979) 'Metamemory through the adult lifespan.' *Developmental psychology, 15,* 543–551.

Maddox, G.L. (1981) 'Measuring the wellbeing of older adults.' In A.R. Somers and D.R. Fabian (eds) *The Geriatric Imperative: An Introduction to Gerontology and Clinical Geriatrics.* New York: Appleton Century Crofts.

McCartney, J.R., Iseman, H., Rogers, D. and Cohen, N. (1987) 'Sexuality and the institutionalized older.' *Journal of the American Geriatric Society, 35,* 331–333.

Maylor, E.A. (1990) 'Age and prospective memory.' *Quarterly Journal of Experimental Psychology, 42,* 471–493.

Melanson, P.M. and Downe-Wamboldt, B. (1987) 'Identification of older adults' perceptions of their health, feelings towards their future and factors affecting these feelings.' *Journal of Advanced Nursing, 12,* 29–34.

Moscovitch, M. (1982) 'A neuropsychological approach to perception and memory in normal and pathological aging.' In F.I.M. Craik and S. Trehub (eds) *Aging and Cognitive Processes* (pp.55–79). New York: Plenum.

Murphy, M.D., Sanders, R.E., Gabrieski, A.S. and Schmitt, F.A. (1981) 'Metamemory in the aged.' *Journal of gerontology, 36,* 185–193.

Palmore, E.B. (1981) *Social Patterns in Normal Aging: Findings from the Duke Longitudinal Study.* Durham, NC: Duke University Press.

Poon, L.W. (1985) 'Differences in human memory with aging: Nature, causes and clinical implications.' In J.E. Birren and K.W. Schaie (eds) *Handbook of the Psychology of Aging* (2nd edition, pp. 427–462). New York: Van Nostrand Reinhold.

Rabbitt, P. and Abson, V. (1991) 'Do older people know how good they are?' *British journal of Psychology, 82,* 137–151.

Rabbitt, P.M.A. (1979) 'Some experiments and a model for changes in attentional selectivity with old age.' In F. Hoffmeister and C. Muller (eds) *Bayer Symposium VII. Evaluation of Change.* Springer.

Rinn, W.E. (1988) 'Mental decline in normal aging: a review.' *Journal of Geriatric Psychiatry and Neurology, 1,* 144–158.

Ryff, C.D. (1989) 'In the eye of the beholder: Views of psychological wellbeing among middle age and older adults.' *Psychology and Ageing,* 4, 2, 195–210.

Salthouse, T.A. (1984) 'Effects of age and skill on typing.' *Journal of Experimental Psychology: General 113,* 345–371.

Salthouse, T.A. (1985) 'Speed of behaviour and its implications for cognition.' In J.E. Birren and K.W. Schaie (eds) *Handbook of the psychology of aging* (2nd edition, pp.400–426) New York: Van Nostrand Reinhold.

Salthouse, T.A. (1982) *Adult Cognition: An Experimental Psychology of Human Aging.* London: Springer-Verlag.

Salthouse, T.A. (1991) *Theoretical Perspectives on Cognitive Aging.* Hillsdale, NJ: Lawrence Erlbaum.

Schaie, K.W. (1996) *Intellectual Development in Adulthood: The Seattle Longitudinal Study.* Cambridge: Cambridge University Press.

Schaie, K.W. and Willis, S.L. (1986) 'Can decline in intellectual adult functioning be reversed?' *Developmental psychology,* 22, 223–232.

Schaie, K.W. (1984) 'Midlife influences upon intellectual functioning in old age.' *International Journal of Behavioural Development,* 7, 463–478.

Schaie, K.W. (1989) 'Individual differences in rate of cognitive change in adulthood.' In V.L. Bengston and K.W. Schaie (eds) *The Course of Later Life: Research and Reflections* (pp. 65–85). New York: Springer.

Schaie, K.W. (1965) 'A general model for the study of developmental problems.' *Psychological Bulletin,* 64, 92–107.

Siegler, I.C. and Costa, P.T. (1985) 'Health behaviour relationships.' In J.E. Birren and K.W. Schaie (eds) *Handbook of the Psychology of Aging* (pp.144–166). Van Nostrand Reinhold.

Slater, R. (1995) *The Psychology of Growing Old: Looking Forward.* Buckingham: Open University Press.

Sterns, H.L., Barrett, G.V. and Alexander, R.A. (1985) 'Accidents and the aging individual.' In J.E. Birren and K.W. Schaie (eds) *Handbook of the Psychology of Aging* (2nd edition, pp. 703–724). New York: Van Nostrand Reinhold.

Stevens, D.P and Truss, C.V. (1985) 'Stability and change in adult personality over 12 and 20 years.' *Developmental Psychology,* 21, 568–584.

Stuart-Hamilton, I. (1991) *The Psychology of Ageing: An Introduction.* London: Jessica Kingsley.

Thurstone L.L. (1938) 'Primary mental abilities.' *Psychometric monographs No 1.*

Tulving, E. (1972) 'Episodic and semantic memory.' In E. Tulving and W. Donaldson (eds) *Organisation of Memory.* New York: Academic Press.

Tulving, E. (1985) 'How many memory systems are there?' *American Psychologist,* 40, 385–98.

Wadeley, A. (1996) 'Adolescence, adulthood and old age.' In M.Cardwell, L. Clark and C. Meldrum (eds) *Psychology for A level.* London: Collins Educational

Wallace, J.B. (1992) 'Reconsidering the life review: The social construction of talk about the past.' *Gerontologist,* 32, 120–125.

Welford, A.T. (1966) 'Industrial work suitable for older people: Some British studies.' *Gerontologist,* 6, 4–9.

Whitehead, M. (1987) *The Health Divide.* London: Health Education Council.

Willis, S.L. (1989) 'Improvement with cognitive training: Which old dogs learn what tricks?' In L.W. Poon, D.C. Rubin and B.A. Wilson (eds) *Everyday Cognition in Adulthood and Late Life* (pp. 545–569). Cambridge: Cambridge University Press.

Zacks, R.T., Hasher, L., Doren, B. (1987) 'Encoding and memory of explicit and implicit information.' *Journal of Gerontology,* 42, 418–422.

PART III

Working with Children
and Young People

Introduction

Issues connected with children attract a high media profile in relation to the decisions of social workers and other social care professionals. This probably reflects our concerns about the vulnerability of children, about the way that we perceive that their life course can be damaged by circumstances, and concerns about the proper role and responsibility of families. The inconsistent and conflicting views about the way that children should be treated, as well as media attention to these issues all point to there being uncertainty and conflict about childrearing.

Given these concerns, it is important that professionals know and understand the implications of findings from psychological research. This section starts with the topic adult–child attachment, and the consequences of separation of children from their parents. Understanding the formation of attachment is clearly relevant to those working with young children in deprived circumstances, and those concerned with issues of adoption. In addition, decisions about whether children should be separated from their parents need to be informed by an understanding of the effects of this process on children at different ages.

The second chapter of this section, by Alan and Ann Clarke, emphasizes the flexibility and resilience of some children in the face of adversity. A number of chapters in this section show how adverse family circumstances are associated with children being at risk for later problems. However, such studies are dealing with the probability of an outcome, they show a high number of children will be at risk, but the studies also show that there are some children who do not follow this pattern. The chapter by the Clarkes provides an important alternative perspective about the way that early adversity does not always result in later problems.

Some professionals work with families who have children with physical and learning disabilities. The next two chapters in this section consider both these topics. The chapter by Vicky Lewis provides information about children with physical disabilities, visual impairment and hearing impairment. In each of these disabilities there are important issues about which professionals need to be aware. The chapter on learning disabilities discusses a number of significant concerns ranging from issues of definition and communication, to sexuality and empowerment.

The next two chapters discuss child abuse, a topic of major concern of those who are involved in making decisions about children. The first of the two chapters summarizes theories that provide explanations of why children are abused, thereby providing important information for the understanding of such cases. The second chapter discusses issues connected with various forms of child abuse and outlines several forms of treatment.

Adolescence is the last topic in this section. Leo Hendry shows that problems of adolescence need to be viewed in relation to both biological changes and the wider cultural pressures on adolescents. He also emphasizes that adolescence is not necessarily a time of difficulties for all young people. In addition, the chapter provides information about some of the important psycho-social issues of this period of life: risk taking; body image and dieting; sexuality; drug use, and leaving home.

Thus, the chapters in this section examine issues which are directly relevant to the concerns of social workers and other social care professionals. Rather than summarizing the psychological view of developmental processes (which is available in many texts), we have sought to provide information about issues which are likely to figure prominently in the concerns of many professionals.

CHAPTER II

Communication, Bonding, Attachment and Separation

David J. Messer

Introduction

In their dealings with children, social care professionals are often faced with issues about attachment and separation of a child from his or her family. To provide the basis for an informed decision about such practical issues, this chapter considers both these topics, but it also provides an overview of related work concerning communication, which helps the understanding of attachment and separation processes.

Effective communication is crucial to most aspects of life; its study is relevant to working with children and obtaining information from them. The communication between children and parents also is thought by many to provide the basis for the development of attachment. This relationship between children and their parents (usually the mother) has been, and still is, an issue of interest to developmental psychologists. The attachment of child to mother was regarded by Freud as fundamental to the later development of other relationships, and the issue of separation from parents came to prominence as a result of concerns during and after World War II. Today, issues of attachment and separation continue to be topics of concern to parents and professionals.

In this chapter, I will first examine the development of communication. This is followed by a consideration of bonding which is usually considered to be the relationship of mothers to their babies. Then the pattern of attachment of infants to their mothers will be outlined. This is followed by a discussion of theories about the formation of attachment relationships. Finally, the effects of children being separated from their parents are considered.

Communication

The development of communication

What is communication? Most people accept that communication involves the transmission of information. This simple statement conceals a number of difficult issues, should non-intentional actions, such as the cry of a new-born or the nervousness of a person in an interview, be considered as communication? Should we be concerned about whether information is accurately received (e.g. when a parent changes a nappy in response to crying but the baby needs a feed)? There are no agreed answers to these questions, but it is important to be aware of these and similar issues when thinking about communication.

What are the important milestones in the development of communication? Important communicative abilities are present from birth. Both crying and smiling are signals that let carers know when a baby is distressed or is enjoying something. Crying is present from the first few moments after birth, and is a powerful signal which is especially aversive to humans (Frodi, 1985). Indeed, so powerful is the signal that unremitting crying can be a precipitating factor in child abuse (Frodi, 1985). Different types of cry (e.g. pain, hunger and tiredness) can be identified from an early age (Wasz-Hockert et al., 1968). Crying typically results in adult attention, and in attempts to remove the cause of the crying. Before speech is established, crying is one of the main signals that inform parents and professionals that something is wrong with a young child.

Reliable smiling in response to people and things does not typically emerge until about 2–3 months after birth. Before this, smiles are produced, but they are not as reliable as later ones, and these early smiles have often been attributed to the effects of 'wind'. Smiling, like crying, is a powerful signal for adults. Adults will work very hard, engaging in all sorts of unusual facial expressions and voices, to get a smile from a baby.

During the first half year of life, babies and adults tend to engage in social interaction which only concerns the participants themselves. Typical interaction involves body games, such as peek-a-boo and talk about emotions and feelings (Dockrell and Messer, 1998). This early form of interaction may help to provide a basis for the development of attachment.

We, as adults, usually modify our actions with young infants, moving closer to them and exaggerating our movements and voice in ways which are likely to maintain infant interest (see Messer, 1994). Often, simple games such as looking at the child and then hiding your eyes is sufficient to engage their attention. After about six months, infant interest in the environment becomes noticeable, and adults often follow infants' interest in objects and events (Trevarthen, 1982). At about nine months, there are important developments in communication, with the use of conventional gestures such as pointing, the use of babbling, and occasionally the beginnings of one word speech (i.e. the production of words like 'dada'). At this age, and sometimes earlier, infants start to show wariness of strangers, and this can make communication with them and enlisting their co-operation more difficult.

During the second year, children's ability to understand the speech of adults gradually increases, and they can put their single word speech to more and more different uses such as commenting on, or requesting something. At about 18 months there are advances in a range of abilities. Children's vocabularies appear to expand rapidly. They start to produce two-word utterances, and they begin to engage in pretend play. It seems likely that these achievements are due to children being able to form abstract and arbitary representations about their world, but the precise nature of this cognitive advance is still the subject of discussion.

Following these communicative advances, children begin to produce 'telegraphic speech' which consists of words essential for the message, words which are less important for meaning are still omitted (e.g. a, the, very, there, here). At about two years, children start to include the grammatical endings of words and to use 'functional' words (e.g. him, her, it, them), and this begins their acquisition of the grammar of language which continues for many years. This increase in verbal abilities means that between 24 and 30 months, one can begin to be reasonably confident that children can understand simple verbal messages.

A later development which has attracted a lot of recent interest is the idea that at about four years children start to develop a 'theory of mind', the ability to understand that other people may have different thoughts to oneself. This has been tested by stories similar to the following. A child called Sue puts her chocolates in a green cupboard and then goes out to play. Her mother tidies up and takes the chocolates out of the green cupboard and puts them in a blue cupboard. Sue comes in from playing. Where do you think Sue will look for the chocolates? Children below four years typically think Sue will look in the blue cupboard, whereas those above four years think Sue will look in the green cupboard. These and similar stories seem to be able to identify children's ability to understand that people's thinking may not always reflect reality. Some studies suggest that these 'theory of mind' abilities can occur earlier than four years, and there is debate about how significant such skills are for the development of communication. Interestingly, children with autism are usually unsuccessful with this task and they also have difficulty communicating and interacting socially. However, the important point is that four-year-olds have a clear appreciation that people can have different intentions from themselves and this type of knowledge means that they can start to relate to people in different and more sophisticated ways. Such abilities have also been related to children's capacity to be able to deceive and lie.

The role of context and non-verbal communication

When interacting with children of any age, it is important to recognize that they often give greater weight to non-verbal communication than to speech; they may be trying to provide the answers they think the adult wants to hear rather than trying to say what they themselves think and feel. Many of the claims Piaget made about the age that children are able to understand and carry out cognitively complex tasks have been criticized because his methodology failed to take these two factors into account (see Box 11.1 for an outline of his stages).

For example, Piaget and Inhelder (1956) claimed that children are not able to understand the perspective of another person until about eight years; instead children seem to simply assume that people think and see in the same way as themselves. One experiment which appeared to confirm this claim was the 'three mountains problem'. In this task, a child was seated at a table on which there were three model mountains; at another side of the table an adult was seated. The child was asked to identify from a set of pictures what the adult could see. Typically, children below six years identified the view that they could see, and not the view that could be seen by the adult.

The same type of abilities were tested using a task which was made more simple and meaningful to children. In this task, children were asked to tell the experimenter whether a policeman could see a thief (see Donaldson, 1978). The children were given a model policeman and a model thief, and the thief could hide behind brick walls which were shaped as a cross when viewed from above. Even some four-year-old children could give accurate answers in this task. Other experiments have found that children are more likely to change their answer

Age-in-Years	Stage	Cognitive abilities
		Box 11.1 Piaget's Stages of Development (see Flavell, 1963)
0–2	Sensorimotor	The baby's understanding of the world is through sensations and motor acivities. The baby is unable to enage in abstract thought.
2–6	Preoperational	Children are able to think about symbols and use language. Children often lack appreciation of other's perspectives, as in the 'three mountains task'.
7–12	Concrete operations	Children are much better at thinking in a logical manner. They are able understand reversible operations, e.g. when water is poured from a tall to a short glass they now understand there was the same amount in both containers despite differences in shape.
12+	Formal operations	The person has the ability to use scientific reasoning to think about the world.

if asked the same question again, presumably because they infer that the first answer was incorrect (Rose and Blank, 1974).

These and other studies have given a dramatic illustrations of the power of non-verbal and contextual cues on children's responses to questions. Although some of this research took place in an experimental context, it has important implications for dealing with children. Questions should be presented in a child-centred way as far as possible, and the context made to appear neutral in terms of the demand characteristics of the situation (the non-verbal and contextual cues which suggest a certain answer is 'correct'). Accurate answers depend upon building up trust and then taking great care to avoid giving clues about the answer that you expected. Not only should leading questions be avoided, but it is equally important not to give non-verbal cues (e.g. by looking pleased that the child has given a particular answer). Similarly, making a young child anxious about the accuracy or importance of an answer is unlikely to make it possible to obtain more reliable information. Often, young children will feel more comfortable answering questions if they are engaged in play or some other activity at the same time.

Discussion point

   ° Think about the strategies you would use to gain the trust of a child and ask them about the cause of a physical injury that they have.

In this section we have seen that during the first years of life, children make dramatic advances in their ability to communicate. Furthermore, during the pre-school and early school years, children rely on non-verbal information to help them understand communication and will often try to give the answer they think the adult wants to hear. As a result, professionals need to be careful not to prompt children, and to provide an open context for communication. In addition, the communication of children and their co-operation will often be influenced by their feelings of security. The topic of attachment and security is considered in the next sections.

Bonding

The issue of bonding, the relationship of the mother to the child, has attracted attention and controversy. Until the 1970s, the usual hospital practice in the western world was to separate newborn infants from their mothers after birth had taken place, and to reunite them for their first feed. This was supposed to give the mother time to recover from labour. Today, hospital practice is very different; unless there are medical reasons for the separation, mother and baby are usually left together (with father) until the mother is taken to the maternity ward.

These changes can partly be attributed to the research work of Klaus, Kennell and their colleagues (1976). In one study they were able to *randomly* allocate mothers to either a treatment group, which had extra contact with their infant after birth, or to a control group, which followed the normal hospital procedure of separation until the first feed. When the two groups were seen at later ages, various positive features were noted about the way the mothers in the treatment group reacted towards their children. These included: holding the baby closer; looking into the infants' eyes more often; more kissing; a more relaxed style of cuddling; being more likely to continue breast feeding, and at two years the mother using a greater proportion of questions.

Discussion point
- ° Was the treatment group disadvantaged? Was the control group disadvantaged? Consider the ethics of the study.

The findings of Klaus and Kennell created great interest. Klaus and Kennell pointed out that in other species such as goats and sheep, the early exposure of the baby animal to the mother is necessary for her to bond to the infant. If this exposure does not take place, then the mother is likely to reject the infant animal. By implication, it was being suggested that a similar process may occur in humans.

In the years following this work, hospital procedures were changed to allow for contact after birth. In addition, the findings began to be interpreted as indicating that those mothers who did not experience early contact, perhaps for medical or other reasons, would be disadvantaged in developing a relationship with their baby, and that a failure to 'bond' would have detrimental consequences for a child's development. It was even suggested that lack of this early bond might be a contributory factor to child abuse.

Subsequent work has questioned the role of early experience in bonding. One point that has often been made is that the social context of birth varies across human cultures, and has varied across historical time. In the Efé of Zaire, infant babies are often given to another mother to breastfeed for the first few days. It is also the case that generations of mothers have successfully taken care of their children despite separation at birth. Further, some mothers, particularly those who experience a painful childbirth, may feel distant from their baby until some weeks after the birth, but they go on to develop strong bonds with their babies. More importantly, a number of studies failed to replicate the findings of Klaus and Kennell (e.g.

Svejda, Campos and Emde, 1980; Carlsson *et al.*, 1979), and where replications have been successful they tend to have been with mothers who are less well educated and of lower social class; it may well be that these mothers feel less confident in hospitals and gain more benefit and confidence from the early contact (Vietze and O'Connor, 1980). Further, parents who have adopted a child and who have not experienced early contact often report strong positive relationships with the child.

In a review of this material, Schaffer (1990) criticizes the idea of bonding as 'super-glue'. He argues that the experimental studies do not provide support for the idea that early contact enhances long-term mother–infant bonds, and that the claims of Klaus and Kennell fail to make allowance for the complexity of human relationships as well as the possibility of changing relationships during development. The findings about bonding illustrate the dangers of over-interpreting the findings from research investigations.

The Development of Attachment from Infant to Mother

The first section about this topic presents evidence that soon after birth infants show a special preference for adults, and in particular their mother. These preferences may well allow the development of attachment, a topic considered in the following section.

A preference for adults

Recent research has revealed that infants prefer the *sound, sight,* and *movement* of adults to other comparable stimuli (see Messer, 1994). When we speak to young children we tend to use a higher pitch (similar to a higher musical sound), a more sing-song voice and shorter utterances. Newborns prefer to listen to this adult-to-child speech than to normal adult-to-adult conversation. Young infants find human faces attractive, and this seems to be because human faces contain many general visual properties which make stimuli attractive for infants (high contrast between dark and light areas, vertical symmetry, movement and curved rather than straight lines). Some investigators claim that infants may have a genetic pre-disposition to find human faces attractive. Infants are also interested in the movements of adults. Bertenthal and Proffitt (1986) attached light points to a person's limbs, and recorded their movements in a darkened room. A computer was used to generate an equivalent set of movements which would not be possible for a human to make. Three-month-old infants preferred to watch the actual human movements rather than the computer-generated ones. Thus, research investigations have discovered that the sounds, sight and movement of human adults are special to very young infants. As a result, they are attentive to the things people do and say, and this may be of assistance to the development of relationships with people. However, as we will see in the next section, infants are also especially attracted to their mother from a very early age.

Interest in the mother

In the last 10 years there have been a series of investigations which have revealed that newborn infants show a preference for the *sound, sight* and *smell* of their mother. Day old infants will suck harder and more frequently on a teat to hear their mother's voice rather than the sound of a stranger's voice (DeCasper and Fifer, 1980). This seems to be a result of *pre-natal* learning. Newborns show preferences for various sounds that they heard before their birth. These include nursery-rhymes, speech transformed so that it sounds similar to what would be heard inside the womb, and even the theme tune to the popular television soap 'Neighbours' (presumably a consequence of maternal interest in this programme during pregnancy! Hepper, 1991).

Even more remarkably, Bushnell, Sei and Mullin (1989) found that newborn infants, who were less than 24 hours old, looked longer at their mother than another woman. This occurred even when all they could see were the adults' faces and when they were unable to smell their mother. The mechanism of this process still remains a mystery.

Infants are also attracted to the odour of their mother. MacFarlane (1975) placed, either side of babies' heads, one breast pad from their mother and one from another mother. By 10 days after birth infants showed a preference by turning towards the breast pad from their mother. The precise mechanism of this process is not yet clear, but it seems that familiarity with odours may result in preferences. Infants who were in a crib scented with either ginger or mint later on showed a preference for the scent they had experienced.

These findings indicate that infants within the first two weeks of life already show a preference for their mother. At present the indications are that this preference may be a result of familiarity – in this case familiarity does not lead to contempt. However, it is important to emphasize that these preferences do *not* constitute attachment. Infants prefer the stimuli produced by their mother, but they are not necessarily distressed if she leaves them, nor, as we will see later, does it appear that these preferences are necessary for the development of close relationships with other adults.

The development of attachment

Infants are usually considered to be *attached* to someone when they show the following characteristics: distress at separation; an orientation to the person which involves responses such as gazing, following and vocalizing; as well as seeking the person in moments of stress.

At about 6–8 months, infants start to show distress at the departure of familiar people and to seek their contact. However, the full range of attachment behaviours is not usually seen until about 8 or 9 months of age (most studies report quite a range of ages at which the characteristic develops). In addition, children often show fear and wariness of strangers at about the same age. One of the first detailed studies of attachment revealed that, although the mother was usually the main attachment figure, this was not always the case. Attachments were also formed to fathers, grandparents and others adults (Schaffer and Emerson, 1964). Obviously, in older children attachment to parents will continue, but the behaviours which mark this attachment change; as verbal understanding increases so children are better able to cope with separations if they are told about and prepared for the events.

The Attachment Process

Theories of attachment

Why do children become attached to their parents? Often we accept this process as being such a natural part of development that we do not think about the reasons why attachment develops. Even in cases of early abuse or neglect, children will show attachment to their parents. In the past an influential theory about attachment was derived from learning theory (see Chapter 1). It was supposed that because mothers provided relief from hunger, thirst and cold, that they became associated with rewarding circumstances and were valued in her own right. A similar idea is contained in Freud's description of the growth of attachment. Here the focus was on the way feeding provides oral gratification which in turn provides a basis for the development of attachment. However, the basis of these theories was shown to be inadequate in the late 1950s and 1960s. Two studies which were very influential in changing views about attachment are given in Box 11.2.

Box 11.2 Care and Attachment

The first, and perhaps most famous, study to show attachment is not based on the supply of food was conducted by Harlow and Zimmerman (1959) on infant monkeys. The infant monkeys were placed in a cage with two wire mesh cylinders. On one cylinder the baby monkey could obtain milk from a teat, while the other cylinder was covered with cloth. If food was the cause of attachment then one would expect the monkeys to form an attachment to the bare cylinder which supplied the milk. In fact, the monkeys spent most of their time on the cloth covered cylinder and would jump on this cylinder when frightened. The study, which would now be considered unethical, indicated that simply supplying food is not sufficient for the formation of attachment.

A second important study was conducted by Schaffer and Emerson (1964). They saw a group of 60 children every month during their first 12 months of life. Observations were conducted in the children's homes. Not only did the study reveal that children formed multiple attachments with mother, father, grandparents and other adults, but the study also revealed that attachments were formed when these other adults took little or no care of the infants' basic needs. Instead, attachments seemed to be formed to individuals who were prepared to play, be responsive and interact socially with the child.

Another interesting study was conducted by Fox (1977) in the kibbutzim of Israel. In the kibbutz, during the day, children are in a group with a metaplet who is a trained carer. The children have contact with their parents in the late afternoon and in the evening. Thus, the metapelet provided training and care in a group setting, and the parents provided individual affection and attention. The attachment of the children to both the metaplet and the mother was assessed. The findings revealed that the children were attached to both individuals, but that in reunions after a separation the children showed a stronger affection for the mother. Thus, attachment developed to both individuals even though they provide different types of care.

The demise of learning theory explanations was accompanied by a growth of interest in Bowlby's theory about attachment. Bowlby (1958, 1969) believed that attachment is the result of evolutionary selection pressures. Young animals that stay close to their mother are more likely to avoid dangers such as becoming lost, being injured or attacked and, as a result, they are more likely to survive.

A powerful example of attachment in non-human species is *imprinting*, which occurs in ducks and geese. Shortly after hatching, chicks will follow the first moving object that they see, whether this is their mother, another animal such as a human or even a dog. The chicks will seek this object when frightened and when adult, sometimes display sexual behaviour towards it.

Findings from studies of animal behaviour were a significant influence on Bowlby's thinking. However, although he believed that there was a strong biological basis to human attachment formation, he did not believe that the process was automatic as in some other species. Rather, he reasoned that the biological need for security has resulted in infants possessing a number of attachment behaviours, such as crying, following, proximity seeking, smiling, clinging and sucking. He also believed that these are powerful stimuli in terms of their ability to gain an adult response. Important to his theory was the idea that mothers provides a secure base for exploration, and that as the infants' feelings of security increase so they are more prepared to move away from the mother (think about the difference in a young child's activities when at home and when they visit a strange environment).

A controversial aspect of Bowlby's work was his belief that mothers should be the most important carer and that this care should be provided on a continuous basis. An obvious implication is that mothers should not go out to work. There have been many attacks on this claim. One criticism has been that a wider perspective reveals that mothers are the exclusive carers in only a very small percentage of human societies (Weisner and Gallimore, 1977). Similarly, van Ijzendoorn and Tavecchio (1987) argue that a stable network of adults can provide adequate care, and that this care may even have advantages over a system where a mother has to meet all a child's needs. In addition, there is evidence that children develop better with a mother who is happy in her work, than a mother who is frustrated by staying at home (Schaffer, 1990). It has also been found in studies such as those by Suwalsky and Klein (1980) that one-year-olds' behaviour is not necessarily related to the number of separations or the different forms of care.

Assessing the quality of attachment

One problem with studying attachment was the need to devise a way to measure it. Furthermore, an assessment of attachment is needed to enable factors that help and hinder its development to be identified. For instance, when children are prepared to wander away from their mother, does this indicate weak attachment, or that the children have a secure relationship with their mother? Does the amount of crying on separation indicate a weak or strong attachment? Preliminary attempts to measure attachment in this way, and treat it as a *quantity*, like the temperature of a person, were largely unsuccessful.

Ainsworth's strange situation

An important advance in measurement came from an investigation by Ainsworth and Wittig (1969) that indicated that there were different forms of attachment to a parent. Rather than measure the amount of attachment, Ainsworth observed the organization of attachment behaviour. The observations were made in a laboratory room (see Box 11.3) and have been used to classify children into one of three groups: *secure* (also known as type B), and two types of insecure attachment, *avoidant* (type A), and *ambivalent* (type C). In American samples, the proportion of children in these three groups is approximately 70 per cent, 15 per cent and 15 per cent respectively. More recently, a further form labelled *disorganized* has been identified (type D).

There have been a considerable number of studies which have used the strange situation to investigate attachment. Originally, Ainsworth and Bell (1970) supposed that secure attachments were the result of mothers being responsive to children's needs. Their study claimed to show relations between responsiveness and the three types of attachment. However, there were flaws in this study. For example, the raters of maternal responsiveness knew about the eventual type of attachment developed by the child. As a result, their scoring of behaviour may have been biased (these raters should have been *blind* (i.e. unaware) of the attachment classification).

More recently, a better controlled study by Isabella, Belsky and von Eye (1989) has claimed to find a similar relationship between responsiveness and attachment as predicted by Ainsworth. In particular, mothers and infants who tended to interact socially with each other at the same time at one month and at later ages were more likely at 12 months to have a secure relationship. Those that had a more one-sided pattern of interaction tended to have insecure relationships. More surprisingly, Fonagy and his colleagues have found that mothers' pre-natal reports of their own relationship with their mother (concerning parental responsiveness, feelings, etc.) predict the security of attachment their child will have to them (Fonagy, Steele and Steele, 1991). It is important to realize that this finding concerns a mother's *perception* of her relationship with her mother, and that this may or may not correspond to the reality of the relationship. Further research by this group has also revealed that mothers who are reflective about themselves and show inter-personal sensitivity are more likely to have securely attached children, whereas those who are non-reflective are likely to have insecurely attached children (Fonagy *et al.* 1994).

Thus, it would seem that attachment patterns can, at least partly, be predicted from maternal characteristics and behaviour. Such predictability provides evidence for the validity (see Chapter 1) of the Strange Situation Classification (SSC), as behaviour is related to attachment in a way that was predicted from Ainsworth's attachment theory. Another set of studies provides a different type of evidence about validity. These have found that the SSC is related to children's reactions when they are separated in more natural circumstances such as when a child is left with a baby sitter (e.g. Smith and Noble, 1987).

Other investigations have reported that the security of attachment predicts children's later abilities. Secure infants appear more co-operative with their mother at two years (Matas *et al.*, 1978). In addition, infants classified as secure in their second year have been found to be later rated by their nursery school teachers as being more popular; having more initiative, higher in self-esteem; less aggressive, and being social leaders. Secure children were also rated as more popular by other children (Sroufe, 1983). The children in Sroufe's study were also seen again at 11 years. The secure infants were rated as higher in social competence, self-confidence and self-esteem (Elicker, Egeland and Sroufe, 1992). These and similar studies support the claim that the SSC is measuring a psychologically important characteristic; the findings have an implication about the way different children will react to stressful events, and point to a complicated social process which provides a basis for these attachment patterns.

Box 11.3 The Strange Situation

The strange situation takes place in a laboratory with a set arrangement of attractive toys and furniture. The infants have to be mobile and the assessment is typically made with infants between 12 and 18 months of age.

In the strange situation the following sequence of events takes place. All the sessions, except the first one, are supposed to take three minutes:

  (i)   the mother and child are introduced to the room

 (ii)   the mother and child are left alone and the child can investigate the toys

(iii) a stranger enters and stays

(iv) the mother leaves the child alone with the stranger, and the stranger interacts with the child

 (v) the mother returns to greet and comfort the child

(vi) the mother leaves the child with the stranger

(vii) the stranger tries to engage the child

(viii) the mother returns.

There is a detailed coding scheme to assign children to one of the three categories of attachment. In broad terms, *securely attached* infants tend to explore the unfamiliar room; they are susbdued when the mother leaves and greet her positively when she returns. In contrast, *avoidant* infants do not orientate to the mother while investigating the toys and room; they not seem concerned by her absence, and they show little interest in her when she returns. The *ambivalent* infants often show intense distress particularly when the mother is absent, but they reject the mother by pushing her away, often this occurs when the mother returns.

A further group of children has subsequently been identified, and this classification group is referred to as disorganized (Type D; Main and Cassidy, 1988). These children show inconsistent behaviour, confusion and indecision. They also tend to freeze or show stereotyped behaviours such as rocking. The methodology used in the strange situation has also been developed to assess attachment in the pre-school and school years (Cassidy and Martin, 1989; Main and Cassidy, 1988).

In general, studies have found that for a particular child the Strange Situation Classification (SSC) is usually the same at different ages (i.e. reliable). When differences occur these are often associated with changes in the type of care children experience (Melhuish, 1993). Two studies have even found similar types of attachment at one year and six years (Main and Cassidy, 1988), and a study conducted in Germany found 78 per cent of the children were classified in the same way at these two ages (Wartner, Grossman, Fremmer-Bombik and Suess, 1994).

Evaluation of the Strange Situation Classification (SSC)

At first sight, all these findings about the strange situation suggest we should accept this perspective without further question. However, it is important to note that there have been criticisms of some of the claims. It has been argued that behaviour in the strange situation is the result of children's inborn characteristics such as their temperament. For example, Kagan has suggested that avoidant infants are difficult to upset, ambivalent infants are easy to stress, and that secure infants are somewhere between these two (see Campos *et al.*, 1983). Evidence to support the idea of infant temperament as the cause of the differences in behaviour in the strange situation come from a number of studies. It has been found that newborns who are less able to orient to people and objects are more likely to have insecure attachments at later ages (Waters, 1978). Similarly, low Apgar scores (an assessment of physiological status at birth) are associated with later insecure relationships. In addition, there are findings which suggest that providing support for parents with more difficult infants can result in secure patterns of attachment (Crockenberg, 1981). Thus, there is still controversy about whether infant temperament contributes to later attachment.

Another criticism of the SSC has been that, according to the culture being studied, there is variation in the proportion of children assigned to the three categories. Grossman *et al.* (1985), working in Germany, found a higher proportion of avoidant children (i.e. showing independence), and it was suggested that this may be a result of the greater value placed on this characteristic by parents in this culture. More worrying for the SSC are the findings from Japan, where infants very rarely leave their mother and the strange situation is therefore an unusual and particularly stressful event. Many infants simply could not cope with the strange situation, and therefore their behaviour was very different to that seen in other studies (Miyake, Chen and Campos, 1985). Similarly, there is discussion of whether the SSC can be meaningfully applied to children who have extensive non-parental care (Belsky and Rovine, 1988). Together, these findings indicate that we should not assume that secure attachments, as diagnosed by the SSC, are optimal for all cultures and it also seems to be the case that sometimes children react in ways not covered by the SSC.

Recent ideas about attachment

More recently, many investigations of attachment have been concerned with the claim that the security of attachment is one part of a child's *working model* of themselves and of their parents, involving conscious and unconscious thoughts (Bowlby, 1973; Main, Kaplan and Cassidy, 1985). According to this formulation, the SSC provides an assessment of the child's expectations about the way a parent will react during stressful events and their own feelings of security about being separated. It is also supposed that the working model that develops with the primary caregiver is likely to be extrapolated to other adults.

Bretherton, Ridgeway and Cassidy (1990) suggest that secure children have developed a positive working model of themselves based on their feelings of security derived from a carer who is sensitive, emotionally available and supportive. In contrast, avoidant children have a carer who is rejecting which results in their having a working model of themselves as unacceptable and unworthy. Ambivalent children have carers who are inconsistent, and consequently the children have a negative self-image of themselves and exaggerate their emotional responses as a way to obtain attention. This hypothesis provides one explanation of the fact that early patterns of attachment are related to later child characteristics. The claim about the working model is not without controversy as any predictability could simply be due to certain positive or negative family characteristics having a continuing impact on attachment and later competencies. In a similar way arguments have been made that continuing child characteristics (e.g. adaptability and sociability) might be responsible for relationships between attachment and later abilities.

Research into the SSC has produced an impressive array of findings which suggest early attachment is a result of both parental and child characteristics. Findings also indicate that the SSC is a good predictor of later child characteristics. There still remains some uncertainty about the direction of causality (from infant or parents), but we now have a wealth of evidence about the psychological importance of this dimension of behaviour. These findings provide ideas about the complexity of attachment patterns and the different forms they may take.

Discussion point

Is it reasonable to think that different children have different types of attachment to their main caregiver? What evidence supports your view? What implications does this work have for social care professionals?

The Effects of Separating Children from their Families

Most of us assume that unless it is necessary, young children should not be separated from their mother when, for instance, she has to go into hospital. This is such a prevailing assumption that it is easy to forget that 30 years ago attitudes were very different. Parental hospital visits were restricted, children were often placed in unfamiliar day nurseries when their mother was absent, and there was little concern about the effects of these separations. One reason for these policies might have been the frequent disruption and anguish at the end of any brief contact with their mother (e.g. at the end of a hospital visit). However, as we will see later, much can be done to minimize distress, and some upset may be preferable to the effects of a complete separation.

The investigations conducted on the effects of separations have provided a scientific basis for the changes in child-care practice. Much of the research was conducted some time ago when these separations were common, but the findings still have relevance to issues of today. The short- and long-term effects of separation have usually been studied separately.

Short-term effects of separation

Research has revealed that the immediate effects of separation on a young child are influenced by the age of the child and the type of care that is provided. As we have already seen, infants below about five months of age appear able to identify their mother, but do not show a marked preference for her presence. Therefore it is unsurprising that separations before this age do not seem to have a marked effect. For example, Schaffer and Callender (1959) observed few signs of distress in infants below seven months when they were admitted to hospital, but above this age there was crying, together with disturbances in sleeping and feeding. In cases of complete separation because of adoption, some effects may occur at an even earlier age. Yarrow and Goodwin (1973) collected information about the reactions of infants who were being adopted into a new home. Their conclusion was that few infants show a reaction before three months; that between three and six months there is an increasing proportion of infants who show a reaction (e.g. sleep and feeding disturbances, emotional reactions), and that between 7 and 16 months all infants showed some reaction. On the basis of these and other studies we can have confidence that at about seven months of age, there is an increase in disturbed behaviour following separation (Tennes and Lampl 1966).

What are young children's reactions to separation? Robertson and Bowlby (1952) observed that there are three progressive reactions: *protest, despair* and *detachment*. The 1–4-year-old children in the study were placed by the parents in residential nurseries. The initial *protest* involved crying, grizzling and calling the name of the mother, with the children appearing distraught and panic stricken. These behaviours lasted from several hours to about a week. Protest reactions typically gave way to *despair* where children were apathetic, uninterested in their surroundings, cried occasionally and had a continuing need for their mother. This in turn was followed by *detachment* as the child cried less and became more alert and interested. The detachment, at first sight, appeared to indicate recovery, but the recovery seems to have been at the cost of suppression of feelings for the mother; when the mother returned the child responded to her with a lack of interest, and often was angry and rejecting. If a child reacts in this way it is important to reassure the parents that a recovery in the relationship can take place, but patience, reassurance and support are required. Subsequent work has confirmed that children from about six months to just before school age exhibit these reactions, but the process is somewhat variable and a range of behaviours are shown by children. It is interesting that Bowlby believed that these grief reactions are similar to those of bereaved adults (see Chapter 24).

In the past, very little used to be done to help the children adjust to their new surroundings. An important study by Robertson and Robertson (1971) showed that given appropriate preparation and care, children could adjust to separation from their mother. The Robertsons were successful in minimizing the distress of four children whom they cared for on separate occasions in their own home (i.e. they acted as foster parents).

Discussion point
- ○ List the techniques the Robertsons might have used to help children adjust to separation in their temporary home (answers are given at the end of the chapter). List current practices which help to minimize the effects of separation.

The long-term effects of separation
Concern about the long-term effects of separation were provided with a focus by Bowlby's (1946) report that delinquency was associated with young children's separation from their mother and claims that prolonged separation might lead to later inability to form relationships. However, Bowlby's study of delinquent boys was flawed. He found that most had been separated from their mother during early childhood, and supposed that this was the cause of the delinquency. What he failed to do was find out whether a similar rate of separations occurred in similar adolescents who were not delinquent.

A later study by Bowlby *et al.* (1956) effectively showed that separations do not necessarily lead to later problems such as delinquency. The study concerned children below four years who had been isolated in TB units. In the units the children were not seen more than once a week by their parents, the nursing regimes tended to be strict, and the care was impersonal. Information was obtained about these children when they were between 7 and 14 years old. A control group of children who had not been in the clinics was also studied. There were differences between the two groups, but they were not large and involved characteristics such as the tubercular group showing more daydreaming, being less sociable and less attentive. No differences were found in terms of delinquency or problems in forming social relationships.

A slightly less optimistic picture has been provided by Douglas (1975), who compared a large group of children admitted to hospital during their first five years with a group who had not been admitted. The time spent in hospital was usually about three weeks. Data collected in adolescence indicated that the children who had *repeated* hospital admissions had a higher rate of delinquency, poorer reading and more job changes. Clarke and Clarke (1976) have questioned whether there was a causal connection between repeated hospital admissions and later problems, using an analysis of Douglas' own data. Another analysis by Rutter (1976) of a different set of data revealed that repeated hospital admissions was a marker for disadvantage, and this rather than the separations themselves could account for the higher developmental risk. Thus, in itself separation from parents does not necessarily lead to later problems, rather the available evidence points to family stress and disruption as being the cause.

In some circumstances, children are removed from their parents and are then looked after by several foster parents or other forms of care are provided (see also Chapter 3 about adoption issues). It is very difficult to be sure about the precise effects of such experience as they are often accompanied by other problems. A study by Tizard (1977) provides important clues. The children, from the first weeks of life, were cared for by a large number of people in an institution and adopted at a later age (between two and seven years). At four and eight years, most parents reported that the adopted children were attached to them. This finding has been widely quoted as evidence that children can develop attachment relationships with adults even if they have not experienced a constant carer during their early years. However, the study did indicate that the children had a tendency to be overfriendly and affectionate to strangers. Some of the children were seen again at the age of 16 (Hodges and Tizard, 1989). Although the children continued to show satisfactory relationships with their parents (by this age, there were both adopted and some biological parents caring for the children), they tended to be less popular with young people of the same age, as well as being more quarrelsome and bullying. The study also suggested that the better adjusted individuals had parents who were more involved and motivated to care for their child as well as being more tolerant and understanding. In some cases children who had adoptive parents showed better adjustment than those who were returned to less committed biological parents. These findings have a number of implications both regarding the selection of foster and adoptive parents, as well as the need to minimize the number of different caregivers a child experiences.

Summary

We have seen in this chapter that the ability to comunicate develops rapidly in the first years of life. Communication is important for many reasons, one of which is that it is implicated in the development of attachment. In the case of early baby to mother bonding, it is apparent that the more extreme claims made have not been supported by reasearch findings. Clear signs of attachments of the infant to the mother develop at about eight months, although infants can discriminate their mother from other adults from birth. These attachments seem to differ in terms of their characteristics – secure, avoidant, ambivalent. Furthermore, there is evidence that these types of attachment are related both to earlier characteristics of the baby and mother, as well as to later characteristics of the child. The reasons for these associations is still the topic of debate. The findings about the short-term effect of separations of children from adults to whom they are attached are reasonably clear. If young children are not given adequate support, then there follows protest, despair and detachment. The longer term effects are less clear, but the findings indicate that children should receive the best support possible when they are separated for any appreciable length of time from people to whom they are attached.

Seminar Questions

1. Think about the studies of bonding. When should practice be changed in the light of research findings? When can we be confident about research findings?

2. Does separation of a child from his or her mother usually result in psychological harm to the child?

3. Describe what could be done to help children adapt to a placement in a foster home.

Answers to Discussion Point on Page 303

(List the techniques that the Robertsons might have used). Meeting the child before the separation; introduction of the child to the Robertsons' home; keeping as far as possible to the same routines; taking bed, blankets, clothes, cuddly toys, and photograph of the mother to the Robertsons' home; talking to the child about the mother during the separation; and fathers visited as often as they could.

Further Reading

Schaffer, H.R. (1990) *Making Decisions about Children.* Blackwell: Oxford.
A comprehensive review of the issues of separation, coupled with a concern for the issues which face health professionals.

Messer, D. (1994) *The Development of Communication.* Wiley: Chichester.
A good coverage of issues of early communication.

References

Ainsworth, M.D.S. and Bell, S.M. (1970) 'Attachment, exploration, and separation: illustrated by the behavior of one-year-olds in a strange situation.' *Child Development, 41,* 49–65.

Ainsworth, M. and Wittig, B.A. (1969) 'Attachment and exploratory behaviour of 1-year-olds in a strange situation.' In B.M. Foss (ed) *Determinants of Infant Behaviour, 4.* London: Methuen.

Belsky, J. and Rovine, M.J. (1988) 'Nonmaternal care in the first year of life and the security of infant–parent attachment.' *Child Development, 59,* 157–167.

Bertenthal, B.I. and Proffitt, D.R. (1986) 'The extraction of structure from motion: Implementation of basic processing constraints.' Paper presented at the International Conference on Infant Studies, Los Angeles, 1986. (Abstract in *Infant Behaviour and Development 9,* 36.)

Blacher, J. (1984) 'Attachment and severely handicapped children.' *Journal of Development and Behavioural Pediatrics, 5,* 178–183.

Blakemore, J.E.D., La Rue, A. and Olejnik, A.B. (1979) 'Sex-appropriate toy preferences and the ablity to conceptualize toys as sex-role related.' *Developmental Psychology, 15,* 339–340.

Bowlby, J. (1946) *Forty-Four Juvenile Thieves: Their Characters and Home-Life.* London: Bailliére, Tindall and Cox.

Bowlby, J. (1958). 'The nature of the child's tie to his mother.' *International Journal of Psycho-Analysis, 39.*

Bowlby, J. (1969) *Attachment and Loss Vol.1. Attachment.* London: Hogarth Press.

Bowlby, J. (1973) *Attachment and Loss, Volume 2: Separation: Anxiety and Anger.* London: Hogarth Press.

Bowlby, J., Ainsworth, M., Boston, M. and Rosenbluth, D. (1956) 'The effects of mother–child separation: a follow-up study.' *British Journal of Medical Psychology, 29,* 211–47.

Bretherton, I., Ridgeway, D. and Cassidy, J. (1990) 'Assessing internal working models in the attachment relationship: an attachment story completion task for 3 year olds.' In M.T. Greenburg, D. Cichetti, and E.M. Cummings (eds) *Attachment During the Preschool Years.* Chicago: University of Chicago Press.

Bushnell, I.W.R., Sai, F. and Mullin, J.T. (1989) 'Neonatal recognition of the mother's face.' *British Journal of Developmental Psychology 7*, 3–15.

Campos, J.J., Caplovitz Barrett, K., Lamb, M., Goldsmith, H.H. and Stenberg, C. (1983) 'Socioemotional development.' In P. Mussen (ed.) *Handbook of Child Psychology*. New York: Wiley.

Carlsson. S.G., Fagerberg, H., Horneman, G., Hwang, C.P., Larson, K., Rodholm, M. and Schaller, J. (1979) 'Effects of various amounts of contact between mother and child on the mother's nursing behaviour: a follow up study.' *Behaviour and Development 2*, 209–214.

Cassidy, J., Martin, R. and the MacArthur Working Group on Attachment (1989) 'Attachment organization in three and four year-olds: Coding guidelines.' Unpublished manuscript, University of Virgina and Pennsylvania State University.

Clarke, A.M. and Clarke, A.D.B. (1976) 'Studies in natural settings.' In A.M. Clarke and A.D.B. Clarke (eds) *Early Experience: myth and evidence*. London: Open Books.

Crockenberg, S.B. (1981) 'Infant irritability, mother responsiveness, and social support mother-infant attachment.' *Child Development, 52*, 857–865.

DeCasper, A.J. and Fifer, W.P. (1980) 'Of human bonding: Newborns prefer their mothers' voices.' *Science 208*, 1174–1176.

Dockrell, J. and Messer, D. (1998) *Children's Language and Communication Difficulties*. London: Cassell.

Donaldson, M. (1978) *Children's Minds*. Glasgow: Fontana Press; William Collins.

Douglas, J.W.B. (1975) 'Early hospital admissions and later disturbances of behaviour and learning.' *Developmental Medicine and Child Neurology 17*, 456–480.

Dunn, J., Kendrick, C. and MacNamee, R. (1981) 'The reaction of first-born children to the birth of a sibling.' *Journal of Child Psychology and Psychiatry, 22*, 1–18.

Elicker, J., Egeland, M. and Sroufe, L. A. (1992) 'Predicting peer competence and peer relationships.' In R.D. Parke and G.W. Ladd (eds) *Family–Peer Relationships: Modes of Linkage*. Hillsdale, NJ: Erlbaum.

Flavell, J.H. (1963) *The Development Psychology of Jean Piaget*. Princeton, NJ: Van Nostrand.

Fonagy, P., Steele, H. and Steele, M. (1991) 'Maternal representations of attachment during pregnancy predict the organisation of infant-mother attachment at one year of age.' *Child Development, 62*, 891–905.

Fonagy, P., Steele, M., Steele, H., Higgitt, A. and Target, M. (1994) 'The Emanuel Miller Memorial Lecture 1992. The theory and practice of resilience.' *Journal of Child Psychology and Psychiatry, 35*, 215–230.

Fox, N. (1977) 'Attachment of Kibbutz infants to mother and metapelet.' *Child Development 48*, 1228–1239.

Frodi, A. (1985) 'Variations in parental and nonparental responses to early infant communication.' In M. Reite and T. Field (eds) *The Psychobiology of Attachment and Separation*. New York: Academic Press.

Goldberg, S., Morris, P., Simmons, R.J., Fowler, R.S. and Levison, H. (1990) 'Chronic illness in infancy and parenting stress: A comparison of three disease groups.' *Journal of Pediatric Psychology, 15*, 347–358.

Grossman, K., Grossman, K.E., Spangler, G., Suess, G. and Unzer, L. (1985) 'Growing points in attachment theory and research.' In I. Bretherton and E. Waters (eds) *Monographs of the Society for Research in Child Development*. Serial No. 209, 50, 3–35 monograph.

Harlow, H.F. and Zimmerman, R.R. (1959) 'Affectional responses in the infant monkey.' *Science 130*, 421–432.

Hepper, P.G. (1991) 'An examination of fetal learning before and after birth.' *Irish J. Psychology, 12*, 95–107.

Hodges, J. and Tizard, B. (1989) 'IQ and behavioural adjustment of ex-instiutional adolescents.' *Journal of Child Psychology and Psychiatry, 30*, 53–76.

Isabella, R.A., Belsky, J. and von Eye, A. (1989) 'Origins of infant-mother attachment: an examination of interactional synchrony during the infant's first year.' *Development Psychology, 25*, 12–21.

Klaus, M.H. and Kennell, J.H. (1976) *Parent-Infant Bonding*. St Louis, Michigan: Mosby.

MacFarlane, A. (1975) 'Olfaction in the development of social preferences in the human neonate.' In Ciba Foundation symposium (ed.) *Parent–Infant Interaction* New York: Elsevier.

Main, M., Kaplan, N. and Cassidy, J. (1985) 'Security in infancy, childhood and adulthood: a move to a level of representation.' In I. Bretherton and E. Waters (eds) *Growing Points of Attachment Theory and Research. Monographs of the Society for Research in Child Development, 50* (1-2 Serial No. 209).

Main, M. and Cassidy, J. (1988) 'Categories of response to reunion with the parent at age six: predicted from infant attachment classifications and stable over a one-month period.' *Development Psychology 24*, 415–426.

Matas, L. Arend, R.A. and Sroufe, L.A. (1978) 'Continuity of adaptation in the second year.' *Child Development, 49*, 547–556.

Melhuish, E.C. (1993) 'Behaviour measures: A measure of love? An overview of the assessment of attachment.' *ACPP Review and Newletter, 15*, 6, 269–275.

Miyake, K., Chen, S.J. and Campos, J.J. (1985) 'Infant temperament, mother's mode of interaction, and attachment in Japan: an interim report.' In I. Bretherton and E. Waters (eds) *Growing Points of Attachment Theory and Research. Monographs of the Society for Research in Child Development, 50* (1-2, Serial No. 209).

Piaget, J. and Inhelder, B. (1956) *The Child's Concept of Space.* London: Routledge and Kegan Paul.

Robertson, J. and Bowlby, J. (1952) 'Responses of young children to separation from their mothers.' *Courier Centre International L'Enfance, 2,* 131–142.

Robertson, J. and Robertson, J. (1971) 'Young child in brief separation.' *Psychoanalytic Study of the Child, 26,* 264–315.

Rose, S.A. and Blank, M. (1974) 'The potency of context in children's cognition.' *Child Development 45,* 499–502.

Rutter, M. (1976) 'Parent–child separation: psychological effects on the child.' In A.M. Clarke and A.D.B. Clarke (eds) *Early Experience: myth and evidence.* London: Open Books.

Schaffer, H.R. (1990) *Making Decisions about Children.* Oxford: Blackwell.

Schaffer, H.R. and Emerson, P.E. (1964) 'The development of social attachments in infancy.' *Monographs of the Society for Research in Child Development, 29,* 3, Serial No. 94.

Schaffer, H.R. and Callender, W.M. (1959) 'Psychologic effect of hospitalisation in infancy.' *Pediatrics 24,* 528–539.

Smith, P. and Noble, R. (1987) 'Factors affecting the development of caregiver–infant relationships' In L.W.C. Tavecchio and M.H. van Ijenddoorn (eds) *Attachment in Social Networks.* Amsterdam: Elsevier Science.

Sroufe, L.A. (1983) 'Individual papers of adaption from infancy to preschool.' In M. Perlmutter (ed.) *Minnesota Symposium on Child Psychology.* Hillsdale, NJ: Lawrence Erlbaum.

Steward, R.B., Mobley, L.A. and Van Tuyl, S.S. (1987) 'The firstborn's adjustment to the birth of a sibling: a longitudinal assessment.' *Child Development 58,* 341–355.

Suwalsky, J.T.D. and Klein, R. (1980) 'Effects of natural-occurring nontraumatic separations form mother.' *Infant Mental Health Journal, 1,* 3, 196–201.

Svejda, M.J., Campos, J.J. and Emde, R.N. (1980) 'Mother-infant "bonding": failure to generalise.' *Child Development, 51,* 775–759.

Tizard, B. (1977) *Adoption: A Second Chance.* London: Open Books.

Tennes, K.H. and Lampl, E.E. (1966) 'Some aspects of mother-child relationship pertaining to infantile separation anxiety.' *Journal of Nervous and Mental Diseases, 143,* 426–437.

Trause, M.A., Voos, D., Rudd, C. Marshall Klaus, M.D., Kennell, J. and Boslett, M.(1981) 'Separation for childbirth: the effect on the sibling.' *Child Psychiatry and Human Development 12,* 1, 32–39.

Trevarthen, C. (1982) 'The primary motives for cooperative understanding.' In G. Butterworth and P. Light (eds) *Social Cognition.* Brighton: Harvester.

van IJzendoorn, M.H. and Tavecchio, L.W. (1987) 'The development of attachment theory as a Lakatosian research programme.' In L.W.C. Tavecchio and M.H. van IJzendoorn (eds) *Attachment in Social Networks.* Amsterdam: North Holland.

Vietze, P.M. and O'Connor, S. (1980) 'Mother-to-infant bonding, a review.' In N. Kretchmer and A. Brasel (eds) *Biomedical and Social Bases of Pediatrics* pp.95–113.

Wartner, U.G., Grossman, K., Fremmer-Bombik, E. and Suess, G. (1994) 'Attachment patterns in South Germany at age 6.' *Child Development 65,* 1014–27.

Wasz-Hockert, O., Lind, J., Vuorenkoski, V., Partanen, T. and Valanne, E. (1968) 'The infant cry: A spectrographic and auditory analysis.' *Clinics in Developmental Medicine 29.* London: Spastics International Medicine Publishing.

Waters, E. (1978) 'The reliability and stability of individual differences in infant-mother attachment.' *Child Development, 49,* 483–494.

Weisner, T.S. and Gallimore, R. (1977) 'My brother's keeper: Child and sibling caretaking.' *Current Anthropology, 18,* 2, 169–190.

Yarrow, L.J. and Goodwin, M.S. (1973) 'The immediate impact of separation: reactions of infants to a change in mother figures.' In L.J. Stone, H.T. Smith and L.B. Murphy (eds) *The Complete Infant.* New York, NY: Basic Books.

CHAPTER 12

The Prediction of Individual Development

Ann Clarke and Alan Clarke

Introduction

In reading this chapter heading, and perhaps flicking through a few pages, you made an implicit prediction. It might have been 'This will be boring', or 'I suppose I'm meant to read this', or even, 'It looks quite interesting'. Predictions over brief and sometimes over lengthy periods are part-and-parcel of our daily lives, and much social work practice involves implicit or explicit predictions about individuals.

The situation is much more formal in the exact sciences, where inevitable, predictable and accurate cause-effect sequences can be established. The so-called softer sciences, dealing with living and changing organisms, rely much more on probabilities rather than inevitabilities. It is probable, but not certain, that we shall die before the age of 90. This or that disease has a high risk of recurring, but it does not in 20 per cent of cases. In fact, clinical medicine has many points in common with psychological science.

The evidence in this chapter will indicate that prediction of individual development involves complex uncertainties. Following the introduction, a brief account will be given of risks, vulnerabilities and resilience, as well as of the uncertainties in normal development. Four areas of atypical development, of special relevance to social work, will be sampled, namely the effects of extreme adversity, childhood sexual abuse, early developmental problems and, lastly, social disadvantage. Finally, the theme of prediction and its relevance to social work will be discussed.

Why are our behavioural predictions probabilistic? (See Chapter 1 for a discussion of probability.) In the short term, our psychological processes (e.g. mood) may alter. Over longer periods there may be fluctuations or clear trends (e.g. following minor maladjustment there is a shift to emotional stability). All these can arise from the complex interactions which characterize our lives. Take the following problem: here is a disturbed adolescent, living under poor circumstances. He is in trouble. What factors dictate our recommendations? We must take account of the individual with his history, his particular characteristics, his problems (including their severity and duration), his family and general environment, the resources which might be made available and his ultimate prospects. We would draw upon our own experience, upon discussion with colleagues and upon published studies on this sort of client. No wonder our predictions will need to be probabilistic; there are uncertainties all down the line!

To look at the bases for confident predictions, we need to analyze major influences upon development: these are the biological trajectory, the social environmental trajectory, interactions and transactions, and finally, chance events. The term *trajectory* is used to indicate that developmental processes follow particular life paths; these may be straight, or winding or come to a major junction, or even to a dead end. The life path is the result of the combined interaction of all four influences, unfolding as the individual develops. This point will become clearer below as each of these major influences is reviewed.

Biological trajectory

Biological factors include genetic as well as environmentally acquired influences, for example, brain damage from head injuries which may limit a person's normal functioning (see Chapter 23). Genetic aspects of behaviour are often entirely misunderstood. To a greater or lesser extent, they interact with the environment. In most cases they do not dictate a precise outcome, but rather a range of possibilities. Depending upon the process, this range may be very large, or in other cases very small. For example, genetic dwarfism allows a very small range of growth if one compares those raised under enriched nutrition versus those reared with impoverished nutrition. On the other hand, for those with a normal potential for stature, a period of poor nutrition has a marked effect, but if followed by proper diet the individual's growth may be considerably augmented.

A further point about genetics is that the action of genes switch on and switch off during development. Taking stature again as an example, the adolescent growth spurt, lasting two or three years and then gradually tailing off, must involve the sudden switching on of extra growth genes which later switch off completely and growth ceases. On the other hand, genetic influences upon intelligence increase during adolescence. In one important study there was no resemblance between the IQs of the adopted children and their adoptive parents with whom they had lived for many years, but there was a resemblance between the biologically related offspring and their parents. This latter finding has been repeated in many studies (Scarr, 1992), and is clear evidence for a genetic factor in IQ.

The so-called nature–nurture problem raises complex issues. Assume, for example, that a group of individuals has been raised under 'perfect' conditions. Differences between them will still be apparent, but will arise almost wholly from genetic factors, because the environment in this example is perfect for all, so variation must be due to heredity. If, on the other hand, one is comparing people from vastly different environments, then the latter differences will appear more powerful in accounting for variation. So it depends upon the sample studied whether nature appears more important than nurture, and *vice versa*; obviously, both are involved in most characteristics.

In summary, genetic programmes unfold at different rates throughout life, they do not in most cases dictate a precise outcome, because they are modified (i.e. enhanced, stabilized or depressed) by other factors. They possess a range of possible outcomes.

Social-environmental trajectory

Turning to the second major headline in development, the social environmental trajectory, we again see an unfolding, this time of environment influences. Think of your own environments at ages 5, 10, 15 and 20; these were each different in the form and type of influences bearing upon your own development. While there are common elements across time for many, for others there may have been radical changes, for good or ill, from one period to another.

Interactional/transactional trajectory

This brings us to the third major process, the way in which the interactional/transactional factors play a part throughout life. The overall genetic/environmental interactions have already been discussed, but what about *transactional* influences? These relate to the effect of the person's own qualities upon the social environment. The shy child (or adult) will try to avoid new situations, will make friends less easily than others, and thus will be reinforced in social withdrawal. Or again, the aggressive person will be more often avoided by others than the non-aggressive, and may maintain an angry personality. A further example may be found in schools; bright children ask more questions than the less gifted, gaining more teacher attention. In summary, transactional processes cause us unwittingly to affect our own development in a feedback manner, and it may well be that these processes are at their most potent when the individual's personal characteristics are extreme.

Chance

Finally, we come to the chance event or chance encounter which can sometimes radically alter the direction of the life path. Such events might be biological (e.g. head injury) or social (e.g. bereavement). While it could be argued that such events might be subsumed under one or other of the first two major influences, we prefer to keep chance as a main category in view of its unpredictability. Consider the disturbed adolescent in the fourth paragraph of this chapter, and think about the past, present and future uncertainties in his life path.

Summarizing, all four major influences on development (biological, social environmental, transactional and chance) interact and involve degrees of unpredictability.

Discussion point

○ Think of a shy child you know. How do you think the four major and interacting influences on development will affect his/her life path?

Risks, Vulnerabilities and Resilience

From the moment of conception, the developing individual is potentially or actually at risk from a variety of hazards, be they genetic influences, or infections, injuries or adverse social or familial factors. Indeed, some as yet to be conceived individuals are at risk from their parentage, socially or genetically, even before their origin. They will be born into hazardous situations.

Linked with the notion of risk is the problem of vulnerability. The same adversity, for example, may crush some while leaving others unscathed. There are wide differences between people in the extent to which they succumb – or do not – to environmental hazards. Those who do not, or who, given a chance, recover from almost unbelievable cruelty or neglect, are termed *resilient*, and there is growing evidence for the importance of the latter recovery processes.

Recently, attempts have been made to classify the various environmental stressors (risk factors) which singly or in combination may influence the developing child. Van Goor-Lambo *et al.* (1990) have produced a useful list, (abbreviated as follows, and with considerable overlap between categories – see Box 12.1).

Box 12.1 Risk Factors

Abnormal family situation (e.g. lack of warmth in parent–child relationship)

Family mental disorder, deviance or handicap (e.g. severely depressed parent)

Inadequate or distorted communication (e.g. silent parent)

Abnormal qualities of upbringing (e.g. parental overprotection)

Abnormal immediate environment (e.g. isolated family)

Acute life events (e.g. loss of love relationship)

Societal stressors (e.g. adverse discrimination)

Chronic stress related to school or work (e.g. discordant peer relationships)

Stressful events or situations resulting from child's disorder or disability (e.g. institutional upbringing)

The headings in Box 12.1, based on research, enable accurate diagnostic coding to be achieved for individuals exhibiting problem behaviour, and are likely to add to our understanding of causal factors. Each category is, of course, subdivided further into four or five sub-categories.

Obviously, the more risk factors a child encounters, the more likely an adverse outcome. Perhaps these risks are additive. However, there is also evidence that outcome can be the result of a multiplicative effect. Thus, Rutter *et al.* (1975) reported from the well-known Isle of Wight study that, in comparison with a matched control group, one risk had no significant effect. Where *two* risk factors were identified, a *four-fold* increase in emotional or conduct disorders resulted. With four adverse influences, a *ten-fold* increase had occurred.

During the last few decades it has become increasingly clear that, despite adversities, some children escape an otherwise gloomy prediction, achieving normality. Evidence for the existence of those who seem to escape their destiny will be found later in this chapter. The processes which encourage these possibilities lie both within the individual and in the immediate and long-term environment, including support from social care professionals. We have outlined such factors as follows:

Protective Factors

- individual attractiveness
- problem solving ability
- an internal locus of control

- a capacity for purposeful planning
- networks of social support
- schools where children are valued and encouraged
- peer group which is prosocial.

Conversely, factors which may militate against escape are individual irritability, low IQ, low emotional security, few emotional ties and chaotic family (Clarke and Clarke, 1992). We should add to these a gender effect; boys are more vulnerable than girls up to puberty, and *vice versa* thereafter. Perhaps the term *locus of control* above requires explanation; some people feel 'in charge of themselves', that is, they who possess an internal locus of control, while others feel themselves at the mercy of outside events, having an external locus of control.

There are, of course, interactions between internal and external factors in determining resilience or vulnerability. Often, one good starting point may be followed by another, and one unfortunate quality leads to further disadvantage. For example, a disturbed child is withdrawn from a chaotic family, fostered, the fostering breaks down, enters a children's home, fails to improve and on leaving gets into 'bad company' and so on. Major troubles lie ahead.

Summarizing, it has been shown that individuals exhibit considerable variation in their vulnerability to the same risks, and many of the factors underlying vulnerability and resilience have been outlined.

Discussion point

- ° Discuss some of the important factors in the placement of a child 'at risk' for problematic development. Why do you think that these should have a multiplicative effect?

The Prediction of Normal Development

Social care professionals will be less interested in those who grow up under typical conditions and whose development is undisturbed than in clients with problems. So we will discuss normality rather briefly. It is, however, important to offer some evidence on the course of normal growth before embarking on an outline of research findings relating to atypical development. This provides a base line from which predictions about life paths may be evaluated.

Two general rules apply to predicting individual development. First, the earlier in a child's life a prediction is made, the less accurate it is likely to be. This is because in the early years, physical and psychological characteristics are unfolding almost as one watches, with limited signs of stability. Furthermore, many psychological processes such as abstract thinking or social attitudes which one might like to predict have yet to appear, so a basis for prediction is missing. The second general rule is that, regardless of the age at which prediction is attempted, the longer the time span over which the forecast is made, the less the probable accuracy. So a one-year prediction is likely to be more accurate than a five-year, and a five-year better than a ten-year. The earlier discussion of interactions between major influences upon development gives good reasons for the operation of this general rule. Yet for centuries there has been a view that an individual's development is constant, that is, varies little with respect to age peers. In a word, people do not change. In the present century this view has been expressed by Freud (e.g. 1910), Watson (1928) and Bowlby (1951) for emotional development, and by Spearman (1904) for intellectual growth. If this were taken literally, it would imply that an emotionally damaged child would never recover, or a backward individual would remain equally so, whatever the circumstances.

A further point about prediction is that much will depend upon whether it is couched in broad terms (e.g. 'I would expect this person to be of university calibre') or much more precise (e.g. 'I would expect this university applicant to gain First Class Honours'). The broader the prediction, the more accurate it is.

We can now offer a few examples of evidence from normal development of personality. By *personality* we mean the sum total of an individual's psychological and biological characteristics. Some, however, use this term to relate only to motivational/emotional traits. We prefer, on the other hand, to divide personality into two interacting aspects, *temperament*, the general emotional nature of the person, and *intelligence*, the capacity for information processing and problem solving.

A well-known study by Block (1971) analyzed data from two earlier long-term researches on the development of children. His main information came from psychological and physiological measures of personality, taken at ages 15, 18 and 33. He showed that some individuals remained very constant in personality, while others had changed considerably. One commentator who had been responsible for one of the two data sets commented with surprise 'Many of our most mature and competent adults had severely troubled and confusing childhoods and adolescences. Many of our highly successful children and adolescents have failed to achieve their predicted potential ... but we were not always wrong! We did have several small groups whose adult status fulfilled theoretical expectations', that is their personality did not alter and was therefore predictable (Macfarlane, 1964). For a further discussion of this statement see Clarke and Clarke (1984) and Block (1980).

So far we have noted that some people show constancy of personality over long periods while others show changes. What can we make of these differences? Notable research by McGue *et al.* (1993) compared identical (same genes) with non-identical twins over the ages of 20–30. Complex analyses suggested that stability of personality was dictated by genetic factors, while change was largely the result of environmental influences. Read again the quotation from Macfarlane above, and perhaps you will infer that for those who changed in personality some marked environmental events may have occurred.

Kagan has identified the temperamental dimension of early shyness as possessing strong continuities at least to mid-childhood and maybe later. Nevertheless, he points out (Kagan and Snidman, 1991) that 'At least half of the children selected as uninhibited at twenty-one or thirty-one months were not extremely shy or timid at 7½ years of age, and 10 per cent of the uninhibited children had become shy. We presume these changes were the result of intervening experiences ... the child's biology is not deterministic' (p.20). A similar study by Kerr *et al.* (1994) confirmed Kagan's findings, but stability of shyness was greater for those children who had been extremely rather than moderately shy.

If excessive shyness is apparent in *late* childhood, then continuities are likely to be greater. Using information from the Berkeley Guidance Study (directed by Macfarlane mentioned earlier and analyzed by Block, 1971), Caspi *et al.* (1988) studied the data on such children, following them up to ages 30 and 40. Very significant associations were found, especially for men, with delayed marriage, delayed fatherhood as well as delayed entry to a stable career. The authors indicate the likelihood that childhood shyness leads to the avoidance of novel situations, especially at life transitions, and point to the transactional processes which can maintain a particular behaviour. Although the differences between the adult outcomes for shy and non-shy children are often striking, the data make clear that predictions from late childhood are imperfect, with overlaps between these two groups.

We turn now to another major aspect of personality, namely intelligence, as measured by IQ tests. There remains a good deal of prejudice against IQ tests, perhaps originally based upon their misuse. One can only say that those who still hold these views cannot be familiar with the research literature (see, for example, Scarr, 1992; Plomin, 1994). The IQ test, when properly administered, remains the best *single* predictor of many aspects of life. Of course, it is imperfect, like other single predictors; many interlocking factors dictate the life path, so multiple predictors are better than single ones.

Thousands of studies have shown that changes in IQ are common (see Clarke and Clarke, 1984), but many of these represent transient fluctuations without any necessary long-term implications. It is easy to be misled when two measures across time show differences; these may represent before and after fluctuations in different directions, so that if the first is downward and the second upward, an increment may be inferred where none really exists. For example, suppose a school boy under functions on, for him, a 'bad day' but later scores adequately, an IQ improvement may be inferred erroneously.

Recent work, using Wechsler tests (these being among the most commonly used IQ tests, covering pre-school, childhood and adulthood age ranges) has shown that children, reared in a wide range of ordinary environments, show few long-term trends up or down, although common fluctuations arising from minor changes in motivation, small ebbs and flows of intellectual growth, and so on. Yule *et al.* (1982), in the important Isle of Wight study, assessed children at age 5 and a half and again at 16 and a half. Only 10 per cent changed by more than 13 points. What is more, in this study the IQ score was quite successful in predicting school achievement. More recently Moffitt *et al.* (1993) assessed 794 children at ages 7, 9, 11 and 13. While IQ change was common, these most often seemed to represent fluctuations around a personal average. 'IQ seems to be elastic rather than plastic' (p.496).

Only in a minority of children, we emphasize, in relatively ordinary, humane environments, are sequential increments or decrements recorded. Differences within this range of environments appear to have little effect on IQ. Putting it differently, the IQ seems to be buffered against minor social differences. The intellectual demands of ordinary life allow the achievement of genetic potential (e.g. Scarr and Weinberg, 1981). The situation is entirely different, as we will see, where children are reared under conditions of adversity where the environment can depress development markedly.

To summarize, it has been shown that in the normal development of temperament and intelligence there is a degree of constancy in some individuals, and variability in others. Temperament can be more variable than IQ and fairly accurate, broad predictions can be made for the latter. Thus, the accuracy of prediction of individual development will also depend on the characteristics being assessed.

Discussion point

- ° Has your temperament remained constant over the years or have you changed? If the latter, why and in what ways?

The Prediction of Atypical Development

We turn now to the studies which have an immediate bearing upon the work of most social care professionals. What is the likely outcome of serious childhood problems? We will see that much will depend upon the type of problem, its history in the individual, its duration and the type of support to be offered. There are several viewpoints from which predictions can be made: first, from some sort of constancy model, that is, that people do not change with respect to age peers as they develop, an ancient notion supported by Freud (1910) or Bowlby (1951), among others, for emotional development, and Spearman (1904) for intellectual growth. Secondly, prediction may be based on knowledge of the natural history of particular conditions (e.g. autism), and thirdly, from an awareness of the common effects of particular interventions (e.g. imprisonment, adoption).

Extreme adversity

Children exposed over long periods to grossly adverse conditions of rearing, such that one is sometimes surprised at their mere survival, might well, following Bowlby (1951), be given a bleak prognosis. Reviews by Clarke and Clarke (1976) and especially by Skuse (1984), show that such a prediction would be wrong, provided strong remedial action is undertaken, and the child's response rapid. In Box 12.2 we offer a brief account of the best documented and lengthiest follow-up in the scientific literature. Apply the three viewpoints mentioned at the end of the previous section, and you will note that the constancy model is negated, and that responsiveness to strong intervention is confirmed. Likewise, compare these three predictions with the other studies to be reviewed later in the chapter.

Skuse (1984) reviewing cases like these concludes that 'in the absence of genetic or congenital anomalies ... victims of such deprivation have an excellent prognosis ...' provided, of course, that appropriate and long-term remedial action is undertaken. Note Skuse's firm prediction, the exact opposite of that provided by received wisdom!

Cases like these have profound implications for the thousands of children languishing in dreadful orphanages in, for example, Romania, Albania and other eastern countries, as well as for children subject to very adverse conditions nearer to home. Sadly, such implications are in the majority of cases unlikely to be fulfilled. Lack of resources, financial and human, lack of will, bureaucratic inertia, political instability, sheer ignorance represent the interlocking reasons for such failures and inactions.

Box 12.2 The Koluchova Study

A Czech psychologist, Koluchova (1972, 1976, 1991, together with the author's personal communications to us), has outlined the following case history, a fascinating story presented here in barest form. Identical twin boys, born in 1960, lost their mother shortly after birth, were cared for by a social agency for a year and then fostered by a maternal aunt for a further six months; their development was normal. Their father, who may have been intellectually limited, remarried and the twins returned to live with him, but his new wife proved to be excessively cruel, banishing the twins to the cellar for the next five and a half years and beating them from time to time. Neighbours were frightened of this woman, and were aware that all was not well. On discovery at the age of seven the twins were dwarfed in stature, lacked speech, suffered from rickets and failed to understand the meaning of pictures. The doctors who examined them confidently predicted permanent physical and mental handicap. Legally removed from their parents, they first underwent a programme of physical remediation, and entered a school for the severely learning disabled child. After some time they were legally adopted by an exceptionally dedicated woman and her sister. Scholastically, from a state of profound disability they caught up with age peers and achieved emotional and intellectual normality. After basic education they went on to technical school, training as typewriter mechanics, but later undertook further education, specializing in electronics. Both were drafted for national service, and later married and had children. They are said to be entirely stable, lacking abnormalities and enjoying warm relationships.

Childhood sexual abuse

By now there is a vast literature on this problem, and no one can underestimate its seriousness (see Chapters 15 and 16). There is a widespread belief that adverse psychological consequences are inevitable. Such a view is understandable in the light of both the incidents themselves, and the probable type of family context in which much abuse occurs.

There is a problem with several of the published studies, common to much research into causal factors in later abnormal behaviour. These start from the recognized atypical behaviour, and look back to find what might be relevant in the case histories. This strategy is flawed because it does not allow for those unknown number of people, with similar factors in their childhood background, who *do not* grow into atypical adults. Those seriously affected may not be wholly representative of all cases of childhood sexual abuse. Two recent studies illustrate this point (see Box 12.3).

Turning to the other half of the problem, there is a widespread belief that perpetrators of child sexual abuse have themselves inevitably been abused as children. If this were so, then very precise predictions might be made. Again, there may have been a reporting bias leading to such beliefs. An important three-year Scottish study by Waterhouse, Dobash and Carnie (1994) indicates, among other things, that the conventional view is simplistic and to be incorrect.

The first part of the study considered around 500 cases of child sexual abuse, but was marred by the uneven amount of information available on the childhood backgrounds of the abusers. The second part of the research is much more revealing about our theme, that the abused do not necessarily become abusers.

It used one–to two-hour skilled, in-depth interviews with 53 abusers, mainly in prison, a reasonably representative sample of this population. A large amount of important information emerged. Here we note only that almost half described their childhoods as 'unhappy'.

Box 12.3 The Studies of Mullen *et al.* (1993, 1994)

Postal questionnaire sent to 2250 New Zealand women. Very detailed information was obtained from a wide range of questions. From the responses to the questionnaires, two groups were selected for detailed interviews.

- Group 1. 298 who had reported childhood sexual abuse.
- Group 2. 298 who did not so report.

While a history of child sexual abuse was associated with increased risk of psychiatric problems 'it should not be overlooked that many victims gave no account of significant psychiatric difficulties' (1993, p.728). The authors go on to state that 'The overlap between the possible effects of sexual abuse and the effects of the matrix of social disadvantage ... were so considerable as to raise doubts about how often, in practice, it operates as an independent causal element.'

The 1994 report indicated that only 53.8 per cent of the women attributed long-term effects directly to the abuse. Where such effects were present, they included lack of trust, fear of men, damage to self-esteem and self-confidence, and in some cases, sexual problems. These could sometimes be indirect effects and therefore potentially preventable.

Offences of the abusers were either classified as 'familial' (48 per cent) or 'extra-familial' (52 per cent). The childhood backgrounds of the latter group were generally quite different from those abusing within the family. They were more likely to have grown up in disrupted families in which significant parental violence towards them was noted, or where a parental mental health problem existed. Those who abused from outside the victim's family were more likely to have experienced prolonged separations or to have grown up in institutions. They were much more likely to have suffered sexually abusive behaviour as children than were those who had abused members of their own families. However, of the total sample of abusers interviewed (53) only 22 (41 per cent) reported early sexual abuse, while 31 did not. As noted, the former tended to come from more disrupted families than those who had not so suffered.

The findings of this study confirm, yet again, that for complex behaviour, the search for single causes is unlikely to be successful. In this, as in other fields, there exists a web of interrelated factors which indicate probabilities of varying strengths, not certainties. The view that abusers have *inevitably* been themselves abused is here shown to be incorrect.

Early developmental problems

Those with certain conditions involving genetic or constitutional disorders (e.g. the more severe forms of learning disability, autism, etc.) have very poor prospects in adulthood of leading a really independent life, although in the case of autism there is a small rate of marginal adult adjustment. Hence predictions can be quite accurate. Even so, one notes in Carr's (1994) follow-up study from birth of a cohort of Down's persons a 60-point IQ range at adulthood; this is an exceedingly large variation between individuals, and therefore a degree of uncertainty about outcome. This range implies some who function as profoundly learning disabled at one extreme, while some others may be on the borders of dull normality.

There is a vast literature on prediction from child or adolescent abnormal personality, with some hundreds of longitudinal studies (e.g. Mednick and Baert, 1981). Here we examine just three which have a particular interest for our theme. A Swedish longitudinal study by Von-Knorring *et al.* (1987) provided information on a large sample for the first 24 years of life. Their criterion for inclusion in the study was psychiatric referral during childhood or early adulthood, presumably this cut out minor disorders. The findings endorse those from other studies; of 28 children exhibiting anxiety and emotional disorders before the age of nine, only three remained in psychiatric care in early adulthood, whereas a quarter of a large group with onset between 10 and 14 years were still in psychiatric care when aged between 20–24. So early emotional disorders had a quite good prognosis.

Rodgers (1990) used a 36-year follow-up of a national birth cohort to study associations between childhood behaviour and affective disorders (omitting conduct disorders) of personality in adulthood. The adult criterion was the score on the Present State Examination (an evaluation of current psychiatric status). The author regarded accuracy of prediction as unimpressive (p.411). In a few cases, however, prospects proved to be especially poor, notably for those who bed-wetted frequently at age six, or who frequently truanted at age 15 and had speech problems at the same age. However, in the main, even groups of children who had experienced multiple risk factors failed to produce in adulthood a high number of psychiatric cases.

Another study which repays close reading has been reported by Esser, Schmidt and Woerner (1990). In a rather brief longitudinal research on a large cohort of children between the ages of eight and thirteen, at age eight around 16 per cent exhibited moderate or severe psychiatric disorders. The same percentage was found at age thirteen, with a remarkable increase in conduct disorders, with similar rates for girls as for boys. For us the most interesting finding was the fairly common switch from no disorders at age eight to disorders at age thirteen, and from disorders at age eight, to no disorders at age thirteen. Specifically, one half of the disordered eight-year-olds were similarly rated at thirteen, while half were not. Adverse family situations and learning disabilities were associated with newly arising conduct disorders. However, more accurate prediction for emotional disorders were the number of life events and adverse family situations. At one extreme, three-quarters of those with conduct disorders at age eight were persistently disordered at age thirteen, but, at the other extreme, many children with early neurotic disorders were likely to become better. Such findings are amply supported by previous work.

Summarizing, research indicates that some early developmental problems remit after a time, while others such as conduct disorders exhibit a high degree of continuity, doubtless because in this latter case there is likely to be a perpetuation of very disturbed backgrounds. Remember, too, that transactional processes ('give a dog a bad name') may also reinforce individual problems.

Social disadvantage

It is all too easy to stereotype those who, legitimately, are described as living in conditions of social disadvantage, and to assume that children in such situations are doomed to repeat the lives of their parents. It is perhaps less obvious that a wide range of families come under this rubric, ranging from those where abuse, cruelty and neglect are rife, to those who, while struggling to provide for their children, manage to maintain high standards. This was a problem studied by Wedge and Prosser (1973) as part of the National Child Development Study (NCDS). They had available data on children at age 11, and drew attention to

> the massive accumulation of burdens affecting disadvantaged children and their families ... it should cause no surprise that many of these children fail to 'behave', fail to 'learn' and fail to succeed ... one in sixteen, the disadvantaged group, suffered adversity after adversity, heaped upon them from before birth; their health was poorer, their school attainment lower and their physical environment worse in almost every way than that of ordinary children. (p.59)

Did all these children fail?

This study was later continued (Essen and Wedge, 1982). It concerned the NCDS children identified as socially disadvantaged at either 11 or 16 or at both 11 and 16. Although the findings show some continuities between 11 and 16, marked discontinuities were also present. Of all the disadvantaged children at either age, about a quarter were disadvantaged at both ages, half at age 11 only, and a quarter at age 16 only. It is therefore clear that a larger group suffered disadvantage at some stage in childhood than is indicated by 'snap-shots' at either age 11 or 16. So important changes can take place in these children's lives, some bad and some good. But multiple disadvantages at either age are equally damaging to the children's life chances.

As a further contribution to the study of the NCDS sample, Pilling (1990) followed an educationally successful, formerly disadvantaged group at age 26/27. Comparing these 'escapees' with an NCDS comparison group, it emerged that the former had been somewhat less disadvantaged than the latter, and certain parental and adolescent higher aspirations for the future seemed relevant. The strongest predictor of later success was parental interest in the child's education, and of course educational achievement is an important, probably the most important, key to a better adult life.

Kolvin et al. (1990) carried out a follow-up of the well-known Newcastle Thousand Family Study of disadvantage which had been initiated in 1947. As with the NCDS sample, there emerged degrees of movement into and out of deprivation. Using data from age five as a baseline, the authors established that only about 44 per cent of the children as adults remained in the same situation, the remainder having shifted to lesser degrees of adversity, and 13 per cent had escaped completely.

Other studies show the same sorts of outcome; there is both escape from, and recruitment to, social disadvantage. As Ferguson et al. (1994) put it:

> with the passage of time young people with serious problem behaviours grow out of these problems ... having left their original family environments they may be exposed to further life and socialisation experiences which may overwrite their social learning processes accumulated during childhood. (p.1137)

Summarizing, in the four areas discussed (extreme adversity, childhood sexual abuse, early developmental problems, social disadvantage), varying proportions of children escape their apparent destinies. The relevance of these findings is evaluated in our final discussion.

Discussion point

- ° Discuss the factors which appear relevant to enabling 'escape' from disadvantage. See also the section on risks, vulnerability and resilience.

Discussion

In reviewing a number of areas in this chapter, we have indicated that there are both constancies and changes in individual development. Sometimes the changes are of negligible importance, but where clear trends occur, they may have a role, good or bad, in altering the individual's life path.

It is increasingly clear that throughout the life span internal and external influences are at work and changing. We are no longer alone in advancing this view. Yet, as Kagan (1992, p.993) points out, 'The indefinite preservation of a young child's salient qualities, whether intellectual ability or a secure attachment, remains an ascendant assumption in developmental work... There is an inconsistency between the contemporary commitment to the importance of the local context which changes, and the capacity of early encounters to create immutable structures which will be preserved'. In other words, there is a continuing belief that people do not change. Even Bowlby (1988), in what must have been one of his last contributions, developed a life-span viewpoint, rejecting the idea of an early and necessary predetermination of development, and instead emphasizing ongoing interactions throughout life. Rutter (1989) has also been clear that constancies as well as changes are common, especially at life transitions where psychological changes are likely, and where a reinforced life pathway may continue or a new one may be established.

In an earlier publication we have argued that, in general, there are likely to be greater constancies where abnormal conditions are concerned than in normality. There are a number of reasons for this, including transactional ones ('give a dog a bad name' may lead to reactions that ensure that the dog continues to be bad). Or again, some problems seem to have an inbuilt progression, genetic in origin (Clarke and Clarke, 1988). Werry (1992) has reviewed abnormal conditions, outlining those with a heightened risk of continuation. These include eating disorders, schizoid personality, psychosis, conduct disorders, obsessive-compulsive problems and attention deficit/hyperkinetic conditions. We would add to these many types of severe learning disability and autism. Yet predictions of poor outcome are probabilistic, and probabilities are not certainties so that there is usually an 'escape' from such predicted outcomes for some individuals, especially in some forms of mild learning disability and in early adjustment disorders (Clarke and Clarke, 1988).

As with other caring professions, professional social care practice often involves predictions about individuals in the light of their current characteristics, the severity of their problems, their history, the social background and its future, the resources for assisting them and the constraints upon various options. Clearly, perfect prediction in the light of all these interacting variables is unlikely except in markedly damaged individuals.

Professionals have to cope with these uncertainties and the gap between what should, and what could, be done for a particular client. Consider what might well have occurred to the twins described by Koluchova had they been consigned to a typically poor Czech children's home. While their intellectual development might well have progressed, they would surely have remained severely disordered emotionally, and as a result, fostering would have been unlikely. Thus, their grossly distorted development would have been maintained. Their histories reveal in an amplified form how a total, strong intervention may radically alter development. Such ideal solutions are rare, one of the frustrations from which social workers suffer. So research sometimes yields information on what *could* be done as opposed to what *can* be done. Resources, both human and financial, very rarely permit interventions so effective as those reported by Koluchova.

Although very difficult in practice, predictions about individuals need to be kept under review in the light of the uncertainties to which this chapter has drawn attention. We have summarized our viewpoint in an earlier (Clarke and Clarke, 1992) publication: 'we see development as a series of linkages in which characteristics in each period have a probability of linking with those in another period. But such probabilities are not certainties, and deflections for good or ill, are possible, but always within limits imposed by genetic, constitutional and social trajectories' (p.54). Social care professionals are often engaged in trying to modify unfortunate linkages. From time to time we have urged that development is *potentially somewhat open ended*. The italicized words are important; the first indicates that often people get locked into a life path from which they have neither the need, nor the desire, nor even the ability or temperament, to escape. The second points out that there are clear constraints to change, whether from genetic 'ceilings', from ageing effects or from social pressures. What is perhaps surprising is that radical departures from broad, predicted outcomes are for most people unusual, but occur sufficiently often to make us aware of uncertainties.

Discussion point

° How may social workers be misled by an over-reliance on their own personal experience?

Summary

Prediction of individual life paths has been considered with reference to fundamental, interacting influences on development: biological, social environmental, transactional and chance events. Individual differences in vulnerability to, and resilience in the face of, social disadvantage were stressed. Towards the end of the chapter we gave a summary of some studies showing apparently spontaneous recovery from the effects of adverse social environments. The salient features of severe psychosocial deprivation were presented, together with the essential factors needed for recovery to take place. Research on normal and abnormal development was presented, including studies of severe environmental adversity early in life, and of child sexual abuse.

Seminar Questions

1. Discuss the concepts of 'vulnerability' and 'resilience', drawing on your own experience.

2. Are early experiences over-rated?

3. Why is it unwise to predict that anyone who has suffered childhood sexual abuse will later become an abuser?

Further Reading

Schaffer, H.R. (1990) *Making Decisions about Children: Psychological Questions and Answers*. Oxford: Blackwell.
This book shows the clear link between research findings and practice, offering details of typical studies, evaluating them and their implications.

Rutter, M. and Rutter, M. (1993) *Developing Minds: Challenge and Continuity across the Life Span*. Harmondsworth: Penguin.
Arguing that there are both discontinuities and continuities in development, this book gives a clear picture of life-span development, stressing both the complexities and also the individualities of varied life paths. Challenging reading.

Clarke, A.M. and Clarke, A.D.B. (eds) (1976) *Early Experience: Myth and Evidence*. London: Open Books.
This multi-authored book was the first major challenge to the idea that early experience sets for the individual a predetermined life path.

References

Block, J. (1971) *Lives Through Time*. Berkeley, CA: Banford Books.

Block, J. (1980) 'From infancy to adulthood: a clarification.' *Child Development*, 51, 622–623.

Bowlby, J (1951) *Maternal Care and Mental Health*. Geneva: World Health Organization.

Bowlby, J. (1988) 'Developmental psychiatry comes of age.' *American Journal of Psychiatry*, 45, 1–10.

Carr, J. (1994) 'Long-term outcome for people with Down's syndrome.' *Journal of Child Psychology and Psychiatry 35*, 425–439.

Caspi, A., Elder, G.H. and Bem, D.J. (1988) 'Moving away from the world: life course patterns of shy children.' *Developmental Quarterly*, 24, 824–831.

Clarke, A.D.B. and Clarke, A.M. (1984) 'Constancy and change in the growth of human characteristics.' *Journal of Child Psychology and Psychiatry*, 25, 191–210.

Clarke, A.M. (1982) 'Developmental discontinuities: an approach to assessing their nature.' In L.A. Bond and J.M. Joffee (eds) *Facilitating Infant and Early Childhood Development*, 58–77. Hanover: New England University Press.

Clarke, A.M. and Clarke, A.D.B. (1976) (eds) *Early Experience: Myth and Evidence*. London: Open Books.

Clarke, A.M. and Clarke, A.D.B. (1988) 'The adult outcome of early behavioural abnormalities.' *International Journal of Behavioural Development*, 11, 3–19.

Clarke, A.M. and Clarke, A.D.B. (1992) ' How modifiable is the human life path?' *International Review of Research in Mental Retardation*, 18, 137–157.

Essen, J. and Wedge, P. (1982) *Continuities in Childhood Disadvantage*. London: Heinemann.

Esser, G., Schmidt, M.H. and Woerner, W. (1990) 'Epidemiology and course of psychiatric disorder in school age children – results of a longitudinal study.' *Journal of Child Psychology and Psychiatry*, 31, 243–263.

Ferguson, D.M., Horwood, L.J. and Lynskey, M. (1994) 'The childhood of multiple problem and adolescents: a 15-year longitudinal study.' *Journal of Psychology and Psychiatry*, 35, 1123–1140.

Freud, S. (1910) 'Infantile sexuality. Three contributions to the "Sexual theory",' (trans. A.A. Brill) *Nervous and Mental Disease Monographs*, No. 7.

Kagan, J. (1992) 'Yesterday's premises, tomorrow's promises.' *Developmental Psychology*, 28, 990–997.

Kagan. J. and Snidman, N. (1991) 'Temperamental factors in human development.' *American Psychologist*, 46, 856–862.

Kerr, M., Lambert, W.W., Stattin, H. and Klackenberg-Larsen, I. (1994) 'Stability of inhibition in a Swedish longitudinal sample.' *Child Development*, 65, 138–146.

Koluchova, J. (1972) 'Severe deprivation in twins: A case study.' *Journal of Child Psychology and Psychiatry*, 13, 107–111.

Koluchova, J. (1976) 'A report on the further development of twins after severe and prolonged deprivation.' *Journal of Child Psychology and Psychiatry*, 17, 181–188.

Koluchova, J. (1991) 'Severely deprived twins after 22 years observation.' *Studia Psychologica, 33*, 23–28.

Kolvin, I., Miller. F.J.W., Scott, D. McL., Gatzanis, S.R.M. and Fleeting, M. (1990) *Continuities of deprivation?: the Newcastle Thousand Family Study.* Aldershot: Gower House.

MacFarlane, J.W. (1964) 'Perspectives on personality consistency and change from the Guidance Study.' *Vita Humana, 7*, 115–126.

McGue, M., Bacon, S. and Lykken, D.T. (1993) 'Personality, stability and change in early adulthood: A behavioural genetic analysis.' *Developmental Psychology, 39*, 96–109.

Mednick, S.A. and Baert, A.E. (eds) (1981) *Prospective Longitudinal Research: an Empirical Basis for the Primary Prevention of Psychosocial Disorders.* Oxford: Oxford University Press on behalf of the WHO regional Office for Europe.

Moffitt, T.E., Caspi, A., Harkness, H.R. and Silva. P.A. (1993) 'The natural history of change in intellectual performance: who changes? How much? Is it meaningful?' *Journal of Child Psychology and Psychiatry 34*, 455–506.

Mullen, P.E., Martin, J.L., Anderson, J.C., Romans, S.E. and Herbison.G.P. (1993) 'Childhood sexual abuse and mental health in adult life.' *British Journal of Psychiatry 163*, 271–332.

Mullen, P.E., Martin, J.L., Anderson, J.C., Romans, S.E. and Herbison, G.P. (1994) 'The effect of child sexual abuse on social, interpersonal and sexual function in adult life.' *British Journal of Psychiatry 165*, 35–47.

Pilling, D. (1990) *Escape from Disadvantage.* London: Falmer Press.

Plomin, R. (1994) 'Genetic research and identification of environmental influences: Emanuel Miller Memorial Lecture.' *Journal of Child Psychology and Psychiatry, 35*, 817–834.

Rodgers, B. (1990) 'Behaviour and personality in childhood as predictors of adult psychiatric disorder.' *Journal of Child Psychology and Psychiatry, 31*, 393–414.

Rutter, M. (1989) 'Pathways from childhood to adult life.' *Journal of Child Psychology and Psychiatry 30*, 23–51.

Rutter, M., Yule, B., Quinton, D., Rowlands, O., Yule, W. and Berger, M. (1975) 'Attainment and adjustment in two geographical areas: III. Some factors accounting for area differences.' *British Journal of Psychiatry 126*, 520–533.

Scarr, S. (1992) 'Developmental theories for 1990's: Development and individual differences.' *Child Development 63*, 1–19.

Scarr, S. and McCartney, K. (1983) 'How people make their own environments: a theory of genotype-environments effects.' *Child Development 54*, 424–435.

Scarr, S. and Weinberg, R.A. (1981) 'The influence of "family background" on intellectual attainment.' In Scarr, S. (ed) *Race, Social Class and Individual Differences in IQ.* Hillsdale, N J: Lawrence Erlbaum.

Skuse, D. (1984) 'Extreme deprivation in childhood. II. Theoretical issues and a comparative review.' *Journal of Child Psychology and Psychiatry, 25*, 543–572.

Spearman, C. (1904) 'General intelligence: objectively determined and measured.' *American Journal of Psychology, 115*, 201–292.

Van-Goor Lambo, G., Orley, J., Poustka, F. and Rutter, M. (1990) 'Classification of abnormal psychosocial situations: preliminary revision of a WHO scheme?' *Journal of Child Psychology and Psychiatry, 31*, 229–241.

Von-Knorring, A.L., Anderson, O. and Magnusson, D. (1987) 'Psychiatric care and course of psychiatric disorders from childhood to early adulthood in a representative sample.' *Journal of Child Psychology and Psychiatry, 28*, 329–341.

Waterhouse, L., Dobash, R.P. and Carnie, J. (1994) *Child Sexual Abuse.* Edinburgh: The Scottish Office Central Research Unit.

Watson, J.B. (1928) *Psychological Care of Infant and Child.* New York: Norton.

Wedge, P. and Prosser, H. (1973) *Born To Fail?* London: Arrow Books.

Werry, J.S. (1992) 'Child psychiatric disorders: Are they classifiable?' *British Journal of Psychiatry, 161*, 472–480.

Yule, W., Gold, D.R. and Busch, C. (1982) 'Long-term predictive validity of the WPPSI: an 11-year follow-up study.' *Personality and Individual Differences, 3*, 65–71.

CHAPTER 13

Physical and Sensory Disabilities in Childhood

Vicky Lewis

Introduction

As someone working in social care you are likely to come into contact with families with children who have many different disabilities; some children will be severely affected psychologically, while others will be developing normally. Your contact will vary depending on the nature of your work. It may be in hospital with a family and their newborn baby, or when the family returns home. It may be as a community worker involved with children and families at home. You may be involved in the placement of children into foster care. You may be attached to a surgery or school. Whatever your involvement, I have tried in this chapter to give you some idea of how a disability may affect development, and to indicate some of the implications for families and professionals.

First, I shall raise some issues relevant to all children with disabilities. I shall then consider some consequences for psychological development of physical disability, Visual Impairment (VI) and Hearing Impairment (HI). Finally, I shall examine some of the implications for professionals who work with children with disabilities and their families.

General Issues Relevant to the Psychological Development of all Children with Disabilities

Childhood is a period characterized by rapid psychological development and, although babies are surprisingly competent (e.g. Bremner, 1994), a great deal of change occurs over the first seven or eight years of life. Not surprisingly, a disability can affect this development. Box 13.1 lists some general issues which are relevant to the impact of a disability on psychological development (see also Chapter 14).

Discussion point

    ° Think of a child you know with a disability and consider how each issue applies to him or her and the family.

Children with a particular type of disability, such as VI, tend to be grouped together and as a result the individuality of each child and family, and the context in which the child is growing up may be overlooked. For professionals working with such children and their families, it is

---

Box 13.1 General Issues

Onset time
An acquired disability will have less effect on psychological development than an equivalent disability present from birth or shortly after. For example, HI acquired after speech has developed will affect communication less than either congenital HI or HI acquired before the onset of spoken language.

Cause
The cause of a disability is often unknown and parents may worry that something they did or did not do was responsible. Knowing the cause can provide a focus for parents' anger and distress. If a disability is inherited, development may proceed more smoothly than if the impairment is acquired, since the parents may have personal experience of the disability and will have come to terms with it. Also a child of a parent with a known inherited disability is more likely to be given tests (e.g. for HI), and earlier diagnosis and support may therefore occur.

Nature of the disability
This varies enormously and may differ greatly in children with ostensibly the same disability: three children may have a Visual Impairment (VI), but one may be unable to see anything, another may have light perception and the third may have a narrow field of central vision. In addition, many children have more than one disability: 33 per cent of children with either VI or HI and most children with moderate to severe motor problems have some additional disability.

Effect on development
This is very varied and a disability in one area may affect many aspects of psychological development. However, all children grow up in different environments and have different experiences: these differences will influence how a particular disability affects development. Having a disability does not remove the individuality of a particular child: children with the same disability will have more in common with members of their own families than another child with the same disability.

Society's view
Western society in particular places great value on normality and often expresses negative attitudes towards people with disabilities. As a result, when parents discover their child has a disability they may mourn the normal child they have lost, and initially may reject their child. Society also holds limited expectations of people with disabilities and often makes unjustified assumptions. Thus, people with limited spoken language are often assumed to be intellectually disabled. Such assumptions may restrict opportunities for development.

---

crucial to be aware of individual differences. Nevertheless, an awareness of how a disability may or may not affect psychological development is of obvious use, and in the next three sections I have provided an overview of the psychological impact of three types of disability.

For any given child it is important to try and understand how a disability may alter how the child experiences the environment. In many cases, although a child's behaviour may initially appear inappropriate, when the behaviour is considered in the context of that child's experiences, the behaviour may be more easily understood. An example of such a behaviour is cited by Landau and Gleitman (1985), who report that, when asked to look up, a three year-old with severe VI reached her arms above her head, whereas blindfolded sighted children tilted their heads back. For the child with severe VI, 'look' meant explore with your hands; for the sighted child, 'look' meant explore with your eyes. Families often need to be helped to understand their child's development in the context of how the child experiences the environment.

Physical Disability

Many children have some form of motor impairment, although the actual incidence is uncertain. The sorts of problems that children with physical disabilities have vary enormously, although a difficulty with some aspect of motor skill or means of acting on the environment is obviously a characteristic. Some children may have problems with gross motor skills, such as walking; others may have difficulties with fine motor skills such as picking up small objects. These difficulties, whether with gross or fine motor movements or some combination, may result from a number of different motor problems, including inability to move the body part involved in the required action, an inability to coordinate and/or control the separate movements involved in the action, or the absence of a body part.

In some cases there may be a specific neurological diagnosis, such as Spina Bifida (SB) or Cerebral Palsy (CP). In other children there may be no identifiable neurological problem, for example children described as clumsy. In addition, a small number of children are born with other types of physical disability and others will become physically disabled as a result of an accident. Box 13.2 lists some of the main types of CP and SB, their causes and consequences for motor ability.

Box 13.2 Cerebral Palsy and Spina Bifida

Cerebral Palsy

In about 90 per cent of cases the brain is damaged at birth, usually because of insufficient oxygen reaching the brain (although it has been suggested that the brain may be damaged before birth and the damage causes the asphyxia at birth, rather than *vice versa*). Other causes include rhesus incompatibility, maternal rubella and, postnatally, meningitis, encephalitis and various traumas. There are three types of CP, all characterized by uncontrolled movements, which may co-occur:

- spastic (50 per cent of cases) – characterized by abnormal posture and rigidity of one or more limbs;

- athetoid – characterized by writhing, involuntary unco-ordinated movements. Often the muscles involved in speaking are affected;

- ataxic (relatively rare) – balance, co-ordination and ability to integrate spatial information affected.

Spina Bifida

SB results from incomplete closure of the spina column somewhere along its length during the first two months of pregnancy. The cause is uncertain, but may involve a genetic predisposition plus some environmental factor, possibly maternal diet, before and during early pregnancy. In SB occulta the vertebrae do not fuse completely but the spinal cord and surrounding tissue are undamaged, and development is usually normal. In SB cystica the cord is involved. There are two types of SB cystica:

- meningocele (15 per cent of cases). The spinal cord is undamaged but the meninges and cerebrospinal fluid protrude into a sac-like cyst on the back. This has little or no effect on motor ability;

- myelomeningocele (85 per cent of cases). Part of the cord and associated nervous tissue protrudes into the cyst with serious consequences for motor ability. Since muscles innervated by nerves originating below the lesion are usually paralyzed, the higher up the spine the damage, the more extensive the paralysis.

The incidence of SB is about 20 per 10,000 (less than 1 per cent) of the school population, although SB occulta, which normally has no consequences for psychological development, may affect as many as 1000 per 10,000 (10 per cent). The incidence of CP is about 25–35 per 10,000 (less than 1 per cent), whilst clumsiness may affect 700 to 1000 per 10,000 (7–10 per cent) of the school population.

Psychologists have been interested in children with motor impairments because their development should illuminate the role of action in thinking and cognition. However, the study of children with physical disabilities is fraught with problems. Even those children who are very severely disabled physically can usually act on the environment in some way and, if development is impaired, this may be a consequence of an additional disability rather than the physical impairment.

In terms of impaired motor skills, children identified as clumsy probably form the largest group. These children, mainly boys, have motor impairments but no known intellectual, sensory or neurological impairments, although it has been suggested that they may have minimal brain damage and perhaps lie on the CP continuum. Their motor impairments involve difficulty with skilled purposive movements resulting in problems with fine motor tasks (e.g. writing and drawing), gross motor tasks (e.g. running and jumping), throwing and catching, and with general balance and posture (e.g. Hulme and Lord, 1986; Smyth, 1992). By late childhood their motor skills may show a delay of four to five years. These problems are likely to persist into adolescence, by which time they may show below average verbal IQs, low academic achievement and increased social and emotional problems (e.g. Losse et al., 1991).

Since the mid-1980s, a number of studies have examined possible explanations for these difficulties, in particular the relationship between clumsiness and visual perception and movement perception (kinaesthesis). Although the relationship is not clear (e.g. Hulme and Lord, 1986) there is some evidence that training kinaesthetic ability can improve motor ability (e.g. Laszlo and Sainsbury, 1993).

In contrast, children with SB or CP are likely to have problems additional to their motor impairments. In CP, the motor problems result from brain damage and therefore there is an increased likelihood of sensory and intellectual impairments. In about 85 per cent of people with myelomeningocele SB, hydrocephalus occurs which, if not treated surgically quickly and effectively, can result in brain damage.

The presence of additional disabilities makes it difficult to examine the consequences of physical disabilities for psychological development. However, since some very severely physically disabled people are intellectually very able, it is clear that a physical disability does not necessarily lead to intellectual impairments. Box 13.3 gives extracts of Selfe and Stow's (1981) account of a boy with quite severe physical problems who achieved several 'O' level passes. Others with even more severe physical problems may achieve a great deal more, for example Stephen Hawking.

Most children with SB and CP are delayed in reaching major motor milestones, and some children may never be able to carry out certain actions. For example, Hewett (1970) reports that less than half of a group of children with CP could walk by five. They may have problems with fine motor movements, especially if athetoid. Interestingly, poor fine motor control has

---

Box 13.3 John (Selfe and Stow, 1981)

John was born after a protracted labour. He was found to be blue at birth and had to be resuscitated; it was feared that he had cerebral palsy. He was very ill for many weeks after birth and was diagnosed as suffering from hemiplegia affecting the left side of his body and diplegia affecting both his legs… John was able to walk with the aid of a wheeled frame by the age of two-and-a-half years…. He had difficulty controlling his tongue and throat musculature but, as he was attempting to communicate, speech therapy was arranged.

At the age of four John … was now speaking in short sentences and was able to communicate with his mother although strangers had some difficulty in understanding him. By the age of six … [h]e had acquired a small sight vocabulary as a basis to reading… He was also able to write with his right hand…. John is now sixteen. He has obtained three 'O' level passes and is hoping to attend a Manpower Services Residential Training School for vocational training in clerical employment.

---

also been reported for children with SB whose arms are not affected. This is possibly because they use their arms to help maintain balance while sitting, etc., and so have fewer opportunities to develop fine motor control.

Children with physical disabilities may have perceptual difficulties. Many children with spastic CP and children with SB and hydrocephalus appear to have problems understanding spatial relationships (e.g. Anderson and Spain, 1977; Abercrombie, 1964). They may orient letters and copy designs incorrectly, misplace parts of the body when drawing a person, misjudge distances and have difficulties dressing (e.g. putting the wrong arm in a sleeve). Given that these sorts of difficulties are seldom found in children with athetoid or ataxic CP, it seems possible that the stiff and jerky movements characteristic of spastic CP may limit a child's understanding of space.

If action is important for understanding, children with physical problems should be impaired cognitively. However, the literature indicates that even a profound physical impairment need not impair cognitive development (e.g. Lewis, 1987). Nevertheless, the majority of children with CP and SB do have below average IQs. This may result from brain damage or reduced experiences because of the physical limitations. Thus any intellectual impairment is unlikely to result directly from an inability to act on the environment.

Discussion point

- ° Discuss the types of social and intellectual experiences that may be denied to a child with CP or SB.

Many children with CP have poor speech which, if understood at all, may be understood by only a few people. Such children, even if of average intelligence, may be presumed to be of below average ability. This was well illustrated by the television documentary of Joey Deacon who had athetoid CP. No-one except his mother, who died when he was young, and Ernie, a friend he made many years later when institutionalized, understood him. For many years of his life, from when his mother died until he met Ernie, Joey was not thought to be able to communicate because no-one understood what he was saying. Eventually, Joey wrote a book about his life (Deacon, 1974), and the way in which this was done illustrates some of the problems which arise when someone who is fairly able wants to communicate and has things to communicate but is not understood. Joey was helped by Ernie and others living in the same institution: Joey spoke a sentence; Ernie, who understood Joey but could not write, repeated the sentence; another friend, who could write, wrote it down; a nurse corrected the friend's spelling; Joey read the corrected text, saying out loud each letter and punctuation in turn; Ernie repeated each letter and punctuation, and yet another person typed the letters and punctuation as Ernie said them.

The opposite may occur in children with SB. Their verbal skills may seem quite good and in advance of other areas of development. Nevertheless, when listened to carefully, it often appears that, although speaking fluently, what they say is inappropriate to the context. They have a tendency to remember and repeat utterances and phrases they have heard in other situations, which may have quite a complex syntactic structure, but whose content is not relevant in the present situation (e.g. Anderson and Spain, 1977).

These communication problems are likely to make interaction with the child difficult. This, plus society's generally negative attitude towards people with physical disabilities, particularly those whose speech is unintelligible and who move in uncontrolled ways, may make acceptance of the disability by both the family and the child difficult. All of this may contribute to children and young people with physical impairments having low self-esteem, something which is often more marked in girls than boys especially when the disability affects their physical appearance (e.g. Appleton *et al.*, 1994).

Visual Impairment

About four per 10,000 of the school population have a VI. Some will have had impaired vision from birth, others will have acquired their impairment. However, the majority will be able to see something. There are many different causes of VI, although in possibly 50 per cent of congenital VI the cause is unknown. Box 13.4 lists some of the main types of VI, their causes and effect on vision.

Vision may be impaired in many ways and, with the exception of conditions such as anopthalmia, no two children are likely to have exactly the same impairment. Also in many cases (e.g. macular degeneration, retrolental fibroplasia), the impairment may go undetected for some time and, even if suspected, the nature of the impairment may be unknown for many months.

Although VI can restrict experiences and opportunities throughout life, it is in childhood that many of the major difficulties occur. The child has to learn about the environment through the intact senses. As with all disabilities, any residual ability can make a marked difference. However, in the following discussion, I shall concentrate on the development of children with little or no sight from birth.

An account of the early development of a child by Selma Fraiberg, from her excellent book *Insights from the Blind* (1977), is given in Box 13.5. If you know a young child with severe VI compare your observations.

Fraiberg's observations are fairly representative of children with profound VI but no other problems (Warren, 1994). They can be bright, responsive children although they may show

---

Box 13.4 Visual Impairment

Congenital cataract
The lens of the eye is cloudy. This condition can be inherited or caused by the mother having rubella in early pregnancy. An extremely opaque lens may be removed and glasses provided. However, the resulting vision is likely to be poor.

Congenital glaucoma
This is usually inherited and results from a build up of vitreous humour within the eye which destroys retinal cells from the periphery inwards.

Albinism
This inherited condition results in a partial or total absence of pigmentation. The child is very light sensitive since the irises cannot screen out bright light, but may be able to read print.

Congenital atrophy of the optic nerve
This is seldom inherited, and the effect on vision depends upon the number and location of the damaged fibres.

Macular degeneration
The cells in the central portion of the retina are destroyed by disease or fail to develop resulting in peripheral vision.

Anopthalmia
Complete absence of one or both eyes often caused by some environmental factor affecting early foetal development.

Retinoblastoma
A malignant tumour on the retina which can be inherited. Not necessarily congenital. The eye is removed to prevent the tumour from spreading.

Retrolental fibroplasia
An excess of oxygen in the newborn period causes the retinal blood cells to grow abnormally. This occurred frequently in premature babies 50 years ago who were administered high levels of oxygen to minimize brain damage. Since not all the retina is affected equally the child may have restricted vision.

Box 13.5 Toni (Fraiberg, 1977)

She was five months old.... When her mother went over to her and called her name, Toni's face broke into a gorgeous smile, and she made agreeable responsive noises. I called her name and waited. There was no smile.... [A]t eight months ... [s]oon after she heard our voices, strange voices, she became sober, almost frozen in her posture. Later, when I held Toni ... she began to cry, squirmed in my arms, and strained away from my body.... At ten months Toni demonstrated for the first time her ability to reach and attain an object on sound cue alone.... Between eight and ten months ... we would see Toni stretched out on the floor, prone on the rug, and for long periods of time lie quite still, smiling softly to herself.... [A]t ten months... [s]he was still unable to creep ... [A]t thirteen months ... she began walking with support – and now also creeping ... she had a small and useful vocabulary, she was using her hands for fine discriminations, and she was now expert in reaching and attaining objects on sound cue. ... [B]eginning in the second year... [w]hen Toni became anxious ... she would fall into a stuporous sleep. ... In all other respects she was a healthy, active little girl, able to ride a trike, play ball, join in children's games. Her speech was good ...

odd behaviours (e.g. Toni falling asleep when anxious). Nevertheless, they develop attachments with familiar people, recognizing their voices and how they hold them, etc. By five months, Toni discriminated between her mother and strangers. However, she may not have shown other features of attachment – holding up arms to be picked up, distress when a familiar person leaves (e.g. Tröster and Brambring, 1992). In the absence of vision, these behaviours depend on children understanding that they are surrounded by objects and people. This understanding is difficult without sight.

Sight continuously provides information about the environment. Touch indicates nothing about out-of-reach objects (such as what objects are available and how far away they are) and sounds are seldom continuous. However, it is through these senses that children with VI have to understand their world. This more difficult route can explain the delayed reaching and mobility characteristic of many children with VI (e.g. Bigelow, 1986). Sighted children see something and reach or crawl towards it. Children with VI do not have this incentive and, until they realize that objects and people are permanent and continue to exist, they will not seek them out. The tactual experiences of the child with VI can also explain some intriguing observations made by Bigelow (1992). She reports that when one of two blind brothers aged four and six was asked to show an object to his brother, he would hand the object to his brother. However, when asked to show an object to a sighted relation the brothers behaved differently: if the object was within five feet of the other person the blind boys realized that the person could see the object; if the object was more than five feet from the sighted person the brothers moved it closer; if the object was more than five feet away and they could not move it closer, they said it could not be seen. The boys' experience of touch appeared to have guided their understanding of the visual system.

It is often suggested that the intact senses of people with sensory impairments are more acute. However, there is no clear evidence for this (e.g. Warren, 1984). In reality, children with VI are often poor at discriminating sounds and tactile patterns, although this improves with age (Gomulicki, 1961). It may be that with experience they get better at using their intact senses, which may give the impression that their intact senses are more acute. A good example of this is evident in Braille reading. A sighted person with no previous experience of Braille will find it extremely difficult to discriminate between Braille letters on the basis of touch alone, whereas an experienced Braille reader will be able to read fluently, albeit more slowly than a sighted person can read print.

Interestingly, reliance on intact senses may explain the limited play of children with VI (Rogers and Puchalski, 1984). Sighted children perceive dolls or toys as miniature versions of people or objects. For children with VI, the doll does not feel, smell or sound like a person; children with VI may have felt the door, window and seat of a car and heard the engine, but have no overall impression which matches a toy car. For children with VI, toys may not represent real objects, and this may explain their reduced play.

Unlike children without a disability, young children with VI may appear to show little interest in their environment with lowered, silent, blank faces (e.g. Fraiberg, 1977). However this posture, which might indicate boredom in sighted children, may indicate the opposite in children with VI: they may be concentrating on listening, trying to comprehend the noises.

Children with VI may also indicate interest in other ways. Fraiberg noted that during the first year, children with VI made small hand movements towards objects they had dropped or towards sounds.

Being unable to see also influences interaction with others. We rely heavily on vision to initiate and regulate interactions. We signal interest in something by pointing or looking and sharing attention. Children with severe VI cannot respond to the visual interest of others, and cannot convey interest in things to others in this way (e.g. Preisler, 1991). Such difficulties will be apparent in all the interactions a child with severe VI has, and may present particular difficulties when the child goes to school or moves into any new environment.

Because children with severe VI appear to show less interest in their environment, it is perhaps not surprising that the language which is spoken to them differs from the language spoken to young sighted children. Whereas parents of sighted young children are likely to elaborate on what is happening, describing objects and events, the parents of young children with VI are more likely to ask questions and give instructions to their children (e.g. Anderson et al., 1993).

When sighted children begin to talk, their first words are usually associated with what can be seen: naming and requesting objects, commenting on events, etc. These opportunities are less available to children with VI and, because of this, some may be delayed in starting to talk, although any delays are usually made up quickly once language begins. However, their language may differ from that of sighted children in various ways. For example, certain words may have different meanings, although the meanings may be appropriate to the children's experience (e.g. Tobin, 1992). For example, Urwin (1981) reports a child with VI describing a coal shed as 'dark'. For her, dark meant 'Sort of still. And cold. Like when it's raining'. Landau and Gleitman (1985) observed a child with VI manually exploring an object when asked to 'look' at the object, but just touching the object when asked to 'touch but not look'.

Other differences include asking many questions or repeating what others have said. Interestingly, both of these may be a way of establishing and maintaining contact with others (e.g. Urwin, 1981). They may be using language to check who is present and what is happening. Another frequently reported difference is a delay in the correct use of personal pronouns: when asked 'would you like a biscuit?', children with VI may reply 'you would like a biscuit' (e.g. Fraiberg, 1977). Their difficulty probably reflects the fact that they have not experienced other people's nonverbal signals which often accompany pronouns and indicate the person referred to.

It is clear that children with severe VI and no other disability can become able and competent individuals. Nevertheless, because they experience their environment without the benefit of sight, much of their development follows different routes from that of sighted children (e.g. Ittyerah and Samarapungavan, 1989). The challenge for parents and for professionals working with such children is to tap into these routes to maximize development.

Hearing Impairment

There are two main types of chronic HI in childhood: conductive, due to an abnormality of the middle ear; and sensorineural, resulting from damage to the sensory hair cells of the inner ear or to the auditory nerve. The incidence is about nine per 10,000. Some of these children will have had impaired hearing from birth; others will have acquired their impairment, either before or after they have learned to talk. Most will be able to hear something, although they may be unable to make sense of spoken language using sound alone. In addition, as many as two-thirds of all children may experience at least one episode of otitis media (inflammation of the middle ear, often called glue ear, which makes hearing more difficult) before the age of three years, resulting in transient HI. However, this seldom has any long-term effect on psychological development (e.g. Schilder et al., 1993).

There are many different causes of HI, although in many cases (possibly 40 per cent) the cause is unknown. Box 13.6 lists the main types of HI, known causes and consequences for hearing.

Box 13.6 Hearing Impairment

Sensorineural loss
The most common type. In about 50 per cent of cases caused by inheritance of a recessive gene from both parents. Also caused by the mother having rubella in early pregnancy, by incompatibility in the rhesus factors in maternal and foetal blood and by the baby experiencing an oxygen deficiency at birth. After birth sensorineural damage can result from severe viral infection, notably meningitis. In all cases the HI is severe and permanent.

Conductive loss
Caused by an air bone gap in the middle ear, usually because of recurrent bouts of otitis media during childhood. Unless the infections are frequent and untreated, the loss is seldom total and usually reversible. Nevertheless, during and immediately after an infection, children may experience marked variations in hearing.

Auditory pathway damage
This is relatively infrequent. However, it can be caused by exposure to a teratogen during early pregnancy, such as was the case with the thalidomide tragedy of the late 1950s.

Sounds are described in terms of amplitude and pitch and HI is assessed by presenting sounds of different pitch/frequencies (measured in Hertz, Hz) at different amplitudes (measured in decibel, dB) and noting responses. As with VI, assessment is difficult with very young children and, unless a HI is anticipated (as in 10 per cent of cases where one or both parents have a HI), it may go undetected for many months. Nevertheless parents may suspect something. Fletcher (1987) comments '... there is something not quite right, but the feeling is vague, unspecific, confirmed by nothing visible, though we watch him very closely'. Her son, Ben, had profound bilateral HI which was finally diagnosed at ten months. However, developments such as the auditory response cradle may enable an earlier diagnosis. This is based on the observation that when a baby hears a sound his or her movements may alter: if moving around, the baby may stop moving on hearing the sound; if lying still, a sound may cause the baby to begin to move. The baby lies in a specially designed cot and sounds of various frequencies and intensities are presented. Any changes in the baby's movements are detected through movements of the cot. In this way, the range of sounds which can be heard can be examined.

Perfect hearing is defined as a 0dB loss across the normal frequency range of 20–20,000Hz. Losses of up to 25dB have negligible effect, but beyond this increasing problems will arise, especially when the frequency range for speech (250–4000Hz) is affected. If the loss exceeds 55dB, little will be heard and spoken language will be understood primarily via lip reading. However, the loss may differ across the frequency range and, since consonants give more information about spoken language than vowels and have frequencies above 1000Hz (vowels have lower frequencies and also have a 15dB advantage so are easier to hear), a high frequency loss impairs speech perception more than a low frequency loss. Hearing aids can assist particularly if the loss is under 50dB or occurs after spoken language has been acquired. Unfortunately, hearing aids are of little use to children with losses above 70dB which are either congenital or acquired pre-lingually.

Box 13.7 describes a child who acquired severe HI after beginning to talk. If you know a young child with severe HI compare your observations.

Joe's acquired HI affected subsequent language development. Not surprisingly, acquiring spoken language can be very difficult for children with severe pre-lingual HI. In the rest of this section, I shall concentrate on such children.

Box 13.7 Joe (Selfe and Stow 1981)

Joe had meningitis at twenty-one months. Before his illness his language was developing well and he was a bright, alert child. He had a large vocabulary of single word utterances. After his illness he relapsed into a passive baby-like state for many months. By... two-and-a-half he was beginning to take an alert interest in the world around him again but the language ... had disappeared altogether. Motor co-ordination ... had returned completely, and he was agile and curious.

By the age of three Joe was attempting to vocalize, but his words were very poorly articulated ... he had a 70 decibel bilateral hearing loss ... a sensorineural deafness associated with his early illness.

He was fitted with hearing aids and his language ability improved dramatically although his articulation remained poor. From the age of four Joe was given intensive help from a peripatetic teacher of the deaf... [O]n ... psychological tests [he] was found to be above average on visual/spatial skills, just below average in verbal comprehension, but well below average on any task that required verbal expression.... His spoken language slowly improved and he learned to lip read and to use his residual hearing to the best possible advantage. He learned to read ... Socially he has become withdrawn and shy...

Children with severe HI and no other disability attain early motor milestones at about the same time as children who can hear, although they may not be as good at tasks requiring certain types of co-ordination (e.g. Wiegersma and Van der Velde, 1983). Also, like children with VI, there is no clear evidence that their intact senses are more acute.

The cognitive abilities of children with HI have received much attention from psychologists because it was thought that they could answer the enduring question of whether understanding precedes language, or *vice versa*. However, this assumes that children with HI do not develop language. While some children with HI do not develop speech, many do, and others will acquire sign language. Sign languages, such as British Sign Language (BSL), are now accepted as real languages, each with its own grammatical features distinct from other spoken or signed languages (e.g. Kyle and Woll, 1985). This is in contrast to some sign systems which follow the grammar of a spoken language (e.g. Signed Exact English, Makaton). Despite this, the effect of HI on cognition is still an important issue.

Children with HI develop a similar understanding of people and objects as hearing children although they will not know certain things (e.g. the noises particular objects or animals make). Their play is similar (e.g. Gregory, 1976), although as they get older they may engage in less joint play, primarily because of communication difficulties. On intelligence sub-tests of visual and spatial ability, provided they have no additional problems, they perform within the normal range (e.g. Conrad and Weiskrantz, 1981). However, and not surprisingly, they perform below average on sub-tests of verbal ability.

The early language environments of children with profound HI markedly affect language acquisition. If one or both parents have HI, interaction from early on seems to proceed more smoothly (Gregory and Barlow, 1989). If the parents sign, the children begin to use signs earlier than hearing children start to talk, although in other respects acquisition of the two languages is fairly similar (e.g. Schlesinger and Meadow, 1972).

However, most children with congenital HI have hearing parents and spoken language acquisition will be painfully slow. Gregory and Mogford (1981) describe two children with less than 10 words by the age of four, compared with an expected vocabulary for hearing children of 2000. Hearing children add new words every day, whereas each new word is a struggle for children with HI. Also, adults talk less to children with HI, providing information and answers rather than asking questions and seeking opinions. Parents may have difficulties explaining things, such as plans for the future, or why children cannot do something (Gregory, 1976). Interestingly, Wood et al. (1986) found that when teachers focused more on the communicative intent of children with HI and less on correcting their speech, the children spoke more.

Reading can also present problems. Conrad (1979) found that only 2.5 per cent of school leavers with profound HI had reading ages comparable with their chronological ages, compared with 50 per cent for hearing school leavers. Conrad also reported that over half of the school leavers with HI had reading ages below eight years. Wood et al. (1986) suggest that this depressing finding may be because, as with speech production, teachers focus on reading accuracy rather than comprehension.

Unlike children with VI who have to discover alternative routes, there is a readily available route for children with profound HI, namely sign language. However, unless one or both parents already sign, this language is not usually easily available. The Fletchers (Fletcher, 1987) did not sign themselves, and eventually obtained the help of a native signer when their son was four. As Fletcher writes:

> So many parents emerge tearstained from their deaf child's diagnosis, feeling a tragedy has oc-
> curred. So many profoundly deaf children reach the age of five with little or no language. This
> need not and should not happen. The tragedy is not that some people are born deaf, but that
> they are denied a means of communication appropriate to their needs.

This view is borne out by Gregory et al. (1995). In the 1960s, Gregory (1976) interviewed over 100 hearing families with a young child with HI. In all cases the parents were adopting an oral only approach. In follow up interviews with many of the original families in the 1980s, about two-thirds of the young deaf people used signing some or all of the time, and just under half the parents had learned to sign. This suggests that signing should be given priority. However, although many deaf children will have access to both oral language and signing, the Total Communication approach, the emphasis is often on encouraging spoken language if at all possible, primarily because so many of the people with whom deaf children come into contact early on, will communicate with spoken language rather than signs. This 'normalization' may not be in the best interests of the deaf child, and is often opposed by the deaf community who argue that there is a perfectly adequate language which is much more accessible to deaf people than spoken language. The same controversy surrounds the use of cochlear implants which are aimed at improving the deaf child's ability to communicate orally. Unfortunately, although cochlear implants may have some small benefits for the language acquisition of young deaf children, the benefits are not great (e.g. Robinshaw, 1996), hence the controversy and need for caution.

Given the problems with communication, it is perhaps not surprising that many children with HI have social and behavioural problems (Denmark et al., 1979). If these problems are a consequence of their communication difficulties, it follows that children who have access to a sign language should have fewer problems.

Implications for Professionals Attached to Families with a Child with a Disability

The material I have discussed in this chapter has many implications for professionals who come into contact with families with a child with a disability.

Discussion point

  ° Review what you have learned about children with (i) a physical disability, (ii) a VI, (iii) a HI. What do you think are the implications for professionals attached to a family with a child with each of these disabilities? For example, what needs might arise for such a family bringing their new baby home from hospital? How might you try to provide these needs? What factors do you need to take into account?

One of the important implications is that we all acknowledge that we are part of society and as such have our own views of and attitudes towards disability. If you are to be able to help and support children with disabilities and their families, you need to explore your own attitudes and how you react or might react towards people with disabilities.

How parents react to the news that their baby or child has a disability obviously varies. Those who have feared something very serious was wrong may actually feel relieved by the diagnosis (e.g. Gregory, 1991). For others, such as parents with HI which their child inherits, the diagnosis may present little problem. However, those families where the diagnosis is not expected often, though not always, go through phases which have been characterized as shock, denial, sadness and anger, adaptation and reorganization (Drotar et al., 1975). The length and nature of these phases may vary. Nevertheless, sadness almost inevitably accompanies the news, and this may interfere with the parents' comprehension of what they are told.

How this period is handled by the professionals involved may influence parents' reactions to the news and to their child (e.g. Cunningham *et al.*, 1984). As a result of a survey of how parents with young children with Down's syndrome were told of their child's disability, in which over half expressed dissatisfaction, Cunningham *et al.* developed the following guidelines. The parents should be told as soon as possible by a relevant professional and given plenty of time. The baby or child should be present, preferably held by the parents or a professional. Although information should be given on this first occasion, it is crucial that other opportunities are arranged within a day or two for the parents to ask questions and have the information repeated. The information which is given needs to be realistic but balanced. The paper also evaluated these guidelines by examining the satisfaction of parents following the introduction of the guidelines at a hospital. Of the 11 babies with Down's syndrome born, the parents of seven were told in accordance with the guidelines and all were satisfied. For the other four the guidelines were not followed, and two of the families abandoned the baby in the hospital. It seems clear from this that everyone involved needs to be very careful what they say to families at this very difficult time.

Although some disabilities are diagnosed at the time of birth or very shortly afterwards, others do not become apparent until later. In general, those disabilities which affect the physical appearance of the child in some way are likely to be diagnosed early on, while those which affect the child psychologically may be diagnosed much later, simply because the behaviour of infants is unpredictable. Nevertheless, during this time the parents may suspect that something is wrong. They may share their worries with professionals or may keep them to themselves. It is important that professionals encourage parents to share any worries. Most of these worries will turn out to be unfounded and reflect the normal variability of development; some may indicate a disability. All should be taken seriously.

One of the difficulties for you as someone working within social care is that you are likely to see children with a wide range of disabilities, some having a minor effect on development, others having a profound effect. Nevertheless, for a family, any disability, however minor it may seem to you, may cause distress and require some readjustment. It is important that you see the disability from the family's point of view, rather than from your own wider perspective on disability. Only if you can empathize with the family will you gain their trust and be able to help them. Similarly, some disabilities are much more frequent than others. You should not let this influence your reaction. The diagnosis of clumsiness in a child may be just as distressing to a family as the diagnosis of some less frequent but more severely limiting physical disability. For each family the problems are very real and unique. However, families and their reactions vary, and professionals need to be sensitive to these differences.

Discussion point
- If you have any family, friends or colleagues who have a physical or sensory disability and who are prepared to talk to you about this, ask them about their childhood experiences. Compare notes with your fellow students. How might the knowledge you have gained from this activity influence how you would work with a family with a child with a disability?

Support for families is crucial to help them come to terms with their child's disability. This is essential if they are to develop a positive attitude towards their child. If the disability is not accepted, it is difficult to help parents help their child. Some may turn to professionals for support; others may have their own support mechanisms. Even if your main focus is the welfare of the family, rather than the psychological development of the child, your advice may be sought about psychological development. Perhaps the main implication of the material covered in this chapter is that there are many routes to development. A conventional route may not be available because of a disability; despite this the child may still develop, albeit by a different route. Awareness of this is important for all professionals. Similarly, it is important to be aware that a psychological ability may be present, but be expressed in a different way in a child with a disability. It is also important for professionals to facilitate ways of helping children to express themselves, and not to assume that lack of expression of an ability means absence of that ability. Parents of a child with a disability need to be encouraged to think about how their child experiences the environment and how to relate to this experience. This is particularly relevant to children with a physical or sensory disability. However, it is also important to be aware that not only will the children you see differ from one another, but the families will also differ from one another. Respect for the individual child and for the individual family is paramount.

Summary

This chapter has examined the impact on psychological development when a child has a physical disability, severe visual impairment or profound hearing impairment. Although different children may be identified as having the same disability, it is argued that it is important to consider each child as an individual, with unique experiences and opportunities, being brought up in his or her own unique environment. Some of the implications for professionals attached to families with children with disabilities are examined. In particular, the professional's own attitude to disability, the reactions of the child's family to the disability and the possibility of development occurring via a number of different routes are identified as important factors.

Seminar Questions

1. How does a physical or sensory disability in children affect their relationships with other people?

2. In what ways does a physical or sensory disability in a child affect the child's perception and understanding of objects?

3. Design a policy to support families who have recently discovered that their child has a disability. How could this be implemented by a multidisciplinary team?

Further Reading

Bishop, D. and Mogford, K. (1988) *Language Development in Exceptional Circumstances*. London: Churchill Livingstone.
Examines the development of language in children with a range of disabilities, including the three types of disability discussed in this chapter.

Delight, E. and Goodall, J. (1990) 'Love and loss: Conversations with parents of babies with SB managed without surgery, 1971–1981 *Developmental Medicine and Child Neurology,* Supplement No. 61.
Reports interviews with 44 families whose child with SB myelomeningocele died before five months. The interviews were retrospective, carried out between five and 15 years after the child had died. Useful for professionals working with families with children with different disabilities.

Gregory, S., Bishop, J. and Sheldon, L. (1995) *Deaf Young People and their Families: Developing Understanding.* Cambridge: Cambridge University Press.
A longitudinal follow up of deaf young people and their families, drawing on interviews with the parents when the deaf people were young children and interviews, about 18 years later, with the young deaf people and their families.

Fletcher, L. (1987) *Language for Ben: A deaf child's right to sign.* London: Souvenir Press.
A hearing parent's account of the development of her profoundly deaf son who learnt to sign. Whilst giving a very positive view of disability, this book also illustrates many of the problems and challenges facing parents with a child with a disability.

Fraiberg, S. (1977) *Insights from the Blind.* London: Souvenir Press.
One of the best accounts of the development of children with VI.

Lewis, V. (1987) *Development and Handicap.* Oxford: Blackwell.
Describes and discusses in some detail the consequences of different disabilities for psychological development and examines the practical and theoretical implications.

Warren, D.H. (1994) *Blindness in Children: An Individual Differences Approach.* Cambridge: Cambridge University Press.
A useful account of research findings with children with VI.

References

Abercrombie, M.L.J. (1964) *Perceptual and Visuo-Motor Disorders in Cerebral Palsy.* Little Club Clinics in Developmental Medicine No. 11. London: Spastics Society and Heineman.

Anderson, E.M. and Spain, B. (1977) *The Child with Spina Bifida.* London: Methuen.

Anderson, E.S., Dunlea, A. and Kekelis, L.S. (1993) 'The impact of input: language acquisition in the visually impaired.' *First Language, 13,* 23–49.

Appleton, P.L., Minchom, P.E., Ellis, N.C., Elliott, C.E., Böll, V. and Jones, P. (1994) 'The self-concept of young people with spina bifida: a population-based study.' *Developmental Medicine and Child Neurology, 36,* 198–215.

Bigelow, A.E. (1986) 'The development of reaching in blind children.' *British Journal of Developmental Psychology, 4,* 355–366.

Bigelow, A. (1992). 'Blind children's ability to predict what another sees.' *Journal of Visual Impairment and Blindness, 86,* 181–184.

Bremner, J.G. (1994) *Infancy* 2nd edition. Oxford: Basil Blackwell.

Conrad, R. (1979) *The Deaf School Child: Language and Cognitive Function.* London: Harper and Row.

Conrad, R. and Weiskrantz, B.C. (1981) 'On the cognitive ability of deaf children of deaf parents.' *American Annals of the Deaf, 126,* 995–1003.

Cunningham, C.C., Morgan, P.A. and McGucken, R.B. (1984) 'Down's Syndrome: is dissatisfaction with disclosure of diagnosis inevitable?' *Developmental Medicine and Child Neurology, 26,* 33–39.

Deacon, J.J. (1974) *Tongue Tied: Fifty Years of Friendship in a Subnormality Hospital.* London: National Society for Mentally Handicapped Children.

Denmark, J.C., Rodda, M., Abel, R.A., Skelton, U., Eldridge, R. W., Warren, F. and Gordon, A. (1979) *A Word in Deaf Ears. A Study of Communication and Behaviour in a Sample of 75 Deaf Adolescents.* London: Royal National Institute for the Deaf.

Drotar, D., Baskiewicz, A., Irvin, N., Kennell, J. and Klaus, M. (1975) 'The adaptation of parents to the birth of an infant with a congenital malformation: A hypothetical model'. *Pediatrics, 56,* 710–717.

Fletcher, L. (1987) *Language for Ben: A Deaf Child's Right to Sign.* London: Souvenir Press.

Fraiberg, S. (1977) *Insights from the Blind*. London: Souvenir Press.

Fraiberg, S. and Adelson, E. (1975) 'Self-representation in language and play: observations of blind children.' In R. Lenneberg and E. Lenneberg (eds) *The Foundations of Language Development: Multi-disciplinary approach, 2*. New York: Academic Press.

Gomulicki, B.R. (1961) 'The development of perception and learning in blind children.' *The Psychological Laboratory, Cambridge University*. (Cited by J. Juurmaa, 1973: 'Transposition in mental spatial manipulation: a theoretical analysis.' Research Bulletin, American Foundation for the Blind, 26, 87–134.)

Gregory, S. (1976) *The Deaf Child and his Family*. London: George Allen and Unwin.

Gregory, S. (1991) 'Challenging motherhood: mothers and their deaf children.' In A. Phoenix, A. Woollett and E. Lloyd (eds) *Motherhood: Meanings, Practices and Ideologies*. London: Sage.

Gregory, S. and Barlow, S. (1989) 'Interaction between deaf babies and deaf and hearing mothers.' In B. Woll (ed) *Language Development and Sign Language*. Monograph No. 1, International Sign Linguistics Association, Centre for Deaf Studies, University of Bristol.

Gregory, S. and Mogford, K. (1981) 'Early language development in deaf children.' In B. Woll, J.G. Kyle and M. Deuchar (eds) *Perspectives on BSL and Deafness*. London: Croom Helm.

Gregory, S., Bishop, J. and Sheldon, L. (1995) *Deaf Young People and their Families: Developing Understanding*. Cambridge: Cambridge University Press.

Hewett, S. (1970) *The Family and the Handicapped Child: A Study of Cerebral Palsied Children in their Homes*. London: Allen and Unwin.

Hulme, C. and Lord, R. (1986) 'Clumsy children – a review of recent research.' *Child: Care, Health and Development 12*, 257–269.

Ittyerah, M. and Samarapungavan, A. (1989) 'The performance of congenitally blind children in cognitive developmental tasks.' *British Journal of Developmental Psychology, 7*, 129–139.

Kyle, J.G. and Woll, B. (1985) *Sign Language: The Study of Deaf People and their Language*. London: Cambridge University Press.

Landau, B. and Gleitman, L.R. (1985) *Language and Experience: Evidence from the Blind Child*. Cambridge, Massachusetts: Harvard University Press.

Laszlo, J.I. and Sainsbury, K.M. (1993) 'Perceptual-motor development and prevention of clumsiness.' *Psychological Research – Psychologische Forschung, 55*, 167–174.

Lewis, V. (1987) *Development and Handicap*. Oxford: Basil Blackwell.

Losse, A., Henderson, S.E., Elliman, D., Hall, D., Knight, E. and Jongmans, M. (1991) 'Clumsiness in children – Do they grow out of it? A 10-year follow-up study.' *Developmental Medicine and Child Neurology, 33*, 55–68.

Preisler, G. (1991) 'Early patterns of interaction between blind infants and their sighted mothers.' *Child: Care, Health and Development, 17*, 65–90.

Robinshaw, H.M. 1996) 'Acquisition of speech, pre-cochlear and post-cochlear implantation: Longitudinal studies of a congenitally deaf infant.' *European Journal of Disorders of Communication, 31*, 121–139.

Rogers, S.J. and Puchalski, C.B. (1984) 'Social characteristics of visually impaired infants' play.' *Topics in Early Childhood Special Education, 3*, 52–56.

Schilder, A.G.M., van Manen, J.G., Zielhuis, G.A., Grievink, E. H., Peters, S.A.F. and van der Broek, P. (1993) 'Long-term effects of otitis media with effusion on language, reading and spelling.' *Clinical Otolaryngology, 18*, 234–241.

Schlesinger, H. and Meadow, K. (1972) *Sound and Sign: Childhood Deafness and Mental Health*. Berkeley, CA: University of California Press.

Selfe, L. and Stow, L. (1981) *Children with Handicaps*. Sevenoaks: Hodder and Stoughton.

Smyth, T.R. (1992) 'Impaired motor skill (clumsiness) in otherwise normal children: a review.' *Child: Care, Health and Development, 18*, 283–300.

Tobin, M. (1992) 'The language of blind children: Communication, words, and meanings.' *Language and Education: An International Journal, 6*, 177–182.

Tröster, H. and Brambring, M. (1992) 'Early social-emotional development in blind infants.' *Child: Care, Health and Development, 18*, 207–227.

Urwin, C. (1981) 'Early language development in blind children.' *The British Psychological Society Division of Educational and Child Psychology Occasional Papers, 5*, 78–93.

Warren, D.H. (1984) *Blindness and Early Childhood Development. Second edition*. New York: American Foundation for the Blind.

Warren, D.H. (1994) *Blindness in Children: An Individual Differences Approach*. Cambridge: Cambridge University Press.

Wiegersma, P.H. and Van der Velde, A. (1983) 'Motor development of deaf children.' *Journal of Child Psychology and Psychiatry, 24*, 103–111.

Wood, D., Wood, H., Griffiths, A. and Howarth, I. (1986) *Teaching and Talking with Deaf Children.* Chichester: Wiley.

CHAPTER 14

People with Learning Disabilities

Julie Dockrell, Nicola Grove and Pat Hasan

Introduction

The focus of this chapter is children and adults who are often described as 'mentally handicapped'. The term 'mental handicap' is applied to a group of individuals who show a wide range of intellectual functioning and social skills. Recently there has been an attempt to dispense with terms that have pejorative overtones, such as 'mentally retarded', 'mental handicap' and so forth, and to use the term 'learning disabled' in Britain. This is also the term that is preferred by service users themselves. This is now, generally speaking, the accepted term in service provision and is used in this chapter. However, you will find that education authorities and the Code of Practice for Special Educational Needs use the term 'learning difficulties' to refer to preschool and school aged children who, as adults, would be identified as having a 'learning disability'.

Box 14.1 Charles and Katrina's Life Opportunities

Charles
Charles is four years old. He was brought to the attention of the consultant paediatrician at the age of 18 months. At this point he was diagnosed as developmentally delayed. Regular assessments have continued. His most recent assessment suggests that his cognitive and social skills are equivalent to those of a two-year-old and his language and communication skills are further delayed. His IQ score is 55. Charles is not toilet trained and he has difficulties in feeding himself. He shows no interest in books and when given a crayon manages a wild scribble. It has been recommended that he attend a developmental nursery.

Katrina
Katrina is 37; she lives at home with her parents in a small village. Katrina has Down's syndrome. As a child Katrina was slow to develop a range of skills. She did not walk until she was four. She started using words about the same time and even now her communication skills are limited. Katrina is very happy in her village. All the residents know her. She goes out by herself and shops locally, provided there is help with the payments. Twice a week Katrina joins her friends at the local adult training centre some 25 miles away. She is particularly fond of one young man at the centre. She has no special friends in the village and much of her leisure time is spent with her parents or watching TV.

Stockdale (1995) has demonstrated that the general public represent 'mental handicaps' negatively – 'those whom society deems mentally handicapped commonly evoke a negative reaction – fear apprehension and avoidance'. Such views have a profound influence on the lives of people with learning disabilities. As the chapter unfolds, the impacts of such views are highlighted. During their lives people with learning disabilities undergo the same life transitions as other people. These life transitions are often accentuated because of problems with communicating and with the need to learn new ways of coping. This chapter describes the impacts of experiencing a learning disability, and concludes by highlighting the role that social care professionals can play in empowering people with learning disabilities.

Learning disabilities are usually identified for the first time in childhood as Charles' case illustrates (see Box 14.1). As we shall see in this chapter, the nature and extent of a learning disability can vary substantially. Yet for the majority of individuals with learning disabilities, the impacts of their problems continue into adulthood and can have quite marked effects on life opportunities, as Katrina's case shows (see Box 14.1). Charles and Katrina have very different needs, which are determined both by their intellectual limitations and their chronological age. In 1971 the United Nations adopted a declaration of rights that stated:

> the mentally retarded person has the same basic rights as other citizens of the same country and the same age … each mentally retarded person has a right to such education, training, habilitation and guidance as will enable him (her) to develop his (her) ability and maximum potential.

The principles of normalization guide professionals in this task (Wolfensberger, 1972; O'Brien and Tyne, 1981). *Normalization* refers to the use of culturally valued activities and resources for enabling people to cope and behave in culturally valued and appropriate ways. Recently, the term 'social role valorization' has become more prevalent. The principle of normalization entails that we offer people with learning disabilities the same types of services and facilities that we ourselves would like and value; services that will encourage individuals to behave and respond in a socially appropriate fashion, and services that reflect a typical community life. To do this effectively it is important to understand the nature of the problems experienced by the individual with learning disabilities, and how an individual's needs will change over the life cycle.

For these reasons, in the subsequent sections we will consider: prejudice and disability; the nature of learning difficulties and their impact on learning; communication; and social skills. Prejudice is a constant factor for individuals with learning difficulties, and unless we are aware of these negative perceptions it is easy to overlook individual strengths and needs. Yet is important to understand the range and kinds of needs experienced by individuals with learning disabilities, and the chapter provides details on these issues. The translation from research results to practice is often complex. A section which addresses issues which are relevant to practice is included to help practitioners draw out the implications from the empirical literature.

Discussion points

- ° At this point you should consider the professional contact you have had with people with learning disabilities. List the features you think characterizes a learning disability.

- ° How has your training so far prepared you for understanding the needs of people with learning disabilities and their families?

- ° What knowledge do you need to gain to be effective in this area of work?

Prejudice and Disability

The nature of prejudice

> A handicap is generally conceived of as a disability, disadvantage, insufficiency or lack; where the individual has difficulty doing things , is restricted and constrained and not able to live life to the full; as an affliction which means that the individual is separated and alienated from society (Stockdale, 1995, p.33)

There are many myths that surround people with learning disabilities (McConkey, 1996; Wolfensberger, 1975). Negative attitudes often stem from inaccurate information. The language we use has a powerful effect: using a phrase like 'the mentally handicapped' suggests that everyone so described is the same, and as the chapter will demonstrate, this is not accurate. Social care professionals will often deal with negative attitudes in relation to their clients and their families. It is important to realize that simply giving more information does not create positive attitudes (Stockdale, 1995), and changing people's beliefs and attitudes is a complex endeavour (see Chapters 8 and 9).

Cultural factors and learning disabilities

People with learning disabilities come from all sections of society and from different racial and ethnic backgrounds. There is a lack of information on good services for people with learning difficulties who come from black and ethnic minority groups. Black people with learning disabilities concurrently experience different types of oppression. Public agencies have a responsibility to ensure that neither direct nor indirect discrimination is taking place. Yet much racism is hidden with organizational structures and service beliefs. Baxter *et al.* (1990) report an exercise carried out by a community learning difficulty team which demonstrated that what white staff valued for themselves, in many cases, conflicted with what black service users valued. Mainstream community care organizations may not cater to the needs of black people. Addressing cultural preferences is an important element of individual care planning. For example, the high value that is placed on independent living is not held by all.

Moreover, it is important to address the extent to which the assessment procedures may be biased – either in terms of the materials used or the assessment situation itself. Many standard test procedures and equipment are based on white middle-class values and experiences. Such materials may underestimate an individual's level of competence (Chaudhury, 1988). Equally, an assessment situation where interpreters are not available seriously limits a family's ability to understand the issues. Even when family members are used as interpreters, technical terms may not be understood and or/privacy may be invaded.

Responding to prejudice

Baxter's work (1990) has highlighted that 'there are clear tensions between a moral stance that emphasizes rights and entitlements and an organizational and managerial approach concerned with efficient delivery of services'. Yet it is undoubtedly the case that clearly targeted resources which meet the needs of the relevant clients should result in efficient service development. This may mean that preparatory work in the community is essential before a new resident is moved into a flat. Equally, the validation and support of black and ethnic voluntary organizations to enable them to negotiate contracts is another possible measure. Towards the end of the chapter, ways of empowering individuals with learning disabilities are discussed.

What are Learning Disabilities?

Definition and IQ

When individuals are diagnosed as having a learning disability this does not mean they all experience the same type or degree of problem. Nor is a learning disability an illness or a disease. Learning disabilities, however, may be caused by illness or disease, such as rubella. When individuals have a learning disability they have some difficulty in acquiring and using information. Learning disabilities are often distinguished by the level of their severity – mild, moderate or severe (often measured by IQ tests) – and in addition, problems experienced with the demands of daily living also are assessed. The American Association on Mental Deficiency (AAMD) has provided a very influential definition of 'mental retardation' as 'significantly subaverage general intellectual functioning existing concurrently with deficits in adaptive behaviour, and manifested during the developmental period'. Subaverage general intellectual functioning is defined by a score on an intelligence test. See Box 14.2 for a details of the notion of IQ and some examples of test items. Individuals with an IQ score below 70 are usually classified as learning disabled. This does not mean that individuals with scores below 70 behave in a qualitatively different way from individuals above 70. The division point is motivated by statistical rather than behavioural or psychological reasons.

The two most influential classification schemes (that of the AAMD and DSM-IV) classify by IQ scores. However, there are limitations in placing too much emphasis on an IQ score. Intelligence test scores provide a measure of current intellectual functioning. These scores do not tell us which cognitive processes are affecting an individual's performance, nor do they address what adaptive problems may be experienced. Moreover, IQ scores can change over time although the precise extent of this change may not be as great as originally assumed (Moffitt *et al.*, 1993). For practitioners, the critical aspect is whether the score says anything important about behaviour and the individual's needs. The observation that many academically disadvantaged individuals functioned adequately in society after their school years led clinicians in the 1960s to move away from using IQ as the sole criterion of 'retardation' and to include social and practical as well as academic disabilities. Thus, learning disabilities are now viewed as both a significant impairment in the ability to learn *and* adapt to the demands of society.

There is considerable debate about what makes up adaptive behaviour (see Coulter and Morrow, 1978 for a discussion) and whether it is a valid concept. Two consistent elements

---

Box 14.2 IQ Scores and Related Measures

IQ is the standard abbreviation for intelligence quotient. It is a score derived from an individual's performance on set of tests designed to measure intelligence.

What is measured?

The definition of intelligence continues to be a problem. There are many different definitions of intelligence and these differences are reflected in the ways tests are constructed. Intelligence tests commonly contain different subtests which summed together give a score that is used to calculate an intelligence quotient. It is possible to get the same overall score on an intelligence test by either being very good at some items and very poor at others or by scoring in the same range on all the items. For example, if there were 10 tests and a score of 5 out of 10 on all of the subtests, the average score would be five. An average score of 5 would also be achieved if the child scored 9 on five tests and 1 on five tests. Carefully designed tests of intelligence take these issues into account in the way the final score is derived.

How the score is derived

The IQ is a standard score with a mean of 100 and a standard deviation of 15. (The normal curve can be used to interpret scores thoughout the scale.) An IQ score of 115 is one standard deviation above the mean and an IQ score of 70 is two standard deviations below the mean. This cutoff point, 2 standard deviations below the mean, marks the point for learning disabled in many classification systems and is a statistical rather than functional criterion.

Mental ages (MA)

Before IQs were in usage, mental age was the common measure in assessing an individual's performance on intelligence tests. An eight year old performing with an MA of four is thought to be performing at the same level generally as a child who is four years of age. It is important to realize that, since these scores are made up by the child's result on a collection of tests, there is no reason to assume that the pattern of results will be the same across the age levels. For example, a four-year-old child with an MA of four is likely to have a fairly even profile of results across the subtests. In contrast, an adult with an MA of four may perform in a different fashion, having some very low scores on some subtests and higher ones on other subtests. Many factors will need to be taken into account in interpreting MA scores.

Example: The Wisc III, a commonly used IQ test, requires children to solve a number of verbal and non-verbal tasks including oral arithmetic problems, word definitions, putting puzzles together and identifying missing parts of pictures.

---

which are present in most definitions of adaptive behaviour are personal independence and social responsibility. Identifying appropriate measuring devices is difficult. For example, the Vineland Social Maturity scale, which is a measure of adaptive behaviour, includes a variety of items including locomotion, communication and self-help. Yet some of the individual items (e.g. cutting paper) may not be relevant to the demands placed on an adult in the community. In effect, adaptive behaviour is rarely used as a criterion by researchers for identification of groups or in the diagnostic process by clinicians. This is partly a result of the uncertainty surrounding their reliability and validity (see Chapter 1). However, it can play a central role in considering the likelihood of successful integration into mainstream school for children. It is more important to know whether an individual can maintain themselves in the community and abide by socially acceptable standards of behaviour than it is to know their IQ score. The IQ score does not provide the descriptive information necessary for decisions about appropriate support in the community. The new definition of mental retardation proposed by the American Association on Mental Retardation (Luckasson, 1992) rejects individual classification of types of retardation such as mild, severe or profound in favour of describing the amount and types of support a person needs. This means that it is important to consider both living contexts and the ways in which individuals can interact. As such, this chapter emphasizes both issues surrounding interaction and communication and the contexts in which individuals now live.

Prevalence, aetiology and classification

Discovering the number of people with a learning disability is a very difficult task (Mittler, 1979). Prevalence studies need to consider the population at large, not simply children and adults in special centres or hospitals. For example, some people never come to the attention of the services until their carer dies and statutory services become involved. Several studies have used standardized assessment devices and considered the child population at large (Drillien *et al.*, 1966; Rutter *et al.*, 1970). The general population estimate of children with IQs less than 70 is somewhere between 2 and 2.5 per cent. While there is a consensus about which individuals are experiencing severe learning disabilities, the situation with respect to milder problems is not always clear cut (Gillham, 1986; Mittler, 1979). The National Child Development Study (Kellmer-Pringle *et al.*, 1966) found that at the age of seven years, 0.4 per cent of the children in the survey were attending special schools; 5 per cent were receiving help in the ordinary classroom because of educational or 'mental' backwardness; while there were a further 8 per cent who, their teachers considered, would benefit from some help. The *Warnock Report* (Warnock, 1978) suggests that children who have 'limited ability' and children who are 'retarded' by other conditions would amount to approximately 10 per cent of the school population. This figure excluded those with severe learning problems. Thus, the range of children who might be included in such a category is broad, and harder to define than a criterion based on IQ would suggest.

A distinction is frequently drawn between those individuals whose difficulties are of organic origin and those whose difficulties are of unknown aetiology. Over the last 30 years, advances in biomedical research have greatly increased our ability to identify some causes of general learning disabilities. Grossman (1983) notes that there are now 200 identified causes of 'mental retardation'. For those individuals experiencing *severe* learning disabilities (roughly IQ of less than 50) aetiological causes can be identified in 85–90 per cent of the cases (Fryers, 1984). Organic insults are generally of three kinds: those occurring before birth, such as genetic abnormalities or problems in utero; those occurring at the time of birth, such as anoxia (lack of oxygen); those occurring postnatally, such as childhood encephalitis.

By contrast, for those individuals experiencing *mild* or *moderate* learning disabilities aetiological implications are less clear. IQ levels of this group tend to fall in the moderate to mild range, 50–70. For many individuals who are diagnosed as 'mentally retarded' there are no obvious organic aetiologies. Zigler and Hodapp (1986) estimated that 45 per cent were of unknown aetiology. This figure is continually changing due to advances in identification procedures, and the increased numbers of infants being kept alive despite serious CNS damage. The mild level of learning difficulty is viewed primarily as academic dysfunction, or a deficiency in learning ability with aetiology unknown, while severe learning difficulty (IQ below 50) is often viewed as a physiologically caused handicap.

Patterns of development will vary across individuals with learning disabilities. The milder problems may result in a child being described as a 'slow learner' and falling behind their peers at school. In contrast, children with moderate learning difficulties, as a group, are delayed in the development of mobility, motor co-ordination, vision and hearing, typically cognitive and social development are more markedly delayed, and linguistic and scholastic attainments even more severely affected. In these children there is no major area of development which is unaffected, but the pervasive abnormalities of development vary in severity. The most severely learning disabled may not be able to sit unsupported, or stand, walk, feed or toilet themselves. This does not mean that there is no awareness of other people or preferences for the people they know. Other individuals with severe learning disabilities can acquire basic self-help skills and possess cognitive and linguistic skills which will be on a par with the average preschool child.

Deciding whether an individual is experiencing a learning disability is not always straightforward. The more severe problems are easy to identify and this generally occurs in the first year of life. However, the diagnosis of milder problem is much more complex and depends on the community where the individual lives and the demands that exist in that specific context. Generally, diagnosis happens in the preschool years or at school. However, some individuals remain undetected until adulthood possibly until they come under the purview of the criminal justice system (see Dockrell et al., 1993).

The recognition that special educational provision needs to be made for children with learning disabilities is of comparative recent origin (Pritchard, 1963). A statement of Special Educational Needs (in Scotland it is called The Record of Needs) is a formal document drawn up which specifies the educational provision required to meet a child's needs (see Stow and Selfe, 1989). The concept of educational need has superseded earlier categorization schemes based on IQ or type of school attended. Integration with non-disabled peers is seen as an important element of special provision but provision covers the full range from children who are supported in ordinary classrooms; various part-time arrangements between special and ordinary schools; or full-time segregated facilities where a child's needs cannot be met in mainstream school.

Although the general aim has been to avoid categorization, the terms 'mild' , 'moderate' and 'severe' are used to refer to the children's teaching and curricular requirements. Children with severe learning difficulties are defined as those who require a developmental curriculum which cover a range of educational experiences and is more selectively and sharply focused on the development of personal autonomy and social skills. Children with moderate learning difficulties are defined as those who need a modified curriculum with similar objectives to that provided in ordinary schools. This means altering the curriculum to make it accessible to these children (see Grove and Park (1996) as an example of how this can be done). Children with mild learning difficulties should cope with the normal curriculum and most are likely to manage with normal support in the ordinary classroom. The national curriculum should be used in all schools and all children have the right to a full curriculum.

Cognition, Communication and Social Skills

One of the defining characteristics of people with learning difficulties is intellectual impairment. Yet, there is still much uncertainty about the nature of the specific skill deficits that accompany learning difficulties. In the past many practitioners have felt let down by theoretical models. These models were not easily translated into practice and often emphasized unmodifiable aspects of cognition. Contemporary models are more relevant to practitioners because they emphasize aspects of thinking and communication that can be modified through instruction.

Cognitive skills

Intelligence tests can serve as a useful screening device, but they do not tell us about the nature of the cognitive problems. Nor, do they necessarily direct predictions of what sorts of other difficulties may exist, for example, in language. Researchers have attempted to clarify the types of difficulties experienced by examining the ways in which individuals process information (Weiss, Weisz and Bromfield, 1986). Persistent problems have been identified in several different cognitive areas including speed of information processing, memory and strategic behaviour (see Dockrell and McShane, 1993 for a review). There are marked difficulties in identifying and maintaining attention to the relevant stimulus dimensions (Owens, 1989). These problems have direct implications for assessing learning disabilities and language skills in particular (Kahmi and Masterson, 1989) and for designing intervention programmes. At the most basic level, it must be established that the individual with learning disabilities is actually focusing on the relevant task dimensions. In addition, there has been extensive work on memory (Campione, Brown and Ferrara, 1982) which shows that individuals with learning disabilities fail to employ strategies that help in learning new material. Individuals can be taught to employ strategies and are most likely to generalize a new strategy if they understand the reasons for its use. Such problems of generalization can have important implications for interventions. For example, if an individual is taught the meaning of a word in one situation, e.g. death, it may need to be relearnt and reinforced each time it occurs in a different context. This could be very important for successful adaptation. While memory performance can be improved by training, difficulties are likely to remain and there is some indication that the speed at which information is retrieved from memory is a limiting factor in general cognitive performance (Kail, 1990). Most findings concern individuals experiencing mild learning disabilities; the evidence that exists suggests that extrapolating from the findings to individuals with severe learning disabilities may be inappropriate (Broman et al., 1987). Nonetheless, these problems highlight the complexities of cognition and the need to be clear about which skills are being tapped in any specific situation. To date, more similarities than differences have appeared when children with general learning disabilities have been compared with normal children on cognitive tasks. General reviews of the relevant research conclude that children categorized as 'cultural-familial' (learning difficulties where there is no known cause) have similar cognitive structures to their normally developing peers whereas organically retarded children do not (Weiss et al., 1986). Such conclusions are still contentious. Children with mild, moderate, and severe learning disabilities are a heterogeneous group and therefore it is difficult to generalize between individuals. An important element to consider in task success is motivation. Low self-esteem and low expectations can result in a lack of motivation to succeed. In the case of children with learning difficulties the initial problems may make the child feel that they will not succeed and they stop trying. For example, recent investigations of children with Down's syndrome suggest that these children have quite specific motivational problems. It has been noted that children's performance is unstable and there is avoidance of difficult tasks (Hasan and Messer, 1997; Pitcairn and Wishart, 1994). Given the range of difficulties that may be experienced, it is important to be sensitive to the different ways these problems may manifest themselves. When dealing with a client who has a learning disability. It is important to establish that:

- they have remembered any new information you have provided
- new skills that are learnt are used in a range of situations
- complex or abstract ideas are presented in a clear and straightforward fashion
- sufficient time is allowed to finish tasks and support is provided to complete complex tasks.

Box 14.3 Aspects of Language and Communication

- Understanding (receptive language). The ability to comprehend the language of other people.
- Expression (productive language). The ability to formulate a message and convey it to others.
- Vocabulary. Words and word meanings.
- Grammar. The system of rules which determines how the form of words changes to indicate different meanings (morphology) and how words combine to form sentences (syntax).
- Articulation (intelligibility).The clarity and accuracy of the motor production of a message (speech sounds or manual signs).
- Social use (pragmatics). The appropriate use of language in different contexts to achieve different goals.

Language and communication

It has been recognized for some time that people with learning disabilities have problems with language and communication. It has been estimated that up to half of this population may show a severe language deficiency, disorders in speech production, or a combination of the two (Enderby and Davies, 1989; Rutter et al., 1970). Partly this is because of the effects of (a) brain damage, (b) impairments to hearing, sight and/or motor skills on the ability to understand, recall and express information. In general terms, there is an association between the severity of cognitive and language difficulties. Thus, people with profound learning difficulties are limited in their understanding and production of language, and tend to rely more on tone of voice, touch and the cues provided by social routines to understand what is going on, or to communicate their intentions. For people with impairments in the range of mild to severe, it is less easy to predict the level of their achievements in language; some people will use only single words, whilst others are very competent communicators. When we talk of language and communication we actually need to think of different aspects which interact with one another, and may be affected in different ways by a learning difficulty.

Discussion point

  ° What is the difference between understanding and communicating? Consider the different criteria you might use for assessing understanding and communication.

People with severe cerebral palsy and learning disabilities may be able to understand quite a lot of what is said to them, but be unable to express themselves effectively because of motor impairments affecting their speech (articulation) and/or their use of gestures or points to pictures. People with Down's syndrome seem to have most problems in developing grammatical structures, as opposed to vocabulary or pragmatics (Beeghly and Cicchetti, 1987). Some people may show autistic-like behaviour, being able to construct long and complex sentences (grammar) but have problems in using their language appropriately (social use) (Wing, 1988). It is especially important to be aware of difficulties in understanding – people may give the impression of responding to what you say, but may actually have grasped little more than your tone of voice. There are also indications that parents may use functionally different language towards a child with disabilities, and are less likely to follow the child's initiative. This latter point highlights the need to consider the interaction of environmental factors and communicative potential (van der Gaag and Dormandy, 1992). The level of skill shown by people with learning disabilities is very dependent on the kind of opportunities that are provided to share new information, make requests and choices and interact socially. When life is dominated by routines, and conversations consist of being told what to do, there is little incentive to make much use of language (Harris, 1988). It is also important to realize that language is not the same as speech. Deaf people use sign language, which has been shown to have all the characteristics of a language system (e.g. grammatical rules), but is not spoken (see Kyle and Woll, 1985). We can think of language as a system for representing the world to ourselves and others, whereas speech is a means of transmitting that system (as is writing).

Box 14.4 Modalities of communication

Eye gaze

Facial expressions

Body position and movement

Vocalizations

Gestures

Spoken words

Hand signs

Pointing to pictures or objects

Discussion point

- ° Think of a person whom you know with a learning disability. How would you investigate how well this person (a) understands your verbal language, and (b) understands the gestures that you might use?

We all use nonverbal communication to accompany our spoken language – facial expressions, body posture, eye gaze and gestures. These are all different modalities of communication (see Box 14.4). People with learning disabilities are likely to rely as much or more on additional modalities to speech to express their meanings. The terms Augmentative and Alternative Communication (AAC) refer to the use of other modalities than speech as a means of expression or a cue to comprehension, for people who are experiencing difficulties in their use of spoken language (Beukelman and Mirenda, 1992; von Tetzchner and Martinsen, 1994). A vocabulary corresponding to spoken words can be taught through gestures and manual signs, usually taken from the sign language of Deaf people (e.g. the Makaton Vocabulary), or pictures and graphic symbols (e.g. Rebus, Bliss symbolics) which are displayed on a board or book for a person to point to. These may be associated with computerized technology with voice output, so that when someone touches the key with a symbol for 'drink' the device says 'May I have a drink please'. Pictures and symbols may also be used to create communication books about a person and their life, and to represent schedules of daily activities. They provide a powerful and simple way of helping people to understand about significant events and share information with others. Sets of common objects ('objects of reference') may be used with people who have profound learning difficulties, who do not respond to pictures.

A common anxiety among parents (and some staff) is that use of AAC systems will stop someone talking, but there is no evidence at all that this is the case, provided that all attempts to communicate (including vocalization) are reinforced. Indeed, the early use of nonvocal systems can help to prevent the occurrence of negative behaviours which may result from frustration at a failure to communicate or understand. There are specialist centres which will assess children and adults, and advise on the most appropriate AAC system. Further information can be found in the handbook produced by Allen *et al.* (1992). The guiding principles for use of AAC systems are that:

- all modalities which are useful to an individual should be exploited

- those who interact with the individual should try to use their system, in order to provide good models of communication, and a sense of value.

When interacting with a person who has a learning disability you should always consider:

- Whether the person genuinely understands what you are saying. Talk simply, but without being patronizing

- Whether the person has rich experiences to talk about, and has opportunities to communicate actively with other people

- Whether the person is making active use of different modalities of communication.

Speech and language therapists will advise on assessment and intervention for communication difficulties if needed.

Facilitated communication

Facilitated communication has been conceived by some as a way of releasing people's ability to communicate. It is an extremely controversial area with professionals in the area. Facilitated communication comprises a series of techniques that 'assist a communication impaired person in pointing at a traditional communication board with letters, graphic signs or pictures, or writing on an electronic communication aid or a computer' (Von Tetzchner 1997). Effectively, the facilitator provides support to the hands, wrist or arm of the client. Facilitated Communication involves two distinct elements: an attitudinal dimension that requires 'faith and trusting' and a set of specific practices (Biklen, 1990, p.307). Considerable debate exists as to whether it is really the client who is communicating or the facilitator. There is an open discussion surrounding these issues in the spring 1997 issue of the *European Journal of Disorders of Communication* (1997).

Social skills

As we have seen, cognitive and language limitations have been core components of diagnostic criteria since the original classification systems were formulated, the inclusion of social and 'adaptive skills' is more recent. The use of the term 'adaptive skills' in the 1992 AAMR definition reflects an attempt to provide an array of competency areas, rather than relying on a more generic concept of adaptive behaviour. Included in this list are social skills – 'Social interchange with others, including initiating and terminating interactions, responding to social cues, recognizing feelings, regulating own behaviour, assisting others and fostering friendships'. As more and more individuals with learning disabilities strive to live independent lives in the community an added emphasis has been placed on social skills. Inappropriate responses or lack of social responsiveness can lead to isolation for the individual. To some extent this has been tackled by the development of specialized social skills training packages. The role of monitoring such educational programmes and liaising with the relevant institutions will sometimes fall to social workers. When considering an individual's social skills it is important to analyze in detail both the skills required in a particular situation and the individual's motivation to learn such skills. The skills required for personal competence will not necessarily be the skills required for community competence. It may be possible to help an individual learn a particular social routine which they do not possess, but the use of this routine in the community will be guided by a complex range of social and pragmatic factors.

An example will serve to illustrate this point. Paul is a 21-year-old man with a mild learning disability. He was having difficulties with his personal relationships with young women. With his needs in mind a psychologist helped teach Paul the skills for asking someone out. These skills included being friendly, giving compliments and discussing interests. These sessions culminated in Paul learning the appropriate words to use to suggest an evening meeting. When these sessions had finished Paul was very satisfied and felt he had learnt a lot. Shortly after this Paul caused some upset at church. Apparently after church he saw a young lady he was attracted to and approached her. Everything he learnt was put into practice in a few minutes. He had never met the young lady before. Paul was very upset by the response. He had, after all, done everything he was taught.

The issue of communication is also important in relation to legal processes. Individuals living in the community may come into contact with the forces of law and order, either as a suspect or as a victim of crime. One question which needs to be considered is how reliable their reports of a particular incident will be (see also Chapter 5). Preliminary evidence suggests recall is poorer among groups of individuals with learning disabilities (Clare and Gudjonsson, 1993), they are more susceptible to leading questions and more acquiescent in their responses. As a result, people with learning disabilities are more vulnerable than their average ability peers. It becomes particularly important when questioning an individual in such situations that the use of all facilities to support an accurate reporting of an incident be made and that an advocate be present. Reporting can be enhanced for example, by using recognition rather than recall procedures. That is rather than recounting a particular incident the individual chose the best pictorial representation from a set. Issues surrounding the reliability and validity of reporting become particularly problematic whenever communication has to be channelled through another form of action, as in facilitator or advocate.

Understanding cognitive, communicative and social factors is fundamental to the successful integration and childhood support of individuals in the community. The extent to which these problems limit an individual's life opportunities often will be influenced by the immediate and wider context in which the individual finds themselves.

Issues for Social Care Professionals

The psychological needs of people with learning disabilities and their families and carers will vary. To some extent, this will be related to the nature of the learning disability, but it is also essential to consider the personal circumstances and life changes that an individual and their carer are experiencing. In this section we consider some of the key life events that can raise particular dilemmas, and proceed to consider the ways in which support can be empowering for the individual(s) concerned. Specific solutions to the problems are not provided; however, we hope the information discussed should provide the basis for either appropriate decision making or identifying sources for further help. Ultimately, these will be determined by the individuals involved, the resources provided locally and the wider social and political constraints at the time.

The years before adolescence

Family concerns about learning disabilities can be raised before a child is born. Amniocentesis (which is carried out at approximately 15–16 weeks gestation) and Chorionic Villus Sampling (carried out even earlier), to detect Down's syndrome and other potential organic abnormalities in the developing foetus present parents with a range of important decisions. Professionals may be involved in counselling parents both before and after these sensitive clinical procedures.

Prenatal screening also can detect certain maternal diseases that, if transmitted to the foetus *in utero*, could result in learning disabilities. Specific examples include rubella, alcoholism which may cause foetal alcohol syndrome and, more rarely nowadays, syphilis. Even severe malnutrition in the mother during pregnancy may affect the infant's learning potential. It is important to realize that learning disabilities may result from causes associated with the labour and delivery process itself. Trauma associated with the birth of the infant may cause damage to certain areas of the brain. Anoxia or prolonged deprivation of the oxygen supply is particularly dangerous. The degree of severity will obviously depend to a certain extent on the nature of the trauma, but prediction of future potential and lifestyle is not straightforward.

Parents are often first told that their child has a learning disability shortly after birth or perhaps sometime later when the diagnosis is more certain. Richards and Reed (1991) state 'the way in which parents are told of their children's condition affects the way they adjust to the situation, the way they treat the child and their attitudes to future service provision'. One line of research has focused on the psychological responses of parents to information of such an emotive and sensitive nature. MacKeith (1973) suggests that a complex set of 'feelings' are invoked which may include almost instinctive 'biological' reactions such as the desire to protect the helpless infant, or conversely, a revulsion at the 'abnormal' aspect of the birth. In addition, in terms of reproduction and childbearing, the parents may feel that they have failed and are inadequate due to their apparent inability to produce a perfect child. This may mean that they view the situation as the 'loss' of the perfect baby which they had hoped for and therefore psychological processes normally associated with loss and bereavement become relevant in this context (see Paul March and Clare Doherty in Chapter 24, this volume). Most research uses models which describe various stages of adaptation by which parents come to terms with the child's disability, e.g. denial, anger, depression, acceptance. There seems to be a consensus in the literature that a stage like models such as this is the most efficient way of conceptualizing parental responses and most researchers provide some variation on this basic theme with models which vary from three to five stages (Dale, 1996; Drotar et al., 1975; Mattson, 1972). The fact that there may be a 'denial' stage when the news is first broken to them, explains in part why parents often need to be told the same information on several occasions before it really 'sinks in'. While they are busy 'denying' that the situation is really happening to them and their child, they are unable to process and internalize the information efficiently. However, it is possible that parental reactions may not always develop through such rigidly defined stages and particularly not within clearly definable time constraints, e.g. Gath (1978) found that 90 per cent of parents of children with Down's syndrome were still grieving over the birth of their child six years later (see Maxwell, 1993 for a personal description of the sense of loss and the needs of the parents).

Obviously, any one of the psychological responses mentioned above is likely to result in particular behavioural outcomes which will affect the parents' relationship with their child, e.g. acceptance, over protection, over pressure or rejection, of which the first two are the most common (Bowley, 1967; Sheridan, 1965). In any event, consequences of feelings such as guilt, self blame and anxiety may disturb the pattern of parent–infant interaction (Bentovim, 1972).

Some research has addressed the issue of which factors might mediate the nature and intensity of the parental reaction and the subsequent degree of adaptation. Goddard and Rubissow (1977) suggest that parental shock is greater and recovery slower when the affected child is their first-born. Steinhauer et al. (1974) suggest that a variety of factors including prognosis affect parental adaptation. This finding presents additional problems because in many cases of learning disability a precise and accurate prediction of the child's potential cognitive and adaptive functioning cannot be made at birth. For example, children with

Down's syndrome appear to be a fairly homogenous group in terms of organic aetiology, but there are considerable individual differences between them in the level of functioning which they achieve. Therefore although parents seek reassurance or at least demand the 'truth', a realistic assessment of prognosis often, unfortunately, cannot be made at the same time as the initial information concerning the child's learning disability is conveyed to them.

Many families with children with learning disabilities have been disadvantaged by a wide range of social and economic factors in their environment (Russell, 1996). The services to alleviate these problems are sparse and often hard to identify. The need for information and advice or counselling is ongoing, but becomes more crucial at critical transition periods. Yet as Baldwin and Carlisle (1994) note, there is no connection between stress and support at periods of transition. As families often complain, services are rarely there when you need them. Moreover, the fragmentation of services often makes access difficult and can lead to feelings of disempowerment. Families encounter major difficulties in everyday life and for many respite care is an important and clearly identified need. Although one should note that respite care which involves removing an individual from their home environment might not be the best option. Nonetheless, only about 4 per cent of parents of disabled children receive respite care – despite the universally expressed wish for respite services in surveys of such families. Robinson (1987) argues that service providers need to offer a wider and more flexible range of services to the families of children with learning disabilities.

When considering the support systems that are offered to families with disabled children, Baldwin and Carlisle (1994) argue that the following four key questions need to be considered:

1.   Is there sufficient information for the families to make an informed choice?

2.   What are the feelings of the parents during assessments and interviews? It is important to recognize the emotional and social context of such encounters.

3.   What is the level of ongoing stress for the parents and families?

4.   What are the ways of involving those parents whose personal circumstances make it difficult for them to use parent networks and other community support systems for information, advice and practical help without additional support?

Discussion point
   °   At this point you should list the information you would collect and evaluate to identify suitable respite care for a profoundly disabled 12-year-old living in the community with their mother and two younger siblings. How would you collect the information to answer your questions?

Adolescence and issues of sexuality
The move from childhood to adulthood places a range of new demands on young people with learning disabilities. Having left full-time education, many young people with learning disabilities depend for their daily activities on segregated facilities, such as day centres and for their social lives on their parents (Aull, Davies and Jenkins, 1993). In general, these young people's lives are much more uniform than would be expected from their non-disabled peers.

Adolescence brings with it changes in physical maturity. The vast majority of young people will develop secondary sex characteristics and will need help in understanding these changes (e.g. menstruation and masturbation; see Fegan, Rauch and McCarthy, 1993). More individuals with learning disabilities are living in the community, marrying and raising children (Dowdney and Skuse, 1993). Education, counselling and support will be needed to help develop personally satisfying and socially acceptable relationships. Furthermore, recognizing that people with learning disabilities have sexual experiences with other people means recognizing there is a risk of contracting a sexually transmitted disease, including HIV.

One of the major problems facing young people with learning disabilities is having to come to terms with their growing awareness of their sexuality (McKinlay, 1996). As a result of their cognitive skills, people with learning disabilities are often regarded as perpetual children, therefore any expression of sexuality is seen as inappropriate. The sexuality of service users throws up tensions and ambiguities for staff and services as a whole. It often appears that family and professionals are colluding to protect these young adults from the normal expression of sexual feelings and behaviour (Fairbrother, 1983). However, as Craft and Craft (1985) note, 'Sexual ignorance is not bliss: it opens people to damaging and exploitative situations'.

Contraceptive needs also must be addressed. Occasionally individuals have been subjected to sterilization at the request of their carers, apparently without the informed consent of the individual concerned (e.g. Fairburn and Bowen, 1994). At present, the usual requirement is for the surgeon to satisfy him/herself that the patient understands what is involved in the procedure and what is known about the consequences of the intervention. This should occur for all medical interventions experienced by people with learning disabilities. The only exception to this ruling is when the patient is a minor. There may, of course, be situations when sterilization is the preferred course of action (after MacLean, 1979), but this should only be considered in the light of the individual's needs and appropriate counselling. Some individuals will choose to have children. Parents with learning disabilities are increasing as a group and their needs are often invisible to service providers. Parental competence will be significantly influenced by the decisions of professionals who support rather than inhibit positive parenting (Booth and Booth, 1993).

Although the numbers are small some people with learning difficulties have been infected with HIV. McCarthy and Thompson (1994) have argued that responsible safer sex education should not be conducted in isolation, but 'should ensure that people with learning disabilities have general information and skills regarding sex and sexuality'. Such situations require the practitioner to collect a variety of kinds of information to draw appropriate conclusions. A needs risk assessment is needed as is a detailed understanding of how the individual sees their sexual lives. Of course, as in all issues where choice is a component the client themselves will need to support to be empowered. As Fruin (1994) states, 'To deny or to attempt to hide the sexual needs, drives and feelings of people with learning disabilities is to repress a significant element of their personalities and to retreat to regarding them as second class citizens' (p.245). Reported rates of sexual abuse of children with disabilities and sexual assaults of adults with disabilities are high (Sobsey and Varnhagen, 1990). Once again, there is the need to understand special factors that contribute to the vulnerability of this group. Cultural beliefs, physical environments and factors related to the victim will all play an important role. Defencelessness, poor communication skills and lack of power are critical factors. Prevention is a major challenge for service providers.

Challenging behaviour

Challenging behaviour is the term that has come to replace 'behaviour problems'. There were sound ideological reasons for this change in terms. Effectively the problem is shifted from the individual to the service providers. A widely accepted definition is to be found in the King's Fund Report, *Facing the Challenge* (1987):

> severely challenging behaviour refers to behaviour of such intensity, frequency or duration that the physical safety of the person or others is likely to be placed in serious jeopardy, or behaviour which is likely to seriously limit or delay access to and frequent use of ordinary community facilities.

Estimates of the prevalence rates of difficult and disruptive behaviours vary considerably. Some authors suggest that 10–15 people with learning disability per 100,000 of the population present a serious challenge to services in the UK (Kiernan, 1987; Lewis *et al.*, 1987, cited in Emerson *et al.*, 1987), while others estimate rates of 31 per 100,000 (Kushlick, Blunden and Cox, 1973). Harris and Russell (1989) found evidence of 45.5 per 100,000 displaying aggressive behaviour in their district health authority survey. Problems of definition and a reliance on the records of service agencies have made accurate estimates difficult to establish. There is some evidence that the term challenging behaviour covers two quite different categories of behaviour: 'problem' and 'dangerous' behaviours. Problem behaviours tend to be frequently experienced but to pose few serious difficulties, e.g. verbal abuse, indecent exposure. Dangerous behaviours (e.g. arson, physical violence) are qualitatively different and fit into the first clause of the definition. These behaviours pose serious difficulties, but are relatively infrequent. Many such dangerous behaviours come within the powers of the criminal justice system and, as such, reflect a societal and consensual definition of the unacceptable. In fact, the presence of a learning disability increases the probability of an offending behaviour. In contrast, those problem behaviours that may limit the 'use of community facilities' are generally manageable within the local services. The management of problem behaviours requires a consistent approach from all professionals who work with an individual. Programmes should not be implemented in an *ad hoc* fashion as this may simply increase the existing problem. It may take a long time to see any effect so an agreed upon recording and evaluation is an essential part of any programme. Dangerous behaviours, sometimes, are outside the range of experience and skills of a local facility. It is for these behaviours that specialist inputs may be necessary (Hastings, Remington and Hopper, 1995; McGill, Clare and Murphy, 1996).

Ageing with a learning disability

Better provision means that more individuals are surviving into old age. This raises concerns for families, especially for parents where a son or daughter might survive them, and for social and medical services. As yet we have very little knowledge about the needs of elders who have a learning disability. Their needs will have to be addressed both in the community and in sheltered and residential accommodation.

In fact, the fastest growing group among people with a learning disability is that represented by the elderly. This group have been described as having a double jeopardy, that of age and learning disability. Anderson (1988) noted that the trend toward an increasingly aged population of individuals with learning disabilities is expected to continue well into the future, and this will have a marked impact on the models of residential care and support services provided.

There are very few studies of this population, perhaps surprisingly, because there are special problems for people aging with a learning disability. Older people with learning disabilities have higher mortality rates than their age matched contemporaries. There is suggestive data that indicates that there is an increased likelihood of decreased motor functioning, mobility and daily living skills in this population; also hearing loss (Cooke, 1988) and fractures (Jancar, 1989). Much of the data that exists reflects the patterns of ageing and the needs of a population that spent the majority, if not all of their lives in an institutional setting. More information will need to be collected to address the needs of individuals who live in the community using normalized services. Nursing services and nursing homes for older people will need to widen their range of skills and expertise to cope with these needs. In addition, preparing the individual for some of the changes of the later years, which include the loss of parents or primary carers, and possible moves to new settings, will demand special skills (Seed, 1996).

Care in the community

In many countries the large institutions that have traditionally provided living accommodation for people with learning disabilities have been replaced by the provision of residential accommodation within the community, with access to the facilities and resources offered in local areas (see Korman and Glennester (1990) for a British example). In the sections above the assumption has been that individuals with learning disabilities live in the community. Yet this is a relatively recent occurrence. Over the last 20 years there has been a gradual reduction of hospital-based support with a parallel development of community-based services. The shift from hospital-based to community-based living has forced providers to consider their clients' needs in a much broader fashion, and these needs are met in a multiplicity of different ways. The social system through which resources and personal support are made available to people with learning disabilities is diffuse and complex. At least three levels of provision are involved:

- formal, through statutory agencies like social work
- informal, through churches, lunch centres, etc.
- benefits, such as financial aid through care allowances.

The relationships between these levels causes serious gaps in service provision, and it is the client and their family who miss out. Comprehensive community-based services are still in their infancy. They need to be carefully supported if individuals are to lead as full a life as possible. Social workers often play a central role in the creation of plans for individuals and the development of community-based resources. Access to social networks is particularly important, and may need to be specifically structured, for example through the use of volunteer groups such as 'Circles of Friends' (Richardson and Ritchie, 1989). Increasingly, there are opportunities for people with learning disabilities to live independently, to work, to attend college courses and clubs in addition to segregated day centres (Seed, 1996). Yet often, people are not aware that these opportunities exist, and the identification of the appropriate resources at the appropriate times becomes a critical issue.

Discussion point

° List the advantages and disadvantages of providing community care for people with learning disabilities. What procedures could you, as a social care professional, develop to ensure that your area team provided appropriate and accessible community resources for people with learning disabilities and their families?

It should be clear from this review that a social care professional's career will inevitably lead to contact with an individual with learning disabilities. This may occur at all stages of the life span, from birth to old age. The consequences of the disability and the individual's needs will change according to their age, as illustrated in Table 14.1.

Table 14.1 Behavioural Characteristics of Learning Disabled People Throughout the Life Span

| Type | *Characteristics from birth to adulthood* | | |
	Birth through Five	Six through Twenty	Twenty-one and Over
Mild (IQ 53–69)	Often not noticed as delayed by casual observer but is slower to walk, feed him- or herself, and talk than most children	Can acquire practical skills and master reading and arithmatic to a third- to sixth-grade level with support. Can be guided toward social conformity.	Can usually achieve adequate social vocational and self-maintenance skills, may need occasional guidance and support when under unusual social or economic stress.
Moderate (36–52)	Noticeable delays in motor development, especially in speech; responds to training in various self-help activities.	Can learn simple communication, elementary health and safety habits, and simple manual skills; does not progress in functional reading and maths.	Can perform simple tasks under sheltered conditions; participate in simple recreation; can travel alone in familiar places; usually incapable of self-maintenance.
Severe (20–35)	Marked delay in motor development; little or no communication skill; may respond to training in elementary self-help, such as self-feeding.	Usually walks, barring specific disability; has some understanding of speech and some response, can profit from systematic habit support.	Can conform to daily routines and repetitive activities; needs continuing direction and supervision in protective environment.
Profound (below 20)	Gross disability; minimal capacity for functioning in sensorimotor areas; needs nursing care.	Obvious delays in all areas of development; shows basic emotional responses; may respond to skillful training in use of legs, hands, and jaws; needs close supervision.	May walk, need nursing care, have primitive speech, usually benefits from regular physical activity; incapable of self-maintenance.

If work is to be done effectively, it is important that professionals understand both the criteria for diagnosing a learning disability and the social and cognitive consequences of such a diagnosis.

Empowering People with Learning Difficulties

People with learning disabilities have traditionally been marginalized in the communities in which they live. Their day-to-day experiences have been restricted by social expectations and social structures, as well as their own individual patterns of impairment. To increase opportunities for people to realize their potential and take a full part in society, it is necessary to change aspects of physical and social environments, as well as the skill levels of individuals. This means that consideration must be given to ways in which the community is organized to support the participation of people with learning disabilities. Nowadays, development and evaluation of community services are commonly based on the 'five accomplishments' identified by O'Brien and Tyne (1981): the development of competence and choice, relationships, community presence, and respect and dignity. The advocacy movement (Whittaker, 1996) has been very influential in promoting the direct involvement of users in determining the course of their own lives, and monitoring service provision. Pressure groups such as 'Values into Action' and 'People First' have identified priorities for action as:

- speaking out and taking control of our lives
- a home of my own
- holidays
- jobs and money
- making friends. (Speake and John 1994)

Advocacy

- Self-advocacy and citizen advocacy offer ways of supporting people in achieving these goals

    Self-advocacy: People involved in self-advocacy groups empower each other in developing the skills to make their wishes known, often including training in assertiveness and social skills.

    Citizen-advocacy: Citizen advocates formally represent people with learning difficulties who are unable to communicate independently. Their task is to get to know the person, and try to establish what they want to happen in any given situation.

Advocating for yourself or for someone else is not straightforward, and there are a number of obstacles to be overcome. There is often a degree of conflict to be resolved when the course of action demanded by an individual or group goes against the views of parents or staff. Care also needs to be taken that someone who is advocating for another person is not inappropriately projecting their own needs. It can be seen that two factors are fundamental to the success of advocacy: the ability to communicate effectively, and positive experience in making choices and expressing personal autonomy. This should begin as early as possible in the life of a child with a learning disability. Several practical approaches may be found in Coupe O'Kane and Smith (1994) and Sands and Wehmeyer (1996).

There is increasing recognition that people with learning difficulties should have the opportunities to lead rich and fulfilling lives, actively participating in the community through supported employment, leisure pursuits and exercising citizenship. For example, the organization 'Values into Action' recently ran a conference (*Making it Happen*) to explore how people have become involved in tenant participation schemes, and in complaints procedures. There are many artistic and drama projects run locally and nationally, which develop people's creativity (Hogg and Cavet, 1995; Segal, 1990).

The ability to participate actively is crucially dependent on *access*, both in a physical sense (to transport and buildings) and in the sense of information. In many areas, people are experimenting with providing information about services in graphic symbol form for people who cannot read text. In the Somerset Total Communication Project, the authority is working across disciplines to develop an integrated policy in communication, with basic training in signing and use of symbols for all care staff. Use of computer software such as *Writing with Symbols* (produced by Widgit) has made this process more feasible. A conference run jointly by Mencap and Westminster College (*Getting it Clear*, May 1996) made recommendations that symbol use be developed more widely across the country.

The role of technology

Advances in technology are making an increasing contribution to enabling people with learning disabilities to be actively involved in the community and controlling their own lives (Bozic and Murdoch, 1996). Environmental controls allow electrical equipment to be operated via remote switch control, multimedia on computers provide access to information, and imaginative ways of putting people in touch with one another are being explored via the Internet and video newsletters. Specialized software involving combinations of symbols, pictures and words, and talking word processors provide ways for people to express their ideas in writing (Carpenter and Detheridge, 1994). Video is also increasingly being used to inform people about a range of issues, from citizenship to relationships, to basic practical skills (see resource list).

The Social Care Professional's Role Revisited

Learning disabilities are characterized by difficulties in cognition, language and social adaptation. The presence of a learning disability carries with it a range of associated risks. These risks include prejudice, limited choice and vulnerability. Social carers have both a professional and statutory duty to address the associated risks. The statutory duty is enshrined in the *Children's Act* (1989). The *Children's Act* restored the leadership in providing services to children and their families to social services departments, and requires that 'every local authority shall have services designed to: minimize the effect on disabled children within their area of disability, and to give such children the opportunity to lead lives which are as normal as possible' (1989, schedule 2, paragraph 6). The professional responsibility covers the range of needs experienced by individuals and their families. For these duties to be met, it is important to consider both the specific difficulties that may be experienced and the wider dilemmas that might ensue from these difficulties. Such a problem solving approach requires that practitioners be aware of potential points of vulnerability (such as adolescence) and the range of services that are provided and that can be developed.

Summary

The ability for professionals to enhance the life opportunities of clients with learning disabilities depends upon both general and specific competencies. In relation to clients with learning difficulties, it is important that social care professionals understand the range of client needs and have access to the resources to develop their skills and expertise. In this chapter we have outlined factors that impinge on the lives of children and adults with learning disabilities. The nature of the difficulties experienced in cognition, language and social skills were discussed and the possible impact of these difficulties on daily living considered. How these factors change over the life-span and in different contexts was examined. The possible roles of the social care professional were outlined and a list of resources to help meet these complex and varied roles is provided at the end of the chapter.

Directory of Resources

British Institute of Learning Disabilities (BILD) Wolverhampton Rd, Kidderminster, Worcs. D410 3PP
Training, publications, information on all aspects of learning disability.

Council for Disabled Children, 8 Wakley St, London, EC1V 7QE
Part of the National Children's Bureau. Promotes the interests of children with disabilities and SEN.

Disabled Living Foundation, 380–384 Harrow Rd, London W9 2HU
Provides up-to-date information on all aspects of living with a disability. Database – living equipment.

Down's Syndrome Association, 155 Mitcham Rd, Tooting, London, SW17 9PG
Support for new parents. Advice. Sets up local groups.

ENABLE (formerly SSMH), 6th Floor, 7 Buchanan St, Glasgow, G1 3HL
Information, publications, legal advice, advocacy services, community services, i.e. holidays, employment support, etc.

The Family Fund Trust, P O Box 50, York, YO1 2ZX
Makes grants to families with children under 16 with severe disabilities. Funded by government.

Norah Fry Research Centre, 3 Priory Road, Bristol, RS8 1TX
Promoting family-based STC for children and adults. Information service, conferences, lobbying.

Gateway – National Federation of Gateway Clubs, 123 Golden Lane, London, EC1Y 0RT

Makaton Vocabulary Development Project, 31 Firwood Drive, Camberley, Surrey, GU15 3QD
Training courses, resource materials, research information user membership.

Mencap, 123 Golden Lane, London, EC1Y 0RT
Promotes awareness. Activities include campaigning, services, information publications.

Mencap – Profound Intellectual and Multiple Disabilities Section, Yewing School, Central Rd, West Didsbury, Manchester, M20 4ZA
Publications, information, advice, training (Maggie Morgan – Co-ordinator).

National Autistic Society, 276 Willesden Lane, London, NW2 5RB

Information, advice and support. Improve awareness, training, research, educational and support services.

NAPSAC Department of Learning Disabilities, E Floor, South Block, Notts University Medical School, Queens Medical Centre, Nottingham, NG7 2UH
Protection from sexual abuse of adults and children with LD. To provide a national voice on this issue.

PAMIS (Profound and Multiple Impairment Service), White Top Research Unit, Frankland Building, The University, Dundee, DD1 4HN
Information and training for parents and professionals.

People First London Boroughs, Instrument House, 207–215 King's Cross Rd, London, WC1X 9DB
Promotes self-advocacy and empowerment. Information, training and advice.

Anthony Quinn and Co, 21 Southampton Row, London, WC1
Lawyers for persons with a learning disability – wills, trusts, education and civil rights.

Respond 3rd Floor, 24–32 Stephenson Way, Euston, London, NW1 2DP
Therapeutic service for people with LD who have been sexually abused and those who sexually offend.

SCOPE, 12 Park Crescent, London, W1N 4EQ
National charity for people with cerebral palsy. Local groups. Freephone helpline 0800 626216.

Sense – National DeafBlind Rubella Assoc, 11–13 Clifton Terrace, Finsbury Park, London, N4 3SR
Family/professional support. Magazine, holidays, residential rehab centres and long-term group homes.

Skill – National Bureau for Students with Disabilities, 336 Brixton Rd, London, SW9 7AA
Dedicated telephone number 0171 978 9890, Mon–Fri 1.30–4.30pm. Advice for students with disabilities. Newsletter.

SPOD, 286 Camden Rd, London, N7 0BJ
Association to aid the sexual and personal relationships of people with a disability.

Values into Action Oxford House, Derbyshire St, London, E2 6HG
Campaigning group for the rights of people with learning disabilities. Internet: http://www.demon.co.uk/via/

Web Sites

http://www.familyvillage.wisc.edu/ (American, but has good information of a variety of syndromes)
http://www.bris.ac.uk/depts/NorahFry/ (latest research)
http://www.peoplefirst.org.uk/ (Northampton 'people first' and good links to other 'people first' sites)
http://www.shef.ac.uk/nhcon (mental health and learning disabilities)
http://www.open.gov/doh/dhhome.htm (Department of Health)

Access Technology and Special Needs in General

NCET, Fastforward Project Widgets, 102 Radford Rd, Leamington Spa, Coventry, CV31 1LF.
The Advisory Unit, Computers in Education, 126 Great North Road, Hatfield, Herts, AL9 5JZ.

Augmentative and Alternative Communication

ISAAC: The International Society of Alternative and Augmentative Communication. British Section (Communication Matters) ansaphone 01254-673303. Membership, c/o Caroline Grey, ACE Centre, Ormerod School, Waynfleete Road, Headington, Oxford.

Technology: Multimedia and video projects; Fast Forward c/o Mental Health Media Council, 356 Holloway Road, London N7 6PA.

Extending Horizons – ideas for using educational technology for pupils with learning difficulties. Available from Imagination Technology Publications, Sterndale House, Litton, Derbyshire, SK17 8QU.

Further Reading

Drew, C., Hardman, M. and Logan, D. (1996) *Mental Retardation.* Englewood Cliffs, NJ: Prentice Hall.
Seed, P. and Kaye, G. (1994) *Handbook for Assessing and Managing Care in the Community.* London: Jessica Kingsley.

References

Allen, J. Cockerill, H., Davies, E., Fuller, P., Jolleff, N., Larcer, J., Nelms, G. and Winyard, S. (1992) *Augmentative Communication: More than just Words.* ACE Centre, Ormerod School, Waynfleete Road, Headington, Oxford.

Anderson, D. (1988) 'Elderly mentally retarded persons: policy issues and trends.' *VIIIth Congress of IASSMD.* Dublin.

Aull, D.C. and Jenkins, R. (1993) 'Young people with learning difficulties: the transition to adulthood.' *Social Care Research Findings, 35.*

Baldwin, S. and Carlisle, J. (1994) *Social Support for Disabled Children and their Families: A Review of the Literature.* Social Work Service Inspectorate. Edinburgh: HMSO.

Baxter, C., Nadirshaw, Z., Poonia, K. and Ward, L. (1990) *Double Discrimination. Issues and Services for People with Learning Difficulties from Black and Ethnic Minority Communities.* London: King's Fund Centre/Commission for Racial Equality.

Beeghly, M. and Cicchetti, D. (1987) 'An organisational approach to symbolic development in children with Down Syndrome.' In D. Cicchetti and M. Beeghly (eds) *Symbolic Development in Atypical Children. New directions for child development.* San Francisco, CA: Jossey Bass.

Bellugi, U., van Hoek, K. Lillo-Martin, D. and O'Grady, L. (1988) 'Disassociation between language and cognitive functions in Williams Syndrome.' In D. Bishop and K. Mogford (eds) *Language Development in Exceptional Circumstances.* Edinburgh: Churchill Livingstone.

Bentovim, A. (1972) 'Handicapped pre-school children and their families: effects on child's early emotional development.' *British Medical Journal, 3,* pp.634–637.

Beukelman, D. and Mirenda, P. (1992) *Augmentative and Alternative Communication: Management of Severe Communication Disorders in Children and Adults.* Baltimore, MD: Paul Brookes.

Bicklen, D. (1990) 'Communication unbound: Autism and praxis.' *Harvard Educational Review, 60,* 291–314.

Booth, T. and Booth, W. (1993) 'Parenting with learning difficulties: lessons for practitioners.' *British Journal of Social Work, 23,* 459–480.

Bowley, A. (1967) 'A follow up study of 64 children with cerebral palsy.' *Development Medicine and Child Neurology, 9,* 172–182.

Bozic, N. and Murdoch, H. (1996) *Learning through interaction: technology and children with multiple disabilities.* London: David Fulton.

Broman, S., Nichols, P., Shaughnessy, P. and Kennedy, W. (1987) *Retardation in Young Children.* Hillsdale, NJ: Erlbaum.

Campione, J.C., Brown, A.L. and Ferrara, R.A. (1982) 'Mental retardation and intelligence.' In R.J. Sternberg (ed.) *Handbook of Human Intelligence.* Cambridge: Cambridge University Press.

Carpenter, B. and Detheridge, T. (1994) 'Writing with symbols.' *Support for Learning, 9,* 27–32.

Chaudhury, A. (1988) 'How special is special?' *Issue.* Spring.

Clare, I.C.H. and Gudjonsson, G.H. (1993) 'Interrogative suggestibility, confabulation and acquiescence in people with mild learning disabilities (mental handicap): Implications for reliability during police interrogations.' *British Journal of Clinical Psychology, 32,* 295–301.

Cooke, L. (1988) 'Hearing loss in the mentally handicapped: a study of its prevalence and association with ageing.' *British Journal of Mental Subnormality, 34,* 112–116.

Coulter, W.A. and Morrow, H.W. (eds) (1978) *Adaptive Behaviour: Concepts and Measurement.* New York: Grune and Stratton.

Coupe O'Kane, J. and Smith, B. (1994) *Taking Control: Enabling People with Learning Difficulties.* London: David Fulton.

Craft, A. and Craft, M. (1985) 'Sexuality and personal relationships.' In M. Craft., J. Bicknell and S. Hollins (eds) *Mental Handicap: A Multidisciplinary Approach.* London: Balliere Tindall.

Dale, N. (1996) *Working with Families of Children with Special Needs: Partnership and Practice.* London: RKP

Dockrell, J.E., Gaskell, G., Rehman, H. and Normand, C.E.M. (1993) 'Service provision for people with mild learning disabilities and challenging behaviour.' In C. Kiernan (ed.) *Research to Practice? Implications of Research on the Challenging Behaviour of People with a Learning Disability.* Avon: BILD.

Dockrell, J.E. and McShane, J. (1993) *Children's Learning Difficulties: A cognitive approach.* Oxford: Blackwell.

Dowdney, L. and Skuse, D. (1993) 'Parenting provided by adults with mental retardation.' *Journal of Child Psychology and Psychiatry, 34,* 25–47.

Drillien, C.M., Jameson, S. and Wilkson, E.M. (1966) 'Studies in mental handicap, Part 1: Prevalence and distribution by clinical type and severity of defect.' *Archive of Disease in Childhood, 41,* 528–538.

Drotar, D., Baskiewicz, I.N., Kennell, J. and Klaus, M. (1975) 'The adaptation of parents to the birth of an infant with a congenital malformation: a hypothetical model.' *Pediatrics, 56,* 5, 710–717.

Emerson, E., Barrett, S., Bell, C., Cummings, R., Toogood, A. and Mansell, J. (1987) *Developing Services for People with Severe Learning Difficulties and Challenging Behaviours.* University of Kent at Canterbury, Institute of Social and Applied Psychology.

Enderby, P. and Davies, P. (1989) 'Communication disorders: planning a service to meet the needs.' *British Journal of Disorders of Communication 24,* 301–332.

Fairbrother, P. (1983) 'The parent's viewpoint.' In A. Craft, and M. Craft, (eds) *Sex Education and Counselling for Mentally Handicapped People.* pp.95–109. Tunbridge Wells: Costello Press.

Fegan, L. Rauch, A. and McCarthy, W. (1993) *Sexuality and People with Intellectual Disability. Second edition.* Sydney: Maclennan and Petty.

Fairburn, G. and Bowen, M. (1994) 'Harm, self-harm and hysterectomy.' *SLD Experience, 8,* 13.

Fruin, D. (1994) 'Almost equal opportunities ... developing personal relationships guidelines for social service department staff working with people with learning disabilities.' In A. Craft (ed) *Practice Issues in Sexuality and Learning Disabilities.* London: Routledge.

Fryers, T. (1984) *The Epidemiology of Severe Intellectual Impairment: The Dynamics and Prevalence.* London: Academic Press.

Gath, A. (1978) *Down's Syndrome and the Family: The Early Years.* London: Academic Press.

Gillham, L.B. (1986) *Handicapping Conditions in Children.* London: Croom Helm.

Goddard, J. and Rubissow, J. (1977) 'Meeting the needs of handicapped children and their families.' *Child: Care, Health and Development, 3,* 261–273.

Grossman, H. (ed) (1983) *Classification in Mental Retardation. Third edition.* Washington DC: American Association of Mental Retardation.

Grove, N. and Park, K. (1996) *Odyssey Now.* London: Jessica Kingsley.

Harris, J. (1988) *Language Development in Schools for Children with Severe Learning Difficulties.* Beckenham: Croom Helm.

Harris, P. and Russell, O. (1989) *The Prevalence of Aggressive Behaviouramong People with Learning Difficulties (mental handicap) in a Single Health Authority: Interim Report.* University of Bristol: Norah Fry Research Centre.

Hasan, P. and Messer, D. (1997) 'Stability or instability in early cognitive abilities of children with Down's Syndrome.' *British Journal of Development Disabilities, 43,* 93–107.

Hastings, R., Remington, B. and Hopper, G. (1995) 'Experienced and inexperienced health care workers' beliefs about challenging behaviours.' *Journal of Intellectual Disability Research, 39,* 474–483.

Hogg, J. and Cavet, J. (1995) *Leisure Activities for People with PMLD.* London: Chapman Hall.

Jancar, J. (1989) 'Fractures in older people with mental handicap.' *Australia and New Zealand Journal of Developmental Disabilities, 15,* 321–327.

Kahmi, A. and Masterson, J. (1989) 'Language and cognition in mentally handicapped people: Last rites for the difference-delay controversy.' In M. Beveridge, G. Conti-Ramsden and I. Leudar (eds) *Language and Communication in Mentally Handicapped People.* London: Chapman Hall.

Kail, R. (1990) *The Development of Memory in Children. Third edition.* New York: Freeman.

Kellmer-Pringle, M., Butler, N.R. and Davie, R. (1966) *11,000 Seventeen Year-Olds.* London: National Children's Bureau.

Korman, N., and Glennester, H. (1990) *Hospital Closure.* Milton Keynes: Open University Press.

Kushlick, A., Blunden, R. and Cox, G. (1973) 'A method of rating behaviour characteristics for use in large scale surveys of mental handicap.' *Psychological Medicine 3,* 466–478.

Kyle, J. and Woll, B. (1985) *Sign Language: The study of deaf people and their language.* Cambridge: Cambridge University Press.

Luckasson, R. (1992) *Mental Retardation. Definition, Classification and System of Supports. Ninth edition.* Washington, DC: American Association on Mental Retardation.

MacKeith, R. (1973) 'The feelings and behaviour of parents of handicapped children.' *Developmental Medicine and Child Neurology, 15,* 524–527.

MacLean, R. (1979) 'Sexual problems and family planning needs of the mentally handicapped in residential care.' *British Journal of Family Planning, 4,* 4, 13–15.

McCarthy, M. and Thompson, D. (1994) 'HIV/AIDS and safer sex work with people with learning disabilities.' In A. Craft (ed.) *Practice Issues in Sexuality and Learning Disabilities.* London: Routledge.

McConkey, R. (1996) 'Seen through a glass darkly.' In P. Mittler and V. Sinason (eds) *Changing Policy and Practice for People with Learning Disabilities.* London: Cassell.

McGill, P., Clare, I. and Murphy, G. (1996) 'Understanding and responding to challenging behaviour: From theory to practice.' *Tizard Learning Disability Review. 1,* 9–20.

McKinlay, I. (1996) 'Discussion: Parental concerns about puberty and sexuality in young people with severe learning disability.' In J. Coupe O'Kane and B. Smith (eds) *Whose Choice? Contentious Issues for those Working with People with Learning Difficulties.* London: David Fulton. pp.38–47.

Mattson, A. (1972) 'The chronically ill child: A challenge to family adoption.' *Medical College of Virginia Quarterly, 8,* 171–175.

Maxwell, V. (1993) 'Look through the parents' eyes: helping parents of children with a learning disability.' *Professional Nurse,* 200–202.

Messer, D. (1994) *The Development of Communication: From Social Interaction to Language.'* Chichester: Wiley.

Mittler, P. (1979) *People Not Patients: Problems and Policies in Mental Handicap.* London: Methuen.

Moffitt, T.E., Caspi, A., Harkness, A.R. and Silva, P.A. (1993) 'The natural history of change in intellectual performance: Who changes? How much? Is it meaningful?' *Journal of Child Psychology and Psychiatry, 34,* 455–506.

O'Brien, J. and Tyne, A. (1981) *The Principle of Normalisation: A Foundation for Effective Services.* London: CMH.

Owens, R. (1989) 'Cognition and language in the mentally retarded population.' In M. Beveridge, G. Conti-Ramsden and I. Leudar (eds) *Language and Communication in Mentally Handicapped People.* London: Chapman Hall.

Pitcairn, T. and Wishart, J. (1994) 'Reactions of young children with Downs Syndrome to an impossible task.' *British Journal of Developmental Psychology, 12,* 4, 485–489.

Pritchard D.G. (1963) *Education of the Handicapped. 1760–1960.* London: Routledge and Kegan Paul.

Richards, C. and Reed, J. (1991) 'Your baby has Down's Syndrome.' *Nursing Times. 87,* 46, 60–61.

Richardson, A. and Ritchie, J. (1989) 'Developing friendships: enabling people with learning difficulties to make and retain friends.' London: Policy Studies Institute.

Robinson, C. (1987) 'Key issues for social workers placing children for family based respite care.' *British Journal of Social Work, 17,* 257–284.

Russell, P. (1996) 'Parents' voices: developing new approaches to family support and community development.' In P. Mittler and V. Sinason (eds.) *Changing Policy and Practice for People with Learning Disabilities.* London: Cassell.

Rutter, M., Tizard, J. and Whitmore, K., (eds) (1970) *Education, Health and Behaviour.* London: Longman.

Sands, D. and Wehmeyer, M. (1996) *Self-Determination Across the Life Span: Independence and Choice for People with Disabilities.* London: Paul Brookes/Jessica Kingsley.

Seed, P (ed.) (1996) *Day Services for People with Learning Disabilities.* London: Jessica Kingsley.

Segal, S. (ed) (1990) *Creative Arts and Mental Disability.* Oxford: AB Academic Publishers.

Sheridan, M.D. (1965) *The Handicapped Child and His Home.* London: National Children's Home.

Steinhauer, P.D., Mushin, D.N. and Rae-Grant, Q. (1974) 'Psychological aspects of chronic illness.' *Pediatric Clinics of North America, 21,* 4, 825–840.

Sobsey, D. and Varnhagen, C. (1990) 'Sexual abuse, assault and exploitation of individuals with disabilities.' In C. Bagley and R.J. Tomlinson (eds) *Child Sexual Abuse: Critical Perspectives on Prevention, Assessment and Treatment.* Toronto: Wall and Emerson.

Speake, B. and John, H. (1994) 'Increasing the personal effectiveness of adults in the community.' In J. Coupe O'Kane and B. Smith (eds) *Taking Control: Enabling People with Learning Difficulties.* London: David Fulton.

Stockdale, J.E. (1995) 'The self and media messages: match or mismatch?' In I. Markove and R.M. Farr (eds.) *Representations of Health, Illness and Handicap.* Switzerland: Harwood Academic Publishers.

Stow, L. and Selfe, L. (1989) *Understanding Children with Special Needs.* London: Unwin Hyman.

Van der Gaag, A. and Dormandy, K. (1992) *Communication and Adults with Learning Disabilities: New Map of an Old Country.* London: Whurr.

Von Tetzchner, S. (1997) 'Historical issues in intervention research: hidden knowledge and facilitating techniques in Denmark.' *European Journal of Disorders of Communication 32,* 1–18.

Von Tetzchner, S. and Martinsen, H. (1994) *An Introduction to Sign Teaching and the use of Communication Aids.* London: Whurr.

Warnock, H.M. (1978) *Special Educational Needs: Report at the Committee of Enquiry into the Education of Handicapped Children and Young People.* London: HMSO.

Whittaker, A. (1996) 'Self-advocacy.' In P. Mittler and V. Sinason (eds) *Changing Policy and Practice for People with Learning Disabilities.* London: Cassell.

Weiss, B., Weisz, J. and Bromfield, R. (1986) 'Performance of retarded and non retarded persons on information processing tasks: further tests of the similar structure hypothesis.' *Psychological Bulletin, 100,* 157–175.

Weisz, J., Yeates, K.O., and Zigler, E. (1982) 'Piagetian evidence and the developmental-difference controversy.' In E. Zigler and D. Balla (eds) *Mental Retardation: The Developmental-Difference Controversy.* Hillsdale, NJ: Erlbaum.

Wing, L. (1988) 'The autistic continuum.' In L. Wing (ed.) *Aspects of Autism: Biological Research.* London: Gaskell.

Wolfensberger, W. (1972) *Normalization: The Principles of Normalization in Human Services.* Toronto: National Institute of Mental Retardation.

Wolfensberger, W. (1975) *The Origins of our Institutional Models.* Syracuse, NY: Human Policy Press.

Zigler, E. and Hodapp, R.M. (1986) *Understanding Mental Retardation.* New York: Cambridge University Press.

CHAPTER 15

Child Abuse

Theories and Research

Dorota Iwaniec

Introduction

Since Henry Kempe and his colleagues drew attention to the Battered Child Syndrome in 1962, theorists, researchers and clinicians have explored the causes of child abuse and neglect. As a result, many explanations have been put forward from different schools of thought, each taking a rather narrow view and trying to fit this complicated phenomenon into a particular theoretical orientation. For a considerable time the medical-psychiatric model of the causation and treatment of child abuse was favoured, attributing the blame for its occurrence to the pathological personality structure of the mother and her history of being abused as a child. As time went on and better understanding of child abuse was acquired, it was realized that the causations of child maltreatment had many routes and could not be explained in a single way. New theories began to emerge embracing social, environmental, personal, interactional and child factors in the attempt to produce a realistic integrated explanation of the causation of child maltreatment. Practitioners, of whatever persuasion, operate within a certain theoretical framework, and use methods of intervention which derive from those theories (see Box 15.1). It is therefore imperative to understand how different theories explain the causation of child abuse especially as theories differ in the role they give to the abused, abuser, their families and the communities in which they live. Such differences have important implications for understanding and for the use of intervention methods (see Chapter 16). Each of the theories identified in Box 15.1 is reviewed in the following sections. These theories are frequently used by social workers and related professionals to explain child abuse. The discussion of theories moves from a description of models of individual processes to models which are concerned with the systems that influence individual behaviour, and finally integrative models are outlined.

Traditional Theories and their Link to Child Abuse

Psychodynamic theory

Many social workers and other professionals describe their theoretical orientation as being psychodynamic. The term covers theories of personality, and unconscious mental processes and therapies that concern themselves both with identification of motives and assume the

Box 15.1 Theories and Causes of Child Abuse	
Theory	*Causation*
Psychodynamic	pathological personality of the mother and history of being abused as a child
Attachment	hostile, rejective, or indifferent mothering
Interactionist	special and difficult child's characteristics (e.g. temperament) make child difficult to rear and enjoy
Social learning	faulty reinforcement and modelling of aggressive behaviour is learned and transmitted from one generation to another. Faulty perceptions, attribution attitudes towards the child
Personal construct	parents construe the child as wicked, deliberately annoying, in need of punishment
Family dysfunction	lack of coherent organization, faulty attribution-distribution, and breakdown of communication. Abuse of power, violence
Social/ecological	social/environmental factors, poverty, unemployment, lack of resources, single parents, punitive child rearing
Feminist	gender/power imbalance, male dominance over female and children
Children's rights	violation of the basic human rights
Integrated model	Situational and structural stresses, insecure and anxious relationships, early social experiences and being abused as children, personality traits, culture and community values

significance of transference relationships (emotional contact and communication between people). The main argument is that people mentally adapt their instinctive drives to the demands and requirements of their social circumstances. Through this process they develop certain personality characteristics for life which influence their relationships with other people. According to Freud, personality is the pattern of thoughts, emotions and intellectual skills that makes a person unique. He believed that much of personality is unconscious and these hidden parts are responsible for the 'errors' and 'slips' which result in maladaptive behaviour.

A key concept in understanding how personality develops is libido, an instinctual source of energy. Libido is sexual energy, a life-force that propels people to act in ways for purposes of reproducing the species. Freud firmly believed that sexual energy was what prompted people to care for one another, even if the caring did not appear 'sexual' as such: throughout life the source of all actions is libido, and the aim is always to relieve tension. Freud thought that personality consisted of three parts: the id, ego and superego:

- the id is present in infancy as a primitive drive

- the ego emerges later, operating according to the reality principle, consisting of rational activities like learning, thinking, perceiving and evaluating

- the superego is the moral watch-dog over the entire personality. This is the centre of individual conscience as well as the model of a well-developed personality (sometimes called the 'ego ideal').

It is said that both the conscience and the ego ideal are formed by parental teaching. It is postulated that child abuse is the result of excessive superego demands and the breakdown of internal self-control. Green *et al.* (1987) and Steele and Pollock (1968) argued that abused children are not encouraged and attended to, and, as a result, do not go through all the psycho-sexual stages, with the consequence that they are prevented from developing a healthy personality and are unable to relate appropriately to others. It is said that the mother has failed to identify with the mothering attribution, and instead directs the anger felt towards her parents at her child.

The internal organization (personality structure) is considered to be the most important factor for the child's development and safety. If that personality is disorganized the functioning of the parent might be at fault and can lead to child maltreatment. Such a person might deny or justify his/her action as a defence to protect the ego. The ego (or self) construct is seen by contemporary psychodynamic theorists as the central integrating aspect of a person, and any threat to its valuation and function is a vital threat to the very being of the individual. As a result several 'devices' (or mechanisms) are gradually accumulated by the self so as to soften anxieties and failure thereby protecting the integrity of the ego by increasing feelings of personal worth. All people use defence mechanisms, but when they are used inappropriately or to excess, with too great intensity or too inflexibly, they become maladaptive (see Box 15.2). To a great extent this is an unconscious process and is used to reduce tension. The reduction of immediate

---

Box 15.2 Defence Mechanisms

Abusive parental behaviour is believed to be linked in various ways to defence strategies. Emotional isolation, projection displacement, reaction formation and fantasy are some of them.

- *Emotional isolation.* The care-giver reduces the tension of need and anxiety by withdrawing into a shell of numbness and passivity, by lowering expectations, and by remaining emotionally uninvolved and detached. Abused children often use this escape to avoid further hurt. Emotionally neglectful parents are in a state of passivity and withdrawal from a child.

- *Projection* (so often seen in abusive-dysfunctional families). The feelings arising from parents' difficulties are unjustifiably attributed to the child. Projection helps parents to avoid conflict and guilt by finding a scape-goat and ascribing obnoxious, intolerable, and therefore unacceptable behaviour to the child, so the child carries the blame for all ills in the family.

- *Reaction formation.* Those who, for example, obsessively condemn sexual behaviour in others may well be having trouble with their own sexual inclinations. This can be seen in some child sexual-abuse cases. In children, the 'don't care' independent attitude may mask a craving for love, nurturance and a need for dependency.

- *Fantasy.* Helps to cope with stressful circumstances by denying reality and creating a world of fantasy. Children who day-dream a lot may be trying to compensate for or escape from unacceptable and painful realities of their lives, for example, caused in parental maltreatment.

---

discomfort increases the use of defence mechanisms. These processes allow an individual to make choices and carry out actions in order to avoid anxiety, pain, and other distress (Herbert, 1989).

Psychological treatments deriving from this theory are psychotherapy and counselling for parents aiming to help them develop better insight and understanding of what is going wrong in their lives, and to direct them to personality and behaviour change. Such change arises from the therapist–client relationship over a period of time. Helping children usually involves play-therapy, group-discussions and activities, and direct individual exploration of painful feelings and facilitation of healing processes.

Discussion points

- ° It is said that people with little insight do not respond to counselling. What methods would you use to increase parental awareness of their children's developmental needs?

- ° This theory blames the mother for the child's maltreatment. What arguments are being used to support such statements?

Attachment Theory

Attachment theory was first introduced by Bowlby in 1951, and further expanded and elaborated by him (1969, 1980). He hypothesized that the integration of early relationship experiences into an overall organization of attachment occurs through a representational or internal working model.

When Mary Ainsworth and her colleagues (1963) began to study child-to-mother attachment they hypothesized that individual differences in maternal sensitivity and emotional availability during the first year of life would be related to differences in the infant's security of attachment at one year. Attachment of child to mother was assessed in a situation unfamiliar to the child in the presence of the mother, and the child's reaction to separation from, and reunion with, the mother (see Chapter 11). As a result of extensive research carried out, secure attachment and two patterns of insecure attachment have been identified: anxious-avoidant and anxious-resistant pattern.

Anxious-avoidant infants treat the mother and stranger alike, and avoid the mother upon reunion. These children, it is said, have experienced hostile and rejective mothering (Belsky *et al.*, 1984). Anxious resistant infants show little curiosity about their surroundings, and they often struggle or become rigid when being comforted. It is suggested that both forms of anxiously attached infants are more difficult to care for, and in turn, their mothers have been found to be less sensitive and less responsive to their babies. In addition, it is known that abused and neglected children cling to their mothers and/or show negative effects like screaming, fear, apprehension and rigidity. Some research studies found that maltreatment during infancy produces an insecure attachment over a period of time that adversely affects the child's later intellectual and socio-emotional development (Ainsworth, 1980; Belsky *et al.* 1984). Insecure attachment sometimes predicts subsequent behavioural problems, control problems, conflict and struggles with care-givers, and creates seriously problematic peer relationships (Stroufe, 1983). Maltreated children with a history of insecure attachment, studied in the nursery, were noted by Stroufe (1983) to be less empathic, to have lower self-esteem, to be less socially competent, and to be less ego-resilient than children with the history of secure attachment. A study by Gaensbauer and Sands (1979) indicated that maltreated infants and toddlers exhibited sadness, apprehension, lethargy, irritability and other aspects of emotional withdrawal, inconsistent and unpredictable signals, indiscriminate sociability, ambiguity and ambivalence to engage with people and in activities, and were prone to anger and distress. These distorted effective communications were said to be the results of poor attachment which led to neglect and abuse.

A new pattern of attachment of the disorganized/disoriented type has been described by Main and Solomon (1986). This fourth type of attachment seems to be more prevalent in samples of high-risk infants. They found that some infants previously classified secure, avoidant or resistant, met criteria for the disorganized/disoriented group. These findings helped to resolve some of the unanswered questions such as why 40–50 per cent of abused and neglected infants were classified securely attached to their maltreating parents. The child here shows conflict behaviours, fear of the care-giver, confusion, disordered temporal sequences and stereotypes or other anomalous behaviour. Main and Hesse (1990) have proposed that disorganized attachment results from extremely unpredictable care-giver interactive behaviour. Conflict behaviour results because the source of security for the infant is also a source of fear. Crittenden and Bonvillian (1984) found that abusive mothers are active and interfering, whereas neglectful mothers are uninvolved and passive. The pattern of attachment in early infancy matches the pattern of maternal care with maltreated infants showing a high level of insecurity, indicated by their avoidance of the mother or their resistance behaviour towards her.

There is, however, no general agreement amongst theorists and researchers regarding validity of the 'strange situation test' (see Chapter 11) to measure secure and insecure attachment. In view of the studies by Thomas and Chess (1977), which emphasize that babies have individual temperamental characteristics that tend to persist, and of studies showing the clear effects of cultural patterns upon childhood responses to strange situations, the causal relationship claimed to have been found between parenting style and child's behaviour in a strange situation is not persuasive (Sutton, 1994). Crockenberg (1981) has investigated the effects upon the baby of two interacting variables: the infant's temperament and the degree of the support available to the mother. She found that insecure attachment was likely to occur only when the mother had both an irritable baby and perceived that she had low social support from family and friends.

Discussion point
- How do you think child care policies were influenced over the years by attachment and bonding theories? Discuss positives and negative effects of this doctrine.

Individual Interactionist Theory

Interactionist theorists explain child abuse and neglect in terms of aversive parent–child interaction. This involves demanding and often anger- provoking behaviour or special characteristics of the child. Accompanying such infant behaviour are inappropriate hostile or passive parental reactions when dealing with their child. It is assumed that parent–child interaction is a two-way process which powerfully affects the way parents and children relate to each other, perceive each other and influence each other's behaviour. The quality and quantity of mutual interaction is not only determined by parental behaviour towards the child, but also by the child's input (whether positive or negative). Many research findings demonstrate that children, by the nature of their physical or psychological make-up, can exert an influence on their parents' interactions and feelings (Gil, 1970; Schaffer and Emerson, 1964; Lynch and Roberts, 1977; Berkowitz, 1988; Iwaniec, 1995). Gil (1970) was the first to suggest that children who were abused by their parents may possess some characteristics which either attract abuse or make them more vulnerable to abuse. Lynch and Roberts (1977) in their study found prematurity and low birth-weight to be associated with abuse. Iwaniec's (1995) study on children of psychosocial short stature (i.e. whose growth and development are seriously curtailed due to severe emotional maltreatment) found their demanding and disturbed behaviour made them particularly vulnerable to parental rejection. Furthermore, these children were perceived by hospital, nurseries and school staff as unappealing and unrewarding. Friedrich's and Boroskin's (1976) review of complex reasons why a child may not fulfil the parents' expectations or demands, suggested that the child may in some way be regarded as 'special' and therefore coping with him or her is difficult. For example, the child may be perceived as suffering from a handicap, illness, prematurity, poor sleeping and eating pattern, excessive crying, physical unattractiveness and difficult to care for.

It is postulated that mismatch of temperamental attributes between parents and child may lead to interactional clashes, and over time to maltreatment (Herbert, 1989; Wolfe, 1985). Parents who have low stress tolerance and quick negative reactivity, when caring for a persistently crying and wakeful baby, may be at potential risk of abusing their child. An easy child is unlikely to produce similar reactions from parents, and will be perceived as rewarding to rear and enjoyable to be with. The child's characteristics and its responses can arouse pride, or alternatively, resentment, guilt or helplessness in parents, and what might have started (in some cases) as a willing and well-motivated parenthood might end up in abuse and neglect. This theory does not see the causation of child abuse as parental personality problems, early experiences or faulty learning, but rather as the current problematic interactions and relationships influenced by difficulties in bringing up, for one reason or another, a demanding child.

Learning Theories

Social learning theory owes its origins to the work of Albert Bandura (1977). This theory built on, and expanded, both operant conditioning theory developed by Skinner and the classical conditioning theory of Pavlov. These theorists adhered strictly to the study of how behaviour, whether adaptive or maladaptive, is learned and maintained. Their main explanation of how behaviour is learned is the external environment (see Box 15.3).

Box 15.3 Operant and Classical Conditioning

In *operant conditioning*, behaviour occurs in response to stimuli, events, cues or signals that tell the individual that a particular response (behaviour) is likely or not likely to be rewarded and whether favourable consequence will be forthcoming. The pattern and frequency of responses is conditional on the presence of stimuli in the environment which promises the delivery of rewards to the individual or the removal of aversive stimuli (i.e. negative reinforcement). Favourable responses will increase behaviours, while unfavourable responses will decrease behaviours. Operant conditioning is now a well-established framework which explains some human behaviour and which informs therapeutic methods. Operant conditioning theory has relevance to child physical-abuse cases. For example, parents who punish a child because of irritating and anger-provoking behaviour, might be unwittingly reinforcing the very behaviour that they are concerned and angry about, because parental attention may be a form of positive reinforcement.

Stimulus-contingent reinforcement, a model of learning developed by Pavlov (1927) is well known and is referred to as *classical conditioning*. A stimulus (e.g. food, the unconditioned stimulus) is presented and reflexly elicits a response (e.g. the production of saliva at the sight of food). A previously neutral stimulus (e.g. a bell) is repeatedly paired with the first stimulus and gradually acquires its response eliciting properties. In this way the response of the organism can be conditioned to the second stimulus (the conditioned stimulus). Emotional reactions of phobic intensity can be brought about by classically conditioned aversive stimuli. This theory provides useful information on how fears, avoidance behaviour and acute anxiety can be developed and maintained in some child abuse cases (e.g. a child might develop food-avoidance behaviour due to harsh handling, force-feeding, screaming and shouting, smacking, and the high level of parents' anxiety during the process of feeding). The child associates (pairs) eating with painful, anxiety-provoking experiences, and reacts to eating with panic, refuses to eat and, as a consequence, fails to thrive. Equally, women who were brutally sexually abused as children would associate a sexual relationship with painful experiences, and freeze when exposed to sexual activity.

Negative reinforcement involves the increase in the frequency of behaviour which avoids an unpleasant event. Unlike punishment, it activates a response rather than deactivates a response.

Social-learning Theory

Social learning as conceived by Bandura (1977) embraces both operant and classical conditioning, but unlike other traditional learning theorists, Bandura opened the so-called 'black box' of the mind to report on cognitive processes. Bandura's expansion of learning theory included the role of cognition, abstraction and integration. This emphasis led him to include observational learning and modelling as active components in development, learning and behaviour. He considered that observation and modelling were key learning elements in these bi-directional interactional processes between a person, his or her behaviour and others' behaviour, and the environment. He conceptualized the mechanisms of observational learning as attention, retention, motor-reproduction and motivation. The cognitive processes of thinking, perceiving, observing, information storage and retrieval and decision-making are firmly grounded in Bandura's conceptualization of learning processes. He postulated that the control over behaviour shifts from sources external to the individual to internally controlled (so-called 'locus of control') which can be self-regulated.

Social-learning theorists postulate that harsh and abusive parenting styles can be transmitted across generations. They argue that such parenting influences the next generation through a process of modelling and reinforcement. Patterson (1982) has provided convincing evidence that parenting style characterized by aggression, threats and hostility tends to train children in the use of aggressive behaviour by modelling such action. These children learn to be aggressive by being exposed to an aggressive model of parenting. The child's environment in these families is characterized by many examples of aggressive behaviour, manifesting itself in physical and verbal abuse between members of the family. The parents' control of the child's behaviour is also often inappropriate in that their response to deviant (including aggressive) behaviour in the child is not only likely to involve physical punishment (which will be imitated), but also to be inconsistent and ineffective.

Thus, aggressive and undesirable interactions are not reduced in this type of environment. The child also learns that he or she can control the punishing behaviour of the parents by delivering punishment of his or her own. The result is a style of family interaction that is characterized by the trading of responses that are unpleasant for other family members, so called aversive behaviours, rather than by more subtle controls such as withdrawal of privileges or love. This style of interaction is called the *coercive* family system. The aversive behaviours range in intensity from the relatively mild to the sort of intense punishment that are classified as child abuse.

Using this theoretical model in relation to physical abuse, Reid *et al.* (1981) conducted a study using abusive, non-abusive but distressed, and normal families. They found that abusive families had highly aversive parent–child interactions. All family members in abusive households showed higher rates of aversive behaviour than in the two other groups. When these data were analyzed in more detail, they showed that the abusive and aggressive interactions were more often between parent and child. Furthermore, child-abusive parents reported routinely employing more serious forms of physical punishment than non-abusive parents.

Application of cognitive theory principles to the understanding of child abuse has been debated (Azar and Siegal, 1990; Iwaniec, 1995). It is argued that unrealistic parental expectations and misattributions lead to abusive situations. Parents who perceive a child's behaviour as deliberately directed at them to hurt or to annoy will see the child as wicked and therefore in need of punishment. Physical abuse is related to the parental misinterpretation of the situation, inability to control anger and aversive parent–child interaction. Unrealistic expectations of the child's ability to perform or understand various tasks can lead to emotional and physical abuse. There are many examples of therapeutic procedures which arise from these broader perspectives and provide further understanding of the child abuse cases. Therapeutic methods within behavioural and cognitive psychotherapy include: stress-management, self-control, relaxation training, cognitive restructuring, modelling, rehearsal, reinforcement procedures, contract work, systematic desensitization and problem-solving. Gough (1993), in the review of research literature on physical abuse, reported some encouraging results when behavioural approaches were used. More recently, successful outcomes have been reported from studies of emotional abuse and non-organic failure-to-thrive (Iwaniec, *et al.* 1985b, 1991, 1995; Batchelor and Kerslake, 1990). Parent training of abusive parents is well documented (Callias, 1994). Behavioural approaches have also been used with sex offenders (Kelly, 1982; Maletzky, 1991).

Discussion point

- ° How does social-learning theory differ from those early learning theories of classical and operant conditioning?

Personal Construct Theory

The personal construct model developed by Kelly (1955) describes how people individually construe their lives and events around them (see also Chapter 18). This theory postulates that individuals are constantly trying to understand and predict events and make interpretations of what is happening and why. Kelly argues that if individuals are able to make sense of the world they live in, then they can make the necessary adaptations to changing circumstances. This means that each and every individual constructs in his or her thought-processes a model of events. The ways in which a person is construing or interpreting events and people lead to either appropriate, or with faulty constructs, inappropriate actions. The term 'personal construct system' emphasizes that every individual lives in his or her own unique world. People might appear to have similar construing processes, but essentially they are different, as each person's experiences and interpretations are also unique and only fully understood by that individual. This theory provides a better understanding of why people react differently to the same situation. Kelly argues that people are not necessarily in the same psychological situation: it only appears to the observer that this is the case. The experience may feel different according to the individual's construing system. Each may be reacting (as they see it) appropriately in the case of his/her individual situation as he or she interprets it. This theory has particular bearing on understanding and dealing with child abuse cases. For example, if parents construe a child as bad, deliberately behaving in a difficult way to hurt them, then they might construe smacking, shaking, shouting, etc. as an appropriate socialization method or punishment for coping with frustrating behaviour. Again, if parents construe a youngster as provocative and unworthy in sexual abuse cases, then it can lead to a sense of helplessness in the child and rejection of the child by parents. The constructs used by the parents might have originated from their own upbringing or recent experiences, forming their perceptions and understanding of a child's behaviour.

Discussion point

- ° Using the material in the previous sections, draw a table giving the name of each theory of perspective, who is mainly responsible for causing the abuse and why the abuse occurs.

Family Dysfunction Theory and Family Violence

In contrast to the previous explanations of abuse, family dysfunction theory emphasizes the process of family dynamics involving the behavioural interplay of each member of the unit and the way that these affect family unity and functioning. This family process perspective, exemplified by the model of intervention known as family therapy, shifts the focus for understanding problems from the individual's behaviour to the relationship within the family. In this view, many problems have their source in family behaviour patterns that are faulty or self-defeating (dysfunctional) in different ways. The family system approach based on Minuchin's (1974) theorizing has been adopted by contemporary family therapists (see also

Chapters 6 and 24). Systems-approach in family therapy derives from the concept of mutual causality or mutual influence, the relationship of events within the given framework, and from the familiar notion that the whole is greater than the sum of its parts. A system can be defined as an organized arrangement of elements consisting of a network of inter-dependent and co-ordinated parts that function as a unit. This arrangement is often referred to as the *coherence* of the family.

Of two sub-systems, one refers to the parents and the other to the children. Both emphasize the need for boundaries between parents and children to maintain a healthy climate for all family members. Improving communications and examining the relationships within the systems are the major therapeutic objectives. This model of thinking has particular implications in understanding and preventing child sexual abuse. In sexual abuse the boundaries between children and parents are crossed, and communication is arrested as a result of threats and general disorganization in family functioning. Bentovim *et al.* (1988b), on the basis of their work and research with sexually abusive families, postulate that child sexual abuse serves the function of keeping families together that would otherwise be separated. They further argue that it is possible for a sexual relationship of a father with his teenage daughter to compensate for the lost sexual and emotional relationship with his wife. They also acknowledge that the wife can be aware of what is happening but pretends that she is not. This collusion gives her a freedom to avoid responsibility for taking action which enables the family to remain intact.

Family therapy aims to bring situations into the open, in order to discuss implication for the whole family, and to free people to take their own decisions regarding their future. Feminist theorists, however, oppose this view, arguing that the gender-power relationship is not addressed, that most women are unaware of their partner's conduct, and that the family work is inappropriate (Dominelli, 1986; Nelson, 1987).

The notion of a child as 'scape-goat', where a family attaches blame to a child for all the family problems, is another example of family dysfunction, often indicating emotional abuse and rejection of the child. Violence is common in dysfunctional families. In some homes violence is treated as a 'norm'. Abusing families are particularly distinguished from non-abusing families by their lack of affectionate relationships, and by the abuse of power by the strong over 'the weak': for example, children, the frail, the elderly and others who are susceptible to being scape-goated for frustrations experienced by the abuser may be defined as among 'the weak'. Browne (1988b) states that a secure relationship between the family members will 'buffer' any effects of stress and facilitate coping strategies on behalf of the family. By contrast, insecure or anxious relationships will not 'buffer' the family under stress and 'episodic overload', such as a quarrel, may result in a physical or emotional attack. Individual coping skills, self-confidence and personal strengths also mitigate the influence of stress, and make violence less rather than more likely as a response to frustration and misery.

Discussion points

- ° What are the main differences between psychodynamics and family disfunctional theories of child abuse?

The Feminist Perspectives

Feminist perspectives about child abuse began to surface as a result of widespread recognition of the way power relations in the family and society might influence abusive behaviour, given that abusers are predominantly male and that sexual abuse is linked to general family violence, especially against women. It has been argued that a patriarchal social structure encourages men to control women and to exert power over a weaker female adult or a child (Dominelli, 1986; Macleod and Saraga, 1988). Such perspectives discount individual or family pathology as a cause of the child abuse, but put the blame on institutionalized male power over females. It is argued that men abuse children because of the general power imbalance, and because of the way men are brought up and socialized, and not as a result of some personality disturbance or deprivation of emotional and sexual relationship with their partners. Furthermore, women are often blamed for child abuse, and discrimination against mothers is widespread (see the Further Reading section). The treatment of abuse by many practitioners, including social workers, involves children and adults, and treatment of the family itself. However, the assumptions of much family work have been criticized by gender/power theorists. Macleod and Saraga (1988) argue that family function explanations of abuse implicitly remove much responsibility from the offender (often the adult male) and place responsibility with the child and non-abusing parent. They argue that this approach also leads to an over-emphasis on maintaining the family as a functioning unit, and places children at risk of further abuse. The feminist perspectives in relation to child abuse put forward two solutions. First, that change is needed at the societal level regarding the gender-related structural inequalities; and second, at an individual level (in particular with child sexual abuse cases), investigation and intervention should be more gender-sensitive and empower mothers to deal with the trauma in self-help mothers' groups instead of relying on professional treatment (Dempster, 1996).

Discussion point
- ° What are the main differences between psychodynamic and feminist perspectives about child abuse?

The Children's Rights Perspectives

Another perspective which stresses the importance of looking beyond individual processes concerns that of children's rights. As knowledge of the causes of child abuse and neglect became better understood, it was generally realized that children had few rights. To safeguard and protect children, the United Nations Convention on the Rights of the Child was set up. Its recommendations were adopted by the General Assembly in 1989. The Convention established the rights of children and young people to care and protection, to the provision of services to meet their basic needs, and to be active participants in the society in which they live. With the signing of the Convention on the Rights of the Child, there has been a growing acceptance that if the children were independent beings with their own political rights rather than the property of their parents, this should minimize the level of abuse (Newell, 1992).

The Convention puts forward 41 articles which define the rights of children and the responsibilities of those providing facilities and services to ensure those rights are realized.

There are rights and duties relating to involvement in society at every level: health and development; education and leisure activities; the provision and quality of care; and protection from harm and abuse. There is also recognition of the role of the state to support parents and carers in order to help them bringing-up children. Additionally, the government has a duty to make the principles and provision of the Convention widely known to children and adults. Many local authorities are now using the Convention to inform their policy and practice. Some have designated officers, to oversee and advocate for children and young people.

There are two main schools of thought on children's rights: the protectionist and the liberationist (Freeman, 1983). The protectionist viewpoint is that children's rights to protection from their parents and carers, where their health, development, and well-being are at risk involves the child protection and welfare services. The liberationist perspectives state that children should have the same rights as adults, regardless of age. Holt (1974), argues that children are oppressed by parents and are powerless to take any action themselves. The liberationists disregard the issue that children are dependent on parents, both physically and emotionally, and are too immature to make informed decisions.

The Cleveland Report (1988) and the introduction of the Children Act (1989) shifted official thinking about children's rights. The Cleveland enquiry criticized the way children were treated during the investigations, and emphasized that the child is a person not an object of concern. They stated that there is a danger that in looking to the welfare of children believed to be the victims of sexual abuse, the children themselves may be overlooked. Corby (1993) suggested that following the events in Cleveland and introduction of the Children Act, the general position adopted regarding children's rights is a half-way house between the protectionist and liberationist stand. Children's views should be taken into consideration but not exclusively. The Children's Rights Convention was not ratified in the United Kingdom until 1991, and as Newell (1992) points out, as long as society accepts that children can be beaten by their parents the pattern of child maltreatment will continue and children's rights will be violated. There is a need to promote alternative methods of discipline and control of children, and this, he argues, can be achieved by parent training.

Social Ecological Theories

In response to various psychiatric views regarding causation of child abuse and neglect, sociologists such as Gelles (1973) and Garbarino and Sherman (1980) argued that it is essential to take into account the social structural characteristics of families and communities in order to fully understand child maltreatment. Sociologically-minded theorists argued that poor living-conditions, unemployment, social isolation, a high proportion of single parents and societal values that encouraged interpersonal violence within the family and community (and specifically corporal punishment) play a central role in the aetiology of child abuse and neglect (Zigler, 1978).

Ecological theories as advocated by Garbarino and Gilliam (1980) indicate the importance of a stable and healthy environment for a child which will provide necessary nurturing, guidance and facilities for good development. They suppose (on the basis of reported child-maltreatment cases) that families where abuse takes place tend to come from deprived areas, be of low employment rate, have a high proportion of single mothers and a high level of movement. In addition, they postulated that these environmental factors produce extra psychological stress on families, already overwhelmed with problems, that trigger off irrational parental behaviour towards their children. Ecological theories were further expanded and elaborated by Belsky and Vondra (1989) and Dubowitz (1993). They have promoted a view that the failure to meet children's basic needs is at the core of child maltreatment, rather than abuse being caused by deliberate and intentional parental behaviour. Consequently, they argue that child abuse and neglect should be seen as a social construct in the context of the society where it occurs, and in the context of the life of the child. Provision of care is seen as operating on a continuum, ranging from very good provision of nurturance from society, the local community, friends and the family to very poor care, attention, resources, policies, or neglect. It is believed that if the family and societal systems are deficient in promoting and facilitating sensitive and adequate nurturing, then the child is exposed to harm on a short- and long-term basis. To minimize child abuse and neglect, parent training both on an individual and group-work basis is proposed. It is claimed that training parents in more effective child-rearing practices would reduce stress and consequently improve parent–child interaction and would strengthen parent–child relationships. They emphasized the need for appropriate provision of services which should be tailored to the needs of that community and individuals requiring specific help and support. They argued that it was unhelpful to house people together who culturally support physical punishment of children and generally behave in a violent way.

Belsky (1988) has argued that child maltreatment is determined by many factors, and that an integrative framework is needed to underscore the role of the child, the parent, the family, the community and the societal context in which parent–child relationships are embedded. Reflecting what was clearly the emerging consensus in the field, he postulated that abusing parents enter the microsystem of the family with developmental histories possibly predisposing them to treat children in an abusive or neglectful manner (antigenic development), and that stress-promoting forces both within the immediate family (i.e. the characteristics of children, and marital problems in the microsystem) and outside it (i.e. social network, and the place of work in the exosystem) increase the probabilities of parent–child conflict. He argued that such stress and conflict generate child abuse stemming from the parents' own experiences as children and the values and child-rearing practices characteristic of the society or sub-culture in which the individual, family and community are embedded (i.e. the macrosystem). Even though child maltreatment may not be inevitable under certain conditions, its probability of occurrence was expected to increase. A similar theory known as the Transactional Model has been developed by Cicchetti and Risley (1981).

Discussion point
- What are the major components of the social ecological theories, and how they might have inform policy and practice?

Integrated Models

It can be said that parent–child social interactions and relationships are central to understanding of the problems of child abuse and neglect. In an attempt to take account of this, Gelles (1987a) produced a complex model of the causes of child abuse that combines psychological, cultural, social and structural explanations. He proposed that violence in the family is determined by:

1. Situational stresses, such as distorted family relationships and family dysfunction, low self-esteem, unwanted children, or children who are resistant to socialization.

2. Structural stresses, such as poor housing, overcrowding, unemployment, social isolation, financial and health problems, and threats to parental authority.

Browne (1988b) expanded on Gelles's (1973) original formulation, postulating that these situational and structural stressors which trigger child abuse and family violence are mediated by and depend upon the interactive relationships within the family. He argued that a secure relationship between family members will protect them from any effect of stress and facilitate coping strategies on behalf of the family. Insecure or anxious relationships will not protect the family under stress, so when stress accumulates it overloads an already volatile ability to cope, and may result in a physical and emotional attack. This, he suggests, will have a negative effect on the existing interpersonal relationships and reduce any protective effects even further, making it easier for the stressors to overload the system again. The viscious cycle is created which leads to systematic overload, where constant stress leads in turn to physical and verbal lashing-out resulting in abuse. As can be seen, this situation becomes progressively worse if intervention is not in place in time. These models suggest that complex influences result in child abuse and neglect. For example, to prevent physical injury, some abusive parents may revert to physical and emotional neglect as a coping strategy to deal with their angry feelings. Other problems occur when an individual fails to control anger arousal. Rutter (1985) suggests that people of low self-esteem, with poor relationships and low levels of stress-management are unable to control anger. Furthermore, the quality of relationships and stress-management in the family will depend upon the personal as well as on character traits and their pathology. This may be a result of early social experiences which indirectly affect parental investment in the child. Patterson (1982) convincingly describes how aggressive behaviour is learned within the family, and how the process of reinforcement and modelling becomes a norm of aggressive parent–child interactions. Many research findings indicate an association between being abused and being abusive (Egeland et al., 1988). It is believed that the culture to which people belong, their values, as well as their social and educational status, influence child-rearing attitudes and family relationships. Integrated models offer a way to deal with such diverse factors as stress, personal characteristics, family characteristics and family environment.

Summary

This chapter has discussed the general principles of various theories and their explanations as to the causes of child abuse. It would appear that there are certain clashes between theorists, each holding on to their own views as to why child abuse occurs: feminist and family dysfunction perspectives, for example, contain specific views about the aetiology of sexual abuse, while psychodynamic theories claim maternal pathology as a cause, and social/environmental theories hold that social deprivation is the major reason triggering child abuse. In spite of strong evidence that the causation of child abuse is multi-factorial, individuals still adhere to a specific theory, and different schools of thought still operate within a single theoretical framework, both of which occasionally lead to tragic outcomes for the child. Attempts to integrate the different approaches to child abuse are being made, and are discussed under the heading of ecological and integrated theories. It is apparent that to protect children and prevent abuse, the professionals involved in this work should have wide theoretical understanding as to the causations of child abuse. By adopting this philosophy they will be able to act appropriately. Furthermore, it would free them to choose methods of intervention and treatment suitable to a particular family and set of circumstances that led to abuse.

Seminar Questions

1. What are the strengths and weaknesses of the theories discussed in explaining child abuse?

2. Discuss how far theories of child abuse can inform everyday practice.

3. What are the advantages of using an integrated theory of child abuse?

Further Reading

Corby, B (1993) *Child Abuse: Towards a Knowledge Base.* Milton Keynes: Open University Press.
This book provides an extensive review of theories, practice, and policy issues which are relevant to social-work practice.

Waterhouse, L. (1996) *Child Abuse and Child Abusers. Protection and Prevention.* (ed) London: Jessica Kingsley Publishers.
Good research studies and theoretical discussions in relation to all forms of abuse.

Patterson, G.R. (1982) *Coercive Family Process.* Eugene, OR: Castalia.
This is an essential book as it explains clearly how aggressive behaviour is acquired within the family and its short- and long-term consequences for the child.

O'Hagan, K. and Dillenburger, K. (1995) *The Abuse of Women within Child Care Work.* Milton Keynes: Open University Press.

References

Ainsworth, M.D.S. (1963) 'The development of infant–mother interaction among the Ganda.' In B.M. Foss, *Determinants of Infant Behaviour* (pp.67–104) New York: Wiley.
Ainsworth, M.D.S. (1980) 'Attachment and child abuse.' In G. Gerner, C.J. Ross and E. Zigler (eds) *Child Abuse: An Agenda for Action.* pp.35–47. New York, NY: Oxford University Press.
Azar, S. and Siegal, B. (1990) 'Behavioural treatment of child abuse: A developmental perspective.' *Behaviour Modification, 14,* 279–300.
Bandura, A. (1977) *Social Learning Theory.* Englewood Cliffs, New York, NY: Prentice-Hall.
Batchelor, J. and Kerslake, A. (1990) *Failure to Find Failure-to-Thrive.* London: Whiting and Birch.
Belsky, J. (1988) 'Child maltreatment and the emergent family system.' In K. Browne, C. Davies and P. Stratton (eds) *Early Prediction and Prevention of Child Abuse.* Chichester: Wiley.
Belsky, J. and Rovine, M. (1988) 'Non-maternal care in the first year of life and the security of infant-parent attachment.' *Child Development, 59,* 157–167.

Belsky, J. and Vondra, J. (1989) 'Lessons from child abuse: the determinants of parenting.' In D. Cicchetti and V. Carlson (eds) *Child Maltreatment. Theory and Research on the Causes and Consequences of Child Abuse and Neglect.* New York, NY: Cambridge University Press.

Belsky, J., Rovine, M. and Taylor, D. (1984) 'The Pennsylvania infant and family developmental project III: the origins of individual differences in infant-mother attachment: Maternal and infant contributions.' *Child Development, 55,* 718–728.

Bentovim, A., Elton, A., Hildebrand, J., Franter, M. and Vizard, E. (eds) (1988) *Child Sexual Abuse within the Family: Assessment and Treatment: the work of the Great Ormond Street Team.* London: Wright.

Berkowitz, L. (1988) 'Laboratory experiments in the study of aggression.' In J. Archer and K.D. Browne (eds) *Human Aggression: Nationalistic Approaches.* London: Routledge.

Bowlby, J. (1951) *Maternal Care and Mental Health, Bulletin of the World Health Organization.* Geneva.

Bowlby, J. (1969) *Attachment and Loss, Volume 1.* London: Hogarth Press.

Bowlby, J. (1980) *Attachment and Loss: Loss.* New York, NY: Basic Books.

Browne, K.D. (1988a) 'The naturalistic context of family violence and child abuse.' In J. Archer and K.D. Browne (eds) *Human Aggression: Naturalistic Approaches.* London: Routledge.

Browne, K. (1988b) 'The nature of child abuse and neglect.' In K. Browne, C. Davies and P. Stratton (eds) *Early Prediction and Prevention of Child Abuse,* Chichester: Wiley.

Callias, M. (1994) 'Parent Training.' In M. Rutter, E. Taylor and L. Hersov (eds) *Child and Adolescent Psychiatry: Modern Approaches,* pp.918–935. Oxford: Blackwell Scientific Publications.

Cicchetti, D. and Risley, R. (1981) 'Developmental perspectives on the aetiology of intergenerational transmission, and sequelae of child maltreatment.' *New Directions for Child Development, 11,* 31–55.

Cleveland County Council (1988) *Report of the Inquiry into Child Abuse in Cleveland 1987.* DHSS Cmnol. 412. London: HMSO.

Corby, B. (1993) *Child Abuse Towards a Knowledge Base.* Buckingham: Open University Press.

Crittenden, P. and Bonvillian, J. (1984) 'The relationship between maternal risk status and maternal sensitivity.' *American Journal of Orthopsychiatry, 54,* 250–262.

Crockenberg, G.S.B (1981) 'Infant irritability, mother responsiveness, and social support influences on the security of infant-mother attachment.' *Child Development, 52,* 857–865.

Dempster, R.H.L. (1996) 'The aftermath of child sexual abuse, women's perspectives.' In L. Waterhouse (ed.) *Child Abuse and Child Abusers: Protection and Prevention.* London: Jessica Kingsley Publishers.

Dominelli, L. (1986) 'Father–daughter incest: patriarchy's shameful secret.' *Critical Social Policy, 16,* 8–22.

Dubowitz, A. (1993) 'A conceptual definition of child neglect.' *Criminal Justice and Behaviour, 20,* 1, 8–26.

Egeland, B. (1988) 'Breaking the cycle of abuse.' In K. Browne, C. Davies and P. Stratton (eds) *Early Prediction and Prevention of Child Abuse.* Chichester: Wiley.

Freeman, M. (1983) *The Rights and Wrongs of Children.* London: Francis Pinter.

Friedrich, W.N. and Boroskin, J.A. (1976) 'The role of the child in abuse: a review of the literature.' *American Journal of Orthopsychiatry, 46,* 4, 580–590.

Gaensbauer, T.J. and Sands, M. (1979) 'Distorted affective communications in abused/ neglected infants and their potential impact on caregivers.' *Journal of the American Academy of Child Psychiatry, 18,* 236–250.

Garbarino, J. and Gilliam, G. (1980) *Understanding Abusive Families.* Lexington, MA: Lexington Books.

Garbarino, J. and Sherman, D. (1980) 'High-risk neighborhoods and high-rise families: the human ecology of child maltreatment.' *Child Development, 512,* 188–198.

Gelles, R.J. (1973) 'Child abuse as psychopathology: a sociological critique and reformotation.' *American Journal of Orthopsychiatry, 43,* 611–621.

Gelles, R.J. (1987a) *Family Violence, Sage Library of Social Research No. 84.* Beverly Hills, CA: Sage.

Gil, D.G. (1970) *Violence Against Children.* Cambridge, MA: Harvard University Press.

Gough, D.A. (1993) *Child Abuse Interventions. A Review of the Research Literature.* London: HMSO.

Green, W.H., Deutsch, S.I. and Campbell, M. (1987) 'Psychosocial dwarfism: psychological and aetiological considerations.' In C.B. Nemeroff and P.T. Loosen (eds) *Handbook of Psychoneuroendocrinology.* New York: Guilford.

Herbert, M. (1989) *Working with Children and their Families.* Chicago, IL: Lyceum Books Inc.

HMSO (1995) *Child Protection. Messages from Research.* London: HMSO, Studies in Child Protection.

Holt, J. (1974) *Escape from Childhood.* Harmondsworth: Penguin.

Iwaniec, D. (1995) *The Emotionally Abused and Neglected Child. Identification, Assessment and Intervention.* Chichester: Wiley.

Iwaniec, D. (1991) 'Treatment of children who fail to grow in the light of the new Children Act.' *Newsletter of the Association for Child Psychology and Psychiatry, 13* 3, 21–27.

Iwaniec, D., Herbert, M. and McNeish, A.S. (1985b) 'Social work with failure-to-thrive children and their families – Part II: Social work intervention.' *British Journal of Social Work 15*, 375–389.

Kelly, G.A. (1955) *The Psychology of Personal Constructs.* New York, NY: Norton.

Kelly, R.J. (1982) 'Behavioural reorientation of pedophiliacs: Can it be done?' *Clinical Psychology Review, 2*, 387–408.

Lynch, M. and Roberts, J. (1977) 'Predicting child abuse.' *Child Abuse and Neglect, 1*, 491–492.

Macleod, M. and Saraga, E. (1988) 'Challenging the orthodoxy: towards a feminist theory and practice.' *Feminist Review, 28*, 15–55.

Main, M. and Hesse, E. (1990) 'Parents' unresolved traumatic experiences are related to infant disorganized attachment status: is frightened and/or frightening parental behaviour the linking mechanism?' In M.T. Greenberg, D. Cicchetti and E.M. Cummings (eds) *Attachment in the Preschool Years*, pp.161–184. Chicago, IL: University of Chicago Press.

Main, M. and Solomon, J. (1986) 'Discovery of an insecure, disorganized/disoriented attachment pattern: procedures, findings and implications for the classification of behaviour.' In M. Yogman and T.B. Brazelton (eds) *Effective Development in Infancy*, pp.95–124, Norwood, NY: Ablex.

Maletzky, B.M. (1991) *Treating the Sexual Offender.* Newbury Park: Sage.

Minuchin, S. (1974) *Families and Family Therapy.* Cambridge, MA: Harvard University Press.

Nelson, S. (1987) *Incest: Fact and Myth.* Edinburgh: Strathmullion.

Newell, P. (1992) *Introduction in Radda Barnen Organization Ending Physical Punishment of European Children.* London: Epoch Worldwide.

Patterson, G.R. (1982) *Coercive Family Process.* Eugene, OR: Castalia.

Pavlov, I.P. (1927) *Conditioned Reflexes* (trans. G.V. Annep) Oxford: Clarendon Press.

Reid, J.B., Taplin, P.S. and Lorber, R. (1981) 'A social interactional approach to the treatment of abuse families.' In R. Stuart (ed.) *Violent Behaviour: Social Learning Approaches to Prediction, Management and Treatment.* New York, NY: Brunner/Maxel.

Rutter, M. (1985) 'Resilience in the face of adversity: protective factors and resistance to psychiatric disorder.' *British Journal of Psychiatry, 147*, 598–611.

Schaffer, H.R., and Emerson, P.E. (1964) 'Patterns of response to physical contact in early human development.' *Journal of Child Psychology and Psychiatry, 5*, 1–13.

Steele, B.F., and Pollock, C.B. (1968) 'A psychiatric study of parents who abuse infants and small children.' In R.E. Helfer and C.H. Kempe (eds) *The Battered Child.* Chicago, Il: University of Chicago Press.

Stroufe, L.A. (1983) 'Infant-caregiver attachment and patterns of adaptation in preschool: the roots of maladaption and competence.' In M. Perlmutter (ed.) *Minnesota Symposium in Child Psychology, 16*, 41–81. New York, NY: Erlbaum.

Sutton, C. (1994) *Social Work Community Work and Psychology.* Leicester: The British Psychological Society.

Thomas, A. and Chess, S. (1977) *Temperament and Development.* New York, NY: Brunner/Mazel.

United Nations (1989) *The UN Convention on the Rights of the Child.* New York, NY: United Nations.

Wolfe, D.A. (1985) 'Child-abusive parents: an empirical review and analysis.' *Psychological Bulletin, 97*, 462–482.

Zigler, E. (1978) 'Controlling child abuse in America: an effort doomed to failure.' In R. Bourne and E. Newberger (eds) *Critical Perspectives on Child Abuse.* Lexington, MA: Health.

CHAPTER 16

Child Abuse

Parenting, Identification and Treatment

Dorota Iwaniec

Introduction

Child abuse and neglect and child protection work have become a major preoccupation for child care social care professionals and their managers. Numerous public enquiries into children's deaths and the ways in which some sexual abuse cases have been dealt with brought about public concerns and put enormous pressures on those who legislate and those who protect. *The Children Act* (1989) and 20 major research projects commissioned by the Government were the results of growing dissatisfaction as to how child abuse cases were dealt with, and of an increasing awareness that serious research into these complex problems was necessary to reassess child protection work. Although our knowledge about child abuse and neglect has increased, there is still a lot that we do not understand and with which we struggle. We still do not have workable operational definitions of various forms of child abuse, and only a vague understanding of what causes the maltreatment of children. We are still developing intervention and treatment methods and are just beginning to evaluate their effectiveness. This chapter will address three questions:

1. What factors led to the problematic parenting?
2. How are various types of abuse defined and how they can be identified?
3. What psychological treatment methods have been used to help the abused and the abuser?

Children's Needs and Parenting Style

Child abuse is considered as parental failure to meet the basic needs of children as outlined in Chapter 15. Those needs are of two kinds: physical and psycho-social. Physical needs include food, shelter, clothing and all the other necessities for survival. Psycho-social needs include love, security, acceptance, recognition, education, attention, new experiences, praise and belongingness. If these needs are not responded to promptly, consistently and appropriately, then the children will be at risk of physical and emotional harm. In addition, if children are to become well-adjusted and prepared for life, they must also acquire a vast amount of information about the environment in which they live, the culture to which they belong, and the prevailing moral code. Thus, a child's socialization process will depend upon parental ability, awareness, willingness to give the necessary information, to provide an appropriate model for behaviour, and to supervise and guide social-learning in order to lay the foundation for a future life and well-being.

Adequate parenting requires a number of skills that are far from simple – part common sense, part intuition and part empathy. Most parents successfully carry out the complex tasks involved in child-rearing, using a variety of methods in very diverse family, cultural and social circumstances. Some, however, find bringing up children difficult, frustrating and anger-provoking. Contemporary parents are often inexperienced in the care of children. They may be unaccustomed to infants because they were brought up in small families and were not given responsibilities for caring for their younger siblings, as older children of yesteryear had to do. They may have been brought up themselves in neglectful and uncaring homes, and have had no opportunities to acquire a better parenting style and understanding of children's developmental needs. They might be living in adverse social and economic circumstances that may affect the quality of everyday child-care. Lack of support and guidance, as well as social isolation brought about by diminished extended-family and community resources (from where, traditionally, help was provided), contribute to inadequate and ill-informed parenting. Growing numbers of single, young and immature mothers (often living in poverty), who are socially isolated and unsupported, are unprepared for the demands of child-rearing, and therefore unable to provide basic physical and emotional nurturance for their offspring. Additionally, some children are hard to rear due to their individual characteristics such as difficult temperamental attributes, prematurity, handicap or chronic illness. They tend to be vulnerable to parental mismanagement and often resentment.

Most parents who maltreat their children have difficulties in controlling frustration and anger when dealing with a child's difficult behaviour (e.g. crying, disobedience, temper-tantrums, refusal to eat or to sleep, toileting, and so on), so they physically or verbally lash out. This sort of behaviour is self-reinforcing because it brings immediate (although momentary) relief. As time goes on, parents more frequently and intensely scream, and use degrading language with greater passion, or smack, believing this is the only way to make children behave. Child-rearing problems often lead to faulty attribution, negative attitudes towards the child, and unrealistic expectations of the child's behaviour and performance. The accumulation of stresses of various kinds, immature personality, and deficiency in child-care skills, often lead to child abuse and neglect (Belsky and Vondra, 1989; Dubowitz, 1993). Parents who are depressed, on the other hand, tend to be uninvolved, detached and unable to tune in to the children's nurturing needs: they are therefore unwittingly neglectful.

Types of Abuse, Definitions and Identification

To deal confidently and appropriately in child abuse cases, practitioners need to have a reasonably clear operational definition as to what constitutes child maltreatment. However, there are many definitions in the legal and research-led literature which are rather global and difficult to operationalize, and therefore not always helpful to practitioners. *Child Protection: Messages from Research,* in Studies in Child Protection (HMSO, 1995), emphasized that child abuse has to be seen as the failure to meet children's needs by poor parenting style and various psycho-social factors that might influence child-rearing practices that might lead to child maltreatment. Child protection workers are urged to reconsider the thresholds of child abuse investigation. It is recommended that less attention should be paid to a single abusive incidence in the context of a warm and supportive parenting style, and more to the damaging consequences for children who live in families which are 'low in warmth and high on criticism'. Although there are various types of abuse, they are often interrelated. The association between types of abuse is illustrated in Farmer and Owen's (1995) study. They found that the existence of secondary concerns was a factor significantly related to the placement of a child's name on the protection register. For example, in a third of cases where the main concern was neglect, there were also concerns about physical abuse; in a fifth of cases where the main concern was physical abuse, there were also concerns about neglect; in a quarter of cases where the main concern was sexual abuse, there were also concerns about neglect; in a sixth of cases where the main concern was sexual abuse there were also concerns about physical abuse; and in a quarter of cases where the main concern was physical abuse there were also concerns about emotional abuse.

Physical Abuse

Physical abuse in western culture implies harmful action and some kind of physical injury directed against the child (Box 16.1).

Box 16.1 Definition of Physical Abuse, Neglect and Sexual Abuse

---

In the 1991 DoH guidelines physical abuse is defined as 'actual or likely physical injury to a child, or failure to prevent physical injury (or suffering) to a child including deliberate poisoning, suffocation and Munchausen's syndrome by proxy'. Sexual abuse is defined as 'any sexual contact between an adult and a sexually immature child for the purposes of the adult's sexual gratification: or any sexual contact to a child made by the use of force, threat or deceit to secure the child's participation; or sexual contact to which a child is incapable of consenting by virtue of age or power differentials and the nature of the relationship with the adult' (Finkelhor and Korbin, 1988).

Physical injuries that may indicate that a child has been the victim of non-accidental abusive acts include: bruises, weals, lacerations and scars, burns and scalds, bone and joint injuries, brain and eye injuries and internal injuries. Physical abuse definition is in line with the *Children Act* (1989) requirement, and includes 'likely physical injury' which was absent in the 1988 guidelines, and includes more recently discovered forms of abuse such as suffocation and Munchausen's syndrome by proxy (see below for an explanation). It is argued that the above definition leaves child-protection workers in a difficult situation, as it does not specify less obvious physical injuries (such as minor bruising) or exceptionally harsh disciplining. The seriousness of physical abuse in terms of protective action is judged according to whether the child is suffering, or is likely to suffer, significant harm; whether injury was accidental or not accidental; whether parents (due to negligence) failed to protect children from accidental injury; and whether the parental action was deliberate in order to harm the child.

Since social care professionals, especially social workers, are in the front line of child-protection work, familiarity with newly-identified varieties of physical abuse (such as Munchausen's syndrome by proxy and deliberate suffocation) also is necessary. Munchausen's syndrome by proxy is described in terms of how the mother (usually) may fabricate illness in her child or children and presents her arguments to doctors, and the child is persistently brought for medical investigation. However, the alleged symptoms are not apparent when the child, separated from the parent, is seen by the doctor, and denies being ill or having any symptoms of the alleged illness. Bools *et al.* (1992) found that 39 per cent of siblings had themselves been subjected to fabricated illnesses, and 1 in 10 had died in suspicious circumstances, while failure-to-thrive and non-accidental injuries also were associated with this syndrome.

A number of reports of deliberate suffocation of children come to child-protection attention: it is sometimes alleged that the parent (as a rule the mother) smothers the child by putting a pillow on its face. Suffocation has been linked with cot-death or so-called Sudden Infant-Death Syndrome (SIDS). Emery and Taylor (1986) estimated that about 10 per cent of all cases of SIDS are due to deliberate suffocation, and warned that in such cases there may be increased risk to the siblings of the victims. Such claims, however, are strongly refuted by numerous researchers, and by parents who have lost their children in such circumstances.

Physical abuse can have an immediate somatic effect (such as brain damage due to shaking or beating), while burning and scalding can result in lifelong disfigurement. In addition, malnutrition due to neglect or emotional abuse can cause stunting of physical growth and may seriously impair cognitive and psychomotor development.

Not all children, however, suffer long-term effects from physical abuse. Some are more resilient to traumatic events and cope better than others. The protective and compensatory factors according to studies by Mrazek and Mrazek (1987) and Lynch (1988) are associated with the child's personality, above average intelligence, formation of positive relationships with people outside the family, and provision of good educational, leisure and health facilities. Angoustinos (1987) points out that these factors are important, providing that abuse is not persistent, severe and of long duration. Early identification of abuse and provision of appropriate intervention and treatment strategies are likely to produce best outcomes. There is some evidence (see Chapter 12) that even severe and prolonged maltreatment, if responded to appropriately, can produce positive outcomes in the long term.

Discussion point
  ° Poor parenting style and lack of understanding children's developmental needs, can lead to physical abuse. Identify and discuss possible factors which may contribute to ill-informed parenting and consequently abuse.

Sexual Abuse

Most definitions of child sexual abuse do not specify the nature of the sexually abusive acts, but these may range from exhibitionism and fondling to forced penetrative acts. Peters *et al.* (1986) divided sexually abusive acts into contact acts (e.g. sexual intercourse, oral and anal sex, fondling of breasts and genitals) and non-contact acts (e.g. exhibitionism, exposure to pornography and solicitation to engage in sexual activity). Baker and Duncan (1985) showed that 51 per cent of those who reported abuse had experienced non-contact abuse, and only 5 per cent had experienced anal or vaginal intercourse. In the clinical sample of children referred as sexually abused, however, penetrative acts were the most common (over 50 per cent) (Monck *et al.*, 1993). It would appear that only the most severe cases are identified as abusive and requiring protection and treatment. Sexual abuse accounts for an estimated 16 per cent of registrations in England and Wales (Department of Health, 1991), 23 per cent in Scotland (Gough, 1992) and 29 per cent in Northern Ireland.

Box 16.2 Signs of Child's Possible Sexual Abuse

Behavioural signs

1. Difficulties in trusting adults and fear of a particular individual
2. Poor peer relationships
3. Running away from home
4. Sudden changes in behaviour
5. School problems including truancy, delinquency, inability to concentrate or sudden drop in school performance, or conversely being a model pupil
6. Strong need for love and affection sometimes expressed in physical terms which might appear seductive
7. Poor self-image and low self-esteem
8. Inappropriate awareness of sexual behaviours
9. Displays of the extremes of sexual behaviour – either promiscuity or revulsion of sex
10. Isolation/withdrawal
11. Precocious sex play with peers, toys; excessive masturbation and sexual drawings
12. Self-destructive tendencies including suicide attempts, self-mutilation, anorexia nervosa, and drug/alcohol and solvent abuse
13. Depression or anxiety
14. Aggressive behaviour including hostility, irritability and defiance of authority figures
15. Psychiatric disorders

Physical /medical

1. Sleeplessness, nightmares and fear of the dark
2. Bruises, scratches, bite marks
3. Depression/suicide attempts
4. Anorexia nervosa
5. Eating disorders or change in eating habits
6. Difficulty in walking or sitting
7. Pregnancy – particularly with reluctance to name the father
8. Recurring urinary tract problems
9. Vaginal infections or genital damage
10. Venereal disease
11. Bed wetting
12. Vague pains and aches
13. Itching or soreness

Evidence of the high prevalence of sexual abuse has arisen from population surveys of adults who were sexually abused as children. Kelly *et al.* (1991) reported prevalence rates (for under 16 year olds) of 18 per cent for men and 43 per cent for women for all abusive experiences. Nevertheless, there are many difficulties in estimating the rate of prevalence because of a lack of precise and generally agreed definition of what constitutes sexual abuse. The very intimate nature of sexual activity inhibits people from disclosing their real feelings or experiences in order to provide an accurate overall picture. Identification of sexual abuse is not easy, as many of the signs shown in Box 16.2 and particularly the behavioural signs, are associated with the child under emotional stress, and do not necessarily indicate in isolation that a child is sexually abused or has been abused in the past. However, awareness of these indicators will enable the social worker to consider sexual abuse as a possibility. Sudden changes of behaviour which exclude other possibilities of emotional stress may indicate sexual abuse.

Effects of sexual abuse

The adverse psychological effect of abuse comes from clinical case descriptions of abused children and retrospective studies of adults who were abused as children. A number of studies (e.g. Berliner, 1991; Briere, 1992) have shown that parents of abused children report significantly more behaviour problems than matched comparisons, but these differences have been more difficult to detect using child self-report measures (Mannarino *et al.*, 1991). Additionally, as many as 21 per cent of children in a study by Conte and Schuerman (1988) showed no symptoms on a 38-item check-list. Studies on adult survivors (Egeland, 1988; Bagley and Ramsay, 1986) report much higher rates of psychological symptoms, including lack of self-esteem, depression, marital difficulties (especially in sexual relationships), sleeping problems, passivity, drug- and alcohol-abuse, anxiety and eating disorders. However, victims coming from very deprived environments may not suffer the same effects as those coming from more stable and caring backgrounds. Since behavioural and emotional symptoms tend to be activated later in the victims' lives, some researchers (Wolfe *et al.*, 1989) argue that they fit a pattern of Post-Traumatic Stress Disorder (PTSD) as manifested by victims of acute disaster or war.

Discussion points

○ Sexual abuse has received more attention in the last decade than any other form of abuse. Why do you think this is the case?

○ Why do the physical and behavioural signs of sexual abuse have to be considered with caution?

Emotional Abuse and Neglect

Emotional abuse refers to 'hostile or indifferent parental behaviour which damages a child's self-esteem, degrades a sense of achievement, diminishes a sense of belonging, and stands in the way of healthy, vigorous, and happy development' (Iwaniec, 1995). Emotional abuse as a separate form of child maltreatment was only recognized in England and Wales by legislators in the 1980s, although in the United States it has been on the Statute book in several states since 1977.

The definition of emotional abuse at a general and operational level is far from clear and explicit, posing great dilemmas for the child-protection workers. The major deterrent in bringing cases of emotional abuse to the courts of law is the difficulty in quantifying and proving that emotionally harmful parental behaviour has affected a child's development and social adjustment to the point of significant harm (Iwaniec, 1995; Skuse and Bentovim, 1994). It has been recognized that there are a significant number of children on the Child-Protections Register for whom the main concern is a fear of emotional abuse, but for the purposes of registration, the discovery of a simple unexplained bruise may be much more convincing than making a case for emotional abuse on its own (Sluckin, 1987).

Defining features

Parents and carers who *persistently* criticize, shame, rebuke, threaten, ridicule, humiliate and put down a child, who induce fear and anxiety in a youngster, and who are never satisfied with the child's behaviour and performance, are emotionally abusive and cruel. Equally, those who distance themselves from the child – by ignoring signals of distress, pleas for help, attention, comfort, reassurance, encouragement and acceptance, are abusive. Their behaviour towards the child can be described as overtly abusive, actively painful and developmentally and cognitively damaging. A negatively-charged interaction between a child and its carers can induce pain, anxiety, confusion and cognitive distortion, and therefore can be described as emotionally harmful (Garbarino *et al*, 1986; Iwaniec, 1995).

When examining emotionally abusive parental behaviours (across all sections of society), the behaviours in Box 16.3 can be considered as emotional abuse if they occur often and persistently, (Iwaniec, 1995). In Box 16.3, 'Often' is a negative measure, 'Almost Never' represents positive/ caring, and 'Occasional' suggests parting is satisfactory but could be helped by advice.

Emotionally abused children show a pattern of behaviour which indicates fear, apprehension and, uneasiness when in the parents' company (Iwaniec *et al.*, 1985b, Iwaniec, 1997). Behaviours that are 'almost never' observed suggests that the child may be emotionally maltreated. If the behaviour occurs, this 'Often' indicates a positive/caring approach to the child.

Emotional abuse and neglect affect children in many different ways and to varying degrees: some children are shy, nervous, anxious, unsure of themselves, lacking self-confidence and self-esteem, while others are developmentally and educationally retarded or present severe behavioural and emotional problems such as destructiveness, self-harming behaviour, fire-setting, bed-wetting, soiling and smearing, running away from home, attempted suicide, anorexia nervosa, bulimia and extreme conduct problems (Garbarino *et al.*, 1986). Acute emotional abuse and rejection can seriously affect children's physical growth, so-called psycho-social short stature, and is associated with severe and prolonged failure-to-thrive. Not all children who are emotionally maltreated are affected in the same way. Some survive relatively unscathed and often the stronger for their experiences (Osborne, 1985; see Chapter

12). Children who live at homes which are low on warmth and high on criticism might be emotionally compensated, by friends at school, teachers and adults who might take an interest in them, thereby providing emotional support, acceptance and a sense of belongingness, thus minimising the emotional upheaval experienced at home.

Box 16.3 Parental Emotionally Abusive Behaviour (Source: Iwaniec, 1995)			
Parental Abusive Behaviour	*Often*	*Occasionally*	*Almost Never*
1. Child not included in the family circle			
2. Ignored, not taken notice of			
3. Not allowed to play an active part in family activities			
4. Seldom spoken to in an easy way			
5. Persistently deprived of privileges and treats as a means of discipline			
6. Frequently punished for minor misbehaviour			
7. Persistently ridiculed and criticized			
8. Never praised			
9. Not acknowledged or reinforced in any good behaviour or positive action			
10. Shamed and put down in front of peers, siblings, and other people			
11. Disregarded in any attempts to please care givers			
12. Ignored and discouraged when attempting to attract attention or affection			
13. Not allowed to mix with peers			
14. Socially isolated			
15. Told he/she is disliked or unloved			
16. Blamed when things go wrong in the family			
17. Not properly supervised or guided			
18. Mis-socialized in various ways			
19. Encouraged in prejudices such as religious, racial, cultural or other hatreds			
20. Not allowed to get physically close to care giver			
21. Not permitted to show emotions			
22. Unrealistic developmental expectations			

Box 16.4 Child's Reactive and Proactive Behaviour (Source: Iwaniec, 1995)

	Often	Occasionally	Almost Never
1. Playing freely			
2. Laughing/smiling			
3. Running			
4. Talking freely			
5. Coming for help			
6. Coming for comfort			
7. Cuddling up to parents			
8. Responding to affection			
9. Responding to attention			
10. At ease when parents are near			
11. Joining in activities with other children			
12. Not frightened when approached by parents or corrected			

Discussion point

    °   Why is emotional abuse so difficult to prove in Courts of law?

Failure-to-Thrive

Failure-To-Thrive (FTT) is associated with poor physical growth and development in infancy and early childhood for either organic or psycho-social reasons, or a combination of both. This concept has become a popular term to describe infants and young children whose weight, often height, head-growth and general psycho-social development are below age-expected norms, and whose well-being causes concern. It is often associated with organic illnesses, inadequate calorific intake for normal growth, acute feeding difficulties, disturbed mother-child interaction (especially during feeding time), insecure attachment, family dysfunctioning and poverty (Iwaniec *et al,* 1985; Hanks and Hobbs, 1993). Types of FTT are described in Box 16.5. Non-organic FTT should be of particular concern for social workers, as it requires social work intervention.

The hypothesis of a psychological aetiology for the non-organic FTT syndrome has its roots in the extensive research on the effects of institutionalization, hospitalism, and maternal deprivation in children (Bowlby, 1951; Spitz, 1945; Widdowson, 1951).

In the 1960s and 1970s, studies of growth-failure and developmental delays (similar to those of institutionalized children) were replicated in infants and young children living at home. Failure-to-thrive in these early studies was associated with maternal personality problems stemming from the mother's early background and family dysfunctioning. Other psychological problems have been found in the way mothers nurture their small infants (Coleman and Provence, 1957; Barbero and Shaheen, 1967; Leonard, Rhymes and Solnit,

---

Box 16.5 Types Of Failure-To-Thrive

1. *Organic failure-to-thrive* – the child fails to grow and develop because of some identified physical illness, e.g. pyloric stenosis, hernia, chronic infection, malabsorption, and other illnesses.
2. *Non-organic failure-to-thrive* – related to insufficient food-intake, low weight-gain due to acute feeding difficulties, neglect, inadequate parenting, rejection, poverty and immature personality of mother.
3. *Combined failure-to-thrive* – occurs when organic and non-organic factors merge. This combination is more common than previously was thought, and is apparent when treatment of what had seemed to be a clear-cut organic condition does not produce an expected improvement. Emotional overlays and/or secondary gains are known to complicate so-called 'psychosomatic' disorders, not least those which have a clear organic basis. Additionally a child who has FTT because of illness might also be rejected, neglected, and severely deprived of attention and care, so the primary cause of FTT, that of illness, is exacerbated by parental maltreatment.

1966). More recent studies (Iwaniec, 1983, 1985; Powell, Low and Speers, 1987; Hanks and Hobbs, 1993; Wolfe, 1988; Batchelor and Kerslake, 1990) have indicated a range of associated factors: problematic parent–child interaction (especially during the process of feeding), acute feeding difficulties, heightened stress and worries about a child's poor weight-gain and developmental performance, low self-esteem, deficiencies in child-rearing skills, inadequate provision of help and support, and environmental stresses (such as poverty, unemployment, social isolation, and neglect). Furthermore, it often appears that these factors are more important in the causation of FTT than character disorders in the carers.

Low weight gain, physical appearance and psychological expressions are very striking in such children and when they are spotted they need to be investigated as a matter of prevention to stop further deterioration and subsequent harm. Severe and prolonged FTT can lead to serious stunting of growth, delays in psycho-social development and behavioural and emotional disturbances.

Emotional stunting of growth

Children with a long and severe history of FTT are, almost always, rejected, emotionally abused and cruelly treated by their families. There are striking behavioural characteristics of these children, such as bizarre eating-patterns, disturbed toileting, destructiveness, defiant hostility and self-harming behaviour. Distorted behaviour around food tends to emerge at an older toddler stage, and is expressed by excessive hunger drive, hoarding, begging food from strangers, eating non-food items, getting up at night in search of food, and hiding it, scavenging food from waste-bins, eating left-overs from other people's plates and excessive drinking. Children so affected tend to eat quickly and voraciously, to the point of gorging and vomiting.

Attachment between these children and their mothers is usually insecure and avoidant and relationships are mutually antagonistic. Discipline is harsh and cruel, and may involve getting rid of a favourite toy or pet, locking up a child in the dark cupboards, frequently withdrawing food as a punishment for minor misdemeanours, and making a hungry child watch others eat.

Disturbed toileting behaviour such as deliberate urination and smearing of faeces over the bed furniture and toys, as well as in public places, and persistent bed-wetting, are common amongst these children.

Children so affected are exceptionally small for their chronological age and developmentally retarded in all areas. Children presenting such patterns of behaviour require immediate professional attention and case conferencing. The prognosis for effective treatment at home is very poor, and alternative provision of care may be required to prevent further harm (Skuse, 1992; Skuse *et al.* 1996; Blizzard and Bulatovic, 1993; Iwaniec, 1995).

Box 16.6 Profile of Non-Organic Failure-to-Thrive (Iwaniec, 1995)

Growth retardation

- child falls below the expected norms, for their chronological age, in weight and often in height and head circumference

Developmental retardation

- motor development
- language development
- social development
- intellectual development
- emotional development
- cognitive development

Physical description

- wasted body, thin arms and legs
- large stomach
- red, cold, and wet hands and feet
- thin, wispy, dull, and falling hair
- dark circles around the eyes

Psychological description and behaviour

- sadness, withdrawal, and detachment
- expressionless face
- general lethargy
- tearful
- frequent whining
- minimal or no smiling
- diminished vocalisation
- staring blankly at people or objects
- lack of cuddliness
- unresponsiveness
- insecure attachment
- passivity

Physical symptoms

- refusal to take feeds
- vomiting
- refusal to chew and swallow
- diarrhoea
- frequent colds and infections
- anxious ambivalent or avoidant attachment

Aetiology – physical and emotional neglect, insufficient calorific intake, inadequate attention to and understanding of children's emotional and physical needs.

Discussion point
- What signs of the child's growth and development indicate failure-to-thrive, and what are the short- and long-term implications for the child and the family?

Treatment of Child Abuse

There is no single or simple way to help abused children and abusive parents. Intervention and treatment strategies can take many steps and forms, follow different routes, and may require several methods and approaches to deal effectively and appropriately with the parents' behaviour and attitudes towards the child, and the child's outcomes. The selection of methods will depend upon individual needs, the nature of abuse, severity, type of family and the ability and capacity to work towards the solution of the problems. The greater the range of therapeutic methods the better, as intervention strategies need to be tailored to the specific requirements of the individual families and circumstances. However, it is worth pointing out that some parents do not engage in the therapeutic work, and continue to abuse their children. In those situations children have to be removed from home to ensure their protection and safety. A few therapeutic methods are described below.

Counselling

Social care professionals use counselling as a main therapeutic method when working with abusive parents. The primary aim in this therapy is the production of constructive behavioural and personality change. The professional tries to help parents to reflect on the problems they are experiencing, and direct them to a better understanding of themselves and their reactive behaviours towards their children and others. Thus, counselling involves rigorous exploration of presenting problems, clarifying conflicting issues, confused assumption and searching for alternative ways of describing and understanding their dilemmas, and then dealing with them.

In the Rogerian 'client-centred' approach the goal of the intervention is to work in a non-intrusive manner in order to remove the incongruence the person has developed between the experiencing inner-self and the self that person presents to others. By addressing those issues it is hoped to increase positive self-regard and self-direction. Rogerian theory is based on the notion that a person is essentially good, rational, realistic, social and forward-looking, but some may need help with their basic impulse to grow. The assumption is that people have within themselves not only the ability to solve the problems, but also growth impulse to better themselves which can make their behaviour more mature, responsible and satisfying. The therapeutic process with abusive parents aims to facilitate education and socialization, and is seen as a freeing of growth capacities, which enables them to develop empathy, understanding and control of their behaviour towards their children. Reflective counselling with parents who were abused as children, and who abuse their own children, can play an important role in bringing feelings and memories of those events to the surface, and link them to their children's feelings as being abused. Parents are asked to put themselves into their children's position in order to understand how they may feel and how they may suffer. The aim is to raise empathy, awareness, and change of behaviour towards their children.

However, some abusive parents who have little insight, limited intellectual capabilities and lead a highly dysfunctional life are unlikely to benefit from counselling, They may need more practical and structured help in order to produce some change.

Attachment work

As indicated in the previous chapter, abused children tend to be insecurely attached to their mothers, as a result of hostility, lack of attention or indifference. There are numerous ways in which children with attachment disorders can be helped, and in which parent–child bonding can be strengthened. In infancy it would involve proactive and sensitive maternal behaviour during feeding, bathing, changing and responding to the child's signals of distress promptly, consistently and appropriately. Nugent (1996) suggests following techniques to increase secure attachment between children and mothers. Mothers are asked to hold infants while feeding in a gently comfortable way, talk to them while being fed, establish eye contact and smile at baby upon eye contact. They are advised to refuse bottle until baby gives eye contact, and when it does they should give bottle immediately, smile and talk to the baby reassuringly at the same time. They should stroke baby's head, cheek and let baby grasp mother's fingers. When child is resistant and stiff, mother is asked to hold it gently and closely to her body and use a rocking chair while holding it for several minutes every day. Mothers should use a 'snuggle' carrier as much as possible to increase physical togetherness. When changing or bathing a child, mother should show pleasure and reassurance, by patting, kissing, smiling and talking in a warm way.

Older children who are insecurely attached tend to be fearful, apprehensive and tense when in the parents' company. Parents, on the other hand, are dismissive, cold and distant. To reduce mutually avoidant behaviour, and bring parents and children closer together, structured, carefully planned interactions increasing in time should be introduced, such as play and other activities. Parents are shown how to interact and relate to the child, and how to create an atmosphere which is warm, encouraging and anxiety free. The therapist practises with parents the tone of voice they should use, the manner of playing and giving instructions, ways of showing pleasure in the child's achievements, praising, showing attention, and so on, (Iwaniec et al. 1985b, Fahlberg, 1991).

Parents are advised to sit a child on the lap, holding it in a gentle reassuring way two to three times a day, while reading a story or simply watching television. It takes time before the child begins to feel at ease and comfortable in the close physical proximity with the parents, and parents with the child. Repetition of these activities, conducted in a warm caring fashion over time, can bring children and parents closer together (Iwaniec, 1995).

Developmental counselling

The primary aim of developmental counselling is to educate parents about the developmental needs of children, and how those needs can be facilitated. It is important to give information as to what is normal or appropriate to the child's age, sex and level of ability, and to suggest to parents what are reasonable expectations for the child. Unrealistic expectations on the part of parents as to what the child should, or should not do, often leads to parent–child interaction and relationship problems and maltreatment. When pressure is put on a child to perform certain tasks which it is not developmentally ready to perform, then the child will get anxious, confused and nervous, which in turn may bring about behavioural and emotional problems and a sense of helplessness. Knowledge concerning the developmental stages of children can be achieved by: giving examples and explanations of why the child behaves in certain ways at a given developmental stage (e.g. temper-tantrums at 2–3 years of age); pointing out that this is perfectly normal behaviour at that age, due to inner frustration of trying to do things independently, learning new skills, and making sense of the environment they live in, in their own way. Toddlers' endless energy, exploration, questions, display of negativism, temper-tantrums and ambivalence are often perceived by parents as sheer naughtiness, leading to interactional problems and often abuse. Parents need education in the child's psycho-social development, explanation and advice as to how to handle difficult behaviour. Quite often a simple reassurance that a particular behaviour is normal for a certain age is enough to reduce anger and anxiety.

There are a variety of ways that parents can be helped: they can be given a simply written script as a preparation for discussions and clarification; developmental charts can be drawn, e.g. developmental ladder, pointing out what is the time-span for a child to acquire certain skills, underlining individual differences in the speed of development; and developmental quizzes can be played which are both educational and enjoyable. An important part of this work includes modelling by means of showing parents how to promote optimal development of their children and how to improve developmental delays. This includes: learning to play with children, engaging them in meaningful activities, answering questions, helping them to learn new skills, reasoning and guiding them in what is right and wrong, and praising when they accomplish a task or behave in a pro-social way (Iwaniec, 1983, 1997).

Children who present more serious developmental delays and those whose social adjustment has been significantly affected by parental abuse, may require day-care services such as nursery, family centre or daily minder, to repair and to speed-up developmental deficits. Whenever possible, parents should be asked to spend some time in the family centre to learn new child care and behaviour management skills along-side nursery nurses.

Family therapy

Family therapy is concerned with helping dysfunctional abusive families to move from established habits of abusive behaviour and interactions (which precludes them from problem solving) to more open and honest appraisal of their daily lives and mutual relationships. They are encouraged by a variety of therapeutic strategies and homework tasks to think, feel and act differently. Members of the family are encouraged to look at themselves from fresh perspectives and try to work out together solutions to their predicaments. There are several 'schools' of family therapy approaches, such as analytic, strategic and structural.

Minuchin's structural family therapy model focuses its attention on the developmental tasks of each member of the family of various stages of their life-span and it is seen as a system. The family system is seen as a total functioning of three sub-systems – spouses' parents and children and children alone – all contained within a defined boundary and operating within a social cultural context. The patterns of relationship, communication and interaction of all family members are observed and analyzed which forms a therapeutic process and agenda. Herbert (1989) describes structured family therapy techniques as follows:

- Enactment. Clients are encouraged, where appropriate, to talk directly to one another, rather than the therapists.

- Boundary clarification. The clarification of boundaries between family members is the major feature of this work. Therapy is focused on examining the nature of current boundaries and on improving communication between family members. The aim is to bring into the open conflict and the powerful nexus of relationships that the family may be sheltering such as sexual abuse within the family. Family members are asked to talk openly on how they are being treated by different members of the family, and whether they perceive that as fair or unacceptable.

- Changing space. Asking clients in the therapy room to move about can intensify an interaction or help to interpret their relationship with different members of the family. For example; parents who use a child as a mediator or channel of communication to avoid speaking directly to each other, tend to sit with a child in the middle. The therapist blocks that manoeuvre (called triangulation) by moving the child from between them, and asks the parents to talk directly to each other.

- Refraining. The objective of this technique is of helping clients change in a covert, less directed manner. It is an alteration in the emotional or conceptual viewpoint in relation to which situation is experienced. It simply means that people can refrain from thinking about themselves in a self-defeating or destructive way to a more positive way. For example, a mother who thinks that she is useless because she cannot control her two-year-old child's behaviour, might feel better when she is told that children at this age are demanding and oppositional.

Behavioural / cognitive methods

OPERANT PROCEDURE

The most common triggering factor of physical abuse is parental dissatisfaction with their children's behaviour and inability to teach their youngster's pro-social behaviour. Training parents in effective child- behaviour management can reduce the incidence of harsh disciplining and abuse.

Behavioural methods are very much concerned with rules and routines in child and family life, and how those rules are communicated and applied in everyday functioning. Persistency, clarity, consistency, fairness and sensitivity are the key components in the behavioural approach to problem solving. There are numerous behavioural methods and techniques, which lend themselves to help abusive parents and abused children (see Herbert, 1989). Because of limited space, two examples of operant methods will be discussed: one on strengthening pro-social behaviour; and one on reducing anti-social behaviour.

STRENGTHENING PRO-SOCIAL BEHAVIOUR

Helping strategies would involve the provision of various types of reinforcement to increase and strengthen desirable behaviours. Parents are advised to pay attention when a child is behaving well, and to withdraw attention by means of ignoring when a child is behaving badly. Most abusive parents' interactions with children consists of screaming, shouting, smacking and telling-off. Thus, the only time such children receive any attention and personal contact is when they misbehave. Pro-social behaviours are usually ignored (or not taken notice of). Paradoxically, parents unknowingly reinforce the very behaviour that brings a lot of aggravation and concerns, and by ignoring desirable behaviours, they unwittingly reduce the occurrences of good conduct. To reverse the process of learning and to motivate children to behave well, a system of social, symbolic and tangible rewards can be introduced as a treatment programme:

- Social reward/reinforcement. Parents are asked to praise the child each time something praiseworthy has been done, or the child has behaved in a pro-social manner. They should smile, hug, kiss and make a lot of fuss to show their pleasure in the child's behaviour.

- Symbolic reward/reinforcement. This type of reinforcement is particularly helpful for young children as it provides visible signs of achievement for everyone to see, and to make positive comments about how well the child is doing. Symbolic rewards are usually organized in the form of charts, which should be displayed in some prominent position, such as the kitchen door, for everyone to see. A picture or a sticker is put on a chart (in conjunction with the social reward) after each positive behaviour. To make the process exciting and educational for the child, a variety of pictures featuring the child's interests could be used, e.g. animals, cars, aeroplanes, fairy-tale characters, and so on.

- Activity rewards/reinforcements. These rewards are mostly used to improve parent–child interaction and relationship. They provide an opportunity to do things together and to make the enjoyment of each other's company a possibility. As a result of good behaviour the child can earn an extra story at night, play a special game with the parents, have a trip to the park, swimming pool, football match, enjoy a milkshake and hamburger in McDonald's, or have some other treat or activity that parents can afford (Iwaniec, 1995).

REDUCING ANTI-SOCIAL BEHAVIOUR

Time-out from positive reinforcement is the method used to reduce the frequency of troublesome behaviour by a reduction in the opportunity to get reinforcement or reward. When the child behaves in a disruptive manner, and does not respond to parental requests to stop that behaviour (in order to reduce destructive interaction of screaming, arguing and smacking), the child is asked either to leave a room for a few minutes to calm down, or is asked to withdraw from the activities, such as playing with other children, as a mild punishment for being disruptive.

If the mother finds it difficult to use 'time-out' for a child, she should take herself away from the anger-provoking and confrontational situation, to stop a stream of abusive language and harsh disciplining. The time-out technique, which is designed to eliminate inappropriate or undesirable behaviour, is unlikely to succeed unless supplemented by the reinforcement of an alternative and more appropriate behaviour pattern (Schaefer and Briemeister, 1989).

Stress management and anger control

Experiencing occasional anger towards a child is not unusual, and it is a natural part of being a parent. Maltreating parents, however, have difficulties in controlling frustration and anger, so they lash out physically and verbally at the child. Those parents need to learn strategies on how to control anger arousal. The first task will be to explore with parents what leads to the outburst of anger and what are the consequences of that behaviour. The second task is to explore the ways in which behaviour might be changed. Parents are encouraged to reconceptualize anger as a state which is aggravated by self-presented thoughts about the child. Attention is paid to identify and then to alter irrational beliefs (e.g. the child is just lazy, is doing it purposely to annoy me, is wicked and needs to be punished).

Coping strategies, such as self-instruction and thought-stopping, are very effective in reducing anger arousal and irrational thoughts. Parents are instructed how to interfere with anger-provoking thoughts as soon as they begin to occur, and to instruct themselves as to how they are going to deal with the problems. Types of self-instruction that may be used include those that encourage a focus on the task to be accomplished (for example, 'I must keep calm', 'I can manage', 'I must not lose my temper'), and those that encourage other incompatible behaviour such as getting a cup of tea, relaxing, or simply taking a deep breath in order to calm down. It is useful to role-play a scenario with parents, to give them confidence and understanding on how to cope in similar situations. For example, bed- wetting leads to much anger, quite often resulting in physical and emotional abuse. If parents managed to stop themselves getting angry (because a child wet the bed) they can tell themselves 'We have managed that quite well. This is not the end of the world. I will just change the bed. He is quite young, so it is not unusual, he/she is not doing it on purpose, she/he cannot help it'. Such self-talk helps the parents to feel better, be more in control, thus reducing physical and verbal lashing of the child (Novaco, 1975; Meichenbaum, 1977; Iwaniec, 1997).

Cognitive restructuring

Among the commonest characteristics of abusive parents are their self-defeating thoughts and beliefs about their abilities to cope effectively with different life-tasks. These dysfunctional thoughts lead to dysfunctional feelings, and consequently, to negative outcomes for parents and children. Many parents who experience difficulties in child-rearing tend to run themselves down, saying that they cannot cope, are useless and ineffective as carers. The aims of cognitive work with those parents are to help them to begin viewing things in ways which generate positive thoughts, beliefs and feelings about their capabilities of evolving problem-solving strategies, and to generate emotional energy to take action, based on the conviction that they are able to produce change. This therapy points to successful aspects of parents' lives, so that they can take comfort from those aspects and redirect their thinking to their strengths and build on them, in order to prepare them to tackle difficult problems.

The first task of the therapist is to identify accurately any damaging thoughts, and to demonstrate their link with negative feelings and unhappy outcomes. Parents are asked to record unhelpful thoughts that seem to recur frequently, and to link them with feelings in order to create a realization of how such thoughts may influence behaviour and well-being, and how exaggerated they are at times. These beliefs and feelings often prove to be untrue as they stand, because they are falsely linked to other areas of life (e.g. 'I am useless as a mother because I cannot even feed the child'). Being ineffective in one area, or with one child, however, does not mean that the mother is useless at everything. She might be a good cook, manager or a good home-maker. Parents are asked to produce a balance-sheet of positive and negative aspects of their functioning for elaboration with the therapist, and to work out step-by-step strategies to produce the desired outcome (Scott, 1989; Neville *et al.*, 1995).

Summary

This chapter began by describing and defining various forms of child abuse and neglect based on various research studies. It went on to explore the thorny questions of definitions and difficulties associated with identification and evidence provision. Some indicators and manifestations of physical, sexual, emotional and non-organic failure-to-thrive were presented and supported by research findings, and a few treatment methods were discussed.

Seminar Questions

1. It is argued that emotional abuse is at the core of other forms of child maltreatment. Identify how it might be linked to physical abuse, sexual abuse and failure-to-thrive.

2. Physical and emotional neglect is associated with non-organic failure-to-thrive children. What other factors seem to be common in maintaining this problem?

3. Omission of meeting children's basic needs is linked to inadequate parenting and various environmental and personal stresses. What helping strategies can you devise to alleviate these problems?

4. Is it necessary to know about the causes of child abuse in a particular family (Chapter 15) to decide on a method of intervention?

Further Reading

Buchanan, A. (1996) *Cycles of Child Maltreatment: Facts, Fallacies and Interventions.* Chichester: Wiley.
The latest book about various theories of child abuse and neglect and their application to everyday practice.

Chess, S. and Thomas, A. (1989) 'Issues in the clinical application of temperament.' In G.A. Kohnstamm, J.E. Bates and M.K. Rothbart (eds), *Temperament in Childhood*, pp.337–386. Chichester: Wiley.
A chapter both detailed and concise describing easy, difficult, and slow-to-warm-up children's temperaments.

Gough, D.A. (1993) *Child Abuse Interventions: A Review of the Literature,* London: HMSO.
A summary of 225 intervention programmes when dealing with physical abuse of children.

References

Angoustinos, M. (1987) 'Developmental effects of child abuse.' *Child Abuse and Neglect 11*, 15–27.

Bagley, C. and Ramsay, R. (1986) 'Disrupted childhood and vulnerability to sexual assault: long term sequelae with implications for counselling.' *Social Work and Human Sexuality, 4*, 33–48.

Baker, A.W. and Duncan, S.P. (1985) 'Child sexual abuse: a study of prevalence in Great Britain.' *Child Abuse and Neglect, 9*, 457–467.

Barbero, G.J. and Shaheen, E. (1967) 'Environmental failure-to-thrive: a clinical view, *Journal of Pediatrics, 71*, 639–644.

Batchelor, J., and Kerslake, A. (1990) *Failure to Find Failure-to-thrive.* London: Whiting & Birch.

Belsky, J. and Vondra, J. (1989) 'Lessons from child abuse: the determinants of parenting.' In D. Cicchetti and V. Carlson (eds) *Child Maltreatment. Theory and Research on the Causes and Consequences of Child Abuse and Neglect.* New York: Cambridge University Press.

Berliner, L. (1991) 'Treating the effects of sexual assault.' In K. Murray and D.A. Gough (eds) *Intervening in Child Sexual Abuse,* Edinburgh: Scottish Academic Press.

Blizzard, R.M. and Bulatovic, A. (1993) 'Psychological short stature: a syndrome with many variables.' *Bailliere's Clinical Endocrinology and Metabolism, 6*, 3, 687–712.

Bools, C.N., Neale, B.A. and Meadow, S.R. (1992) 'Co-morbidity associated with fabricated illness (Munchausen syndrome by proxy).' *Archives of Disease in Childhood, 67*, 77–79.

Bowlby, J. (1951) *Maternal Care and Mental Health.* Geneva: Bulletin of the World Health Organisation.

Briere, J.N. (1992) *Child Abuse Trauma: Theory and Treatment of the Lasting Effects.* Newbury Park: Sage.

Coleman, R. and Provence, S. (1957) 'Environmental retardation (hospitalism) in infants living in families.' *Pediatrics, 19*, 285.

Conte, J. and Schuerman, J.R. (1988) 'The effects of sexual abuse on children: a multidimensional view.' In G.E. Wyatt and G.J. Powell (eds) *Lasting Effects of Child Sexual Abuse.* Newbury Park: Sage.

Department of Health (1991) *Working Together under the Children Act 1989.* London: HMSO.

Dubowitz, A. (1993) 'A conceptual definition of child neglect.' *Criminal Justice and Behaviour, 20*, 1, 8–26.

Egeland, B. (1988) 'Breaking the cycle of abuse.' In K. Browne, C. Davies and P. Stratton (eds) *Early Prediction and Prevention of Child Abuse.* Chichester: Wiley.

Emery, J.L. and Taylor, E.M. (1986) *Letter in New England Journal of Medicine, 315*, 1676.

Fahlberg, V.I. (1991) *A Child's Journey through Placement. (UK edition).* London: British Agencies for Adoption and Fostering.

Farmer, E. and Owen, M. (1995) *Child Protection Practice: Private Risks and Public Remedies – Decision-making, Intervention, and Outcome in Child-Protection Work,* London: HMSO.

Finkelhor, D. and Korbin, J. (1988) 'Child abuse as an international issue.' *Child Abuse and Neglect, 12*, 2–24.

Garbarino, J., Guttmann, E. and Seeley, J.W. (1986) *The Psychologically Battered Child.* San Francisco, CA: Jossey-Bass.

Garbarino, J. and Sherman, D. (1980) 'High-risk neighborhoods and high-rise families: the human ecology of child maltreatment.' *Child Development, 51*, 188–198.

Gough, D.A. (1992) 'Survey of Scottish child protection registers.' In Directors of Social Work in Scotland, *Policy, Practice, Procedures, and Protection. An Overview of Child Abuse Issues and Practice in Scotland.* Edinburgh: HMSO.

Gough, D.A. (1993) *Child Abuse Interventions. A Review of the Research Literature.* London: HMSO.

Hanks, H. and Hobbs, C. (1993) 'Failure to thrive – a model for treatment.' *Bailliere's Clinical Paediatrics, 1*, 1, 101–119.

Herbert, M. (1989) *Working with Children and their Families.* Chicago, IL: Lyceum Books Inc.

HMSO (1995) *Child Protection. Messages from Research.* Studies in Child Protection London: HMSO.

Iwaniec, D. (1983) 'Social and psychological factors in the aetiology and management of children who fail to thrive.' *PhD Thesis.* Department of Psychology, University of Leicester.

Iwaniec, D., Herbert, M. and McNeish, A.S. (1985b) 'Social work with failure-to-thrive children and their families – Part II: Social work intervention.' *British Journal of Social Work, 15*, 375–389.

Iwaniec, D. (1995) *The Emotionally Abused and Neglected Child. Identification, Assessment, and Intervention.* Chichester: Wiley.

Iwaniec, D. (1997) 'Evaluating parent training for emotionally-abusive and neglectful parents: comparing individual versus individual group intervention.' *Research on Social Work Practice, 7*, 3, 329–349.

Kelly, R.J. (1982) 'Behavioural reorientation of pedophiliacs: can it be done?' *Clinical Psychology Review, 2*, 387–408.

Kettle, J. (1990) *Survey of Treatment Facilities for Abused Children and of Treatment Facilities for Young Sexual Abusers of Children.* London: National Children's Home.

Leonard, M.F., Rhymes, J.P. and Solnit, A.J. (1966) 'Failure to thrive in infants.' *American Journal of Diseases of Children, 111,* 600–612.

Lynch, M. (1988) 'The consequences of child abuse.' In N. Browne, C. Davies and P. Stratton (eds) *Early Prediction and Prevention of Child Abuse.* Chichester: John Wiley and sons.

Mannarino, A.P., Cohen, J.A., Smith, J.A. and Moore-Motily, S. (1991) 'Six and twelve month follow-up of sexually abused girls.' *Journal of Interpersonal Violence, 6,* 4, 494–511.

Meichenbaum, D.H. (1977) *Cognitive Behaviour Modification. An Integrative Approach.* New York: Plenum Press.

Monck, E., Bentovim, A., Goodall, G., Hyde, C., Lewin, K. and Sharland, E. (1993) *Child Sexual Abuse: A Descriptive and Treatment Study.* London: HMSO.

Mrazek, P. (1980) 'Sexual abuse of children.' *Journal of Child Psychology and Psychiatry 21,* 91.

Neville, D., King, L., and Beak, D. (1995) *Promoting Positive Parenting.* Aldershot: Arena Publications.

Novaco, R.W. (1975) *Anger Control: The Development and Evaluation of an Experimental Treatment.* Levington, MA: D.C. Health & Co.

Nugent, O. (1996) 'Issues of bonding and attachment.' *Child Care in Practice, 2,* 4, 24–28.

Osborne, Y. (1985) 'A retrospective study of self-identified victims of psychological child abuse.' Unpublished. Louisiana State University, Baton Rouge.

Peters, S.D., Wyatt, G.E. and Finkelhor, D. (1986) 'Prevalence.' In D. Finkelhor (ed.) *A Sourcebook on Child Sexual Abuse.* Beverly Hills, CA: Sage.

Powell, G.F., Low, J.F. and Speers, M.A. (1987) 'Behaviour as a diagnostic aid in failure to thrive.' *Journal of Developmental and Behavioural Pediatrics, 8,* 18–24.

Schaefer, C.E. and Briemeister, J. (1989) *Handbook of Parent Training: Parents as Co-Therapists for Children's Behaviour Problems.* New York: Wiley.

Scott, M. (1989) *A Cognitive-Behavioural Approach to Clients' Problems.* London: Routledge.

Skuse, D. (1992) 'The relationship between deprivation, physical growth, and the impaired development of language.' In P. Fletcher and D. Hall (eds) *Specific Speech and Language Disorders in Children.* London: Whurr.

Skuse, D., Albanese, A., Stanhope, R., Gilmour, J. and Voss, L. (1996) 'A new stress-related syndrome of growth failure and hyperphagia in children, associated with reversibility of growth-hormone insufficiency.' *The Lancet, 348,* 9024, 353–357.

Skuse, D. and Bentovim, A. (1994) 'Physical *and* emotional maltreatment.' In M. Rutter, E.D. Taylor and L. Hersov, *Child and Adolescent Psychiatry,* Oxford: Blackwell.

Sluckin, A. (1987) *Report of the Department of Psychology.* University of Leicester, Topic Group on Emotional Abuse. (Unpublished paper.)

Spitz, R.A. (1945) 'Hospitalism: an inquiry into the genesis of psychiatric conditions in early childhood.' *Psychoanalytic Study of the Child, 1,* 53–74.

Widdowson, E.M. (1951) 'Mental contentment and physical growth.' *The Lancet, 260,* 1316–1318.

Wolfe, D.A. (1988) 'Child abuse and neglect.' In E.J. Mash and L.G. Terdal (eds) *Behavioral Assessment of Childhood Disorders.* New York: Guilford Press.

Wolfe, V.V., Gentile, G. and Wolfe, D.A. (1989) 'The impact of sexual abuse on children: a PTSD formulation.' *Behavior Therapy, 20,* 2, 215–228.

CHAPTER 17

Adolescents and Society

Leo B. Hendry

Introduction

The characteristics of today's society – consumerism, the state of the family, the training and employment situation, rising homelessness, drugs, the threat of AIDS and lawlessness – bring into focus reflections of the adult world that young people face in their journey across adolescence. Today, the adolescent experience is unlike that of previous generations. Adolescence starts five years earlier, marriage takes place six or seven years later than it did 100 years ago, and co-habitation, perhaps as a prelude to marriage, is a rapidly growing trend (Coleman and Hendry, 1999). At the same time, compulsory schooling has been extended and there are pressures on the workforce to become more highly skilled, thus putting a premium on continuing education. The delay in acquiring an income is just one of the factors which may defer the young person's passage to adulthood. The number and type of adjustments and changes young people face have often been perceived to be at the root of so-called 'storm and stress' of the teenage years (Lloyd, 1985).

The social conventions of recent years have given adolescents greater self-determination at steadily younger ages. Yet this greater freedom for adolescents does carry with it more risks and greater costs when errors of judgement are made: 'dropping out' of school, being out of work, teenage pregnancy, sexually transmitted diseases, being homeless, drug addiction and suicide, are powerful examples of the price that some young people pay for their extended freedom.

In this chapter I shall first provide an overview of major issues in adolescence: growing up in present day society and lifestyle development. This will provide you with an understanding of general issues that face adolescents. This leads on to a consideration of more specific issues which social workers and related professionals may encounter. Throughout the chapter you are challenged to relate these research findings and theoretical perspectives to your own professional philosophy and practice.

Growing up in Present Day Society: Issues of Lifestyle

Over the last 15 years or so we have seen the growth of consumerism and the primacy of the market-place, and their influence on young people's development. In Britain and elsewhere there is increasing scrutiny of the behaviour of adolescents by policy-makers and, despite a focus on the need to protect young people's legal rights, there has been an erosion of autonomy.

Western societies have become more affluent, and the old social attitudes relating to age, class and gender have broken down. As a result, it can be argued that we are freer to 'appropriate' meanings into our lives from wherever we choose. Social networks are formed around soccer teams, discos, pubs, night clubs, youth organizations, raves and so on. Yet for some young people involvement in these 'tribal' networks and lifestyles can be difficult because of lack of opportunities and cash. The networks can also be influenced by what Matza and Sykes (1961) in a different context called 'subterranean' social class values. Such 'embedded' social class values can still influence attitudes, tastes, choices and overall lifestyles, even though adolescents from all walks of life can, and do, converge on the same leisure contexts such as raves, pop concerts and night clubs (Hendry et al., 1993).

The problematic pattern for youth of work training schemes and unemployment has implications for adolescent transitions (e.g. Roberts and Parsell, 1990). Hendry and Raymond (1983), for instance, highlighted connections between work and leisure from the adolescents' perspective. Unemployed young people cut off from the culture of work also had their leisure activities curtailed. If they continued to visit pubs, clubs and cafes they had to restrict their spending. Local discos replaced city-centre nightspots. When they went out they usually remained in the neighbourhood, yet local youth club attendance was perceived as 'childish'. The major impact of unemployment seemed to be its effect on the transition from adolescence to adulthood with exclusions from certain 'tribal' contexts. Unemployment appeared to create a bleak landscape for some adolescents in which leisure, with all its concomitant social opportunities, lessened or vanished (Coleman and Hendry, 1999).

Abel and McQueen (1992) operationalized the concept of lifestyle as a complex patterning of three basic elements: behaviours, orientations and resources. *Behaviours* are the actions and activities individuals perform in everyday life; *orientations* include attitudes, values, tastes and beliefs; while *resources* consist of the characteristics – either material (e.g. having wealthy parents) or psycho-social (e.g. being female, or living in a 're-constituted' family), which an individual possesses because of his/her social position. The first two of these are elements of choice while the third is related to structural factors. These basic dimensions interact to form an individual's way of life. However, it is also the case that structural constraints at a societal level affect behaviours, orientations and resources. Hence, the influence of structural constraints and individual characteristics results in the emergence of general lifestyles; but variations in these influences for particular adolescents give rise to that adolescents specific lifestyle.

Discussion point
   ° In what ways do you consider adolescence to be a different experience for young people today by comparison with your own adolescence?

Changing Relationships in Adolescence
Adolescence as a transitional period from childhood to adulthood requires changes from child–parent relationships to young adult–parent relationships. This may not necessarily be easy for either young people or their parents. Family settings can affect individual development, depending on the degree of self-agency the adolescent possesses and the life events parents are facing.

There is quite a bit of evidence that the support of the family is crucial to adolescents, and that those who do not have strong support from parents are more likely to become involved in undesirable behaviours. (Noller and Callan, 1991, p.123)

During adolescence, greater significance is given to peers, as providers of advice, support, feedback and companionship, as models for behaviour and as sources of comparative information concerning personal qualities and skills. Relationships with parents alter in the direction of greater equality and reciprocity (e.g. Coleman and Hendry, 1999; Hendry *et al.*, 1993) and parental authority comes to be seen as an area which is itself open to discussion and negotiation (Youniss and Smollar, 1990).

In Hendry *et al.*'s (1993) longitudinal study, parents were a first choice over friends in such areas as discussing progress at school, careers, problems at school, but not necessarily in more personal matters. Mothers were preferred over fathers as confidantes in all areas except that of careers and sex as far as boys were concerned, and not surprisingly, for both sexes where problems with mother were concerned. The majority of girls chose to confide in their mother over problems with friends and nearly half the boys preferred to speak to their mother about such matters. Similarly, doubts about their own abilities would be voiced to their mother by nearly half the girls and one third of the boys. Figures like these point to a disengagement by fathers. Girls tend to be very uncomfortable talking to their fathers about pubertal issues across adolescence, and learn almost nothing about puberty from their fathers (Brooks-Gunn, 1987). What this all points too, as Youniss and Smollar (1985) have noted, is that a mother's role in enforcing family rules brings her into conflict with her children more readily, but she is still viewed as being supportive and tender, not 'distanced' in the way that fathers are seen to be.

Adolescent friendships normally exist within the larger social structure of peer relationships. In this larger social setting each adolescent has a more or less well-defined peer status. Close friendships are not independent of such status. Friends tend to be similar in their positions within the larger group. As the individual adolescent seeks to grow more independent of the family, peer groups and friendship groups become important points of reference in social development. Peer groups and friendships provide social contexts for shaping the day-to-day values, even though these may be similar to parental values in some instances. Hendry *et al.* (1993) showed that patterns of friendships change across adolescence, with same-sex friendships being mainly independent of relationships with boy-friends/girl-friends. Further, in the formation of heterosexual partnerships in later adolescence, young women are more likely to be in advance of young men, even if it occurs at the expense of best (same-sex) friendships. This move towards 'serious' heterosexual partnerships emphasizes the earlier social sophistication of young women at all stages of adolescence.

Social class differences are apparent in the perceived value of individuality in relation to popularity with friends and peers, with middle class adolescents being more likely to subscribe to this as a worthwhile characteristic. Peer pressure lessens across adolescence, perhaps as a manifestation of growing self-confidence and independence. This can be linked to findings that self-perceptions associated with friends and peers show that 'having many friends' is most potent in mid-adolescence.

These findings highlight the importance of peer pressures in adolescence. Peer pressures transmit group norms and maintain loyalties amongst group members. However, conformity to the group is the price that has to be paid for approval and acceptance by peers. A component of perceived peer popularity involves conformity to the peer group with respect to behaviours such as 'drinking and smoking', 'being straight' or 'going out with the opposite sex' (Hendry *et al.*, 1993). Brown (1982) asked adolescents to report on the expectations of friends, and discovered that a disapproval of drinking in early adolescence shifted towards a raised pressure to drink in mid-adolescence, whereas pressures to use drugs and have sexual intercourse were strongest in later adolescence. However, Brown also noted that adolescents often actively discouraged such activities. The results of the Hendry *et al.* study agree with these findings. For instance, peer pressure to 'drink and smoke' was greatest at 15–16 years of age in mid-adolescence, but at the same time, many adolescents did not perceive such behaviours as particularly relevant to acceptance by the peer group.

Discussion point
- ° What major aspects of peer and friendship groupings do social care professionals need to understand in working with adolescents?

Theoretical Perspectives

The adolescent years are a period when great adjustments have to be made by young people to changes both within themselves and in society, and in relation to the expectations which society places on them. Many young people make the transitions to adulthood with relative ease, but some are handicapped by economic and structural forces which make their passage to a worthwhile adult status very difficult. Others have the misfortune to have to cope with too many challenges to their self-esteem and identity at one time.

As Coleman and Hendry (1999) have outlined, there seems little doubt that some of the most important events to which young people have to adjust are the multitude of physiological and morphological changes which occur during early adolescence, and which are associated with what is generally know as puberty. Puberty is the process by which children reach reproductive maturity, and it consists of a number of interdependent biological processes, ranging from the purely physiological (e.g. hormonal) to the physical (e.g. pubic hair growth, and vaginal or testicular development) to the psycho-social (i.e. changes visible to others, such as breast growth or facial hair and which have social meaning). The psychological impact of these changes will vary with the social context and the reaction of others.

In considering theoretical explanations of the way adolescents cope with these transitions, three different approaches are presented (see Boxes 17.1 and 17.2). Briefly, Coleman and Hendry (1999) suggested that various 'relational' issues come into focus sequentially across adolescence, declining from a peak of concern as the individual develops the psycho-social skills to resolve particular issues (see Figure 17.1).

Coleman and Hendry (1990) suggested that concern about gender roles and relationships with the opposite sex declines from a peak around 13 years; concerns about acceptance by or rejection from peers are highly important around 15 years; while issues regarding the gaining of independence from parents climb steadily to peak around 16 years and then begin to tail off.

Such a theory may provide some insight into the amount of disruption and crisis implicit in adolescence, and the relatively successful adaptation among most adolescents. The majority of teenagers cope by dealing with one issue at a time. Adaptation covers a number of years, with the adolescent attempting to solve one issue, then the next. Thus, any stresses resulting from the need to adapt to new models of behaviour are rarely concentrated all at one time. Those who, for whatever reason, do have more than one issue to cope with at one time are most likely to have problems of adjustment.

The onset of puberty coincides with the first of these three focal issues, namely adolescents' concern with seeking a gender identity and the commencement of more adult-like social relationships. The young person then moves on to a second 'rehearsal' stage involving social skills, roles and strategies, mostly associated with peer acceptance and peer involvement before testing their acceptance in adult society. The third focal 'step' sees the young person being more accepted into, and more comfortable in, various adult social contexts and settings such as

---

Box 17.1 A Focal Theory of Adolescence

Coleman's 'focal theory' reasons that the transition between childhood and adulthood cannot be achieved without substantial adjustments of both a psychological and social nature. Nevertheless, despite the amount of overall change experienced, most young people are extremely resilient and appear to cope with adjustments without undue stress.

'Focal theory' offers a reason or rationale for this apparent contradiction in that at different ages particular sorts of relationship patterns come into focus, in the sense of being most prominent, but that no pattern is specific to one age only. Thus the patterns overlap, different issues come into focus at different times, but simply because an issue is not the most prominent feature at a particular age does not mean that it may not be critical for some individuals. These ideas, derived from empirical findings, combine to suggest a symbolic model of adolescent development where each curve represents a different issue or relationship.

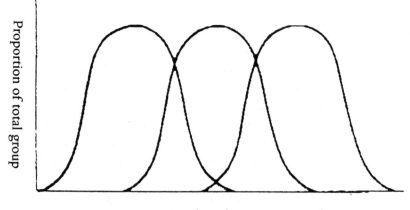

Figure 17.1 Coleman's Focal Theory

clubs and pubs, entering the labour market, having longer term 'responsible' relationships, and developing a maturity of outlook. Coffield *et al.*'s (1986) model reminds us of the broader social and cultural factors which impact on the transition to adulthood in the various developmental domains (see Figure 17.2).

Coffield *et al.* are right to draw attention to the social circumstances of the individual, for these will obviously contribute in a substantial way to the adolescent's psychological adjustment. There can be little doubt that in situations of economic hardship it will be more difficult to manage the adolescent transitions in a satisfactory manner.

On the other hand, Lerner (1985) in discussing lifespan developmental psychology stresses the dynamic interactions in the socialization process and draws attention to the way

---

Box 17.2 An Integrating Model

Coffield *et al.* (1986) offer an integrating model, derived from their experience of carrying out research in the North-East of England with young people, many of whom were unemployed, all of whom were living at the periphery of British society. In their model, class and patriarchy are seen as all-pervading influences which determine, to a large extent, the options and choices available to young people in this under-privileged section of society (see Figure 17.2). As they write:

> Class and patriarchy are means whereby some gain advantages over others; they are best thought of as relationships between people which accord power, wealth and status to some and deny it to others. Our argument is that all of the main factors in our model tend to interact vigorously, creating different patterns of problems and opportunities for individuals.... In contrast to Coleman and Hendry, who argue that young adults cope with one issue at a time, we would claim that most of them are struggling to cope with all these different aspects of life, which impinge upon them simultaneously. (Coffield *et al.*, 1986, pp.213–214)

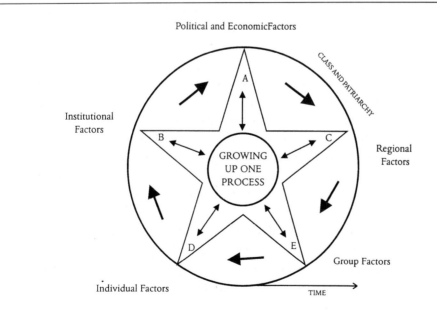

Figure 17.2 Coffield et al.'s (1986) Integrating Models

adolescents are involved in three modes: as a stimulus (eliciting different reactions from the social environment); as a processor, in making sense of the behaviour of others; and as an agent, shaper and selector, by doing things, making choices and influencing events.

These ideas concerning reciprocal influences and individual young people as 'active agents' in their own transition process from childhood to adulthood are important concepts in gaining an understanding of young people in present-day society. Furthermore, the theoretical orientations provide a useful base from which to view particular behaviours which are a feature of adolescence. These are considered in the next section.

Psycho-Social Issues and Young People

> Up until some twenty or thirty years ago, many people viewed adolescence as an age period necessarily characterised by emotional turmoil and disturbance... Paradoxically just as it was being appreciated that most adolescents did not manifest psycho social disorders ... there has been a marked rise in psycho-social problems in young people – criminal activities, suicidal behaviour, alcohol and drug abuse, depression and eating disorders. (Rutter, 1995, p.ix)

There are a variety of psycho-social 'tasks' to be achieved in the adolescent transition – personal development, social relationships, leaving school, seeking qualifications and employment (or unemployment), leisure pursuits, creating a particular lifestyle, becoming mature and independent – and all are important to understand. According to person-environment 'fit' theory (Eccles and Midgley, 1989), behaviour, motivation and mental health are influenced by the 'goodness of fit' between the characteristics individuals bring to their social environments and the demands of these social environments. However, there are a variety of individual 'biological factors', psycho-social factors, and wider ecological factors which interact to disrupt this 'goodness of fit' equation. A similar perspective is contained in the 'ecological model' (Bronfenbrenner 1979), which considers individual development as the result of a series of ongoing interactions and adaptations between the individual and a set of overlapping social systems that relates both to the individual and to each other (Bronfenbrenner 1979).

It should also be recognized that adolescents may not be as counter-cultural as it is often depicted nor are they uniformly hedonistic and self-centred. In fact, peers often support traditional parental attitudes and beliefs and can work in concert with, rather than in opposition to, adult goals and achievements. Nevertheless, peer influences may become more critically important for young people whose access to parental influences is impaired. Youth appears to reflect societal values and behaviours. For example, adolescent drug and alcohol use and sexual activity seem to be interconnected with shifts and attitudes among the adult population, yet issues of timing and modes of transition for such attitudinal shifts are not particularly well understood.

The disjunction between physical capabilities, socially approved independence and power and the ambiguities of their current status can be stressful for young people. Five aspects of adolescent life are discussed in this section: risk-taking and delinquency; body image; sexuality; drugs (both legal and illegal); and leaving home. The aim is to help you understand the background to these issues.

Risk-taking and delinquency

Though risk-taking has been one of the attributes of youth since adolescence became recognized as a distinctive period of the lifespan, the concept remains ill-defined. Are young people at risk because they pursue different courses of action to adults? Or do they pursue very similar courses of action to adults, but are more vulnerable because they lack the experience to resolve situations to their advantage? From where does this supposed predilection for risk taking derive? Is it part of the psychological make-up of youth – a thrill-seeking stage in a developmental transition – a necessary rite of passage *en route* to the acquisition of adult skills and self-esteem? There also are questions as to whether the supposed problems of adolescence can be attributed to risk taking and the need for excitement.

It is important to understand the very positive attraction of thrilling and dangerous behaviours for some adolescents. Many young people in their teenage years seek out thrills, excitement and risks as earnestly as they did in childhood, perhaps to escape from a drab existence, to exert some control over their own lives, or to achieve something. Once we start to make the journey into adulthood there are fewer legitimate venues for risk taking, and the ones left open to us as adults often bear serious consequences. Consequently, those who see juvenile crimes only as a protest of the underprivileged deny the real thrill that such delinquent activities can inspire. Thus, various anti-social activities can (potentially) provide therapeutic effects. Yet little is known of the properties, contexts and motivations which generate emotional effects for young people in present-day society. Though the majority of young people are hard-working, law abiding and conventional, some adolescents exhibit rebellion both in their self-presentation and in their behaviour.

Risk taking and delinquency can be seen as inter-related phenomena (see also Chapter 19). Boys make up the biggest proportion of juvenile offenders and enter the justice system at an earlier age than do girls. In 1961 the peak age for male offenders was 14 years. By 1989 the peak age had increased to 18 years mainly because of changes in the system of juvenile justice. Many of the crimes reflect the age and gender of the perpetrators. Much media attention, for instance, has focused recently on the fad for 'joy riding' – stealing cars and performing stunt tricks in them. More threateningly, in 1981, 1985 and early in the 1990s, many inner city areas of Britain witnessed events, variously described as riots, disturbances and uprisings.

A number of theorists have emphasized the role of identity processes in determining delinquent behaviour (Emler and Reicher, 1995). The desire to identify with a peer group especially in mid-adolescence (Coleman and Hendry, 1999) requires adherence to particular types of behaviour and roles which imposes a group conformity even when anti-social actions may result. Adolescents are, by their very nature, heavily influenced by peer group norms, prone to risk-taking and likely to be thrill-seeking.

In addition, general developmental predictors of delinquency (and drug misuse) can be cited: disturbed family background, school disaffection, poor social skills, peer associations, precocious social behaviour, and so on (see Farrington (1994) and Chapter 19). Interestingly, Rutter (1995) has pointed out that, while we know a great deal about the factors statistically associated with anti-social behaviour, we know less about the mechanisms and processes involved.

To these views should be added a perspective that crime and delinquency in our society are in some measure the cost of certain kinds of social development. It has been argued that the predominant ethic of our society is acquisitiveness and desire for success. But not everyone can be rich or successful legitimately. The values underlying juvenile delinquency may be far less deviant than is commonly assumed. Furthermore, the relationship between social deprivation, status frustration and race has moved juvenile crime to centre stage in policy matters.

It would also appear that the quest for excitement and violence is symbolic in the sense that young people 'use' these behaviours to identify, however misguidedly, with adult patterns of behaviour. Research has focused, especially, on drug and alcohol use, cigarette smoking, sexual behaviour and delinquency (e.g. Jessor and Jessor, 1977). Most of these behaviours would not be so alarming if seen in adults but are perceived as inappropriate for young people in the process of growing up. Silbereisen et al. (1987) have proposed that a number of so-called anti-social activities are in fact purposive, self-regulating and aimed at coping with aspects of adolescent development. They can play a constructive developmental role at least over a short term. Early sexual activity and early child-bearing or the experiences of living through parental divorce may have similar functions in providing positive roles, goals and experiences in young people's lives, even though on the surface they appear to be negative experiences (Petersen et al., 1987).

Like adults, teenagers typically adopt behaviours in the belief that they will help achieve some desired end such as giving pleasure or gaining peer acceptance. In doing so they are likely to ignore or discount evidence that particular behaviours may pose a potential threat to them. Many of the explanations regarding adolescent risk behaviour thus rest on accounts of the development of the individual. Both Irwin (1989) and Jack (1989) for instance, consider that risk-taking is a normal transitional behaviour during adolescence. Indeed risk-taking is seen as fulfilling developmental needs related to autonomy and the need for mastery and individuation (Irwin and Millstein, 1986).

Discussion point
  ° Identify protective factors and risk factors in relation to delinquency. What can be done to increase protection and decrease risk?

Body image and dieting
An understanding of adolescence needs to take account of the physiological changes of puberty which inevitably exercise a profound effect. The body alters radically, and it is not surprising that many adolescents experience clumsiness as they attempt to adapt to these changes. The body also alters in function with new and sometimes worrying physical experiences such as the girl's first period, or the boy's nocturnal emissions. Perhaps most important of all, however, is the effect that such physical changes have upon identity. The development of the individual's identity requires not only the notion of being separate and different from others, but also a sense of self-consistency, and a firm knowledge of how one appears to the rest of the world. Dramatic bodily changes seriously affect these aspects of identity, and represent a considerable challenge in adaptation for even the most well-adjusted young person. Adolescents observe these changes, evaluate them, attempt to integrate them in

a personal 'style' and invite (sometimes even challenge) others, more or less consciously, to be involved in the quest for identity, since identity is not just 'for oneself', but also 'for others' (e.g. Goffman, 1971; Rodriguez-Tomé, 1972).

Amongst others, Davies and Furnham (1986) have shown that the average adolescent is not only sensitive to, but often critical of their changing physical self. Because of sexual and gender development young people are inevitably confronted, perhaps for the first time, with cultural standards of beauty and attractiveness in relation to evaluating their own 'body image'. Direct influences may come, for instance, via media images or by the reactions of others (e.g. Eagly *et al.*, 1991).

Concerns about weight are frequently accompanied by dieting practices, and sometimes by serious eating disorders (Greenfeld *et al.*, 1987; Ledoux *et al.*, 1991). Some adolescents are particularly self-conscious about certain aspects of their 'shape', and their self-perceptions of their bodies may be closely related to their leisure pursuits (e.g. disco dancing) and relationships with the opposite sex. Dieting behaviour in adolescence coincides with the generally heightened awareness of appearance common to this age group. This concern about 'body image' may be a refusal to 'grow up', 'a rejection of femininity', or a reaction to criticism and ridicule. In extreme examples this can set adolescents – and especially young women – on the pathway to anorexia nervosa. Most adolescents with anorexia nervosa report initial efforts to control dietary intake not different from others engaging in transient restrictive dieting. Crisp (1980) and Bruch (1985) stated that many develop the 'binge' syndrome of bulimia nervosa, and other authors have reported that half of their bulimic patients have a history of anorexia (Lacey, 1983; Hsu and Holder, 1986). Further, anorexic young women who are caught up in conflictual and confused family situations, which can include sexual abuse (Palmer *et al.*, 1990), often talk in 'pseudo-psychological' terms about 'something inside which stops me eating', turning some real and highly conflictual problems in family life, into a solely 'internal' conflict. Emotional and cognitive changes cannot be considered divorced from physical development at any time, but particularly not in adolescence.

Sex and sexuality

Adolescent sexual behaviour has always been a cause of concern to adults in society. Fears about sexual activity leading to unwanted pregnancy are coupled with a desire to protect the younger adolescent from exploitation and pressure to become sexually active before they have the emotional or social maturity to cope. In recent years, of course, the spread of HIV through sexual activity has caused increased focus to be put on young people's activities (see Chapter 21).

Ford (1987) identified the important indicators of patterns of heterosexual activity as age at first intercourse, the level of pre-marital sex, the number of sex partners and the proportion using a condom. Johnson *et al.* (1994) have shown that the age for first heterosexual intercourse reveals a pattern of decreasing age at occurrence compared to the past (see also Farrell, 1978; Ford and Bowie, 1989), together with some convergence in the behaviour of young men and young women over time. In the past four decades, the median age at first heterosexual intercourse has fallen from 21 to 17 years for women and from 20 to 17 years for men, while the proportion reporting its occurrence before the age of 16 has increased from fewer than 1 per cent of women now aged 55 years and over to nearly one in five of those now in their teens.

Apart from age and gender, variables such as socio-economic status, nationality, ethnic origin and cultural background will, to some extent, play their part in determining sexual behaviour. The broad social trends described above also need to be considered in the light of other studies which have highlighted the different experience of young people in urban and rural settings (Johnson et al., 1994). Ford and Bowie (1989) found 56 per cent of youngsters in rural areas were sexually experienced compared with 70 per cent of their counterparts in urban and semi-urban areas.

Although teenagers are more likely to be sexually experienced than they have been in the past, there is no evidence that they are more likely to have casual sex relationships. Ford and Morgan (1989) claim that over 70 per cent of teenagers have intercourse only within a committed, loyal relationship. Bury (1984) and Wellings and Bradshaw (1994) have characterized adolescent sexual relationships as being 'serial monogamy'. Other studies seem to confirm this pattern (Abrams et al., 1990). Johnson et al. (1994) also report that first intercourse is now often associated with more planning and less spontaneity than formerly. They state that the majority of young people have their first experience of sexual intercourse within an established relationship. Young women are usually initiated by an older male partner, whilst young men's first partners tend to be age peers. It is uncommon, and increasingly so, for first intercourse to take place within marriage, and very rare for young men's first sexual intercourse to be with a prostitute.

A small proportion of young people do have multiple sexual partners, and it is a behaviour possibly associated with emotional deprivation or serious psychological problems (Hein et al., 1978). Studies which have focused on 'sexually delinquent' youth (those who have committed sexual offences against other persons) and runaways emphasize the very high-risk pattern of sexual activity common in some groups which require very targeted and specific health education interventions (Rotheram-Borus et al., 1991). MORI (1990) reports that 11 per cent of 16–19 year olds had four or more sexual partners in the previous year. Although some of these sexual encounters may have been serially monogamous and not undertaken in a promiscuous fashion at the time, there is clearly room for debate about the impact of such activities.

The beginnings of sexual activity means that masculinity and femininity have to be renegotiated in adolescent terms (Bancroft, 1990). Sexual identity is intimately connected to how gender identity is perceived within the culture. It is not, therefore, surprising that young people may try a number of different sexual roles, the nature of which will be closely connected to their attempts to develop some separate identity in the context of, and sometimes in opposition to, their families. Experimentation often includes, at least in fantasy, experimenting with gender roles. From a developmental point of view, sexual variations, including homosexuality or 'crushes' on admired adults by girls and boys are not necessarily to be taken seriously. They may be best considered in terms of the young person exploring which 'elements' of sexual orientation are to become his or hers. In certain settings peer pressure may create a conflict between what the individual adolescent believes and what many of his or her friends are doing. Because peers play such an important role in the lives of adolescents, social acceptance and social relations are likely to be urgent concerns for most young people. For example, in relation to safer sex, carrying condoms can be perceived as inappropriate and likely to suggest a girl was 'looking for it', thus leaving her open to abuse. As one young woman said in Hendry *et al.*'s (1991) study, 'You'll get AIDS and cancer if you use the pill and slagged off if you carry a condom'.

Contraceptive use amongst teenagers has increased in line with the rise in those claiming sexual experience in teenage years, but such use has been shown in numerous studies to be inconsistent. The condom is the only contraceptive which assists in the prevention of sexually transmitted diseases and the HIV virus (see Chapter 21). Ford and Bowie (1989) suggest that about a third of sexually active young people use condoms, but almost all claim to use them for contraceptive rather than disease prevention purposes (Hendry *et al.*, 1991). Despite the campaigning for condom use, a complex web of cultural and social factors conspire to make them unappealing and unusable for many young people, especially when other forms of contraception are available (Wight, 1990). Despite the fact that contraception is difficult for many young people to access or negotiate with a partner, the evidence of data relating to teenage pregnancies indicates that young women are no more likely now than in the past to conceive children at this early stage in their lives (Johnson *et al.*, 1994).

All of the foregoing relates to heterosexual activity. Very little is known about rates of homosexual activity amongst adolescents. Kent-Baguley (1990) notes that 'not surprisingly, the majority of young lesbians and gays feel marginalised, isolated and unhappy at school, often feeling obliged to participate in "queer-bashing" talk to avoid self-revelation'. Little wonder that the extent of the phenomenon is so unclear. Also in question is the extent to which homosexual practices place young people at risk. Widespread assumptions about the nature of sexual acts or the levels of promiscuity in this subgroup too often reflect simple stereotypes and prejudices. Young people themselves are particularly confused about the nature of the AIDS danger in relation to homosexuality, since there is almost no discussion within health education about sexuality *per se* and homosexuality in particular.

Drugs: alcohol and illegal substances

The literature on young people drinking describes such behaviour as part of the socialization process from child to adult (Stacey and Davies, 1970; Sharp and Lowe, 1989). In England and Wales, the majority of adolescents have had their first 'proper' drink by the age of 13 (82 per cent of boys, and 77 per cent of girls). In Scotland, schoolchildren are introduced to alcohol a little later (71 per cent of 12-year-old boys and 57 per cent of girls), but catch up with their English and Welsh peers by the age of 15 (Marsh *et al.*, 1986). Lest these young drinkers cause great concern, it needs to be pointed out that most only drank alcohol a few times a year. Most adolescents' early drinking is done at home with parents. Only as they grow older does the context for their drinking spread to parties, then clubs and discos and lastly pubs. Scottish adolescents are much less likely than their English and Welsh counterparts to drink in pubs (Marsh *et al.*, 1986).

Most young people's drinking is done at weekends, as diary evidence shows. In relation to quantities, girls in every age group drank less than boys (Marsh et al. ,1986). Boys' consumption grows annually, with some very high levels being reached by age 17, whereas girls' consumption peaks in the last year of compulsory schooling. Pub-going seemed to peak in the late teens and thereafter tail off.

The majority of adolescents associate drinking with positive reactions, but Marsh et al. (1986) noted that linked to such specific bouts of drunkenness were not only the inevitable physical symptoms, but also drinking-related problems such as vandalism, attracting the attention of the police and so on. Coffield (1992) in a study of young people in the North-East of England, makes the following comment:

> The pattern of weekend 'binges' appears to be widespread among both young men and young women and underage drinking seems to be endemic throughout the region. As a result of drinking too much, boys become involved in fights among themselves, with other male groups and with the police; they also damaged themselves and others in accidents with motorbikes and cars; their relationships with parents became strained, and some became more willing to experiment with illicit drugs after drinking heavily. If any of the girls became involved with the police, it was in connection with drink-related offences. Among the young people we met, the non-drinker is the deviant and talk of sensible drinking is openly ridiculed. Our young people reported very few hangovers, although they were often sick as a result of excessive drinking. They tend to dismiss any possible health risks because they 'bounce back' so quickly and with-out any apparent ill-effects. (Coffield, 1992, pp.2–3)

British studies (Ives, 1990a) suggest that between 4 and 8 per cent of secondary school pupils have tried solvents, and that sniffing peaks around ages 13–15 (third and fourth year of secondary schooling in England, second and third year of schooling in Scotland). In Davies and Coggans' (1991) sample, nearly 11 per cent of the sample had used solvents at least once, although less than 1 per cent reported using solvents once a month or more frequently. Most of those who had used solvents had used them only once or a few times. However, despite the low incidence of continued misuse, it is clear that the fashion for solvent misuse has not gone away despite attracting less media attention in recent years. The number of solvent-related deaths give some indication of the problem's continuation. In 1983, when concern was at its highest, deaths totalled 82. In 1988 there were 134 deaths, more deaths per annum than are attributed to the misuse of any other illegal drug in the adolescent population (Wright, 1991). Part of the concern rests in the fact that published guidelines to retailers on the sale of glues – the most well-known solvent – have led to a trend towards misuse of more dangerous products such as aerosols (Ives, 1990b; Ramsey, 1990).

More common in usage amongst adolescents is cannabis, ranking third behind alcohol and cigarettes as a preferred drug. Davies and Coggans (1991) note that, although 15 per cent of their sample of school-age children had tried cannabis at least once, only 2 per cent carried on using it about once a month or more frequently. The study revealed a low incidence of other illegal drugs in school-age populations. Six per cent reported having used LSD at least once. Figures for heroin and cocaine were 1 per cent. Ecstasy was recorded at below 1 per cent, although more recent surveys might highlight the fashion in use of such designer drugs in dance settings. Amphetamines or 'speed' have, however, replaced 'E' as a popular choice with young people, at least in the Edinburgh area (Fast Forward, 1994). However, Davies and Coggans comment:

> Data of this sort are reassuring for parents worried about the probability of their children taking drugs, but it should be said that this low level of probability is not evenly spread throughout society. (Davies and Coggans, 1991, p.36)

Cannabis is not in itself addictive and, although linked with short-term memory problems and other minor symptoms, is not associated with any significant long-term damage to health. It is, however, an illegal substance, and thus most of the problems associated with its use stem from social rather than medical causes. There is some evidence that young people view cannabis in quite a different light from those offering health education (Hendry *et al.*, 1991). Those concerned with health promotion are often bound by professional guidelines to group cannabis with other illegal drugs and must effectively prohibit its use. Young people's own culture, however, denies that cannabis is harmful – it is often seen as less dangerous than alcohol. The association of cannabis with other illegal substances diminishes the validity of the message that health educators promote.

As we noted in the opening sections of the chapter, young people today are living in a post-modern consumer-orientated culture, where, through the powers of mass media advertising the pleasure principle and instant gratification are emphasized as aspects of adult society. By contrast, health education and health promotion seem to be based on a rationalist view of social conduct. Given these conflicting 'messages' about social 'mores', it is perhaps not to surprising that adultist perspectives on adolescent drinking and drug usage are both overly moralistic – and hypocritical – and that some young people from time to time make the transition from their everyday world to a hedonistic leisure sphere via the exciting, mood-altering effects of alcohol and/or illegal drugs.

Leaving home

Part of the process of transition to adult status involves disengagement from parental influence. For most young people in the UK this is a gradual process. Hendry *et al.* (1993) found that only 6 per cent of 17–18 year olds had left their parental home. After this age gender differences appear. Girls are much readier to 'fly the nest' than their male counterparts. Even by 23–24 years half of the male population are still living with parents while a third of the girls are in this situation. Only a small proportion of young people feel that parents forced them to leave, and these are mostly in the younger age groups (17–18 years) and amongst those from manual households. Other studies have shown that the majority of young people moving away from the parental home continue to live locally, often deriving help from an extended kin network (Harris, 1993). It is those who do not enjoy this family support who are at risk of homelessness. The pervasive influence of unemployment has created a shifting population of homeless people who have inhabited the 'cardboard cities' in the streets of central London and other cities. Voluntary organizations estimate that 200,000 young people experience homelessness in Britain each year. (Killeen, 1992).

Jones (1995) has also pointed out the differing perceptions of leaving home of the adolescent (e.g. risk of the loss of security, claiming the rights of adult citizen, excitement and fear) and of the parents (e.g. easing a conflict situation, the departure of children and the resulting 'empty nest'). She went on to indicate another aspect of leaving home, namely the competing images in wider society about homeless young people. On the one hand, homeless youth are seen as a problem for society, rather than a problem of – and created by – society, hence homelessness becomes defined in the media as a problem for those who witness it, rather than for those who have to experience it (Jones, 1995). On the other hand, organizations seeking more housing provision may stress the 'normality' of homeless young people. Hostel staff may also do this as far as the outside world is concerned, but Liddiard and Hutson (1991) have shown that agencies may operate on internal gate- keeping systems which re-creates deviancy stereotypes, by distinguishing between 'deserving' and 'understanding' cases for hostel provision.

State support for the transition to adulthood has been withdrawn so that the responsibility of families to provide avenues for young people's development of citizenship has been stressed and extended. As Jones and Wallace (1992) stated, young people's access to an employment income or access to the state safety net of social security, access to family support and access to independent housing all interact with the young person's 'personal resources' (Abel and McQueen, 1992) to affect the transition to independence. Consequently, young people experiencing family conflict; living in deprived areas; having 'special needs'; leaving school 'early' with poor qualifications; or leaving 'care', are particularly 'at risk' in progressing towards independent living and securing accommodation.

Working with Adolescents: The roles of adults

The transition from childhood to adulthood presents new psycho-social issues. What factors influence an adolescent's response to these issues?

Box 17.3 shows the way that social workers and other social care professionals will come into contact with adolescents in a variety of circumstances and come into contact with adults who have important relationships with the young people.

It has been suggested by Galbo (1986) that, during adolescence, the importance of non-parental adults is likely to increase because of the adolescent's need to differentiate himself or herself from parents and the teenager's widening social contacts. Another aspect of this is the growing unavailability of parents in the hurly-burly of modern society. Hamilton and Darling (1989) identified four major dimensions of the *mentoring* role that a relationship with adults can provide:

- a mentor being seen as a role model
- as a teacher by pointing out areas where protégés can improve performance
- by being a challenger
- and by sharing his/her own experiences with the protégé(s).

It emerged from Hamilton and Darling's study that parents and unrelated adults were the most likely to assume a mentoring role, with non-parental mentors complementing rather than substituting for parental mentors. This supports the work of Galbo (1986), who claimed that adolescents continue to regard their parents as the most important people in their lives, even as their social networks expand. Most interestingly, it gives a warning that adult mentors are 'unlikely by themselves to fill the gap left by absent or unavailable parents' (Hamilton and Darling, 1989).

As yet, there is little understanding of how the mentoring process works from the young person's perspective. Recently, Philip and Hendry (1996) have looked at mentoring relationships 'through young people's eyes' and found that varying forms of mentoring are significant for different groups of young people. All young people in their sample stressed the importance of long-term relationships where trust was assured and negotiation was possible. Those young people who had experienced important 'life events' were especially clear about

---

Box 17.3 Services for Young People

- joint strategic planning and co-ordination between agencies, especially social work, education and housing;
- the availability of a wide range of services, particularly:

  individual and family counselling;
  varied forms of group work;
  befriending;
  specialist education;
  residential schools with flexi-care arrangements;
  residential units which encourage staff continuity;
  foster care schemes with specialist training and support.

- careful assessment of the young person's needs, relationship patterns, schooling and behaviour to match these with suitable services;
- joint setting and reviewing of expectations, aims and methods of work by social workers, young people, parents and other key parties;
- flexible use of field, residential and group work staff to respond to individual circumstances and needs;
- social workers' acquisition and exercise of mediation and conflict resolution skills in work with young people, parents, carers and schools;
- social workers and carers taking time to build trust with young people and parents, then challenging unhelpful attitudes and behaviour;
- preparation and support to young people (and parents) for participation in decisions which affect them;
- recognition that for some young people living away from home is a positive move which offers respite, shared care or, in extreme cases, long-term protection from risk;
- external monitoring of decisions for young people to return home or move to 'independence';
- ensuring that care or supervision ends only when systems are in place which provide continuity of support for young people.

(Triseliotis et al., 1995)

---

the need for support which was rooted in the mentor's ability to empathize with the young person. Such findings raise important questions about social care services for young people.

In addition to these shared elements of mentoring, several important variations were evident. In particular, the process of mentoring appeared to be highly gendered: young men were less likely than young women to identify mentoring or the need for mentoring as salient in their lives. This is in line with research which suggests young men are unlikely to seek help in relation to emotional issues (Mac an Ghaill, 1994). Where they did perceive mentoring as important in their lives, they mostly referred to the 'classic' one-to-one style. However, it could be suggested that in the present social climate the traditional model is of diminishing significance: for young women particularly in this study, elements of mentoring were highlighted within overlapping groups of relationships, where identities are constantly reworked in relation to shifting sets of standards and contradictions (Lees, 1993). Thus, young people themselves identified a range of 'ideal types' of mentoring relationships – including professional youth workers operating in small teams, the use of best (same sex) friend, groups of peers, and adults with experience of long term 'risk' behaviours.

What approaches should social care professionals take in working with young people? Coles (1995) and Hendry et al. (1995) have recommended a variety of macro-social interventions focusing on changing systematic features of community institutions and contexts such as schools and youth organizations, individual counselling, as well as group and peer interventions. The intentions behind these strategies with this client group are: to provide information and empower non-judgementally; to enable the development of social competence; problem-solving skills; autonomy and self-identity; the ability to act independently to exert some control over situations; and to gain a sense of purpose and future orientation. Triseliotis et al. (1995) have outlined elements of successful social work interventions from the adolescents' perspective:

- having a say in the type and choice of specific placement
- some openness and congruence in the setting of expectations
- planned individual and family work
- resolution of conflict within reasonably supportive families
- liking for the nature of schooling offered on a residential basis or by day attendance at a residential school
- close, confiding relationship with the social worker or key worker
- happy match between young person and residential or foster carers
- shared goals and approach by social worker and family in relation to home supervision.

Additionally they presented the perceived qualities of adults that teenagers could relate well to and co-operated with;

- were informed in approach (e.g. were easy to talk to; took the young person out)
- respected the young people, listened to what they said, tried to understand and did not lecture them

- could recognize the difference between being frank and sometimes challenging from being 'pushy' and 'nagging'
- were available, punctual and reliable
- kept confidences
- did practical things to help
- carried out their promises.

Triseliotis *et al.*'s list closely matches the qualities of successful mentors.

Summary

In present-day society, adolescents' transitions towards adulthood need not necessarily be beset by problems, though particular challenges may make some young people especially vulnerable and put them 'at risk'. Developmental considerations together with relatively new economic circumstances (e.g. the job situation) and societal health risks (e.g. HIV/AIDS) create a context whereby young people perceive the need for a range of support networks, agencies and services, including adult mentors, to access as they require them.

It was argued, that despite suggestions about the existence of a wide-ranging culturally transient society, social class values still exert a powerful influence on lifestyle development in adolescence. Such ecological factors interact with relational changes and the psycho-social effects of biological puberty to 'shape' the developing adolescent.

The findings from research studies on various aspects of potentially risky and risk-taking behaviours, including excessive dieting, sex, the use of various types of legal and illegal drugs, delinquent activities and homelessness were outlined. The chapter concluded by examining mentoring relationships in adolescence, and came to the conclusion that the present-day needs of young people require a variety of mentoring networks to be available should adolescents perceive the necessity for such support on their road to maturity.

Seminar Questions

1. In what ways to you consider adolescent transitions to be different for young men and young women, and for ethnic minority groups, in present day society?

2. What is your personal professional approach to working with young people? (Give reasons for your viewpoint.)

3. Should social care professionals discuss such issues as gay love, HIV/AIDS or using 'hard drugs' with underage teenagers? If so, what approaches could/should be used?

4. How could meaningful support networks be created for young people by social care professionals and other youth professionals?

Further Reading

Coleman, J.C. and Hendry, L.B. (1999) *The Nature of Adolescence.* London: Routledge.
A useful general textbook on aspects of adolescent development. Covering such chapters as: physical development, sexuality, thinking and reasoning, self identity, the family, peers and the transitions from school to adult society.

Coleman, J.C. and Warren-Adamson, C. (1992) *Youth Policy in the 1990's: The Way Forward.* London: Routledge.
This book deals with many important issues for social workers regarding youth policies in the UK, including youth employment and training, youth work and informal education, health and mental health, empowerment and child welfare, juvenile justice, leaving home and adolescents as consumers.

Hendry, L.B., Shucksmith, J., Love, J. and Glendinning, A. (1993) *Young People's Leisure and Lifestyles.* London: Routledge.
Outlines a large seven year longitudinal study of adolescence, looking at schooling, employment transitions, family and peer relationships, sport, leisure and health. The findings are interpreted within a lifestyle development framework

Hendry, L.B., Shucksmith, J. and Philip, K. (1995) *Educating for Health: School and Community Approaches with Adolescents.* London: Cassell.
An easy-to-read book which looks at theoretical health models and approaches to practice in school and community. It also considers alternative approaches in reaching young people and explores young people's rights and the relevance of health education approaches for youth.

References

Abel, T. and McQueen, D. (1992) 'The formation of health lifestyles: a new empirical concept.' *BSA and ESMS Joint Conference on Health in Europe.* Edinburgh 18–21 September.

Abrams, D., Abraham, C., Spears, R. and Marks, D. (1990) 'AIDS invulnerability: relationships, sexual behaviour and attitudes amongst 16–19 year olds.' In P. Aggleton, P. Davies and G. Hart (eds) *AIDS: Individual, Cultural and Policy Dimensions.* London: Falmer Press.

Bancroft, J. (1990) 'The impact of socio-cultural influences on adolescent sexual development: further considerations.' In J. Bancroft and J.M. Reinisch (eds) *Adolescence and Puberty.* Oxford: Oxford University Press.

Bronfenbrenner, U. (1979) *The Ecology of Human Development.* Boston, MA: Harvard University Press.

Brooks-Gunn, J. (1987) 'Pubertal processes and girls' psychological adaptation.' In R. Lerner, and T.T. Foch (eds) *Biological-Psychosocial Interactions in Early Adolescence: A Lifespan Perspective.* Hillsdale, NJ: Lawrence Erlbaum.

Brown, B.B. (1982) 'The extent and effects of peer pressure among high school students: a retrospective analysis.' *Journal of Youths and Adolescence, 11,* 121–133.

Bruch, H. (1985) 'Four decades of eating disorders.' In D.M. Garner, P.E. Garfinkel (eds) *Handbook of Psychotherapy for Anorexia Nervosa and Bulimia.* New York: Guildford Press.

Bury, J. (1984) *Teenage Pregnancy in Britain.* London: Birth Control Trust.

Coffield, F. (1992) 'Young people and illicit drugs.' *Summary Research Report.* Northern Regional Health Authority and Durham University.

Coffield, F., Borrill, C. and Marshall, S. (1986) *Growing Up at the Margins.* Milton Keynes: Open University Press.

Coleman, J.C. and Hendry, L.B. (1999) *The Nature of Adolescence. 2nd Edition.* London: Routledge.

Coles, B. (1995) *Youth and Social Policy.* London: UCL Press

Crisp, A.H. (1980) *Anorexia Nervosa: Let Me Be.* London: Plenum Press.

Davies, J. and Coggans, N. (1991) *The Facts About Adolescent Drug Abuse.* London: Cassell.

Davies, E. and Furnham, A. (1986) 'Body satisfaction in adolescent girls.' *British Journal of Medical Psychology, 59,* 279–287.

Eagly, A.H., Ashmore, R.D., Makhijani, M.G. and Longo, L.C. (1991) 'What is beautiful is good, but…a meta-analytic review of research on the physical attractiveness stereotype.' *Psychological Bulletin, 110,* 109–128.

Eccles, J.S. and Midgley, C. (1989) 'State/environment fit: developmentally appropriate classrooms for early adolescents.' In R.E. Ames and C. Ames (eds) *Research on Motivation in Education, 3,* 139–186. San Diego: CA: Academic Press.

Emler, N. and Reicher, S. (1995) *Adolescence and Delinquency.* London: Blackwell.

Farrell, C. (1978) *My Mother Said…The Way Young People Learned About Sex and Birth Control.* London: Routledge and Kegan Paul.

Farrington, D.P. (1994) 'Interactions between individual and contextual factors in the development of offending.' In R.K. Sibereisen and E. Jodi (eds) *Adolescence in Context.* Berlin and New York: Springer-Verlag.

Fast Forward (1994) *Headstrong? Peer Research Project Annual Report.* Edinburgh: Fast Forward Positive Lifestyles Ltd.

Ford, N. (1987) 'Research into heterosexual behaviour with implications for the spread of AIDS.' *British Journal of Family Planning, 13*, 50–54.

Ford, N. and Bowie, C. (1989) 'Urban-rural variations in the level of heterosexual activity of young people.' *Area 21*, 3, 237–248.

Ford, N. and Morgan, K. (1989) 'Heterosexual lifestyles of young people in an English city.' *Journal of Population and Social Studies, 1*, 167–182.

Galbo, J.J. (1986) 'Adolescents' perceptions of significant adults: implications for the family, school and youth servicing agencies.' *Children and Youth Services Review, 8*, 37–51.

Galbo, J.J. (1989) 'Non-parental significant adults in adolescents' lives.' *National Biennial Meeting of the Society for Research in Child Development*. Kansas City, April.

Glendinning, A., Love, J., Shucksmith, J. and Hendry, L.B. (1992) 'Adolescence and health inequalities: extensions to McIntyre and West.' *Social Science and Medicine ,35*, 5, 679–687.

Goffman, E. (1971) *The Presentation of Self in Everyday Life*. Harmondsworth: Pelican.

Greenfield, D., Quinlan, D.M., Harding, P., Glass, E. and Bliss, A. (1987) 'Eating behaviour in an adolescent population.' *International Journal of Eating Disorders ,6*, 99–111.

Hamilton, S.F. and Darling, N. (1989) 'Mentors in adolescent lives.' In K. Hurrelman and U. Engel (eds) *The Social World of Adolescents*. New York: De Gruyter.

Harris, C. (1993) *The Family and Industrial Society*. London: Allen and Unwin.

Hein, K., Cohen, M.I. and Mark, A. (1978) 'Age at first intercourse among homeless adolescent females.' *Journal of Paediatrics, 93*, 147–148.

Hendry, L.B. and Raymond, M. (1983) 'Youth unemployment and lifestyles: Some educational considerations.' *Scottish Educational Review, 15*, 1, 28–40.

Hendry, L.B., Shucksmith, J., Philip, K. and Jones, L. (1991) 'Working with young people on drugs and HIV in Grampian Region.' Report of research project for Grampian Health Board, University of Aberdeen, Department of Education.

Hendry, L.B., Shucksmith, J., Love, J.G. and Glendinning, A. (1993) *Young People's Leisure and Lifestyles*. London: Routledge.

Hendry, L.B., Shucksmith, J. and Philip K. (1995) *Educating for Health: School and Community Approaches with Adolescents*. London Cassell.

Hsu, L.K.G. and Holder D. (1986) 'Bulimia nervosa: treatment and short term outcome.' *Psychological Medicine, 16*, 6570.

Irwin, C.E. (1989) 'Risk-taking behaviour in the adolescent patient: are they impulsive?' *Paediatric Annals 18*, 122–133.

Irwin, C.E. and Millstein, S.G. (1986) 'Biopsychosocial correlates of risk-taking behaviours during adolescence.' *Journal of Adolescent Healthcare 7*, 825–965.

Ives, R. (1990a) 'Sniffing out the solvent users.' In Ashton, M. (ed) *Drug Misuse in Britain: National audit of drug misuse statistics, 1990*. London: ISDD.

Ives, R. (1990b) 'The fad refuses to fade'. *Druglink 5*, 5, 12–13.

Jack, M.S. (1989) 'Personal fable: a potential explanation for risk-taking behaviours during adolescence.' *Journal of Adolescent Healthcare 7*, 825–965.

Jessor, R. and Jessor, S.L. (1977) *Problem Behaviour and Psychological Development*. New York, Academic Press.

Johnson, A.M., Wadsworth, J., Wellings, K. and Field, J. (1994) *Sexual Attitudes and Lifestyles*. London: Blackwell.

Jones, G. (1995) *Leaving Home*. Buckingham: Open University Press.

Jones, G. and Wallace, C. (1992) *Youth, Family and Citizenship*. Buckingham, Open University Press.

Kent-Baguley, P. (1990) 'Sexuality and youth work practice'. In T. Jeffs and M. Smith (eds) *Young People, Inequality and Youth Work*. London: Macmillan.

Killeen, D. (1992) 'Leaving home.' In J.C. Coleman and C. Warren-Adamson (eds) *Youth Policy in the 1990's*. London: Routledge,

Lacey, J.H. (1983) 'Bulimia nervosa, binge eating and psycho-genetic vomiting: a controlled treatment study and long-term outcome.' *British Medical Journal, 286*, 1609–1613.

Lees, S. (1993) *Sugar and Spice: Sexuality and Adolescent Girls*. London: Penguin.

Ledoux, S., Choquet, M. and Flament, M. (1991) 'Eating disorders among adolescents in an unselected French population.' *International Journal of Eating Disorders ,10*, 81–89.

Lerner, R.M. (1985) 'Adolescent maturational changes and psychosocial development: a dynamic interactional perspective'. *Journal of Youth and Adolescence, 14*, 355–372.

Liddiard, M. and Hutson, S. (1991) 'Homeless young people and runaways – agency definitions and processes.' *Journal of Social Policy, 20*, 3, 365–388.

Lloyd, M.A. (1985) *Adolescence.* London: Harper and Row.

Mac an Ghaill, M. (1994) *The Making of Men.* Milton Keynes: Open University Press.

Marsh, A., Dobbs, J. and White, A. (1986) *Adolescent Drinking.* OPCS Social Survey Division, London: HMSO.

Matza, A.D. and Sykes, G. (1961) 'Juvenile delinquency and subterranean values.' *American Sociological Review, 26,* 712–719.

MORI (1990) 'Young Adult's Health and Lifestyles.' Research conducted for Health Education Authority, London: MORI.

Noller, P. and Callan, V. (1991) *The Adolescent in the Family,* London: Routledge.

Palmer, R., Opperneimer, R., Dignon, A., Chalones, D. and Howells, K. (1990) 'Childhood sexual experience with adults. Reported by women with eating disorders.' *British Journal of Psychiatry, 156,* 699–703.

Petersen, A.C., Ebatta, A.T. and Graber, J.A. (1987) 'Coping with adolescence: the functions and dysfunctions of poor achievement.' *Biennial Meeting of the Society of Research in Child Development.* Baltimore: Maryland.

Philip, K. and Hendry, L.B. (1996) 'Young people and mentoring – towards a typology?' *Journal of Adolescence, 19,* 189–201.

Ramsey, S. (1990) 'Dangerous games: UK solvent deaths 1983–1988.' *Druglink,* 55, 8–9.

Roberts, K. and Parsell, G. (1990) 'Young people's routes into UK labour markets in the late 1980s'. ESRC 16–19 Initiative Occasional Paper No. 27. London: City University.

Rodriguez-Tomé, H. (1972) *Le Moi et l'Autre dans las Conscience de l'Adolescent.* Neuchâtel: Delachaux et Niestlé.

Rotheram-Borus, M.J., Becker, J.V., Koopman, C. and Kaplan, M. (1991) 'AIDS knowledge and beliefs, and sexual behaviour of sexually delinquent and non-delinquent (runaway) adolescents.' *Journal of Adolescence, 14,* 199–244.

Rutter, M. (1995) *Psychological Disturbances in Young People.* Cambridge: Cambridge University Press.

Sharp, D. and Lowe, G. (1989) 'Adolescents and alcohol – a review of the recent British research.' *Journal of Adolescence 12,* 295-307.

Silbereisen, R.K., Noack, P. and Eyferth, K. (1987) 'Place for development: adolescents, leisure-settings, and developmental tasks'. In R.K. Silbereisen, K. Eyferth and G. Rudinger (eds) *Development as Action in Context: Problem Behaviour and Normal Youth Development.* New York: Springer-Verlag.

Stacey, B. and Davies, J. (1970) 'Drinking behaviour in childhood and adolescence: an evaluative review.' *British Journal of Addiction, 65,* 203–212.

Triseliotis, J. Borland, M., Hill, M. and Lambert, L. (1995) *Teenagers and the Social Work Services.* London, HMSO.

Wellings, K. and Bradshaw, S. (1994) 'First heterosexual intercourse.' In A.M. Johnson, J. Wadsworth, K. Willings and J. Field (eds) *Sexual Attitudes and Lifestyles.* London: Blackwell.

Wight, D. (1990) 'The impact of HIV/AIDS on young people's sexual behaviour in Britain: a literature review.' Working Paper No. 20. Glasgow: Medical Sociology Unit.

Wright, S.P. (1991) 'Trends in deaths associated with abuse of volatile substances 1971–1989.' London: St George's Hospital Medical School.

Youniss, J. and Smollar, J. (1985) *Adolescent Relations with Mothers, Fathers and Friends.* Chicago, IL: University of Chicago Press.

Youniss, J. and Smollar, J. (1990) 'Self through relationship development.' In H.A. Bosma, and A.E. Jackson (eds) *Coping and Self-concept in Adolescence.* Heidelberg: Springer-Verlag.

PART IV

Working with Clients

Specific Issues

Introduction

This final section of the book deals with a number of particular issues and specific adult client groups in more detail. These chapters provide information relevant to the training of social care professionals, but also include quite detailed and specific information, for example, about the effects of different addictive drugs, or the detailed classifications of mental illness. These are likely to form a useful and convenient source of reference for practising professionals.

The first chapter, by David Winter, provides a balanced appraisal of a range of approaches to psychological problems which should help the social care professional assess the validity of different approaches, as well as aiding communication with professionals who view problems from different perspectives.

Criminal behaviour, like the psychological problems discussed by David Winter, can also be understood from a number of perspectives. Clive Hollin, chapter demonstrates how longitudinal studies which follow individuals over their lifespan have shed important light on the complex causation of criminal behaviour. The discussion of the effectiveness of different treatment regimes may also provide pointers for working with offenders. One particular behavior which frequently brings people into contact with both the legal system and social care professionals is that of substance use and abuse. Richard Hammersley's chapter is likely to be invaluable to the professional who works with people with drug or alcohol problems. The chapter questions the traditional, over-simplistic approach which divides drug users into addicts and non-addicts. He presents a succinct account of theories of dependence and a useful review of intervention approaches. He also highlights the difficulties experienced by social care professionals in dealing with this client group.

The next few chapters move the focus from behaviour to some specific issues of health and disability and ultimately the issue of death and bereavement. The areas selected are not exhaustive, but have been selected as particularly relevant or topical for social care professionals. For example, while issues to do with adapting to terminal illness in general are discussed in the chapter on dying and bereavement, only the disease of HIV is singled out for detailed discussion. This reflects the recency of work in this area and the fact that it has raised new issues which may cause additional concerns for professionals working in these areas. HIV is a relatively recent focus of medical and social work intervention, and as such has attracted considerable new research to which professionals may not have easy access. The chapter by Barbara Hedge provides an up-to-date discussion of the issues surrounding working with those suffering from HIV.

Medical advances have meant increasing survival rates and rehabilitation of people with brain damage, caused either by accidents or strokes. Social care professionals are likely at some time to have contact with clients with a range of types of brain damage. Some basic understanding of the problems for both clients and their families is likely to be crucial. Jane Pierson's chapter provides a clear explanation of the causes and effects of brain damage as well as a basic introduction to the structure of the brain. This theme is continued in the following chapter by Judith Thomas and John Done in the discussion of dementia in older people. This chapter not only discusses brain pathology but offers clear advice on how to apply psychology to aid communication with demented clients.

The final chapter deals with the important issues of death and bereavement placing a particular emphasis on issues for the professional social worker. Dealing with the dying and the bereaved is one of the most challenging issues for those in both the medical and social services professions, and one in which it is easy to feel useless. Yet effective interventions based on an understanding of the processes of grieving can do a great deal to alleviate suffering.

CHAPTER 18

Psychological Problems

Alternative Perspectives on their Explanation and Treatment

David A. Winter

Introduction

John was concerned that he might contaminate other people if they were to touch objects which he had touched after going to the toilet. Consequently, he washed his hands repeatedly, often as many as a hundred times, after using the toilet.

Jyothi became increasingly anxious as the summer approached. This anxiety stemmed from a fear of butterflies, as a result of which she rarely left the house during the summer, kept windows firmly closed, and avoided any television programme in which there was a likelihood of her seeing a butterfly.

Stephen had been sleeping poorly for some time. Therefore, it was no surprise to his wife not to find him in bed when she woke. However, she then discovered his body in his car, which had a hose leading into it from the exhaust pipe. Despite what appeared a successful career and a loving family, he had repeatedly maintained that he was worthless and that life was, and would continue to be, futile.

Mary was admitted to psychiatric hospital after being discovered hiding in her neighbours' garden. The neighbours had called the police, whom she told that assassins had been sent by the CIA to kill her and that she was hearing messages that they would 'get her'.

George, a respected public figure, was faced with disgrace after being arrested for exposing himself to a group of schoolgirls. It transpired that he had been engaging in this behaviour for several years, but felt unable to stop himself.

All of the above people might at some stage have come to the attention of a psychiatrist, clinical psychologist and/or social care professional. Many will first have contacted their general practitioner, and indeed, it has been estimated that psychological problems are the second most common reason for a woman, and the fourth most common reason for a man, to consult a general practititioner (Goldberg and Huxley, 1980). How are we to understand these people's difficulties, and how might they be treated? Is it possible to adopt a consistent approach to such understanding and treatment, despite the diversity of the problems involved? These are the main questions which will be addressed in this chapter.

After considering the systems of diagnosis used by psychiatrists, I shall discuss seven major ways of understanding the possible causes of, and treating, psychological problems. You may encounter all of these approaches in your contacts with other professionals and may employ some of them in your own work. You are likely to find that each of them is particularly appropriate to use with certain types of client. Finally, I shall examine the relevance of socio-cultural factors and gender to the diagnosis and treatment of psychological problems.

Psychiatric Classification

A first step in understanding, and deciding upon the appropriate treatment for, psychological problems is often to classify these. Numerous diagnostic systems have been devised, most by psychiatrists, and currently the most favoured is the *Diagnostic and Statistical Manual 4* (DSM-IV) (American Psychiatric Association, 1994). Before considering the details of DSM-IV, I shall discuss some of the problems faced by psychiatric diagnostic systems, particularly in relation to the concept of schizophrenia.

At the time of writing, it is the one hundredth anniversary of this concept, or at least of Kraepelin's (1896) concept of *dementia praecox*, later renamed schizophrenia by Bleuler. Despite the longevity of the concept, several writers have noted that the kind of cases described by Kraepelin and Bleuler are almost never seen today, explanations for this including the effect of major tranquillisers on the course of the disorder. A more radical explanation is provided by Boyle (1990), who notes that many of Kraepelin's and Bleuler's descriptions of cases of schizophrenia are virtually identical to descriptions of the infectious disease, encephalitis lethargica. Boyle takes the view that the concept of schizophrenia is a 'scientific delusion', and that the behaviours claimed to be symptoms of schizophrenia are the result of various different factors.

Box 18.1 Can the Sane be Differentiated from the Insane?

Rosenhan (1973) cast severe doubt on the validity of psychiatric diagnosis by a study in which eight people with no history of psychiatric problems presented at American hospitals reporting that they were hearing voices, but otherwise behaving as they normally would. They were all admitted to hospital, at which point they stopped complaining of hearing voices. Psychiatric staff did not recognize the deception, and on discharge from hospital all the 'stooges' were given a diagnosis of schizophrenia in remission.

After disclosing his results, Rosenhan challenged a hospital to identify a number of stooge psychiatric patients who would present at the hospital over a three-month period. The hospital staff identified over a fifth of their 193 referrals in this period as stooges. Rosenhan, however, had in fact not sent any stooges to the hospital! His challenge, therefore, in effect made the staff more aware of normal aspects of the behaviour of individuals who might otherwise have received a psychiatric diagnosis.

To be useful, a diagnostic system needs to be both *valid*, being able to identify accurately those conditions which it is meant to identify, and *reliable*, providing the same diagnoses when applied by different clinicians to the same individuals. There are various different aspects of the validity of a diagnostic system. One of these, *construct validity*, essentially concerns whether a diagnostic category is made up of a set of symptoms that go together. This was not so in

Kraepelin's and Bleuler's original descriptions of schizophrenia, and subsequent studies have tended to find that it is still not the case in that there is overlap in symptoms between clients assigned to different diagnostic categories and indeed no clear distinction between schizophrenic and normal traits (see Box 18.1).

Another major aspect of validity is predictive validity, the ability of a diagnosis to predict outcome and the types of treatment which are likely to be successful. Although Kraepelin believed that schizophrenia always had a chronic, deteriorating course, recent studies have found outcome to be extremely variable and to depend largely upon socio-economic factors, with about a 25 per cent rate of complete recovery (Warner, 1985). Response to treatment is also difficult to predict, research suggesting that only a small proportion of clients diagnosed as schizophrenic benefit from the 'neuroleptic' drugs often considered the treatment of choice for this condition, and that there are minimal differences between those given these drugs and those on no medication. Furthermore, clients with mood disorders (e.g. mania) also benefit from such medication, while schizophrenics may benefit from lithium, which is usually considered a specific treatment for some mood disorders, and benzodiazepines, which are usually used to treat anxiety disorders.

Early studies tended to find psychiatric diagnosis to be unreliable, particularly cross-nationally, and it has been suggested that some of the differences between the diagnostic practices of psychiatrists in different countries are due more to social, economical, and political factors than to 'scientific' or medical considerations. For example, the greater frequency of diagnosis of schizophrenia in the USA than in the UK, where diagnoses of mood disorders are more common, has been explained as due to pressures by drug companies on psychiatrists to make the former diagnosis because of the greater profits derived from the major tranquillisers used to treat schizophrenia than from lithium, used to treat mood disorders. A similarly high frequency of diagnoses of schizophrenia in the former USSR has been explained as due to the use of this diagnosis as a means of controlling political dissidents.

The development of diagnostic systems such as DSM-IV, with precise criteria for particular diagnoses, is, of course, an attempt to increase the reliability of diagnosis. However, it should be remembered that DSM-IV is one amongst several diagnostic systems, and that there is little correlation between the diagnoses arrived at by users of the different systems. That such systems are at least as heavily influenced by social constructions of what constitutes a psychiatric problem as by scientific considerations was graphically illustrated when homosexuality was dropped as a diagnostic category during the third revision of the DSM system. Johnstone (1989, p.245) describes this as 'perhaps the most spectacular instant cure achieved by modern psychiatry'.

DSM-IV is a multiaxial system for the diagnosis of psychiatric disorders, the first two axes (or dimensions) of which encompass a range of diagnostic groups, as indicated in Box 18.2. It should be apparent from this list that the system attempts to be comprehensive. Indeed, to ensure that this is so, and to allow for the fact that people do not always neatly fit into diagnostic categories, it includes in each diagnostic group a 'Not Otherwise Specified' category for cases in which there are symptoms characteristic of the diagnostic group concerned but the individual does not meet the criteria of a specific disorder (e.g. Psychotic Disorder Not Otherwise Specified).

Box 18.2 Disorders Included in Axes I and II of DSM-IV

Axis I (Clinical Disorders)

Disorders Usually First Diagnosed in Infancy, Childhood, or Adolescence: these largely involve abnormal development and maturation, e.g. communication disorders such as stuttering; attention-deficit disorders such as hyperactivity.

Delirium, Dementia and Amnestic and Other Cognitive Disorders: these involve impairment of cognition which appears to be caused by substances or medical conditions.

Mental Disorders Due to a General Medical Condition: these include any such disorder apart from those included in other DSM-IV diagnostic groups. Examples include personality change due to a medical condition such as temporal lobe epilepsy.

Substance-Related Disorders: these are characterized by adverse social, behavioural, psychological or physiological effects of seeking or using substances.

Schizophrenia and Other Psychotic Disorders: these involve either distorted perception of reality; impaired capacity to reason, speak and behave rationally or spontaneously; and/or impaired capacity to respond with appropriate affect or motivation. They occur in the absence of impaired consciousness or memory.

Mood Disorders: these are characterized by depression, mania, or both.

Anxiety Disorders: these include the frequent experience of intense anxiety; and of avoidance, ritual acts, or repetitive thoughts to protect the sufferer from this experience.

Somatoform Disorders: these include persistent complaints or worry about physical symptoms or illnesses that are not supported by physical examination; and exaggerated concerns about minor physical deficits.

Factitious Disorders: these involve an attempt to feign physical illness or psychiatric disorder.

Dissociative Disorders: these may involve amnesia, feelings of depersonalization, or multiple personalities.

Sexual and Gender Identity Disorders: these include sexual dysfunctions (e.g. premature ejaculation); paraphilias (e.g. paedophilia); and confusions about gender identity.

Eating Disorders: these include obsessive concern about becoming overweight; distorted body image; inability to control food intake appropriately; and fluctuation of self-evaluation dependent on perceived body shape or weight.

Sleep Disorders: these involve disturbance in the process of sleep (e.g. difficulty in initiating or maintaining sleep).

Impulse-Control Disorders not Elsewhere Classified: these involve repeated impulsive acts leading to physical or financial damage of the individual or another person.

Adjustment Disorders: these involve emotional or behavioural symptoms developed in response to stress.

Axis II (Personality Disorders and Mental Retardation)

Personality Disorders: these involve pervasive and enduring patterns of maladaptive behaviours, responses, and thoughts that begin by early adulthood, often interfere with interpersonal relationships, and are distressing or impair functioning. Examples include paranoid personality disorder.

As a social care professional, you will certainly come across descriptions of clients in terms of diagnostic categories such as those of DSM-IV. You will also hear clients being described in terms of the broad distinctions of whether they are 'neurotic' or 'psychotic'. Essentially this concerns whether they are in or out of touch with reality, which may be regarded as a major consideration when assessing whether they are likely to be a danger to the self or others. You may find that diagnostic categories help you and your colleagues to make better sense of the clients' experiences and to decide how they might best be helped. However, you should remember that diagnostic systems are only aids to understanding, not necessarily descriptions of real disease entities, that they can never provide a total picture of the person who is your client, and indeed, carry the danger that sometimes they may cause you to take a blinkered view of the client's situation.

Discussion point

° What does the need to include a category of 'Not Otherwise Specified' in DSM-IV imply about the usefulness or otherwise of this or any diagnostic system?

Models for Understanding and Treating Psychological Problems

A glance at a library shelf on psychiatry or clinical psychology will confront the reader with numerous alternative perspectives on psychological problems and their treatment. The confusion which this may cause is similar to that which may be faced by the person suffering from a psychological problem, who, in the course of their encounters with a range of mental health professionals, or even with the same professional, may find their problem being explained and treated in several different ways, some of these seemingly incompatible. Let us now consider the major ways of understanding, or models of, psychological problems.

The medical model

Within psychiatry, the most influential approach to psychological problems has been the medical model. This views the person presenting such problems as a patient with a mental illness, the possible causative factors and treatment of which are essentially no different from those in the case of a physical illness. One of the benefits often claimed for such an approach is that it has led to more humane treatment of people with psychological problems, who are no longer seen as being responsible to any great degree for their sometimes strange or socially unacceptable behaviour. This behaviour may be seen as evidence of madness but not of badness.

However, the approach is not without limitations, not least the absence of evidence for a physical causation of most psychological problems. Some initial optimism for the eventual discovery of such causation was provided by the finding that general paresis of the insane, a condition suffered by many hospitalized psychiatric patients in the early 1900s, was caused by syphilitic infection. The introduction of effective treatments for syphilis virtually eradicated this condition. Considerable research efforts have, however, generally failed to identify the physical causal factors in other psychiatric conditions. For example, Bentall (1990, p. 23) notes that 'almost every variable known to affect human behaviour has, at one time or another, been held to be important in the aetiology of schizophrenia'.

Variables used to explain schizophrenia include abnormalities of brain structure or biochemistry, genetic factors, diet, season of birth, and viral infection, in addition to a range of environmental factors. One particular hypothesis is that schizophrenia is due to dysfunction in the right cerebral hemisphere, this resulting in specific deficits in such psychological functions as attention, thinking, perception, language and emotion (Cutting, 1985). In relation to genetic factors, although most clinicians would accept that these contribute to the causation of schizophrenia, there are flaws in several of the studies which have provided evidence for this (Marshall, 1990) (see Box 18.3).

Box 18.3 Problems in Genetic Studies of Schizophrenia

These studies are of two types: studies of twins; and studies of adoptees. In twin studies, if the genetic hypothesis is correct, a higher concordance rate for a diagnosis of schizophrenia (i.e. the likelihood that if one twin is schizophrenic, the other will also suffer from the condition) would be expected in monozygotic twins, who are genetically identical, than in dizygotic twins, who are no more alike genetically than any other pair of siblings. In studies of adoptees, if the genetic hypothesis is correct, children of schizophrenic parents who are separated from these parents at birth, and adopted by non-schizophrenic foster parents should have a higher rate of being diagnosed schizophrenic than the natural children of non-schizophrenic parents.

Amongst the problems of such studies is that the diagnoses, either of twins or adoptees, have in some cases been made by the researcher, who is hardly likely to be unbiased: for example, if one of a pair of monozygotic twins is diagnosed as schizophrenic, the researcher may be biased towards also diagnosing the other twin as schizophrenic. In some cases, even diagnoses other than schizophrenia in such a twin, or in the adopted child of schizophrenic parents, have been used as evidence of a genetic component in schizophrenia. A further problem in several studies is that their findings are equally explicable in terms of the influence of genetic or of environmental factors.

Explanations in terms of the medical model are not confined to psychotic conditions, those in which the sufferer is regarded as being out of touch with reality. Let us briefly consider how the model may account for a neurotic complaint, agoraphobia, the explanation of which in terms of other models will be discussed in subsequent sections of this chapter. A principal physiological factor which has been implicated in medical explanations of agoraphobia (and also, as we shall see, in some psychological explanations) is a high level of arousal, a genetic basis for which has been suggested. Various other medical factors have also been proposed as contributing to agoraphobic symptoms, including hyperventilation and cardiac disease.

The treatment methods derived from the medical model are known as physical treatments, and are essentially of three types. *Pharmacotherapy* involves the use of medication, for example to correct the assumed biochemical imbalance associated with a particular problem. *Psychosurgery*, which is now rarely employed but not entirely extinct, involves the surgical removal or destruction of parts of the brain. *Electroconvulsive therapy (ECT)* consists of the brief passage of an electrical current through the brain.

There is little doubt that physical treatments may provide some alleviation of the distress which an individual is suffering, for example by making him or her feel less depressed or anxious, or by controlling hallucinations. However, whereas in physical medicine treatment may be directed at the cure of a disease, physical treatments in psychiatry are likely only to remove or reduce symptoms, and these effects may persist only as long as the treatment lasts. Consequently, a person may, for example, remain on medication for many years, as is often the case with those diagnosed as schizophrenic. Such reliance on a physical treatment may, in some cases, reduce the individual's use of their own inner resources to solve their problems.

Although they may be effective in alleviating symptoms, the mechanism of action of many physical treatments is unclear. This is particularly exemplified by ECT, the reasons for the effects of which are barely any better understood now than when it was developed as a result of observations of the effect of electric shocks on pigs in an abattoir. Indeed, although the research evidence is inconsistent, there have been reports of the effectiveness of 'pseudo-ECT', in which the patient is given anaesthetic and muscle relaxant, connected to electrodes, but not administered an electric shock (e.g. Lambourn and Gill, 1978). Such apparent *placebo effects* are generally considered to be due to the patient's belief that they will be helped by the intervention. Perhaps because of uncertainties regarding their modes of action, physical treatments are often not applied solely to the types of patient for whom they were specifically developed, as we have seen when considering schizophrenia. Even ECT, long regarded as a treatment for depression, is sometimes used with patients with other diagnoses, including schizophrenia.

A final, and perhaps the major, difficulty with physical treatments is that they almost invariably have side-effects. These may require the patient to take another type of physical treatment to counteract the side-effects of the first, and even treatments to counteract the side-effects of the treatment which is counteracting the initial side-effects!

Since physical treatments are based on a view of people with psychological problems as being ill, it is not surprising that such treatments may involve admission to hospital. In the past, this was often for a lengthy period, sometimes resulting in patients becoming so institutionalized that it was difficult for them to cope in the outside world even if their 'illness' were successfully treated. Current community care policies attempt to prevent such occurrences, and there are now a number of alternatives to psychiatric hospitalization, including day centres, therapeutic communities, residential homes and hostels.

The psychodynamic model

The psychodynamic model derives from the work of Freud, the founder of psychoanalysis. The psychoanalytic view of the etiology (causation) of psychological problems is that their basis can usually be traced back to crises which the individual experienced early in life, generally in the relationship with his or her parents. Indeed, Freud considered that all such problems are essentially the result of experiences within the first six years of life. Furthermore, the nature of an individual's problem is believed to depend upon the stage of their psychosexual development at which any unresolved crisis occurred and at which they may become *fixated*, or stuck. These stages were viewed by Freud as involving the particular bodily zone on which the sexual drive is focused at different ages. For example, the anal stage is characterized by conflicts between the child and his or her parents concerning toilet training, and unresolved conflicts at this stage were considered by Freud to be likely to result in obsessive-compulsive symptoms (such as those of John, described above) later in life. As we have seen in Chapter 7, the psychodynamic model also considers that the symptoms presented by a person with psychological problems may involve some indirect expression of unconscious wishes or impulses. For example, a man who ejaculates prematurely could be unaware of his anger towards women, but this anger could be expressed indirectly in his symptom, which in effect deprives his partner of pleasure.

Post-Freudian developments in psychoanalysis, such as object-relations theory (e.g. Klein, 1984), attachment theory (Bowlby, 1969) and self-psychology (Kohut, 1977), have questioned the emphasis in classical Freudian theory on the gratification of instinctual drives, and placed greater emphasis on the individual's relationships with significant others. However, the central importance of early childhood experiences, and particularly of the parent–child relationship, is retained.

Just as there are several variations on the psychodynamic model, there are also several psychodynamic explanations of particular psychological problems. For example, phobias are viewed in classical psychoanalysis as involving the translation of an internal danger into an external one with a symbolic meaning. Agoraphobia is seen as due to fears of the sexual, aggressive or dependency urges aroused by meeting people when the individual goes out, these urges being dealt with by *projecting* them onto (i.e. attributing them to) others, who are thereby seen as dangerous, as is the whole outside world. Other variants of this formulation focus on the agoraphobic's ambivalent feelings towards his or her mother (Deutsch, 1929), and on the 'anxious attachment' of the individual who fears the loss of attachment figures (Bowlby, 1969, 1973).

The classical psychoanalytic treatment method involves the client lying on a couch and being asked to say whatever comes into his or her mind, a process known as *free association*. The analyst will make *interpretations* which may, in effect, help to make conscious what was previously unconscious. There may also be a *corrective emotional experience*, in which the client replays in the relationship with the analyst some past conflict, which may thereby be resolved. For example, the client who feels that by expressing anger they damaged one of their parents, and who imagines that this anger will have a similar damaging effect on other people, may discover that the analyst is not damaged when anger is expressed in the therapy session. Such experiences may involve a process of *transference*, in which the client transfers onto the analyst feelings which belong in another relationship, notably that with a parent when the client was a child. To facilitate this process, analysts typically reveal very little information about themselves, thus offering a 'blank screen' onto which the client can project fantasies derived from past experience.

This classical analytical procedure is very time-consuming, generally involving sessions as many as five times a week over a period of several years. It is, therefore, hardly viable in a National Health Service setting, and in a private setting will only be affordable by affluent clients. It has been modified in psychodynamic psychotherapy, in which the frequency of sessions is only once or twice per week and therapy is generally relatively short-term, often lasting no more than a year and sometimes only a few months. The brevity of the therapy may be facilitated by an approach which focuses on particular conflict areas. Psychoanalytic concepts, such as transference, have also been usefully employed in psychodynamic approaches to social casework (Preston-Shoot and Agass, 1990). An alternative modification to the analytic procedure has been the development of group approaches to psychotherapy (see Chapter 7), many of which draw on psychoanalytic principles although group therapies have also been developed from virtually every other psychodynamic model. A further development in the psychodynamic model, as in all other psychological models, is that it may be practised in the form of counselling as well as psychotherapy. Although the distinction between these two approaches is somewhat blurred, the focus of counselling is likely not to be as 'deep' as that of psychotherapy, and it is likely to be more concerned with specific problem areas and issues at a conscious level of awareness.

Research evidence for psychodynamic explanations of psychological problems and their treatment is limited. Although there have been attempts to investigate psychodynamic theory experimentally (Fonagy, 1982), much of the evidence relies on retrospective accounts of childhood or on psychological tests of questionable reliability. We shall now consider a model of psychological problems which its proponents contrasted with the psychoanalytic model in that it was viewed as being firmly based on experimental evidence.

The behavioural model

The behavioural model essentially regards psychological problems as bad habits, behaviours which have been learnt by the person who has these problems.

Applying the model to a phobia, such as agoraphobia, the phobic person is viewed as having learnt their fear because the object of their phobia has been associated with some traumatic event by a process of classical conditioning (see Chapter 1). Then, by a process of operant conditioning, the person learns that avoiding the phobic object reduces their anxiety. However, there are numerous difficulties with this explanation (see Box 18.4). Most of these, and variations on them in learning theory explanations of other psychological problems, cannot be addressed without taking into account at least the thoughts, if not also the feelings, of the people concerned as well as their behaviour.

Behaviour therapy, the treatment approach developed from the behavioural model, stands in marked contrast to psychoanalysis in that it is generally very practical, and in the pure behavioural approach it focuses solely on the client's symptoms without any consideration of the thoughts, feelings, or conflicts which might underlie these. Psychological problems being viewed as a result of the individual's learning experiences, behavioural treatment of these problems involves relearning.

The approach employed with problems involving fear, such as phobias, is the exposure of the client to the feared object since without such exposure the client will never learn that this object need not be feared. Exposure may be carried out in the client's imagination or in real life (*in vivo*), as by the agoraphobic client, perhaps accompanied by the therapist, being encouraged to travel on a bus or enter some other situation which he or she has previously avoided. This exposure may be gradual, as in *systematic desensitization*, or for prolonged periods with very little preparation, as in *flooding*. It may involve the therapist modelling exposure to the phobic object (for example, entering a butterfly farm while being watched by Jyothi, who was described above); and, as in some treatment packages for agoraphobics, the provision of a manual to the client to guide the exposure programme. The client's relatives may also be enlisted to assist in such a programme, this sometimes reversing a previous pattern in which they have helped the client to avoid feared situations. Although training in relaxation was initially a major component of systematic desensitization, research has suggested that it is unnecessary. As indicated in Box 18.4, research also questions whether, as originally assumed, flooding is only effective if the client remains in the feared situation until their anxiety diminishes.

The applicability of behaviour therapy is by no means limited to anxiety-related disorders. Socially unacceptable behaviour (such as that of George, described above) and psychotic symptoms have been treated by operant conditioning involving the manipulation of rewards or punishments. For example, hallucinating clients (such as Mary, described above) have been given social approval when they refer to their hallucinations as thoughts rather than voices; or exposed to 'white noise' as an aversive stimulus following reports of hallucinations (Slade, 1990).

Box 18.4 Problems with the Behavioural Explanation of Phobias

1. If asked, very few phobic people can remember an experience in which a traumatic event was associated with their phobic object, as might happen in classical conditioning.

2. Even when a conditioning experience is remembered, as with the dog phobic who remembers being bitten by dogs, it is usually possible to find other people who have undergone the same experience but have not developed phobias. This has forced learning theorists to offer explanations based on personality differences between people.

3. Phobias are more easily acquired to some objects than others. For example, it would be most unusual for someone to be phobic of lemons whereas phobias of snakes are relatively common. This has been explained by suggesting that phobias of certain objects are more likely to develop because they have an evolutionary significance (Seligman, 1971).

4. Experimental attempts to condition phobic responses have met with little success, perhaps fortunately for the individuals concerned.

5. There is no evidence of a substantial increase in the incidence of phobias following natural traumas.

6. The operant conditioning explanation for avoidance behaviour cannot accommodate evidence that such behaviour is sometimes acquired and maintained in the absence of fear: a person may, for example, avoid walking under ladders although he or she may experience little or no fear if faced with a situation of having to do so.

7. Learning theory explanations predict that the avoidance response should gradually disappear, or extinguish, when the traumatic event is no longer present. To accommodate the fact that this does not generally occur, modifications to the model have had to be developed (Eysenck, 1979).

8. The model also suggests that phobics who are exposed to an anxiety-provoking situation and instructed to remain there until their anxiety decreases would show greater improvement than those instructed to leave as soon as their anxiety increases to a certain level (in whom leaving the situation would reduce their anxiety, which would be expected to reinforce their phobic avoidance behaviour). However, this is not the case (de Silva and Rachman, 1983).

9. While the model predicts that exposure to the phobic object is a necessary condition for anxiety reduction, this is not always so. For example, anxiety may in some cases be reduced by the provision of information.

As Hudson (1989, p.76) has described in relation to the treatment of agoraphobia, 'social workers can readily be taught to use behaviour therapy techniques'. Such techniques can provide rapid symptom relief without the side-effects associated with physical treatments. However, it has been suggested that, like the latter, behaviour therapy fails to resolve the problems which underlie the symptoms.

The cognitive model

The inadequacies of purely behavioural accounts of human experience resulted in a 'cognitive revolution' in psychology. Cognitive models view psychological problems in terms of errors in thinking which may be manifested in irrational beliefs.

Such models are perhaps best known for their applications to the understanding of depression. For example, Seligman's (1975) learned helplessness theory asserted that experiences of inability to control events lead to expectancies that events are independent of the person's responses and a resulting failure of depressed people to initiate responses. This model was later modified to take into account the individual's attributions, or beliefs concerning the causation, of these experiences. Depression was considered to be more likely to result if the cause was perceived as being internal, global (affecting many situations), and stable (Abramson, Seligman and Teasdale, 1978). For example, a person may become depressed following rejection for a job if he or she views this as being due to a personal failure (an internal cause) resulting from their own general (global) and unchangeable (stable) incompetence. This was the type of thinking shown by Stephen, described earlier.

Another cognitive model of depression was developed by Beck (1967), who described a 'cognitive triad' of negative views of the self, the world and the future in depressed people. Beck considered that these beliefs are contained in *schemata*, cognitive structures which may be triggered by life events congruent with them. 'Cognitive distortions' in the way in which the individual processes information serve to maintain these schemata. For example, there may be selective attention to information which is consistent with negative schemata, and the person may overgeneralize from isolated negative incidents. It has been demonstrated that depressed people are more likely than non-depressed people to recall negative material relating to the self (Bradley and Mathews, 1983). Biased information processing is not specific to depressives, however, and indeed there is evidence that the cognitions of non-depressed people may be biased towards an unrealistic optimism whereas the pessimism of depressed people is more realistic (Alloy and Abramson, 1982).

When using this approach, it is assumed that in psychological problems involving anxiety, schemata concerned with danger are overactive. This view is supported by research evidence that anxious people tend to attend selectively to threatening stimuli (Mathews and MacLeod, 1986). In agoraphobics, their overactive schemata concerning dangers may result in unrealistically high expectations of threats to the person's physical well-being, loss of control, and inability to deal with external danger. An illustration of various other types of cognition which are relevant to psychological problems is provided by explanations of phobias and other problems involving anxiety. One such cognition is the individual's view of his or her coping resources, for example beliefs about *self-efficacy* (Bandura, 1977). These beliefs, which concern whether people expect that they can successfully carry out some behaviour, have been found to predict performance, for example that of an agoraphobic who is attempting to enter somewhere which he or she would normally avoid. Other relevant cognitions are the causal beliefs, or attributions, which individuals hold about the physical sensations of arousal which they experience when under stress. In those who experience panic attacks, there may be catastrophic misinterpretation of these physical sensations, for example that they are symptoms of a heart attack, and a vicious circle of increased anxiety and further consequent physical sensations may ensue.

As a social care professional, you may observe or be involved in cognitive therapy, which attempts to change the client's thoughts as well as their behaviour. In cognitive-behavioural approaches, as the name implies, a combination of cognitive and behavioural techniques is used. For example, in Meichenbaum's (1977) self-instructional training, identification of the negative internal self-statements (e.g. 'I am useless') which a person makes, and their replacement by coping self-statements (e.g. 'I can pass the test if I persevere'), may be tagged onto the use of techniques such as desensitization.

The 'rationalist' cognitive therapies, rather than simply trying to modify isolated cognitions, are also concerned with teaching the client to think rationally and correcting the 'cognitive errors' which the client is assumed to make, thereby distorting their experiences. In Beck's (1976) approach, a particular focus is on monitoring, and then examining the evidence for, negative automatic thoughts (i.e. those which occur continuously and normally go unchallenged). Homework assignments will often be given in order to test hypotheses derived from the client's thoughts. For example, the client who believes that assertiveness leads one to be rejected by others may test out this hypothesis by experimenting with being assertive in particular situations.

The development of cognitive therapy has provided an approach which, for example in terms of brevity and effectiveness, carries many of the benefits of behaviour therapy, and which, at least in its cognitive-behavioural form, has been considered particularly valuable for social workers to employ (Sheldon, 1995). Unlike behaviour therapy, as well as relieving symptoms, it may be considered also to address underlying structures and processes. However, it generally pays little attention to the history of the client's cognitions. A further criticism which has been levelled at several cognitive therapy approaches is their assumption that a particular way of thinking is correct and rational: a successful therapeutic outcome may be considered to involve accepting the therapist's view of the world!

The humanistic model

In the mid-twentieth century, there was increasing dissatisfaction with aspects of the dominant models applied to psychological problems. In particular, there was concern that these models were *mechanistic*, treating people as if they were machines; *reductionist*, viewing people in terms of their component parts, for example their behavioural responses or drives, rather than as whole people; and *deterministic*, seeing people's actions as determined by their biochemistry, by instinctual forces, or by their history of rewards and punishments rather than as a result of choices. Such dissatisfactions led to the development of the humanistic movement in psychology, which burgeoned in the 1960s.

There are numerous alternative humanistic approaches, but most consider that the person experiencing psychological problems has been unable to actualize his or her self, to be the person he or she truly wishes to be. As described by Carl Rogers (1961), this may be a result of the person having been exposed to 'conditions of worth', for example being told that their parents will only love them if they behave in a particular way. Their resulting state is likely to be one of *inauthenticity*, an area on which existential psychologists have particularly focused. The person may not be fully aware of their own needs and of how these differ from the demands of others. As a result, the person's needs are unlikely to be met, and this is considered by some humanistic psychologists, for example Gestalt therapists (Perls, Hefferline and Goodman, 1974), to result in a blockage of energy.

The rejection of mechanistic and reductionist aspects of other models has resulted in a de-emphasis of diagnosis by humanistic psychologists. There are, therefore, few humanistic models of particular types of psychological problem. However, a broad distinction is sometimes made between the neuroses and the psychoses. The former are generally seen as manifestations of inauthenticity, as in the agoraphobic woman who has denied her need for independence because of the demands of her family. The psychoses may be seen in terms of the individual trying to be authentic but in the process denying external reality entirely. If you come into contact with humanistic therapies, you will find that they generally involve a more democratic relationship between the therapist and client than in most other therapies, and one in which emphasis is placed upon the client's autonomy. While there are numerous humanistic therapy approaches, they share, to varying degrees, common features which have been listed by Rowan (1981) (see Box 18.5). One of the most influential of these approaches has been Rogers' person-centred therapy. The basic assumption of this therapy is that facilitative therapeutic conditions enable a client to actualize their potential. These conditions are determined more by the therapist's personal characteristics than by the techniques which he or she uses. In particular, it has been shown that if the client sees the therapist as non-possessively warm, empathic and genuine, therapy is likely to be effective (Watson, 1984). Person-centred therapy involves a non-directive therapeutic approach, in which the therapist essentially reflects back to the client what he or she is saying. There are some similarities with existential psychotherapy, but in the latter there is greater emphasis on such issues as death, freedom, isolation and meaninglessness (Yalom, 1980). Another influential humanistic approach, Gestalt therapy, makes more use of techniques. One of these which research has shown to be particularly effective is the *two-chair technique*. In this, the client successively sits and talks in two chairs which may represent conflicting parts of the client or the client and a person with whom he or she is in conflict.

While humanistic approaches generally do focus on helping the client to pursue their own personal goals, attaining these goals may not always assist social adjustment. A further difficulty with these approaches is that, partly because of their rejection of conventional diagnostic practices, in some cases they have adopted a rather cavalier approach to the selection of clients for what may be very powerful forms of therapy. As a result, vulnerable clients may become 'casualties' of therapy, which may precipitate suicide attempts or psychotic breakdowns (Lieberman, Yalom and Miles, 1973).

The constructivist model

Constructivist approaches in psychology were pioneered by George Kelly (1955) with his development of personal construct theory. This shared some of the underlying assumptions of the humanistic model, but placed much more emphasis on diagnosis (although not necessarily using traditional diagnostic categories) and more emphasis on research evidence. As with all constructivist approaches, the theory was based on the view that people actively construct their worlds. Their constructions may be validated or invalidated by events, and are revised accordingly if the person is functioning optimally. Such a person will be in a good position to anticipate subsequent events. Psychological problems occur when a person fails to change their ideas despite persistent invalidation (lack of confirmation) of some constructions.

Box 18.5 Common Features of the Humanistic Approach as Compared to Psychoanalytic and Behavioural Approaches

Comparisons	Psycho-analysis	Behaviourism	Humanistic Psychology
1. Psychodynamic approach – looking for what is behind surface behaviour.	YES	NO	YES
2. Action approach – looking at actual conduct of client, trying new things.	NO	YES	YES
3. Acknowledgement of importance of interpretation, transference, resistance, countertransference, etc.	YES	NO	YES
4. Use of guided fantasy and imagery.	NO	YES	YES
5. Use of groups as well as one-to-one.	YES	NO	YES
6. Emphasis on therapy for therapist.	YES	NO	YES
7. Emphasis on the body. Touching.	NO	NO	YES
8. Emphasis on gratification, joy and ecstasy.	NO	NO	YES
9. Belief in the real self.	NO	NO	YES
10. Medical model of mental illness.	YES	YES	NO
11. Encouragement of transference.	YES	NO	NO
12. Mechanistic approach to client.	NO	YES	NO
13. Old paradigm research methods.	YES	YES	NO

(Reproduced from Rowan, 'Humanistic therapy', *New Forum*, March 1991, 63-64, by permission of C. Newnes)

In Kelly's view, each person develops a unique system of personal constructs in order to anticipate their world. He regarded these constructs as bipolar: for example, if an individual construes their mother as kind, he or she will also be viewing her as not cruel, or whatever might be the individual's own particular contrast to being kind. Consideration of such contrasts may make more comprehensible a person's choices, including the sometimes apparently self-destructive choices of people presenting psychological problems. This and other aspects of Kelly's theory are increasingly being found useful in social work settings (Maitland and Brennan, 1992). For example, Browning (1988) describes how she was able to understand a young man's behaviour of shutting himself in his bedroom when she discovered that, while she contrasted this behaviour with desirable opportunities, his own contrast to it was suicide.

Other constructivists have drawn upon both cognitive and psychodynamic models. For example, Guidano and Liotti (1983) view people as developing 'emotional schemata', the nature of which is dependent on their early experiences, particularly those concerning attachment.

The constructivist model gives explanations, many of which are based upon research evidence, of the bases for particular types of psychological problem (Winter, 1992). For example, some clients diagnosed as schizophrenic have poorly organized personal construct systems. Agoraphobics often have a low level of awareness of constructions of interpersonal conflict, and as a result, situations of potential conflict may be unpredictable and anxiety-provoking for them. In their model, Guidano and Liotti also emphasize that the agoraphobic's view of the world involves a contrast between a need for protection and a need for total independence, perhaps as a result of childhood experiences of inhibition of their exploratory and autonomous behaviour by the ostensibly loving attentions of a parent.

Constructivist therapies have some commonalities with both humanistic and cognitive therapies. However, they place more emphasis than do most humanistic approaches on tailoring therapeutic techniques to the characteristics of the individual client. Unlike most cognitive approaches, they are less concerned with the validity of the client's view of the world than its viability. While they encourage the client to experiment, this is more to enable the client to discover that there are alternative ways of seeing the world than to lead him or her towards a particular viewpoint.

The initial stage of constructivist therapy generally involves exploration of the client's constructions of their world, of the implications of these, and possibly also of how they developed. In personal construct psychotherapy, use is often made of *enactment*, brief role-playing, both to facilitate exploration and to encourage experimentation with alternative ways of viewing events and behaving. One particular role-playing approach developed by Kelly is *fixed-role therapy*, in which the client is asked to enact for two weeks in their daily life a role portrayed in a character sketch written by the therapist. This sketch will not be of someone who is the complete opposite of the client, but rather will provide some new theme which the client might usefully explore. The aim is not to transform the client permanently into the new character, but to provide 'one good, rousing, construct-shaking experience' (Kelly, 1955, p.412), which will show the client that he or she need not be trapped in one particular role and corresponding set of reactions from other people. A further concern in personal construct psychotherapy may be to 'loosen' a client's constructs in an area in which they are very 'tight' or rigid, or conversely to tighten a very unstructured part of the client's construct system. Techniques may be borrowed from other types of therapy, but these will always be used with the aim of facilitating certain types of change in the client's construing.

Constructivist therapies take seriously clients' views of the world, while at the same time equipping them with the skills to enable them to view events from different perspectives. An occasional criticism of the constructivist model is that it takes insufficient account of the social, as opposed to the individual's own personal, construction of reality. This has been the major concern of *social constructionism*, and of the approaches to psychological problems developed from it (McNamee and Gergen, 1992).

Discussion point

  ° The following constructs were each used by a person referred for psychological therapy. How might they explain the problems and dilemmas with which each of these people was faced?

  - One client contrasted being self-destructive with being egotistical

  - Another contrasted being depressed with being aggressive

  - A third contrasted being assertive with being calmly logical.

The systemic model

The criticism that focusing on the psychological problems of the individual may exclude consideration of the wider context in which these problems occur has been directed at all the models described so far. By contrast, the systemic model views an individual's symptoms as reflecting a problem, or an attempted solution to a problem, in a broader system, for example a family or a society. This problem may essentially be one concerning the structure of the system (Minuchin, 1974). An example is an 'enmeshed' relationship, in which the boundary between the people concerned is diffuse, as in an unusually close relationship between a parent and child. It may be a problem of communication, as in the *double-bind*, first described in the families of schizophrenics, in which there are two conflicting communications, often one verbal and the other non-verbal (Bateson *et al.*, 1956). A mother may, for example, tell her daughter that she loves her although her facial expression is one of hatred.

Using the systemic model to explain agoraphobia might involve seeing the condition as a way of preserving the equilibrium of a marital system. For example, a husband may only be able to see himself as strong as long as his wife is dependent upon him by virtue of her phobia (Hafner, 1977).

The systemic model may be applied in any context. It provides a useful perspective on a wide range of systems (e.g. teams, agencies) impinging on social care (Preston-Shoot and Agass, 1990). However, it is in family therapy that it has been most fully elaborated. There are numerous schools of family therapy, but the defining feature of those which can be classed as systemic is that it is the family as a whole, rather than the individuals within it, that is being treated.

In the *structural* family therapy approach (Minuchin, 1974), the therapist is primarily concerned with modifying boundaries between subsystems within the family, or between the family and the outside world. If, for example, there is an enmeshed relationship between a child and a parent, and a clear boundary between this subsystem and the other parent, the therapist might address remarks to the parents as a unit, perhaps also asking them to sit together in sessions at some distance from the child. Approaches to family therapy based on *communications theory* are mainly concerned with clarifying the communications, at both verbal and non-verbal levels, within the family (e.g. Watzlawick, Beavin and Jackson, 1967). In *strategic therapies* (e.g. Palazzoli *et al.*, 1978), the therapist uses indirect strategies in an attempt to solve the family's problems. For example, in reframing a new meaning is provided for some aspect of the family's situation, as in a child's delinquent behaviour being viewed as a means of increasing the closeness between his or her parents. Paradoxical techniques are also often used in strategic therapy. One of these is to prescribe the symptom, as in the case of the child with temper tantrums whose family is told that there should be a certain number of tantrums at defined times during the day. Finally, the *narrative* approach to family therapy views problems as stories created by the family, and therapy involves the generation of alternative stories (White and Epston, 1990). While systemic therapies may result in fundamental change in that they influence the context in which a problem occurs, they may be easily sabotaged by the refusal of relevant individuals to participate in therapy. The manipulative nature of some systemic techniques is also a cause of concern for a number of therapists.

What type of therapy should be used?

In selecting a therapeutic approach, one might imagine that its relative effectiveness, compared to that of other approaches, would be the primary consideration. However, although the research evidence consistently indicates that psychological therapy, whatever its underlying model, is more effective than no treatment, and as effective or more effective than pharmacological treatment, little difference has been found in the effectiveness of different forms of therapy (Roth and Fonagy, 1996). Furthermore, there is evidence that the primary ingredient of an effective therapy is the quality of the client–therapist relationship rather than specific therapeutic techniques (Orlinsky, Grauwe and Parks, 1994). Particular aspects of the quality of this relationship which have been found to be significantly related to therapeutic outcome include the extent to which client and therapist are engaged in the process of therapy, their collaboration, the client's expressiveness, and the therapist's empathy and warmth. In general, clients' perceptions of the therapeutic relationship have been found to be more highly predictive of outcome than have therapists' perceptions.

Although therapies for psychological problems are generally effective, there is also evidence that they may occasionally have adverse effects (Lambert and Bergin, 1994). This highlights the importance of practitioners receiving appropriate training and supervision in the models which they employ. Addresses of organizations which will provide details of accredited training courses in the United Kingdom may be found at the end of this chapter.

The overall similarity in the effectiveness of different therapies does not imply that these therapies are equally effective with all clients. It may be, for example, that a behavioural or cognitive approach is more appropriate with the client who presents with a very specific symptom which he or she wishes to be removed, whereas the client who wishes to gain insight into the childhood roots of his or her problems may be best treated by psychodynamic therapy. There is some evidence of such relationships between clients' expectations of therapy and the types of treatment to which they are likely to respond (Caine, Wijesinghe and Winter, 1981).

As well as the similarity in their effectiveness, there is perhaps less difference in the practice of alternative psychotherapies than was once the case. Indeed, over a third of psychological therapists regard themselves as eclectic (Norcross, 1986), applying a range of different approaches. Others attempt to integrate two or more forms of therapy.

Discussion point

- ° If you were seeking treatment for a psychological problem, what therapeutic approach would you prefer? Why? Is this the same approach which you would prefer to use in your own therapeutic practice?

Race, Class, Gender and Psychological Problems

The diagnosis and treatment of psychological problems is not independent of the socio-cultural background and gender of the person presenting such problems. For example, black people in Britain are more likely to be diagnosed as schizophrenic, to be compulsorily admitted to psychiatric hospital, and to be given major tranquillisers or ECT than are white people (Fernando, 1988). All ethnic minorities are less likely to be referred for psychotherapy than are indigenous white people. Similar differences in psychiatric diagnosis and treatment have been reported between working class and middle class people, and women are also more likely to receive psychiatric diagnoses than are men (Johnstone, 1989). Differences in diagnosis are sometimes explained as due to the greater stress suffered by blacks, immigrants, working class people and women, and sometimes even in terms of genetic differences between socio-cultural groups. Differences in the therapies offered to these groups are occasionally explained in terms of the need for verbal articulacy in order to be able to benefit from psychotherapy. However, an equally viable explanation for such diagnostic and therapeutic differences is that general practitioners and psychiatrists, who are predominantly white, middle class and male, may be biased against, or insufficiently sensitive to the cultural and social situations of, black, working class or female clients. For example, behaviour which may appear indicative of insanity in a white, middle class subculture may be perfectly normal in the culture of the person exhibiting the behaviour. Clinicians and social care professional would do well to bear this in mind when faced with clients from whom they differ along socio-cultural dimensions.

Summary

Psychological problems may manifest themselves in many forms, which have been classified in terms of various diagnostic systems, one of the most currently favoured of which is DSM-IV. Questions have been raised regarding the reliability and validity of such systems.

Numerous models have been used to explain and treat psychological problems, the most influential being the medical, psychodynamic, behavioural, cognitive, humanistic, constructivist and systemic models. Each of these models, and corresponding therapies, has particular advantages and limitations. While there is little difference in the overall effectiveness of the therapies concerned, some therapies may be particularly suitable for certain types of clients. Both the diagnosis and treatment of psychological problems may be influenced by issues of race, social class and gender.

Seminar Questions

1. Is it useful to apply a diagnostic category to a client presenting with psychological problems? Why?

2. Consider one of your clients who has a psychological problem. How might this problem be explained and treated in terms of each of the models described in this chapter?

3. Can any one way of conceptualizing or treating psychological problems be considered more correct than the others?

4. What aspects of a social care professional's background might influence the way in which he or she views and works with different types of client? What are the mechanisms by which such influences might occur?

Further Reading

Davison, G.C. and Neale, J.M. (1996) *Abnormal Psychology.* New York: Wiley.
Provides an introduction to the causes of, and interventions for, psychopathology. Specific disorders are covered in detail.

Dryden, W. (ed.) (1991) *Individual Therapy: A Handbook.* London: Open University Press.
Provides descriptions, with case examples, of 11 therapeutic approaches.

Bergin, A.E. and Garfield, S.L. (eds.) (1994) *Handbook of Psychotherapy and Behavior Change.* New York: Wiley.
The 'bible' of research on the psychological therapies.

Psychotherapy and Counselling Courses and Organizations in the UK

The United Kingom Council for Psychotherapy, 167–9 Great Portland Street, London W1N 5FB (Tel. 0171 436 3002) will provide details of its member organizations, which encompass analytical psychology; behavioural and cognitive psychotherapy; experiential constructivist therapies; family, couple, sexual and systemic therapies; humanistic and integrative psychotherapy; hypnopsychotherapy; psychoanalytic and psychodynamic psychotherapy; and psychoanalytically-based psychotherapy with children. Many of these organizations provide training course in psychotherapy, completion of which is generally a prerequisite for inclusion on the National Register of Psychotherapists (United Kingdom Council for Psychotherapy, 1997).
Details of accredited counselling courses may be obtained from the British Association for Counselling, 1 Regent's Place, Rugby, Coventry CV1 2PJ (Tel. 01788 578328), which is also collaborating on the production of a register of counsellors.

References

Abramson, L.Y., Seligman, M.E.P., and Teasdale, J.D. (1978) 'Learned helplessness in humans: Critique and reformulation.' *Journal of Abnormal Psychology, 87*, 49–74.

Alloy, L.B. and Abramson, L.Y. (1982) 'Learned helplessness, depression, and the illusion of control.' *Journal of Personality and Social Psychology, 42*, 1114–1126.

American Psychiatric Association (1994) *Diagnostic and Statistical Manual of Mental Disorders, 4th Edition.* Washington, DC: American Psychiatric Association.

Bandura, A. (1977) 'Self-efficacy: Toward a unifying theory of behavioral change,' *Psychological Review, 84*, 191–215.

Bateson, G., Jackson, D.D., Haley, J., and Weakland, J. (1956) 'Toward a theory of schizophrenia,' *Behavioral Science, 1*, 251–64.

Beck, A.T. (1967) *Depression: Clinical, Experimental and Theoretical Aspects.* New York, NY: Hoeber.

Beck, A.T. (1976) *Cognitive Therapy and the Emotional Disorders.* New York, NY: International Universities Press.

Bentall, R.P. (1990) 'The syndromes and symptoms of psychosis,' in Bentall, R.P. (ed) *Reconstructing Schizophrenia.* London: Routledge.

Bowlby, J. (1969) *Attachment and Loss. 1: Attachment.* London: Hogarth Press.

Bowlby, J. (1973) *Attachment and Loss. 2: Anxiety and Anger.* London: Hogarth Press.

Boyle, M. (1990) *Schizophrenia: A Scientific Delusion?* London: Routledge.

Bradley, B. and Mathews, A. (1983) 'Negative self-schemata in clinical depression'. *British Journal of Clinical Psychology, 22*, 173–81.

Browning, H. (1988) 'Speculative adventures: the social work setting.' In G. Dunnett (ed) *Working with People: Clinical Uses of Personal Construct Psychology.* London: Routledge.

Caine, T.M., Wijesinghe, O.B.A. and Winter, D.A. (1981) *Personal Styles in Neurosis: Implications for Small Group Psychotherapy and Behaviour Therapy.* London: Routledge and Kegan Paul.

Cutting, J. (1985) *The Psychology of Schizophrenia.* Oxford: Blackwell.

de Silva, P. and Rachman, S. (1983) 'Exposure and fear-reduction.' *Behaviour Research and Therapy, 21*, 151–152.

Deutsch, H. (1929) 'The genesis of agoraphobia.' *International Journal of Psychoanalysis, 10*, 51–69.

Eysenck, H.J. (1979) 'The conditioning model of neurosis,' *Behavioral and Brain Sciences, 2*, 155–99.

Fernando, S. (1988) *Race and Culture in Psychiatry.* London: Croom Helm.

Fonagy, P. (1982) 'The integration of psychoanalysis and experimental science: a review.' *International Review of Psychoanalysis, 9*, 125–45.

Goldberg, D. and Huxley, P. (1980) *Mental Illness in the Community: The Pathway to Psychiatric Care.* London: Tavistock.

Guidano, V.F. and Liotti, G. (1983) *Cognitive Processes and Emotional Disorders.* New York, NY: Guilford.

Hafner, R.J. (1977) 'The husbands of agoraphobic women: assortative mating or pathogenic interaction?' *British Journal of Psychiatry, 130*, 233–9.

Hudson, B.L. (1989) 'Social factors and the role of social workers.' in K. Gournay (ed) *Agoraphobia: Current Perspectives on Theory and Treatment.* London: Routledge.

Johnstone, L. (1989) *Users and Abusers of Psychiatry: A Critical Look at Traditional Psychiatric Practice.* London: Routledge.

Kelly, G.A. (1955) *The Psychology of Personal Constructs.* New York, NY: Norton.

Klein, M. (1984) *Contributions to Psycho-Analysis, 1921–1945.* London: Hogarth Press.

Kohut, H. (1977) *The Restoration of the Self.* New York, NY: International Universities Press.

Kraepelin, E. (1896) *Psychiatrie, 5th. Aufl.* Leipzig: Barth.

Lambert, M.J. and Bergin, A.E. (1994). 'The effectiveness of psychotherapy.' In A.E. Bergin and S.L. Garfield (eds) *Handbook of Psychotherapy and Behavior Change.* New York, NY: Wiley.

Lambourn, J. and Gill, D. (1978) 'A controlled comparison of simulated and real ECT.' *British Journal of Psychiatry 133*, 514–519.

Lieberman, M.A., Yalom, I.D., and Miles, M.B. (1973) *Encounter Groups: First Facts.* New York, NY: Basic Books.

McNamee, S. and Gergen, K.J. (eds) (1992) *Therapy as Social Construction.* London: Sage.

Maitland, P. and Brennan, D. (eds) (1992) *Personal Construct Theory, Deviancy and Social Work.* London: Inner London Probation Service and Centre for Personal Construct Psychology.

Marshall, R. (1990) 'The genetics of schizophrenia: Axiom or hypothesis?' In R.P. Bentall (ed) *Reconstructing Schizophrenia.* London: Routledge.

Mathews, A. and MacLeod, C. (1986) 'Discrimination of threat cues without awareness in anxiety states.' *Journal of Abnormal Psychology, 95*, 131–8.

Meichenbaum, D. (1977) *Cognitive-Behavior Modification: An Integrative Approach*. New York, NY: Plenum.

Minuchin, S. (1974) *Families and Family Therapy*. Cambridge, Massachusetts: Harvard University Press.

Norcross, J.C. (1986) 'Eclectic psychotherapy: An introduction and overview.' In J.C. Norcross (ed) *Handbook of Eclectic Psychotherapy*. New York, NY: Brunner/Mazel.

Orlinsky, D.E., Grawe, K. and Parks, B.K. (1994) 'Process and outcome in psychotherapy – noch einmal.' In A.E. Bergin and S.L. Garfield (eds) *Handbook of Psychotherapy and Behavior Change*. New York, NY: Wiley.

Palazzoli, M.S., Boscolo, L., Cecchin, G. and Prata, G. (1978) *Paradox and Counterparadox*. New York, NY: Jason Aronson.

Perls, F.S., Hefferline, R.F. and Goodman, P. (1974) *Gestalt Therapy*. Harmondsworth: Penguin.

Preston-Shoot, M. and Agass, D. (1990) *Making Sense of Social Work: Psychodynamics, Systems and Practice*. Basingstoke: Macmillan.

Rogers, C.R. (1961) *On Becoming a Person*. Boston: Houghton Mifflin.

Rosenhan, D.L. (1973) 'On being sane in insane places.' *Science, 179*, 250–8.

Roth, A. and Fonagy, P. (1996) *What Works for Whom? A Critical Review of Psychotherapy Research*. New York, NY: Guilford.

Rowan, J. (1981) 'Humanistic therapy.' *New Forum*, March, 63–64.

Seligman, M.E.P. (1971) 'Phobias and preparedness.' *Behavior Therapy 2*, 307–20.

Seligman, M.E.P. (1975) *Helplessness: On Depression, Development and Death*. San Francisco: Freeman.

Sheldon, B. (1995) *Cognitive-Behavioural Therapy: Research, Practice and Philosophy*. London: Routledge.

Slade, P.D. (1990) 'The behavioural and cognitive treatment of psychotic symptoms.' In R.P. Bentall (ed) *Reconstructing Schizophrenia*. London: Routledge.

Warner, R. (1985) *Recovery from Schizophrenia: Psychiatry and Political Economy*. London: Routledge and Kegan Paul.

Watson, N. (1984) 'The empirical status of Roger's hypotheses of the necessary and sufficient conditions for effective psychotherapy.' In R.F. Levant and J. Shlien (eds) *Client-Centered Therapy and the Person-Centered Approach: New Directions in Theory, Research and Practice*. New York, NY: Praeger.

Watzlawick, P., Beavin, J.H., and Jackson, D.D. (1967) *Pragmatics of Human Communication*. New York, NY: Norton.

White, M. and Epston, D. (1990) *Narrative Means to Therapeutic Ends*. New York, NY: Norton.

Winter, D.A. (1992) *Personal Construct Psychology in Clinical Practice: Theory, Research and Applications*. London: Routledge.

Yalom, I.D. (1980) *Existential Psychotherapy*. New York, NY: Basic Books.

CHAPTER 19

Crime and Crime Prevention

Clive R. Hollin

Introduction

The past decade has seen several important advances in both the development of our under-standing of crime and methods applied to crime prevention. This chapter will outline some of the more recent research that has informed current thinking on the aetiology of criminal behaviour. The impact of this research will be discussed with reference to the increasing polar-ization of opinion on the thorny topic of crime prevention. Needless to say, the policies and practice that flow from the debate that surrounds the research will affect all practitioners work-ing with offenders. In considering crime prevention there are three approaches that at present are particularly important. The first is to act to prevent crime by changing the environment, an approach popularly known as situational crime prevention. The second approach is to deliver harsh punishment to offenders in order to deter them from committing more crime. The third is to attempt to work with offenders in a constructive manner to enable them to develop the skills to avoid reoffending. This latter approach is, of course, generally known as a rehabilita-tive or treatment approach.

The aims of this chapter are therefore twofold: first, to present an overview of recent research that increases our understanding of the development of criminal behaviour; second, to set this research against the three popular strands of crime prevention detailed above. In introducing the research we begin with a question: who commits crime?

Who Commits Crime?

In the time it takes you read this chapter two events can be guaranteed to have been taking place on a very large scale. The first certainty is that many crimes will have been committed. Crime surveys, such as the British Crime Survey (Mayhew, Maung and Mirrlees-Black, 1993), strongly suggest that most of these crimes will be relatively trivial in nature, including minor offences such as petty vandalism, minor thefts and fiddling of trifling amounts of money from tills, expense accounts and tax returns. However, some crimes will be highly serious, involving substantial financial cost and serious damage to both public and private property; other crimes will leave victims with serious personal injuries, or with the physical and psychological pain of sexual humiliation, or even loss of life.

The second absolute certainty is that hundreds, even thousands, of new human beings, will have arrived screaming and kicking to open their eyes to face the future. While these infants will grow and develop in many different ways, there is one more thing that is certain: some of these new born children will grow up, perhaps in not too many years time, to become the people who steal from cars, burgle houses, mug people late at night, set fires, rape, sexually assault children and kill.

As we consider these two events, so they begin to overlap to form the million-dollar question: as we look at all those new born infants, nestling and suckling, which of them will become the criminals? Who commits crime? Of course, this question is not idle academic speculation: the children who grow into criminals are the very people who will demand social work and probation services, and who will produce the victims who often need professional help and support.

The next section therefore considers what we know about the social and individual characteristics of children who become adolescent and then adult offenders.

The development of criminal behaviour

In seeking to understand the crucial factors in the development of criminal behaviour, the strongest evidence comes from studies that follow individuals over their life-span. This type of study is called a 'longitudinal' study. As Loeber and Farrington (1994) note, longitudinal studies in the study of the development of antisocial behaviour are informative at three levels: (1) the prediction of later outcomes from earlier information; (2) identifying developmental sequences and patterns; and (3) providing knowledge of the impact of critical periods and life events on development (see Box 19.1).

Box 19.1 Longitudinal Research

Briefly, a prospective longitudinal study first identifies a large sample, or cohort, who are followed forward into their futures. From childhood to adulthood the cohort, with their consent, is regularly tested and interviewed and official records are also monitored. This design gives researchers the advantage that from the outset they are able to define what information is to be gathered, they can use sophisticated measures of behaviour, and they are able to chart accurately the experiences of the cohort as they age. There is little doubt that when conducted properly this type of design gives extremely high quality information.

Despite the advantages of longitudinal studies in terms of quality of information, there are practical problems in carrying out this type of research. Longitudinal research necessarily extends over a long period of time and therefore demands great continuity among the researchers engaged in the study. In addition, longitudinal studies are financially expensive in requiring extensive long-term funding. Despite the practical and financial difficulties, there are a number of longitudinal studies – across a range of fields such as temperament and personality, schizophrenia, and drug use (Robins and Rutter, 1990; Rutter and Smith, 1995) – with the twin aims of investigating the stability of behaviour from early to later life, and searching for childhood predictors of adverse outcomes in adolescence and adulthood.

A recent study by Loeber *et al.* (1995) provides a perfect illustration of a longitudinal study. Loeber *et al.* were concerned to learn more about the predictive factors for the onset of conduct disorder, itself an established risk factor for later delinquency, in males between the ages of 8 and 17 years. A sample of 177 pre-adolescent boys was followed for six years, with data being gathered on a range of psychological, psychiatric and social factors. The findings showed that parental substance abuse, low socioeconomic status, and the child's resistance to discipline were important factors in his or her eventual progression to diagnosed conduct disorder. Other psychiatric diagnoses, primarily attention-deficit hyperactivity disorder, were important with respect to time of onset. Thus, in agreement with other studies (e.g. Farrington, Loeber, and van Kammen, 1990; Lahey *et al.*, 1995), a complex interaction between specific aspects of the child's psychological functioning and particular patterns of parental behaviour, set against a background of socioeconomic disadvantage, are seen as providing the setting conditions for the development of childhood behaviour problems (see also Chapter 12).

Thus, there are strong arguments for a longitudinal approach to the study of criminal behaviour and, indeed, several relevant longitudinal studies have been reported in the literature. These studies have illuminated our understanding of many criminological issues including the relationship between age and crime, predictors of juvenile delinquency, and patterns of adult crime.

Juvenile delinquency

With regard to the relationship between age and offending, it is established that for the adolescent population delinquency rates consistently increase from about eight years of age, reach a peak at about 16–17 years of age, then rapidly decline into the late teens and early twenties (e.g. Farrington, 1986). However, is the relationship between age and crime, known to be similar for both males and females, due to increasing prevalence, i.e. more young people committing crimes; or is it due to a rise in incidence, i.e. the young people who commit crimes committing more offences as they grow older?

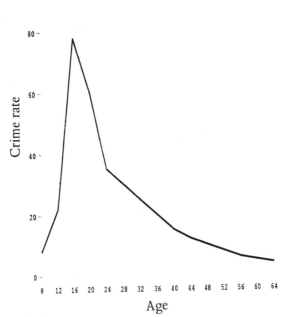

Figure 19.1 Age and crime

It is difficult for researchers to disentangle prevalence and incidence rates, but there is general agreement that the rise in rates of offending with age reflects a rise in prevalence not incidence. Thus, from their longitudinal study carried out in the United States, Wolfgang, Thornberry and Figlio (1987) reached the conclusion that the peak in rates of offending at 16–17 years of age is due 'almost entirely to an increase in the number of active offenders and not to an increase in their annual "productivity"' (p. 44).

Figure 19.1 illustrates the age–crime relationship typically found in research studies. In this graph the term 'crime rate' refers to the prevalence, in terms of a percentage, of offending among the population: that is, the percentage of people of specific ages who are committing offences. Thus, around 20 per cent of all 12 year olds are committing offences, around 80 per cent of all 16 year olds are offending, 20 per cent of 36 year olds, 8 per cent of 52 year olds, and so on.

Thus, to consider the question 'who commits crime', a part of the answer is that juveniles are known to commit far more than their fair share of offences. However, to place this statement in context, most but not all of juvenile crime is relatively trivial in nature, including large numbers of status offences. When discussing juvenile crime, it is important to be aware of the distinction between status offences and index (or notifiable) offences. Status offences are those acts which apply only to young people and not to adults – acts such as truancy, drinking alcohol and driving a motor vehicle under age. Index offences, on the other hand, are serious offences – such as murder, rape and sexual assault, burglary, arson, robbery – which are criminal acts regardless of the age of the perpetrator. Young people do commit both status and index offences but status offences are more frequent (Farrington, 1987). For a further discussion and different perspective on delinquency, see Chapter 17 by Leo Hendry.

The age–crime relationship also reveals that most crime is, to use Moffitt's (1993) term, 'adolescence limited'. The general message that emerges from the longitudinal research on age and offending is that most young people 'grow out' of delinquency by the time they reach 18 years of age. However, this is not the case for all juvenile offenders. Another valuable contribution of the longitudinal studies is that they have identified a number of factors associated with longer-term offending or, as Moffitt (1993) calls it, 'life-course persistent' offending.

Discussion point

- ° If the majority of adolescent offenders will 'grow out of crime', what implications does this developmental pattern have for practice in social care?

Predictors of long-term offending

One of the benefits of longitudinal research is that once data have been collected, the investigators can look back and try to identify any early factors or significant life events that are associated with persistent offending. While there are longitudinal studies from different countries, the Cambridge Study in Delinquent Development is the most widely cited longitudinal study conducted in Great Britain.

The Cambridge Study in Delinquent Development began in 1961 with a cohort of 411 young males, then aged 8–9 years, and is currently in progress with more than 90 per cent of the sample still alive as they pass into their forties. The Cambridge Study has involved repeated testing and interviewing of not only the males in the cohort, but also their parents, peers and school teachers; in addition, the researchers have had access to official records. This methodology has allowed a vast range of data to be collected on the individual members of the cohort, parental child-rearing practices, economic factors, school behaviour, and so on. Summaries of the many findings from this study have been provided by Farrington and West (1990) and Farrington (1995). It is important to note at the outset that as the cohort used in this study consisted entirely of males, its findings are restricted to male patterns of behaviour.

Looking first at offending, approximately 20 per cent of the cohort in the Cambridge Study were actually convicted as juveniles, with about 33 per cent convicted up to the age of 25 years. Self-reported delinquency proved to be a reasonable match with official convictions: that is, the males who were convicted also self-reported the greatest intensity of delinquent acts. Thus, it proved possible at each stage of the study to compare the worst offenders with the remainder of the cohort. The important point here, of course, is that such a comparison will highlight the critical factors in the development of chronic long-term offending.

With regard to childhood experiences – childhood being defined as up to their 10th birthday (the age of criminal responsibility in England and Wales) – there were marked findings that distinguished the future long-term offenders. As Farrington and West (1990) note:

> The future juvenile delinquents were more likely to have been rated troublesome and dishonest in their primary schools. They tended to come from the poorer families, to come from the larger-sized families, to be living in poor houses with neglected interiors, to be supported by social agencies, and to be physically neglected by their parents. However, they did not tend to come from low socio-economic status families (as measured by occupational prestige) or to have working mothers. The delinquents were more likely to have criminal parents and delinquent older siblings. (p. 118)

For the future long-term offender there emerges a picture of a childhood characterized by broken homes and harsh parenting; of early behaviour seen as troublesome (impulsive, hyperactive, attention deficit, daring, unpopular with peers) by authority figures; and poor attainment on intelligence and educational tests. In addition, those young males committing their first serious offence around the age of 13 years, and those adolescents who accumulate more than six criminal convictions, were at greatest risk of progressing to an adult criminal career (Farrington, 1983). As shown in Box 19.2, Farrington (1995) notes that the most important distinguishing characteristics, observed at age 8–10 years, of later delinquency (whether measured by convictions or self-report) fell into six main categories.

In summary, the findings of the Cambridge Study strongly suggest that a range of adverse features in early life are associated with social difficulties and the onset of antisocial behaviour and later criminal behaviour. The intensity and severity of such personal and social disadvantage in childhood appear to be predictive of chronic offending in adolescence and adulthood.

One further advantage of longitudinal research is that it is possible to look not only at broad patterns of development, but also at the impact of life events on those patterns. Farrington

Box 19.2 Distinguishing Childhood Characteristics of Long-Term
Offenders (based on Farrington, 1995).

1. Antisocial childhood behaviour, including troublesomeness in school, dishonesty and aggressiveness
2. Hyperactivity-impulsivity-attention deficit, including poor concentration, restlessness, daring and psychomotor impulsivity
3. Low intelligence and poor school attainment
4. Family criminality, including convicted parents, delinquent older siblings, and siblings with behaviour problems
5. Family poverty, including low family income, large family size and poor housing
6. Poor parental child-rearing behaviour, including harsh and authoritarian discipline, poor supervision, parental conflict and separation from parents.

(1995) notes the influence of several such life events. Thus, age at first conviction, school attended, unemployment and moving to a more prosperous area were all related to patterns of criminal activity in adolescence. Some developmental studies have focused specifically on aggression and violent conduct, finding a similar pattern of predictors to those noted above for frequent offending (e.g. Kingston and Prior, 1995).

However, it would not be wise to divorce childhood antisocial behaviour and adolescent delinquency from other problems. Stattin and Magnusson (1995) examined the relationship between the onset of official delinquency and other educational, behavioural and interpersonal problems. They found clear relationships between a range of social and behavioural problems and delinquency: 'The age at onset of offending is intimately connected in time with the emergence of problem behaviour generally' (p.440). Further, as Farrington, Barnes and Lambert (1996) have shown, these problems cluster and are concentrated in specific families. Farrington *et al.* report that in their sample of 397 families, half the total convictions in the whole sample were accounted for by 23 families! This concentration of criminal behaviour could not be simply explained by co-offending.

In conclusion, it would be wrong to think that the stage has been reached when it is possible to construct an exact model of a criminal career. There are as yet too many unanswered questions to begin to be so bold as to assume to predict human behaviour. For the present, while the findings of the longitudinal surveys are important in describing the conditions associated with the onset of criminal behaviour, they also demand an explanation of how they cause delinquent behaviour.

Long-term offenders

When data are collected over a lengthy period, it is possible to look closely at those children and adolescents who progress to the status of chronic long-term, adult criminals. By comparing the characteristics and circumstances of the adult offenders with the non offenders even more details about the pathway to adult crime can be uncovered.

By the time the people in the Cambridge Study of Delinquent Development had reached the age of 18 years, the long-term offenders in the cohort had taken to a lifestyle characterized by heavy drinking, sexual promiscuity, drug use and minor crimes involving motor vehicles or group violence and vandalism. The long-term offenders were highly unlikely to have any formal qualifications, they held unskilled manual jobs, and had had frequent periods of unemployment. By age 32 years, the long-term offenders were unlikely to be home owners, had low paid jobs, tended to have physically assaulted their partner, and used a wide range of drugs. These chronic offenders had an extensive history of fines, probation and prison sentences. It was clear from their life histories and current circumstances that the adult offenders were leading a socially dysfunctional existence.

Similar findings for a general offender population are reported by Nagin, Farrington and Moffitt (1995), and specifically for physical aggression by Windle and Windle (1995).

In terms of frequency of criminal behaviour, the long-term offenders in the Cambridge Study committed more offences while unemployed rather than while in employment. Interestingly, the types of crime committed while unemployed were for financial reward – theft, burglary, fraud – not crimes against the person. The formation of close relationships in early adulthood was found to be related to a decrease in offending. Specifically, those offenders who married showed a decrease in offending – with the proviso that their partner was not a convicted offender.

Farrington and West (1990) paint a bleak picture of the life of those men who had continued to offend and be convicted as adults. The factors noted previously as prevalent at age 18 years, continued into later life:

> Convicted men differed significantly from unconvicted ones at age 32 in most respects of their lives: in having less home ownership, more residential mobility, more divorce or separation from their wives, more conflict with their wives or cohabitees, more separation from their children, more unemployment, lower take-home pay, more evenings out, more fights, more heavy smoking, more drunk driving, more heavy drinking, more drug-taking, more theft from work, and more other types of offences ... While convicted and unconvicted men were significantly different in many respects, it should not be concluded that all convicted men were more deviant than all unconvicted men. The two groups overlapped significantly. (p. 126)

'Social failure', to use Farrington's (1990) expression, does not it seems irredeemably lead to conviction, but it does massively increase the risk of criminal behaviour. Nor should it be thought that a disadvantaged background inevitably leads to crime (see also Chapter 12): Farrington and West (1990) note the phenomenon of 'good boys from bad backgrounds'. Such males, for whom all the signs indicated a criminal career, appeared to be characterized during adolescence by their shyness, and as adults by their social withdrawal and isolation, spending most of their leisure time at home. However, while not following a life of crime, these particular unconvicted males were experiencing relationship problems with their parents or partners.

As noted above, Moffitt (1993) has advanced the view that with respect to offending there are two distinct categories of individual: (1) an 'adolescence- limited' group who are antisocial only during adolescence; and (2) a 'life-course-persistent' group who engage in antisocial behaviour at every stage of their lives. Moffitt advances the thesis that: 'The two groups differ in etiology, developmental course, prognosis, and, importantly, classification of their behavior as either pathological or normative' (p. 679). In other words, the persistent offenders will be differentiated from the adolescent-limited offenders by a range of social and psychological factors (see Box 19.2).

Nagin and Land (1993) provide some empirical support for Moffitt's view. They found that life-course-persistent offenders were characterized by a constellation of school and family problems, chronic interpersonal problems, high job instability, and high levels of self-harming behaviours such as heavy drinking and drug abuse. However, the range and intensity of these child and adolescent factors were much more extensive for the chronic adult offenders.

In summary, the criminal career research has generated a wealth of data on both the aetiological factors important with respect to the development of criminal behaviour, and in the distinguishing characteristics of different groups of offenders. However, there are still many issues that remain to be resolved. We know rather more about the development of male offending than we do about female offending. We know remarkably little about the role of mental health and mental illness in the development of criminal behaviour. Further, most but not all criminals begin offending in adolescence, but what about those people who begin to commit crime when they are adults? Is the genesis of 'white collar' crime the same as for 'blue collar' crime?

As empirical knowledge of the type discussed above accumulates, so our understanding of crime increases. It is true to say that we now know a great deal about levels of crime and the factors associated with its onset and maintenance. The issue that follows is the extent to which that knowledge can be applied to prevent crime. However, this is not a simple issue of application of knowledge, there are powerful philosophical arguments and political forces to consider.

Discussion point

° Before reading on, consider the research described so far and discuss what measures should be taken to reduce crime in the light of the research findings. Do you think the measures you suggest would be politically acceptable?

Crime, Opportunity and Punishment

While we can offer descriptions of the development and circumstances of offenders, a description is not an explanation. When it comes to explanation, there are two distinct philosophies at work. The first view is of the individual as a rational agent possessing free will, so that an individual's circumstances reflect their choices in life. The second position is that we are all, to a greater or lesser extent, products of our environment (Honderich, 1993).

If the first philosophy is translated into action, it means that offenders are people who choose of their own free will to commit crime (Roshier, 1989). If this stance is taken, then two policies follow: first, give as few opportunities as possible for the choice of a criminal act; second, when people are caught, make the consequences as painful as possible to deter that individual from future offending. Alternatively, it follows from the second explanation that if environmental conditions are implicated in the cause of crime then change is needed in the environment. Further, the adverse effects on the individual resulting from the environment need to be addressed. The policy implications that flow from this stance are that changing the environment, primarily the social structure, and working constructively with the individual offender must be of central concern.

In practice, this issue crystallizes into the debate on the relative effectiveness of the punishment and treatment in preventing crime. (The term 'treatment' is problematic given its associations with medical models and hence apparently implying a model of crime that infers psychopathology. For lack of a better word, the term treatment is used here in the broad sense of making attempts to change constructively either a social system or an individual's functioning.) However, the relative merits of punishment and treatment are not left to philosophical debate or even empirical investigation. Crime is a hot political issue, and politicians of all persuasions invariably express their intention to be strong on crime. Tough stances in the field of criminal justice invariably translate into punitive policies to deliver harsh penalties and deter criminals from a life of crime. The intention is clear, so how are harsh penalties delivered and, perhaps more importantly, do they prevent crime?

The next section moves to look first at the crime prevention strategy of reducing opportunity, and then at the effectiveness of punishing offenders. As the policy and practice espoused by this approach currently offers a considerable challenge to the more client-centred stance typically taken in social and probation work, it is both informative and instructive to consider these approaches in some detail.

Situational crime prevention

If we follow the view that crimes are the end result of criminals seizing the opportunity to make a personal, usually financial, gain, then why not look at the opportunity as well as the criminal? This is precisely the approach taken by situational crime prevention: analyzing and changing the environment in an effort to prevent crime. Since the early 1980s, a string of studies have been published that are summarized in a number of texts (e.g. Clarke, 1992; Cornish and Clarke, 1986; Heal and Laycock, 1986). Indeed, situational crime prevention, in both a theoretical and practical sense, has become something of a speciality in its own right. Briefly, situational crime prevention has two major strands: (1) reducing the opportunity for successful crime; and (2) increasing the risk of detection:

1. *Reducing Opportunity.* There are several ways to reduce the opportunity for crime, but the most straightforward are removing the target and hardening the target. Target removal is seen in crime prevention strategies such as replacing telephone coin boxes with phone cards, or introducing night transport systems to ensure the safety of late night workers as they go home. Target hardening is seen in strategies such as car alarms and immobilizers and home security systems.

2. *Increasing the Risk of Detection.* There are various approaches that can be taken to signal to offenders that the risk of detection has been increased. One such strategy is to increase levels of formal surveillance at sites where there is an opportunity for crime. Most obviously, this type of prevention can be achieved through an increased police presence at venues such as football matches and city centres as pubs close.

Technology can also be used to increase formal surveillance, as seen in the now ubiquitous use of closed circuit television, and the electronic 'tagging' of offenders to monitor their movements. The issue of tagging has, of course, stirred considerable debate within the probation service (Nellis, 1991).

Informal surveillance methods can be achieved quite simply as, for example, in positioning coin operated public telephones in open locations such as shops and launderettes. On a more organized basis, Neighbourhood Watch is an excellent example of the mobilization of communities to be aware of suspicious events and so take steps to reduce crime.

DETERRENCE OR DISPLACEMENT?

One of the principles underpinning situational crime prevention is that when crime becomes less likely to succeed, so would-be offenders are deterred from committing a criminal act. The evidence from the outcome studies suggests that there is some evidence in support of this position. However, the unresolved question is whether situational crime prevention measures actually reduce crime or simply displace it to other victims, times or situations. The question of civil liberties is also important when discussing situational crime prevention. For example, as discussed by Nellis (1991), electronic tagging of known offenders has the potential for a profound social impact in terms of state surveillance and control of members of society. While this should be of concern to all citizens, those who work with offenders in a professional capacity must be aware of this debate.

Despite reservations, it is likely that situational crime prevention is here to stay. The deterrence approach that it espouses is also to be found in an approach that seeks to deliver harsh punishment to deter offenders from future offending. While manifest in many forms, from fines to capital punishment, this approach attracts a high profile in relation to austere prison regimes.

Punitive prison regimes

It is reasonably well established that, across the board, reconviction rates of persons discharged from prisons in England and Wales lies between 54 and 70 per cent (Lloyd, Mair and Hough, 1994). The exact figures vary according to type of offender, length of follow-up, date of study, and so forth. To attempt to lower this base rate of reconviction, various types of prison regimes have been designed of which harsh, punitive orientated regimes are a topical example.

Punishment orientated regimes seek to make the experience of imprisonment particularly aversive so as to deter the offender from reoffending. There are several examples of this type of regime, such as the 'short, sharp, shock' regime (Thornton *et al.*, 1984), and 'scared straight' programmes (Homant, 1981; Lewis, 1983). Restitution programmes, often favoured by victims, are certainly seen as highly unpleasant by offenders (Blagg, 1985), and there is some evidence for their effectiveness in terms of reducing reoffending (Schneider, 1986; Schneider and Schneider, 1985). Restitution programmes are typically conducted in community settings rather than in prisons. There is, however, a particular form of punishment regime, the 'boot camp', which is set be used in England and Wales. This regime has attracted a reasonably strong research literature, and it is possible to make some informed statements about its effectiveness in terms of crime prevention.

Boot camps

As MacKenzie and Souryal (1995a) note:

> The public and policy makers appear to expect boot camps to accomplish spectacular results. Boot camps provide a short term of incarceration in a strict military environment with a rigid daily schedule of hard labor, drill and ceremony, and physical training. There is obviously a hope that this tough punishment will deter offenders from continuing their criminal activities (p. 2).

Clearly such an overtly punitive approach will raise moral and philosophical objections (Mathlas and Mathews, 1991; Morash and Rucker, 1990; Sechrest, 1989), but what about effectiveness?

PROCESS MEASURES

MacKenzie and Shaw (1990) compared adjustment and attitude change in inmates sentenced either to traditional incarceration or to a boot camp. They found that the boot camp inmates were more positive about their experience of imprisonment, were more positive about their future, and held more prosocial attitudes. Indeed, MacKenzie and Souryal (1995b) list a range of positive process outcomes, including inmates being drug free and physically healthy, inmates believing that the programme has helped them, and an overall positive impact on the families of offenders. However, as MacKenzie and Souryal (1994) note, the finding that boot camp inmates become less antisocial during incarceration may be a selection effect. The offenders were different from the general prison population in that they were convicted of nonviolent crimes and had less serious criminal histories.

RECIDIVISM

A string of studies has looked at the impact of boot camp regimes on recidivism (e.g. MacKenzie *et al.*, 1995; MacKenzie and Shaw, 1993), as well as adjustment during community supervision (MacKenzie and Brame, 1995). The picture emerging from these studies is not a simple one: the findings show some fluctuation according to the location of the boot camp regime, the actual measure of reoffending, and the offenders' situation after release. Thus, for example, MacKenzie *et al.* (1995) found that in four states there was no impact of boot camps on recidivism, in one state there was an increase in recidivism after the boot camp, and in three states there were mixed findings regarding recidivism. Further, it is possible that success is related to intensity of supervision after release (MacKenzie and Brame, 1995). Nor can it be assumed that all boot camp regimes are similar, leaving the possibility that these differences are related to varying outcomes. As MacKenzie *et al.* (1995) note, the more successful boot camp programmes, in terms of reducing recidivism, 'devoted a comparatively large amount of time to therapeutic activities' (p.353).

MacKenzie *et al.* (1995) offer the conclusion that:

> It is hardly surprising in our research that offenders were positively affected by their experience in the boot camps that had components characteristic of effective treatment programs but that the recidivism of boot camp releasees was actually higher than for the comparative groups in the camp that emphasized physical activity and military deportment without any therapeutic programming. Certainly, there is little past research to suggest that the physical exercise,

military atmosphere, and hard labor aspects of these programs would successfully change the behavior of the offenders if, at the same time, the criminogenic needs of the offenders are not being addressed (pp.353–354).

The marked lack of success of overtly punitive strategies in terms of crime prevention is perhaps not so startling when set against the findings of the longitudinal studies. Farrington (1995) suggests that the findings from longitudinal research point to the need for strategies to improve young people's school achievement and interpersonal skills, improve parental child-rearing practice and reduce poverty. Such a far-reaching strategy to prevent crime clearly sets a wide agenda, cutting across political, economic, social and psychological boundaries. It is far beyond the scope of this chapter to cover the broad range of crime prevention strategies that seek to work through large-scale social change (Tonry and Farrington, 1995). Indeed, in a psychology book it is appropriate to focus on the contribution of work that is primarily psychological in orientation, although as it is ultimately difficult to disentangle social and psychological influences. In this light, the next section turns to the recent research on the effectiveness of working with young offenders.

Discussion point

- ° What role, if any, should social care professionals have in crime prevention methods that rely on punitive approaches?

Offender Treatment: Still Not Working?

There is a vast literature on the topic of working with offenders (e.g. Hollin, 1996) that would be impossible to cover in a book, let alone a chapter. The aim here, therefore, is first to offer a brief overview of approaches to the treatment of offending behaviour. Following this overview of the literature, the second aim of this chapter is to look at current thinking with regard to 'what works' in treatment programmes with offenders. While this literature tends to have a focus on young offenders (e.g. Hollin and Howells, 1996), it is certainly not the case that the principles apply exclusively to young offenders. The following should therefore be read as applying both to young and adult offenders.

Programmes and settings

PROGRAMME STYLE

It is difficult to think of a therapeutic approach that has not been used with offenders. Forensic psychotherapy has a long history (e.g. Aichhorn, 1925/1955), and continues to engage the attentions of many practitioners (e.g. Cordess and Cox, 1995; Welldon and Van Velsen, 1997). Behaviour therapy also has a relatively long history of application with offenders (see Blakely and Davidson, 1984; Gordon and Arbuthnot, 1987; Milan, 1996). While techniques such as social skills training, incorporating elements such as modelling, role-play, and discussion, have enjoyed spells of popularity (e.g. Hollin, 1990a), cognitive-behavioural programmes currently engage the attention of many practitioners. A cognitive-behavioural approach is marked by an increased emphasis on understanding the role of social factors, alongside a focus on changing affect and cognition as well as overt behaviour.

A range of cognitive-behavioural programmes for young offenders has been reported in the literature (Hollin, 1990b). Examples of such approaches, applicable with adult as well as young offenders, include increasing self-control through self-instructional training (Goldstein and Keller, 1987; Snyder and White, 1979), sometimes specifically focused on anger control (Feindler and Ecton, 1986; McDougall et al., 1987; Lochman, 1992). Social problem-solving skills, including sensitivity to interpersonal problems; the ability to choose a desired outcome of a social exchange ('means-end thinking'); considering the likely outcomes of one's actions ('consequential thinking'); and generating different ways to achieve the desired outcome ('alternative thinking'), have been another target for change in working with young offenders (Hains, 1984; Spivack, Platt and Shure, 1976). These cognitive change methods have been applied with success in work with adult offenders (e.g. Ross, Fabiano and Ewles, 1988).

Given the link between immature moral reasoning and juvenile delinquency (Nelson, Smith and Dodd, 1990), several cognitive- behavioural programmes have been designed to increase moral reasoning in young offenders (e.g. Gibbs, 1996).

Some approaches have blended a variety of the methods discussed to form a multimodal programme. For example, Aggression Replacement Training uses three main approaches to changing young offenders' violent behaviour: structured learning training, including SST and social problem-solving training; anger control training; and moral education (Glick and Goldstein, 1987; Goldstein and Glick, 1996). Similarly, the Reasoning and Rehabilitation programme developed by Ross and Fabiano (1985) also incorporates several methods to enhance thinking and problem solving skills.

Institution and community

Within penal institutions a range of approaches has been used: however, behavioural techniques, most often a token economy programme, have a long history (Milan, 1987). The most recent moves in prison-based treatment are towards the adoption of formal treatment programmes, such as the Reasoning and Rehabilitation programme (e.g. Garrido and Sanchis, 1991).

In less secure residential establishments a wide range of work is conducted with young offenders (Schaefer and Swanson, 1988). The successful Achievement Place style of residential provision, incorporating 'teaching-parents' and the use of behavioural methods of change, generated a great deal of interest in the 1970s and 1980s (Braukmann and Wolf, 1987; Burchard and Lane, 1982). More recently, Hagan and King (1992) described a successful intensive treatment programme conducted in a residential facility for young offenders. This programme combined a range of interventions, including individual cognitive and psychotherapy, a residential management programme, education, family therapy and an independent living programme. Similar examples of successful residential outcomes, even with the most difficult and disadvantaged young people, are sprinkled throughout the literature (e.g. Bullock et al., 1990; Epps, 1994; Haghighi and Lopez, 1993).

Within the community there are many examples of programmes aimed at reducing crime among young offenders. These programmes include both school-based interventions (e.g. Burchard and Lane, 1982), and family-based intervention to increase parental child management skills (Bank *et al.*, 1987; Kazdin, Siegal and Bass, 1992) and to aid constructive family functioning (Henggeler *et al.*, 1993; Kazdin, 1987; Welch, 1985).

For apprehended young offenders, there are initiatives aimed at diversion from custody and so, it is argued, away from the detrimental effects of the criminal justice system (e.g. Leger *et al.*, 1996). In the probation services, behavioural casework went through a period of popularity (Hudson, 1986; Remington and Remington, 1987). More recently, the STOP Project conducted by Mid-Glamorgan Probation Service in Wales (Raynor and Vanstone, 1994), based on the Reasoning and Rehabilitation Programme, was successfully used with offenders. The use of intensive probation and supervision schemes, sometimes incorporating treatment elements, as an alternative to custody is currently a focus of attention (Gendreau, Cullen and Bonta, 1994).

This brief overview of the treatment literature raises the crucial issue of effectiveness: given the time, effort, and money expended on working with offenders, does treatment work to reduce offending and prevent crime?

Does treatment work?

In the field of offender rehabilitation we are faced with many different types of intervention, conducted in different settings, with different measures of 'success'. As there are literally hundreds of outcome studies, how can meaningful conclusions be drawn from this literature about what works, for whom, and under what conditions?

There have been several meta-analytic studies (see Box 19.3 for an explanation of the term 'meta-analysis') of the offender treatment literature (Andrews *et al.*, 1990; Garrett, 1985; Gottschalk *et al.*, 1987; Lipsey, 1992; Lösel and Koferl, 1989; Izzo and Ross, 1990; Roberts and Camasso, 1991; Whitehead and Lab, 1989), with a number of summaries also available

---

Box 19.3 Narrative and Meta-analytic Reviews

The traditional approach to making sense of a large body of research evidence is for a reviewer to conduct a narrative or qualitative literature review. Such a narrative approach often uses the tactic of polling the positive and negative results of several hundred studies and 'vote counting'. Some narrative reviews of offender rehabilitation are pessimistic in concluding that little or nothing works (Lipton, Martinson, and Wilks, 1975; Martinson, 1974); while other narrative reviews claim that successful intervention is possible (e.g. Gendreau and Ross, 1979, 1987; Ross and Gendreau, 1980).

As several authors note (e.g. Cook *et al.*, 1992; Gendreau and Andrews, 1990), a narrative approach to understanding the messages embedded in a large empirical literature has some disadvantages, not least because of the demanding intellectual task of attempting to balance and judge the effects of different studies, with different strengths, employing different methods, and conducted in different settings. However, the development of the quantitative technique of meta-analysis has gone some way towards providing a means by which to produce a standardized summary of a large number of studies.

As Izzo and Ross (1990) explain, meta-analysis is

'A technique that enables a reviewer to objectively and statistically analyse the findings of each study as data points.... The procedure of meta-analysis involves collection of relevant studies, using the summary statistics from each study as units of analysis, and then analysing the aggregated data in a quantitative manner using statistical tests' (p.135).

(Gendreau and Andrews, 1990; Hollin, 1994; Lipsey, 1995; Lösel, 1995a, 1995b, 1996). The broad conclusion from these analyses is that there is an overall gain of about a 10 per cent reduction in recidivism when treated offenders are compared with no treatment controls. However, there is a large variability in effect: some programmes produce a negative effect (i.e. they increase recidivism); others produce no effect; while others lead to significant reductions in recidivism. Lipsey (1992) suggests that the high effect programmes can produce decreases in recidivism of 20–40 per cent above the baseline levels from mainstream criminal sanctioning of offenders.

Principles for effective services

A summary of the main points from the meta-analysis are listed in Box 19.4. These are taken mainly from the two most recent meta-analytic studies reported by Andrews *et al.* (1990) and by Lipsey (1992). It is important to note that these conclusions refer to reduced offending as an outcome of the intervention. This says nothing about personal change, although it is clear that psychological, educational, and behavioural treatment programmes are effective in bringing about such change (Lipsey and Wilson, 1993). Interestingly, the meta-analyses suggest that punishment orientated regimes seem to make matters worse not better.

As the findings from the meta-analyses have become more widely disseminated, so they have been formulated into principles, relevant to both managers and practitioners, to guide the development of effective services for working with offenders. In the rest of this section the principles identified in Box 19.4 are considered in more detail.

The risk principle, as suggested by Andrews and Bonta (1994), states that an important predictor of success is that offenders assessed as medium to high risk of recidivism (by criminal history or a standardized measure) should be selected for intensive programmes (see Chapter 4 for a discussion of risk).

Box 19.4 Markers for the Design of Effective
Programmes to Reduce Reoffending

1. Indiscriminate targeting of treatment programmes is counterproductive in reducing recidivism: medium to high risk offenders should be selected, and programmes should focus on criminogenic areas.
2. The type of treatment programme is important, with structured and focused treatments approaches more effective than nondirective methods.
3. The most successful studies, while behavioural in nature, include a cognitive component in order to focus on the attitudes, values and beliefs that support antisocial behaviour.
4. With respect to the type and style of service, Andrews *et al.* (1990) suggest that nondirective client-centred therapies are not the optimum approach with mainstream offenders.
5. Treatment in the community has a stronger effect on delinquency than residential programmes.
6. The most effective programmes have high 'treatment integrity' in that they are carried out by trained staff and there is effective management of the intervention.

Lipsey (1992) comments that: 'More structured and focused treatments (e.g. behavioral, skill-orientated) and multimodal treatments seem to be more effective than the less structured and focused approaches (e.g. counseling)' (p.123). Andrews *et al.* (1990) suggest that some therapeutic approaches are not suitable for general use with offenders. Specifically, they argue that 'Traditional psychodynamic and nondirective client-centred therapies are to be avoided within general samples of offenders' (p.376). This leads Andrews and Bonta (1994) to the responsivity principle: the need to deliver programmes in a way that is in keeping with the style of service delivery to which offenders will be likely to respond.

While behavioural in orientation, treatment programmes that successfully reduce offending include a cognitive component to focus on changing the 'attitudes, values, and beliefs that support anti-social behaviour' (Gendreau and Andrews, 1990, p.182). In other words, as well as gaining the skills to keep out of trouble, it is desirable that interventions help offenders reassess and change their antisocial thinking. For example, offenders may have little thought for their victims, so helping offenders gain a sense of empathy may be an important goal in working to reduce offending.

Roberts and Camasso (1991) also stress the importance of working with families to reduce recidivism. As noted previously, the longitudinal studies clearly point to the role that families play in the development and maintenance of offending.

A focus on offending is in keeping with the need principle, as Andrews and Bonta (1994) explain:

> Many offenders, especially high-risk offenders, have a variety of needs. They need places to live and work and/or they need to stop taking drugs. Some have poor self-esteem, chronic headaches or cavities in their teeth. These are all 'needs'. The need principle draws our attention to the distinction between criminogenic and noncriminogenic needs. Criminogenic needs are a subset of an offender's risk level. They are dynamic attributes of an offender that, when changed, are associated with changes in the probability of recidivism. Noncriminogenic needs are also dynamic and changeable, but these changes are not necessarily associated with the probability of recidivism. (p.176)

Finally, the meta-analyses strongly suggest that the most effective programmes have high 'treatment integrity'. The integrity principle maintains that the programmes are conducted by trained staff, while those individuals responsible for the management and supervision of treatment are involved in all the operational phases of the programme (Hollin, 1995; Hollin, Epps, and Kendrick, 1995; Lösel and Wittmann, 1989).

The principles outlined above are not the only points to be drawn from the meta-analyses. For example, with respect to setting, treatment programmes conducted in the community are likely to have stronger effects on delinquency than residential programmes. While residential programmes can be effective, they should be structurally linked with community-based interventions. Further, programmes that help the offender to gain real employment in the community have a significantly enhanced chance of success. Several attempts have been made to bridge the research-practice divide by distilling the complexities of the meta-analysis into blueprints for the design of effective programmes for working with offenders (Antonowicz and Ross, 1994; Coulson and Nutbrown, 1992; Gendreau, 1996; Hollin, 1994; Lösel, 1995b, 1996).

The assertion can now be made with confidence that treatment with offenders can have an impact on a range of target behaviours, including criminal behaviours. It is more a case of 'what works' rather than 'nothing works' when it comes to the treatment of offenders (McGuire, 1995). The impact of this message can be seen in several areas. There has been a willingness to reassert the potential effectiveness of intervention and to place rehabilitation of offenders back on the political agenda (e.g. Palmer, 1992). There is also a new firmness in both questioning sentencing practices (Andrews, 1990) and in promoting effective policies (Leschied and Gendreau, 1994).

Adult sex offenders

While the points made above apply to a wide range of offenders, both young and old, the treatment of adult sex offenders is currently the cause of a great deal of public concern and professional debate and activity. As detailed by Hanson *et al.* (1991), there are many technical and methodological difficulties in assessing treatment outcome for sex offenders. The position is summed up neatly in a statement taken from a report of a Canadian working group looking at the effectiveness of sex offender treatment:

> The research literature on sexual offending provides no tidy or conclusive findings that can easily direct the design of correctional treatments. Despite a substantial and steadily growing level of knowledge in the field, there remains considerable speculation about what motivates these individuals to commit their offences, and considerable uncertainty about how best to treat or manage those who seem to pose the greatest risk. (Solicitor General Canada, Working Group, Sex Offender Treatment Review, 1990, p.9)

The sentiments expressed by the Canadian Working Group are almost as valid in 1995 as at the time they appeared in print (see also Furby *et al.*, 1989). However, the word *almost* is important: since 1990 there have been several important publications that lead to some qualification of the views expressed in the above quotation (e.g. Marshall, 1993; Marshall *et al.*, 1991; Marshall and Pithers, 1994; Pithers, 1993; Quinsey *et al.*, 1993).

Before looking at this newer information, it is important to distinguish different measures of treatment outcome. See Box 19.5 for a brief explanation of the difference between process and outcome measures.

Box 19.5 Measures of Treatment Outcome

There are two classes of measure that must be held conceptually distinct. The first of these are process measures: that is, those targets for change specifically addressed by treatment programmes, such as sexual arousal, attitudes towards women and social skills. The second type of measure is an outcome measure: that is, the effect of the treatment on sexual offending, which is typically measured using recidivism. While the former is necessary and important, both in terms of fine tuning treatment programmes and enhancing our understanding of outcome findings, recidivism rates are the acid test of treatment effectiveness.

From their review of the literature, with a clear focus on recidivism as an outcome measure, Marshall *et al.* (1991) draw a rather more optimistic message with regard to treatment effectiveness. Marshall *et al.* reviewed a range of outcome studies from several different treatment philosophies.

Marshall *et al.* begin with the effectiveness of physical treatments. They identify three types of physical treatment used with sex offenders: psychosurgery, castration and administration of pharmacologic agents. They conclude that there is little supportive evidence for the first two, but that the third holds promise. Specifically, Marshall *et al.* suggest that the combination of the hormonal analogue cyproterone acetate and psychological treatment is of potential value in reducing sex offending.

Moving to nonbehavioural treatments, Marshall *et al.* discuss the outcomes of several studies that employed a variety of approaches such as emotional release therapy, psychoanalytic treatment and humanistic self-help programmes. They find little in the way of supportive evidence for the effectiveness of these approaches specifically in reducing sex offending.

Finally, Marshall *et al.* consider outcome studies where the treatment, in both institutional and outpatient settings, has been behavioural and cognitive-behavioural in orientation. They reach the view that:

> Evaluations of outpatient cognitive/behavioural programs, then, are definitely encouraging. While there is not an extensive body of outcome literature, what there is suggests that at least child molesters and exhibitionists can be effectively treated by these comprehensive programs. However, as with the institutionally based programs, outpatient programs are not uniformly effective and none of them as yet have demonstrated effectiveness with rapists. (p.480)

Quinsey *et al.* (1993) took issue with Marshall *et al.*'s conclusion on the grounds that 'the approach taken in Marshall *et al.*'s review is unable to provide satisfactory answers to questions concerning treatment efficacy' (p. 513). Essentially, Quinsey *et al.* question whether the research evidence is strong enough to allow the type of conclusion drawn by Marshall and his colleagues. In his defence of his position, Marshall (1993) argues that expectations of levels of high methodological rigour are unrealistic in a newly developing field. Pithers (1993) and Marshall and Pithers (1994) rehearse the same arguments, and also reach the conclusion that treatment can be effective in reducing sex offending.

The basic issue in this debate is the level of satisfactory proof that one is willing to accept regarding treatment outcome. Marshall embodies a belief held by one camp of practitioners that treatment can be effective and, at this stage in the development of the field, we should be aiming to build on that foundation. On the other hand, Quinsey and his colleagues take a more rigorous scientific stance, demanding high quality empirical evidence before making a commitment to treatment effectiveness. Quinsey *et al.* (1993) suggested that the field is in desperate need of a meta-analysis, an approach that, as noted above, has had profound effects in other areas of treatment work with offenders.

Hall (1995) has recently reported just such a meta-analysis, and reaches the conclusion that sexual offenders who complete treatment show a modest but significantly lower rate of reoffending than untreated sex offenders. With regard to type of treatment, Hall concludes that treatment is most effective when conducted 'with outpatient participants and when it consists of hormonal or cognitive-behavioral treatments' (p.808). As with general offending, the force of the literature is to suggest that effective work with sex offenders is also possible.

Barriers to success of treatment programmes for offenders

It would be wrong, however, to assume that there is a consensus with all concerned pulling in the same direction to develop effective services for offenders. There are three key barriers to success: these are institutional resistance, resistance to treatment integrity, and social resistance.

INSTITUTIONAL RESISTANCE

This refers to the obstacles, in either a community or residential setting, that block the progress that might be made with a properly implemented treatment programme. Laws (1974) described the barriers he faced when developing a residential behavioural programme with offenders. The barriers were about control over admission to the programme, offenders leaving the programme before its completion, control over finances, and control over staff training. Laws, as have others, documented professional clashes both with administrators and fellow practitioners. Overcoming institutional resistance implies a need for greater political and organizational awareness and ability by behavioural practitioners. Burchard and Lane (1982) made the point that advocates of offender treatment 'Who do not recognize that much of their time will be spent trying to change the behavior of staff and policy and administrators are in for a rude awakening' (p.616).

RESISTANCE TO TREATMENT INTEGRITY

Any treatment programme, whatever its theoretical base, can only stand a chance of being successful if it is properly implemented. Effective programmes require planning for both content and resources, trained personnel to conduct assessments and deliver treatment, and the flexibility to cope with the varying demands presented by different clients. The literature is full of examples of how organizations can work to produce low treatment integrity and lose any positive effects of treatment (Hollin, 1995).

SOCIAL RESISTANCE

Two strands to social resistance can be identified: the first is public and political resistance; the second is academic resistance, variously referred to as 'knowledge destruction' (Andrews and Wormith, 1989) or 'theorecticism' (Gendreau, 1996). Both types of resistance seek to dismiss the idea of effective work with offenders as it does not suit a favoured political or academic opinion.

Conclusion

A substantial body of research evidence, including the longitudinal studies, has highlighted the complexities of the economic, social, situational and individual factors involved in the development of criminal behaviour. While a grand theory of crime remains to be articulated, the position is emerging where the relationship between the environment and the individual might be seen in the following way. Close social conditions, such as parenting, peer group, and schooling, in turn influenced heavily by economic factors, can engender and reinforce individual factors conducive to crime. These individual factors may be a combination of the skills to commit crime and the formation of attitudes supportive of criminal behaviour.

It follows that attempts to prevent crime can focus on the environment, the individual, or both. Of course, given the interrelationship between the factors, no one approach is ever going to achieve a complete success rate. Considering the crime prevention strategies of the type discussed above, we can see that following the above analysis some effect of situational crime prevention would not be unexpected. Indeed, the research shows some effect of situational approaches. In the same way, we can see the overlap between the criminogenic factors highlighted by the longitudinal research and the treatment targets indicated by the meta-analyses. Thus, treatment work focused on these targets would be predicted to be of limited success and, again, that is precisely what the literature shows.

Crime prevention based on punishment and deterrence receives rather less conceptual and empirical support. If some, perhaps most, mainstream offenders have spent their lives being socially and economically punished, then more punishment for offending might be expected to produce more of the same. While not conclusive, the literature suggests that this analysis may have some substance.

In conclusion, effective strategies for crime prevention will demand a radical reappraisal of current practice. There are pockets of good, effective practice, but it is hard to resist the conclusion that without political leadership crime prevention will remain fragmented and fail to reach the potential that may well be achievable.

Seminar Questions

1. What implications do the findings on effective work with offenders have for the training of professionals working in this area?

2. To what extent should policy and practice in working with offenders be reliant upon the findings of empirical research?

References

Aichhorn, A. (1955) *Wayward Youth (trans.)*. New York, NY: Meridian Books. (Original work published in 1925.)

Andrews, D.A. (1990) 'Some criminological sources of anti-rehabilitation bias in the report of the Canadian Sentencing Commission.' *Canadian Journal of Criminology, 32*, 511–524.

Andrews, D.A. and Bonta, J. (1994) *The Psychology of Criminal Conduct*. Cincinnati, OH: Anderson Publishing Co.

Andrews, D.A. and Wormith, J.S. (1989) 'Personality and crime: Knowledge destruction and construction in criminology.' *Justice Quarterly, 6*, 289–309.

Andrews, D.A., Zinger, I., Hoge, R.D., Bonta, J., Gendreau, P. and Cullen, F. T. (1990) 'Does correctional treatment work? A clinically relevant and psychologically informed meta-analysis.' *Criminology, 28*, 369–404.

Antonowicz, D.H. and Ross, R.R. (1994) 'Essential components of successful rehabilitation programs for offenders.' *International Journal of Offender Therapy and Comparative Criminology, 38*, 97–104.

Bank, L., Patterson, G.R., and Reid, J.B. (1987) 'Delinquency prevention through training parents in family management.' *The Behavior Analyst, 10*, 75–82.

Blagg, H. (1985) 'Reparation and justice for juveniles.' *British Journal of Criminology, 25*, 267–279.

Blakely, C.H. and Davidson, W.S. (1984) 'Behavioral approaches to delinquency: a review.' In P. Karoly and J.J. Steffan (eds) *Adolescent Behavior Disorders: Foundations and Contemporary Concerns*. Lexington, MA: Lexington Books.

Braukmann, C.J. and Wolf, M.M. (1987) 'Behaviourally based group homes for juvenile offenders.' In E.K. Morris and C.J. Braukmann (eds) *Behavioral approaches to crime and delinquency: A handbook of application, research, and concepts*. New York, NY: Plenum.

Bullock, R., Hosie, K., Little, M. and Millham, S. (1990) 'Secure accommodation for very difficult adolescents: some recent research findings.' *Journal of Adolescence, 13*, 205–216.

Burchard, J.D. and Lane, T.W. (1982) 'Crime and delinquency.' In A.S. Bellack, M. Hersen and A.E. Kazdin (eds) *International Handbook of Behavior Modification and Therapy.* New York, NY: Plenum.

Clarke, R.V.G. (ed) (1992) *Situational Crime Prevention: Successful Case Studies.* Albany, NY: Harrow and Heston.

Cook, T.D., Cooper, H., Cordray, D.S., Hartmann, H., Hedges, L.V., Light R.J., Louis, T.A. and Mosteller, F. (eds) (1992) *Meta-analysis for explanation: A Casebook.* New York, NY: Russell Sage Foundation.

Cordess, C. and Cox, M. (1995) *Forensic Psychotherapy: Crime, Psychodynamics and the Offender Patient.* London: Jessica Kingsley.

Cornish, D.B. and Clarke, R.V.G. (eds) (1986) *The Reasoning Criminal: Rational Choice Perspectives on Offending.* New York, NY: Springer-Verlag.

Coulson, G.E. and Nutbrown, V. (1992) 'Properties of an ideal rehabilitative program for high-need offenders.' *International Journal of Offender Therapy and Comparative Criminology, 36*, 203–208.

Epps, K.J. (1994) 'Treating adolescent sex offenders in secure conditions: the experience at Glenthorne Centre.' *Journal of Adolescence, 17*, 105–122.

Farrington, D.P. (1983) 'Offending from 10 to 25 years of age.' In K. Teilman Van Dusen and S.A. Mednick (eds) *Prospective Studies of Crime and Delinquency.* The Hague: Kluwer-Nijhoff.

Farrington, D.P. (1986) 'Age and crime.' In M. Tonry and N. Morris (eds) *Crime and Justice: An Annual Review of Research, vol. 7.* Chicago, IL: University of Chicago Press.

Farrington, D.P. (1987) 'Epidemiology.' In H.C. Quay (ed) *Handbook of Juvenile Delinquency.* New York, NY: Wiley.

Farrington, D.P. (1990) 'Implications of criminal career research for the prevention of offending.' *Journal of Adolescence, 13*, 93–113.

Farrington, D.P. (1995) 'The development of offending and antisocial behaviour from childhood: key findings from the Cambridge Study in delinquent development.' *Journal of Child Psychology and Psychiatry, 36*, 929–964.

Farrington, D.P., Barnes, G.C. and Lambert, S. (1996) 'The concentration of offending in families.' *Legal and Criminological Psychology, 1*, 47–63.

Farrington, D.P., Loeber, R. and van Kammen, W.B. (1990). 'Long-term criminal outcomes of hyperactivity-impulsivity-attention deficit and conduct problems in childhood.' In L. Robins and M. Rutter (eds) *Straight and Devious Pathways from Childhood to Adulthood.* New York, NY: Cambridge University Press.

Farrington, D.P. and West, D.J. (1990) 'The Cambridge Study in delinquent development: a long-term follow-up of 411 London males.' In H.J. Kerner and G. Kaiser (eds) *Criminality: Personality, Behaviour, and Life History.* Berlin: Springer-Verlag.

Feindler, E.L. and Ecton, R.B. (1986) *Adolescent Anger Control: Cognitive-Behavioral Techniques.* New York, NY: Pergamon Press.

Furby, L., Weinrott, M.R. and Blackshaw, L. (1989) 'Sex offender recidivism: A review.' *Psychological Bulletin, 105*, 3–30.

Garrido, V. and Sanchis, J.R. (1991) 'The cognitive model in the treatment of Spanish offenders: theory and practice.' *Journal of Correctional Education, 42*, 111–118.

Garrett, C.J. (1985) 'Effects of residential treatment on adjudicated delinquents: a meta-analysis.' *Journal of Research on Crime and Delinquency, 22*, 287–308.

Gendreau, P. (1996) 'Offender rehabilitation: what we know and what needs to be done.' *Criminal Justice and Behavior, 22*, 144–161.

Gendreau, P. and Andrews, D.A. (1990) 'Tertiary prevention: What the meta-analyses of the offender treatment literature tells us about "what works".' *Canadian Journal of Criminology, 32*, 173–184.

Gendreau, P. and Ross, B. (1979) 'Effective correctional treatment: Bibliotherapy for cynics.' *Crime and Delinquency, 25*, 463–489.

Gendreau, P., Cullen, F.T. and Bonta, J. (1994) 'Intensive rehabilitation supervision: The next generation in community corrections?' *Federal Probation, 58*, 72–78.

Gibbs, J.C. (1996) 'Sociomoral group treatment for young offenders.' In C.R. Hollin and K. Howells (eds) *Clinical Approaches to Working with Young Offenders.* Chichester: Wiley.

Glick, B. and Goldstein, A.P. (1987) 'Aggression replacement training.' *Journal of Counseling and Development, 65*, 356–367.

Goldstein, A.P. and Glick, B. (1996) 'Aggression replacement training: methods and outcome.' In C.R. Hollin and K. Howells (eds) *Clinical Approaches to Working with Young Offenders.* Chichester: Wiley.

Goldstein, A.P. and Keller, H. (1987) *Aggressive Behavior: Assessment and Intervention.* New York, NY: Pergamon Press.

Gordon, D.A. and Arbuthnot, J. (1987) 'Individual, group and family interventions.' In H.C. Quay (ed) *Handbook of Juvenile Delinquency.* New York, NY: Wiley.

Gottschalk, R., Davidson, W.S., Gensheimer, L.K. and Mayer, J. (1987) 'Community-based interventions.' In H.C. Quay (ed) *Handbook of juvenile delinquency.* New York, NY: Wiley.

Hagan, M. and King, R.P. (1992) 'Recidivism rates of youth completing an intensive treatment program in a juvenile correctional facility.' *International Journal of Offender Therapy and Comparative Criminology, 36,* 349–358.

Haghighi, B. and Lopez, A. (1993) 'Success/failure of group home treatment programs for juveniles.' *Federal Probation, 57,* 53–58.

Hains, A.A. (1984) 'A preliminary attempt to teach the use of social problem-solving skills to delinquents.' *Child Study Journal, 14,* 271–285.

Hall, G.C.N. (1995) 'Sexual offender recidivism revisited: a meta-analysis of recent treatment studies.' *Journal of Consulting and Clinical Psychology, 63,* 802–809.

Hanson, R.K., Cox, B. and Woszczyna, C. (1991) 'Assessing treatment outcome for sexual offenders.' *Annals of Sex Research, 4,* 177–208.

Heal, K. and Laycock, G. (eds) (1986) *Situational Crime Prevention: From Theory into Practice.* London: HMSO.

Henggeler, S.W., Melton, G.B., Smith, L.A., Schoewald, S.K. and Hanley, J.H. (1993) 'Family preservation using multisystemic treatment: long-term follow-up to a clinical trial with serious juvenile offenders.' *Journal of Child and Family Studies, 2,* 283–293.

Hollin, C.R. (1990a) 'Social skills training with delinquents: a look at the evidence and some recommendations for practice. *British Journal of Social Work, 20,* 483–493.

Hollin, C.R. (1990b) *Cognitive-behavioural Interventions with Young Offenders.* Elmsford, NY: Pergamon Press.

Hollin, C.R. (1994) 'Designing effective rehabilitation programmes for young offenders.' *Psychology, Crime & Law, 1,* 193–199.

Hollin, C.R. (1995) 'The meaning and implications of "programme integrity".' *In J. McGuire (ed) What works: Effective Methods to Reduce Reoffending.* Chichester: Wiley.

Hollin, C.R. (ed) (1996) *Working with Offenders: Psychological Practice in Offender Rehabilitation.* Chichester: Wiley.

Hollin, C.R., Epps, K.J. and Kendrick, D.J. (1995) *Managing behavioural treatment: Policy and practice with delinquent adolescents.* London: Routledge.

Hollin, C.R. and Howells, K. (eds) (1996) *Clinical Approaches to Working with Young Offenders.* Chichester: Wiley.

Homant, R.J. (1981) 'The demise of JOLT: The politics of being "scared straight" in Michigan.' *Criminal Justice Review, 6,* 14–18.

Honderich, T. (1993). *How Free Are You?: The Determinism Problem.* Oxford: Oxford University Press.

Hudson, B.L. (1986) 'Community applications of social skills training.' In C.R. Hollin and P. Trower (eds) *Handbook of Social Skills Training, Vol. 1: Applications Across the Life Span.* Oxford: Pergamon Press.

Izzo, R.L. and Ross, R.R. (1990) 'Meta-analysis of rehabilitation programs for juvenile delinquents: A brief report.' *Criminal Justice and Behavior, 17,* 134–142.

Kazdin, A.E. (1987) 'Treatment of antisocial behavior in children: current status and future directions.' *Psychological Bulletin, 102,* 187–203.

Kazdin, A.E., Siegel, T.C. and Bass, D. (1992) 'Cognitive problem-solving skills training and parent management training in the treatment of antisocial behavior in children.' *Journal of Consulting and Clinical Psychology, 60,* 733–747.

Kingston, L. and Prior, M. (1995) 'The development of patterns of stable, transient, and school-age onset aggressive behaviour in young children.' *Journal of the American Academy of Child and Adolescent Psychiatry, 34,* 348–358.

Lahey, B.B., Loeber, R., Hart, E.L., Frick, P.J., Applegate, B., Zhang, Q., Green, S.M. and Russo, M.F. (1995) 'Four-year longitudinal study of conduct disorder in boys: Patterns and predictors of persistence.' *Journal of Abnormal Psychology, 104,* 83–93.

Laws, D.R. (1974) 'The failure of a token economy.' *Federal Probation, 38,* 33–38.

Leger, R.E., Schillo, B.A., Speth, T.W. and Davidson, W.S. (1996) 'Diversion programs.' In C.R. Hollin and K. Howells (eds) *Clinical Approaches to Working with Young Offenders.* Chichester: Wiley.

Leschied, A.W. and Gendreau, P. (1994) 'Doing justice in Canada: YOA policies that can promote community safety.' *Canadian Journal of Criminology, 36,* 291–303.

Lewis, R.V. (1983) 'Scared straight – California style: Evaluation of the San Quentin Squires Program.' *Criminal Justice and Behavior, 10,* 209–226.

Lipsey, M.W. (1992) 'Juvenile delinquency treatment: A meta-analytic inquiry into the variability of effects.' In T.D. Cook, H. Cooper D.S. Cordray, H. Hartmann, L.V. Hedges, R.J. Light, T.A. Louis and F. Mosteller (eds) *Meta-Analysis for Explanation: A Casebook.* New York, NY: Russell Sage Foundation.

Lipsey, M.W. (1995) 'What do we learn from 400 research studies on the effectiveness of treatment with juvenile delinquents?' In J. McGuire (ed) *What Works: Reducing Reoffending.* Chichester: Wiley.

Lipsey, M.W. and Wilson, D.B. (1993) 'The efficacy of psychological, educational, and behavioral treatment: Confirmation from meta-analysis.' *American Psychologist, 48,* 1181–1209.

Lipton, D.N., Martinson, R. and Wilks, D.(1975) *The Effectiveness of Correctional Treatment.* New York, NY: Praeger.

Lloyd, C., Mair, G. and Hough, M. (1994) *Explaining Reconviction Rates: A Critical Analysis.* London: HMSO.

Lochman, J.E. (1992) 'Cognitive-behavioral intervention with aggressive boys: three-year follow-up and preventive effects.' *Journal of Consulting and Clinical Psychology, 60,* 426–432.

Loeber, R. and Farrington, D.P. (1994) 'Problems and solutions in longitudinal and experimental treatment studies of child psychopathology and delinquency.' *Journal of Consulting and Clinical Psychology, 62,* 887–900.

Loeber, R., Green, S.M., Keenan, K. and Lahey, B.B.(1995) 'Which boys will fare worse? Early predictors on the onset of conduct disorder in a six-year longitudinal study.' *Journal of the American Academy of Child and Adolescent Psychiatry, 34,* 499–509.

Lösel, F. (1995a) 'The efficacy of correctional treatment: A review and synthesis of meta-evaluations.' In J. McGuire (ed) *What Works: Reducing Reoffending.* Chichester: Wiley.

Lösel, F. (1995b) 'Increasing consensus in the evaluation of offender rehabilitation? Lessons from recent research syntheses.' *Psychology, Crime and Law, 2,* 19–39.

Lösel, F. (1996) 'Working with young offenders: The impact of the meta-analyses.' In C.R. Hollin and K. Howells (eds) *Clinical Approaches to Working with Young Offenders.* Chichester: Wiley.

Lösel, F. and Koferl, P. (1989) 'Evaluation research on correctional treatment in West Germany: A meta-analysis.' In H. Wegener, F. Lösel and J. Haison. (eds) *Criminal Behaviour and the Justice System: Psychological Perspectives.* New York, NY: Springer-Verlag.

Lösel, F. and Wittmann, W.W. (1989) 'The relationship of treatment integrity and intensity to outcome criteria.' In R.F. Conner and M. Hendricks. (eds) *International Innovations in Evaluation Methodology: New Directions for Program Evaluation, No 42.* San Francisco: Jossey-Bass.

MacKenzie, D.L. and Brame, R. (1995) 'Shock incarceration and positive adjustment during community supervision.' *Journal of Quantitative Criminology, 11,* 111–142.

MacKenzie, D.L., Brame, R., McDowall, D. and Souryal, C. (1995) 'Boot camp prisons and recidivism in eight states.' *Criminology, 33,* 327–357.

MacKenzie, D.L. and Shaw, J.W. (1990) 'Inmate adjustment and change during shock incarceration: The impact of correctional boot camp programs.' *Justice Quarterly, 7,* 125–150.

MacKenzie, D.L. and Shaw, J.W. (1993) 'The impact of shock incarceration on technical violations and new criminal activities.' *Justice Quarterly, 10,* 463–487.

MacKenzie, D.L. and Souryal, C. (1994) *Multisite Evaluation of Shock Incarceration.* Washington, DC: US Department of Justice.

MacKenzie, D.L. and Souryal, C. (1995a) 'A "Machiavellian" perspective on the development of boot camp prisons: a debate.' Unpublished symposium presentation.

MacKenzie, D.L. and Souryal, C. (1995b) 'Inmates' attitude change during incarceration: A comparison of boot camp with traditional prison.' *Justice Quarterly, 12,* 501–30.

McDougall, C., Barnett, R.M., Ashurst, B. and Willis, B. (1987). 'Cognitive control of anger.' In B.J. McGurk, D.M. Thornton and M. Williams (eds) *Applying Psychology to Imprisonment: Theory & practice.* London: HMSO.

McGuire, J. (ed)(1995) *What Works: Reducing Reoffending.* Chichester: Wiley.

Marshall, W.L. (1993). 'The treatment of sex offenders. What does the outcome data tell us? A reply to Quinsey, Harris, Rice, and Lalumiere.' *Journal of Interpersonal Violence, 8,* 524–530.

Marshall, W.L. and Pithers, W.D. (1994) 'A reconsideration of treatment outcome with sex offenders.' *Criminal Justice and Behavior, 21,* 10–27.

Marshall, W.L., Jones, R., Ward, T., Johnston, P. and Barbaree, H.E. (1991) 'Treatment outcome with sex offenders.' *Clinical Psychology Review, 11,* 465–485.

Martinson, R. (1974) 'What works? Questions and answers about prison reform.' *The Public Interest, 35,* 22–54.

Mathlas, R.E. and Mathews, J.W. (1991) 'The boot camp program for offenders: Does the shoe fit?' *International Journal of Offender Therapy and Comparative Criminology, 35,* 322–327.

Mayhew, P., Maung, N.A. and Mirrlees-Black, C. (1993) *The 1992 British Crime Survey.* London: HMSO.

Milan, M.A. (1987) 'Basic behavioral procedures in closed institutions.' In E.K. Morris and C.J. Braukmann (eds) *Behavioral Approaches to Crime and Delinquency: A Handbook of Application, Research, and Concepts.* New York, NY: Plenum.

Milan, M.A. (1996) 'Working in institutions.' In C.R. Hollin and K. Howells (eds) *Clinical Approaches to Working with Young Offenders.* Chichester: Wiley.

Moffit, T.E. (1993) 'Adolescence-limited and life-course – persistent antisocial behavior: A developmental taxonomy.' *Psychological Review, 100*, 674–701.

Morash, M. and Rucker, L. (1990) 'A critical look at the idea of boot camp as a correctional reform.' *Crime and Delinquency, 36*, 204–222.

Nagin, D.S., Farrington, D.P. and Moffitt, T.E. (1995). 'Life-course trajectories of different types of offenders.' *Criminology, 33*, 111–139.

Nagin, D.S. and Land, K.C. (1993) 'Age, criminal careers, and population heterogeneity: Specification and estimation of a nonparametric, mixed Poisson model.' *Criminology, 31*, 327–362.

Nellis, M. (1991) 'The electronic monitoring of offenders in England and Wales.' *British Journal of Criminology, 31*, 165–185.

Nelson, J.R., Smith, D.J. and Dodd, J. (1990) 'The moral reasoning of juvenile delinquents: A meta-analysis.' *Journal of Abnormal Child Psychology, 18*, 231–239.

Palmer, T. (1992) *The Re-emergence of Correctional Intervention.* Newbury Park, CA: Sage.

Pithers, W.D. (1993) 'Considerations in the treatment of rapists.' In G.C.N. Hall, R. Hirschman, J.R. Graham and M.S. Zaragoza (eds) *Sexual Aggression: Issues in Etiology, Assessment and Treatment* (pp.167–196). Washington, DC: Taylor and Francis.

Quinsey, V.L., Harris, G.T., Rice, M.E., and Lalumiere, M.L. (1993) 'Assessing treatment efficacy in outcome studies of sex offenders.' *Journal of Interpersonal Violence, 8*, 512–523.

Raynor, P. and Vanstone, M. (1994) *STOP: Straight Thinking on Probation, Third Interim Evaluation Report.* Bridgend, Mid-Glamorgan: Mid-Glamorgan Probation Service.

Remington, B. and Remington, M. (1987) 'Behavior modification in probation work: A review and evaluation. *Criminal Justice and Behavior, 14*, 156–174.

Roberts, A.R. and Camasso, M.J. (1991) 'Juvenile offender treatment programs and cost-benefit analysis.' *Juvenile and Family Court Journal, 42*, 37–47.

Robins, L. and Rutter, M. (eds) (1990) *Straight and Devious Pathways From Childhood to Adulthood.* New York, NY: Cambridge University Press.

Roshier, B. (1989). *Controlling Crime: the Classical Perspective in Criminology.* Milton Keynes, Bucks: Open University Press.

Ross, R.R. and Fabiano, E.A. (1985) *Time to Think: A Cognitive Model of Delinquency Prevention and Offender Rehabilitation.* Johnson City, TN: Institute of Social Sciences and Arts.

Ross, R.R., Fabiano, E.A. and Ewles, C.D. (1988) 'Reasoning and rehiabilitation.' *International Journal of Offender Therapy and Comparative Criminology, 32*, 29–35.

Ross, R.R. and Gendreau, P. (1980) *Effective Correctional Treatment.* Toronto: Butterworths.

Rutter, M. and Smith D.J. (eds) (1995) *Psychosocial Disorders in Young People: Time Trends and Their Causes.* Chichester: Wiley.

Schaefer, C.E., and Swanson, A.J. (eds) (1988) *Children in Residential Care: Critical Issues in Treatment.* New York, NY: Van Nostrand Reinhold.

Sechrest, D.K. (1989) 'Prison 'boot camps' do not measure up.' *Federal Probation, 53*, 15–20.

Schneider, A. (1986) 'Restitution and recidivism rates of juvenile offenders: Results from four experimental studies.' *Criminology, 24*, 533–552.

Schneider, A.L. and Schneider, P.R. (1985) 'The impact of restitution on recidivism of juvenile offenders: An experiment in Clayton County, Georgia.' *Criminal Justice Review, 10*, 1–10.

Snyder, J.J. and White, M.J. (1979) 'The use of cognitive self-instruction in the treatment of behaviorally disturbed adolescents.' *Behavior Therapy, 10*, 227–235.

Spivack, G., Platt, J.J. and Shure, M.B. (1976) *The Problem-Solving Approach to Adjustment: A Guide to Research and Intervention.* San Francisco, CA: Jossey-Bass.

Stattin, H. and Magnusson, D. (1995) 'Onset of official delinquency: Its co-occurrence in time with educational, behavioural, and interpersonal problems.' *British Journal of Criminology, 35*, 417–449.

Thornton, D.M., Curran, L., Grayson, D. and Holloway, V. (1984) *Tougher Regimes in Detention Centres: Report of an Evaluation by the Young Offender Psychology Unit.* London: HMSO.

Tonry, M. and Farrington, D.P. (eds)(1995) *Building a Safer Society: Strategic Approaches to Crime Prevention.* Chicago IL: University of Chicago Press.

Welch, G.J. (1985) 'Contingency contracting with a delinquent and his family.' *Journal of Behaviour Therapy and Experimental Psychiatry, 16*, 253–259.

Welldon, E.V. and Van Velsen, C. (eds) (1997) *A Practical Guide to Forensic Psychotherapy.* London: Jessica Kingsley.

Whitehead, J.T. and Lab, S.P. (1989) 'A meta-analysis of juvenile correctional treatment.' *Journal of Research in Crime and Delinquency, 26*, 276–295.

Windle, R.C. and Windle, M. (1995) 'Longitudinal patterns of physical aggression: associations with adult social, psychiatric, and personality functioning and testosterone levels.' *Development and Psychopathology, 7,* 563–585.

Wolfgang, M.E., Thornberry, T.P. and Figlio, R.M. (1987) *From Boy to Man, From Delinquency to Crime.* Chicago IL: University of Chicago Press.

CHAPTER 20

Substance Use, Abuse and Dependence

Richard Hammersley

Aims and Objectives

This chapter aims to improve your understanding of drug and alcohol problems, their effects, their treatment and their outcome. By the end of the chapter you should be able to distinguish between the concepts of addiction, substance abuse and substance dependence. You should be able to list the most important factors that determine dependence and describe commonalities between dependent and criminal careers. In addition, I hope you will be able to describe the most common treatments for dependence and be aware of the difficulties both of treatment and of dealing with substance dependent people.

Addiction, Dependence and Abuse

The concept of addiction

Until recently, the study and treatment of drug problems were organized around the concept of addiction. According to this view, people who had problems with their substance use had problems because they were addicted to the drug. An addict was someone who was compelled by a physiological need to continue taking the drug, who experienced horrible physical and psychological symptoms when trying to stop and who, as a result of their addictive need, would continue taking the drug despite the many problems that they had experienced. Furthermore, they would become psychologically altered for the worse by their addiction, commit crimes to pay for the drug, neglect their normal social roles to take the drug and upset, even harm, the people around them. Among offenders and clients of social services, sadly it is easy to find many people who fit this description rather well; not only drug addicts, but also people addicted to alcohol or gambling.

Some drugs, it is supposed, are much more addictive than others. Heroin, tobacco and crack cocaine are supposedly addictive in that most users will become addicts if they go beyond mere experimentation. Alcohol, benzodiazepines like valium, ativan and temazepam, glues, solvents and butane gas, and amphetamines have some users who are not addicted, but a number become addicted – perhaps as many as 10 per cent. Cannabis, hallucinogenic drugs like LSD, ecstasy and psilocybin mushrooms lead to addiction more rarely. For gambling, which shares many properties of substance addictions, there is no 'addicting' substance at all (Brown, 1987).

Other behaviours, such as over-eating, also have some common features with addiction (see Orford, 1985).

The key idea, however, is that substance users can be divided into addicts, with problems, and non-addicts, who have no problems due to their substance use. One of the defects in the concept of addiction is that this division is too simple (Peele, 1985; Davies, 1992). These days, most professionals who deal with people with any kind of problem, medical, criminal, educational or social, will have seen many clients who are not exactly addicts, but whose drug or alcohol use seems to have contributed to or worsened their other problems. Some examples will illustrate this.

Cigarette smoking, aside from its health risks, does not generally cause major problems. Most cigarette smokers are addicted to cigarettes, but it is a relatively benign addiction compared to alcoholism or heroin addiction. Still, smoking can be a major drain on the finances of people on low incomes. It is also a common cause of fires, which can have catastrophic effects. Less obviously, cigarettes often provide young adolescents with their first experience of consuming an addictive drug, breaking the law to do so (as they are typically under 16). Young smokers are often also doing badly at school, have poor social skills and an inclination to be delinquent (e.g. Goddard, 1990). For many clients, smoking may be the least of their problems, but it can nonetheless be a problem.

Does that not confirm the concept of addiction? Is it not just that society has until recently accepted tobacco addiction as normal? What about alcohol? Many people get into difficulties with alcohol without being alcoholic. They can simply spend more than they can afford on alcohol, whether that is a person who occasionally spends most of their benefit cheque on alcohol, or the student who does the same to their grant cheque. They then have to go short or get into debt to survive until the next cheque. Drunken misbehaviour is another common source of problems, even among people who are not remotely 'alcoholic'. Misbehaviour can vary from the merely embarrassing, such as sleeping with people whom one would normally avoid, or quarrels with family or friends, to the hazardous, such as failing to use condoms when drunk, to the criminal (Collins and Schlenger, 1988). Also, many people can become violent or irrational after a lot to drink. Drunken driving is another problem. Alcohol problems are not restricted to alcoholics.

Cannabis has now been tried by at least 40 per cent of people under 30 (Ramsay and Percy, 1996). Cannabis may be generally less harmful than alcohol, tobacco or most other illegal drugs. Compared to other drugs and alcohol, about the same proportion of cannabis users (10 per cent) become dependent, although that dependence is less severe than for some other drugs and whether or not it is a genuine 'dependence' remains contentious. Even when not dependent, people can get into financial difficulties with cannabis, or, if they use it heavily, have their judgement clouded for long periods of time. It is hard to find people who have got into trouble because of what they did while stoned, although cannabis probably contributes to many road and other accidents. It is also easy to find people whose problems are worsened by being prosecuted for possessing or supplying cannabis, or who seem to be using cannabis as a way of escaping from other problems. People with mental health problems use cannabis as often as anyone else. This is not an area that has been well researched, but clinical impressions are that cannabis use often worsens the mental health of people who have existing problems. Cannabis may also cause anxiety and a negative mood in some novice users (Commentaries, 1996).

Until the late 1980s, most studies of heroin users studied people who had sought help with their heroin addiction – not surprisingly they seemed to be addicted (see Davies, 1992). Since HIV was identified there has been more interest in heroin users who do not seek help. Perhaps surprisingly, not all heroin users, not even all injectors, fit the addict mould. A large number of people smoke or inject heroin a couple of times a week, typically at the weekends, or less often (see Zinberg, 1984). Although they are not 'addicted' this can cause them problems, most obviously the risk of becoming infected with HIV or hepatitis viruses (Department of Health, 1991). Heroin use is viewed very negatively by society and they may be labelled as 'junkies', which makes it hard for them to fit in. Would you employ a heroin user? Not surprisingly, many casual heroin users conceal their behaviour (Zinberg, 1984). On top of that, even occasional heroin use can be expensive, and it is viewed as serious illegal behaviour. The occasional heroin user who has been caught faces a dilemma. She or he can either own up to their 'addiction' and get help that they perhaps do not need, or they can deny that they have a problem. Denial will not be viewed sympathetically by most courts, or by many professionals trying to help them. Professionals dealing with heroin users need to be aware that the safest route is often for the user to plead that they are addicted, even when this is untrue (Davies, 1992), or when the user has no intention of attempting to change their drug using behaviour (Weppner, 1981).

Cocaine use has only become extensive in the UK within the past decade. Even now, it has not reached American levels. As with heroin, if one looks only at people who seek help for cocaine addiction then it seems like a monstrous problem. Looking at cocaine users outside treatment, the drug seems less problematic than heroin. Studies around the world have found that there are many cocaine users who do take cocaine for a while in a way that causes them problems, usually they have spent too much on cocaine, but unlike heroin, most users seem to be able to stop or reduce cocaine use without major difficulties. However, many cocaine users go through a period when their cocaine use is excessive, at least in terms of its cost. If they are in contact with probation or social services during this time then they may seem like addicts. The difference is that most cocaine users will get over their drug problem without professional help. For cocaine, the trick is to separate the truly dependent user from the user who has taken a lot of cocaine, but for whom this drug will not be a long-standing problem (see Ditton and Hammersley (1996), for further review and discussion).

The concept of addiction is not helpful because it ignores the problems of people who are not addicted, and because it tends to force people with drug-related problems into the addict mould. The more modern view is to see drug problems as two-fold: substance abuse and substance dependence (e.g. DSM-IV, American Psychiatric Association, 1994). 'Addiction' is now usually used to refer to a field of study, covering substance use, abuse and dependence, rather than to a theory of why people become dependent.

Before going on to describe the more modern view, why is it that the concept of addiction remains so popular? One way of understanding why people have a belief, such as a belief in addiction, is to ask what benefits they get out of that belief (Davies, 1992). Many groups in society benefit from a belief in addiction. This includes people who have been substance dependent, who can be released from some of the blame for the behaviour. Law enforcement and caring agencies see a concrete problem that can perhaps be tackled. Furthermore, social workers, probation officers and others who see alcohol or drug dependent clients often see people with such extensive behavioural problems that the idea that they are compelled by the drug to act that way makes intuitive sense. It is easy to forget that anyone who can cope with dependence unaided, or has no problems, is not likely to reach your office or clinic. Often, clients and those dealing with them both see substance dependence as the key to all the clients' problems. In fact, people who are dependent on drugs or alcohol can also have problems that are little or nothing to do with their dependency and might have occurred anyway, although dependence does usually make other problems worse. Including alcohol and tobacco, it will be quite unusual for a social care professional to see a client where substance use is neither a problem for him or her, nor for anyone in their family.

Substance use and abuse

Box 20.1 shows the DSM-IV classification of substance abuse. This is the most widely used and validated classification of mental disorders, although it is not as popular in the UK as it is in the USA. Abuse is using a substance in a harmful or risky manner, without medical sanction. The latter must be added because some prescribed medicines can be harmful and risky – but worth the chances of a cure. The concept of 'abuse' is something of a compromise because it is debatable whether any use of a substance is entirely risk-free. The concept of abuse suggests that some risks are negligible, others substantial. The health risks of tobacco smoking now seem so substantial that all smoking is probably abuse – there is no negligible-risk use of tobacco. Most other drugs can be used in ways that make risks negligible.

Box 20.1 DSM-IV Criteria for Substance Abuse

- A maladapative pattern of substance use leading to clinically significant impairment or distress, as manifested by one (or more) of the following, occurring within a 12-month period:
    1. recurrent substance use resulting in a failure to fulfil major role obligations at work, school or home (e.g. repeated absences or poor work performance related to substance use; substance-related absences, suspensions, or expulsions from school; neglect of children or household);
    2. recurrent substance use in situations where it is physically hazardous (e.g. driving an automobile or operating a machine when impaired by substance use);
    3. recurrent substance-related legal problems (e.g. arrests for substance-related disorderly conduct);
    4. continued substance use despite having persistent or recurrent social or interpersonal problems caused or exacerbated by the effects of the substance (e.g. arguments with spouse about consequences of intoxication, physical fights).
- The symptoms have never met the criteria for Substance Dependence for this class of substance (see Box 20.2).

Box 20.2 DSM-IV Criteria for Substance Dependence

- A maladapative pattern of substance use leading to clinically significant impairment or distress, as manifested by three (or more) of the following, occurring at any time in the same 12-month period:

1. Tolerance, as defined by either of the following:

   (a) a need for markedly increased amounts of the substance to achieve intoxication or desired effect;

   (b) markedly diminished effect with continued use of the same amount of the substance.

2. Withdrawal as manifested by either of the following:

   (a) the characteristic withdrawal syndrome for the substance (varies from substance to substance);

   (b) the same (or a closely related) substance is taken to relieve or avoid withdrawal symptoms.

3. The substance is often taken in larger amounts or over a longer period than was intended.

4. There is a persistent desire or unsuccessful efforts to cut down or control substance use.

5. A great deal of time is spent in activities necessary to obtain the substance (e.g. visiting multiple doctors or driving long distances), use the substance (e.g. chain-smoking), or recover from its effects.

6. Important social, occupational, or recreational activities are given up or reduced because of substance use.

7. The substance use is continued despite knowledge of having a persistent or recurrent physical or psychological problem that is likely to have been caused or exacerbated by the substance (e.g. current cocaine use despite recognition of cocaine-induced depression, or continued drinking despite recognition that an ulcer was made worse by alcohol consumption).

Specify if:

- *With physiological dependence:* evidence of tolerance or withdrawal (i.e. either Item 1 or 2 is present).

- *Without physiological dependence:* no evidence of tolerance or withdrawal (i.e. neither Item 1 nor 2 is present).

Many people drink alcohol without abuse. So the idea that alcohol can be used is not contentious. Can controlled drugs (drugs whose general use outside medicine is illegal) also be used without abuse? The DSM-IV criteria, which are based on research and clinical experience, suggest that they can. Many drug users use drugs occasionally, with no recurrent problems.

Substance dependence

The concept of dependence is based around a constellation of symptoms and problems, not just on the idea of physiological need for a drug. Box 20.2 shows the DSM-IV classification of dependence. It can be seen that only criteria 1 and 2 refer to physiological dependence. Anyone who fits three or more of these criteria (out of seven possible) would be diagnosed as substance dependent. This illustrates the fact that dependence is quite varied. Few people will fit all seven possible criteria.

Most substance-dependent people have tried to give up the substance several times, always returning to use after weeks, months, or even years. They often report strong craving or desire for the substance and are at risk of resuming use particularly when experiencing strong feelings such as when stressed, anxious, depressed, angry or happy. They often also feel that they have difficulty controlling the amount of substance they take, once they start to use it. When they relapse, they often return very rapidly to their old, often destructive, habits.

Some substance dependent people can stay dependent for long periods of time without suffering any other problems. This particularly applies to people who otherwise fit well into society and who have not experienced financial, legal or health problems as a result of their use. Many tobacco smokers are like this. Some people drink very heavily for years while only damaging their livers. Even some heroin and cocaine users fit this pattern.

Nonetheless, one of the most striking things in the counselling of substance dependent people is that they will continue to use the substance even when they have suffered very severe problems as a result. People who have been to jail several times and suffered hypothermia, head injury and liver damage may keep drinking. People who have lost a limb to gangrene may keep injecting heroin. People whose hearts have failed while taking cocaine may keep taking it. People who have become psychotic while smoking cannabis may continue to take it.

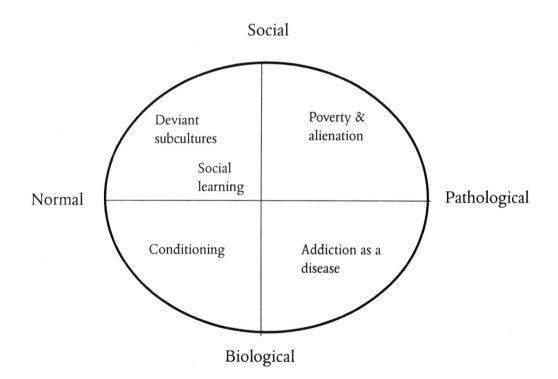

Figure 20.1 Main dimensions of theories about addiction. Five types of theory are shown for illustration inside the circle.

Discussion point

    ° What is the difference between dependence and addiction?

Theories of Dependence

Dependence is a complicated behaviour that takes several years to develop, so it is unlikely that one theory or factor will explain all of it. Most researchers think that social, personal, family and lifestyle factors are important, as well as the action of the drugs themselves, but we do not yet understand fully how they work and interact.

There are many theories of addiction or dependence. In understanding these theories it can be useful to regard thinking about addiction as having two dimensions. First, there is the extent to which dependence is supposedly caused biologically, rather than by social phenomena. Second, there is the extent to which dependence is the result of abnormal or pathological processes or is the extreme end of normal processes. Figure 20.1 shows these dimensions, with some types of theory added for illustration. Deviant subculture theories (e.g. Pearson, 1987) suggest that dependent behaviour is defined as normal within specific subcultures. Poverty and alienation theories suggest that dependence is motivated by these problems and provides meaning to lives which would otherwise be empty (e.g. Agar, 1973). Conditioning theories (e.g. Donovan and Marlatt, 1993) suggest that dependence is learned because substance use is associated with reinforcement. Disease theories suggest that dependence is caused by some abnormal reaction between the body's biochemistry and the drug of dependence (e.g. Vaillant, 1995). Social learning theories (e.g. Zinberg, 1984; Davies, 1992) suggest that dependence is learned because this behaviour and self-ascription is reinforced and maintained by social settings and other people. The difficulty is that all these theories (and many others) appear to play a role in dependence. The alternative to devising a simple theory of dependence is to adopt what is known as multifactorial approach. In medicine this is sometimes called the 'biopsychosocial' model. The multifactorial approach recognizes that no single theory will explain dependence, but rather that many different factors contribute (e.g. Edwards, 1986). The hope is that eventually it will be possible to integrate these diffferent factors into a coherent theory. In the meantime, beware of people who claim that they have the simple answer to the problems of substance use.

Social factors

People who are poor, badly educated and have few opportunities in conventional society do not use substances more, but seem to have more dependence problems than those who fit better into conventional society and are more affluent (Ramsay and Percy, 1996). Maybe the disadvantaged have less to lose by becoming dependent, maybe their other problems make them cope less well in general and maybe they are alienated from society.

Personal factors

Some people seem more predisposed to dependence than others. Dependence itself is not inherited in any simple way, but some genetic factors can make it more likely. The only established example is that the sons of alcoholics tend to be less sensitive to alcohol and hence able to drink more without hangover (see Valliant, 1995). Similar biological factors are currently being sought for other substances. There is also much research on the brain mechanisms that underlie dependence.

At the psychological level, people with behavioural problems as children may also be more at risk for dependence as adults. People who were exceptionally well adjusted as children seem able to avoid problems, even when family and social factors are against them. Substance dependence does not seem to be caused by any single set of psychiatric or other problems, although many such problems are more likely to be found among the substance dependent (Lavelle, Hammersley and Forsyth, 1993; Newcomb and Bentler, 1990).

Family factors

Coming from a poorly functioning family is a risk factor (see Conger, 1991, Chapters 6 and 11). Families that function poorly are either excessively permissive in parenting style, or excessively authoritarian, or inconsistent (both latter styles are correlated with physical abuse of children). Most external family factors that are correlated with substance abuse seem to have their effect through parenting style. It is not single parents, or having a parent in prison, or a substance abusing parent itself that automatically causes problems, but the potential for this causing poor parenting. Additionally, substance use among parents also directly predicts substance use by children. It should, however, be emphasized that a poorly functioning family predicts problems in general, not drug or alcohol problems in particular.

Drug lifestyle factors

The following factors seem to lead to greater risks of dependence, whatever the person's background (see Conger, 1991; Elliott, Huizinga and Ageton, 1985; Newcomb and Bentler, 1990):

- Starting young (under 11 for tobacco or alcohol, under 14 for other drugs)
- Using larger quantities of a substance, more frequently
- Being delinquent or deviant in other ways
- Having other mental health problems including depression, anxiety or stress-related problems
- Using the substance to avoid negative feelings
- Being labelled by society as an 'addict'
- Associating mainly with other substance users
- Trading in a drug, whether as bar staff, or drug dealers.

Drug factors

As Table 20.1 shows, different drugs are not all equally problematic. However, there is no black and white distinction between dangerous and safe drugs. All drugs can cause problems and most can lead to dependence, but some are more likely to do so than others. The problems caused by different drugs, and the nature of dependence on them also vary. For further information, see Ghodse (1995), Glass (1991) or any other detailed book on drug abuse or addiction.

Table 20.1 The Effects of Commonly Used Substances				
Drug	Main acute problems	Health risks	Abuse and dependence	Crime
Alcohol	Accidents, violence, overdose	Liver, heart and circulation, cancers	1/10 drinkers may abuse alcohol	Particularly violent crime
Tobacco	Fires	Cancer, heart and circulation, respiratory diseases	Most smokers are dependent	No causal links
Solvents, glues and gases	Accidents, violence, sudden death	These vary with the substance	Occasional dependence, most users are young and 'mature out' of use	Delinquency, rather than crime
Cannabis	Accidents, impaired memory, occasional psychoses, anxiety, lack of productivity	Not clear – respiratory disease, probably cancer	Dependence is rare relative to number of users, but perhaps as common as with alcohol	No causal links, but youth may steal to buy cannabis
Amphetamines	Occasional overdose, anxiety and agitation, other acute problems very rare (but see Ecstasy)	Mostly psychological and injecting risks	Dependence is rare relative to number of users, but can cause major problems	Delusional or violent behaviour can occur after prolonged use
Ecstasy	Death through overheating, acute toxic reaction.	Possibly liver and brain damage.	No evidence of dependence, prolonged use may have amphetamine like effects	Makes users sociable, but may steal to buy this expensive drug
LSD and other hallucinogens (e.g. psilocybin mushrooms)	Delusions and psychoses, occasional accidents, suicides.	None shown	No evidence of dependence. Maybe psychological effects (negative or positive).	No connections with crime.
Benzodiazepines (e.g. temazepam, valium, ativan)	Amnesia, drunk-style behaviour, violence, problems when injected.	None shown, but extreme injecting risks	Dependence with regular use, often used by heroin injectors.	Violence a particular problem.
Cocaine and crack	Occasional heart failure, overdoses, anxiety, accidents, foolish or grandiose behaviour.	Heart disease, respiratory disease, nasal problems, injecting risks.	Dependence with regular use. but less severe than opiate or benzo. dependence.	Expensive, leading to crime to finance use. Perhaps links with violence among heavy users.
Heroin and other opiates	Overdose, vomiting, accidents, neglect of other activities.	Diseases of neglect, serious constipation, also injecting risks.	1/10 may become dependent.	Crime to pay for drugs.
Drug injecting	Tissue damage, overdose	HIV, Hepatitis, Gangrene, other infections, physical damage (e.g. limb loss).	Smoking and injecting seem more likely to lead to dependence	Among the most dependent, injectors tend to be criminals also.

Developmental factors

Adolescent delinquency and substance abuse share common developmental predictors (Jessor and Jessor, 1977; Elliott, Huizinga and Ageton, 1985). Delinquents/substance abusers tend:

- to have disrupted family backgrounds
- to do poorly in school/truant
- to have poor social skills
- to associate with delinquents
- to have been in care (and later on remand or in prison)
- to have a history of age inappropriate behaviour (doing things younger than approved of by society)
- to have been sexually or physically abused
- to have low psychological well-being (depressed, anxious, low self-esteem etc.).

Not surprisingly, many criminals are substance dependent, and many substance dependent people are criminal. Longitudinal research has concluded that the question of whether drugs cause crime is ill-conceived because both develop together. Drug use can often increase the amount of crime someone commits, but having criminal skills (hence high disposable income for one's age) can increase the amount of drugs someone can take (Hammersley *et al.*, 1989). However, strong causal statements are not supported by research evidence. In particular, drugs do not 'cause crime' in any straightforward way, nor does prison or a criminal record 'create drug users'. There is no ideal research world where we can remove the drug use history from drug users and study what they would have become without drugs. Yet, politicians and the media tend to presume that drug users would have had no problems without drugs. However, on the basis of drug dependent people's psychological and demographic characteristics alone, one would guess that many of them would have been criminal anyway, or perhaps have become dependent on some other substance.

Features of dependent and criminal careers

As a criminal or drug user grows up and ages, they continue to share common problems that can make getting out of drugs or crime difficult. These include the following.

STIGMATIZATION

Both are often viewed negatively by society, even if they have reformed, and they may have difficulty being accepted back into society.

LEGAL INVOLVEMENT

Both may have criminal records which limit the kinds of employment that are possible for them and cause them other problems, such as difficulties getting insurance or other financial services. Another problem can be the use of drugs in prison. With the introduction of mandatory drug testing in prison, many prisoners risk lengthening their sentences by the use of drugs, most commonly cannabis. Drug use has become so prevalent among young people, especially delinquents, that most criminals these days will have taken illegal drugs at some time or other.

Even if they show no particular signs of substance dependence or substance problems, their breaking the law by drug use can have serious implications for their rehabilitation, in prison, on probation or in supported accommodation or other rehabilitation schemes.

EFFECTS ON THE FAMILY

Both dependence and a criminal career can disrupt family life in many ways. If it is a parent with the problem, then the parent may be absent for periods of time and may be a neglectful, inconsistent or excessively permissive parent when present. Children of dependent people may be forced to adopt caretaking roles, looking after themselves and the intoxicated parent. Or, children may have to play the role of go-between for parents in conflict over substance use. Not surprisingly, the children of dependent parents are at high risk of becoming dependent themselves in later life, although most do not (e.g. Vitaro et al., 1996).

A substance dependent teenager or young adult is very likely to have disputes with parents. They may also steal from parents, fail to adhere to house rules and otherwise be problematic. As they get older, they may continue to be reliant on parents in some ways, while in conflict with them in other ways. For parents or children, the dilemma of living with a substance dependent family member is that they are torn between love of the person and extreme dislike of some of their behaviours. A cyclical pattern of rejecting and accepting the substance dependent person is very common, and often rotates at the same time as the person's attempts to moderate or cease drug or alcohol use.

PSYCHOLOGICAL CORRELATES OF DEPENDENCE

People with dependency problems tend to be impulsive and somewhat anti-social (willing to violate the rights of others for one's own ends). Not surprisingly, these traits tend to apply also to offenders (see Lavelle et al., 1993).

DUAL DIAGNOSIS PROBLEMS

As well as these general personality traits, both offenders and the drug dependent tend to be more likely to have other psychological problems. Neurotic disorders, such as anxiety and depression, are more common than in the general population (Lavelle et al., 1993). So are most rarer psychiatric problems. There has been considerable debate about whether dependence causes psychological problems, such as depression, or whether substance use can be a kind of self-medication for psychological problems. There does not seem to be a simple answer, but treating dependence first when possible seems to give better outcome. Few dependent people can address their other problems while still drug dependent.

MID-LIFE ONSET PROBLEMS

Some people do not develop alcohol problems until in mid-life. As drug use becomes more common in society, it is likely that an increasing number of drug users also will become dependent in mid-life. Offending and imprisonment can be reasons for developing mid-life dependence. It is, however, more common for dependence to cause previously law-abiding people to acquire criminal records.

When dealing with probation or social work clients, it is a mistake to neatly divide them into 'addicts' and non-addicts, for many will have some level of substance problem themselves or in their family, whether you know about it or not. Ideally, all those who would benefit from treatment for dependence should receive such treatment as a first priority. The benefits of treatment are modest but demonstrated. For criminal behaviour, dependence treatment seems to reduce the chances of reoffending more than does prison. However, the treatment of dependence often includes examination of offending behaviour as a problem area for the client.

Discussion point

- ° What is meant by the statement that for adolescents drug use and crime occur in 'a common causal configuration'?

Prevention

Stopping substance dependence is a daunting task, consequentally there is much call for its prevention. Few other goals in this society are endorsed by all political party leaders, police chief constables, educationalists, social workers and clients themselves. Sadly, at this time, enthusiasm has not led to demonstrable success. There are a number of reasons for this absence of success, which will have to be addressed in future prevention work. Before discussing problems, three basic means of prevention should be outlined. These are supply-side measures, education and community initiatives.

Supply-side measures

These include laws to restrict the supply of legally available drugs in terms both of hours and location of availability (no alcohol on Sundays before noon, no drinking in the street) and age of legal use (no tobacco to the under-16s). They also include attempts to limit or eliminate the supply of controlled drugs by customs, police and even military efforts (for example, military interventions in cocaine-producing countries). The major spying agencies, such as the CIA and MI5 are also getting more involved in counter-drugs operations.

At best, supply-side measures can only have a modest effect on supplies. The most optimistic estimates are that 10 per cent or less of controlled drug supplies are intercepted although effects are difficult to estimate (Murji, 1991). Strict supply reduction tends to generate a black market in the drug, or in the supply of the drug (for example, to minors). Even those who favour talk of the 'war on drugs' and 'stamping out drugs' now recognize that supply-reduction will not work alone. Such measures will always be part of prevention, but never more than a limited part. However, much more money is spent on supply-side measures than on other aspects of prevention.

Education

This is to-date the main vehicle of drug prevention. In theory, drugs education should be able to reduce drug dependence. In practice, educational programmes have either failed to have any effect at all, or have even increased substance use amongst young people (Hawthorne, 1996). The best results achieved in evaluated programmes (and many programmes are not evaluated at all) are small short-term changes in attitudes. It is far from clear that short-term attitude shifts prevent substance use in the long-term. As will be discussed, current educational packages are highly deficient (Coggans *et al.*, 1991; Dorn and Murji, 1992).

Community initiatives

Such initiatives have developed around Britain and many other countries. They have been further encouraged by area drug teams, which comprise relevant senior managers from the health, social service, police and other sectors. The idea behind community initiatives is to develop a concerted community effort according to local problems. For example, in a run-down area of high rise flats, a concierge system may be introduced to keep drug injectors from using the stairs as a shooting gallery. At the same time, the police may try to arrest the key local dealers, general environmental improvements may be introduced, an educational theatre programme be run in local secondary schools, and the local drugs agency may increase the number of detached workers operating in the area. Such a concerted effort may clean up the area, but it may simply drive drug injectors elsewhere. Some prisons have introduced the internal equivalent of community initiatives, with voluntary drug free areas, supported by counselling and drug testing. It is too early to assess the long-term effects of such initiatives.

Problems with prevention

The agenda and goals of prevention often fail to move beyond appealing slogans like 'Just say no to drugs' and 'Choose life not drugs'. Such slogans handicap prevention because they fail to acknowledge the complexity of substance using behaviour and discuss any use of any drug as if it was equivalent to heroin dependence (Coggans *et al.*, 1991; Dorn and Murji, 1992). They also set a goal for prevention that may not be achievable – to stop young people using substances at all. The more modest goal of stopping young people coming to harm through substance use is controversial, but may at least be achievable (e.g. Gilman, 1990).

To date, most preventative programmes remain biased towards complete avoidance of substance, particularly drug, use. In an effort to achieve this goal programmes tend to use fear messages, emphasizing the harm caused by drugs, to be biased against drugs, failing to consider any positive benefits for the user (although these benefits are what entice users), to paint a picture of drug use at odds with most users' experiences and to prescriptively advise against drug use, rather than providing unbiased information to allow young people to make up their own minds. Programmes tend also to confuse different substances, so that cannabis is discussed as if it, at very least, usually led on to 'harder stuff'. This goes against the fact that 21 per cent of adults in England and Wales have tried cannabis but only 3 per cent (that is one of every seven who have tried cannabis) have even tried opiates or cocaine (Ramsay and Percy, 1996). The people delivering preventative programmes can include teachers, drug workers, the police, ex-users (usually ex-addicts) and trained peers. The more sophisticated deliverers may be obliged to deliver a programme that they know to be biased and inaccurate, while those who accept the programmes' messages may know less about drugs than the young people they are trying to influence. Generally, a message that is unbiased and credible is more likely to be believed (see Coggans *et al.*, 1991; Dorn and Murji, 1992), which is a prerequisite for the message to be acted upon. Biased messages presented by adults who lack street credibility are unlikely to succeed with drug users or those contemplating drug use. A few organizations have broken away from this mould (see Gilman, 1990), at the risk of being accused of going soft on drugs, or even of promoting their use. The problem remains that exaggerated fear messages about drugs may find most favour with parents and other people who do not use drugs and have no intention of doing so.

To sum up, it has yet to be shown that it is possible to prevent drug abuse. Future prevention may have more focused objectives and use a more sophisticated approach. For example, it might be possible to reduce the proportion of cannabis users who abuse the drugs, but the best way of accomplishing this may not be by reducing the number of users. A huge need continues for well-designed, carefully evaluated, successful preventative programmes.

Discussion point
- What might a successful drug education programme consist of?

Interventions and Outcome

Without successful prevention, there is a massive need to treat or address the problems of dependent people. Most treatment regimes have not been well evaluated, but a number of major attempts have been made to identify what makes effective treatment for dependency problems (see for example *Addiction*, 1996; Leukefeld and Tims, 1988; Tims and Leukefeld, 1986). These studies suggest that treatment is, at best, only moderately effective. A year after treatment, a programme is doing very well if more than 30 per cent of its clients are still abstinent or moderate in their substance use. Most dependent people will give up and return to dependence several times over the course of several years, before finally managing the problem. Treatment can significantly speed up that process, but it cannot 'cure' dependence overnight.

Many treatment programmes promise rapid effective cures with success rates of 70 per cent or more. How do they achieve this? There are several methods all of which are suspect. First, only 'treat' people who are not dependent. If cannabis users who are caught are compelled to attend drug treatment, then most of them will 'get better' because there was nothing wrong with them that would hinder them stopping cannabis use, when that is required. Second, only take people into treatment who have already stopped using drugs. In other words, people who have already cured themselves. Third, throw out of treatment anyone who fails, and throw them out of your statistics as well. That way, all the people who complete the programme will get better. Fourth, don't follow people up for very long. Leaving the door of the clinic or prison, most people will be abstinent. Rates will be lower a week later and usually down to about 20 per cent a year later. One can also exaggerate treatment effectiveness in other ways. For a critical and amusing account of the defects of treatment evaluation, see Miller and Sanchez-Craig (1996). A final factor is that many substance dependent people try several different treatments. Once better, they often feel that only the last one worked. In reality, their improvement may have been due to all the different treatments together.

Thus, it is important to be cautious in accepting claims for the success of specific treatments. This section will consider the general factors that make for effective treatment and the issue of abstinence, before going on to outline the main different approaches to treatment that are in current use.

General factors which make for effective treatment

A good relationship between the client and counsellor based on empathy and trust seems to be most important for outcome, rather than the ideology and theory of treatment. For dependent people, treatment often needs to be of medium-length (lasting months, rather than weeks) and to involve the examination of the client's entire life situation, rather than just their substance use (Leukefeld and Tims, 1988; Tims and Leukefeld, 1986).

Client characteristics also make treatment success more likely. For alcohol treatment, clients who are more socially stable (more affluent, employed, living in a family home) and have less severe problems (less symptoms of dependence, fewer medical and other problems) are more likely to respond well to treatment (Miller and Sanchez-Craig, 1996). The same probably applies to treatment of any dependence. These features of treatment and client are probably more important than the specific treatment philosophy being used by a particular agency.

Abstinence or moderation?

The most hotly debated issue in treatment is whether dependent people can and should be allowed to moderate their behaviour and use substances moderately (see Marlatt, 1996; also Robertson *et al.*, 1987). The alternative is that dependent people should abstain entirely from the substances that caused them problems, and probably all other psychoactive substances too, although most abstinence-oriented programmes tolerate tobacco and caffeine use.

There is a moral dimension to this debate. Is intoxication morally unacceptable, or is it part of human nature? Ignoring this, the facts appear to be that some dependent people have such severe problems and such difficulty managing their substance use that abstinence is the first ethical option to suggest. Nonetheless, some people will not manage to abstain, however severe their problems. At the other end of the spectrum, some problem substance users are not dependent. They may need to change their substance-using behaviour, rather than abstain. Somewhere between these extremes lie most people who will seek help for substance use, or whose use is a major component of their problems. Judgement about the individual must be used to decide whether abstinence or moderate would be appropriate.

Alcoholics Anonymous and its relatives

Alcoholics Anonymous consists of groups of recovering alcoholics who provide mutual support and aim at complete abstinence from alcohol (see Vaillant, 1995). Narcotics Anonymous is a similar organization for drug problems. Strictly speaking, neither is a treatment at all and AA/NA do not endorse any particular approach to treatment. The philosophy is the famous 12-steps approach (see Box 20.3), which requires that the alcoholic surrender to a higher power (or God), admit their wrongs and try to rectify them. This requires some spiritual feeling, accepting abstinence as a goal, and usually works better for those who were heavily dependent. There are also professional residential programmes that offer a 12-steps approach and this approach is sometimes called the 'Minnesota Model'. 12-steps

---

Box 20.3 The 12-Steps of Alcoholics Anonymous

Step 1   We admitted we were powerless over alcohol – that our lives had become unmanageable

Step 2   Came to believe that a Power greater than ourselves could restore us to sanity

Step 3   Made a decision to turn our will and our lives over to the care of God as we understood Him

Step 4   Made a searching and fearless moral inventory of ourselves

Step 5   Admitted to God, to ourselves, and to another human being, the exact nature of our wrongs

Step 6   Were entirely ready to have God remove all these defects of character

Step 7   Humbly asked Him to remove our shortcomings

Step 8   Made a list of all persons we had harmed, and became willing to make amends to them all

Step 9   Made direct amends to such people whenever possible, except when to do so would injure them or others

Step 10 Continued to take personal inventory and when we were wrong promptly admitted it

Step 11 Sought through prayer and meditation to improve our conscious contact with God as we understood Him, praying only for knowledge of His will for us and the power to carry that out

Step 12 Having had a spiritual awakening as the result of these steps, we tried to carry this message to alcoholics, and to practise these principles in all our affairs.

See Vaillant (1995) pp.254–265. Other organizations, such as Narcotics Anonymous, use similar steps recorded to apply to other substances or problems.

---

seems to work best for people who attend meetings regularly and get actively involved in the organization – indeed that is part of the AA ethos (Vaillant, 1995).

Recovered AA/NA members can be enthusiastic advocates of the 12-steps approach, particularly if they have also been through Minnesota Model treatment, and they sometimes denigrate other options. They can also be opposed to providing help about moderation, because they believe that the addict has to 'hit bottom' before they are ready to stop drinking or drug use. In their view, moderation merely prolongs the problem. On the other hand, moderation can stop some people becoming dependent at all and may at least prolong life for others. Despite the extreme position of some '12-steppers', the basic philosophy is neutral about the issue of whether abstinence is for everyone. Many people have benefited from AA or NA membership, and those who do not like the approach tend to rapidly give up going. Groups exist in most towns and cities. Therefore, AA can be a useful option to suggest that clients try, as long as it is not presented as the only treatment possibility.

Detoxification

The most naive disease model of addiction sees 'the problem' as lying entirely with the drug. Medically supervised detoxification programmes used to simply wean dependent people off their drug, then discharge them. Detox. can be helpful, particularly for alcohol and the benzodiazepines, where withdrawal can be dangerous, and for people who find withdrawal very upsetting. However, long-term counselling after detox. is generally also provided. Detox. is usually only the start of treatment, not its end (Mattick and Hall, 1996). It is important to emphasize this because both substance dependent people and their families sometimes think that 'getting off' will sort out their problems without further effort. They may even resist or resent other therapeutic approaches.

Residential rehabilitation

The practical issues discussed in this section are derived from numerous conversations over the years with people conducting drug and alcohol treatments. They belong more to the oral traditions of service provision than to treatment textbooks and manuals. The success of residential programmes may have more to do with these practical management issues than with the different treatment philosophies employed.

Many treatment programmes take dependent people into residence. The philosophies behind residential programmes vary, although many are 12-steps, or modified versions of that approach. Most include group work, examining group members' lives and attitudes, as well as other therapeutic activities. Residential programmes can be successful, but a number of management problems have to be overcome. It can often be difficult to judge the worth of a residential programme without direct knowledge of it.

First, while being on a residential programme can provide a dependent person with a breathing space to make personal changes, there can be an air of unreality about some residential programmes. Clients who normally prowled the inner cities in conditions of extreme poverty are suddenly taken to tranquil country mansions and introduced to healthy outdoor pursuits. Having been abstinent in these benign surroundings, many users relapse when they return to their previous haunts.

Second, any counselling is only as good as the counsellors. Enabling change in clients is difficult, and when a residential programme's counsellors are not up to the task, the programme can simply become a place for time out and entertainment, rather than a treatment programme. Counsellor training can vary from minimal (some counsellors are simply graduates from treatment themselves) to extensive.

Third, particularly if the counselling provided is poor, putting a lot of dependent people together can mean that they reinforce each others' existing attitudes, devise ways to drink or take drugs in the residence, teach each other further bad habits and drug taking skills and otherwise undermine the programme. This can happen to an extent even in well-managed programmes.

Fourth, residential programmes can be problematic for people who are anti-social, disruptive and badly behaved. They are likely to be discharged within a few days of admission. This may be necessary for the management of the programme, but these 'difficult' clients include many of those who most badly need help.

It should be clear that running a residential programme for dependent people is difficult. Not only may some programmes not work, but most programmes probably work sometimes, yet not other times. Most residential programmes will have difficulty managing if a particular group of residents happen to include several highly manipulative, clever and anti-social people who run rings around the staff. Complacency is unwise.

Counselling

Counselling usually involves one-to-one sessions between a substance user and a professional, or lay counsellor. Group sessions may also occur. The quality, training and supervision of counsellors varies so greatly that it is not safe to make generalizations about the merits of counselling for substance problems. At one extreme, counselling can be conducted by people with many years of training in counselling techniques and high standards of professional supervision and monitoring, including psychologists, psychiatrists and others with in-depth psychoanalytic or counselling training. Even then, not all these people will be effective therapists for drug and alcohol problems.

At the other extreme, counselling can be conducted by people with training of only a few months, or even a few weeks. This would include most peer and ex-user counsellors. That people 'know the score' about drug use and have successfully given up themselves does not itself make them competent to effect change in other people.

In the middle, there are many social care professionals including social workers and probation officers, whose jobs include some counselling, some work with substance users, and much else. The extent to which they are trained and qualified to counsel drug users varies. Sometimes, such professionals are expected to work with drug users after perhaps one two-day course on counselling and another on drugs. They then have to pick up further skills on the job.

Counselling substance users often involves attempting to enable substantial life and attitude changes in people who often have major, multiple problems, whose existing attitudes may be highly resistant to change and whose motivation to change may be low. The difficulties of counselling should not be underestimated and it is important that adequate training and supervision are provided for counsellors.

Cognitive-behavioural approaches

There are a number of therapeutic approaches that can be described as cognitive-behavioural (see Miller, 1996, 1980; Donovan and Marlatt, 1993). They differ in detail but they share the following features:

- An emphasis on changing current thoughts and behaviours, rather than dwelling on possible causes from the past

- An approach which systematically examines the client's thoughts and behaviours, identifies problematic ones, and devises specific means of changing these (see Box 20.4)

- A theoretical orientation which holds that thought and behaviour patterns can be dysfunctional in their own right and can be treated by changing them, without reference to any more fundamental unconscious problems.

Many studies have found that cognitive-behavioural therapies work for dependence problems. While other therapies have been evaluated less often, they currently seem less effective (Hodgson, 1994). Cognitive-behavioural approaches cannot be expected to work without the full co-operation of the client. Someone who is unwilling to honestly discuss their thoughts

---

Box 20.4 Example of Problem Behaviors and Thoughts
Underlying Substance Abuse

Jim A is a 35-year-old man with a history of binge drinking and violence while intoxicated which has resulted in his serving two prison sentences. Sober, he is generally quiet and unexpressive. He has little memory for the violent events which occur when he is drunk. He does not consider himself a violent man. When asked if his drinking is a problem, he gets quite annoyed and says 'I am not an alcoholic'. Further discussion suggests that Jim believes the following:

- Alcoholics drink every day

- Everyone is entitled to get drunk from time to time

- Violent people get aggressive for no reason

- As he is not a violent man, his assaults while drunk must have been legitimate responses to other people's behaviour.

Therapy concentrated on

- Getting Jim to see the violence as related to his drinking, without labelling him alcoholic

- Suggesting strategies for having a drink from time to time without getting so drunk

- Teaching non-violent methods of being assertive with other people.

---

and behaviours will gain no benefit (although the same could be said about other therapies). A key issue for such approaches is to consider clients' motivation for change and, if necessary, take steps to reinforce motivation. It may also be useful to tailor counselling according to clients' current motives. The simple idea is that clients who do not want to change will not respond even to the best treatment.

Harm reduction

Some dependent people seem resistant to contemplating change, or have repeatedly failed to change their behaviour. One objective of treatment for this group is for them to manage their behaviour so that they come to the least possible harm until they may be ready to change (Department of Health, 1991). The objectives of harm reduction are to reduce the intensity of substance use if possible, to reduce the health, psychological and social problems caused by substance use, to keep clients in contact with services and to move clients towards contemplating change, if possible. An additional objective might at least be to prevent a gradual increase in the harm caused by substance dependence.

For example, repeated imprisonment might progressively increase a homeless alcoholic's isolation on the outside, hence increase binge drinking and worsen his mental and physical health. Diversion from prison into treatment might slow that increase in harm, even if treatment did not lead to abstinence.

The harm reduction model has been best developed for heroin injectors, but can be applied also elsewhere (Marlatt, 1996). The much-discussed Dutch model of drug controls is based in part on a concept in the constitution of the Netherlands. This concept of justice requires that the enforcement of laws should not cause more harm than their violation. For example, is petty cannabis dealing so harmful that it outweighs the harm caused to the dealer by a custodial sentence?

For heroin injection, harm reduction is immediately aimed to reduce injecting, as well as the harm it causes, and to reduce the expensive consumption of street drugs. Injecting is dangerous to health, often even fatal, while the cost of street heroin can contribute to a chaotic lifestyle of crime and drug abuse. Two methods of reducing harm are the provision of clean injecting equipment, to prevent the spread of HIV, Hepatitis and other infectious diseases, and the provision of oral methadone to reduce the use of street drugs by injection (Department of Health, 1991).

Brief interventions

A number of studies have shown that even very brief interventions can be effective with some people with drug or alcohol problems, particularly those who are less dependent. Interventions that seem to work include simply advising clients or patients to consider cutting down or stopping their substance use and providing brief written information to help (see Heather, 1995; Robertson *et al.* 1986; Miller, 1996). Advice by correspondence and on the telephone may also work. It is easier to achieve success when the aim is reduction or moderation, rather than complete abstinence, the success rates for brief interventions tend to be 10 per cent, sometimes better, which is impressive because the interventions are so simple and cheap. Some studies have found that much more extensive interventions perform no better (see Heather, 1995) and, as already mentioned, any programme that achieves 30 per cent success is doing well.

When clients have multiple presenting problems, of which substance use is perhaps a relatively small part, then such brief interventions may be useful to the social care professional. To illustrate, someone with a history of violence after binge drinking may be able to stop this pattern of drinking, or reduce its frequency by following some very simple suggestions. For example, if they always get into trouble after drinking with the same cronies on a Friday night, perhaps they should avoid drinking with that particular group.

Referral

Social care professionals will often want to refer clients on to specialist addiction services. In most regions there are numerous statutory and non-statutory agencies dealing with substance abuse and addiction. Different agencies tend not to be well networked or integrated, and the matching of client and appropriate service is not well-developed (Heather, 1996). In referring clients, it is useful to try to become aware of all the agencies locally available, as well as the various services that they provide. It is also useful to remember that treating dependence is difficult. If a particular service seems to have done badly with a client, this does not guarantee that they will also fail with the next one you refer. On the other hand, success for some clients does not guarantee future success for all. The client's wishes are probably most important as referral can be pointless if the client does not take up the referral, does not stay with the service offered, or participates insincerely to satisfy probation. Most agencies now offer a range of services. At this time one cannot state that any particular treatment is the best, nor that any treatment is worthless. The claims of treatment staff in this regard should be considered cautiously and an agency that claims an implausibly high success rate is perhaps less desirable than one with a more realistic approach.

Another concern in referring clients to drug treatment is that many substance dependent people who become clients of probation or social services will have ambiguous feelings about their need for help. On the one hand, the circumstances that led them to probation or social services may suggest to them that they need to deal with their substance use problem. On the other hand, they may resent social workers and probation officers as interfering and wish to return by the easiest and most rapid route to their old ways. They may also strategically play-up, or play-down, their substance problems to achieve their own ends. They may, for example, see drug treatment as preferable to prison (although some prefer to serve their time unbothered by troublesome counsellors), or preferable to losing custody of their children. In other circumstances, or simply when confronted by a different worker, they may play down their problems in the hope of avoiding the need for treatment also (see Weppner, 1981 for a good description of how users can play the system).

Fortunately, the dilemma of whether to refer or whether to dispute clients' sincerity is eased by the finding that even compulsory referral to treatment as an alternative to prison does not reduce treatment's (modest) success rates (Leukefeld and Tims, 1988). Sometimes treatment can effect change even in people who had no initial desire to change.

To sum up, treatment of dependence is a difficult and imprecise business where much can go wrong and with low success rates. On the other hand most available treatment options may be worth a try. Three broad avenues of treatment may be useful:

1. Self-help organizations like AA benefit many, but not all, dependent people

2. Dependent people also benefit from extended treatment aimed at effecting major life changes

3. Dependent people not yet ready to change, as well as the non-dependent, can also benefit from brief interventions aimed to reduce the harm caused by their substance use by, for example, changing their use patterns.

Still, really successful treatments for addiction remain too good to be true.

Discussion point

- How would you honestly present the difficulties of drug treatment to a client without putting them off?

Caring for the Counsellors

Few professionals get their degrees and diplomas with the intention of working with substance dependence, drug and alcohol problems. Most get involved either by moving into a job that includes such work, by gradually getting interested, or by realizing that many clients who are ostensibly seen for other reasons have drug and alcohol problems. While the pervasiveness of alcohol, and increasingly other drugs, means that it can be unrealistic to separate off 'drug addicts' or 'alcoholics' as special groups, there can be a number of difficulties when dealing with drug and alcohol problems. These include:

- *Lack of specialized training.* Although by now most professional training includes some information on substance abuse and dependence, this is a recent development and the training can be quite cursory. Some professionals continue to hold stereotypical or otherwise inappropriate beliefs about drug users or alcoholics, which can be unhelpful when dealing with them. They may also feel afraid and incompetent to deal with them.

- *Client manipulativeness.* Alcoholics, heroin users and other people with drug problems are often viewed negatively by general medical, social and legal services. They are seen as people who have caused their own problems, who are immoral, weak and wicked, who will do 'anything' to get their drug of choice, who are pathological liars and manipulators and who will often create awkward or even dangerous scenes in service premises. There is a small grain of truth in this bleak perception. However, this client group is generally no harder to manage than other clients if there are clear rules about the conduct expected of them, with clear consequences if the rules are broken.

- *Poor outcome.* This client group can be disappointing to deal with. They can take a long time to improve, sometimes seem not to improve at all, often relapse, often fail to stick to treatment or other plans and often seem to do their best to sabotage attempts to help them, despite their claims about wanting to manage their substance use behaviour. There is thus a tendency for those dealing with them to become demotivated and cynical about the possibility of effecting change. It is therefore important that agencies maintain and encourage realistic aims and objectives in dealing with substance problems.

- *Counsellor substance use.* Many professionals (and students) in the addiction field are confronted at some point by uncomfortable feelings of hypocrisy about their own substance use. An old medical aphorism was that 'An alcoholic is someone who drinks more than their doctor' and to some extent this still applies. How can one's own substance use be reconciled with providing professional advice about the resultant problems? It is important that counsellors can reach an acceptable position on this, which does not involve hypocrisy, denial of their own substance use (or boasting of abstinence), a judgmental moral position, or excessive stigmatizing of their clients. The objective use of criteria for dependence and abuse, such as the DSM-IV, may be helpful.

Discussion point

- ○ To what extent are you at risk of abusing drugs or alcohol? What steps might you take to avoid future problems?

Summary

This chapter has examined the outdated concept of addiction and described the nature of substance abuse and substance dependence. Problems relating to substance use can occur without dependence. Some of the types of factors that determine dependence are social, personal, family, drug lifestyle, drug pharmacology and developmental factors. The career of a substance dependent person has a lot in common with a criminal career.

For treatment, the abstinence-moderation debate was discussed, with the suggestion that both goals can be appropriate. Factors that make treatment effective include the duration of treatment, the client–counsellor relationship and that the client is better-functioning, but do not generally include the school of treatment used, although cognitive-behavioural approaches seem to work well. Various important approaches to treatment were described and their practical drawbacks were discussed. Finally, some of the difficulties inherent in working with substance dependent people were described.

It was suggested that many social work and probation clients will be substance abusers or dependent, or have such a person in the family. Problems in dealing with these clients include unrealistic expectations for 'cures', difficulties in choosing agencies for referral and low success rates in treatment. These problems are not dramatically different from those of dealing with other clients. Indeed substance problems are much more common in society than is usually appreciated and people cannot be neatly be divided into 'addicts' who require special care and normal people who do not. Someone's problems with substance use will be one component of many client's case histories.

Seminar Questions

- Is dependence the same whatever the substance?
- To what extent do drugs cause crime?
- Who should provide drugs education for teenagers? Currently it is usually provided by the police, school teachers or, more rarely, peers
- To what extent does harm reduction license or encourage drug use?
- When, if ever, is it ethical for drug users, or heavy drinkers, to counsel others about their substance use?
- Could we have a society without intoxication?

Further Reading

Much of the better work on addiction is psychological or medical. The following books contain material of interest.

Davies, J.B. (1992) *The Myth of Addiction: An Application of the Psychological Theory of Attribution to Illicit Drug Use.* Chur: Harwood Academic Publishers.
This is a contentious but stimulating look at the nature of addiction, suggesting that its biological basis has been exaggerated.

Department of Health (1991) *Drug Misuse and Dependence: Guidelines on Clinical Management.* London, HMSO.
This spells out official policy on drug injecting.

Ghodse, H. (1995) *Drugs and Addictive Behaviour: A Guide to Treatment.* Oxford, Blackwell Science.
This is a comprehensive guide to treatment.

Vaillant, G.E. (1995) *The Natural History of Alcoholism Revisited.* Cambridge, MA: Harvard University Press.
This book reports on longitudinal work on the development and progress of alcoholism and discusses many issues about addiction in depth.

References

Addiction (1996) Special issue: Substance problems: understanding how treatment systems work, *91,* 5.

Agar, M. (1973) *Ripping and Running, A Formal Ethnography of Urban Heroin Addicts.* New York, Seminar Press.

Brown, R.I.F. (1987) 'Pathological gambling and associated patterns of crime: comparisons with alcohol and other drug addictions.' *Journal of Gambling Behavior, 3,* 98–114.

Coggans, N., Shewan, D., Henderson M. and Davies, J.B. (1991) *National Evaluation of Drug Education in Scotland.* ISDD Research Monograph Four, London, Institute for the Study of Drug Dependence.

Collins, J.J. and Schlenger, W.E. (1988) 'Acute and chronic effects of alcohol use on violence.' *Journal of Studies on Alcohol, 49,* 516–521.

Commentaries (1996) 'Comments on Hall *et al.*'s Australian National Drug Strategy Monograph no. 25 "The Health and Psychological Consequences of Cannabis Use."' *Addiction, 91,* 759–773.

Conger, J.J. (1991) *Adolescence and Youth, 4th edition,* New York: Harper Collins.

Davies, J.B. (1992) *The Myth of Addiction: An Application of the Psychological Theory of Attribution to Illicit Drug Use.* Chur: Harwood Academic.

Department of Health (1991) *Drug Misuse and Dependence: Guidelines on Clinical Management.* London, HMSO.

Ditton, J. and Hammersley, R.H. (1996) *A Very Greedy Drug: Cocaine in Context.* Reading: Harwood.

Donovan, D.M. and Marlatt, G.A. (1993) 'Behavioral treatment.' In M. Galanter (ed.) *Recent Developments in Alcoholism, vol 11: ten years of progress,* pp.397–411. New York, NY: Plenum Press.

Dorn, N. and Murji, K. (1992) *Drug Prevention: A Review of the English Language Literature.* ISDD Research Monograph 5. London: ISDD.

DSM-IV, American Psychiatric Association (1994) *Diagnostic and Statistical Manual of Mental Disorders – 4th Edition.* Washington, DC: APA.

Edwards, G. (1986) 'The alcohol dependence syndrome: concept as a stimulus to enquiry.' *British Journal of Addiction, 81,* 171–184.

Elliott, D.S., Huizinga, D. and Ageton, S.S. (1985) *Explaining Delinquency and Drug Use.* London: Sage.

Ghodse, H. (1995) *Drugs and Addictive Behaviour: A Guide to Treatment.* Oxford: Blackwell Science.

Gilman, M.R. (1990) 'A smack in the eye for standard drugs and HIV education.' *British Journal of Addiction, 85,* 1661–1666.

Glass, I.B. (1991) (ed.) *The International Handbook of Addiction Behaviour.* London, Tavistock/Routledge.

Goddard, E. (1990) *Why Children Start Smoking.* London: HMSO.

Hammersley, R.H., Forsyth, A.J.M, Morrison, V.L. and Davies, J.B. (1989) 'The relationship between crime and opioid use.' *British Journal of Addiction, 84,* 1029–1043.

Hawthorne, G. (1996) 'The social impact of Life Education: estimating drug use prevalence among Victorian primary school students and the statewide effect of the Life Education programme.' *Addiction, 91,* 1151–1159.

Heather, N. (1995) 'Interpreting the evidence on brief interventions for excessive drinkers – the need for caution.' *Alcohol and Alcoholism, 30,* 287–296.

Heather, N. (1996) 'Waiting for a match – the future of psychosocial treatment for alcohol problems.' *Addiction, 91,* 469–472.

Hodgson, R. (1994) 'Treatment of alcohol problems.' *Addiction, 89,* 1529–1534.

Jessor, R. and Jessor, S.L. (1977) *Problem Behavior and Psychosocial Development. A Longitudinal Study.* New York: Wiley.

Lavelle, T.L., Hammersley, R.H. and Forsyth, A.J.M. (1993) 'Is the "addictive personality" merely delinquency?' *Addiction Research, 1,* 27–37.

Leukefeld, C.G. and Tims, F.M. (eds) (1988) *Compulsory Treatment of Drug Abuse: Research and Clinical Practice.* NIDA Research Monograph 86. Rockville, MD: NIDA.

Marlatt, G.A. (1966) 'Harm reduction: come as you are.' *Addictive Behaviors, 21,* 779–788.

Mattick, R.P. and Hall, W. (1996) 'Are detoxification programmes effective?' *Lancet, 347,* 97–100.

Miller, W.R. and Sanchez-Craig, M. (1996) 'How to have a high sucess rate in treatment: advice for evaluators of alcoholism programs.' *Addiction, 91,* 779–85.

Miller, W.R. (1980) (ed) *The Addictive Behaviors: Treatment of Alcoholism, Drug Abuse, Smoking and Obesity.* New York, Plenum Press.

Miller, W.R. (1996) 'Motivational interviewing: Research, practice, and puzzles.' *Addictive Behaviors, 21,* 835–42.

Murji, K. (1991) 'Enforcement strategies and retail drug markets.' *British Criminology Conference.* York, July. ISDD: London.

Newcomb, M.D. and Bentler, P.M. (1990) 'Antecedents and consequences of cocaine use: An eight-year study from early adolescence to young adulthood.' In L. Robins and M. Rutter (eds) *Straight and Devious Pathways from Childhood to Adulthood.* Cambridge: Cambridge University Press.

Orford, J. (1985) *Excessive Appetites: A Psychological View of Addiction.* Chichester: Wiley.

Pearson, G. (1987) *The New Heroin Users.* Oxford, Blackwell.

Peele, S. (1985) *The Meaning of Addiction: Compulsive Experience and its Interpretation.* Lexington, Mass: Lexington Books.

Ramsay, M. and Percy, A. (1996) *Drug Misuse Declared: Results of the 1994 British Crime Survey.* Home Office Research Study 151, London: HMSO.

Robertson, I., Heather, N., Dzialdowski, A., Crawford, J. and Winton, M. (1986) 'A comparison of minimal versus intensive controlled drinking treatment interventions for problem drinkers.' *British Journal of Clinical Psychology, 25,* 185–194.

Robertson, I., Spencer, J., Blume, S., Chick, J., Raistrick, D., Sobell, M.B., Sobell, L.C., Glatt, M., Duckert, F., Orford, J. and Heather, N. (1987) 'Is controlled drinking possible for the person who has been severely alcohol dependent?' *British Journal of Addiction, 82,* 237–255.

Tims, F.M. and Leukefeld, C.G. (eds) (1986) *Relapse and Recovery in Drug Abuse.* NIDA Research Monograph 72. Rockville, MD: NIDA.

Vaillant, G.E. (1995) *The Natural History of Alcoholism Revisited.* Cambridge, MA: Harvard University Press.

Vitaro, F., Dobkin, P.L., Carbonneau, R. and Tremblay, R.E. (1996) 'Personal and familial characteristics of resilient sons of male alcoholics.' *Addiction, 91,* 1161–1177.

Weppner, R.S. (1981) 'Status and role among narcotic addicts: implications for treatment personnel.' *International Journal of Offender Therapy and Comparative Criminology, 25,* 233–247.

Zinberg, N.E. (1984) *Drug, Set and Setting: The Basis for Controlled Intoxicant Use.* Yale University Press. New Haven, CT.

Some Interesting Internet Addresses

The following sites contain much material on drugs and alcohol, from many different perspectives. They also have numerous links to all sorts of other sites.

The Addiction Research Foundation, Toronto
http://www.arf.org/

Addiction Resources on the Web
http://easyweb.easynet.co.uk/~acw/websites.htm

alt.drugs Frequently Asked Questions
http://www.cis.ohio-state.edu/hypertext/faq/bngusenet/alt/drugs/top.html

The Center for Alcohol and Addiction Studies, Brown University
http://center.butler.brown.edu/

Dutch Harm Reduction Site
http://www.cts.com/~habtsmrt/hrmtitle.html

European Monitoring Centre for Drugs Addiction
http://www.emcdda.org

Institute for the Study of Drug Dependence
http://www.isdd.co.uk

Marijuana Anonymous
http://www.marijuana-anonymous.org

National Addiction Centre, London, England
http://www.iop.bpmf.ac.uk/home/depts/psychiat/nac/nac.htm

National Clearing House for Alcohol and Drug Information (USA)
http://www.health.org/

National Institute on Alcohol and Alcoholism (USA)
http://www.niaaa.nih.gov/

Rational Recovery (on-line self-help)
http://www.rational.org/recovery/

Stanton Peele Website
http://www.frw.uva.nl/cedro/peele/

The Web of Addictions
http://www.well.com/user/woa/

CHAPTER 21

Psychological Impact
of HIV Disease

Barbara Hedge

Introduction

In the early 1980s reports from the Centers for Disease Control (CDC) first described Acquired Immune Deficiency Syndrome (AIDS), an acute illness in gay men which was usually fatal (CDC, 1981). In 1983 an infectious agent, the Human Immunodeficiency Virus (HIV) was identified as the cause of AIDS. Since then world-wide, more than 7 million people have been diagnosed with AIDS, 4.5 million have died from HIV associated conditions, and probably around 21 million have been infected with HIV.

HIV disease is a chronic condition in which the asymptomatic phase, i.e. without symptoms, may last for many years. Although most medical interventions are directed towards the control of diseases which occur as a result of the lowered immune function, an increasing range of anti-retroviral drugs which inhibit the replication of HIV and thus tackle the virus directly is now available. Undoubtedly, medical advances in the treatment of HIV disease are being made, and many individuals live longer and survive repeated bouts of illness. However, the length of remission which the new anti-retroviral medications might bring is still unclear. The resulting uncertainty in prognosis increases the emotional burden for those with HIV, even in those who are clinically well and asymptomatic; as the headline in a recent publication for people with HIV asked 'False horizon or new dawn?' (King, 1997).

Good care addresses an individual's quality of life as well as its length; it aims to help people live with HIV infection rather than simply wait to die. Since HIV has been recognized as not only a disease of gay men, people with haemophilia and injecting drug-users, but also of heterosexuals, particularly those in sub-Saharan Africa, South America and Asia, the complexity of the psychological and social reactions to the infection has increasingly become apparent.

Comprehensive health care for those with HIV disease which attempts to maximize quality of life, can best be provided by the variety of skills found in a multi-disciplinary team comprising doctors, nurses, psychologists, psychiatrists, dieticians, pharmacists, social workers and a variety of counsellors. It is now essential for all health and social carers to have some knowledge of the psychological and social implications of HIV disease.

This chapter is mainly concerned with the psychological sequelae of HIV disease. As many of these are related to the clinical course of infection, a short introduction to the natural history of infection and disease progression will first be given. The meanings attached to HIV infection and the impact of HIV disease are next discussed. Emotional distress associated with HIV infection is described, and ways in which psychological interventions can improve quality of life are considered, with particular attention to the situations where social carers are involved. Finally, some thought is given to the psychological effects that prolonged caring for people with HIV disease can have on carers.

The natural history of infection and disease

The human immunodeficiency viruses (HIV-1 and HIV-2) are part of a family of retroviruses which infect cells of the immune system; particularly affected are those bearing CD4 receptors (that play a key role in orchestrating the immune system's response to infection), and the monocyte, microglia and macrophage cells in the brain. Infection of the latter can lead to cognitive impairment. The immune system produces antibodies in an attempt to destroy the virus. Initially, a strong immune response may keep the level of virus low, but virus replication continues, particularly in the lymph nodes, and individuals remain infected and potentially infectious for life. The onset of AIDS may be caused by more virulent mutations of the virus, or by a failure of the immune response.

Most of the tests for HIV infection look for the presence of antibodies. As antibodies to HIV are not produced in measurable quantities until some weeks after infection there is a 'window period' during which individuals may be infected but will not test 'antibody positive'. It is common practice to test 12 weeks after a possible exposure to HIV when the antibody can usually be detected.

The most frequent route of HIV transmission is through sexual practices such as penetrative sex between men, or between men and women. HIV can also be transmitted through blood and blood products. This may occur through the sharing of inadequately sterilized needles, syringes or other skin piercing instruments while injecting drugs or occasionally through needle-stick injuries. The virus can also be passed from person to person via donated organs or semen, and from mother to child during pregnancy, at the time of delivery or postnatally through breast feeding (Peckham and Newell, 1990). There is no evidence of the virus being transmitted by everyday, social contact.

A transient, flu like illness may accompany the initial antibody response. However, many individuals remain asymptomatic for ten or more years, although it is now recognized that there is viral activity during this time (Ho et al., 1995). As the virus replicates it destroys the immune system and a variety of symptoms such as swollen lymph glands, night sweats, fatigue and diarrhoea may be experienced. A diagnosis of AIDS is made when HIV has damaged the immune system to such an extent that certain opportunistic infections, tumours or encephalopathy are observed. A commonly used marker of immunosupression is a count of CD4 cells. There is a trend for a decreasing CD4 count to be associated with increasing clinical symptoms of illness, with individuals becoming more vulnerable to particular opportunistic infections and cancers. The CD4 count alone is not a good predictor of an individual's clinical disease pattern.

In 1996 new evidence from the MACS viral load study (Mellors *et al.*, 1996a) indicated that determination of the quantity of HIV in blood, the 'viral load', assisted prediction of disease progression and could be useful in assessing response to anti-retro viral treatments. Individuals with a 'set point' (after infection with HIV for six months) viral load of less than 3000 copies/ml were unlikely to develop AIDS within ten years (Mellors, 1996b). As the set-point viral load increased, so the average time to develop AIDS decreased; those with the highest viral load, over 30,000 copies/ml, developed AIDS on average after 2.8 years. High viral load and other factors such as older age at time of infection and a lack of anti-retroviral treatment before diagnosis of AIDS were associated with poorer rates of survival (Mellors 1996b; Graham *et al.*, 1992).

Neuropsychological complications of disease

The neuropsychological effects of HIV disease are many and varied (Grant, 1990), and can result from either the direct effect of HIV on the central nervous system or from secondary complications of immune deficiency (e.g. cerebral opportunistic infections such as toxoplasmosis, progressive multi-focal leucoencephalopathy and lymphoma).

The progressive dementia directly attributable to HIV in the brain, AIDS Dementia Complex, was first reported by Navia, Jordan and Price (1986). It is characterized by cognitive impairment, decline in motor function, memory loss and behavioural changes. To standardize diagnoses, operationally defined criteria were drawn up by the World Health Organization (WHO 1990a) for HIV associated dementia and for HIV associated minor cognitive/motor disorder (when cognitive impairment exists, but does not meet the criteria for a dementia), that exclude other causes of cognitive impairment that may be seen in HIV disease.

Cognitive impairment has been reported in people with asymptomatic HIV disease but this is unusual, most cases being seen in advanced disease states (McArthur *et al.*, 1993). The pattern of cognitive deficits which emerges in late stage disease shows impairment consistent with some features of subcortical dementia, including memory impairment and decline in fine motor speed, concentration, problem solving and visuo-spacial ability (Navia 1990). The incidence of HIV associated dementia is reported to be around 7 per cent (Janssen *et al.* 1990) and the prevalence cited as ranging from 2.6–16 per cent (Meadows *et al.*, 1993a; McArthur, 1987). Some of this variability is probably due to differences in sampling or in criteria used in judging dementia. It is also possible that the prevalence of dementia is changing over time, as changes occur in the life expectancy of people with AIDS, or with the changing patterns of medical intervention. Generally, the prognosis for people with HIV associated dementia is poor, but there is increasing evidence that some anti-retrovirals such as zidovudine (AZT) and stavudine (d4T) can reduce its frequency and symptomatology (Baldeweg *et al.*, 1995).

Coming to Terms with HIV Disease

Even when people suspect that they may be infected with HIV, confirmation of their positivity can come as a shock. Many parallels can be drawn between the issues faced by people with HIV disease and those faced by people with other potentially fatal illnesses, but the former may have to face additional problems, such as the stigma and discrimination attached to gay sexual behaviours, drug use or racial intolerance (King, 1989a). The uncertainty attached to the course of HIV disease, its poor long-term prognosis and the ever-changing recommendations for optimum medication regimes can cause great distress. Many people are concerned that should they develop symptomatic disease they will not be able to cope with its physical symptoms, nor with the frank explanations or elaborate excuses necessary to explain their condition to friends, relatives or employers. So it does not seem surprising that psychological symptoms are frequently seen in those with HIV disease; indeed, it is more remarkable how well so many people cope for so long.

This section discusses psychological reactions to HIV disease, how these might be related to stage of infection, possible exacerbaters of psychological symptoms such as multiple stressors and issues related to suicide. Adapative coping strategies and the 'buffer' which can be provided by social support are then considered. Finally, the potential effect of stress on immune functioning is outlined.

Table 21.1 Common Symptoms Associated with Anxiety and Depression

Symptoms	Anxiety	Depression
Somatic (physical)	Increased heart rate fast breathing sweating nausea and diarrhoea frequent micturation muscle pains headaches sleep difficulties	sleep disturbance loss of libido anorexia
Cognitive (thoughts)	reduced concentration preoccupation with problems catastrophizing	failure worthlessness unlovable guilt hopelessness
Affective (feelings)	fear loss of control panic	irritability low mood despair
Behavioural (acts)	restlessness avoidance of feared situations	lack of energy reduced activity levels

Psychological reactions to HIV disease

Many intense, negative psychological reactions have been reported in people with HIV disease (King, 1989b; Hedge et al., 1992). Figure 21.1 illustrates the range of reactions seen in those presenting in crisis. It can be seen that anxiety and depression are the most common reaction. Manifestations of anxiety and depression can be catagorized as somatic, cognitive, affective and behavioural as shown in Table 21.1. People often, but not always, experience some symptoms from each category.

Box 21.1 Pre- and Post-Test HIV Counselling

Pre- and post-test HIV counselling has two major aims. The first is to prevent further transmission of HIV by helping the individuals maintain safer sex and drug using behaviours. The second is to minimize the distress attached to a positive result. These aims are intricately related, so counselling aimed towards supporting an individual may well also benefit society in general.

Counselling involves more than simply giving information. Although the provision of accurate, up-to-date information about HIV infection is essential, the counselling process enables people to relate relevant information to their own behaviours and circumstances, and so help them to understand their own level of risk and make informed decisions of whether to test. This can be achieved by guiding people through the problem solving process, i.e. fact finding, exploring options, decision making, accepting consequences, finding practical assistance and providing further support as necessary. The use of leaflets or videos to provide information may be beneficial, but cannot replace discussion.

Pre-test counselling aims to ensure that individuals are fully informed about the meaning of a positive test result and its implications, and are prepared to cope should their result be positive.

Post-test counselling provides an opportunity for patients who test positive to explore ways in which quality of life can be enhanced while living with HIV infection, and for discussion of the prevention of further spread of infection.

The need for confidentiality is of prime importance in testing for HIV, to maintain people's trust, to respect their rights, and to prevent discrimination against them.

Tasks Involved

Pre-test Counselling

- explain what the test means and what it does not tell
- alert to possible ramifications of a positive test result
- assess personal risk
- discuss the advantages and disadvantages of knowing HIV status
- develop coping strategies
- identify social support, who to tell and why to be circumspect
- educate in safer sex and safer injection practices
- explain confidentiality of test result.

Post-test Counselling

- focus on the reason for the session
- give clear, simple, unambiguous information
- clarify the meaning of an HIV positive test
- expect emotional reactions: shock, denial, anxiety, anger
- address individual's immediate concerns
- identify and address issues of immediate importance, e.g. who to and who not to tell; who to use for support; safer sex and injecting practices
- provide a lifeline, e.g. 24-hour helpline telephone number and written information about HIV, giving details of services available
- give a further appointment within a few days.

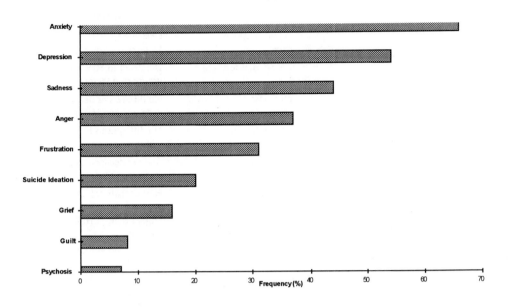

Figure 21.1

Psychological reactions and stage of infection

Psychological symptoms have been documented at all stages of infection. Following a positive HIV antibody test, patients commonly voice many fears and often show symptoms of psychological distress. To prepare people for receiving a positive test result and minimize associated distress, the former Department of Health and Social Security recommended that pre- and post-test counselling (see Box 21.1) be available for all those considering having an HIV antibody test (DHSS, 1985).

It can be seen from Table 21.2 that, although the time of testing is frequently associated with high anxiety, for those who test negative this distress is soon dissipated (Perry *et al,*. 1990). For those who test positive there frequently follows a period of gradual adjustment during which distress and psychological symptoms decrease. However, living with HIV is rarely uneventful; further changes can occur, such as a deterioration in physical health, an AIDS diagnosis, a lowered CD4 count, a high viral load reading or the suggestion that anti-retroviral medication be started. Such events can increase psychological distress, particularly when several occur simultaneously (Hedge *et al.*, 1992).

Table 21.2 Psychological Distress and Stage of HIV Disease

Study (Sample)	Stage of HIV disease	Psychological Distress
Ostrow et al. (1989) (gay men)	HIV test: report negative report positive	Decreased Increased
Perry et al. (1990)	12 months post HIV test	Unrelated to HIV status Related to pre-morbid factors
Pugh et al. (1994) (gay men)	6–12 months post HIV test	No differences between HIV negatives and HIV positives
Williams (1991) (gay men)	Asymptomatic infection	No different to HIV negative controls
Fell (1993) (gay men)	Asymptomatic infection	Anxiety declined as time from result increased
Catalan et al. (1992a) (men with haemophilia)	Asymptomatic infection	Higher than in HIV negative controls
	Symptomatic infection	Higher than in HIV negative controls Higher than in asymptomatic infection
Egan (1992) (injecting drug users)	Asymptomatic infection	No different to HIV negative controls
	Symptomatic infection	No different to HIV negative controls
Chuang et al. (1989) (gay men)	AIDS	Less than in those with pre-AIDS symptomatic disease
Hedge et al. (1992) (gay men)	All	Unrelated to stage of infection

The inconsistencies in reported results, such as whether more distress is seen in people with AIDS or in those with pre-AIDS symptomatic disease (Table 21.1), are difficult explain with any certainty. It is clear that those who request an HIV test shows small but increased distress compare to general population samples. It also appears that injecting drug users show increased psychiatric morbidity regardless of HIV infection, to a greater extent than is seen in samples of gay men or men with haemophilia. However care has to be taken in interpreting studies such as these which use volunteer samples, where it could be that the most mentally healthy HIV-infected individuals and the least mentally robust HIV negative people participate, both seeing advantages in further attention and involvement. The former may expect increased health care, and the latter may seek reassurance that they remain uninfected (Catalan et al., 1995).

The relevance of the early studies must be assessed in a historical context. The meaning attached to HIV infection today is increasingly that of living with a chronic condition which may prove fatal in the long-term, whereas in the 1980s HIV was seen as an acute, infective condition with a life expectancy of around five years. As the profile of HIV disease changes, we must expect to see changes in its impact and the psychological distress experienced.

Suicide ideation and behaviour

Suicidal ideas are relatively common in people with HIV disease. Rabkin *et al.* (1993) found that 38 per cent of gay men with AIDS reported wanting to die at some time since their AIDS diagnosis, and 25 per cent considered suicide a viable option should life become intolerable in the future. For most, such ideas although emotionally significant, appear to be only hypothetical; for some, an act of deliberate self harm will follow. Reports by Marzuk *et al.* (1988) of a 36-fold increase in relative risk of suicide in men with AIDS in New York, and of Gala *et al.* (1992) of an increase in suicides amongst HIV-positive deaths, especially in those with histories of attempted suicide, are consistent with data linking other serious physical illnesses such as cancer within increased risk of suicide (Fox *et al.*, 1982; Allebeck and Bolund, 1991). Studies outside the US (e.g. Pugh *et al.*, 1993; Wedler, 1991) also noticed an increase, albeit lower, suicide risk (10–11 times). However, the methodological problems encountered in assessing the incidents of suicide in any population are enormous; many authors, e.g. Pugh *et al.* (1993) highlight the misclassification and under-reporting of probable cases.

Although the time of testing has been linked with increased thoughts of suicide (Perry, Jacobsberg and Fishman, 1990a), the potential suicide risk of people with HIV infection is high at all times, as many stressors which are associated with an increased suicide risk, e.g. life events, depression, social isolation and cumulative stress, have been documented in those with HIV disease (Paykel, Prusoff and Myers, 1975; Brown, 1979; Slater and Depue, 1981; Schneider *et al.*, 1991). As most carers for people with HIV disease will at some time be faced by individuals contemplating or having attempted suicide, it is important that the risk of suicidal behaviour is recognized and that appropriate care is provided.

Stress, coping skills and social support

A number of models have been proposed to explain how psychological and physical dysfunction are related to induced stress. For example, Lazarus and Folkman (1984) conceptualize coping as 'constantly changing cognitive and behavioural efforts to manage external and/or internal demands that are appraised as taxing or exceeding the resources of the person', and that stress occurs when the perceived biological, psychological and social resources available are not sufficient to meet the demands of the situation. It is well documented that stress, or non-coping, is frequently accompanied by various emotional reactions such as fear, anxiety, depression and anger.

Lazarus and Folkman's model suggests that the costs and benefits of possible coping behaviours are evaluated, and that the coping behaviour perceived as most beneficial is then adopted. There is evidence that an appraisal of the threat presented by a stressor could be 'buffered' by the availability and extent of social support systems (Cohen and Wills, 1985), the individual's perceived control over the situation (Rotter, 1966) and the coping style employed (Lazarus and Folkman, 1984).

According to this model, the way people deal with HIV disease will depend upon their understanding and interpretation of the event, stresses experienced, the coping options they perceive as available, and on meditating factors such as the perceived availability of social support and the coping strategies they finally adopt.

A number of studies provide support for this model. For example, Namir (1986) described social support as being important to people with AIDS for the provision of emotional support, illness-related support and physical contact. Hedge *et al.* (1993) found that while objective measures, such as a CD4 count, were of little predictive value in identifying psychological morbidity, a self-rating of good social support contributed to a profile of psychological well-being. Neither the number of friends nor family involvement was predictive of psychological symptomatology, but the presence of a regular partner or a perceived stable group of close friends was associated with lower levels of psychological distress. About a third of the sample had no partner, and another 17 per cent reported no close friends. Thus, it can be seen that the psychological effects of having little or no significant support is clearly an issue for many individuals.

The role of precipitating factors in reactions to stress is well established (Harris and Brown, 1989). Lovett *et al.* (1993) suggested that life events increase psychological distress in people with HIV disease. Hedge *et al.* (1992), examining individuals presenting in crisis to an HIV psychology service, found the most frequently reported preceding events to be personal illness (39 per cent), bereavement (30 per cent), fears concerning disclosure of HIV status (23 per cent), issues surrounding testing (17 per cent), dilemmas concerning medication (17 per cent) and child difficulties (10 per cent). Eighty-nine per cent of crises were preceded by two or more major events or dilemmas. These data suggest that it is the cumulative stress level which leads to an inability to cope, and emphasize the need to recognize the impact of multiple, concurrent problems even if not all are directly related to HIV.

There is also evidence (Namir *et al.*, 1987; Catalan *et al.*, 1992a; Hedge *et al.*, 1993) that strategies used to cope with HIV disease affect the psychological distress levels experienced. Adaptive coping styles included active coping strategies, such as the seeking of emotional support and problem focused coping, emotional focused coping and the maintenance of a high level of self-esteem. Increased denial, emotional and behavioural disengagement, hopelessness and less positive reframing of experiences were associated with increased psychological morbidity (Leserman, Perkins and Evans, 1992; Kurdek and Siesty, 1990; Lovett *et al.*, 1993).

Stress and the immune system

A key question is whether behaviour or mental health functioning are co-factors in the progression to symptomatic disease, Kemeny *et al.* (1990) linked depression with a steeper drop in CD4 cells, while Perry, Jacobsberg and Fishman (1990b) found that the association between anxiety following the death of a partner and the CD4 count was only transitory. Solomon and Temoshok (1987) reported a better immune profile to be associated with a sense of control over life. However, Temoshok (1988) found a positive relationship between psychological distress and total white cell count – an effect in the opposite direction to that expected. This discrepancy could be attributable to numerous confounding factors, such as susceptibility to infection, or methodological problems, such as the choice of measures of immune function and psychological well-being (see Green and Hedge, 1991), which beset such investigation in a clinical population. Consequently the issue remains a major challenge.

Summary

Psychological distress in response to HIV infection has been documented at all stages of disease. Although most studies have reported on homosexual men, there is evidence that mood disturbance is widespread. Distress can be precipitated by events such as physical illness or bereavement. The level of cumulative stress experienced seems to be important. Suicide can be a risk as many predisposing factors are present in the lives of those who are HIV positive. Identification of 'buffers' such as active coping skills and social support suggests possible avenues for psychological interventions aimed at minimizing stress. It is not yet established whether psychological dysfunction affects the rate of progression to symptomatic disease.

Psychological Intervention Strategies

Given the high levels of psychological distress experienced by individuals with HIV disease, we need to consider ways of minimizing the effects of stressors. In this section I shall explore a cognitive-behavioural model, describe some intervention studies, and consider some common issues and dilemmas which can lead to distress.

Cognitive-behavioural model

There is a substantial body of evidence which suggests that therapy based on Beck's cognitive-behavioural model of treatment (Beck, 1976) can benefit those with psychological symptomatology. This model rests on three assumptions:

- thoughts determine emotions and behaviour
- unrealistic and negative thoughts lead to emotional disorder
- decreasing unrealistic and negative thoughts, and increasing realistic positive thoughts reduce emotional symptomatology.

A common misapprehension is that cognitive behaviour therapy is simply the encouragement of positive thinking. In fact it comprises a number of techniques which address dysfunctional cognitions and behaviours within a structured therapy session (Table 21.3). For example, because many realities for those with HIV infection are negative, the technique of 'decatastrophization' is used. This is a process which attempts to separate the reality from the accompanying global negative feelings, and allow the person to explore coping alternatives, through 'positive reframing'. A thought such as 'I'll never be well enough to return to work' may be realistic when expressed by an individual with HIV disease. If the corollary is 'so I'll never be happy again', then thought depressive could result, whereas the follow-up thought 'so I'll have plenty of time for reading' can be part of a positive, coping strategy. Thus decatastrophization and positive reframing can play a major role in preventing a severe depressive or anxiety response.

Table 21.3 Cognitive-behavioural Intervention

Relaxation training and breathing exercises
Activity scheduling
Thought stopping
Reality testing
Decatastrophization
Positive reframing
Problem solving
Development of long-term and intermediate goals

The problem solving approach aims to support individuals in making informed decisions about their present difficulties, and to equip them with the general skills and strategies necessary for dealing with future problems (Hawton and Kirk, 1989; Selwyn and Antoniello, 1993).

Intervention studies

Although there are many reports of high levels of psychological distress and psychiatric symptomatology in people with HIV infection, there is only limited literature on intervention studies.

George (1988) examined patients with HIV disease 6–12 months after individual, cognitive-behavioural interventions. She found a significant reduction in distress and sustained improvements in anxiety, and depression. Similarly, Hedge *et al.* (1990) reported increases in self-esteem and decreases in anxiety and depression following an intervention aimed at increasing coping skills. A number of group interventions have been successful in reducing stress, improving coping skills and improving quality of life (Fawzy, Namir and Wolcott, 1989; Moulton *et al.*, 1990; Lamping *et al.*, 1993; Kelly *et al.*, 1993). Hedge and Glover (1990) showed that an educational group not only provided information, but also relieved distress and enhanced mutual support.

Box 21.2 Confidentiality and Disclosure

All physicians have an obligation to respect their patient's privacy by preserving their confidences. In the case of HIV, which is spread by specific sexual and drug using behaviours, an argument has been made for the identification of those infected in order to allow those who are uninfected to remain so, and thus limit and eventually eradicate the epidemic. How should individual rights be balanced against public health needs?

Every patient has the right to confidentiality, and the stigma attached to HIV disease increases the need for confidential information to remain within the HIV care team. It is important that the patient understands the need for all members of the multidisciplinary care team to be aware of his or her HIV status and other relevant information, i.e. is made aware of the limits of confidentiality. Ethical problems can arise when a patient refuses to tell a person who is at continuing risk of exposure (such as a sexual partner where unsafe sex is being practised). Experience shows that breaking confidentiality usually does not solve the problem as patients take their care elsewhere, and are unlikely to disclose such information a second time. When confidentiality is respected there is less reason for difficulties to be hidden and for problems to remain unsolved (Pinching, 1994).

Specific issues and dilemmas

Although most psychological interventions are directed at increasing the coping skills of individuals with HIV disease, some issues and dilemmas which may need the support of social care professionals (Hedge *et al.*, 1992) require a special mention and are discussed next. The rights to privacy and confidentiality are considered in Box 21.2.

Discussion point

° Sometimes the dilemmas encountered can be extremely complex. For example, a social worker who had been involved in the rehousing of the family of a man with HIV infection discovered that his wife did not know his HIV status and that she was planning another child once rehoused. Do you think that the woman should be told of her husband's HIV infection or should confidentiality be maintained? If the man died, should confidentiality be maintained after his death? Devise a plan which aims to protect the wife and possible child whilst maintaining the man's confidentiality.

Child-bearing issues

The reported rate of transmission of HIV from mother to child (vertical transmission) varies widely with higher rates seen in the developing world. Other factors increasing the likelihood of vertical transmission are the mother having advanced disease, having a lower CD4 count and breastfeeding the new-born. The European Collaborative Study (1992) reported a vertical transmission rate of 14.4 per cent compared with a rate of 39 per cent in Zambia and Zaire (Hira *et al.*, 1989; Ryder *et al.*, 1988).

The decision of whether to have a baby or to continue with a pregnancy may be difficult to make. The possible negative consequences of child- bearing are:

- an infected, maybe sick child
- a child who dies
- guilty parents
- parents who are too sick to care for the child
- parents who die leaving an orphan
- an adverse effect on the pregnant woman's health.

For these reasons, termination of pregnancy is available for women who are HIV positive. Not all women decide to forgo children; for some, childlessness would be an additional loss to bear, and for others bearing a child avoids negative, cultural reactions directed towards childless men and women.

Recent studies have indicated the effectiveness of caesarean sections (European Collaborative Study, 1994) and of an anti-retroviral drug, zidovudine (AZT) in reducing the incidence of transmission of HIV from mother to baby (Conner *et al.*, 1994). A trial in which women received zidovudine during both pregnancy and labour, and the baby received zidovudine following the birth, showed the infant infection rate to be 8.3 per cent compared with 25.5 per cent in a placebo control group (Conner *et al.*, 1994). Fears of the long-term effects of this treatment on the children (as yet unknown) and the chance of developing zidovudine resistant virus themselves leads to some women to decline the offer of drug interventions during pregnancy.

The possibility of reducing the number of infected infants has led to an increased debate about HIV testing in an ante-natal setting. Some physicians now endorse the mandatory testing of all pregnant women, with or without their consent, while others favour targeting those seen to be at high risk, e.g. injecting drug users and those who are from or may have had sex with a partner from a high risk area overseas such as sub-Saharan Africa.

As testing for HIV in a pregnant woman not only has implications for the baby but also for the woman, her partner and her relationship, it is important to ensure that she is granted the same rights and has the same opportunities for receiving pre- and post-test counselling as men and women seeking an HIV test in other settings. Although a policy of offering an HIV test and counselling to all pregnant women may not be cost effective in terms of the number of infant infections prevented, selective targeting of at risk women is likely to miss some women who are positive, and may well antagonize those who realize that they have been targeted.

When the HIV test is seen to be offered to all women as part of a normal, ante-natal health screen, it is usually found to be acceptable (Barbacci, Repke and Chaissan, 1991; Meadows *et al.*, 1993b). Counselling support at this time will help those with positive test results to maintain their self-esteem, address safer sex and relationship issues, and make informed choices about dilemmas such as continuing with the pregnancy, whether to take zidovudine and whether to have a caesarean section. Although most of the literature on child-bearing focuses on women, the desire to parent is seen in both men and women, heterosexual and gay (Sherr and Hedge, 1989), so access to counselling needs to be available to both prospective parents.

Discussion point

   ° Consider the case for imposing mandatory HIV testing on all pregnant women in order to protect the health of the offspring by implementation of anti-retroviral treatment programmes for mothers, birth by caesarean section and prevention of breast feeding. Should the rights of parents be superseded by the rights of their born or unborn offspring?

Children and families

Around one million children are now infected with HIV world-wide; mother to child transmission accounting for more than 90 per cent of infections. The patterns of illness seen in children with AIDS differ slightly from those seen in adults. The definition of paediatric AIDS (CDC, 1987) has been changed to include a wide range of serious bacterial infections. Neurological changes are often seen, which range from mild developmental delays, through failure to reach milestones, to progressive encephalopathy.

In some children, the rapid progressors, symptomatic illness is seen in the first few months of life. For these, prognosis is poor. Others, the slow progressors, may be free from major symptoms for some years. Those who reach school age before experiencing any HIV related problems will probably be aware of their illness and of any secrecy surrounding it. There is also more chance that their parents will be ill or dying by this time. All children, both those infected and uninfected siblings, who observe their parents becoming weak and unable to care for them may be disturbed and distressed. Seeing children in distress can increase the distress of parents. A thorough assessment of the concerns and needs of all family members may be required to determine what psychological support and practical assistance is required to improve their quality of life.

The multiple difficulties experienced when family members are ill frequently leads to social care professional involvement. Issues which commonly need to be considered are:

- uncertainty of prognosis (parents and children)
- confidentiality of HIV status or disclosure (to whom)
- explanations for the children
- coping with multiple loss
- planning for the future.

It has generally been found (Woolley *et al.*, 1989) that children cope best with illness and death in the family when they are given age-appropriate explanations. This may be hard for parents who are trying to maintain a sense of normality and prefer secrecy, but support with adopting a 'problem solving' approach may enable parents to make decisions of when and what to tell, and help them answer children's questions (Salter Goldie, De Matteo and King, 1997). With support and security children can cope with many distressing experiences (Melvin, 1996).

Provision for children's well-being while parents are unable to care for them or after their deaths, needs to be made. Setting up a package of care before there is a need can be helpful, for example by identifying and meeting a foster family. This enables a new relationship to be established before the child has to cope with a dying parent (Melvin, 1996). Reassurance to parents that their children are well looked after can allow them to give more attention to their own health care. Sadness and guilt that children will grow up not understanding why their parents died can be alleviated by encouraging parents to leave letters, tapes and momentos to be opened when children are older.

A report from the Children and Family AIDS Task Force (1993) suggests that services for families with HIV need to be well co-ordinated, comprehensive, family-centred and, when possible, community-based. Social care professionals often have the important but difficult task of keeping the family together at this time, and may need to be co-ordinators when a formal family service does not exist.

Injecting drug users

As HIV can be transmitted by sharing needles and syringes as well as by sexual behaviours, users need to understand safer injecting behaviours as well as safer sexual practices. There is good evidence (Stimpson, 1991) that, with the availability of needle exchange centres, where clean needles and syringes are readily available, less unsafe injecting behaviour now occurs, although injectors may still share 'works' with their regular partners (Klee, 1993, 1997). Less change has been seen in the sexual behaviours of injecting drug users; many still have unprotected penetrative sex with their regular partners (Stimpson, 1991; Derren *et al.*, 1993).

Individuals who inject drugs and have HIV disease face all the difficulties associated with their HIV and further problems related to their drug use. Gala *et al.* (1993) found that drug users showed a higher pre-HIV psychological morbidity and frequently experienced worse social circumstances (Chiswick *et al.*, 1992), so provision for mental health involvement is essential. As the lifestyle of injecting drug users can be irregular and associated with activities that they might not want to divulge, there is often less uptake of regular medical services. An increase in uptake of HIV and other medical services has been shown when these are linked to drug treatment services (Brettle, 1990; Catalan and Goos, 1991). Where this is not possible, it is essential that there is close collaboration between all medical, social and drug using services in order to optimize care.

Prisons

In prisons HIV can be spread by drug use or sexual activity (Bird *et al.*, 1993). Although the need for prisoners to have access to mental health services and drug treatment programmes has been recognized (WHO, 1990b), these are not always available. Regulations often prevent prisoners having access to clean needles and syringes or condoms, but some prisons unofficially recognize the problems of drugs and make bleach available for cleaning needles. Many prisons have no facilities for programmes educating prisoners about HIV, sex and drugs. When available, these have been shown useful in increasing behavioural intentions to adopt safer behaviours.

Management of neurological problems

HIV-related brain disorder can be the result of the direct effect of HIV on the central nervous system, or due to secondary complications of immune deficiency, such as opportunistic infections and tumours or nutritional deficiencies, drug toxicity, electrolyte imbalance, hypoxia, impaired liver or kidney function. In many cases, improvement of cognitive function is found when the cause is treated. Especially in the later stages of HIV disease, cognitive and behavioural changes may be seen which cannot be completely reversed. In some instances, cognitive dysfunction is a result of major depression, and not infrequently a mood disturbance and an organic dysfunction coexist. This makes the differentiation of functional from organic illness difficult. The identification by neuropsychological testing of cognitive functions which have remained intact and those which show deficits can be useful in guiding the management of the patient. High dose zidovudene has been shown to confer short term improvement in the cognitive performance of people with HIV associated dementia (Tozzi *et al.*, 1993; Sidtis *et al.*, 1993). The efficacy of other anti-retrovirals such as stavudine (d4T), in managing neurological problems is now being investigated. Over the past ten years the prevalence and incidence of HIV associated dementia has fallen. Many have attributed this decrease to the introduction of zidovudine (Portegies, 1994; Janssen *et al.*, 1992) but it could be a secondary gain from the improved physical health seen in those with symptomatic disease, consequent on other changes in treatment which occurred around the same time.

There remains a small but significant number of people (4–15 per cent) with advanced HIV disease who have HIV associated dementia. They may experience problems with memory loss, slowing of thought, apathy, social withdrawal and difficulties with balance, clumsiness, writing, planning and problem solving.

Care of those who are severely impaired can be onerous. The regular hospital and community care services are frequently unable to provide the necessary care for people who are unable to live alone and need help with the tasks of everyday living. Provision of social and emotional support for the carers, family and friends is of great importance (Ostrow *et al.*, 1988). If residential care is not available or is not desired by the family and caregivers, attendance at day centres and intermittent respite care can help to maintain a person in the community.

Discussion point

- ° If a smoker you have been working with develops HIV dementia and severe memory loss and demands to stay in his or her own home rather than move to sheltered accommodation or have a live-in carer, what do you do? Who would be responsible if there was a fire and someone was killed?

Coping with grief

There is no 'correct' way to grieve, nor any set time after which the grieving should have ceased. Models of the normal grieving process (Kubler-Ross, 1970; Parkes, 1970, 1972; Worden, 1992) have been built from descriptions of common reactions to death and the tasks, stages or phases which individuals typically encounter while learning to live with the realities of death (see Chapter 24). However, the reaction of an individual to a particular death will be affected by the circumstances in which it occurs. Consideration of the models suggest that some ways of coping with death may be more beneficial than others.

Bereavement in the context of HIV presents some unique features. For example, those who die are usually young and the highest rate of mortality is in the age range of 20– 40 years. Furthermore, death is often the last of many losses, as HIV infection may have already brought the loss of relationships, sex, employment, control, a future, hope and health. In addition, those bereaved by HIV frequently are themselves HIV-positive. If bereavement or its psychological sequelae has an adverse effect on the immune system, then it could prove hazardous to health. Folkman *et al.* (1994) have described the patterns of distress experienced by caregivers during illness and death. They found that prior to the death of a partner, HIV positive caregivers were less distressed than those not infected, while after the death the infected partners showed more distress. A possible explanation is that those who are HIV positive view the experience as a model of their own death. First, they empathize with the patient; afterwards they realize they may face a similar experience alone, as their own infection makes it less likely that they will find a new partner. Lennon, Martin and Dean (1990) report the intensity of grief during bereavement to be related to the involvement in caretaking during end-stage disease, and to the adequacy of practical and emotional support given to the caregiver during this time.

Most people experiencing grief will not need professional help; the support of friends and relatives and general guidance from the social or health care providers who have given support to the recently deceased will be adequate. Reassurance that it is natural to grieve, together with an explanation that this may involve exploring positive and negative feelings about the deceased, dealing with emotions such as anger, guilt and hopelessness and anticipation of the problems and necessary changes which the death may bring about, can be useful. For people bereaved through HIV, peer support groups for partners, friends and relatives, organized by volunteers and community groups, complement services provided by health professionals and social workers.

When the stigma attached to HIV leads people to fear rejection and so hide their losses, isolate themselves and not make use of available social support, there is an increased chance of abnormal grief response. Abnormal grieving is usually categorized by grief reactions of abnormal intensity which persist over time with little evidence of change. Guided mourning (Mawson, Marks and Ramn, 1981), increasing adaptive coping skills and increasing appropriate social support can assist the grief process. Occasionally, a death will precipitate a frank psychiatric response. Appropriate psychiatric intervention, e.g. for a depressed or psychotic state, as well as grief management will then be necessary.

Another facet of AIDS-related bereavement, the social loss, was described by Dean *et al.* (1988), who reported multiple bereavement in a large cohort of gay men in San Francisco. Ninety-five per cent of the sample reported HIV-related loss, with an average of 6.2 HIV-related deaths each. With increasing numbers of AIDS related deaths, McKusick (1991) reported increasing distress involving:

- psychological and emotional numbness
- shrinking away from friends and resources
- symptoms of complicated bereavement (inordinate guilt, calcified anger, rage, indifference)
- depression.

He described a cycle of negative impact: deaths led to a decrease in the available social support which resulted in higher levels of depression in those with HIV disease, which had the effect of less self-care which increased the likelihood of mortality, etc. To combat the effects of multiple bereavement, McKusick suggested the adoption of a community-wide coping programme to enable people to stay involved rather than distance themselves from the problem, and to find some form of social support which promotes discharge of anxieties and renewal of vigour. The use of public ritual, e.g. annual candlelight ceremonies to mourn the people lost to HIV, can support communities in reaffirming their capability to overcome these feelings of loss and to remain empowered.

Summary

Intervention strategies which address dysfunctional cognitions and behaviours have been found useful in reducing psychological symptomatology in people with HIV disease. Of major importance are interventions aimed at enhancing adaptive coping skills and enabling people to identify and use social support. Particular input is needed by people living with HIV in a family setting or making decisions concerning child-bearing. Social care professionals frequently work in both hospital and community settings, and with both the medical teams looking after the parents and those looking after the children. This enables them to take a key-worker role in alerting the appropriate professional to a family's difficulties so that relevant support can be accessed.

The management of individuals with neurological problems can be considerable, and support may also be required by the carers. Social workers and other professionals may be involved in the co-ordination of appropriate residential or day care for people with HIV associated dementia, or in the provision of respite care for their carers.

Burnout and Coping in Health Carers

This last section considers the issue of caring for the carers by discussing the phenomenon of burnout and some strategies to minimize it. Hortsman and McKusick (1986) reported health care workers to experience enormous stress when caring for persons with HIV disease. Dealing with profound physical and mental deterioration in patients led to feelings of helplessness, frustration and inadequacy at being unable to cure. Carers showed symptoms of anxiety, depression, overwork, fatigue, stress, fear of death and decreased interest in sex. Such occupational stress has been documented in a variety of health care professionals, particularly in those caring for people who have terminal illnesses (Vachon, 1987).

Burnout

The term 'burnout' is used to characterize a syndrome which can develop when stresses are not recognized and addressed (Maslach, 1982). Maslach and Jackson (1981) defined burnout as a combination of emotional exhaustion, depersonalization and a reduced sense of personal accomplishment.

Factors which have been identified as increasing the levels of stress staff experienced while working with people with HIV disease are shown in Table 21.4. The question of whether AIDS presents unique burdens to health care staff is not easily answered (Bennett, Miller and Ross, 1993). Many of the factors contributing to stress are experienced by care workers in other fields such as oncology and cystic fibrosis. However, Bennett, Michie and Kippax (1991) found that the greater patient dependency in HIV units necessitated the need for greater contact between the nurse and patient, and increased the emotional intensity of the work. Bennett et al. (1992) investigated factors which could be associated with burnout. They found grief not to be predictive of burnout, but that greater work-related grief was experienced when carers identified closely with patients. Burnout was associated with an absence of internal coping strategies, and with a reliance on external coping strategies, e.g. excessive alcohol or drug usage. Older, more experienced carers were less likely to experience burnout.

Strategies to minimize burnout

To minimize burnout, strategies are needed to focus on both the individual's coping skills and on the organization's attempt to minimize stressors (see Chapter 1). In line with the findings that intensity of work rather than overall length of time working on an HIV unit contributed to stress levels (Hortsman and McKusick, 1986; Bennett, Michie and Kippax, 1991), time out techniques (e.g. rotating with staff in the genito-urinary medicine clinic) could be adopted. To utilize the coping strategies of those who are older and who have more experience, increasing the opportunities for informal sharing of problems might be beneficial. Alternatively, the provision of staff support groups could facilitate exchange of information and coping strategies between experienced and inexperienced staff.

When patients are seen for a long time by a relatively small group of care staff, close emotional involvement with patients frequently occurs. Specific training in strategies aimed at expressing warmth and empathy while maintaining professional boundaries has been suggested to reduce emotional stress (Bennett *et al.*, 1991).

To facilitate carers in the above, organizational change may be required (Macks and Abrams, 1992). This may include

- assessment of job requirements and available resources
- task planning
- staff development, education and training
- enhancing communication systems
- provision of formal support
- enhancing informal communications and appreciation
- mechanisms
- reviewing job structure and workload.

Attention to either the organization or to individual coping strategies without attention to the other is likely to be ineffectual as stress is a product of both.

Table 21.4 Factors Increasing Staff Stress

1. *Characteristics of patients*

   Younger age

   Under stress

   Dependent

2. *Characteristics of staff*

   Younger age

   Identification with patient

   Involvement with patient

   External coping resources (e.g. alcohol, food, retail therapy)

   Lack of internal coping resources (e.g. knowledge, skills)

3. *Characteristics of work environment*

   Intense patient contact

   Specific hospitals

   Origanizational stressors

   Disagreements over patient treatment

   Stigma of working with HIV disease

Summary

Although it may not be possible to remove the prime stressors – sick patients and their needs – there are ways to lessen the stresses attached to caring for people with HIV disease. Caring for carers requires resources, but this may prove more cost effective than the increased sickness rate and high turnover of staff which can be associated with burnout.

Summary

The emotional reactions to infection with HIV are well documented. HIV is associated with multiple stressors including physical illness, bereavement and medication dilemmas. An individual's ability to cope is associated with the cumulative stress experienced and the perceived available social support. Further work on the interaction between stressors and the functioning of the immune system is clearly needed.

Although there are many questions still to be answered concerning the effect that psychological intervention has on long-term coping behaviours, there is evidence that strategies which develop coping skills and which enable people to mobilize social support are beneficial in the short term. In relation to this, it is important to recognize the effect which bereavement from HIV related deaths is having on communities, traditionally those who have provided social support.

The magnitude of the epidemic, with no end in sight, has resulted in high levels of stress for carers. To minimize the impact of this stress, it appears to be necessary to address the coping skills of carers and to make supportive managerial and organizational changes.

Seminar Questions

1. If you were asked to care for patients with HIV disease, what would be your concerns? Explore your thoughts and feelings concerning HIV infection, emotional distress, homosexuality, and injecting drug use.

2. When do you think that issues concerning death and dying should be raised with a patient? Discuss how this might best be done.

3. Plan a psychological support service for people with HIV disease for a local clinic. What are the practical difficulties you are likely to encounter? How could you overcome them?

Further Readings

Catalan, J., Burgess, A. and Klimes, I. (eds) (1995) *Pyschological Medicine of HIV Infection.* Oxford: Oxford Medical Publications.
A very useful reference book, covering all aspects of psychological and psychiatric manifestations of HIV infection.

Green, J. and McCreaner, A. (eds) (1996) *Counselling in HIV Infection and AIDS (2nd ed.).* Oxford: Blackwell Science.
An easily read text which gives guidance with examples on useful counselling support for people with HIV disease.

Hawton, K., Salkovskis, P.M., Kirk, J. and Clark, D.M. (eds) (1989) *Cognitive Behavioural Therapy for Psychiatric Problems: A Practical Guide.* Oxford: Oxford University Press.

An easily understood, comprehensive account of cognitive-behavioural techniques. The chapters on problem solving, anxiety and depression are particularly recommended.

McKusick, L. (ed.) (1986) *What To Do About AIDS.* Berkeley, CA: University of California Press. Although written early in the AIDS epidemic, this easily readable book gives useful insights into the issues and problems experienced by those with HIV disease and identifies some useful interventions.

References

Allebeck, P. and Bolund, C. (1995) 'Suicide and suicide attemps in cancer patients.' *Pyschological Medicine, 21,* 979–984.

Baldeweg, T., Catalan, J., Lovett, E., Gruzelier, J., Ricco, M. and Howbine, D. (1995) 'Long-term zidovudine reduces neurocognitive deficits in HIV-1 infection.' *AIDS, 9,* 589–596.

Barbacci, M., Repke, J. and Chaissen, R. (1991) 'Routine prenatal screening for HIV infection', *Lancet, 337,* 709–711.

Beck, A.T. (1976) *Cognitive Therapy and the Emotional Disorder.* New York: International Universities Press.

Bennett, L., Michie, P. and Kippax, S. (1991) 'Qualitative analysis of burnout and its associated factors in AIDS nursing.' *AIDS Care, 3,* 181–192.

Bennett, L., Kelaher, M. and Ross, M. (1992) 'Links between burnout and bereavement in HIV/AIDS professionals.' *Quality of Life Satellite Symposium: VIII International Conference on AIDS,* Amsterdam.

Bennett Miller Ross (1993) *Health Workers with AIDS: Research, Interventions and Current Issues in Burnout and Response.* Reading, Berks: Harwood Academic Publishers.

Bird, A., Gore, S. Burns. S. and Duggie, J. (1993) 'Study of infection with HIV and related risk factors in a young offenders' institution.' *British Medical Journal 307,* 228–231.

Brettle, R. (1990) 'Clinical issues of injecting drug users related to HIV.' In I.V.D. Weller (ed.), *Aspects of HIV Management of Drug Users.* Theale: Colwood House Medical Publications.

Brown, G.W. (1979) 'The social etiology of depression - London studuies.' In R.A. Depue (ed.) *The Psychobiology of the Depressive Disorders: Implications for the Effects of Stress.* San Diego, CA: Academic Press.

Catalan, J., Burgess, A. and Klimes, I. (1995) *Psychological Medicine of HIV Infection.* Oxford: Oxford University Press.

Catalan, J., Klimes, I., Day, A., Garrod, A., Bond, A. and Gallwey, J. (1992a) 'The psychological impact of HIV infection in gay men.' *British Journal of Psychiatry, 161,* 774–778.

Catalan, J., Klimes, I., Bond, A., Day, A., Garrod, A. and Rizza, C. (1992b) 'The psychological impact of HIV infection in men with haemophilia: controlled investigation and factors associated with psychiatric morbidity.' *Journal Psychosomatic Research, 36,* 409–16.

Catalan, J. and Goos, C. (1991) 'European symposium on AIDS and drug misuse: providing care for HIV infected drug users.' *AIDS Care, 3,* 203–205.

Centres for Disease Control (1994) 'Strategies to reduce vertical transmission of HIV-1.' *Communicable Disease Report Weekly, 281* 127–130.

Centres for Disease Control (1981) 'Pneumocystis pneumonia.' *Morbidity and Mortality Weekly Report, 30,* 250–252.

Centres for Disease Control (1987) 'Classification system for human immunodeficiency virus (HIV) infection in children under 13 years of age' *Morbidity and Morality Weekly Report, 36,* 225–236.

Chiswick, A., Egan, V., Brettle, B. and Goodwin, G. (1992) 'The Endinburgh cohort of HIV positive drug users: who are they and who cares for them.' *AIDS Care, 4,* 421–424.

Chuang, H.T., Devins, G.M., Hunsley. J. and Gill, M.J. (1989) 'Psychosocial distress and well-being among gay and bisexual men with Human Immunodeficiency Syndrome.' *American Journal Psychiatry, 146,* 876–880.

Cohen, S. and Wills, T.A. (1985) 'Stress, social support and the buffering hypothesis.' *Psychological Bulletin, 98,* 310–357.

Conner, E.M., Sperling, R.S., Gelber, R., Kiselev, P., Scott, G., O'Sullivan, M., VanDyke, R., Bey, M., Shearer, W., Jacobson, R., Jimenez, E., O'Neill, E., Bazin, B., Delfraissy, J-F., Culnana, M., Coombs, R., Elkins, M., Moye, J., Stratton, P. and Balsey, J. (1994) 'Reproduction of maternal-infant transmission of human immunodeficiency virus type 1 with zidovudene treatment. Pediatric AIDS Clinical Trials Group Protocol 076 Study Group.' *New England Journal of Medicine 331,* 1173–1180.

Dean, L., Hall, W.E. and Martin, J.L. (1988) 'Chronic and intermittent AIDS related bereavement in a panel of homosexual men in New York City.' *Journal of Palliative Care, 4,* 54–57.

Derren, S., Paone, D., Friedman, S., Neigus, A., Des Jarlais, D. and Ward, T. (1993) 'IDU's and and HIV/AIDS: interventions, behaviour change and policy.' *AIDS Care ,5*, 503–514.

DHSS (1985) 'Information for doctors concerning the introduction of the HTLV III antibody test.' *AIDS Booklet 2*. London: DHSS.

Egan, V., Brettle, R. and Goodwin, G. (1992) 'The Edinburgh cohort of HIV positive drug users: patterns of cognitive impairment in relation to progression of disease.' *British Journal of Psychiatry, 161*, 522–531.

European Collaborative Study (1992) 'Rise factors for mother-to-child transmission of HIV-1.' *Lancet, 539*, 1007–1012.

European Collaborative Study (1994) 'Caesarean section and risk of vertical transmission of HIV infection.' *Lancet, 343*, 1464–1467.

Fawzy, F.I., Namir, S. and Wolcott, D.L. (1989) 'Structured group intervention model for AIDS patients.' *Psychiatric Medicine, 7*, 35–45.

Fell, M., Newman, S., Herns, M., Durranc, P., Manji, H., Connolly, S., McAllister, R., Weller, I. and Harrison, M. (1993) 'Mood and psychiatric disturbance in HIV and AIDS: changes over time.' *British Journal of Psychiatry, 167*, 604–610.

Folkman, S., Chesney, M., Cooke, M. Boccellari, A. and Collette, L. (1994) 'Caregiving burden in HIV-positive and HIV-negative partners of men with AIDS.' *Journal of Consulting and Clinical Psychology, 62*, 746–756.

Fox, B.H., Stanek, E.J., Boyd, S.C. and Flanney, J.T. (1982) 'Suicide rates among cancer patients.' *Connecticut Journal of Chronic Diseases, 35*, 85–100.

Gala, C., Pergami, A., Catalan, J., Durbano, F., Musicco, M., Riccio, M., Baldeweg, T. and Invernizzi, G. (1992) 'Risk of deliberate self-harm and factors associated with suicidal behaviour among asymptomatic individuals with Human Immunodeficiency Virus infection.' *Acta Psychiatrica Scandinavica, 86*, 70–75.

Gala, C., Pergami, A., Catalan, J., Durbano, F., Musicco, M., Riccio, M., Baldeweg, T. amd Invernizzi, G. (1993) 'The psychosocial impact of HIV infection in gay men, drug users and heterosexuals.' *British Journal of Psychiatry, 163*, 651–659.

George, H. (1988) 'AIDS: factors identified as helpful by patients.' *IV International Conference on AIDS*, Stockholm.

Grant, I. (1990) 'The neuropsychology of human immunodeficiency virus.' *Seminars in Neurology, 10*, 267–274.

Graham, N.M.H., Zeger, S.L., Lawrence, P., Park, L., Vermund, S., Detels, R., Rinoldo, C. and Phair, J. (1992) 'The effects on survival of early treatment of human immunodeficiency virus infection.' *New England Journal of Medicine, 326*, 1037–1042.

Green, J. and Hedge, B. (1991) 'Counselling and stress in HIV infection and AIDS.' In C. Cooper and M. Watson (eds) *Cancer and Stress: Psychological, biological and coping strategies*. Chichester: Wiley.

Harris, T. and Brown, G. (1989) 'Problem solving.' In K. Hawton, P.H. Salkovskis, J. Kirk and D.M. Clark (eds) *Cognitive Behavioural Therapy for Psychiatric Problems: A Practical Guide*. Oxford: Oxford University Press.

Hedge, B., James, S. and Green, J. (1990) 'Evaluation of focused cognitive-behavioural intervention with HIV seropositive individuals.' *VI International Conference on AIDS*, San Francisco.

Hedge, B., Sherr, L. and Green, J. (1991) 'To take or not to take antivirals?: psychological sequelae of the decision making process.' *VII International Conference on AIDS, Florence.*

Hedge, B. and Glover, L.F. (1990) 'Group intervention with HIV seropositive patients and their partners.' *AIDS Care, 2*, 147–154.

Hedge, B., Petrak, J., Sherr, L., Sichel, T., Glover, L. and Slaughter, J. (1992) 'Psychological crises in HIV infection' *VIII International AIDS Conference*, Amsterdam.

Hedge, B., Slaughter, J., Flynn, R. and Green, J. (1993) 'Coping with HIV disease: successful attributes and strategies.' *IX International Conference on AIDS*, Berlin.

Hira, S.K., Kamanga, J., Bhat, G.J. Mwale, C., Tembo, G., Luo, N. and Perine, P. (1989) 'Perinatal transmission of HIV-1 in Zambia.' *British Medical Journal 299*, 1250–1252.

Ho, D., Neumann, A., Perelson, A., Chen, W., Leonard, J. and Markowitz, M. (1995) 'Rapid turnover of plasma virions and CD4 lymphocytes in HIV-1 infection.' *Nature 375*, 123–6.

Hortsman, W. and McKusick, L. (1986) 'The impact of AIDS on the physician.' In L. McKusick (ed) *What to do about AIDS*. Berkeley, CA: University of California Press.

Janssen, R., Nwanyanwu, O., Selik, R. Stehr-Green, J. (1990) 'Epidemiology of Human Immunodeficiency Virus Encephalopathy in the US.' *Neurology, 42*, 1472–1476.

Kelly, J., Murphy, D., Bahr, G., Kalichman, S., Morgan, M., Stevenson, Y., Koot, J., Brosfeild, T. and Bernstein, T. (1993) 'Outcome of cognitive-behavioural and support brief therapies for depressed HIV infected persons.' *American Journal of Psychiatry, 150*, 1679–1686.

Kemeny, M.E., Duran, R., Taylor, S.E., Weiner, H., Visscher, B. and Fahey, J.L. (1990) 'Chronic depression predicts CD4 decline over a five year period.' *VI International Conference on AIDS*, San Francisco.

King, E. (1997) 'False horizon or new dawn?' *AIDS Treatment Update, 48/49*, 1–4.

King, M.B. (1989a) 'Prejudice and AIDS: the views and experiences of people with HIV infection.' *AIDS Care, 1*, 137–152.

King, M.B. (1989b) 'Psychological status of 192 out-patients with HIV infection and AIDS.' *British Journal of Psychiatry, 154*, 237–242.

Klee, H. (1993) 'HIV risks for women drug injectors: heroin and amphetamine users compared.' *Addiction, 88*, 1055–1062.

Klee, H. (1997) 'Amphetamine injecting women and their primary partners: an analysis of risk behaviour.' In J. Catalan, L. Sherr and B. Hedge (eds) *The Impact of AIDS: Psychological and Social Aspects of HIV Infection.* Amsterdam: Harwood Academic Press.

Kubler-Ross, E. (1970) *On Death and Dying.* London: Tavistock.

Kurdek, L. and Siesty, G. (1990) 'The nature and correlates of psychological adjustment in gay men with AIDS-related conditions.' *Journal of Applied Social Psychology, 20*, 846–860.

Lamping, D., Abrahamowicz, M., Gilmore, N., Edgar, L., Grover, S., Tsoukas, C., Falutz, J., Lalonde, R., Hamel, M. and Darsigny, R. (1993) 'A randomised controlled trial to evaluate a psychosocial intervention to improve quality of life in HIV infection.' *IX International Conference of AIDS*, Berlin.

Lazarus, R.S. and Folkman, S. (1984) *Stress, Appraisal and Coping.* New York, NY: Springer-Verlag.

Lennon, M.C., Martin, J.L. and Dean, L. (1990) 'The influence of social support on AIDS related grief reaction among gay men.' *Social Science and Medicine, 31*, 477–484.

Leserman, J., Perkins, D. and Evans, D. (1992) 'Coping with the threat of AIDS: the role of social support.' *American Journal of Psychiatry, 149*, 1514–20.

Lovett, E., Pugh, K., Baldeweg, T., Catalan, J., Riccio, H., and Burgess, A. (1993) 'Psychological morbidity in a cohort of gay men with HIV infection: role of disease stage, coping strategies and life events.' *IX International Conference on AIDS*, Berlin.

Macks, J. and Abrams, D. (1992) 'Burnout among HIV/AIDS health care providers.' In P. Volberding and M. Jacobson (eds) *AIDS Clinical Review* New York, NY: Marcel Decker.

Marzuk, P., Tierney, H., Tardiff, K., Gross, E., Morgan, E., Hsu, M. and Mann, J. (1988) 'Increased risk of suicide in patients with AIDS.' *Journal American Medical Association, 259*, 1333–1337.

Maslach, C. (1982) *Burnout: The Cost of Caring.* Englewood Cliffs, NJ: Prentice Hall.

Maslach, C. and Jackson, S.E. (1981) 'The measurement of experienced burnout.' *Journal Occupation Behaviour, 2*, 99–93.

McArthur, J.C. (1987) 'Neurologic manifestations of AIDS.' *Medicine 66*, 407–37.

McArthur, J., Hoover, D., Bacellar, H., Miller, E., Cohen, B., Becker, J. *et al.* (1993) 'Dementia in AIDS patients: incidence and risk factors.' *Neurology, 43*, 2245–52.

McKusick, L. (1991) 'Multiple loss accounts for worsening distress in a community heavily hit by AIDS.' *VII International Conference of AIDS*, Florence.

Meadows, J., Catalan, J., Singh, A. and Burgess, A. (1993a) 'Prevalence of HIV associated dementia in a central London health district in 1991.' *IX International Conference on AIDS*, Berlin.

Meadows, J., Catalan, J. and Gazzard, B. (1993b) 'HIV antibody testing in the antenatal clinic: the views of the consumers.' *Midwifery, 9*, 63–69.

Mellors, J., Rinaldo Jr, C., Gupta, P., White, R., Todd, J. and Kingsley, L. (1996a) 'Prognosis in HIV-1 infection predicted by the quantity of virus in plasma.' *Science, 272*, 1167–1170.

Mellors, J., Kingsley, L., Rinaldo, C., Todd, J., Hoo, B., Kokka, R. and Gupta, P. (1996b) 'Quantification of HIV-1 RNA in plasma predicts outcome after serocoversion.' *Annals Internal Medicine, 122*, 573–579.

Melvin, D. (1996) 'Counselling issues for children and families living with HIV infection.' In J. Green and A. McCreaner (eds) *Counselling in HIV Infection and AIDS. 2nd ed.* Oxford: Blackwell Science.

Moulton, J., Gorbuz, G., Sweet, D., Martin, R. and Dilley, J. (1990) 'Outcome evaluation of eight week educational support groups, validating the model using control group comparisons.' *VI International Conference on AIDS*, San Francisco.

Namir, S. (1986) 'Treatment issues concerning persons with AIDS.' In L. McKusick, (ed.) *What to do about AIDS.* Berkeley, CA: University of California Press.

Namir, S., Wolcott, D.L., Fawzy, F.I. and Alumbaugh, M.J. (1987) 'Coping with AIDS: psychological and health implications.' *Journal Applied Social Psychology, 17*, 309–328.

Navia, B., Jordan, B. and Price, R. (1986) 'The AIDS Dementia Complex: I clincial features.' *Archives of Neurology, 44*, 65–69.

Navia, B.A. (1990) 'The AIDS dementia complex.' In J.L. Cummings (ed) *Subcortical Dementia.* New York, NY: Oxford University Press.

Ostrow, D.M., Grant, I. and Atkinson, H. (1988) 'Assessment and management of the AIDS patient with neuropsychiatric disturbances.' *Journal Clinical Psychiatry, 49,* 14–22.

Ostrow, D., Joseph, J., Kessler, R., Soucy, J., Tal, M., Eller, M. *et al.* (1989) 'Disclosure of HIV antibody status: behavioural and mental correlates.' *AIDS Education and Prevention, 1,* 1–11.

Parkes, C. (1970) 'The first year of bereavement: a longitudinal study of the reaction of London widows to the deaths of husbands.' *Psychiatry, 33,* 444–467.

Parkes, C. (1972) *Bereavement Studies of Grief in Adult Life.* New York, NY: International Universities Press.

Paykel, E.S., Prusoff, B.A. and Myers, J.K. (1975) 'Suicide attempts and recent life events.' *Archives General Psychiatry, 32,* 327–333.

Peckham, C. and Newell, M.L. (1990) 'HIV-1 infection in mothers and babies.' *AIDS Care, 2,* 205–212.

Perry, S., Jacobsberg, L.B., Fishman, B., Weiler, P.H., Gold, J.W.M. and Frances, A.J. (1990) 'Psychological responses to serological testing for HIV.' *AIDS, 4,* 145–152.

Perry, S., Jacobsberg, L. and Fishman, B. (1990a) 'Suicide ideation and HIV testing.' *Journal American Medical Association, 263,* 679–682.

Perry, S., Jacobsberg, L.B. and Fishman, B. (1990b) 'Relationship between CD4 lymphocytes and psychosocial variables among HIV seropositive adults.' *VI International Conference on AIDS.* San Francisco.

Perakyla, A. and Bor, R. (1990) 'Interactional problems of addressing "dreaded" issues in HIV-counselling.' *AIDS Care, 2,* 325–338.

Pinching, A.J. (1994) 'AIDS: Health care ethics and society.' In R. Gillon (ed) *Principles of Health Care Ethics.* Chichester: Wiley.

Portegies (1994) 'AIDS dementia complex: a review.' *Journal Aquired Immune Deficiency Syndrome, 7,* 2, 538–549.

Pugh, K., O'Donnell, I. and Catalan J. (1993) 'Suicide and HIV disease.' *AIDS Care, 5,* 391–399.

Pugh, K., Riccio, M., Jadresic, D., Burgess, A., Baldeweg, T., Catalan, J., Lovett, E., Howbins, D., Gruzelier, J. and Thompson, C. (1994) 'A longitudinal study of the neuropsychiatric consequences of HIV-1 infection in gay men: II psychological and health status at baseline and 12 months follow-up.' *Psychological Medicine, 24,* 897–904.

Rabkin, J., Remien, R., Katoff, L. and Williams, J. (1993) 'Suicidality in AIDS long-term survivors: what is the evidence?' *AIDS Care, 5,* 401–411.

Rotter, J.B. (1996) 'Generalised expectancies for internal versus external control of reinforcement.' *Psychological Monographs, 80,* 1–28.

Ryder, R.W., Nsa, W., Hassig, S.E., Beheta, F., Rayfield, M., Ekungda, B., Nelson, A., Mulenda, U., Francis, H., Mcoandagadirwa, K., Davaihi, F., Rogers, M., Nzilambi, N., Greenberg, A., Manon, J., Quinon, T.M., Piot, P. and Curnen, J. (1988) 'Perinatal transmission of the human immunodeficiency virus type 1 to infants of serpositive women in Zaire.' *New England Journal of Medicine, 320,* 1637–1642.

Salter Goldie, R., De Matteo, D. and King, S. (1997) 'Children born to mothers with HIV/AIDS: family psycho-social issues.' In J. Catalan, L. Sherr and B. Hedge (eds) *The Impact of AIDS: Psychological and Social Aspects of HIV Infection.* Amsterdam: Harwood Academic Press.

Schneider, S.G., Taylor, S.E., Kemeny, M.E. and Hammen, C. (1991) 'AIDS related factors predictive of suicidal ideation of low and high intent among gay and bisexual men.' *Suicide and Life Threatening Behaviour, 21,* 313–328.

Selwyn, P. and Antoniello, P. (1993) 'Reproductive decision-making among women with HIV infection.' In M.A. Johnson and F.A. Johnstone, (eds) *HIV Infection in Women.* Edinburgh: Churchill Livingstone.

Sherr, L. and Hedge, B. (1989) 'On becoming a mother – counselling implications for mothers and fathers.' *WHO Conference,* Paris.

Sidtis, J., Gatsonis, C., Price, R., Singer, E., Collier, A., Richmand, D. *et al.* (1993) 'Zidovudine treatment of the AIDS dementia complex: results of a placebo-controlled trial.' *Annals of Neurology, 33,* 343–349.

Slater, J. and Depue, R.A. (1981) 'The contribution of environmental events and social support to serious suicide attempts in primary depressive disorder.' *Journal Abnormal Psychology, 90,* 275–285.

Solomon, G.F. and Temoshok, L. (1987) 'A psychoneuroimmunologic perspective in research on AIDS: questions, preliminary findings, and suggestions.' *Journal Applied Social Psychology, 17,* 285–307.

Stimpson, G. (1991) 'Risk reduction by drug users with regard to HIV infection.' *International Review of Psychiatry, 3,* 401–415.

Temoshok, L. (1988) 'Psychoimmunology and AIDS.' In T.P. Bridge (ed.) *Psychological Neuropsychiatric and Substance Abuse Aspects of AIDS.* New York: Raven Press.

The Children and Family AIDS Task Force (1993) *HIV/AIDS in Children and Families in Massachusetts: Recommendations for Policy and Program.* Report to the Commissioner of the Massachusetts Department of Public Health.

Tozzi, V., Narcisco, P., Galgani, S., Sette, P., Balestra, P., Gerace, G. *et al.* (1993) 'Effects of zidovudine in 30 patients with mild to end-stage AIDS dementia complex.' *AIDS, 7,* 683–692.

Vachon, M. (1987) *Occupational Stress in the Care of the Critcally Ill, the Dying and the Bereaved.* New York, NY: Hemisphere.

Wedler, H. (1991) 'Suicidal behaviour in the HIV infected population: the actual situation in the FRG.' In J. Bestow, M. Bellini, J. Faria and A. Kerkhof (eds) *HIV and AIDS Related Suicidal Behaviour.* Bologna, Italy: Monduzzi Editore.

Worden, J. (1992) *Grief Counselling and Grief Therapy: A Handbook for the Mental Health Practitioner.* London: Routledge.

World Health Organization (1988) *Report of the Consultation on the Neuropsychiatric Aspects of HIV Infection. Geneva: WHO Global Programme on AIDS.*

World Health Organization (1990a) *Report of the Second Consultation on the Neuropsychiatric Aspects of HIV-1 Infection.* Geneva: WHO.

World Health Organization (1990b) *Drug Abusers in Prisons: Managing Their Problems.* Regional Publication, no. 27. Copenhagen: WHO.

Williams, J., Rabkin, J., Remien, R., Gorman, J. and Ehrhardt, A. (1991) 'Multidisciplinary baseline assessment of homosexual men with HIV infection.' *Archive General Psychiatry, 48,* 124–130.

Woolley, H., Stein, A., Forrest, G. and Baum, J. (1989) 'Imparting the diagnosis of life-threatening illness in children.' *British Medical Journal, 298,* 1623–1626.

CHAPTER 22

Brain Damage

Jane M. Pierson

Introduction

Damage to the brain, most commonly as a result of a stroke or a traumatic head injury, may have profound physical and psychological effects. The physical effects, such as partial paralysis or loss of vision, are often the immediate focus of concern. However, it is the psychological effects which, in the longer term, are often the most distressing and problematic for brain damaged individuals, their relatives, and others involved in their care and management. Social care professionals, either based in hospitals or in the community, may participate in the care and rehabilitation of brain-damaged people. This may involve assessment of needs, arranging appropriate community or residential care and providing help and support for families. Some knowledge of the psychological effects of brain damage is important to dealing with such issues.

This chapter begins with an outline of some of the structures and functions of the brain. The sections which follow discuss the major causes of brain damage, some of the psychological effects of brain damage, and recovery and rehabilitation of brain-damaged people. The section dealing with the effects of brain damage focuses on stroke and head trauma, and is necessarily selective and clinically-oriented. Each of its subsections emphasizes abnormalities of behaviour which are most likely to complicate long-term care and management, and are thus most relevant to social work and related professions. Details from the case history of a head-injured person are provided in Box 22.1 to illustrate later discussion, and to provide a preliminary reminder of the profound personal tragedy which lies behind the material in this chapter.

Functional Neuroanatomy of the Brain

Figure 22.1 shows the central nervous system (the brain and spinal cord) and some of the major divisions of the brain including the *cerebellum*, the *brain stem*, the *thalamus* and the *cerebral hemispheres*.

While damage to any part of the central nervous system can result in disturbances of function, it is damage to the cerebral hemispheres and closely associated structures which is most often involved in the deficits discussed later in this chapter. The left and right cerebral hemispheres are virtually identical in structure, although, as explained below, they differ somewhat in function. As can be seen in Figure 22.2, each has an outer layer of *cortex* (part of

---

Box 22.1 Head Injury – A Personal Tragedy

In *The Man with a Shattered World* (1972), the eminent Russian neuropsychologist A.R. Luria gives a moving account of one head-injured person's struggle to surmount his difficulties over 25 years. L. Zasetsky was a college student who was called to serve in the army during the second world war and suffered a bullet wound to the brain. What follows are excerpts from Luria's description of his first meeting with Zasetsky, in a rehabilitation hospital, three months after he was wounded.

> I asked how he was getting on, and after some hesitation he replied shyly 'Okay.' What town was he from? 'At home…there's…I want to write but I just can't.' Did he have any relatives? 'There's…my mother…and also – what do you call them?' I then asked him to raise his right hand. 'Right? Right?…Left?…Where's my left hand?' He made a desperate effort to answer my questions and acutely sensed each failure. I (then) suggested 'tell me what you remember about the front.' '…the attack. I clearly remember it…for then, then…then I wounded.' It was painful for him to describe what was still fresh in his memory; he simply could not find the words with which to begin. I asked him if he knew what month it was. 'Now? what's the word?…It's, it's…May!' And he smiled. Finally he had come up with the right word. When I asked him to list the months of the year, he managed to do this with relative ease and again felt reassured. But when I asked him to list them in reverse order, he had endless difficulties. What did these desperate, futile attempts to remember mean? His response to nature was as keen as ever. He enjoyed the quiet and calm of his surroundings, listened intently to the sounds of birds, and noted how smooth the lake's surface became on a still day. He wanted very much to respond, to accomplish whatever was asked of him. Each failure only renewed his sense of loss. He had no trouble listing the months of the year. Why, then, couldn't he tell me what month precedes September, or indicate his left and right hands? Why was he unable to add two simple numbers, recognize letters, write, remember common words, or describe a picture? In short, what type of brain injury had damaged these faculties, yet spared not only his immediate grasp of the world but his will, desire, and sensitivity to experience, allowing him to evaluate each and every failure? (pp. 17–20).

---

the grey matter of the brain) and a number of subcortical structures including the *fibre tracts* (white matter). The fibre tracts can be divided into intrahemispheric fibres which interconnect areas of cortex within each hemisphere and interhemispheric fibres which run between the hemispheres. The major band of interhemispheric fibres is the *corpus callosum*. It is this structure which is severed in the split-brain or commissurotomy operation, performed to control intractable life- threatening epilepsy. A discussion of this operation and the findings of post-operative tests of split-brain patients can be found in Springer and Deutsch (1993) – see Further Reading section.

The cortex, fibre tracts and other underlying structures of each cerebral hemisphere are conventionally divided into four *lobes – occipital, temporal, parietal* and *frontal*. Within each of these lobes are areas of *primary cortex*. Figure 22.3 shows the lobes and the primary cortical areas of the left hemisphere. The locations of lobe boundaries and primary cortical areas are very similar for the right hemisphere.

Knowledge about the different functions in which each lobe is involved has been derived from a number of sources, including the study of brain-damaged people and the correlation of their behavioural deficits with areas of damage seen post-mortem or in a scan of the living brain using *Computerized-axial Tomography* (CT) or *Magnetic Resonance Imaging (MRI)* (e.g. Andreasen, 1988). Other important sources of evidence include studies using cortical

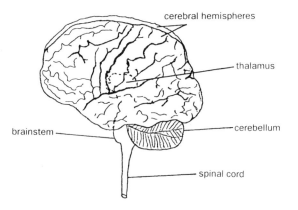

Figure 22.1 The central nervous system

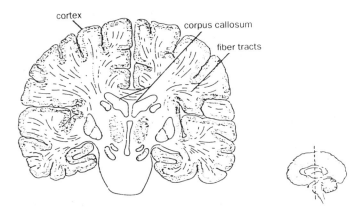

Figure 22.2 A vertical section cut through the middle of the brain

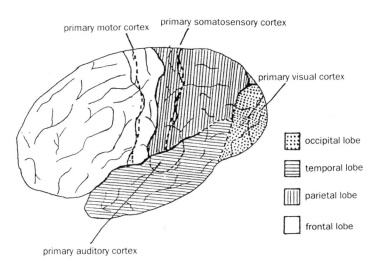

Figure 22.3 A lateral view of the left hemisphere

electrostimulation (Penfield and Jasper, 1954), the Electroencephalograph (EEG), which records the brain's electrical activity via electrodes placed on the scalp, and studies using *Positron-Emission Tomography* (PET), where radioactive tracers are used to image brain activity (for a review, see Raichle, 1994). A summary of the functions associated with each of the lobes of the brain is provided in Box 22.2.

The functions described in Box 22.2 are largely common to both cerebral hemispheres. However, the hemispheres differ in the sources of their sensory input and the targets of their motor output. Each visual cortex receives input only from the opposite half of the visual field. Thus, both visual fields are seen by both eyes, but the right-visual field is represented in the visual cortex of the left hemisphere and the left-visual field in the right-visual cortex. The somatosensory cortex in each parietal lobe receives input only from the opposite side of the body, and the gross motor movements of each side are largely initiated by the motor cortex in the opposite cerebral hemisphere. These crossed arrangements explain why people with brain damage confined to one hemisphere often have paralysis and loss of sensation confined to the limbs on the side of the body opposite to the side of hemispheric damage. They may also have loss of vision which is confined to areas within the opposite visual field. Note that, in contrast with the visual, somatosensory and motor projections, the neural pathways between the ears and the auditory cortices are predominantly bilateral (i.e. each ear is connected to both hemispheres).

Box 22.2 Functions of the Lobes of the Brain

The occipital lobes at the back of the brain are principally involved in vision. The *primary visual cortex* within each occipital lobe receives information from the eyes via subcortical regions including the thalamus. The rest of the occipital lobes are largely responsible for elaboration of visual information.

The lateral (outside) surface of each temporal lobe has a *primary auditory cortex* which is the main target for information coming from the ears via areas within the brain stem. Areas of cortex on the medial (inside) surfaces of the temporal lobes, and a closely associated region, the *hippocampus*, have been linked to some aspects of memory function. However, localization of memory function within the brain is controversial (Squire and Zola-Morgan, 1991; Thompson and Krupa, 1994).

The *primary somatosensory cortex* of the parietal lobes is involved in the sense of touch and receives information (via the thalamus) from sensory receptors close to the surface of the skin and within body tissues. The functions of other areas of the parietal lobes are not well established. They may, however, be involved in processing spatial information such as that conveyed by a map (De Renzi, 1982). Recent research has also suggested that parietal areas may integrate spatial information from the visual, auditory and tactile (touch) senses (Farah *et al.*, 1989; Pierson-Savage *et al.*, 1988). Areas of parietal cortex may also be involved in the orienting of attention (Posner, 1990).

The *primary motor cortex* of the frontal lobes initiates movements of all parts of the body, and functions in conjunction with other brain areas involved in movement control (see Schmidt, 1988). The rest of the frontal lobes, including the *pre-frontal cortex*, seems to be involved in some of the most sophisticated human behaviours. These include the planning of complex sequences of actions, abstract thinking, problem solving and inhibition of behaviour which does not conform to social rules (Pribram and Luria, 1973; Levin, Eisenberg and Benton, 1991).

In addition to the differences between the hemispheres discussed above, there also appear to be differences in the higher, cognitive functions for which each hemisphere is specialized. In most right-handed people, speech production is controlled by an area in the frontal lobe of the left hemisphere adjacent to the primary motor cortex; the corresponding area in the right hemisphere has no apparent role in speech. Other areas of the left hemisphere have been linked to speech comprehension, reading and writing. However, the extent to which the right hemisphere may also contribute to these language processes is controversial (Bishop, 1988; Baynes, Tramo and Gazzaniga, 1992). In contrast to the verbal specialization of the left hemisphere, the right hemisphere is regarded as being relatively specialized for visuo-spatial tasks such as judging the orientation of lines, or appreciating implied three dimensionality in a two-dimensional drawing. The pattern of hemispheric specialization of function outlined here appears to be characteristic of almost all right handers, and also of the majority of left handers (Bradshaw, 1989).

Discussion point

○ Which cerebral hemisphere is likely to be damaged in a person who has right-side paralysis and speech problems?

Causes of Brain Damage

Stroke

A stroke or *Cerebrovascular Accident* (CVA) occurs when there is a sudden disruption of the brain's blood supply. Strokes are often a complication of atherosclerosis ('narrowing' of the arteries) and hypertension (high blood pressure). Thus their frequency of occurrence increases with age. In cases of *cerebral ischaemia*, blood flow is interrupted because a vessel becomes narrowed or blocked by fatty deposits or by a blood clot. In other cases, a vessel may rupture resulting in an *intracerebral haemorrhage*. While the rupture may be a direct consequence of atherosclerosis and hypertension, in other (often younger) people it may be due to a congenital *aneurysm* which weakens part of the vessel wall and makes it liable to burst. Ischaemia and haemorrhage deprive the nerve cells or *neurons* in the affected part of the brain of oxygen and glucose, and the cells die within a few minutes. In cases of haemorrhage, there may be additional disruption of function because the accumulation of blood exerts pressure on adjacent brain tissue.

Head trauma

Traumatic head injury does not have to involve penetration or even fracture of the skull to result in severe brain damage. A *closed head injury* (where there is no skull penetration) may occur when the brain is subjected to strong kinetic forces, e.g. by a direct blow to the head or because of rapid deceleration of a vehicle during a traffic accident. These forces may rotate the brain and tear the protective structures which normally tether it in place, driving the brain against the inside of the skull. In some cases, the force of a blow to one side of the head causes the brain to strike the inside of the skull on the opposite side, resulting in a *contrecoup* injury. Rotation of the brain and its impact with the skull may damage neural tissue directly and also rupture blood vessels. Blood often accumulates in the *sub-dural space* between the *dura mater* and the *arachnoid mater*, two of the *meninges* or membranes which cover the brain. The pressure produced by the accumulated blood damages and disrupts the function of the underlying brain tissue.

The forces produced by rapid deceleration of a motor vehicle (and the blow to the head which often follows) may result in multiple areas of damage. However, the frontal lobes seem particularly vulnerable to damage in these circumstances (Walsh, 1994). The kinetic forces produced by shaking an infant may also result in brain damage. Indeed, brain damage due to shaking is a significant cause of non-accidental injury and death in children under one year of age.

Other causes of brain damage

Tumours may form on the meninges or within the brain itself. Tumours of the meninges or *meningiomas* are usually benign, but they may damage the brain through the pressure they exert on underlying neural tissue. Other causes of brain damage include degenerative diseases such as Alzheimer's dementia, infections such as meningitis, *anoxia* or loss of oxygenated blood to the brain (often as a result of a heart attack), exposure to neurotoxic drugs and over-consumption of alcohol. Some of the psychological consequences of these forms of brain damage and those of strokes and traumatic head injury can be similar. However, the remainder of this chapter will focus on the psychological effects of stroke and head trauma.

Psychological Effects of Stroke and Head Trauma

Accounts of the psychological effects of brain damage usually discuss each of the common syndromes independently of each other. These accounts are based largely on people who have very limited areas of brain damage as a result of surgical removal of brain tissue, a localized tumour, or an ischaemic stroke which affects only a small, circumscribed area of the brain. Such people may, for example, exhibit an isolated problem with one aspect of language or memory function, but have no other obvious cognitive impairments. Cases of this kind are, however, relatively rare. As noted above, those with head injuries often sustain damage to several areas of the hemispheres, and as a consequence, they may have multiple problems with language, memory, attention and social behaviour. A similar clinical picture may also be seen in cases of stroke, particularly where there has been a cerebral haemorrhage.

An appreciation of the multiplicity of inter-related psychological problems which may beset a brain-damaged individual is vital for the development and implementation of effective rehabilitation and care programmes. Nevertheless, understanding the nature of the deficits themselves is aided greatly by examining them separately. This approach is facilitated by classification of syndromes, and in this section some of the common consequences of stroke and head trauma are broadly grouped into changes in personality and emotionality, disturbances of attention, language problems and memory deficits. These groupings are somewhat arbitrary and the distinctions between deficits in each of these categories are not clear cut.

The following discussion of the psychological effects of brain damage, recovery and rehabilitation, is concerned only with acquired brain damage in adults. The consequences of brain damage in children and the degree of recovery of function may differ considerably from the typical adult pattern. Indeed, developmental neuropsychology is essentially a field in itself, and consideration of the effects of brain damage in children is beyond the scope of this chapter. Comprehensive accounts are provided by Spreen, Risser and Edgell (1995) and Snow and Hopper (1994). The latter text also discusses some of the care needs of brain injured children.

Changes in personality and emotionality

Damage to the pre-frontal cortex may be associated with marked changes in personality. So called 'frontal cases', who are often young adult victims of traffic accidents, may become highly irritable and abusive with little or no provocation, and may be unable to cope with routines and rules. They may also experience disinhibition of impulses which profoundly affects their social behaviour. For example, they may swear continually, they may make unwanted sexual advances, or they may urinate in the middle of a corridor. As well as being problematic in itself, such severe behavioural disturbance also complicates attempts to remediate other deficits, such as language or memory problems, even when these are relatively mild. In the longer-term, people with frontal damage may engage in law-breaking behaviour which they cannot inhibit, and may continually reoffend when on probation. The interview extract in Box 22.3 provides examples of some of the typical symptoms of frontal damage, as well as the grief and suffering which such symptoms cause for those who are close to the brain-damaged person.

Box 22.3: The Aftermath of Frontal Lobe Damage

'I just don't know what to do' sobbed Mrs W. 'He's my husband and I love him but I don't reckon I can stand it any longer. It's like he's a .... stranger. Before it (the accident) happened he was always pretty easy going but he always had everything organized. Now he gets angry at the slightest thing and he swears all the .... time – even in front of the kids and he would never have done that before. He's always making these big plans – we'll move to a new house.... we'll go on a holiday and then five minutes later he's changed his mind before he's even thought about the .... details, you know. He's still determined to ride his (motor) bike even though he knows he won't be allowed to and I'm dead scared he'll have another accident. He'd never even been booked for speeding or anything before but now he just doesn't seem to care about the laws and that..... Most of our friends have stopped visiting him and I'm not surprised. Last time C. came he tried to undo her shirt! I was so embarrassed..... I just keep waiting for the old J. to come back but I know he won't, it's his head and it won't get much better that's what they say. Most of the time he doesn't seem to realise he's changed but the other day he was in tears and he said "don't leave me" but what can I do?'

Relatives are usually unprepared for the effects that brain damage may have on a loved one and many report being angered by the lack of support and information available. The crisis surrounding the event may also affect the health of family members, and impact upon family stability and coping ability (Resnick, 1993). Thus, each member of the brain-damaged person's close family may require intensive intervention services to help them deal with their own difficulties, as well as to aid them in their role as caregivers (Florian and Katz, 1991). In addition to other interventions, mutual support groups may be a valuable resource for relatives. Zeigler (1989) reports that such a group for the spouses of head-injured people proved useful in helping members to deal with many of the changes which were a consequence of their spouse's head injury. These included role changes and increased responsibilities, occurrences of unpredictable behaviour and changes in the couple's sexual relationship.

Management of a behaviourally-disturbed, brain-damaged person is extremely difficult, and those with severe problems may have to be placed in psychiatric care. This is unsatisfactory as there are few psychiatric units which provide intensive specialist rehabilitation of cognitive and other deficits. In less serious cases, behaviour modification may help to control outbursts. For example, the person can be ignored when swearing and rewarded when pleasant. However, to be successful, tactics of this kind need to be employed consistently by all members of the care team and in practice this is often difficult to achieve.

Changes in emotionality may appear in conjunction with both stroke and head injury. Several studies reviewed by Heller (1990) reported that up to 60 per cent of people with left-frontal-lobe lesions met the DSM III criteria for diagnosis of depression. (The DSM diagnostic system, including the updated DSM-IV classification, is discussed in further detail in Chapter 18.) While depression may also be evident in some people with right hemisphere damage, others may appear euphoric and unconcerned about the physical and psychological consequences of their brain damage. Such people may also display inappropriate affect, bursting into tears for no reason or being happy when told of a sad event such as the death of a loved one. Such disruption of emotion seems particularly marked when there are lesions in the right-parietal or right-temporal lobe.

Mood disorders in brain-damaged people are not always the direct consequence of damage to areas of the brain which mediate emotional responses. In some cases, they may simply be a reaction to hospitalization and loss of physical and cognitive capacities. The assumption that little can be done about an affective disorder because it is caused by brain damage is a dangerous one. People viewed in this way may be deprived of the understanding and general support which could do much to improve both their mental state and their prognosis during the traumatic and confusing period immediately after a stroke or head injury. However, a study by Towle, Lincoln and Mayfield (1989) raises questions about the value of intensive social care interventions in alleviating stroke related depression in the longer term.

In the Towle *et al.* study, 44 depressed stroke patients, all more than one year post-stroke and living in the community, were assigned at random to one of two groups. Levels of depression, as measured by the Wakefield Depression Inventory, did not differ for the two groups. Those in the first (minimal intervention) group were visited once by a social worker and given a pamphlet which provided information about aids and support services available to stroke survivors. Those in the second (intensive intervention) group received the initial visit and the pamphlet, and were then visited up to twice a week by the social worker for 16 weeks. During these visits the social worker counselled the client and caregiver, advised on services and benefits, and facilitated contact with local day centres. After 16 weeks, levels of depression for both groups were significantly lower than they had been initially, but there was no significant difference between the depression levels of the two groups. Further research is needed to determine if modification of the regime given to the intensive intervention group may produce a greater reduction in level of depression. It is also important to determine if intensive intervention may be more effective if it is commenced sooner after stroke and continued for longer than it was in the Towle *et al.* study.

Disturbances of attention

Difficulty in orienting attention may be seen in some people with brain damage, and may be particularly marked in those with parietal lesions (Posner, 1990). People with parietal damage may fail to turn their head and eyes to pay attention to an event, such as a light flash or the opening of a door, which would invoke an orienting response in a person who is not brain damaged. After brain damage, people may also have problems with attending to a conversation or task for any length of time. In some cases, particularly where there is a considerable degree of frontal-lobe involvement, the person may be highly distractible, having an attention or concentration span of only a few seconds. Such problems in sustaining attention often co-occur with the changes in personality and emotionality which were discussed above. People with difficulties in sustaining attention may become frustrated and easily fatigued when required to do anything which needs extended concentration, and these problems may be particularly marked when an ordered sequence of steps must be followed. However, performance can sometimes be improved if motivation is heightened or if the task is structured in a way which allows frequent short breaks during its completion.

Discussion point

° How might you improve motivation to complete a task and thus help overcome concentration problems stemming from frontal lobe damage?

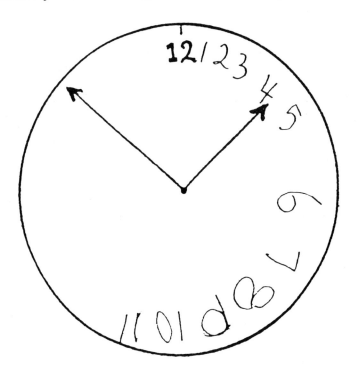

Figure 22.4

When there has been damage to only one cerebral hemisphere people may show signs and symptoms of *hemineglect* (see, for example, Robertson and Marshall, 1993). This syndrome is fairly common and is usually associated with strokes. However, it may also result from traumatic head injury and other types of brain damage. The syndrome may appear after damage to either hemisphere, but it is more common and more severe after right-hemisphere damage, particularly when the right-parietal lobe is involved. The acute behavioural manifestations of hemineglect are quite dramatic as patients fail to respond to objects and events on the side which is opposite the damaged hemisphere. Thus, patients with right-hemisphere damage and left hemineglect may not dress or groom their left sides, and may eat food only from the right side of a plate, leaving food on the left untouched. When asked to copy a drawing or draw from memory they may leave out or distort left-side details or misplace them to the right side of the drawing. Figure 22.4 shows a clock face completed from memory by a patient with damage to the right-parietal lobe and left hemineglect.

While the obvious symptoms of hemineglect usually resolve within a few weeks or months after brain damage is sustained, more subtle manifestations may persist (Pierson-Savage *et al.*, 1988). These include one-sided extinction to bilateral-simultaneous stimulation. In people with this condition as a result of right-hemisphere damage, responses to a single stimulus located in the right or the left side of space are adequate. However, when two stimuli are presented simultaneously, only the stimulus on the right is acknowledged, the stimulus on the left is now neglected. Thus, the left-side stimulus is said to be extinguished by the simultaneously-presented right-side stimulus. Extinction can be problematic for many everyday activities. For example, when crossing a road, a person with left-sided extinction will usually notice a single vehicle approaching from the right or the left. However, if two vehicles approach from opposite directions, the vehicle on the right will usually be noticed but the vehicle on the left may be missed. Any person with a past history of hemineglect should be carefully screened by a clinician or therapist to ensure that they do not show any evidence of extinction.

It can be demonstrated that people with hemineglect or extinction can actually see, hear and feel the objects or events which are nevertheless neglected. Thus, the mechanisms underlying failure to respond to such stimuli are controversial, and there are competing models of hemineglect and extinction (Bisiach and Vallar, 1988; Heilman, Watson and Valenstein, 1993). However, the problem seems to be at least partly attentional in nature. Recent experiments have shown that patients with hemineglect may respond to items on the neglected side if their attention is drawn to them by a cue placed on that side (e.g. Mattingley *et al.*, 1993). These findings suggest that rehabilitation of people with hemineglect can be aided by practices which encourage allocation of attention to the neglected side. For example, a person working with the client could position him or herself on the non-neglected side at the start of a conversation and then gradually move to the neglected side during the course of the interaction.

Discussion point

○ Difficulties in sustaining attention and changes in personality which may arise after brain damage often create profound distress for members of the brain-damaged person's family. If you were the social care professional approached by Mrs W. (Box 22.3), what would you say? What suggestions could you make to help her to deal with her situation?

Language problems

Anomia, or difficulty in finding words when speaking, is often observed in the acutely brain damaged. The problem is illustrated by the interview with Zasetsky in Box 22.1, and is somewhat like the 'tip of the tongue' phenomenon which most people (without brain damage) also experience on occasions. The person clearly knows the word she or he wants to use, but is unable to find it at the appropriate point in a conversation. While such word-finding difficulties often resolve quite quickly after brain damage, they remain a persistent and frustrating problem for some people.

There is a large number of other spoken language deficits or *aphasias* which may be acquired, usually as a result of left-hemisphere stroke or trauma. People with such lesions may have difficulty in producing speech even if they do not have problems in actually controlling movements of the muscles used to produce speech. In some people all speech is slow, effortful and largely devoid of grammatical structure – symptoms which, along with others, are diagnostic of *Broca's aphasia*. In other cases, there may be deficits in speech comprehension and in some people production and comprehension problems co-occur. If people have problems with producing or understanding speech, it might seem sensible to have them write down what they want to say and also to write down instructions for them. While in some cases this does aid communication, people with aphasia may also have acquired *dyslexia* and *agraphia* which result in difficulties with reading and writing, respectively.

Aphasia and dyslexia have been very widely studied, and this work has generated a vast clinical and empirical literature. Clear and accessible accounts of the symptoms of acquired language impairment and strategies for rehabilitation and management can be found in a number of texts. Thus, these topics will not receive further consideration here (for aphasia, see Benson, 1996; for acquired dyslexia, see Ellis, 1993).

Memory deficits

Disturbance of memory is common after brain damage, particularly if it is the result of traumatic head injury. People often fail to remember the accident itself, the events which preceded it and the period immediately afterward. They may also have initial difficulties in retaining new information such as the name of the doctor who is treating them or the number of their ward. In many people such difficulties are relatively transient. However, a subset of both stroke and head-injury cases have permanent memory deficits, or *amnesia*. For some brain-damaged people, persistent memory dysfunction is reflective of an overall decline in cognitive capacity. However, it may also appear in conjunction with relatively normal levels of intellect and awareness. (For discussion of procedures which differentiate memory problems from general intellectual impairment, see Parkin and Leng, 1993.) While amnesia may be apparent after stroke and head trauma, it is more commonly seen in cases of *Korsakoff's syndrome*. In these patients, brain damage is usually a consequence of chronic alcohol abuse.

Amnesia seems to be associated with bilateral damage to a number of closely interconnected structures, including the hippocampus and parts of the medial temporal lobes (Bauer, Tobias and Valenstein, 1993). Amnesia has two key features, *anterograde amnesia* and *retrograde amnesia* which co-occur in most amnesic patients. Anterograde deficits are difficulties in remembering events which have occurred since brain damage was sustained. Retrograde deficits are problems with remembering material acquired in any period before brain damage occurred. Some people with amnesia also *confabulate* or make up fictitious details about themselves, usually when faced with questions they cannot answer. Confabulation may reflect a desire to hide memory difficulties.

Anterograde amnesia seems to reflect a difficulty in transferring material from short-term or working memory (which can retain items for only a few seconds) to a more permanent long-term memory store (Squire and Zola-Morgan, 1991). Such problems in consolidating new information severely hinder rehabilitation and management. When, for example, a brain-damaged person with anterograde amnesia is shown a simple activity, she or he may be able to perform it immediately afterward. However, if questioned minutes later, the person may remember neither the activity nor even the social worker or therapist who demonstrated it!

Discussion point

   ° Patients who fail to complete exercises and activities are often viewed as uncooperative and lacking in motivation. How could you distinguish between non-compliance due to an attitude problem and failure to complete the task due to anterograde amnesia?

Anterograde memory impairments are severe in many people with amnesia and seem to prevent acquisition of a wide range of new material. Experimental studies have, however, shown that there are some types of learning which are relatively unimpaired. These include acquisition of classically conditioned responses (Daum, Channon and Canavan, 1989) and attainment of certain novel motor skills, for example mirror drawing (Milner, 1965). The person may however retain the ability to perform the new motor task but be unable to recall learning it or performing it previously.

Retrograde amnesia is usually far from complete. The very rare cases of total retrograde amnesia, which are sometimes reported in the popular press, involve people with psychological problems unrelated to damage to the brain (Kopelman, 1987). Brain-damaged amnesics usually retain their linguistic knowledge and a basic outline of their life history. However, it is often claimed that in people with retrograde amnesia, their memory for recent events, which occurred not long before the onset of amnesia, may be more impaired than their memory for events which are relatively remote in time (Butters and Cermak, 1986).

The notion that retrograde amnesia may be more pronounced for recent events than for earlier occurring events is controversial. It is based largely on qualitative clinical observations of autobiographical memory, and may be artefactual, reflecting a difference in the relative salience of events from the remote and the more recent past. Important events, which are thus remembered (e.g. marriage and the birth of children) are more likely to have occurred in the relatively remote rather than the recent past for middle-aged and elderly people. A difference in memory for events from the remote and recent past has not been demonstrated in experimental studies where the relative salience of information from these time frames has been carefully controlled. For example, Warrington and McCarthy (1988) tested an amnesic person's memory for non-autobiographical information (the identity of famous people) from a range of time frames. The famous people, whose faces were depicted in the pictures used in the study, were matched for their salience or importance during the time period in which they became famous. The person's memory was found to be impaired for faces from all the time frames used, and there was no evidence that people from the recent past were more poorly remembered than those from the relatively remote past.

The pattern of amnesic deficits discussed above is only one of several patterns of memory disturbance which may appear after brain damage. Memory deficits associated with dementia are discussed in Chapter 23 by Done and Thomas. For a comprehensive account of memory processes and memory deficits, see, for example, Baddeley, Wilson and Watts (1995).

Recovery and Rehabilitation

Cognitive and other problems resulting from stroke or head trauma usually improve somewhat during the first few months after brain damage is sustained. Improvement in function may come more slowly as the time since damage increases, but some people continue to make small gains several years after suffering a stroke or head trauma (Dombovy and Bach-y-Rita, 1988). The extent of improvement in adults varies quite considerably from person to person, and depends in part upon the particular cognitive processes which are affected. For example, as noted above, clinically-evident symptoms of hemineglect usually disappear within six months, although some deficits may still be elicited by subtle testing. In contrast, the language problems of Broca's aphasia often show little improvement.

In some cases of head injury or haemorrhagic stroke, initial improvement in function can be attributed to reduction of pressure when blood accumulations and swelling of the brain subside. The mechanisms underlying more long-term recovery of function after brain damage are not fully understood. In adults, dead neurons are not replaced and damaged parts of neurons within the central nervous system do not appear to regenerate. Empirical neuroanatomical and neurophysiological evidence suggests, however, that undamaged cells adjacent to dead neurons may develop new sprouts or become physiologically more responsive (Cotman and Nieto-Sampedro, 1982; Kaas, Merzenich and Killackey, 1983; Marshall, Drew and Neve, 1983). Nevertheless, it is likely that these changes make only a limited contribution to recovery after brain damage. Improvements in cognitive and other functions are probably the result of some form of compensation for the deficits. In some cases, such compensation may be attributed to the employment of specific strategies taught during rehabilitation.

The specialized topics of neuropsychological assessment and neuropsychological rehabilitation are quickly becoming a literature in themselves, and cannot be given further consideration here. Crawford, Parker and McKinlay (1992) provide a useful discussion of assessment, and there are several texts which describe neuropsychological rehabilitation, including Von Steinbuchel, Van Cramon and Poppel (1992).

Hospitals often include social care professionals as part of a multi-disciplinary rehabilitation team but they may have limited personal involvement with the brain-damaged patient until the latter stages of the rehabilitation process, when preparations are made for discharge and long-term care. Earlier close involvement is, however, desirable and can usually be achieved if arrangements are made to have admission notifications sent to the social work and other relevant departments. Early contact allows the social care professional more time to get to know the patient and the family. It also affords a fuller understanding of the cognitive and other impairments which need to be considered when planning for discharge and further care (Dancer, 1996; Marshall and Dixon, 1996). Moreover, the social care professional can help to broaden the focus of rehabilitation programmes which often concentrate on achieving physical and cognitive improvements rather than social recovery (Carlton and Stephenson, 1990).

Social care professionals have an important role to play in assisting brain-damaged people and their families with the difficult process of psycho-social readjustment after a head injury or a stroke. However, in 1990, Carlton and Stephenson observed that 'Given the incidence of head injury and the severity of its biopsychosocial sequelae, it is surprising that social workers have not published more on the subject.' (p. 5). A survey of the current literature suggests that little has changed since Carlton and Stephenson made this comment. There has also been relatively little published about social care interventions specific to stroke. Clearly, more research and publication is needed to maximize the effectiveness of interventions for brain-damaged people and their families.

Summary

The cerebral hemispheres of the brain are each divided into four lobes which appear to be associated with different functions. Thus, the psychological effects of hemispheric damage depend in part on the lobes involved. Strokes and head trauma are the most common among a number of causes of brain damage. The effects of strokes and head trauma include changes in personality. Patients (particularly those with frontal-lobe damage) may become highly irritable and engage in socially unacceptable behaviour. Concentration may also be impaired, and some patients (particularly those with parietal-lobe damage) may have problems with directing attention to the location of events. Damage to the left hemisphere often results in deficits in producing and understanding spoken and written language. Memory disturbances after brain damage are common and often transient, but some people have permanent memory problems. Some recovery is usual after brain damage, and improvement probably reflects compensation for deficits which may be aided by rehabilitation. Social care interventions need to focus not only on the brain-damaged individual, but on members of his or her family as well.

Seminar Questions

1. Using the Further Reading section as a starting point, consider some of the empirical studies which have examined the psychological effects of brain damage. Outline other studies which could further the investigation of these effects.

2. If you were a social care professional on a multi-disciplinary hospital rehabilitation team, how would you help the team to develop a rehabilitation programme for brain-damaged people which emphasizes social recovery, rather than simply focusing on remediation of physical and cognitive deficits?

3. Budgetary constraints often mean that intensive rehabilitation and other interventions cannot be offered to all who need them. Should someone who habitually drives when drunk and sustains brain damage in a car accident have the same right to these services as someone whose brain damage is due to a ruptured aneurysm?

Further Reading

McCarthy, R.A. and Warrington, E.K. (1990) *Cognitive Neuropsychology*. London: Academic Press. Provides a good coverage of clinical and experimental studies of the psychological effects of brain damage.

Sacks, O. (1985) *The Man who Mistook his Wife for a Hat*. London: Pan Books. Case histories of brain-damaged people narrated in a lively style.

Springer, S.P. and Deutsch, G. (1993) *Left Brain, Right Brain 4th Edition*. New York, NY: Freeman. A very readable account of insights into functional brain asymmetry which have come from research with brain-damaged, split-brain and normal right and left-handed people.

References

Andreasen, N.C. (1988) 'Brain imaging: applications in psychiatry.' *Science, 239*, 1381–1388.

Baddeley, A.D., Wilson, B.A. and Watts, F. (eds) (1995) *Handbook of Memory Disorders*. Chichester: Wiley.

Bauer, R.M., Tobias, B. and Valenstein, E. (1993) 'Amnesic disorders.' In K.M. Heilman and E. Valenstein (eds) *Clinical Neuropsychology 3rd. edition*. New York: Oxford University Press.

Baynes, K., Tramo, M.J. and Gazzaniga, M.S. (1992) 'Reading with a limited lexicon in the right hemisphere.' *Neuropsychologia, 30*, 187–200.

Benson, D.F. (1996) *Aphasia: A Clinical Perspective*. New York: Oxford University Press.

Bishop, D. (1988) 'Can the right hemisphere mediate language as well as the left? A critical review of recent research.' *Cognitive Neuropsychology, 5*, 353–67.

Bisiach, E. and Vallar, G. (1988) 'Hemineglect in humans.' In F. Boller and J. Grafman (eds) *Handbook of Neuropsychology, 1*. Amsterdam: Elsevier.

Bradshaw, J.L. (1989) *Hemispheric Specialization and Psychological Function*. Chichester: Wiley.

Butters, N. and Cermak, L.S. (1986) 'A case study of the forgetting of autobiographical knowledge: Implications for the study of retrograde amnesia.' In D. C. Rubin (ed.) *Autobiographical memory*. Cambridge: Cambridge University Press.

Carlton, T. and Stephenson, M.B. (1990) 'Social work and the management of severe head injury.' *Social Science and Medicine, 31*, 5–11.

Cotman, C.W. and Nieto-Sampedro, M. (1982) 'Brain function, synapse renewal, and plasticity.' *Annual Review of Psychology, 33*, 371–401.

Crawford, J., Parker, D. and McKinlay, W. (1992) *A Handbook of Neuropsychological Assessment*. Hove: Lawrence Erlbaum Associates.

Dancer, S. (1996) 'Redesigning care for the nonhemorrhagic stroke patient.' *Journal of Neuroscience Nursing, 28*, 183–189.

Daum, I., Channon, S. and Canavan, A.G.M. (1989) 'Classical conditioning in patients with severe memory problems.' *Journal of Neurology, Neurosurgery and Psychiatry, 52*, 47–51.

De Renzi, E. (1982) *Disorders of Space Exploration and Cognition*. Chichester: Wiley.

Dombovy, M. L. and Bach-y-Rita, P. (1988) 'Clinical observations on recovery from stroke.' In S.G. Waxman (ed.) *Advances in Neurology*. New York: Raven Press.

Ellis, A.W. (1993) *Reading, Writing and Dyslexia: A Cognitive Analysis, 2nd. edition*. Hove: Lawrence Erlbaum Associates.

Farah, M.J., Wong, A.B., Monheit, M.A. and Morrow, L.A. (1989) 'Parietal lobe mechanisms of spatial attention: modality specific or supramodal?' *Neuropsychologia, 27*, 461–470.

Florian, V. and Katz, S. (1991) 'The other victims of traumatic head injury: Consequences for family members.' *Neuropsychology, 5*, 267–279.

Heilman, K.M., Watson, R.T. and Valenstein, E. (1993) 'Neglect and related disorders.' In K.M. Heilman and E. Valenstein (eds) *Clinical Neuropsychology, 3rd. edition.* New York: Oxford University Press.

Heller, W. (1990) 'The neuropsychology of emotion developmental patterns and the implications for psychopathology.' In N.L. Stein, B. Leventhal, and T. Trabasso (eds) *Psychological and Biological Approaches to Emotion.* Hillsdale, NJ: Lawrence Erlbaum Associates.

Kaas, J.H., Merzenich, M.M. and Killackey, H.P. (1983) 'The reorganization of somatosensory cortex following peripheral nerve damage in adult and developing mammals.' *Annual Review of Neuroscience, 6*, 325–356.

Kopelman, M.D. (1987) 'Amnesia: Organic and psychogenic.' *British Journal of Psychiatry, 150*, 428–442.

Levin, H.S., Eisenberg, H.M. and Benton, A.L. (1991) *Frontal Lobe Function and Dysfunction.* New York: Oxford University Press.

Luria, A.R. (1972) *The Man with a Shattered World. The History of a Brain Wound.* New York: Basic Books.

Marshall, J.C., Drew, M.C. and Neve, K.A. (1983) 'Recovery of function after mesotelencephalic dopaminergic injury in senesence.' *Brain Research, 259*, 249–260.

Marshall, M. and Dixon, M. (1996) *Social Work with Older People, 3rd edition.* London: Macmillan.

Mattingley, J.B., Pierson, J.M., Bradshaw, J.L., Phillips, J.G. and Bradshaw, J.A. (1993) 'To see or not to see? The effects of visible and invisible cues on line bisection judgements in unilateral neglect.' *Neuropsychologia, 31*, 1201–1215.

Milner, B. (1965) 'Visually guided maze learning in man: Effects of bilateral hippocampal, bilateral frontal and unilateral cerebral lesions.' *Neuropsychologia, 3*, 317–338.

Parkin, A.J. and Leng, N.R.C.. (1993) *Neuropsychology of the Amnesic Syndrome.* Hove: Lawrence Erlbaum Associates.

Penfield, W. and Jasper, J. (1954) *Epilepsy and the Functional Anatomy of the Human Brain.* Boston: Little, Brown.

Pierson-Savage, J.M., Bradshaw, J.L., Bradshaw, J.A. and Nettleton, N.C. (1988) 'Vibrotactile reaction times in unilateral neglect.' *Brain, 111*, 1531–1545.

Posner, M.I. (1990) 'Hierarchical distributed networks in the neuropsychology of selective attention.' In A. Caramazza (ed.) *Cognitive neuropsychology and neurolinguistics.* Hillsdale, NJ: Lawrence Erlbaum Associates.

Pribram, K.H. and Luria, A.R. (1973) *Psychophysiology of the Frontal Lobes.* New York: Academic Press.

Raichle, M.E. (1994) 'Images of the mind: studies with modern imaging techniques.' *Annual Review of Psychology, 45*, 333–356.

Resnick, C. (1993) 'The effect of head injury on family and marital stability.' *Social Work in Health Care, 18*, 49–62.

Robertson, I.H. and Marshall, J. (1993) *Unilateral Neglect. Clinical and Experimental Studies.* Hove: Lawrence Erlbaum Associates.

Schmidt, R.A. (1988) *Motor Control and Learning 2nd edition.* Champaign, IL: Human Kinetics Publishers.

Snow, J.H. and Hopper, S.R. (1994) *Pediatric Traumatic Brain Injury.* Thousand Oaks. CA: Sage Publications.

Spreen, O., Risser, A.H. and Edgell, D. (1995) *Developmental Neuropsychology.* New York: Oxford University Press.

Squire, L.R. and Zola-Morgan, S. (1991) 'The medial temporal lobe memory system.' *Science, 253*, 1380–1386.

Thompson, R.F. and Krupa, D.J. (1994) 'Organization of memory traces in the mammalian brain.' *Annual Review of Neuroscience, 17*, 519–549.

Towle, D., Lincoln, N.B. and Mayfield, L. M. (1989) 'Evaluation of social work on depression after stroke.' *Clinical Rehabilitation, 3*, 89–96.

Von Steinbuchel, N., Van Cramon, D.Y. and Poppel, E. (eds) (1992) *Neuropsychological Rehabilitation.* Berlin: Springer Verlag.

Walsh, K.I. (1994) *Neuropsychology, A Clinical Approach, 3rd edition.* Edinburgh: Churchill Livingstone.

Warrington, E.K., and McCarthy, R.A. (1988) 'The fractionation of retrograde amnesia.' *Brain and Cognition, 7*, 184–200.

Zeigler, E.A. (1989) 'The importance of mutual support for spouses of head injury survivors.' *Cognitive Rehabilitation, 7*, 34–37.

CHAPTER 23

Dementia in Older People

John Done and Judith Thomas

What is Dementia?

Dementia refers to a disorder occurring in some 1 per cent of the 65–74 year olds, and 10 per cent of 75+ year olds (Ineichen, 1987). The disorder is characterized by a decline in all aspects of cognition (i.e. memory, thinking, comprehension, problem solving and general intellect), and is the result of a progressive destruction of brain tissue.

The question of whether we all experience a decline in cognition when we get old is addressed by Meldrum in Chapter 22. She draws the tentative conclusion that there does appear to be a decline, although this is probably true for only some cognitive skills and some people. This chapter deals with the group of elderly people who show such extreme cognitive deterioration in intellect and memory that it can be regarded as pathological. Members of this group are considered to suffer from *dementia*.

Since some noticeable cognitive decline often occurs as a normal function of ageing, society tends to hold a somewhat stereotyped view that any loss of memory is a natural part of ageing. It therefore becomes difficult to decide whether an elderly person who is forgetful is in an early stage of a dementing illness or is experiencing something normally expected of someone that age. As a result, there is often a tension, even amongst social workers and health professionals, about whether a person is suffering from dementia (thereby adopting the medical model) or simply forgetful and requiring supports such as a carer who provides reminders (thereby adopting a societal model).

Dementia does not only involve an impairment of intellect and memory, since just about every sphere of psychological functioning can also change or become disrupted in some way. Thus personality, emotional stability, behaviour toward others (e.g. becoming aggressive when previously passive and tolerant), speech and communication and self-care may well change for the worse. Since dementia is normally a progressive disorder in which deterioration occurs over a period of time, the pattern of deterioration and its severity varies depending on the stage of the illness. One can consider there to be three stages of dementia – early, middle and late stages. In the *early stage* of dementia, the most obvious disturbance is the impairment of memory. Difficulty in acquiring new information and retaining it over anything other than a few seconds is probably the most conspicuous sign. Recall of the sufferer's past life may be relatively well preserved compared with memory for recent events. This is often first noticed in the course of a daily activity. For example, a husband may return from a shopping trip without a significant number of important items which he had intended to buy, and on being questioned about this by his wife he may not recall having written a shopping list.

The initial realization that something is not quite as it should be depends upon the *premorbid* abilities and the premorbid personality of the person. That is, there needs to be a degree of change which is noticed by a close friend or relative to be rather more than just absent-mindedness. The changes might not be noticed at first, since sufferers often make excuses to hide these memory defects.

Changes of mood may also occur in this early stage and may involve anxiety, irritability and depression. Thinking becomes slow, impoverished in content, and may well appear to become concrete. That is, dealing with abstract concepts (e.g. discussing a son's attitude toward his wife) may result in an upsettingly impoverished contribution from the dementing person. Not surprisingly, judgement becomes impaired. At an early stage there may also be apparent changes in behaviour. Behaviour may become disorganized, inappropriate, distractible and restless, and there may be few signs of interest or initiative.

Box 23.1 What's it Like to be a Carer?

Olive has been married to Fred for 35 years. Fred now suffers from Alzheimer's disease which has reached a moderate level of severity. This is an extract from Olive's report on how her husband's illness has affected her.

> The children visit and talk on the phone, providing as much support as is possible, given that they have young children themselves. Friends are in scarcer supply. Olive thinks some friends would come over if she invited them, but she doesn't because Freddie's condition is simply too embarrassing. And so she lives without the job she loved, without any hope of a holiday, without trips to concerts and theatres, without adult conversation – and with Freddie. She is an intelligent, mild-mannered, articulate woman who tells the whole story evenly and unemotionally. Until you ask her, ever so gently, does she mind? Then her eyes flash and it pours out. 'Of course I mind! I resent it very much. I do not want to look after this ... person. I've reached this age, I should be having an easier life, doing things I've never done. I'm no saint; you see articles where people say what a wonderful enriching experience it all is and I don't believe them'.

> '... I can look at him and sometimes manage to remember it was someone I had fun with, or an affectionate relationship with. And at other times, he's like a stranger and I'm looking after him through circumstances beyond my control. I think, I do all this for him and all I get back is aggression – what's that speech, "Who will rid me of this troublesome priest?" – it runs through my head. You even get to the thought, well, perhaps he won't wake up tomorrow, and then you feel guilty about thinking it. I don't want to lose my life looking after him. It's like having a child without the joy. I've always been rather squeamish, and to have to do the things I have to do for him is ...oh....'

Olive believes Freddie still recognizes his own home and his dog; 'As long as he has that awareness I shall try to carry on. I can't think 10 years, I think just one more year... and at the end of that year I expect I shall think just another year. It's bloody awful, to be quite truthful.'

Source: The Sunday Times Colour Magazine, 26 May 1991.

It should be emphasized at this point that this early stage may be characterized by any combination of these changes, with some being more marked than others. Sometimes loss of memory is the most striking feature, whereas with others it may be an apparent change in personality, which is most noted when the person becomes antisocial, perhaps becoming sexually disinhibited or committing some petty crime.

Generally speaking, the course of a dementing illness shows progression across a wide range of psychological functions. At a *middling stage* of progression sufferers will not be able to remember their date of birth or how old they are, or be able to recall the names of certain significant others such as their wife, husband, current Prime Minister or the queen. Such forgetfulness becomes not only a social problem, but also it becomes a hazard since going out alone can result in forgetting arrangements to meet up and then forgetting one's own address. Speech at this stage is often very circumlocutory, that is, the speech becomes rambling, not getting to the point and failing to find informative words. Disorientation in time and space occur. Sufferers may forget where they are at the moment, or even the current time of day, which may lead to inappropriate behaviour such as preparing dinner at an absurd hour for a family who left years ago. This disorientation can lead to distress about where they are and concern that they should be somewhere else. Another sign that may be observed at this stage is the blunting of emotions, i.e. there is little expression of either positive (happiness) or negative (sadness) mood, and sudden mood changes may occur without apparent cause (emotional incontinence).

In the *late stage* memory is very poor, sufferers not infrequently have difficulty in remember their own name, or whether they are married or have children. Recognition of familiar others may not occur and emotions are blunted, and personality may not be expressed through lack of communication or behaviour.

This gives a general picture of the decline in cognitive and other psychological functions during dementia. In reality, the stages merge into one another, but it is often convenient for social workers and health care professionals to refer to the stage of dementia that a client has reached. It is also the case that the condition of clients can vary from day-to-day. For example, disorientation can be very marked one day, causing considerable burden on the carer, and then be of little concern the next day. Likewise occasional evidence of improved memory can give rise to the 'halo effect' i.e. you believe that in fact memory is not that bad after all. This is misleading, since some memories can be better preserved than others, which we discuss later. Furthermore, dementia is not a single disorder, and this too makes for considerable variation in this general picture.

Dementia is Not a Single Disorder

Dementia is an umbrella term which covers all syndromes in which there is a marked cognitive decline. AIDS, Huntington's chorea, Parkinson's disease, Wilson's disease, multiple sclerosis and stroke can result in dementia, although this is not always the case. Other disorders that invariably result in dementia are Alzheimer's disease, Creutzfeld Jacob Disease (CJD, thought to be a human equivalent of BSE, popularly known as 'mad cow disease'), and Picks disease.

Henderson (1983) points out that dementia can occur in 100 different diagnoses in which higher brain function is impaired.

Generally speaking, 45 per cent of cases of dementia are cases of Alzheimer's disease, 17 per cent result from disorders of the blood system (often referred to as arteriosclerotic or multi-infarct type dementia), 17 per cent are cases with both Alzheimer's disease and arteriosclerotic cause, and 19 per cent include the rest, e.g. cases of Huntington's, Wilson's and Parkinson's disease who have become demented,.

The focus of this chapter will therefore be Alzheimer's and multi-infarct dementias. Thus, whenever the term dementia is used from here on, it will be referring to Alzheimer's and multi-infarct dementias.

How Does One Diagnose Dementia?

This is an important question. It is necessary to have a test which will allow assessment of memory and intellect which will indicate that someone is demented. However, we return again to the problem that apparent cognitive decline is common in older people who do not have dementia. Someone who may have started premorbidly with a good memory may well be at an early stage of dementia, but score higher on the test than someone with a mediocre memory who does not suffer from dementia. Thus fixed criteria, such as 'a score below 5 on a 10-item memory scale' will either be too strict, and will miss those who used to have a good memory and are now at an early stage, or it will be too liberal and will label as 'demented' those who have always had a poor memory. As a result, a test of memory and intellect has to be judged in the light of (a) the person's premorbid abilities, and (b) how the average person of similar age would perform on the same test. Judgements about premorbid abilities are usually made by reference to occupation, number of years of full time education and social class. However, given that reading aloud remains surprisingly well preserved in mild/moderate dementia, it is possible to derive a measure of premorbid ability from the National Adult Reading Test (Nelson, 1982). It may also be important to find out which type of dementia the person is suffering from, but this in general moves into the realms of medical diagnosis and will not be dealt with here.

Before leaving this topic, related conditions which can result in misdiagnosis should be discussed. Some elderly people who are depressed can have cognitive deficits, together with changes in affect and personality which appear very similar to dementia. This condition, when recognized, sometimes goes by the name of *pseudodementia*. In most such cases, the symptoms of depression precede the onset of the signs of dementia, but in some cases the symptoms of depression begin at about the same time as the cognitive decline, which makes accurate diagnosis difficult. To complicate matters further, it is possible to suffer from both dementia and depression at the same time. Correct diagnosis is important since depression can be treated and the cognitive impairment thereby reduced, while dementia cannot be treated at present. Thus false diagnosis can have major implications.

Another medical disorder masquerading as dementia which will be mentioned here is *acute confusional state (delerium)*, the main features of which are disorientation and confusion. The state mimics dementia, but in fact results from physical causes which include dehydration, acute infection (e.g. urinary infection), drug intoxication, metabolic failure, withdrawal from alcohol and drugs and, in some cases nutritional insufficiency (see Gelder *et al.*, 1989 for more details). It can arise over a 24-hour period, the person being normal one day and utterly confused the next. Thus social care professionals can play an important role here, asking questions of relatives, friends or neighbours about what the person is *normally* like. Since delerium is reversible, it is very important to obtain an accurate history of the person over the previous days and months.

Discussion point

° Deciding whether an elderly person has dementia has important implications for case management. How might you identify someone who is suffering from dementia? With reference to case management, why is it important to differentiate dementia from other disorders?

Box 23.2 The Brain Pathology of Alzheimer's Dementia?

A true diagnosis for Alzheimer's disease is only achieved after death when a post mortem examination is undertaken. *Histopathology* (i.e. the study of cells to discover if some are pathological) of someone who suffered Alzheimer's shows the presence of *neurofibrillary tangles*, tangles for short, and *neuritic plaques*. Both tangles and plaques can be seen under a microscope if the brain tissue has been suitably stained. Tangles consist of a dense aggregate of a particular kind of filament not seen in the normal brain, often referred to as 'paired helical filaments'. Plaques, on the other hand, are extracellular collections of degenerating neural tissue surrounding a core of protein known as *amyloid protein*.

However, tangles and plaques are found in the brain of 'normal' elderly people (Roth, 1994), and hence there was some debate about whether these abnormalities really are responsible for the psychological abnormalities of Alzheimer's disease. The debate was settled by the work of Roth *et al.* (1966) and Blessed, Tomlinson and Roth (1968), who found that, although tangles and plaques are found in the normal ageing population, when they occur in large numbers the person becomes clinically demented. They also found a direct correlation between the degree of cognitive impairment measured with the now famous Blessed Rating Scale and the number of plaques and tangles found in the post-mortem examination.

How Long Does Dementia Last?

In some cases of dementia there may be periods in which there is no further deterioration of psychological functions. However, these periods will be followed by further decline, usually in a gradual progression. In multi-infarct dementia there may be a more step-like deterioration, i.e. a period of fairly rapid deterioration, followed by a period of stability.

Owing to medical factors reducing the physical health of a dementia sufferer, there does appear to be an association with premature death. Some studies show that this is true for early onset dementia, i.e. that occurring before the age of 70 (e.g. Henderson and Kay, 1984), but untrue for those who become demented in their 80s. In the studies of Kay *et al.* (1970) and Maule *et al.* (1984), the majority of sufferers had died within five years of the initial diagnosis, but survival time appears to be increasing (Christie, 1985), perhaps due to advances in care.

However, one can roughly estimate that the period between onset and death is in the order of some seven years, although this can vary from as little as 1–2 years up to 15 years.

How Common is Dementia and What are its Causes?

As mentioned earlier, approximately 1 per cent of 65–74 year olds and 10 per cent of 75+ year olds become demented (Ineichen, 1987). These numbers might suggest that dementia is relatively uncommon, but of course, the disorder is such that contact with social and health services is inevitable. In addition, the condition is likely to become more prevalent as the population of elderly people rises. In the OPCS (1985) survey, it was estimated that by the year 2001 there would be 9 million people in the UK who would be over 65 and 4.5 million who would be over 75. But in some areas in the UK with a high density of elderly people (e.g. Bath), the increase in elderly people making up the population was predicted by Ineichen (1987) to increase by a third by 2001.

Very recently there have been a number of breakthroughs that have suggested that Alzheimer's disease might be caused by the malfunction of genes; there is, however, also the possibility that environmental factors might trigger this malfunction.

It has been known for some time that there is a very high rate of Alzheimer's disease during early middle age in people with Down's syndrome (Oliver and Holland, 1986). Down's syndrome is a genetic disorder which results from an extra copy of chromosome 21. Much molecular genetic research has led many (e.g. St. Clair, 1987), but not all (e.g. Harrison, 1993), to believe that genetic abnormality on this chromosome is central to the cause of Alzheimer's disease.

Research studies have frequently found an association between certain adverse social or environmental factors and Alzheimer's disease. These have included social deprivation, type of job, aluminium in the water, and various other factors, too. However, none of these associations have been reliably found when other people have tried to replicate the findings (Amaducci *et al.*, 1988).

The Psychology of Memory and its Contribution to Understanding Dementia

Memory is considered by many psychologists to be served by a number of different processes. It is considered that there is a need to separate out *encoding, storage* and *retrieval*. Encoding refers to the way information coming in from the outside world is transformed from sensory data into meaning; storage refers to a 'filing cabinet' of memories; retrieval refers to gaining access to this memory that was filed away. So, if you cannot remember what you did on your summer holiday last year it may be because (a) you spent most of the time inebriated, so that you failed to encode much of what was happening around you, (b) the memories you filed away have been replaced, or faded away, or (c) it may be that memories are accurately stored, but without a prompt you cannot recall what happened. The loss of memory that occurs in dementia could result from impairments in any, or all, of the structures and processes responsible for encoding, storage and recall.

Generally speaking, this view of separate encoding, storage and retrieval processes is too simplistic. For example, Godden and Baddeley (1975) asked divers to learn and recall lists of words either on shore or under water. They found that what was learned under water was best recalled under water. Thus, it appears as though the situation you are in when trying to recall something can facilitate, or even hinder, recall. In this case, encoding the situation that would prevail at the time of recall influenced the ability to retrieve memories. Hence there can be considerable interaction between these three processes such that treating them as separate processes is too simple. However, this provides a useful framework to aid the understanding of memory.

It is generally thought that there are three different types of memory store: sensory stores (that hold memories for a very short time, e.g. rather like an after-image); short-term memory stores (such as remembering the telephone number that a friend told you at lunch), and long-term memory (e.g. recalling events at the first school you attended) (see Eysenck and Keane, 1991)

Attempting to remember a telephone number for a few seconds illustrates two key features about short-term memory, namely (a) the limited capacity of this type of memory, and (b) items are lost quickly if you do not repeat them to yourself, or if you get distracted. The limits to the capacity are best measured in terms of the number of *chunks* (a chunk is a familiar unit of information based upon previous learning and experience). Thus, if I try to remember a list of names (say eight first and eight surnames, making a total of sixteen actual names) I will only remember about eight if the individuals are unknown to me. However, if these were the names of friends of mine then I would remember the same number of units, i.e. eight, but the units this time would be a combination of one first and one surname.

In dementia the overall capacity (i.e. number of items that can be stored) is reduced, the rate of forgetting in short-term memory is increased, and this is particularly so when there is distraction or competition from other memories. For example, if you tell a patient suffering from dementia your name and then ask them to say what they had for breakfast, this increases the likelihood that the patient will forget your name within a few seconds.

Quite clearly, there are profound deficits in long-term memory in dementia. Remembering people's names, or personal events in one's own life, or even recognizing objects or people can create problems. Psychologists have made great play out of differences between different types of long-term memories. Some have suggested that there are differences between *episodic memories* that concern personal experiences (such as a visit to Brighton when aged six) and *semantic memories* which are general knowledge such as recognizing that an object is a spoon, not a knife. For these two types of memory there is a clear difference in content (you do not recall a scene and a series of personal events when asked to describe a spoon, as you would if you were asked to describe a trip to the seaside as a child). Some patients with memory disorders (*amnesic* rather than demented patients) have deficits with episodic, but not semantic memory (Parkin, 1982). This is not the case for sufferers of dementia. For them, general knowledge about the world is also impaired. Such impairments are typically held to demonstrate deficits in the semantic memory store. However, Nebes (1989) has suggested that semantic memory stores may remain intact in dementia sufferers, and argues that sufferers are simply unable to retrieve memories from intact memory stores. When they are provided with relevant situational cues recall is possible. Chertkow and Bub (1990) disagree with this theory and have provided evidence to suggest that dementia sufferers not only have difficulty retrieving intact memories, but also stored memories can be lost altogether or else severely corrupted. So the debate about the intactness of semantic memories in dementia continues, although increasingly the evidence points toward deficits in both access of memories as well as damaged memory stores.

There is yet another distinction between different types of long-term memory that is relevant to dementia. This is the distinction between the memory for the performance of a learned activity (e.g. using knife, fork and spoon appropriately) as opposed to conscious recollection (e.g. being able to say what use is made of a spoon). The distinction between these two types of memory has resulted in the labels *implicit* (memory for performance) and *explicit* (conscious recollection). Dementia sufferers can often perform activities (e.g. demonstrate the use of a corkscrew) but are unable to provide explicitly the name or give a verbal description (e.g. say that a corkscrew is used to remove a cork from a bottle). Thus sufferers of dementia show particularly marked impairments for explicit memory. Implicit memories at the early/moderate stages of dementia appear to be intact.

The Application of Psychology to Improve Communication with Sufferers of Dementia

If you want to communicate with someone who is demented, the first step has to be to get their attention. The psychology of attention shows that the most powerful stimulus to attract attention is hearing someone speak your name. Most of us have had the experience of being in a crowded room with quite a lot of noise around us and yet hearing our own name immediately if it is spoken aloud by someone even a good distance away. If saying someone's name is

Figure 23.1 Try to use the appropriate form of address

accompanied by a sensory cue, e.g. giving a light touch, then the alerting power is increased considerably. This may sound a very simple strategy, and indeed it is, but there can be problems in its practical application. First, it is very important to use the right name. A surprising number of people are not known by their given name. In a hospital one often sees name labels on patients' beds with their nickname or familiar name in brackets, and it is obviously really important to discover what these are. Equally important is to establish whenever possible the mode of address preferred by each individual, as many people, particularly elderly people, are not at ease to be called by their first name by those they do not know well. For example, a long-term headmistress who has only ever been addressed by her full title except by very close friends, is not likely to respond to someone using her first name when she is deep in thought remembering her past life in school (Figure 23.1).

A good idea is to try and establish, from the person or their relatives, what they like to be called, and use that mode of address. Remember, too, to tell them your name at the start of a meeting, and to remind them on subsequent meetings. In the early stages of dementia, sufferers are often very aware of their poor memories and worry a lot about it, so on a very first meeting it will put them at their ease to say 'Hallo, Mrs Jones.' Wait to see if you have their attention and continue 'My name is Patti O'Dores. We haven't met before; I have come to talk to you...' If you have met before, just remind them of your name, and don't necessarily expect them to remember. For example 'Hallo, Mrs Smith. I'm Teresa Green – we met last week for a chat'. A light touch on the arm, from the front or side so as not to startle, is usually a good accompaniment to saying someone's name, although there are those who dislike being touched and one would need to be aware of this.

The Form of the Communication

Before you even embark on a communication exercise with someone who is dementing, consider the basic points in Box 23.3.

Box 23.3 Points to Consider about Communication

(a) Hearing aid – is one normally used. If so, is it in, is it correctly placed. Check with family, if possible.

(b) Check whether dentures and spectacles are normally used and are in place.

(c) Reduce surrounding noise as much as possible when communicating. Competing messages, or sounds which can attract attention, can refocus attention away from what you are saying, as well as impairing encoding of incoming message.

(d) Speak a little more slowly than normally to give time for information to be processed.

(e) Watch for signs that your message has not been understood, and repeat or rephrase.

(f) Give time for a response before you assume that repetition is needed.

(g) Don't 'talk down' to the elderly dementing person. Simplifying language structure does not mean patronizing 'baby talk'.

Box 23.4 Strategies to Improve Communication

Patient Behaviour	Carer Strategy
Poor auditory comprehension	Reduce complexity of utterance Reduce use of pronouns
Jargon output (i.e. fluent speech containing inappropriate words/non-words and having little/no meaning)	Look for pragmatic clues (i.e. note context, watch for gesture, note tone of voice, etc. Use 20 question technique (e.g. Is it to do with the garden? or, Are you talking about the children? etc.).
Lack of attention	Gain attention by alerting
Loses attention	Repeat alerters Reduce distractions
Unable to make choices	Avoid complex choices Use 'closed' questions (e.g. 'Do you want tea or coffee?' rather than ' What would you like to drink?').
Perseveration (continued repetition of utterance)	Reply tactfully Distract attention
Word-finding problems	Intelligent guesswork 20 question approach
Rambling, non-proposition speech (thought disorder)	Distract Ignore/Don't try to interpret

---

We have mentioned above that dementia sufferers have short-term memories which are limited in size such that they can store fewer items than normal, and they are also more prone to forgetting material, especially when there is a distraction. Therefore, the structure and content of orally given information needs to be in a form which pays due regard to these limitations. A few basic guidelines to avoid the more obvious pitfalls are:

1. Keep sentences short, so that information can be relayed in manageable 'chunks', e.g., 'Mary ... (pause) ... your daughter, Jane, is worried about you. (Pause) Jane thinks you are not eating enough. You are getting a bit too thin, aren't you? Jane thinks it would be a good idea for you to have 'Meals on Wheels'. Will you try 'Meals on Wheels' for a little while?' This information is easier to assimilate than 'Jane tells me that last time she saw you she noticed how thin you were getting and she thinks you're not getting meals for yourself. She is really worried about this and suggested that 'Meals on Wheels' might solve the problem because she can't get down to see you often enough, now that she hasn't got a car and it's such a difficult journey. What do you think?' It is very likely that 'Mary' will have lost the thread of this suggestion by the time she is asked to respond to the question.

2. Try to avoid the use of too many pronouns. In above example, 'Jane' is mentioned once, at the beginning of the sentence, after which the pronoun 'she' is used. For a person with short-term memory problems, it can be difficult to remember who or what is being discussed. Another example might be 'Mary... (pause)... Helen does your

shopping for you, doesn't she? Well, Helen isn't very well today, so this is Jo. Jo is going to do your shopping just for today. Can you give Jo your list?'

3. Give information in a logical sequence so that the context developed at one stage facilitates the understanding of the next stage. For example, do not say 'As it's quite a long way to go and there's often a lot of traffic on Friday's, I think we'll leave just after coffee to go and look at the nursing home'. Better to say 'We are going to look at that nursing home this morning. We'll leave just after coffee so that we can take our time'.

4. Alert any change of subject or activity and give the person time to make change of 'mental set'. If, for example, you are in someone's home and you have been discussing a carer coming in to help her clean, introduce a new topic with a phrase as 'Mary, now I want to talk to you about food'.

Response to Communication from the Dementing Person

Discussion so far has focused on talking to the dementing person. Equally important is responding to their communication attempts.

Social care professionals with the elderly are often involved in the sensitive area of whether a person in hospital is able to continue to care for him/herself after discharge; also, whether someone caring for a demented relative at home can reasonably be expected to carry on doing so. This can be a vexed enough question with frail elderly people without the additional problems that dementia brings. First, as with any other illness, it is important to have a correct diagnosis. Somebody with jumbled speech may be thought of as being 'demented' when in fact there are many other possible reasons for confused output. For example, a Cerebrovascular Accident (CVA), or 'stroke' can result in damage to the language area of the brain. This can also sometimes lead to reduced ability to understand what is said. It can also sometimes result in the speech of the person who has had a stroke being quite severely affected in its content. This might take the form of the person being unable to retrieve 'content words', i.e. the nouns and verbs of a sentence, so that the sentence starts off well but no actual information is given. Or sometimes the sentences may seem complete and fluent, with preserved intonation patterns, but a lot of wrong words being used, e.g. 'teapot' instead of 'wheelchair' or even words which are not real words at all, with the speaker not realizing that what he/she is saying does not make any sense. This condition, if caused by a stroke or head injury, is called 'dysphasia' and can to the unwary be interpreted as demented output, so be wary. If there is no previous history of dementia, it may be that the person you have been asked to see is dysphasic but not in the least demented. A speech and language therapist would be able to make a differential diagnosis, and if the problem turns out to be dysphasia the speech and language therapist should be involved to advise on the ability of the client to understand what is being said to him/her regarding future plans. This is particularly important if a Power of Attorney (a legal document empowering one person to act on behalf of another), is being considered.

Applications to Social Care Practice

Having established that it is dementia, the social care professionals has the difficult task of organizing the most appropriate ongoing care and trying to balance the client's views, their rights, needs and also the relatives' views/needs. Using the communication techniques outlined earlier, it is important to see the client as many times as possible so that any fluctuations in ability to understand and take part in conversations can be identified. On a first brief meeting, your perceptions of the client may differ widely from your opinion as you see more of him or her. This applies particularly when you see a client at home. One of the authors remembers visiting the wife of a man reported to have quite advanced dementia. The door was opened by him, saying 'Hello, do come in. Come into the sitting room, you'll be more comfortable in here. I'll fetch my wife.' His wife looked amazed and said that he had not uttered as many words in the previous seven days. As the visit progressed he said no more, did not seem aware of my presence and did not respond to my 'goodbye' at the end. It is very important to listen to what relatives say and take this into account when making an assessment. People suffering from dementia can still have good social skills and can rise to the occasion of a visit by a GP or other formal visitor, temporarily masking the cognitive impairment. Relatives often say that they feel that visitors think they are exaggerating the difficulty of caring because during the relatively short visit the behaviour was quite 'normal'. This applies, too, sometimes when close family members who live some way away come for a visit and at the end of it say to their mother 'Dad seems fine – a bit forgetful, yes, but nothing like you describe over the phone'. For the social care professional to be able to get an accurate picture of what is really happening, a great deal of time needs to be spent not only with the client but with the relative, listening and appraising.

The value of respite care to give the carer breathing space cannot be overstated. Of course it is not easy to persuade an elderly person to go away from their home, and often it is difficult to persuade a carer to agree to the suggestion of respite care. Some spouses are amazingly reluctant to accept help and feel it is their duty to keep going in what others would consider impossible circumstances. Given this degree of dedication, and the general philosophy of care in the community rather than in institutions, the more help that can be offered to carers the longer the relationship is likely to survive. Day centres can provide short-term relief for the carer, and once the routine is established both parties seem to benefit, but carers often admit to almost unbearable feelings of guilt at agreeing that they need some time to themselves.

Conversely, one needs to be aware that there will be those who are unable or not prepared to cope with changes occurring in their relative, and at a very early stage are exaggerating the difficulties of caring and asking for placement in a home. Often, with carefully thought out input from social services, a person in the early stages of dementia can manage very adequately in their own home for a long time.

If long-term placement in a home is the only solution at some stage, then choice of home is obviously important but may well be limited by availability. If the client needing such placement is a 'wanderer', always restless and on the go, try and locate a home where there is space to do that without either placing themselves in danger or upsetting the routine of the home.

It may not be easy to feel that one has arrived at the best solution when dealing with arrangements for a person suffering from dementia, but the general social care professional principles apply (e.g. client's best interests are of primary importance when making recommendations, etc.), and it is important to be aware that there are various degrees of dementia, and although Alzheimer's disease is progressive, the rate of progression will vary with different individual people.

Summary

Dementia results from a serious disorder of the brain, which affects every aspect of psychological functioning. The progression of dementia means that psychological and physical needs change over time. For both formal and informal carers this implies a need to be aware of the patient's current abilities and needs. Some psychological functions may be better preserved than others, but perhaps more important is knowing how to work with the client to make these psychological functions most effective. Here we have focused on communication and related psychological theory to techniques which can improve the communication between carer and sufferer.

Seminar Questions

Imagine that you have a client who is suffering from profound dementia.

1. How do you involve your client in making decisions about options for residential or home care? Consider the following areas for discussion:

    (i)   There will be many issues to discuss, requiring repeat visits. What problems does this present?

    (ii) How do you include someone in decision making when their judgement is very impaired?

    (iii) Can you help someone suffering from dementia to make choices?

2. How do you as a social care professional ensure that decisions about particular residential care suit the needs of your client? Consider the following areas for discussion:

    (i)   Your client may be uncooperative so what can you do?

    (ii) To what extent do you bias your judgement according to the views of your client as opposed to those of friends and relatives?

    (iii) How can you ensure that a 'best' decision has been made?

Further Reading

Comer, R.J. (1992) *Abnormal Psychology*. New York: Freeman and Co.
Chapter 20 gives an overview of the clinical aspects of dementia.

Eysenck, M.W. and Keane M.T. (1991) *Cognitive Psychology: A Student's Handbook*. London: Lawrence Erlbaum Associates.
For further developing your knowledge of theoretical psychology.

Huppert, F.A., Brayne, C. and O'Connor, D.W. (1994) *Dementia and Normal Ageing*. Cambridge: University Press.
Contains a number of useful chapters which focus on the nature and causes of dementia.

Miller E. and Morris R. (1994) *The Psychology of Dementia*. Chichester: Wiley.
A contemporary book by two highly respected psychologists which covers the psychological dysfunctions of dementia sufferers.

References

Amaducci, L.A., Lippi, A. and Fratiglioni, L. (1988) 'What risk factors are known?' In A.S. Henderson and J.H. Henderson (eds) *Etiology of Dementia of Alzheimer's Type*. London: Wiley.

Blessed, G., Tomlinson, B.E. and Roth, M. (1968) 'The association between quantitative measures of dementia and of senile change in the cerebral grey matter of elderly subjects.' *British Journal of Psychiatry, 114*, 797–811.

Boddy, J. (1978) *Brain Systems and Psychological Concepts*. Chichester: Wiley.

Chertkow, H. and Bub, D. (1990) 'Semantic memory loss in dementia of Alzheimer's type: what do various measures measure?' *Brain, 113*, 397–446.

Christie, A.B. (1985) 'Survival in dementia: a review.' In T. Arie, (ed) *Recent Advances in Psychogeriatrics 1*. Edinburgh: Churchill Livingstone.

Eysenck, M.W. and Keane, M.T. (1991) *Cognitive Psychology: A Student's Handbook*. London: Lawrence Erlbaum Associates.

Gelder, M., Gath, D. and Mayou, R. (1989) *Oxford Textbook of Psychiatry, 2nd edition*. Oxford: Oxford Medical Publications.

Godden, D. and Baddeley, A.D. (1975) 'Context-dependent memory in two natural environments: On land and under water.' *British Journal of Psychology, 66*, 325–31.

Harrison, P.(1993) 'Alzheimer's disease and chromosome 14: different gene, same process?' *British Journal of Psychiatry, 163*, 2–5.

Henderson, A.S. (1983) 'The coming epidemic of dementia.' *Australian and New Zealand Journal of Psychiatry, 17*, 117–127.

Henderson, A.S. and Kay, D.W.K. (1984) 'The epidemiology of mental disorders in old age.' In D.W. Kay and G.D. Burrows (eds) *Handbook of Studies on Psyhiatry and Old Age*. Amsterdam: Elsevier.

Ineichen, B. (1987) 'Measuring the rising tide: How many dementia cases will there be by 2001?' *British Journal of Psychiatry, 150*, 193–200.

Kay, D.W.K, Foster, E.M., McKechnie, A.A. and Roth, M. (1970) 'Mental illness and hospital usage in the elderly: A random sample followed up.' *Comprehensive Psychiatry, 11*, 26–35.

Maule, M., Milne, J.S. and Williamson, J. (1984) 'Mental illness and physical health in older people.' *Age and Ageing, 13*, 349–356.

Nebes, R.D. (1989) 'Semantic memory in Alzheimer's disease.' *Psychological Bulletin, 106*, 377–394.

Nelson, H.E. (1982) *National Adult Reading Test (NART)*. Windsor: NFER-Nelson.

Oliver, C. and Holland, A.J. (1986) 'Down's syndrome and Alzheimer's disease: a review.' *Psychological Medicine, 16*, 307–322.

Parkin, A.J. (1982) 'Residual learning capacity in organic amnesia.' *Cortex, 18*, 417–440.

Roth M. (1994) 'The relationship between dementia and normal aging of the brain.' In F.A. Huppert, C. Brayne and D.W. O'Connor (eds) *Dementia and Normal Aging*. Cambridge: Cambridge University Press.

Roth, M., Tomlinson, B.E., and Blessed, G. (1966) 'Correlation between scores for dementia and counts of "senile plaques" in cerebral grey matter of elderly subjects.' *Nature, 200*, 109–110.

St. Clair, D. (1987) 'Chromosome 21, Down's syndrome and Alzheimer's disease.' *Journal of Mental Deficiency Reseach, 31*, 213–214.

Dying and Bereavement

Paul March and Clare Doherty

Introduction

By definition, social care involves working with people who are experiencing the psychological consequences of social trauma. Trauma can take many forms, but will always be accompanied by feelings of loss. Social care professionals will come to experience these losses with their clients. The most traumatic and yet universal loss is that of life. In some organizations such as hospitals, nursing homes and hospices, the experiences of death and bereavement will be a central and pervading feature of the work. But whatever the area, be it child protection, drug rehabilitation or the resettlement of the long-term mentally ill, the professional will find the families with whom she or he works inevitably at times touched by death and bereavement. For these reasons it is important for social workers and those in related professions to be sensitive to the emotional reactions of dying and bereaved people, and to be aware of the difficulties that they will experience. In addition to considering theoretical approaches to death and bereavement, the chapter aims to introduce the reader to grief counselling and therapy.

Reactions of Dying and Bereaved People

A number of perspectives have been used to help understand the psychological reactions of dying and bereaved people. Littlewood (1992) summarizes seven models:

1. Illness and disease models (e.g. Lindemann, 1944)
2. Biological models (e.g. Engel, 1962)
3. Psychodynamic models (e.g. Pincus, 1976)
4. Attachment models (Bowlby, 1980)
5. Personal construct and cognitive models (Parkes, 1975)
6. Stress models such as Caplan's (1964) model of crisis intervention
7. Phenomenological and existential models (e.g. Smith, 1976).

All these models present mourning as an active and evolving process, and there is a high level of agreement between them over the descriptions and explanations of likely reactions. So, for the sake of clarity, only one model will be presented here. The model stems from the work of Bowlby on attachment (1969, 1980). It has been used to understand the reactions of both dying and bereaved people. A summary of the theory is given below, and it is also considered by David Messer in Chapter 11.

The attachment model

In attachment theory a person's relationship with his first and primary caregiver provides a template for future relationships. A person who experiences this first relationship as loving and secure will tend to perceive future relationships in the same way. That person will have basic trust in the world and in those around him (Erikson, 1951, 1982) and will have the capacity to give and receive love. When someone whom the person loves dies, the person is left with the contradiction of being attached to someone who is no longer there. Mourning is the process of correcting this contradiction and of overcoming the loss.

The studies outlined below will demonstrate that dying people themselves also suffer losses and have similar reactions to those who are bereaved. Consequently, we will consider the reactions of dying and bereaved people together. Most people who are dying have people around them who are mourning their death. The feelings and behaviour of dying and bereaved people are a function of the relationship between them, and should not therefore be considered in isolation from each other. Indeed, one of the guiding principles of the new hospice movement is that the family is the unit of care.

How does the attachment model help us to understand the reactions to loss? Table 24.1 shows three different versions of the model. Bowlby's model is a general description of the reactions to the loss of an attachment figure. Parkes' model is derived mainly from two longitudinal interview studies of widows and widowers (Parkes, 1972; Parkes and Weiss 1983). The Kubler-Ross (1973) model is derived from interviews of over 200 terminally ill patients. The stages outlined by the models bear close similarities to each other despite the fact that their authors collected their evidence, at least initially, independently and data were collected from quite different populations (see Table 24.1).

Table 24.1 Three Models of the Process of Grieving

Bowlby	Parkes	Kubler-Ross
	Alarm	Denial
	Searching	
Protest	Anger–protest	Anger
		Bargaining
Despair	Apathy–Despair	Depression
Reintegration	New identity	Acceptance

Some people have questioned whether it is appropriate to describe the process of bereavement in terms of a series of stages at all. Corr (1993), for example, argues that a stage model, in which a person proceeds in a linear fashion from one stage to the next, has not been supported by subsequent research. He argues that such a model is a generalization from the experience of some individuals, and that these models lack the flexibility necessary to describe the range of individual reactions. Thus, there are dangers when stage models are interpreted in a rigid and prescriptive way, but both Parkes and Kubler-Ross, as well as others (e.g. Worden, 1991), have made explicit that they are not making such a claim. Another problem is that different cultures prescribe different grieving rituals, and it is not clear the extent to which the findings of Parkes and Kubler-Ross apply to non-Western cultures (see Box 24.1 and Seminar Question 1). However, the research into bereaved and dying people suggests that when you look at a *group* of such people a predictable pattern emerges. Further, it is possible to use this pattern to understand the experiences of bereaved and dying individuals by using this perspective as a framework, whilst at the same time recognizing that there is a huge variability in the ways individuals react. So, when talking with a bereaved or dying person, it is only proper that their experience should be in the foreground of the conversation, with the context at the back (see Seminar Question 2).

Box 24.1 Grief in Other Cultures

Attachment theory attempts to explain the reactions of dying and bereaved people in terms of the personal meaning of loss. However, there are also cultural influences that may determine whether and how grief is experienced or expressed. For example, in a review of anthropological studies of grief, Stroebe and Stroebe (1987) suggest that the length of a grief reaction is culturally prescribed. In traditional Navajo Indian culture, the expression of grief lasts for four days following death. Orthodox Jews grieve for one year. In both cases the bereaved then returns to a normal life. Stroebe and Stroebe (1987) point to studies which demonstrate the positive part that culturally-determined rituals play in moderating the grief reaction, and they suggest that the long-lasting grief and depression encountered in the bereaved in Britain is partly a result of the lack of death and bereavement rituals. One could also argue that British culture allows individuals to grieve indefinitely and does not impose an externally-based end to the process (see seminar question 1).

To a certain extent, cultural differences can be explained by the attachment model. For example, according to Stroebe and Stroebe (1987), Japanese women accept the death of their husbands with equanimity compared with Western women. This can be explained in terms of their strong belief in the afterlife coupled with their view that their ancestors are always with them. Such assumptions lead to there being less to grieve about because they mitigate against feelings of complete loss.

There are other more general issues about the sequence of events described by the model. For bereaved persons who have more warning of an impending death their process of mourning may be shorter or less complicated because they have mourned the death in advance, so called 'anticipatory bereavement'. Although mourning in advance may be helpful for the long-term adjustment of the bereaved it may also cause problems. As loved ones come to accept the inevitability of death they may begin to withdraw from the patient and begin to consider life after the patient's death. This is an understandable reaction, but it may leave the dying patient feeling rejected and isolated. The reverse can also happen; the patient may begin to accept their own death and withdraw from their loved ones who remain overwhelmed by grief. The patient's disengagement may only increase the grief of other family members. The phenomenon of anticipatory bereavement demonstrates the need to give care to the dying and the bereaved together. Loved ones and relatives will mourn in different ways. They will undoubtedly have an influence on each other, sometimes supporting each other but often finding it impossible to provide mutual support because of the consequent increases in their own feelings of loss.

Alarm and Denial

Physiological and behavioural symptoms of alarm are produced in many animals by imminent threat or danger. The news of death can be the cause of an alarm reaction because the world suddenly becomes a threatening and unpredictable place. Parkes (1972) found the alarm reaction to be very common in the first few hours, and up to 10 days following a bereavement. Most of the widows in his study were initially restless, panicky and in a state of high arousal. Two-thirds were jumpy and irritable. Many of the somatic changes these widows reported in the first days such as headaches, muscle tensions, knots in the stomach and dryness of the throat are a result of normal physiological reactions to threat. Appetite loss and insomnia were also experienced by most of the widows.

The task at this early stage is to begin to accept the reality of the loss. Anything that makes this loss unreal such as suddenness, unexpected, bizarre or unusual circumstances is likely to make accepting reality more difficult, and to result in a more prolonged or complicated grief reaction (Parkes and Weiss, 1983). Thus, a loss that goes against the normal life cycle, e.g. of a child or a loss by violence or unusual circumstances, is especially traumatic.

Bereaved people who feel able to see the body of the deceased are likely to find the experience upsetting, but helpful in the long run because it makes the reality of death more apparent. Social care professionals should bear this in mind, but ultimately be guided by the bereaved person's own wishes.

Kubler-Ross (1969) found that almost all of the patients she interviewed initially denied that they had a life threatening illness. Denial means deceiving yourself about something that another part of your mind knows to be true. Kubler-Ross found that only three out of 200 patients remained in a constant state of denial, with the remainder drifting in and out of the state. Denial was more common in patients who had been told their diagnosis or prognosis in an abrupt or insensitive way or were surrounded by family and/or staff who were also denying the seriousness of their condition.

Searching

Parkes (1972) found that initial grief is often characterized by pangs of yearning for the dead person rather than a prolonged depression. These pangs began within a few hours and reached a peak between 5 and 14 days. The bereaved feel an intense wish to be with their loved one and an irresistible urge to search for them. Bowlby and Parkes describe this urge to search as instinctual, and it is also evident in animals (Lorenz, 1963). Bereaved humans usually recognize that, rationally, a search is useless, and so they find their overwhelming need to search as inexplicable, crazy and distressing. Many bereaved people describe very clear and upsetting pseudo-hallucinations of the bereaved person which are explained by Parkes as experiences likely to help in the location of a lost object. Thus, other needs such as sleep and food are ignored. Parkes and Weiss (1983) found that those bereaved persons who experienced a high degree of pining were more likely to experience a prolonged or complicated grief

Box 24.2 Mr and Mrs A

Mrs A was referred to the hospital social worker by her husband's surgeon because of anxiety attacks. Her husband had recently undergone open heart surgery. It had seemed quite likely that her husband would die. In fact he recovered, but instead of feeling better Mrs A felt worse.

Mrs A was in her forties and Mr A was 25 years older. They had been married 20 years. During their marriage Mr A had suffered two previous life-threatening illnesses. Given the age difference, in the normal course of events, we might expect that Mr A would die before his wife. Mr A's illnesses seemed to emphasize this expectation and, at an intellectual level, Mr and Mrs A were quite aware of this reality.

Problems arose, however, because both Mr and Mrs A behaved towards each other as though they were not aware of this reality. When the prospect of Mr A. dying was raised Mrs. A would demand that it should not be talked about because it was not going to happen. Over a few meetings Mrs A learned that, although she tried stopping others talking about it, the discussions continued in her own head anyway. As a result, she began to describe these internal discussions rather than controlling them.

When she first met Mr A she felt that she was worth nothing. He had changed her life and so if he died she believed that she would revert to nothing. She was so convinced by this that she felt that she would want to commit suicide if he did die. Interestingly, as Mrs A became more open, Mr A began expressing the view that he knew that Mrs A would cope when the time came for her to do so, and he felt that there was little value in talking about it until then because it would only be needlessly upsetting.

Mr and Mrs A organized themselves so that Mrs A could cope quite well with life as long as she received regular reassurance from her husband. He also willingly stepped in and took over tasks that she felt she could not manage, even though he believed she could. There appeared to be a magical idea behind this arrangement which might be described as follows: whilst Mrs A was dependent upon Mr A in this concrete way he could not possibly die. Mr and Mrs A did not subscribe to this notion because intellectually they recognized it as magical. In spite of this they behaved as though it was true.

It was the social worker's job to hold up a mirror to this reliance upon magical thinking, and by so doing to present the couple with the issue of whether they would continue to align themselves emotionally with such thinking which underlay much of Mrs A's distress. Initially Mrs A reacted by trying to convince the social worker and Mr A that she really was worthless. Mr A rose to the occasion by being even more solicitous. The social worker then presented Mr A with the dilemma he seemed to be in. Mr A thought that Mrs A could cope with tasks independently but behaved as if this were not so by taking over from her. Perhaps he did not put his money where his mouth was because it felt too cruel to do so to someone who felt so worthless.

Mr and Mrs A's dilemma demonstrates clearly the dynamic between how a person approaches life and how they approach death. The discussions with Mr and Mrs A centred on two options. They might continue living their lives as though they would never end in death, whilst at the same time living under the shadow of death. Alternatively, they might risk facing these fears, and thus become more free to develop their lives.

reaction. Many of these people linked their pining with having been unduly dependent upon their dead partner.

According to Kubler-Ross (1969), a common reaction of patients to the news of their life threatening illness was to look for another opinion or look for reassurance that the information that they were hearing was not true. This is an understandable reaction given the enormity of the news. These patients have been catapulted into an unpredictable world and are desperately trying to change it back into the world they know and understand. They may therefore be very threatened by and dismissive of information or facts, supplied by the social worker or other social care professional, which appear to be self-evident. For example, a client may passively resist any attempt by her social worker to discuss transfer to a hospice.

Anger and guilt

Anger was expressed by most of the bereaved people studied by Parkes. Anger was most commonly felt during the first month and may be seen as a reaction to the threat of a loss that has not been fully accepted. The periods of anger were interspersed with periods of apathy and depression and as the first year progressed these periods of apathy became more common as people moved into the next stage.

Freud (1917) suggested that adaptation to loss is partly determined by the degree of ambivalent feelings the bereaved hold for the dead person. His writings suggest that, in a difficult relationship, the bereaved will sometimes have unconsciously wished for the death of the person. If that wish becomes a reality the bereaved may believe, unconsciously, that they have brought about the death. They will then protect themselves from the arising guilt by blaming others for the death. Parkes and Weiss (1983) provided support for Freud's suggestions. He found high levels of expressed anger and self-reproach were associated with a poorer adaptation. Parkes noted that widows or widowers who had experienced an unhappy or conflictual marriage initially appeared to cope better with their bereavement, but as time went on they seemed unable to progress. Parkes also suggests that these findings may have a more straightforward explanation. Perhaps those bereaved who have experienced a difficult marriage have more to grieve, they mourn 'not only for the marriage that was but also for the marriage that could have been' (Parkes and Weiss 1983, p.122).

Parkes (1972) found a tendency for the widows to blame others for the death. For example, social workers may sometimes feel that they are being blamed. This may be because they have been present and involved, and/or because they are seen as representing an organization such as a hospital which is in a position of power over life and death. Likewise, Kubler-Ross (1969) found that as dying patients began to consider their predicament, they became angry with and envious of the healthy people around them. If the social worker is being sensitive with their client about their terminal illness, then it is important for the social worker not to take these feelings personally. However, it is also essential to consider whether the client has an externally-based reason for being angry. For example, a client who complains angrily that they are not receiving the attention they need may be right. The social worker could indeed be avoiding the client (physically and/or emotionally) because they find being with a dying person uncomfortable.

Bargaining

Kubler-Ross noted that some people used bargaining as a way of controlling the pain involved in accepting their own death. She found that people would try to strike a deal with God, fate, the hospital, etc. They would agree to live an honest life if God reprieved them. Or they would agree to die if they were given the time or energy to accomplish some final task. Kubler-Ross equated this period of bargaining with a child who initially reacts with anger when banned from doing something by her parents. Then, after some consideration she thinks, 'Well, I haven't got what I want from being disagreeable. Let's try asking nicely.'

Kubler-Ross warns about taking these bargains literally. If a social worker can accede to a client's wishes then there is no reason why not. However, do not expect the client to keep their side of the bargain. Whether or not the client accepts it, the fact that he or she is dying is not really under their own control.

Depression, apathy, acceptance and gaining a new identity

Bereavement involves a loss of identity. Our identities are determined by the relationships we have with people and objects. When a husband loses a wife he also loses a large part of the way he (and others) sees himself. He is now a widower, a person he knows nothing about. Parkes found that many bereaved described the loss of their spouse as a loss of part of themselves. It seems that during the first few weeks of bereavement, the bereaved learn that their way of dealing with the world no longer applies. There follows a period of apathy and aimlessness. Some react as if they had never lost their loved one and they avoid situations that will prove otherwise. The rest are caught in a vicious circle. Their apathy makes it difficult to learn a new identity, but they need one in order to interact with the world again.

Kubler-Ross (1969) and Hinton (1972) both found depression to be a common emotional reaction in the dying person. Hinton cites evidence which shows that 18 per cent of people who committed suicide suffered from a serious physical illness and 4 per cent were suffering from an illness that probably would have killed them within six months. Hinton (1972) reports that increased levels of anxiety and depression were more common in younger people, and that anxiety and depression levels increased with the length of their illness. He also found an interesting relationship between anxiety and religious belief. Those who were actively religious or firm non-believers appeared to suffer less anxiety than those who professed belief in God but who did not practise.

Kubler-Ross divides the types of depression experienced into two forms. The first is reactive depression that occurs in response to losses that have already occurred. For example, loss of job due to illness, or loss of part of the body by amputation. In many respects, such losses are likely to result in the sort of bereavement reactions outlined by Parkes and Weiss (1983). The second is preparatory depression. Dying people review their life and mourn, in advance, the loss of different aspects of it. Elderly people who have lived a full life have relatively little to mourn. They have gained much and have lost few opportunities and so they may suffer little preparatory depression. On the other hand, people who review their life and perceive a life of mistakes and missed opportunities may paradoxically have more to mourn as they begin to realize that these opportunities are now lost forever.

Kubler-Ross identified some people who felt neither anger nor depression. They seemed content to spend long periods in silence and appeared somewhat detached from those around them. Kubler-Ross called this stage acceptance. The families of people in this stage often feel rejected, and therefore it may be important to explain that this disengagement is a sign that the person has been surrounded by loving and supportive relatives, friends and staff. Kubler-Ross is at pains to distinguish acceptance from resignation. In many ways, a resigned person will appear similar to one who has reached acceptance. Both will be quiet and still, demanding little. But the stillness of those who have accepted comes from calmness whilst in those who have become resigned it comes from despair. Those in despair cannot accept death, nor can they deny its existence any longer. It is important for those working with the terminally ill to distinguish between a person who is resigned to death and one who has accepted it.

Summary

Bereaved and dying people are faced with an old world that has been destroyed and a new one that is alien and unpredictable. Understandably, they usually react initially with disbelief and then by withdrawing emotionally and behaviourally. Periodically they emerge, sometimes in anger, to tackle the world again. But their expectations of life usually need to change so much that they are left with very few resources to enable them to deal with this new world, and so usually they withdraw again, sad and disorientated. A pattern emerges of frightened withdrawal followed by tentative exploration. Given time, the dying may be able to re-emerge to experience their life with its end in sight, and the bereaved too can begin to learn an identity for themselves without the person they love.

The Origins of Stress in Caring for the Dying and Bereaved

The previous section has outlined the reactions that social care professionals might expect from bereaved and dying people. This section considers the difficulties social workers can experience in this context. These difficulties have been divided into those arising from working in a stressful environment and those arising from the personal attributes of individual professionals. However, as will be clear, these two areas interact.

The stressful environment

The central difficulty in caring for the dying and bereaved appears to be the strong sense that it imparts in carers of being quite unable to help. The following quotations illustrate this.

> The loss of a loved person is one of the most intensely painful experiences any human being can suffer, and not only is it painful to experience, but also painful to witness, if only because we are so impotent to help. (Bowlby 1980)

> Pain is inevitable in such a case and cannot be avoided. It stems from the awareness of both parties that neither can give the other what he wants. The helper cannot bring back the person who's dead, and the bereaved person cannot gratify the helper by seeming helped. (Parkes, 1972)

Despite this, in a large-scale study of death and coping in health professionals, Vachon (1987) found that six of the ten most frequently-cited stressors encountered by staff appeared to have nothing directly connected with issues of death but involved the structure or running of the organization. These stressors included problems of role ambiguity, role conflict, communication problems and inadequate staffing. The following example illustrates some of these stressors.

An 84 year old woman was living alone. Her family contacted the local social services because of increasing concern about her level of confusion and hence her safety. They requested immediate admission for her to a geriatric unit for an assessment which would also give them some respite. A social worker visited the elderly woman and agreed with the family's concern. She attempted to arrange admission to a residential establishment. The community geriatrician, whilst sympathetic to the social worker's concerns, could not make her a priority in view of the high level of family support. Despite some reservations the social worker accepted this. However, four weeks later, the social worker was informed that the woman had died tragically in a fire in her flat caused by her having left the stove on. The social worker was left wondering whether this elderly person would have died if she had communicated her concerns more clearly to the geriatrician.

Like Vachon, Davidson and Foster (1995) highlight the stress caused by working in an area in which there is significant confusion over the role of social workers as distinct from nurses, doctors, psychologists and chaplains. Indeed, they suggest that some social workers may find themselves working in environments where spending time with dying and bereaved people is not valued. This may lead to despondency and demoralization in the social worker. Unlike medicine and nursing, social work is not encumbered by a tradition in which death is a mark of professional failure. But this does mean that social workers may often find themselves alone in trying to tackle the emotional reactions associated with death whilst other staff seem intent upon denying the existence of those same reactions in themselves (except, of course, social workers who work alongside specialist nursing services such as MacMillan nurses). The feelings of helplessness which death can give rise to is perhaps more difficult to tolerate in those organizations and professions where the task is to save life. Davidson and Foster (1995) provide an example that illustrates these pressures but also shows how it is, nevertheless, possible to remain helpful in such situations.

A social worker was distressed when the chief medical resident ceased to visit a young, dying patient who often asked why he did not come. The worker chose not to be angry at the doctor's avoidance but assumed that he cared about the patient but had difficulty knowing what to say to her. When the social worker spoke to him of the client's sadness that he no longer visited her, he said that he could not bear to visit because the patient was a symbol of his failure. The worker understood his feelings of helplessness and guilt but suggested strongly that they go at once to see the client together. After the visit, they talked about the sadness of being unable to prevent 'off-time' deaths that defy normal span of life.

The crucial factor was the social worker's decision not to be angry with the doctor. At first sight, such a decision appears the only obvious one to make, but this would ignore the strength of feeling that might have prompted a more angry reaction. Here is a lonely and frightened young patient who is feeling abandoned by the doctor and asks the social worker all the uncomfortable questions that she feels she cannot ask him because he seems as frightened as her. The social worker might easily feel aggrieved that she has to endure this discomfort only because the doctor (who is probably paid significantly more than her) cannot take responsibility for an important aspect of his own job. The fact that she decides not to be angry suggests that this social worker has come to accept her own mortality, which means that she is not unduly disturbed by the defensive attempts by others to keep mortality at bay. This brings us to the next section.

The vulnerable social worker

Worden (1991) suggests three reasons why working with dying and bereaved people may be personally painful for the social worker. First, contact with a bereaved or dying person may remind social workers of their own previous bereavements. If these bereavements have reached a resolution then that social worker's ability to understand and help others may be greatly improved. However, if grief remains unresolved, caring for a grieving or dying client may be very difficult. This is particularly true if the experience of the client is close to the experience of the social worker. If the social worker suffers from unresolved grief, the experiences of the bereaved or dying client will serve only to remind the social worker of their own pain. As a result the social worker can be lost in his/her own grief and be quite unable to empathize with the client.

Second, the experiences of a bereaved or dying client may correspond with a social worker's own feared losses. For example, a social worker who cannot tolerate holding in his or her mind the thought of losing a child will find it difficult to provide good care to a family whose young son has leukaemia.

Third, contact with dying and bereaved people is likely to present social workers with the reality and inevitability of their own death. Some social workers will find this reality very frightening and attempt to avoid it either literally or emotionally.

A number of writers have suggested that, for some care givers, the need to feel helpful and the subsequent choice of profession is in part prompted by unhappy and unresolved past experiences of caring or being cared for. Malan (1979) calls this the 'helping profession syndrome', and Bowlby (1980) calls it 'compulsive care giving'. Both these authors suggest that some carers are giving what they themselves unconsciously feel that they have missed or need. This behaviour fulfils an important function for these carers and, as such, need not be a bad thing.

Nevertheless, it is important that the less conscious motivation behind carer choice is recognized otherwise it can be used defensively. The feeling that they have not been properly cared for or loved is painful. However, they can avoid these painful feelings by convincing themselves (and others) that they are strong, invulnerable providers of care. This self-deception may be successful, but it depends upon these carers receiving continual reassurance that they are indeed being helpful. But when dealing with death and dying, the overriding feeling is one of helplessness not helpfulness. Consequently, this defence mechanism is likely to break down, with the result that the caregivers begin to re-experience the very feelings they have been trying to avoid; feelings of being unloved and uncared for. The caregivers may then look at the care their clients are receiving from them and become envious because the clients are getting what these caregivers want. It is difficult to give clients care when you are made envious by the very thing you are giving. However these feelings of envy can be avoided if the caregiver is able to distort reality again and perceive clients' genuine needs as unreasonable demands. These complex processes illustrate the types of difficulties social care professionals can face, and also the difficulty of identifying and resolving the conflicts.

Discussion point
- ° What were your reasons for entering your social care profession?
- ° Are any of these reasons likely to make it particularly difficult for you to cope with painful experiences such as the death of clients?

Summary
In summary, this section has presented a picture in which caring for the dying and bereaved is a rewarding but difficult and demanding task which is likely to result in most responsible social care professionals feeling hopeless and useless at some time. Professionals react to this pressure in different ways. For some their own experiences of loss, of illness or of being cared for will make it difficult to look after the dying or bereaved, whilst for others, their experiences, if understood, can enhance their capacity. The next section will examine ways of coping with this difficult task.

Helping the Bereaved Client: Grief Counselling and Grief Therapy

Worden (1991) makes a distinction between a normal and an abnormal grief reaction. Such a distinction is undoubtedly artificial and somewhat arbitrary, but can help in clarifying the aims of therapy or counselling. The most appropriate psychological intervention will depend upon making an assessment of whether the client is facing the inevitable difficulties associated with bereavement, or whether there are some further difficulties either associated with the circumstances of the death (or threat of death), the personality of the client and/or the client's past experiences. If grieving remains relatively uncomplicated by difficult circumstances or personality factors, then the aim of counselling would be threefold.

Grief counselling
1. To provide an opportunity for clients to face the new realities of their lives
2. To reassure the client that, although his/her reactions feel disturbing and crazy, they are nevertheless common and understandable in the context of the massive change in life circumstances
3. To help the client clarify the dilemmas that will reside in day-to-day decision making, for example how to manage finances and the practical problems of living alone.

These aims require that the counsellor principally takes a supportive role in relation to the client, but will also occasionally need to be prepared to challenge the client in terms of a decision the client makes when it becomes apparent that there is a predictable pattern of problems emerging whenever the client tries to move forward. For example, a counsellor may need to help a bereaved elderly woman who complains of loneliness to recognize that a reluctance or ambivalence about joining social activities may be linked to a fear that engaging in new activities and becoming independent may result in losing the attention of her only son and his wife.

Grief therapy

Grief therapy is a term we might reserve for the psychological intervention which should be considered where there are complications. A complicated reaction might be said to be one in which the client has a chronic feeling (conscious or unconscious) that to let grief run its course would lead to such unbearable problems that the grief reaction must be tightly controlled in some way. The consequences of such control will be that the client will compromise the relationship with reality. The mechanism of control can take many forms. For example, it may involve the denial or cutting off from feelings. Alternatively, the client may form an obsessional relationship with the death and ruminate upon the circumstances with the implicit belief that by thought or willpower the 'story' can be made to end differently. These are only examples though, and there are many other ways in which all of us attempt to control matters.

The function of grief therapy is to work towards gaining an understanding of why the client feels it is necessary to control grief. The therapist can help in this matter by providing a forum in which the death can be considered in relation to the manner of dying (whether expected or unexpected, violent or peaceful, etc.), the past experiences of the client, the family situation and immediate social environment. In clients where there are chronic difficulties with grief there is invariably an interaction between these variables which results in an uncompromised view of reality being experienced as devastating. If the client can be helped to understand what interactions are contributing to this feeling of devastation, then the client will be in a clearer position to make a decision about whether they can open themselves to experiences that might feel devastating but which are (in themselves) not fatal. It is also important to keep in mind that the client may decide that these feelings appear so dangerous that they prefer to live in an illusory world, even though this will cause problems, perhaps quite serious problems. See Box 24.2 for an example of this process of therapy.

The role of the social worker in bereavement counselling

Traditionally, bereavement counselling was seen to be within the remit of social work. This is no longer always the case, and social work training may not always provide the necessary training in the area. So individual social workers need to think carefully about their own level of expertise when confronted with these difficult situations. Whilst many social workers may not feel able to work directly with the bereaved, their ability to assess the level of severity is extremely valuable. Good judgement will enable them to make appropriate referrals to specialist psychotherapy units for more complex cases, and to local befriending and counselling services for others.

Coping with the Stress of Caring for the Dying and the Bereaved

The stress of caring needs to be addressed at two levels, the institutional and the personal. For reasons that will be outlined below, the institutional level should be the primary source of input and is considered first.

Institutional

If social care professionals are expected to be helpful to dying and bereaved people then it must be accepted by their employers that they will be involved in upsetting, stressful work which is potentially dangerous to mental health. It is the responsibility of the employers to provide safeguards to ensure that these professionals are not damaged by their work. Davidson and Foster's (1995) view is that social workers are having to meet the challenge of entering into the intimate lives of clients to discuss death and pain, 'in settings where the means to provide caring responses to clients are reduced by fragmentation, poor staffing levels, discontinuity of care and lack of value placed on this work'. They further add that many social workers are distressed and dissatisfied and unless they can 'review their practice, re-examine their core functions and thereby reframe their current activities to be consonant with professional values and goals, they may accept constricted roles or experience a downward spiral of powerlessness'.

A universally suggested solution to this problem is the setting up of support systems (e.g. Worden, 1991; Hines, 1989). It would be fair to say that all professionals who are working in an area in which death occurs regularly should have access, during work time, to a support system. Although the exact nature of the system will vary depending upon the nature of the work and institution, formal support groups are frequently cited as important components of a support system. Hines (1989) stresses that the focus of these groups should not be simply on giving personal support but should be task-oriented. This means the group should aim to improve working practices as well as emotional support and containment.

For example, Davidson and Foster (1995) outline a number of management strategies to ensure staff support and development for social workers:

1. Support programmes that offer confirmation of being valued, feedback about behaviour and effects on others and encouragement to develop new ways of working

2. Staff development programmes to ensure that social workers feel competent through providing current information on technological, legal and ethical developments, such as power of attorney and living wills

3. Encouraging the establishment of peer support groups and team-working to reduce isolation

4. Providing a range of professional development courses to add to social workers' knowledge and competence in dealing with the dynamics of grief and mourning; interpersonal and family relationships; life-stage development; personal concerns that relate to professional functioning and mastery of roles

5. Promoting attendance at conferences and workshops which provide opportunities for continuing staff education, e.g. by providing assistance towards conference fees, travel allowance and release from work duties

Discussion point

° Rank the elements in a support system in terms of their importance to you. If possible discuss these with fellow students.

Personal

As outlined above, individuals enter the social care profession for a variety of reasons, and so past experiences may make caring for some clients difficult or impossible. Consequently, it is important for these professionals to be able to recognize their own limitations, to consider how they cope with inevitably painful feelings, and whether any negative coping methods affect their own life or the care provided to clients. Much of the social work literature (e.g. Davidson and Foster, 1995; Koocher, 1979) emphasizes the importance of coping strategies to avoid feelings of 'burn-out' (see Chapter 2). For instance, Davidson and Foster state that

> 'Social workers often thrive and avoid excessive stress or burn-out by having time protected for vacations, days away from practice and periods of activity away from direct client contact as part of their assignments. They may find it helpful to participate in social and physical activities that balance the emotional intensity of their work.'

Vachon (1987) lists the nine most frequently cited personal coping mechanisms:

1. Having a sense of competence or pleasure from work
2. Having a sense of control over aspects of one's own practice
3. Managing one's lifestyle
4. Having a personal philosophy of illness and death
5. Leaving the work situation if it became too stressful
6. Avoiding or distancing oneself from clients or their families
7. Continuing a programme of education
8. Having a support system outside of work
9. Using humour.

Vachon does not present these as either good or bad, merely as common. Some, of these (e.g. (5) and (6)) which advocate limiting emotional investment, are more controversial and unhelpful to the client. In optimal circumstances, however, the social worker will attempt to be empathic and responsive, yet retain enough emotional distance so as to avoid becoming over-involved and over-identified with the client. The effects of the remainder of the coping mechanisms will depend entirely upon how they are used. For example, humour (9) can be used to convey truth and improve understanding or, on the other hand, to humiliate and demean. (See Chapter 2 for a further discussion about coping with general work stress.)

Discussion point

- ° What coping mechanisms do you use to help you with painful experiences?
- ° Are any of these likely to be damaging to you or your clients?

In this section, we have suggested that the responsibility for helping social care professionals cope with the stress of caring for the dying and bereaved lies primarily with their employers. Formal support systems should be in place which are relevant to the area and which are task oriented. However, research indicates that existing systems are usually of doubtful effectiveness. In addition to the responsibilities of the institution, each individual professional needs to take responsibility for their behaviour, consider their limitations, and how they cope when they are asked to work at or beyond their limit.

Summary

We began by noting that the experience of death and dying is an inevitable part of social work and other related professions. We then considered the reactions of people who were dying or bereaved. Attachment theory was used to demonstrate that there was an understandable pattern of feelings and behaviour in response to the experience of dying or being bereaved. However, individuals find different routes through this pattern.

In the second half of the chapter we examined the stress of dealing with dying and bereaved people. The sources of stress were considered and two important areas identified. The first was the powerful sense of impotence that can be induced in staff who work in this area. The second concerns the motivation for working in the area in the first place. We suggested that some social workers (and others in the caring professions) may be attracted to the work, at least in part because they have unfulfilled needs concerning, for example, unmourned losses. They unconsciously see a possibility of having their needs met but instead find themselves attempting to meet the needs of others and becoming envious and frustrated.

We briefly described the function of grief counselling and grief therapy. A (somewhat arbitrary) distinction was made between therapy and counselling. We described counselling as facilitating a supportive relationship with those who are experiencing a relatively uncomplicated mourning. We understood grief therapy to provide help of a more challenging nature to clients who, for a variety of reasons, may seek to establish long-term control over the mourning process because the experience of uncontrolled mourning feels unbearable.

Finally, ways of coping with this area of work were reviewed. At an institutional level, we suggested that this work posed a potential danger to mental health and so safety mechanisms were necessary in the form of accessible support systems. At a personal level, social care professionals should consider how they cope with the inevitable painful feelings associated with such work and whether their coping mechanisms are adaptive in the long term or likely to result in problems for themselves or for those to whom they give care.

Seminar Questions

1. Do culture and ethnic origin influence bereavement reactions? Are there examples of culturally determined differences within the UK? Can rituals aid recovery?
2. What are the potential dangers of using models of dying and bereavement like the ones described to understand the behaviour of individual clients?

Further Reading

Kubler-Ross, E. (1973) *On Death and Dying*. London: Tavistock Publications.

Parkes, C.M. (1972) *Bereavement. Studies of Grief in Adult Life*. Harmondsworth: Penguin Books.

Parkes, C.M. and Weiss R.S. (1983) *Recovery from Bereavement*. New York, NY: Basic Books.

Worden J.W. (1991) *Grief Counselling and Grief Therapy, 3rd edition*. New York, NY: Springer-Verlag.

These books are useful for those seeking to study this area in greater depth. The first three are seminal texts which provide the basis of much subsequent work. They are well written and readable. The final book (Worden, 1991) is a useful summary of the bereavement process, but will be of particular interest to those social workers who are involved in explicit grief counselling and therapy.

References

Bowlby, J. (1969) *Attachment and Loss Vol. I.* New York, NY: Basic Books.

Bowlby, J. (1980) *Attachment and Loss Vol. III.* New York, NY: Basic Books.

Caplan, G. (1964) *Principles of Preventive Psychiatry.* New York, NY: Basic Books.

Corr, C.A. (1993) 'Coping with dying: lessons we should not learn from the work of Elizabeth Kubler-Ross.' *Death Studies, 17,* 69–83.

Davidson K.W. and Foster Z. (1995) 'Social work with dying and bereaved clients: helping the workers.' *Social Work in Health Care, 21,* 4, 1–16.

Engel, G.L. (1962) *Psychological Development in Health and Disease.* Philadelphia, PA: Saunders.

Erikson, E.H. (1951) *Childhood and Society* New York, NY: Norton.

Erikson, E.H. (1982) *The Life Cycle Completed* New York, NY: Norton.

Freud, S. (1917) 'Mourning and melancholia.' In *Metapsychology – the Theory of Psychoanalysis.* London: Penguin Freud Library.

Hines, N. (1989) 'Care for the carers.' In L. Sherr (ed) *Death, Dying and Bereavement.* Oxford: Blackwell.

Hinton, J. (1972) *Dying.* Harmondsworth: Penguin.

Lindemann, E. (1944) 'The symptomatology and management of acute grief.' *American Journal of Psychiatry, 101,* 141.

Littlewood, J. (1992) *Aspect of Grief: Bereavement in Adult Life.* London: Routledge.

Lorenz, K. (1963) *On Aggression.* London: McEwan.

Koocher, G. (1979) 'Adjustment and coping strategies among the caretakers of cancer patients.' *Social Work in Health Care, 5,* 2, 145–150.

Kubler-Ross, E. (1969) *On Death and Dying.* London: Tavistock Publications.

Malan, D.H. (1979) *Individual Psychotherapy and the Science of Psychodynamics.* London: Butterworths.

Parkes, C.M. (1972) *Bereavement. Studies of Grief in Adult Life.* Harmondsworth: Penguin Books.

Parkes, C.M. and Weiss, R.S. (1983) *Recovery from Bereavement.* New York, NY: Basic Books.

Pincus, L. (1976) *Death and the Family.* London: Faber.

Smith, C.R. (1976) 'Bereavement: The contribution of phenomenological and existential analyses to a greater understanding of the problem.' *British Journal of Social Work, 5,* 1, 75–92.

Stroebe, W. and Stroebe, M. (1987) *The Psychological and Physical Consequences of Partner Loss.* Cambridge: Cambridge University Press.

Vachon, M.L.S. (1987) *Occupational Stress in the Care of the Critically Ill, the Dying and the Bereaved.* Washington, DC: Hemisphere.

Worden, J.W.(1991) *Grief Counselling and Grief Therapy, 3rd edition* New York, NY: Springer-Verlag.

Conclusion

Making Use of Psychology

In the course of their work, social workers and those in related professions are called upon to deal with complex and difficult issues. They frequently have to make important recommendations which have major implications for people's lives, often with unclear evidence on which to base them. The professional has to draw on their own background knowledge derived from theory and research findings, and their own individual observations and experience. Aspects of psychology discussed in this book can contribute to both the underlying knowledge base used by social care professionals in understanding and helping others, but also to an understanding of how the professionals themselves operate, make decisions, function in organizations and are affected by stress. Some chapters have provided background information and theories which may be useful to underpin the work of social workers and those in other social care professions. Others offer more specific practical advice. Sometimes, as in the case of models of dying and bereavement (see Chapter 24 by Paul March and Clare Doherty), there is considerable agreement between the different approaches. However, psychology is a relatively new and fast developing discipline, and sometimes the differing theoretical as well as applied approaches produce conflicting research findings giving a confusing picture. This may make it hard for the new professional trying to apply their knowledge in practice. This final chapter draws on themes emerging throughout the book, and offers some final concluding thoughts on how social care professionals might integrate and apply their knowledge and understanding of psychology. First it, discusses how a practitioner might try to evaluate research evidence and integrate the different theoretical approaches. Then it looks at how they might use psychological insights and approaches to monitor their own practice and evaluate their interventions.

Evaluating research, theory and therapeutic approaches

How is the social care professional to evaluate the diverse theoretical approaches or different types of intervention given the often conflicting evidence? What type of theoretical approach will help them to understand clients' problems and what therapeutic approach will be most effective in helping them? The large number of authors of this book means that some chapters are written by those who clearly favour some particular standpoint or theory whereas others take a more eclectic approach. For example, Chapter 7 on working with groups by Mary Horton draws heavily on the psychodynamic viewpoint whereas David Winter's chapter (Chapter 18) presents the pros and cons of as many as seven different ways of viewing psychological problems. Similarly, Dorota Iwaniec (Chapter 15) offers a range of ways of understanding child abuse. These approaches need not be mutually exclusive and can represent different ways of viewing the same problem. For example, Mary Horton (in Chapter 7) demonstrates how group processes can be framed in both cognitive social psychology terms and in psychodynamic terms. Psychological theories are not yet so comprehensive that reliance on a single approach can encompass all problems. In fact reliance on a single approach may lead to over simplistic interpretations. This is clearly highlighted in Chapter 15, where the dangers of approaching child abuse with a single theoretical explanation in mind are discussed. There is now strong evidence that child abuse, in common with most problems social care professionals address, has multiple causes. Dorota Iwaniec discusses the development of integrated approaches to the causation of child abuse and neglect. However, even where such frameworks exist, professionals are likely to be most effective if they are able to achieve their own integration of a wide range of different approaches which they can bring to bear on the specific problems which they encounter.

To achieve such an integration, social care professionals need to be able to assess and evaluate research findings. This requires an awareness of the flaws present in different types of research. An introduction to such methodological issues was given in the introductory chapter which suggested the need to collect converging evidence from a range of sources. However, it can also be the case that a number of studies taken together may give a biased impression. For example, Richard Hammersley (in Chapter 20) draws attention to the fact that studies of clinical populations may lead to the conclusion that heroin users are all addicted. Ignoring heroin users who do not attend clinics clearly can lead to a distorted view. Similarly, a large number of studies emphasizing the permanent damage caused by disrupted childhoods may lead us to ignore the equally important and interesting fact that many are remarkably resilient (see Chapter 12 by Ann and Alan Clarke). Research studies do a great deal to widen our knowledge and understanding, but students need also to read them with a critical awareness and to bear in mind that limitations of space mean that not all questions can be raised or answered by the authors of this book.

As with the theoretical frameworks, the therapeutic approaches based on them have both strengths and weaknesses, and the skill of the practitioner lies in being able to assess which approach will be most effective in the varying situations they encounter. The starting point would seem to be a good knowledge of a range of options. David Winter (Chapter 18) provides a comprehensive review of therapies, and suggests that different approaches will be useful with different types of clients. You may have noticed that different approaches are discussed in various sections of the book. These should give you some indicators as to the circumstances in which certain methods may be useful. For example, Clive Hollin (Chapter 19) discusses evidence suggesting that psychodynamic therapy may not be suitable for offenders, whereas cognitive approaches may be useful. All this suggests that professional activities will be most effective where there is a knowledge of psychology research and theory which is integrated with experience and professional judgement.

Monitoring and evaluating your own individual practice
While the main focus of this book is working with clients, some chapters also suggest ways in which social care professionals might monitor and evaluate their own practice. Just as the

studies of restricted samples (discussed above) can lead to biased research findings, social care professionals by the nature of their job and the clients with whom they come into contact may also form distorted views of particular client groups. For example, if your only contact with adolescents is in dealing with those who come into contact with social service departments, you may well underestimate how law abiding most of this age group are (see Chapter 17 by Leo Hendry). Similarly, a professional seeing only elderly people in need of help may lose sight of the ways in which ageing can be a positive experience (see Chapter 10 by Claire Meldrum). Chapter 4, by Wendy Middleton *et al.* also demonstrates a number of ways in which we may use heuristics to speed up decision making but which can lead to errors in judgement.

Social care professionals need to be aware of such biases in their own work and attempt to draw on diverse sources of information. Research psychologists and social scientists recognize the need to be objective, but also know the flaws of particular approaches. Consequently, when addressing an issue, they usually attempt to obtain converging evidence from a number of different studies and approaches. Similarly, social workers may also need to be aware of the potential for flaws and errors in their assessments and decision making. This may be facilitated by an openness to varied viewpoints including that of clients themselves, their family and other professionals as well as taking into account a range of theoretical approaches. Other aids to decision making such as the development of risk indicators (described in Chapter 4) may also be a future direction for improving decision making.

Social workers and research

An awareness of the biases and flaws in decision making is just one way social workers, those in related professions can monitor their own practice. However, there may also be a need for more rigorous and objective evaluation of the effectiveness of professional interventions. Focussing specifically on professional social work, it appears that its origins in psychodynamic theory have tended to mean that such evaluation of practice was considered either too problematic or unnecessary. In recent years the need to evaluate any service to justify the financial outlay has become an important part of our society. Unlike social workers, psychologists emphasize the need to quantify and measure behaviour. Assessment of individuals and research into the effectiveness of interventions has for a long time been a major part of their work. It is becoming much more common for trained social workers to go on postgraduate courses in social science research and study for PhDs. Methods used are likely to be similar to those used by psychologists (with the exception that laboratory experiments are less relevant). Increasingly, psychologists working alongside social workers and other social scientists trained in research have a role to play in evaluating social work practice.

As social workers expand their knowledge of research methodology and become increasingly involved in evaluating practice, they will also need to have increased awareness of research ethics. Ethical issues are usually well recognized by social workers in their day-to-day practice with clients. However, they may be less aware of the formal ethical guidelines which are increasingly being developed to protect the participants in research projects (who may themselves be either staff or clients) from any potential harm. Box 1 gives a brief summary of the ethical principles which guide the research of psychologists. Social workers and other social care professionals involved in research should ensure that they are aware of any ethical guidelines governing their research and should check that they have approval from their organizations to conduct the research. This may include approval from a Research Ethics Committee.

Box 1 Ethics for Research

Over the last few years, there has been increasing awareness of the ethical issues involved in research. Researchers based in universities or in other organizations such as the National Health Service who carry out research involving human participants will find that they need to have their research approved by ethics committees. Psychologists conducting research are also bound by their own professional guidelines published by the British Psychological Society (1997). These cover the following issues:

- *Deception.* People taking part in studies should be given as much information as possible and should not be deceived about the purposes of the research unless there is a very good scientific reason. However, some psychological research is impossible if participants are told the purpose of the research in advance. Even so, deception is inappropriate where, once the deception was revealed, the participants are likely to object or be uneasy.

- *Debriefing.* When people have taken part in a research study, it is the responsibility of the researcher to give full information to help the participants to understand the nature of the research. They should check the participant does not suffer from any unforeseen negative effects and take appropriate action should such effects occur.

- *Withdrawal from the investigation.* At the start of any study researchers must make it plain to all participants (including children) that they have a right to withdraw at any time.

- *Confidentiality.* Information about participants is confidential unless otherwise agreed in advance. If information about an individual is published it should not be identifiable. (Researchers also need to take into account the requirements of the Data Protection Act when using computers to store their data.)

- *Protection of participants.* Researchers have a responsibility to protect participants from physical and mental harm. This normally involves not exposing people to risks greater than those experienced in day-to-day life. This includes not exposing them to stress, so for example, if the research touches on areas which may be very private to individuals, they should be assured that they need not answer anything personal if they do not wish to do so.

- *Observational research.* Researchers using observational methods must respect the privacy of individuals. Unless people give consent, they should not be observed except in situations where they might expect to be observed by strangers.

- *Giving advice.* If, during an investigation, a researcher finds evidence of psychological or physical problems which the participant does not know about, they may have responsibilities to advise the participant. This may raise complex and difficult issues which the guidelines discuss in some detail.

- *Colleagues.* Ethical responsibilities are shared by research collaborators, assistants, students and others involved.

Discussion point

  ° Read the above guidelines and then look back at Box 11.3 in Chapter 11. How would you conduct a research study using Ainsworth's strange situation (Ainsworth and Wittig, 1969) so that you were complying with the ethical guidelines described in Box 1.

  ° Refer to the discussion of Milgram's (1994) study in Chapter 7. Do you think this study would get approval from an ethics committee applying the principles outlined in Box 1?

It is apparent that the boundaries for theory, research and application are constantly changing. The development of a research tradition within social care offers a new and more directly relevant perspective on issues that confront the profession. However, much can be gained from cross-disciplinary approaches incorporating an awareness of other viewpoints when dealing with as complex an issue as how people function.

Summary

In conclusion, this book has aimed to provide a broad introduction to a range of aspects of psychology which have been selected as useful to social care professionals. A wide range of excellent books exist to give more detailed information on specific topics. We hope the reader will use the further readings to follow up topics which arouse their interest or which are relevant to their professional development.

References

Ainsworth, M. and Wittig, B.A. (1969) 'Attachment and exploratory behaviour of 1-year-olds in a strange situation.' In B. M. Foss (ed) *Determinants of Infant Behaviour, 4*. London: Methuen.
British Psychological Society (1997) *Code of Conduct, Ethical Principles and Guidelines*. BPS: Leicester.
Milgram, S. (1974) *Obedience to Authority*. London: Tavistock.

Contributors' Affiliations

Alan Clarke, Psychology Department, University of Hertfordshire, College Lane, Hatfield, Herts AL10 9AB

Ann Clarke, School of Education, University of Hull, Hull HU7 7RX

Anthony Clyne, Camden Social Services, East Mental Health Team, 61 Belsize Avenue, London NW3 4BN

Julie Dockrell, Child Development and Learning, Institute of Education, 20 Bedford Way, London WC1H 0AL

Joanna Dodd,

Clare Doherty, North West London Mental Health NHS Trust, Willesdon Centre for Psychological Treatment, Willesden Hospital, Harlesden Road, London NW10 3RY

John Done, Psychology Department, University of Hertfordshire, College Lane, Hatfield, Herts AL10 9AB

Ben Fletcher, Business School, University of Hertfordshire, Mangrove Road, Hertford SG13 8QF

Nicola Grove, Department of Clinical Communication Studies, City University, Northampton Square, London EC1V 0HB

Richard Hammersley, Division of Behavioural Sciences, Department of Psychological Medicine, University of Glasgow Academic Centre, Gartnavel Royal Hospital, 1055 Great Western Road, Glasgow G12 0XH

Peter Harris, School of Social Sciences, University of Sussex, Falmer, Brighton BN1 9QN

Pat Hasan, Psychology Department, University of Hertfordshire, College Lane, Hatfield, Herts AL10 9AB

Barbara Hedge, Infection and Immunity Clinical Group, Group Offices, Frederick Andrewes Unit, St Bartholomews Hospital, London EC1A 4BE

Leo Hendry, Department of Education, King's College, University of Aberdeen, Aberdeen AB9 2UB

Clive Hollin, Senior Lecturer in Forensic Psychology, Centre for Applied Psychology, University of Leicester, University Road, Leicester LE1 7RH

Mary Horton, Psychology Department, University of Hertfordshire, College Lane, Hatfield, Herts AL10 9AB

Dorota Iwaniec, Department of Social Work, The Queen's University of Belfast, 7 Lennoxvale, Belfast BT9 5BY, Northern Ireland

Karen Izod, Karen Izod and Associates, 97 Portsmouth Rd, Guildford, Surrey GU2 5DL

Fiona Jones, Psychology Department, University of Hertfordshire, College Lane, Hatfield, Herts AL10 9AB

Mark Kebbell, Research Fellow, Department of Psychology, Liverpool University, Liverpool L69 3BX

Vicky Lewis, Professor of Education, The Open University, Walton Hall, Milton Keynes MK7 6AA

Paul March, North West London Mental Health NHS Trust, Willesdon Centre for Psychological Treatment, Willesden Hospital, Harlesden Road, London NW10 3RY

Claire Meldrum, 10 Elveden Close, Norwich, Norfolk NR4 6AB

David Messer, Psychology Department, University of Hertfordshire, College Lane, Hatfield, Herts AL10 9AB

Wendy Middleton, Department of Psychology, Royal Holloway, University of London, Egham Hill, Egham, Surrey TW20 0EX

Ann Phoenix, Psychology Department, Birbeck College, Malet Street, London WC1E 7HX

Jane Pierson, National Ageing Research Institute, Parkville, Victoria 3052, Australia

Paul Seager, Psychology Department, University of Hertfordshire, College Lane, Hatfield, Herts AL10 9AB

Judith Thomas, Department of Speech and Language Therapy, Queen Elizabeth II Hospital, Howlands, Welwyn Garden City, Herts, AL7 4HQ

David Winter, Department of Psychology, Napsbury Hospital, Shenley Lane, London Colney, Nr St Albans, Herts AL2 1AA

Richard Wiseman, Psychology Department, University of Hertfordshire, College Lane, Hatfield, Herts AL10 9AB

Anne Woollett, Psychology Department, Stratford Campus, University of East London, Romford Road, London E5 4LZ

List of Contributors

Ann and Alan Clark, Emeritus Professors, have undertaken rehabilitative work with the learning disabled over many years, and have published jointly many articles and several books on developmental psychology and on learning disabilities since 1953. Among a number of honours, they received jointly two international research awards.

Anthony Clyne is a senior practitioner and approved social worker working in mental health services. He has a special interest in risk assessment in social work practice.

Ben (C.) Fletcher is a professor of personal and organizational psychology and Dean of the Business School at the University of Hertfordshire. He has published extensively in the field of occupational stress, including *Work, Stress, Disease and Life Expectancy* (Published by Wiley, 1991).

Judith Dockrell is Professor of Psychology at South Bank University. She is a qualified educational and clinical psychologist and has a special interest in children who have speech and language problems.

Joanna Dodd has worked as a lecturer and conducted research in organizational psychology. She currently works as a freelance consultant in the public sector and construction industry.

Clare Doherty trained at the Tavistock Clinic as an adult psychotherapist and is also a qualified family therapist. She works in a variety of NHS mental health settings. She is also a qualified social worker and has worked for many years in that capacity.

John Done is a principal lecturer at the University of Hertfordshire, his main research interests concern cognition in dementia and schizophrenia together with health services research in relation to mental illness. He has lectured to a range of students about cognitive factors and aetiology in mental health and illness.

Nicola Grove is a lecturer in Clinical Communication studies in the School of Social and Human Sciences at the City University, London. She has particular interests in people with severe and profound learning difficulties using alternative and augmentative communication.

Richard Hammersley is director of the Social Science Research Training Unit, which provides core research training for all PhD students in Social Science subjects. He previously taught medical faculty students at the University Glasgow. His main research interests are in aspects of drug abuse and ingestive behaviour. He has co-authored books on *Cocaine, Ecstasy* (forthcoming) and *Group Communication Skills* (forthcoming).

Peter Harris is a senior lecturer at the University of Sussex. His research interests cover social cognition and health, with a particular interest in risk perceptions in the health domain.

Pat Hasan is a principal lecturer in psychology at the University of Hertfordshire. She has had experience of teaching introductory psychology to students on nursing and social work courses and has conducted a longitudinal study to investigate the relation between communication and cognition in preschool children with Down's syndrome.

Barbara Hedge is Head of the Infection and Immunity Clinical Psychology Service at St Bartholomew's and the Royal London Hospitals. She has specialized in the field of HIV and sexual health since 1987. Over this time she has seen many changes in the treatment of HIV disease and has studied the effects these changes have made to people's mental health and quality of life. Dr Hedge has published widely in these fields and is an organizer of the AIDS Impact conferences.

Leo B. Hendry is Professor of Education, Centre for Educational Research, Department of Sociology, University of Aberdeen, and Professor of Health Psychology, Psychology Institute, Norwegian University of Science and Technology, Trondheim, Norway. His book publications include: *Adolescents and Health Issues: Growing up and Speaking Out* (with Janet Shucksmith, 1998), and *The Nature of Adolescence, 3rd Edition* (with John Coleman, 1999).

Clive Hollin is Professor of Criminal Psychology at the Centre for Applied Psychology, University of Leicester. Alongside academic appointments, at the University of Leicester and the University of Birmingham, he has worked in prisons, the Youth Treatment Service, and at Rampton Special Hospital. He has published widely in the field of criminology and legal psychology, including the text *Psychology and Crime* and edits the journal *Psychology, Crime and Law.*

Mary Horton is a Senior Research Fellow in Social Psychology at the University of Hertfordshire. Her interest lies in showing the relationship between psychoanalytic ideas and social psychology. She is a psychodynamic counsellor and a psychoanalytic psychotherapist in training.

Karen Izod is an Organizational and Business Development Consultant working independently on change projects in public, private and voluntary sectors. She is also a Consultant on the Group Relations Programme, Tavistock Institute, London.

Dorota Iwaniec is Professor of Social Work, Head of Department and Director of the Centre for Child Care Research at The Queen's University of Belfast. She has conducted extensive research and clinical practice into parenting, child abuse, but specifically into failure-to-thrive and emotional abuse of children.

Fiona Jones is a principal lecturer in psychology at the University of Hertfordshire. She has research interests in the areas of occupational stress and health behaviour. She is also a qualified social worker and has worked in a range of social work settings.

Mark Kebbell heads a group researching eyewitness evidence at the Psychology Department of Liverpool University. He is currently on a Research Fellowship funded by the British Academy. His research concerns eyewitness testimony, particularly eyewitness evidence in court.

Vicky Lewis is Professor of Education at the Open University. She is a developmental psychologist with a special interest in the development of children with disabilities and the implications of such studies for our understanding of the processes of development. Much of her research has been with children with autism and with blind children.

Paul March is a clinical psychologist with experience of working in the filed of adult mental health. He is currently working with people with acquired brain injuries.

Claire Meldrum has a wide experience in teaching pure and applied psychology to undergraduate and Access students. Her interests include issues within health and social psychology. While at the University of Hertfordshire, she taught social workers and nurses. Currently Claire is teaching at City College Norwich and is preparing the second edition of the successful textbook, *Psychology for A level.*

David Messer is Professor of Developmental Psychology at the University of Hertfordshire. He has research interests in children's sleeping difficulties and their effect on care givers and children's language difficulties. He has taught on courses for social workers and has published a number of books.

Wendy Middleton has research interests in health psychology, specifically risk perception and risk behaviour. She is currently involved in teaching and researching in the addiction field.

Ann Phoenix works in the Department of Psychology, Birkbeck College, University of London. Her research interests include motherhood and the social identities of young people, particularly those associated with gender, race, social class and adoption. Her current research is an ESRC funded project (joint with Stephen Frosh) on masculinities in 11–14 year old boys.

Jane Pierson works at the School of Public Health, La Trobe University in Australia. She has research and teaching interests in the psycho-social consequences of stroke and neuropychological aspects of stock rehabilitation.

Paul Seager is currently a researcher at the University of Hertfordshire. He is interested in all aspects of deception, and is actively researching ways in which people can become more accurate lie detectors.

Judith Thomas currently works at the Department of Speech and Language Therapy, Queen Elizabeth Hospital, Welwyn Garden City. She is a specialist in voice problems and has a special interest in dementia.

David Winter is Head of Clinical Psychology Services and Co-ordinator of Research for Barnet Healthcare NHS Trust and Visiting Professor in the Psychology Department, University of Hertfordshire. His extensive publications on personal construct psychology and psychotherapy research include *Personal Construct Psychology in Clinical Practice* (Routledge, 1992).

Richard Wiseman currently heads the Perrott Warrick Research Unit, based at the University of Hertfordshire and funded by Cambridge University. This Unit examines unusual areas within psychology including; the psychology of the paranormal, the psychology of deception and lying and the psychology of luck and intuition.

Anne Woollett is a Professor in Developmental and Family Psychology in the Psychology Department at University of East London. Her research interests are in families, family relations and family formation. Currently she is undertaking a study of how children and young people living in East London make sense of family relations and negotiate transitions in their lives.

Subject Index

Author Index